Inside Lotus® 1-2-3® Macros, Revised and Expanded

Richard W. Ridington, Jr.

and

Scott Tucker

Foreword by Jim Seymour

Brady

New York   London   Toronto   Sydney   Tokyo   Singapore

BRADY

Simon & Schuster, Inc.
15 Columbus Circle
New York, NY 10023

Manufactured in the United States of America

3 4 5 6 7 8 9 10

Library of Congress Cataloging-in-Publication Data

Ridington, Richard W. (Richard Warren), 1954-
    Inside Lotus 1-2-3 macros, revised and expanded
    Audience: Adult 1-2-3 users.
    1. Lotus 1-2-3 (Computer program) 2. Macro instructions (Electronic computers) 3. Business—
Data processing. I. Tucker, Scott. II. Title. III. Title: Inside Lotus one-two-three macros, revised and
expanded.
HF5548.4.L67R525 1989   005.36'9   89-38499
ISBN 0-13-463522-1   CIP

About the Authors

Richard W. Ridi...
magazine. He co-...
lease 1A of Lotus 1-... is Resources Editor at *LOTUS*
Using Macros (Brady, ? best-selling book about Re-
editor at *Business Compu...idden Power of Lotus 1-2-3:*
tributor to *PC Magazine.*   was also a contributing
Before joining *LOTUS*, N...magazine and a con-
week-long Business Productivi... founded the
Computer Institute, taught cours...
sity and the University of New Ham... the Summer
training to the Hartford Insurance ... n Univer-
CIGNA.

Mr. Ridington was also president of a ...vided
whose clients included IBM, the state of Con... and
Duracell. He has served as a consultant to pu...
microcomputer videos, books, and training prog.

H. Scott Tucker is Director of Product Design for Lotus
Development Corporation's PC Spreadsheet Division.
In this position, he oversees the feature design and functional specification of future releases of 1-2-3 and Symphony.

Mr. Tucker was one of the principle designers of
Lotus 1-2-3 Release 3 and has been with Lotus since 1985.
Before joining the company he managed the development of more than 50 macro-driven business applications for a major 1-2-3 aftermarket vendor.

Mr. Tucker holds an MBA in Corporate Finance from
Brigham Young University in Provo, Utah. He has co-
authored a book on Lotus Symphony and has written
many articles for *LOTUS* magazine. He is also a regular
speaker before groups of users across the country, in
Europe, and Australia.

Reader's Comments

Dedication

To Dr. Gene Dalton at Brigham Young University, who enlarged my horizons with his inspired teaching and advice.

—S.T.

To Cindy, Russ, and the adventuresome campers at Wesleyan in the summer of '83. It has been fun.

—R.R.

Acknowledgments

Special thanks to Terry Anderson, whose persistence led to the writing of this book; to Milissa Koloski and Susan Hunt, whose consistent support saw it through; to Tom Dillon for its production; and to Judyth Powers, Professor Stephen Turner, and Alan Wichlei, whose manuscript reviews kept you, our readers, in our hearts and minds as we worked.

Limits of Liability and Disclaimer of Warranty

The authors and publisher of this book have used their best efforts in preparing this book and the programs contained in it. These efforts include the development, research, and testing of the theories and programs to determine their effectiveness. The authors and publisher make no warranty of any kind, expressed or implied, with regard to these programs or the documentation contained in this book. The authors and publisher shall not be liable in any event for incidental or consequential damages in connection with or arising out of, the furnishing, performance, or use of these programs.

Trademarks

Contents

Foreword / xvii

Introduction / xx
  Prerequisites / xx

Section I   Introduction to Macros / 1

Chapter 1   An Introduction to Macros / 3
  Overview / 3
  An Overview of Macros / 3
    Why Use Macros? / 3
    Types of Macros / 5
  The One Minute Macro / 7
  A Guide to Using the Book / 9
    Tools / 10
    How to Find Definitions of Words You Don't Understand / 11
    Key Name Conventions / 11
  Next / 12

Section II   Keystroke Macros / 13

Chapter 2   Keystroke Macros / 15
  Overview / 15
  Keystroke Macros: The Quick Course / 16
    Macro Examples / 23
  Keystroke Macros: The Detailed Course / 35
  Three Steps for Writing a Macro / 36
  Three Simple Types of Macros / 36
  Type 1: Macros That Enter Labels / 36
    What To Do If the Macro Did Not Work / 40
    Applications / 41
    Summary / 42
  Type 2: Macros That Enter Values and Formulas / 42
    Label Prefixes and Macros / 45
    Macros That Enter Labels Beginning with a Number / 46
    Writing Formulas with Macros / 48

Optional Exercise / 48
Summary / 50
Type 3: Macros That Enter 1-2-3 Commands / 51
What to Do If the Macro Did Not Work / 53
Summary / 54
Two Ways to Revise Macros / 54
Multiple Line Macros / 55
How Multi-Line Macros Work / 58
Multi-Line Macros as Newspapers / 58
Flow of Control / 59
Summary / 60
Letting 1-2-3 Write Your Macros / 60
How To Build on Existing Macros / 62
Adding Style to Your Macros / 64
Macro Labels Can Be Any Length / 64
Macro Documentation / 66
Assigning Range Names to Macros the Quick Way / 71
Where To Place Your Macros on the Worksheet / 73
How To Reduce the Screen Hopping / 75
Speeding Up Screen Switching with Range Names / 75
Eliminating the Screen Switching with Worksheet Windows / 77
Testing Your Macros / 78
Summary / 81

Chapter 3   Using Special Key Names / 82
Compatibility / 88
Sample Macro for Goto / 88
Applying Key Names To Write Formulas That Point / 90
Saving Time When You Write Macros / 93
Application / 95
Summary / 102

Chapter 4   The {?} Interactive Command / 103
The {?} Interactive Command and the Return Key / 104
Data Entry with the {?} Interactive Command / 106
Macro Testing with the {?} Interactive Command / 108
Applications / 109
Summary / 109
Next / 110

Chapter 5   Macro Libraries / 111
Release 2 and 2.01 Macro Libraries / 111
An Organized Macro Library / 113
  Create Separate Macro Library Worksheets / 114
  Segment Your Macro Library / 115
  Formula Libraries / 117
  Release 2.2 Macro Libraries / 117
  Two Methods of Attaching the Macro Library Manager / 119
A Quick Tutorial / 120
The Macro Library Manager Menu / 124
Macro Library Manager Tips / 126
Summary / 131

Chapter 6   Macro Automation Features / 132
Automated Data Entry / 132
Automatic Macro Activation / 134
Automatic Worksheet Loading / 136
Automatically Loading Macro Libraries in Release 2.2 / 138
Summary / 139

Chapter 7   A Prologue to More Advanced Macros / 140
An Introduction to Loops / 140
  Using Range Names / 142
  Style Guidelines for Range Names in Macros / 145
Another Sample Loop / 147
Terminating a Macro with a Command / 147
Sample Applications of { quit } / 148
Next / 149

Chapter 8   Debugging Your Macros / 150
Prescriptions for Common Macro Problems / 153
  1-2-3 Beeps and the Macro Does Not Run / 153
  The Macro Doesn't Run; 1-2-3 Doesn't Beep / 154
  The Macro-Name Letter Appears in the Control Panel or on the Worksheet / 155
  Characters Appear in the Control Panel Instead of on the Worksheet / 156
  Embedded Spaces in a Macro / 158
Assumptions in Macros / 159
Underlying Problems with Range Names / 161
Next / 163

Chapter 9   Dynamic Code: Self-Modifying Macros / 164
Creating Variables Through Blank Spaces / 165
Creating Variables Through String Manipulation / 166
Writing the String Formula / 167
Numbers in Macro String Formulas / 168
String Formula Limitations / 170
Next / 171

Section III   Macro Programming / 173

Chapter 10   Introduction to Macro Programming / 175
Overview / 175
Benefits / 177
Syntax / 178
A Warning About Certain Range Names / 179
Command Components / 181
   Keywords / 181
   Arguments / 181
   Separators / 184
Form of the Command Definitions / 185
Command Definitions / 186
   Organization of the Commands / 186

Chapter 11   Controlling the Screen / 192
Overview and Introduction to New Concepts / 192
{ Beep } / 192
{ Bordersoff } / 194
{ Borderson } / 194
{ Frameoff } / 195
{ Frameon } / 196
{ Graphoff } / 197
{ Graphon } / 198
{ Indicate } / 199
{ Paneloff } / 201
{ Panelon } / 203
{ Windowsoff } / 204
{ Windowson } / 206

Chapter 12   Allowing Keyboard Interaction / 209
Overview and Introduction to New Concepts / 209
{ Break } / 211
{ Breakoff } / 212
{ Breakon } / 213
{ Get } / 214
{ Getlabel } / 216
{ Getnumber } / 219
{ Look } / 223
{ Menubranch } / 226
{ Menucall } / 230
{ Wait } / 233
{ ? } (Interactive Command) / 235

Chapter 13   Controlling Program Flow / 237
Overview and Introduction to New Concepts / 237
{ } (Subroutine Call) / 238
{ Branch } / 246
{ Define } / 247
{ Dispatch } / 250
{ For } / 252
{ Forbreak } / 256
{ If } / 258
{ Ifkey } / 263
{ Onerror } / 265
{ Quit } / 267
{ Restart } / 268
{ Return } / 270
{ System } / 271

Chapter 14   Manipulating Data / 275
Overview and Introduction to New Concepts / 275
{ Blank } / 276
{ Contents } / 277
{ Let } / 281
{ Put } / 284
{ Recalc } / 287
{ Recalccol } / 289

Chapter 15   File Manipulation / 292
  Overview and Introduction to New Concepts / 292
  { Close } / 298
  { Filesize } / 301
  { Getpos } / 302
  { Open } / 304
  { Read } / 308
  { Readln } / 315
  { Setpos } / 319
  { Write } / 320
  { Writeln) / 324

Chapter 16   Accessing Add-ins / 327
  Overview and Introduction to New Concepts / 327
  { App1 }, { App2 }, { App3 }, { App4 } / 328

Chapter 17   @ Functions Commonly Used in Macros / 331
  Overview and Introduction to New Concepts / 331
  Special Functions / 332
    @cell / 332
    @cellpointer / 334
    @vlookup / 336
    @hlookup / 338
  Logical Functions / 340
    @isaaf / 340
    @isaap / 340
    @iserr / 341
    @isna / 342
    @isnumber / 343
    @isstring / 344
  String Functions / 345
    @left / 345
    @right / 345
    @mid / 346
    @string / 347
    @value / 348
    @find / 348
    @exact / 349
    @lower / 350
    @upper / 350
  Time and Date Functions / 351
    @now / 351

@time / 352
Summary / 353

Chapter 18   Enhancing Existing Macros / 354
Using the Advanced Macro Commands / 354
  Macros for 1-2-3 Release 2.2 / 360
  Next / 364

Chapter 19   Writing Your Own Commands / 365
Adding a Command to Vary the Width of a Range of Columns / 366
Adding a Command to Copy a Range of Relative Formulas As Absolute / 368
  Variation on the Macro / 372
Abbreviating Commands to Freeze/Unfreeze the Screen / 373
Abbreviating Commands to Prompt for Input / 374
Simplifying the {for} Command / 376
Command-Enhancement Summary / 379
Next / 379

Chapter 20   Release 1A Versus Release 2 Advanced Macro Commands / 380
Summary / 381
Next / 382

Section IV   Advanced Techniques / 383

Chapter 21   Introduction to the Advanced Techniques / 385
When To Use Customized Macros / 386
An Overview of the Content of an Application / 390
  User Interaction / 391
  Processing Data / 392
  Output / 392
An Overview of the Processes for Developing an Application / 393
  Application Planning / 393
  Development Tools / 394

Chapter 22   Managing User Input / 396
Single Characters / 397
  Using {get} / 398
  Case Sensitivity / 399
  Disabling the Keyboard / 401

Capturing Special Keys / 401
Implementing a Key Table / 404
Turning Off the Slash Key / 407
Displaying Your Own Menu at the "/" / 407
Displaying Your Own Help Screen at F1—A Release 2.2 Technique / 408
Be Careful of Curly Braces / 408
Generalizing the Curly Brace Test / 410
Embedding the Test in a Formula / 410
Accepting Label and Number Input / 413
Using {getlabel} To Manage Label Input / 413
Using {getnumber} / 417
Custom Prompts with Defaults / 419
Using {?} To Accept Data Entry / 425
Using Range Input / 426
Getting Help During Range Input / 429
Database Records / 431
Defining and Redefining Ranges / 435
Method 1: Helping the User Redefine a Range / 436
Method 2: Using a Macro to Redefine the Range / 438
Associated Ranges / 441
Bounds Checking and Validity Checking / 442
Bounds Checking / 443
Testing for Acceptable Entries / 445
Summary / 448

Chapter 23   Menu Systems / 449
Controlling Menu Responses / 450
Preventing Inadvertent Menu Selection / 450
Disabling the Escape Key / 451
Backing Up Through the Menu Tree / 453
Dynamic Menus / 454
Full-Screen Menus / 460
{If}-List: A Simple Approach to Full-Screen Menus / 461
{Dispatch}: A Fast Approach to Full-Screen Menus / 462
Speeding Up Full-Screen Menu Selections / 465
Full-Screen Menus with a Moving Cell Pointer / 469
{?} Moving Cell Pointer Menu / 470
{Get} Moving Cell Pointer Menu / 471
Query Find Moving Cell Pointer Menu / 475
Drawing Attention to Full-Screen Menus / 481

Chapter 24   Error Avoidance and Recovery / 483
The {?} (Interactive) Command / 484
Dealing with Files / 484
Dealing with Range Names / 487

Chapter 25   Testing Cells for Contents / 489
Overview / 489
Testing for a Specific Label / 490
Maintaining Compatibility with Releases 2, 2.01, and 2.2 / 492
Another Compatibility Issue: Testing for Blanks / 492

Chapter 26   Using the Screen / 493
Introduction / 493
Message at the Top of the Screen / 496
Messages in Windows / 498
A Dynamic Menu / 500
Showing a Message on the Screen / 503
Highlighting an Onscreen Message / 505
Managing Multiple Graphs / 509
Displaying Full-Screen Messages / 513
A Full-Screen Message Using an XY Chart / 518
Displaying Your Own Logo When the Worksheet Loads / 523
Dressing Up Displays Using the ASCII-No LICS-Screen Driver / 524
Using Custom ASCII Drivers / 529

Chapter 27   Help Systems / 532
Basic Systems / 532
Minimizing Memory / 533
   File-Combine Method / 533
   Read Method / 535
Restoring the Screen and Cell Pointer / 535
   Capturing Cell Addresses / 536
   Mid-Formula / 538
   Range Input / 545
   Query Find / 546
Context Sensitivity / 547
   Individual Help Nodes in the Menu Screen / 548
   Context Sensitivity in Full-Screen Menus / 549
   Context Sensitivity from the Worksheet / 549

Chapter 28   Application Design / 552
Using Available Memory Efficiently / 552
Making Your Application Portable to Other Environments / 554
   Portability Across Computing Environments / 554
   Converting the Application for Foreign Use / 556

Chapter 29   Structured Programming / 559
An Introduction to Selected Programming Concepts / 559
The Methods of Structured Programming / 560
  Keep Each Line of the Macro Brief and Meaningful / 560
  Use Variables / 561
  Use Range Names / 561
  Organize Common Actions into a Single Routine / 563
  Segregate Dissimilar Tasks into Separate Routines / 565
  Make Subroutines Independent of Calling Routines / 565
  Set Up the Worksheet Manually / 566
  Separate One-time Instructions from Recurring Instructions / 567
  Plan: How to Use Flow Charts and Pseudo Code / 569

Chapter 30   Macro Development Tips and Tools / 571
Toggling Between Two Files / 573
Navigational Aids / 573
Directory Switcher / 574
Learn Macro / 576
Speedkey Macro / 580
Benchmarking Your Routines / 583
Run Macro / 587
Debugging with {indicate} / 588
Range Name Table Documentor / 589
Protecting Your Macros / 594
Updating an Application Already in Use / 596
Search and Replace / 598
User Macro / 598
Accelerator Keys / 599
Conclusion / 600

Index / 601

Foreword

When Lotus shipped the first copies of 1-2-3 in 1983, the words that opened the chapter in the program's manual on writing and using macro commands didn't make much of them. In fact, it called the whole idea "The Typing Alternative," and used the term "macros" only as a kind of lowercased shorthand. Once you got past the basics, the manual introduced more sophisticated macros and the /X command with a section titled "Do You Sincerely Want to Become a Programmer?" full of dire warnings. In words which now sound quaint, co-developers Mitch Kapor and Jon Sachs revealed their deep apprehension about letting 1-2-3 users run amok in their spreadsheets:

> Allowing the computer to make decisions means there is the possibility it will make a decision you didn't anticipate. Programmers call these unanticipated decisions "bugs." Any programmer can tell you tracking down bugs and getting rid of them can be a tricky business. The additional Typing Alternative capability can open the door to a brave new world, or it can open the lid of Pandora's Box. It's up to you.

Little did they know. While so much of the design, packaging, and marketing of 1-2-3 was far-seeing and prophetic—the program remains remarkably similar, at least externally, even today; and its documentation, packaging, and marketing have built the biggest success story of the 1980s in the software business—those words today make us chuckle, for they are so at odds with what has happened to both 1-2-3 and its users. For macros have become one of the most popular features of the program, perhaps the single feature which most separated 1-2-3 from the other good spreadsheet programs available when it came to market.

The inclusion of a macro programming language—and writing 1-2-3 macros is no less programming than working in the dBASE III programming language, or the COBOL programming language, or the BASIC programming language—was a masterstroke. It turned 1-2-3 into not only a very satisfactory personal-productivity tool, but also into a platform, or "development environment," suitable for constructing sophisticated, self-running systems for many kinds of business and scientific analyses. Because 1-2-3 macros can even replace the program's own moving-bar-cursor menu array across the top of a user's screens, savvy 1-2-3 programmers were able to produce macro-driven applications which called upon the internal mathematical functions, instant on-screen graphing, data-management and file storage and retrieval functions of the program—all without writing traditional program code for those functions.

Better still for 1-2-3 programmers, the program has become so widely respected as a pioneering leap forward in computer software and so widely accepted as a mainstream business tool that those who write models and templates which run under 1-2-3 can be sure their work will share that cachet which attaches to 1-2-3. They can also be sure, with three million or so buyers and at least three times as many users of 1-2-3, that their work will be almost immediately usable, without an undue learning curve. Anyone who doubts the extent of the penetration of 1-2-3 into the U.S. business community need only read through the executive/managerial or secretarial/clerical classified ads in any big-city newspaper on Sundays: a very high percentage of the ads include lines such as "1-2-3 experience required."

But macros, while they have created a subindustry, are misunderstood if they are seen only as the key to turning 1-2-3 into a development environment. From the quick, ad hoc macro written to handle a repetitive task (such as entering a repeating label across a worksheet) to the complex macros that jump users to specific points in big tasks, then pause for data entry (as in large-scale account reconciliation models), macros are first and foremost individual productivity tools. They can make working with 1-2-3 models faster; they can extend the power of 1-2-3 to assistants, secretaries, and clerks who may not themselves know very much about using the program; they can actually make using Lotus more fun. Doubt the last claim? Just watch an experienced, blase 1-2-3 user break into a grin as a macro he or she has written ripples through a worksheet, adjusting column widths or pausing for new entries from the keyboard or recalculating the sheet—or all three.

Unfortunately, there is a dark side to 1-2-3 macros, as well. Over the years since Lotus introduced 1-2-3, countless gurus and self-proclaimed power users have shamelessly brow-beaten their colleagues over their failure to learn and use macros in virtually every spreadsheet, and mocked the computer skills of those who haven't taken the time to learn how to write a 1-2-3 macro. That kind of self-aggrandizing behavior is as embarrassing as it is commonplace in large organizations.

Whether you're a heavy 1-2-3 user who's still trying to dig deeper into the more arcane corners of Lotus macros, or a casual user who's grown tired of having sand kicked in your face by the 1-2-3-guru bullies, this book's for you. Dick Ridington and Scott Tucker have reduced the art of creating 1-2-3 macros to a few simple steps, with explanations and guidance far better than you'll find in the Lotus manuals. Even better, they've subtly shown how and when macros can make a real difference in the time you spend building and manipulating 1-2-3 worksheets. Because that's part of the game, too: knowing when a rewrite of a few 1-2-3 formulas will produce a cleaner, easier to understand, easier to use, faster-calculating worksheet than one driven by a huge, complex macro.

You don't have to learn how to use macros to get a lot out of 1-2-3. Kapor and Sachs, and their successors at Lotus in the continuing evolution of the program, have done a splendid job of making much of the power of 1-2-3 accessible to even the casual user. But if you want to cross that last bridge, and open the last inner leaves of the Lotus blossom, you'll want to master writing and using 1-2-3 macros. This book is the place to start.

Jim Seymour
Austin, Texas

Introduction

Prerequisites

There are a few things you'll need to get the most from this book.

- You'll need Lotus 1-2-3, Release 2, 2.01, or 2.2.

- You can also use 1-2-3 Release 3. The macros you learn here will work very effectively in Release 3. However, since the book was written primarily with Release 2.x in mind, it omits coverage of the key names and keywords unique to Release 3 and of Release 3's macro libraries.

If you are using Lotus 1-2-3 Release 1 or Release 1A, you have two options:
1. Read Chapter 2, which contains information about keystroke macros, and is largely transferrable to earlier releases of 1-2-3. For full coverage of macros in Release 1 or 1A, see *The Hidden Power of Lotus 1-2-3*, Brady, 1985.

2. After reading Chapter 2, read the following chapters on customizing macros. If you want to use the additional capabilities described there, consider upgrading to Release 2.01 or any subsequent release of 1-2-3.

Know the Interactive Use of 1-2-3

You don't need to know anything about macros; this book will teach you that from the beginning. However, you should be comfortable using 1-2-3 to set up a simple worksheet (such as a budget or expense report). If you have yet to learn to do that, we suggest you either attend a training course, or obtain one of the many books on 1-2-3 (Brady's *Lotus 1-2-3 Self Taught on the IBM PC* is one). You might also read LOTUS Magazine, which offers a wide range of tutorials on the use of 1-2-3 (and Symphony).

If you already know how to write a macro, check the table of contents at the beginning of the book and those at the beginning of each chapter to discover the sections that are most relevant to your needs.

Even if you already know 1-2-3, if you don't have a good reference book on the interactive use of 1-2-3, consider getting one. It's not unlikely that as we show you how to automate your work with 1-2-3, we'll mention some commands you are unfamiliar with. A good reference text (such as *Lotus 1-2-3 Self Taught* or the 1-2-3 documentation) will explain them to you.

Section I

Introduction to Macros

1

An Introduction to Macros

Overview

This chapter will introduce you to the subject of macros and how this book can help you learn about them:

What is a macro? Learn what a macro is and how you might use it to enhance your work with 1-2-3.

How can this book help you learn about them? This book is designed to be used in two ways—either as a comprehensive tutorial on macros, or as a quick reference to answer your questions.

What are the prerequisites for reading this book? Here's what we assume you already know, and how to learn those things if you don't already know them.

An Overview of Macros

Why Use Macros?

There are numerous reasons to use macros. 1-2-3 is easier to use with macros than without. The more you use macros, the more effort and time you save.

- Macros can execute an operation more quickly than you can manually. The longer the operation, the more time you'll save. (Just how much depends on the speed of the computer you're using and the 1-2-3 operations the manual keystrokes are performing, but a macro will always be faster than manual keystrokes.)

- Macros can do in only two keystrokes what it would take ten keystrokes or ten thousand keystrokes to do manually.

Here are a few examples of how you might use macros:

- When you have a series of worksheets to print, instead of waiting for each worksheet to print and entering the commands to retrieve and print the next worksheet, you can press two keys and let a macro print the entire series of worksheets unattended.

- If you are keeping data in another program to use with 1-2-3, you can write a macro to handle all the importing and reformatting of your data. Imagine that you keep your accounting files in dBase III Plus. You've exported those files from dBase, whereupon a 1-2-3 macro automatically imports them, reformats them, defines them as a 1-2-3 database, and generates a statistical report.

- You might even write a ready-to-run application to perform your monthly sales analyses, complete with all the prompts, menus, and error checking you'd expect in a standalone program. Someone with scant knowledge of 1-2-3 could then operate the program.

Macros make it possible for more people to use 1-2-3. Because macros reduce the need to remember complex series of commands, they make 1-2-3 accessible to a broader range of people. This has two implications. Because more people can use the program, the productivity of an entire work group can rise significantly, and it frees more experienced users from having to do all the work associated with maintaining a given application. With the assistance of a macro, a novice can post or produce reports from complex worksheets with only minimal training. Particularly in smaller organizations where training time is limited, macros free you to involve more people in the use of a personal computer.

Macros increase your control. Macros allow you to standardize critical operations so they are performed the same way every time, regardless of who performs them. Once an operation has been performed correctly, a macro can ensure the operation will be performed the same way thereafter. For example, a macro can enable a novice to perform the tricky process of combining 1-2-3 worksheets without any prior training.

Macros are fun to write and fun to use. Writing them offers some of the same logical challenge as playing chess while also producing enduring, useful tools. You'll enjoy using 1-2-3 more because macros can remove the tedium, allow others to help with the work, and speed up the work.

Types of Macros

All macros can be classified into two categories:

two kinds
of macros

Those that automatically execute keystrokes.

Those that customize 1-2-3.

Let's review each of those.

Keystroke Macros Are Like Player Pianos

You operate 1-2-3 by pressing keys. For example, to print a report in 1-2-3 you might use the keystrokes */ppagpq*. Those keystrokes consist of the following 1-2-3 operations: press the slash key to display the 1-2-3 menu and select the commands Print Printer Align Go Page Quit.

You use different keys to operate a piano than you do to operate 1-2-3, but the principle is the same: you operate both 1-2-3 and a piano through pressing sequences of keys. Remember the old player pianos? They replayed recorded keystrokes in order to play songs. Likewise, macros replay recorded keystrokes to perform 1-2-3 operations.

keystroke
macros
repeat
keystrokes
verbatim

A macro is just a special kind of label on your 1-2-3 worksheet that stores keystrokes. For example, you might store the keystrokes */ppagpq*. At your command, 1-2-3 will replay those stored keystrokes to repeat the operation they originally performed (in this example, printing a report).

A macro can consist of anywhere from one keystroke to many thousands, so they can repeat all of the things you can do with 1-2-3:

- Enter data and formulas.

- Use function keys (such as the F5 Goto key), directional keys (such as Rightarrow), and editing keys (such as the Escape key).

- Enter commands (such as/Worksheet Column Set-width).

Of course, not only can you write macros that do these things individually, you can combine all of them to make a longer macro that simulates how you work. For example, the macro might:

1. Allow you to enter data in a cell, move the cell pointer to the next cell, and wait for you to enter more data.

2. Write formulas to summarize the data and enter labels to identify it.

3. Save the worksheet and print a report.

Customizing Macros Are Like Programs

In addition to acting like a player piano for 1-2-3, macros enable you to do things with 1-2-3 that you cannot do from the keyboard. For example, you can create prompts of your own design, change the indicator in the top-right corner of your screen, and change the way 1-2-3 responds to errors.

use a macro to develop a program that requires no prior training to use

You can use macros to develop a completely customized 1-2-3 application. So customized, in fact, that the person using it needs to know nothing more than how to turn on the computer. You can decide what someone will see on the screen (regardless of what 1-2-3 would normally show at the time), to solicit information from a user (the macro might ask him for a given month's sales), to have 1-2-3 make decisions based on worksheet conditions (if sales exceed 10%, you can have the macro calculate a bonus to be awarded to the salesperson), to trap errors (if you want someone to enter a number between 0 and 4 and he enters a 5, the macro can ask him to correct the error).

better than a separate language

Use Macros to Enhance Existing Applications. If you compare the features we've just described to those found in standalone programming languages such as BASIC or Pascal, those features don't seem special. After all, any programming language can do those things. What is special about macros is that they not only can do many of the things a programming language can do, they can do them for 1-2-3 applications. The benefits of that are:

build on what you already know

1. You don't have to learn an entirely new program to use them. Compared with the time it would take to learn Pascal, BASIC, or any other programming language, you can learn macros in a relatively short time. Furthermore, you can learn them a little at a time and develop useful macros at each stage in your learning (which is how we'll teach you in this book).

develop quickly

2. You can often develop applications much more quickly with macros than with a separate programming language. Because the basis for any macro application is the powerful engine of 1-2-3, you can save yourself the work of developing those capabilities from scratch with a programming language. That's not to say that such applications don't require substantial work with macros; they do—

but it is still in most cases significantly less work than would be the case with a separate programming facility.

enhance existing worksheets

3. You don't need to build applications from scratch or rewrite your existing worksheets—you can use macros to enhance any of your existing 1-2-3 worksheets.

enhance existing macros as your skills grow

4. Further, as your macro-writing skills evolve, you'll be able to enhance the simple macros with which you began into full-fledged applications. [1]

what does a macro look like?

Shortly, we'll explore in more detail some of the results you can achieve with macros. Before we do, let's take a moment to look at a macro, just as it might appear on your worksheet.

We earlier described the keystrokes required to print a worksheet,/ppagpq (press slash and select Print Printer Align Go Page Quit). Here's how the macro to automate that operation might look on your worksheet:

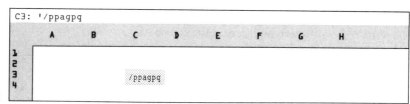

Figure 1-1

If you look in the control panel represented at the top of the screen, you'll see that the macro is a label entry in cell C3. There are other steps you'll need to know before you can use this macro, but you now know what one looks like. Which brings us to our next topic: an exercise in which you can use a macro yourself.

The One Minute Macro

If you've never written a macro and would like to try one, the following exercise is for you. Treat this exercise as an appetizer; we'll save the main course of explanations for later.

---

[1] Such applications, known as turn-key applications, are ones in which the user needs to know nothing about 1-2-3 in order to use them. They customize 1-2-3 so that instead of including the standard 1-2-3 commands and prompts, they provide menus and prompts with which the user is already familiar.

Load 1-2-3 into memory and begin with a blank worksheet. If you already have a worksheet with data on it on your screen, save the file and enter the command /Worksheet Erase Yes to clear the worksheet.

You will next be asked to type a label, the first and last characters of which are a little unusual, but important. The first character is an apostrophe, which is located in the UN-shifted position of the same key as the quotation mark. The last character is a tilde (it looks like a horizontal squiggle; you pronounce it as you do Matilda). Note that the tilde is in the UP-shifted position of its key.

Place the cell pointer in cell A1.

writing
your first
macro

Type: '/wcs30~

Press: Return

Press: /rnc

Type: \a

Press: Return Return

What you'll see on the screen

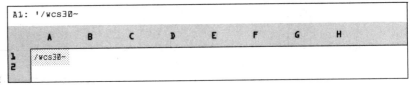

Figure 1-2

check your
work

You've just finished preparing a macro. The mode indicator (in the top right corner of the screen) should now display the word Ready. If it does not, press the Escape key until the word Ready appears, then repeat the preceding steps.

This macro will change the width of a worksheet column to 30 spaces. Observe the current width of column A (the column in which the cell pointer resides).

To prepare to use the macro, locate the key marked "Alt" (it's near the space bar). Watch the screen as you perform the following keystrokes.

activating
the macro

Press: Alt (and hold it down)

Type: a

Release: Alt

Note the change in the width of column A. If you look in the control panel you'll see that column A is now 30 spaces wide. That's what the macro did. You can also use the macro to set the width of any other worksheet column. Move the cell pointer one cell to the right and activate the macro once more (press the Alt key and hold it down, type a, then release the Alt key).

As you've just seen, it's easy to both write and use a macro. In the coming chapters, you'll learn how this macro works and how to write and use other macros.

A Guide to Using the Book

This book is designed to provide you with a comprehensive resource on the subject of macros.

If You Write Macros. Whether you plan to use macros to automate your own worksheet or to develop custom applications for others, this book will show you how. It will help you develop macros that are inherently powerful, easy to learn and simple to use, and structured for ease of maintenance.

If You Supervise Those Who Write Macros. If you're in a position to supervise macro development projects, this book will help you, too. You'll receive a clear explanation of what macros can do, what objectives you should seek from them, and how your organization can maximize its investment in them.

If You Support or Teach Those Who Write Macros. Co-written by a former trainer with curriculum development experience, the book's comprehensive treatment of macros makes it an excellent classroom text. If you've become the expert whom everyone in your department consults for advice, you can use this book to maximize your time. Once you identify what someone needs to know, point out the relevant sections of the book for him to read and apply, then follow up to see if they need help tailoring the solution to their application. Following are some suggestions on how you might put this book to work.

Help with Learning Macros

- For a comprehensive tutorial on macros, read the book from front to back. The book is written both to explain macros and to have you write them, so you'll be spending quite a bit of time with your computer.

- For answers to questions that arise as you use 1-2-3, use the book as a comprehensive reference on macros. Use the tables of contents at the beginning of the book, the overviews at the beginning of each chapter, the liner notes running throughout the text, and the index at the back of the book for quick access to the information you need.

Help with Using Macros on the Job

- The book contains many useful tips and descriptions of a number of undocumented features that can enable you to get your work done faster.

- The book also contains numerous macros. You can reproduce these ready-to-use productivity tools or purchase the optional disk and consolidate them directly into your worksheets.

Help with Using Macros in Organizations

- The book includes standards for controlling the way macros are used in organizations. When more than one person may be responsible for developing or maintaining an application, making the application easy to understand and revise will go a long way toward making it a good investment.

- The book provides a way to explain macros to others you work with. If someone needs to know only a few things about macros, mark those portions of the book for that person to read. To provide a comprehensive course on macros that won't require your time to teach, give that person the entire book.

Tools

The book also contains two tear-out quick reference cards (see inside back cover): one shows how to write a macro for the first time (use it yourself or copy it[2] for beginners you know), the other contains a crib sheet describing the syntax of each of the advanced macro commands.

---

[2] Unlike the other materials in this book and the optional diskette, which are not copyable without written authorization from the copyright holders, you may copy and distribute the reference cards as long as you meet two conditions: *(1)* The copy you distribute must be complete (you may not omit portions of a reference card) and *(2)* you may not incorporate the copied card into other materials for which you charge a fee or otherwise receive remuneration. However, you may distribute the copied reference cards separately along with such materials.

You can also obtain the Inside Lotus 1-2-3 Macros Tutorial Disk, which contains most of the macros used in this book. The Tutorial Disk can save you a great deal of time because it lets you use the macros in the book without keying them in yourself. The Disk presents you with a menu driven macro library from which you can combine macros into your own worksheets. Use the tear-out card bound into this book to obtain the Tutorial Disk. [3]

How to Find Definitions of Words You Don't Understand

You'll find all of the macro-related terms defined when we first use them. If you're skimming the book (as opposed to reading front to back) and encounter an unfamiliar macro term, a quick trip to the index will help you locate where it's defined.

Special terms related more to 1-2-3 in general than to macros in particular (such as *control panel*), appear in the glossary at the back of the book.

Key Name Conventions

guide to the keys described in this text

The keys identified in the following tables refer to keys found on IBM Personal Computer keyboards, and all compatible keyboards (including the AT keyboard, Enhanced AT Keyboard, and the PS/2 keyboard).

Table 1.1. Keys Found on IBM PC and Compatible Keyboards

	Key Name Used in Text	Key That Name Refers To
Function keys	Help:	F1 function key
	Edit:	F2 function key
	Name:	F3 function key
	Abs:	F4 function key
	Goto:	F5 function key
	Window:	F6 function key
	Query:	F7 function key
	Table:	F8 function key

(Continued)

[3] If the card has been removed, send a check for $30 to Ridington & Tucker, P.O. Box 1122, Cambridge, MA 02142. Orders originating in Massachusetts please add $1.50 sales tax. You will receive a 5.25″ disk unless you specify 3.5″ size.

Table 1.1. Keys Found on IBM PC and Compatible Keyboards
(Continued)

	Key Name Used in Text	Key That Name Refers To
	Calc:	F9 function key
	Graph:	F10 function key
Cursor control keys	Rightarrow:	The cursor control key pointing to the right.
	Leftarrow:	The cursor control key pointing to the left (do not confuse this key with the Backspace key, which usually also has a leftward pointing arrow on it, but is physically separate from the cursor control keys).
	Uparrow:	The cursor control key pointing up.
	Downarrow:	The cursor control key pointing down.
editing keys	Backspace:	An editing key usually emblazoned with a leftward pointing arrow (do not confuse it with the Leftarrow key, which is located among the other cursor control keys).

Next

In the next chapter, you'll learn how to write keystroke macros that can enter labels, values, and formulas on the worksheet, move the cell pointer, select function keys, and enter 1-2-3 commands for you. In short, you'll learn to automate through macros everything you now do manually with 1-2-3.

Keep Pace with
Today's Micro-
computer
Technology with:

Brady Books
and
Software

Brady Books and software
are always up-to-the-
minute and geared to
meet your needs:

- Using major applica-
  tions
- Beginning, intermedi-
  ate, and advanced
  programming
- Covering MS-DOS and
  Macintosh systems
- Business applications
  software
- Star Trek™ games
- Typing Tutor

Available at your local
book or computer store or
order by telephone:
(800) 624-0023

///BradyLine

Insights into
tomorrow's technology
from the authors and
editors of Brady Books

You rely on Brady's bestselling computer books for up-to-
date information about high technology. Now turn to
BradyLine for the details behind the titles.

Find out what new trends in technology spark Brady's authors and
editors. Read about what they're working on, and predicting, for the
future. Get to know the authors through interviews and profiles, and
get to know each other through your questions and comments.

BradyLine keeps you ahead of the trends with the stories behind the
latest computer developments. Informative previews of forthcoming
books and excerpts from new titles keep you apprised of what's going
on in the fields that interest you most.

- Peter Norton on operating systems
- Winn Rosch on hardware
- Jerry Daniels, Mary Jane Mara, Robert Eckhardt, and
  Cynthia Harriman on Macintosh development, productivity, and
  connectivity

Get the Spark. Get *BradyLine*.

Published quarterly, beginning with the Summer 1990 issue. Free exclusively to
our customers. Just fill out and mail this card to begin your subscription.

Name _____

Address _____

City _____ State _____ Zip _____

Name of Book Purchased _____

Date of Purchase _____

Where was this book purchased? *(circle one)*

Retail Store   Computer Store   Mail Order

*Mail this card for
your free subscrip-
tion to BradyLine*

F
R
E
E

67-46352

College Marketing Group
50 Cross Street
Winchester, MA 01890

ATT: **Cheryl Read**

Section II

Keystroke Macros

2

Keystroke Macros

Overview

This chapter is about keystroke macros and, in its first part, you can choose from two ways to learn about macros: the Quick course and the Detailed course. Both paths cover the same essentials:

- Automating simple keystrokes (such as labels, values, and commands).

- Incorporating special keys (such as directional, function, and editing keys) in macros.

- Making macros interactive with their user (such as when a macro pauses midstream to enable you to enter data, and then proceeds).

However, the two paths, the Quick and the Detailed courses, are in other ways designed to meet two separate sets of needs. Here are their primary objectives:

acquiring a good set of tools

- The Quick course will give you a brief introduction to the varieties of keystroke macros and provide a host of macros you can immediately put to work on existing worksheets. You'll also learn to modify those macros and write simple variations of them from scratch.

- The Detailed course progresses more slowly but provides you with an expert understanding of how keystroke macros work. You'll learn many useful techniques and general principles that will enable you to write any kind of keystroke macro. If you're planning to write the more sophisticated, soup-to-nuts applications that occupy section IV, you should know that those chapters assume a strong grasp of keystroke macros—a much stronger grasp than the Quick course can provide. Before proceeding to them we recommend that you read, or at least skim, the Detailed course.

options:
when to
read which
course

Naturally, you may read both the Quick course and the Detailed course (the former directly precedes the latter in the text). In any event, if you have difficulty understanding any material in the Quick course, skip directly to the Detailed course. The more rigorous instructions you'll find there should remedy any problems you have with the Quick course. If you skip the Quick course in favor of the Detailed one, return to the Quick course when you've finished to review the many macro examples that appear there.

In the latter portion of this chapter, the two paths unite. There you'll learn:

- How to store your favorite macros in library files and retrieve them from any worksheet.

- How to take advantage of a host of additional automation functions, including how to automate form-oriented data entry, how to have a macro activate itself, and how to designate a file to load itself.

- How to write macros that automatically repeat themselves.

- How to diagnose and solve some of the trickier problems you may encounter in keystroke macros.

- How to write macros that respond to a variety of needs by dynamically modifying themselves.

Keystroke Macros: The Quick Course

Here you'll learn about macros by using them. We'll keep explanations to a minimum to get you moving as quickly as possible. Copy and use these macros verbatim (or, to save time and reduce transcription errors, combine them all at once from the optional disk).

Beginning with a new worksheet, precisely reproduce the following screen.

	A	B	C	D	E	F	G	H
1	\A	Total~						
2								
3	\B	100~						
4								
5	\C	@now~						
6								
7	\D	'100 Elm Street~						
8								
9	\E	/wcs25~						
10								
11	\F	@now~						
12		/rfd2~						
13								

Figure 2-1

Notes:

- Leave blank rows where you see them on the model.

- All macros are labels, so in the examples above you must enter each macro as a label. In cells such as B3, you must force 1-2-3 to regard the entry as a label by beginning it with an apostrophe label prefix.

- The label in cell B7 begins with two apostrophes—you can see but one on the worksheet because the other acts as a label prefix.

- Produce the entries in column A by typing an apostrophe, the backslash, and the appropriate letter. Don't confuse the backslash with the slash— the difference matters.

assign macro range names

Next, you'll assign range names to the macros: Place the cell pointer on cell A1, select / Range Name Labels Right, press the PageDown key, and press Return. Now press the Goto and Name function keys: the range names you just created should appear in the control panel. Select one to verify that it refers to a macro label.

always save your file before activating a new macro

In the next step, you're going to activate the macros. In this case, you're activating macros entered on an otherwise empty worksheet. Normally, your worksheet will also contain data. Although you write macros to help you, if improperly written, they have the potential to do quite a bit of harm, usually in the form of overwriting existing data. To protect yourself from this possibility, make it a habit to save your worksheet before using any new macro for the first time. If any mishap occurs, you can reverse it by retrieving the saved worksheet. We won't tell you to save your file each time we introduce a new macro, but we recommend you do so for your own protection.

In Release 2.2, if you have the / Worksheet Global Default Other Undo command set to Enable, you can use the Undo key (Alt-F4) to reverse the effects of most macros. However, because this method doesn't address all the possible problems you might run across, we recommend you follow the preceding maxim: Save your file before executing a macro.

activating a macro: Alt stands in for the backslash

Move to a blank area of the worksheet and activate the first macro by holding down the Alt key and pressing A (henceforth, we'll refer to that key sequence as Alt-A). You'll see the word Total appear on your worksheet because Alt-A tells 1-2-3 to read the macro stored in cell B1.

In different cells, try each of the next three macros: \B through \D. To activate any macro, substitute the Alt key for the backslash key—so you activate the \B macro with the keystrokes Alt-B.

In Release 2.2, you can choose another way to run macros. Press Alt-F3 (known as the Run key) and 1-2-3 will display a menu of all extant range names. Highlight a name that refers to a cell containing the first line of a macro and 1-2-3 will run that macro. The Run key makes it easier to activate macros for two reasons. It displays a menu of range names, so you don't have to remember those names. It also lets you name macros with any valid range name, so you no longer have to designate macros with a name consisting of a backslash-single letter combination. You can use more meaningful range names.

However, remember that the Run-key menu will show you all extant range names, not just those referring to cells containing macros. For that reason, you may wish to differentiate the names you assign to cells containing macros from those you assign to any other range name. Also note that if you don't name a macro with the backslash-letter combination, you cannot use the Alt-letter keystrokes to run that macro; you must use the Run key.[4]

The last of the preceding macros is a bit unusual in that it starts with a label prefix. Here's why. When you activate a macro, 1-2-3 merely simulates what you would ordinarily type at the keyboard by retyping the keystrokes stored in the macro label. If you were typing a label entry that began with a number, you'd begin the entry by typing a label prefix; in order to have 1-2-3 do the same thing, you put the label prefix in the macro.

---

[4] For that reason, if you want to use macros created in Release 2.2 with Release 2.01 or a lower release of 1-2-3, you should name your macros only with the backslash-letter convention.

a macro that
enters 1-2-3
commands

Let's move on to the next macro, \E. To see what this macro does, key it in manually by typing the keystrokes it contains. Substitute the Return key for the tilde. As you'll see, this macro will set the current column to 25 spaces by selecting the command / Worksheet Column-Set Width, entering 25, and pressing Return. Now use the macro to do the same thing; press Alt-E.

The next macro does two things; it enters a formula (@now) and then formats the current cell as Date Format 2. Move to an empty cell and press Alt-F to try it. Notice that the \F macro is in two successive cells on the worksheet. It's important that there be no empty cells between those two sets of macro instructions in order for 1-2-3 to read them as one macro. Conversely, it's important that the preceding macros be physically separated by at least one empty cell to keep them from being merged into a single long macro.

a single
macro must
be in
successive
cells;
separate
macros
must be
separated
by an
empty cell

You've now written and used macros that enter labels, values, formulas, 1-2-3 commands, and combinations thereof. Now let's write some macros that employ the nonalphanumeric keys (the nonalphanumeric keys encompass such keys as the function keys, the editing keys, and the directional keys).

writing
special key
names in
macros

If you like, save the worksheet to preserve your work, then select / Worksheet Erase Yes to start with a fresh worksheet and reproduce the following screen. Be sure you use braces (which are curly)—not brackets (which are angular) or parentheses—to enclose the word *down* in the macros. Having said that, we should point out that there is an open parenthesis in cell B13 and a close parenthesis in cell B16.

After you've finished creating the worksheet, name the macros (place your cell pointer on cell A1, select / Range Name Labels Right, press PageDown, and press Return).

```
       A         B          C        D        E        F        G        H
  1   \A        10{down}
  2             10{down}
  3             10{down}
  4
  5   \B        10{down 2}
  6             10{down 2}
  7             10{down 2}
  8
  9   \C        10{down}
 10             10{down}
 11             10{down}
 12             \-{down}
 13             @sum(
 14             {up 4}
 15             .{end}{down}
 16             )~
 17
```

Figure 2-2

Move to an empty cell and try macro \A by pressing Alt-A. Note the effect of the {down} command in the macro—it represents the Downarrow key on the keyboard. {Down} is the macro *key name* for the Down-arrow key.

Now try the macro named \B by pressing Alt-B. Notice that when you insert a space and a number in the {down} command, 1-2-3 repeats the key the specified number of times.

Now let's look at a small application that enters three numbers in a column and totals them. Move to an empty cell that has at least four empty cells directly beneath it and press Alt-C. Try reading the macro and keying it in manually to discern the function of each keystroke in the macro. If you like, move to another blank range and reactivate the macro.

how to have the macro repeat a special key

Next, you'll see a new version of the \C macro that allows you to specify the numbers. Add the following macro to the worksheet and, to name it, place your cell pointer on cell A18, select / Range Name Labels Right, and press Return. Once again, make sure you've used braces as enclosures.

a macro that allows you to enter data

	A	B	C	D	E	F	G	H
18	\D	{?}{down}						
19		{?}{down}						
20		{?}{down}						
21		\-{down}						
22		@sum(						
23		{up 4}						
24		.{end}{down}						
25		)~						
26								

Figure 2-3

Move to a blank range and activate the macro. 1-2-3 will seem to have ignored your request, but you'll notice a telltale CMD indicator at the bottom of the screen (that tips you that a macro is indeed running). The macro has paused to allow you to enter some data. Type 25 and press Return. 1-2-3 will move down one cell and pause once again. Enter 50, press Return, enter 25, and press Return.

The new command you used in the \D macro, {?}, is known as the interactive command. When 1-2-3 reads it in a macro, the macro will pause to enable you to use the keyboard as if no macro were running. However, as soon as you press Return, the macro resumes. In the \D macro, there were three {?} interactive commands; therefore, when you activate it, there will be three separate pauses in the macro.

Now add the \E macro shown below and assign to it a range name with the / Range Name Labels Right command.

	A	B	C	D	E	F	G	H
27	\E	/wcs{?}~{right}						
28		/wcs{?}~{right}						
29		/wcs{?}~						
30		{left 2}						
31								

Figure 2-4

a variable macro to set column widths

This macro enables you to set the width of three adjacent columns. Activate the macro by pressing Alt-E. When the macro pauses, enter the number of spaces you wish the first column to occupy and press Return. Repeat that twice (although you may change the number you enter with each entry). The last line of the macro will return the cell pointer to the cell from which it began.

Note that you can use the {?} interactive command in the context of any 1-2-3 operation. In an earlier macro, you used it to enter data; here you used it to complete a command; elsewhere you might use it to move the cell pointer.

Now that you're acquainted with several of the special key names (such as {down} and {left}), let's look at a comprehensive list of those names.

Table 2.1. List of Key Names

Function Key:	Key Name:
F1	{help} [5]
F2	{edit}
F3	{name}
F4	{abs}
F5	{goto}
F6	{window}
F7	{query}
F8	{table}
F9	{calc}
F10	{graph}

[5] In 1-2-3 Releases 2 and 2.01, the Help function key can not be represented in a macro. It is available, however, in Releases 2.2 and 3.

Directional Key:	Key Name:
Tab	{bigright}
Backtab[6]	{bigleft}
Home	{home}
End	{end}
PgUp	{pgup}
PgDn	{pgdn}
Uparrrow	{up} or {u}
Downarrow	{down} or {d}
Leftarrow	{left} or {l}
Rightarrow	{right} or {r}

Editing Key:	Key Name:
Esc	{esc} or {escape}
Backspace	{bs} or {backspace}
Ins	{insert} or {ins}
Del	{del} or {delete}

Note: Releases 2.2 and 3 will recognize either {insert} or {ins} as the Insert key. Releases 2 and 2.01 do not recognize {ins}.

Miscellaneous Key:	Key Name:
Return	~
Tilde	{~}
Left brace	{{}
Right brace	{}}

Note that each of the editing keys except one has two forms. The exception is the Insert key, which you must write {insert}.

It's unlikely that you'll be using any of the Miscellaneous keys except for the tilde. The other keys are useful primarily in advanced applications, which we'll cover later in the book.

---

[6] To use the Backtab key press Shift and Tab. Backtab moves the cell pointer to the left one screen.

Macro Examples

Now that you're familiar with the basics of writing keystroke macros, here are a variety of ready-to-run macros for you to use. In each case, enter the macro as you see it (or combine it directly into your worksheet if you have the optional disk). To assign a name to each macro, place your cell pointer in column A, select / Range Name Labels Right, highlight the labels that appear in column A, and press Return. To activate a macro, check the name that appears to the left of its first cell (that name will consist of a backslash and a single letter). Position the cell pointer to the location where you wish to use the macro, then press Alt and the letter used in the macro name.

If you have difficulty with a macro, take the following steps. Carefully check the macro you've written against the one reproduced here (most macro mistakes result from typographical errors). Try keying the macro's keystrokes yourself and observe carefully what happens (if there's an error in the keystrokes, you should see it). If you can't discover the problem, consult the chapter titled "Debugging Your Macros" on page 150, or read the Detailed course (its meticulous instructions should prevent more problems).

Purpose: Label days of the week

Description: Enters each of the days of the week at the top of the current column and the next six columns to the right.

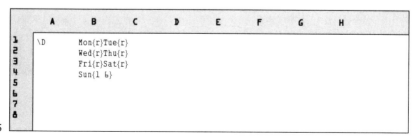

Figure 2-5

Purpose: Widen the current column.

Description: Widens the current column one space at a time. To widen the column by more than one space, hold down the W key when activating the macro.

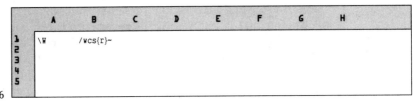

Figure 2-6

Purpose: Set width of a range of columns.

Description: Changes width of a range of columns, pausing for you to highlight the range and set the width.

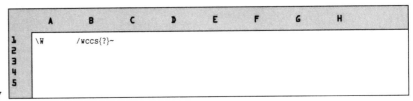

Figure 2-7

Purpose: Reset width of a range of columns.

Description: Changes width of a range of columns back to the global setting.

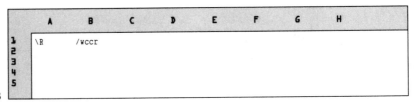

Figure 2-8

Purpose: Clear Worksheet Titles.

Description: Clears the worksheet titles setting (Worksheet Titles Horizontal, Vertical, or Both) currently in effect.

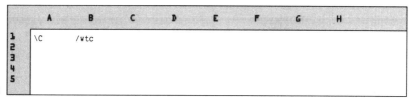

Figure 2-9

Purpose: Unprotect a protected worksheet.

Description: Disables Worksheet Global Protection so that you can make changes to any cell on the worksheet.

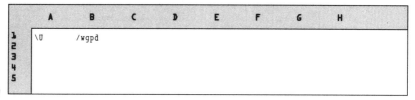

Figure 2-10

Purpose: Protect an unprotected worksheet.

Description: Enables Worksheet Global Protection so that you can change only Range Unprotected cells on the worksheet.

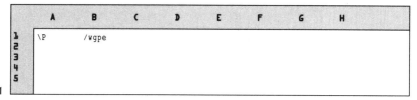

Figure 2-11

Purpose: Turn on Automatic Recalculation.

Description: Changes the worksheet from Manual Recalculation to Automatic Recalculation.

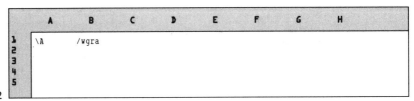

Figure 2-12

Purpose: Turn on Manual Recalculation.

Description: Changes the worksheet from Automatic Recalculation to Manual Recalculation.

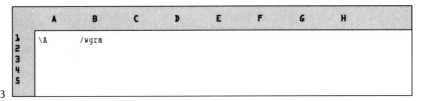

Figure 2-13

Purpose: Copy another cell to the current cell.

Description: Allows you to specify any cell to copy from (either by typing a cell address or by pointing), and automatically copies that to the current cell.

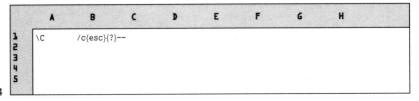

Figure 2-14

Purpose: Move another cell to the current cell.

Description: Place your cell pointer on the destination cell. The macro allows you to specify any cell to move data from (either by typing a cell address or by pointing), and automatically moves that to the current cell.

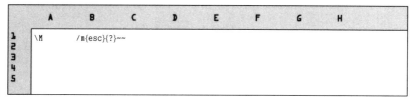

Figure 2-15

Purpose: Justify text.

Description: Justifies any range of text you specify. You may include as many columns and rows as needed.

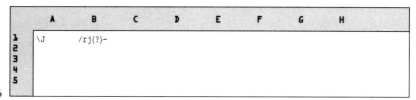

Figure 2-16

Purpose: Search formulas and labels in the worksheet for specified text.

Description: Streamlines the Range Search command introduced in Release 2.2; searches both formulas and labels in the entire worksheet for the string you specify when the macro pauses for input.

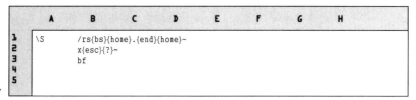

Figure 2-17

Purpose: Shift screen to move current row to top.

Description: Reorients the screen so that the current row will reside on the topmost displayed row.

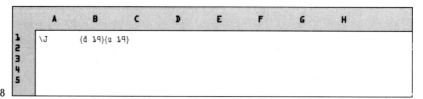

Figure 2-18

Purpose: Set label for 1-2-3 to display in place of zeros.

Description: Instructs 1-2-3 Release 2.2 to display -0- centered in the cell instead of a right-justified 0. Particularly useful since the Global Zero setting is stored neither with the file nor in the 1-2-3 configuration file.

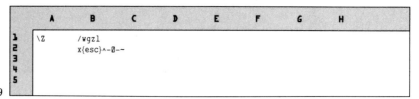

Figure 2-19

Purpose: Print the current print range.

Description: Prints the currently specified print range.

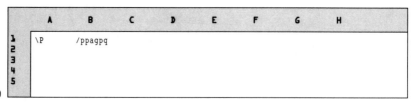

Figure 2-20

Purpose: Alert you when printing is complete.

Description: Prints the current range and, as soon as control returns from the printing operation, alerts you so you can continue your work.

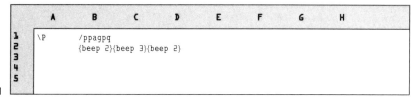

Figure 2-21

Purpose: Print new print range using the current settings.

Description: Cancels any existing print range and allows you to specify a new range (either by pointing or by typing cell addresses). If you want the macro to anchor the cell pointer for you, insert a period directly to the left of the {?} interactive command.

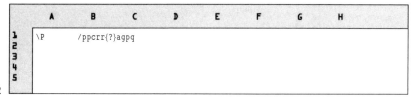

Figure 2-22

Purpose: Select new named print range and print it.

Description: Assuming you have several named ranges, any of which you might want to print, you can select a range from your named ranges and automatically print that range.

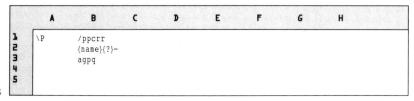

Figure 2-23

Purpose: Print range as displayed, then as formulas.

Description: Print the currently specified range as it's displayed on your screen, then prints the underlying cell contents, including formulas, from the same range.

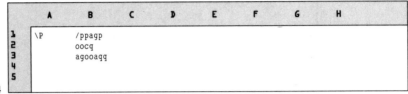

Figure 2-24

Purpose: Input @date formula.

Description: Facilitates entering the year, month, and day arguments used to write an @date function.

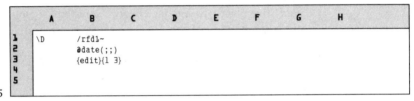

Figure 2-25

Purpose: Rearrange @date formula.

Description: Allows you to enter the three arguments for @date (year, month, and day) in the form month, day, and year. Note: You must press the Return key after entering the month, aftering entering the day, and after entering the year.

	A	B	C	D	E	F	G	H
1	\D	/rfd1~						
2		@date(;;)						
3		{edit}{l 2}{?}						
4		{r}{?}						
5		{home}{r 6}{?}~						

Figure 2-26

Purpose: Date stamp as value.

Description: Places a static date stamp in the current cell (perhaps to mark the last date you posted or revised the model).

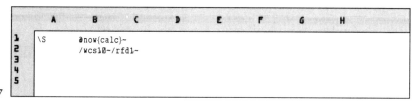

Figure 2-27

Purpose: Create a formatted table of files in the worksheet.

Description: Uses Release 2.2's File Admin Table to populate the worksheet (beginning at the current cell) with the filename, date, time, and size of each worksheet file in the current file directory. Sets appropriate column widths and range formats. This macro assumes that there are two or more worksheet files in the directory.

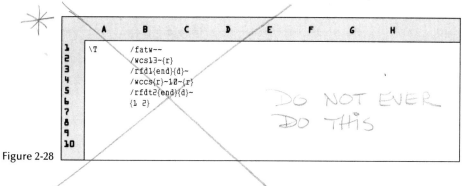

Figure 2-28

Purpose: Define and sort database.

Description: Enables you to redefine the current Data Sort Data-Range and Primary-Key settings, then sort the database in ascending order.

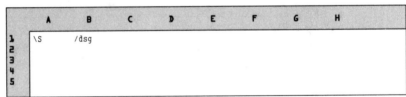

	A	B	C	D	E	F	G	H
1	\D	/dsr						
2		d{?}~						
3		p{?}~						
4		a~g						
5								

Figure 2-29

Purpose: Sort current database.

Description: Sorts the database on the currently specified sort-key(s). Before using this macro, you must have already manually defined a /Data Sort Data-Range and a Primary Key.

	A	B	C	D	E	F	G	H
1	\S	/dsg						
2								
3								
4								
5								

Figure 2-30

Purpose: Sum column of numbers.

Description: Totals a column of numbers and enters separating lines. Place your cell pointer in the cell beneath your bottommost entry in the column and activate the macro.

	A	B	C	D	E	F	G	H
1	\S	\-{d}						
2		@sum({u}{end}{u}.{end}{d})~						
3		{d}						
4		\={u}						
5								

Figure 2-31

Purpose: Refresh the values of all file links in the worksheet.

Description: Assures that your Release 2.2 worksheet calculations are up-to-the-minute by performing a Link-Refresh and a Calc.

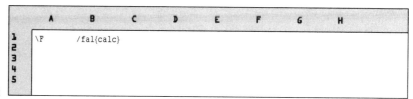

Figure 2-32

Purpose: Format cell as currency with zero decimal places.

Description: Formats the current cell as currency with no decimal places.

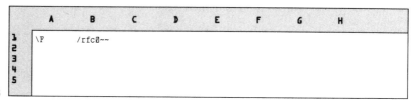

Figure 2-33

Purpose: Format range as C0.

Description: Enables you to format any range as currency with zero decimal places. If you wish to have the macro leave the cell pointer unanchored when it presents you with the prompt "Enter range to format:", place the key name {bs} directly to the left of the {?} interactive command.

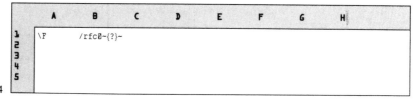

Figure 2-34

Purpose: Make pie graph.

Description: Enables you to specify and display a pie chart. If you don't wish the chart to display in color, change the "c" in line 5 to a "b".

	A	B	C	D	E	F	G	H
1	\G	/grgtp						
2		x{?}~						
3		a{?}~						
4		b{?}~						
5		oc						
6		tf{?}~						
7		ts{?}~						
8		qvq						
9								
10								

Figure 2-35

Purpose: Goto named range.

Description: Enables you to select a range name from a menu and move the cell pointer to that range.

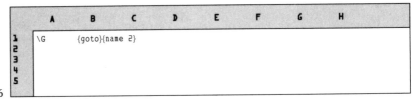

	A	B	C	D	E	F	G	H
1	\G	{goto}{name 2}						
2								
3								
4								
5								

Figure 2-36

Purpose: Save the current worksheet and maintain a backup file.

Description: Release 2.2 macro gives the existing .WK1 disk file a .BAK extension and saves the contents of memory to a .WK1 file, permitting you to revert at any time to the previous version of the file.

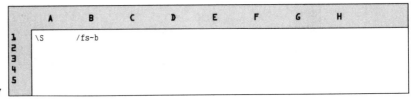

	A	B	C	D	E	F	G	H
1	\S	/fs~b						
2								
3								
4								
5								

Figure 2-37

next

Before proceeding, we suggest you experiment with the foregoing macros for a while. Copy one you're interested in, change the label in column A to a new, unique name, use the / Range Name Labels Right command to assign that name to the macro, and revise the macro. Or, write some macros from scratch.

When you're done, you can either read the Detailed course to learn more about how keystroke macros operate, or skip directly to the section on Macro Libaries.

Keystroke Macros: The Detailed Course

Here you'll learn the fundamentals of how macros work and how to write them. In particular, you'll learn about keystroke macros, the simpler of the two kinds of macros (for information about the two kinds, see Chapter 1).

If you're reading this after having read the Quick course, you already know some of what to do to write a macro. In this section you'll learn how macros work, which will enable you to write a broader range of macros than you've seen to date. Once you understand how 1-2-3 responds to macros, you'll gain a much deeper understanding of them, and that understanding is crucial if you aspire to write sophisticated turn-key applications such as those we'll introduce in the latter portion of the book.

In section one of this course, you'll learn three steps common to writing all keystroke macros. You'll also learn to use those steps to write the three basic kinds of keystroke macros. These tools will enable you to construct an almost endless array of simple macros: worksheet reformatting macros, print macros, worksheet consolidation macros, and a great many more.

In section two, you'll learn to control the power you've been introduced to in this section. You'll learn to comment your macro code to make it easier for others to understand, to structure your macros to make them easier to revise, and to debug your macros to rid them of errors.

In section three, you'll expand your macro skills in two ways: by learning to write multiple line macros and to use the special key names in a macro, and by learning to write macros that are interactive with their user. Because interactive macros can pause during execution and await input of data or commands from the keyboard, they combine the best of both worlds: the speed and automation of macro execution and the control and individuality offered by interactive control of 1-2-3.

One final note before we get started. As we said earlier, although you intend macros to help you, if improperly written, they have the potential to do harm—usually in the form of overwriting existing data stored on the worksheet. To protect against this possibility, make it a habit to save your worksheet before using any new macro for the first time. If any harm occurs, you can reverse it by retrieving the saved worksheet. Note: If you are using Release 2.2, and you have not disabled the Undo function, you can instead press Alt–F4 to reverse the effects of a macro, but you must do so before you do anything else. We won't be telling you to save your file each time we introduce a new macro, but you'd be wise to do so.

In the last chapter, we whisked you through a macro. Here we'll explain in detail the process of writing a macro. In this section, you'll learn to:

- Use the three steps for writing any simple macro.

- Write a macro that enters a label on the worksheet.

Three Steps for Writing a Macro

There are three steps for writing any keystroke macro:

model

1. Model: Manually perform the operation you want the macro to automate. As you do that, record your keystrokes on a piece of paper.

write

2. Write: Using the keystroke record as a guide, write the macro on the worksheet as a label.

name

3. Name: Assign a special range name to the first cell of the macro.

Once you learn these three simple steps, you'll be able to apply them to create different macros, so let's put these steps to work while we learn the three types of keystroke macros.

Three Simple Types of Macros

Type 1: Macros That Enter Labels

Objective: In this exercise, you'll write a macro that types a name on the worksheet.

Step One: Model the Operation

When you do something with 1-2-3—such as entering your name in a cell, you do that by pressing a sequence of keys. For example, if you wanted to enter the name Chris into a cell, you would type **Chris** and press the Return key.

If, instead of writing your name on the worksheet interactively (as we described above), you were to write a macro to perform the same operation, you'd store those keystrokes (we'll describe how to store keystrokes in a moment). Later, when you activate the macro, it will read the stored keystrokes and perform the operation for you.

making your macro accurate

Since a macro is, in effect, a record of the keystrokes needed to perform an operation, it must be accurate and complete. If you record the wrong keystrokes or leave out some of them, when you later activate the macro, it won't properly perform the intended operation.

There's a simple prescription for making sure the macros you write will be accurate and complete: before you write them, you'll model them. Modeling means that you'll perform the operation interactively with 1-2-3 and, on a piece of paper, write down each keystroke as you press it. Because modeling produces an accurate record of keystrokes on which to base your macro, it'll save you a lot of time you'd otherwise spend correcting errors.

steps to perform

Load 1-2-3. If you don't have a blank worksheet on the screen, save whatever you have been working on, then enter / Worksheet Erase Yes to clear the screen. Now follow these instructions:

Move: To cell F1

Type: Chris Johnson

Press: Return

On a sheet of paper, write down the keystrokes you just performed on the worksheet. You should write "Chris Johnson", but you'll recall that you also pressed the Return key, so you must write down that keystroke as well. Because there's no typeable character for the Return key, you'll need some way to symbolize it. When you write macros, you'll use a character called a tilde to do that, so use that character now to represent it on paper. The tilde character looks like a horizontal squiggle (~). Your keystroke record should look like this:

Figure 2-38

Your paper depicts an accurate model of the keystrokes you wish to automate. With that done, you are ready to write the macro itself.

Step Two: Write the Macro

You now have a keystroke record on paper. Your next step is to duplicate that record as a label on the worksheet. That label entry will be a macro.

In the next step, you will type the macro as a label entry. Before you do, locate the tilde on your keyboard. (Note that the location of the tilde varies from one type of keyboard to another.)

all macros
are labels

Move: To cell B3

Type: Chris Johnson~

Press: Return

Look at the new label on the worksheet. Depending on your computer's display adapter, the tilde you've typed may look remarkably like a quotation mark when it appears on the screen. Regardless of the two characters' similar appearances, the tilde and the quotation mark are *not* interchangable. Be sure to type the tilde when you wish to represent the Return key in a macro.

Step Three: Name the Macro

You have a macro label and are now ready to take the last step in writing a macro: assigning to it a special range name.

1-2-3 includes a command, / Range Name Create, which allows you to assign an English–like name to any range on the worksheet. In the case of your macro, that range will be the cell containing the macro. In a moment you'll use that command; but first, a few pointers.

- The name you assign to the macro label must follow a special pattern. Macro range names consist of two characters: a backslash followed by any single letter. For example: \A

Avoid confusing the backslash (\) with the slash (/). If you mistakenly use a slash in place of the backslash, the macro won't work.

- 1-2-3 regards upper and lower case letters as identical in range names, so you may use them interchangably.

- Range names must be unique. No two macros on the same worksheet can share the same range name. However, macros on two different worksheets can share the same range name.

Note: If you have moved the cell pointer, return it to cell B3 now.

naming a
range

Select: / Range Name Create

Type: \A

Press: Return

Note: Look in the control panel. 1-2-3 will specify the address of the cell where the cell pointer resides as the range to receive the name. That is correct, so in the next step, you will accept it.

Press: Return

Now, in anticipation of using the macro, move the cell pointer to cell F5 and, in accordance with our earlier suggestion, save the file.

Move: To cell F5

Select: / File Save

Enter: EX1 (for exercise number one)

You're ready to activate the macro. First you'll depress a special key called the Macro key, then type the letter you included in the macro's range name. The location of the Macro key varies from one computer to another, but on the IBM PC and compatibles, the Macro key is the key marked Alt.

If you are using a computer other than an IBM compatible and it does not have a key marked Alt (it uses some other key as the macro key), consult the 1-2-3 Manual to determine the location of that key. For example, on a Wang computer, use the GL (glossary) key as the Macro key.

As you perform the following keystrokes, watch cell F5.

activating
the macro

Depress: Macro (and hold down)

Type: A

Release: Macro

You should have seen your macro type the name you recorded earlier. However, a macro works so quickly the name probably seemed to materialize on your screen rather than be typed. If your macro did not work as expected, go to the next section entitled "What to Do if the Macro Did Not Work" to discover what went wrong and how to fix it.

In Release 2.2, there's another way to name and run a macro. You can assign *any* valid range name to a macro. Since range names can be up to fifteen characters in length and can include spaces, that gives you a lot more flexibility.

If you use a name for a macro that does not conform to the backslash-single letter convention, you cannot run it by pressing Alt and the letter used in the name.[7] Instead, you must use something known as the Run key. Press the Run key (Alt-F3) and you'll see a menu of all extant range names. Highlight the one that refers to the cell containing the macro you want to run and press Return to run it.

The Run key makes it easier to activate macros for two reasons. It displays a menu for range names, so you don't have to remember those names. It lets you name macros with any valid range name; you no longer have to designate macros with a name consisting of a backslash-single letter combination. However, remember that the Run-key menu will show you all extant range names, not just those referring to cells containing macros. For that reason, you may wish to differentiate the names you assign to cells containing macros from those you assign to any other range name. For example, you might want to begin all macro names with the characters M_. So the macro to enter your name might bear the name M_NAME.

Even if your macro worked you may want to read the next section: you will learn how to correct problems that may occur in the future. If you don't care to do that now, skip directly to the section entitled "Summary."

What To Do If the Macro Did Not Work

If your macro did not work as stated above, here's what to do:

1. If your computer "beeped" when you tried to activate the macro, either you did not assign the range name or you assigned an incorrect range name. To fix it, repeat step three above. If that does not work, either start over or refer to Chapter 8, "Debugging Your Macros" to the portion titled "Underlying Problems with Range Names."

---

[7] For that reason, if you want to use Release 2.2 macros with Release 2.01 or a lower release of 1-2-3, you should name your macros only with the backslash-letter convention.

2. If, after you tried to activate the macro, on the edit line of the control panel you saw multiple backslashes followed by an "A", press Escape. You pressed the backslash key and an A; you should instead have pressed the Alt-A keys.

3. If, after activating the macro, you see the letters "Chris Johnson" in the control panel—but not on the worksheet—and 1-2-3 is in Label mode, then you have probably forgotten to place a tilde (~) at the end of your macro label. Check the macro label and, if necessary, edit it and add a tilde to the end.

4. If you had some other problem, refer to the section on Debugging Your Macros that appears in this chapter.

Applications

You now have the ability to write macros that enter text on the worksheet. You can now write those to enter your name, your company's name, or any other label (such as "Total:") you use repetitively. Labels that begin with a number (such as most street addresses) require special care, and we'll explain that in a moment.

For now, experiment with your new macro writing skills by writing several macros that enter text on the worksheet. As you do, keep the following guidelines in mind:

keep the cell pointer away from the macro itself

- If you activate a macro that writes a label entry while the cell pointer highlights the macro itself, you will overwrite the macro with the label typed by the macro. If that happens, you'll have to rewrite your macro, but the range name will remain intact. For now, pick a column (such as column F) in which to place the cell pointer before you activate your macros.

assign proper range names

- Remember that you must assign a unique range name to each macro you write. Each range name should consist of a backslash and a single letter (such as \B). To activate a macro, move the cell pointer to a blank cell, depress the Macro key, and type the letter you used in the range name.

blank cells

- You must leave a blank cell between each macro and the one above or below it in that column.

- Finally, we suggest you enter those macros in column B (we'll explain the reason for that shortly).

Summary

writing the
macro

As you can see, writing a macro is relatively easy when you follow the three steps for writing any simple macro: Modeling, Writing, and Naming. You applied those three steps to write a macro that enters a label (a name) on the worksheet.

using the
macro

To activate a macro, you depress the Macro key and type the letter used in the macro's range name.

You can activate a macro anywhere on the worksheet, but you should pay attention to the context in which you do so. For example, if you have begun typing a label but have not yet entered it on the worksheet, you should not activate a macro designed to set the width of the current column. Were that to happen, since 1-2-3 would be in label mode when you activated the macro, the keystrokes meant to select commands would instead become part of the label you were in the midst of typing.

Before proceeding to the next chapter, do two things:

wrapping
things up

Use the / Range Erase command to eliminate the entries in column F.

Use the / File Save command to save the completed worksheet so you can use it again.

Type 2: Macros That Enter Values and Formulas

Objectives

In this section, you will learn to:

- Write macros that enter values or formulas on the worksheet.

- Write macros that enter labels beginning with a number.

Prerequisites

You should have reviewed material in the prior section on the three steps for writing a macro and how to execute one.

a macro to
write a
value

Begin with a blank worksheet. If you've got something else on your screen, use the / File Save command to save it, then use the / Worksheet Erase Yes command to clear the worksheet.

In the following exercise, you're going to write a macro that enters a value on the worksheet. Your first macro will enter the number 100 as a value entry. To begin, move the cell pointer to a scratch-pad column.

Move: To cell F1

Step 1: Model the Operation

model the
macro

Now you'll model the operation you want to automate with a macro.

Type: 100

Press: Return

Now, on a sheet of paper, write down the keystrokes you just performed on the worksheet.

Write: 100~

Reminder: The tilde (~) symbolizes the Return key. Since you pressed the Return key after typing the number 100, you must represent it in your model of the operation.

write the
macro

Step 2: Write the Macro

Macros are always stored on the worksheet as labels, even when the macro's function is to enter a value. If you store a macro as a value instead of a label, 1-2-3 will not respond when you attempt to activate it.

You may know that when you begin typing an entry with a number, 1-2-3 assumes you wish it to be a value (you'll see the mode indicator change to VALUE to confirm that). The keystrokes we want to store in this macro begin with a number, but because it's a macro, it must be a label. To force 1-2-3 to enter your keystrokes as a label, you must precede them with a label prefix character (such as the apostrophe, which is the label prefix denoting left hand alignment of the label that follows it).

The apostrophe is located on the same key as the quotation mark. Avoid confusing it with the similar mark on the same key as the tilde. If you do, the macro will not work precisely as you intend.

Move: To cell B5

Type: '100~

Press: Return

name the
macro

Step 3: Name the Macro

Your next step is to assign a range name to the cell containing the macro. Like all macro range names, this one must consist of only two characters, a backslash followed by a single letter. Use the range name \B. Upper and lower case letters are insignificant in range names. You may use them interchangeably[8]. If you have moved the cell pointer, return it to cell B5 now.

Enter: / Range Name Create

Note: 1-2-3 will display a menu of stored range names on the third line of the control panel. If you have any other range names in this worksheet, you should see them displayed there. Do not press Return now, or you will select an existing range name as the name for this macro. Instead, type in the new name.

Type: \B

Press: Return

Note: 1-2-3 will display the current cell as the default range to be assigned the name. That is correct, so you will accept it in the next step.

Press: Return

running the
macro

You're finished writing the macro. In the last section, you learned about the special Macro key (on most computers, that's the key marked Alt). You'll use it again now to activate your new macro. Although you will use the Macro key as before, the letter you type will differ from your last exercise. Type the letter you used to name this macro.

As you perform the following keystrokes, watch the screen carefully.

Move: To cell F7

Depress: Macro

Type: B

Release: Macro

You should have seen 1-2-3 enter the number 100. Once again, it happened so quickly that it seemed to materialize in cell F7 rather than have

---

[8] 1-2-3 stores all range names as upper case no matter what case you use when you create each range name.

been typed. If your macro did not work as expected, refer back to "What To Do If the Macro Did Not Work" (Page 40). Now try it again, this time, in a different location.

Move: To cell F8

Depress: Macro

Type: B

Release: Macro

As you can see from the entry now in cell F8, it doesn't matter where you execute this macro—1-2-3 will type the keystrokes stored in the macro wherever the cell pointer resides.

Label Prefixes and Macros

There is another point to be learned about macros that enter values. With the cell pointer in cell F8, look in the control panel at the entry the macro made in cell F8. Do you see a label prefix? You shouldn't; the macro typed the entry as a value.

Compare what you see in the control panel with the macro itself entered in cell B5.

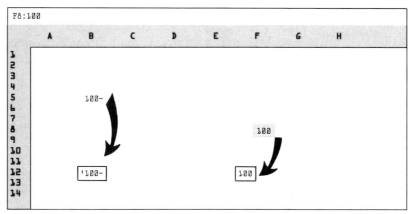

Figure 2-39

macros don't type leading label prefixes

The macro in cell B5 does have a label prefix before it, whereas the resulting value in cell F7 does not. If the label prefix exists in the macro, why didn't 1-2-3 type that character when you activated the macro?

1-2-3 ignores leading label prefixes when it reads a macro. Since all macros must be labels, 1-2-3 assumes the leading label prefix is there because the macro is a label, not because you want it included in the keystrokes stored in the macro.

Why did the "name" macro you used earlier produce an entry with a label prefix preceding it? That macro began typing with the first character of the name you stored in the macro, and that first character was a letter. Any time a letter is the first character entered in a cell, 1-2-3 supplies the leading label prefix automatically. In such cases, 1-2-3 supplies the current Global Label Prefix (you can change the Global Label-Prefix for all subsequent entries with the / Worksheet Global Label-Prefix command).

It's now time for you to practice on your own. Create several macros that enter values, assign valid range names to them, and activate them. As you practice, keep in mind that you must leave a blank cell directly beneath each macro you write.

Macros That Enter Labels Beginning with a Number

You now know how to write a macro that enters a value on the worksheet. However, there will be times when you want a macro to enter a number as a label. For example, "100 Park Avenue" begins with a number, but you do not want 1-2-3 to treat it as a value. For 1-2-3 to accept such an entry, you must force 1-2-3 to regard it as a label.

If you type "100 Park Avenue," 1-2-3 will attempt to treat the entry as a value. When you press Return to enter it on the worksheet, 1-2-3 will sound a beep and revert to Edit mode. In order to enter "100 Park Avenue" on the worksheet, you must force 1-2-3 to treat the entry as a label by preceding it with a label prefix. How will you arrange things so that your macro enters this label prefix for you?

You already know that when a macro executes, it ignores the leading label prefix character found in the macro label and begins by typing the next character.

when to use two label prefixes in a macro

The solution to this challenge is to place a second label prefix in the macro label before the number 100. This second label prefix will be the first visible character in the macro label on the worksheet. The following keystrokes will create a macro demonstrating this principle (note that the second line of keystroke instructions begins with *two* label prefixes):

Move: To cell B7

Type: "100 Park Avenue~

Press: Return

Assign a range name to the macro.

Select: / Range Name Create.

Note: 1-2-3 will display a menu of stored range names on the third line of the control panel. Do not press Return now, or you will select an existing range name as the name for this macro. Instead, type in the new name:

Type: \C

Press: Return

Note: 1-2-3 will display the current cell as the default range to be assigned the name. That is correct, so you will accept it.

Press: Return

Move: To cell F9

Now move to a cell and activate the macro.

Depress: Macro

Type: C

Release: Macro

Examine the resulting entry in the control panel and note the label prefix preceding it.

Writing Formulas with Macros

You can use the same principles to write macros that enter formulas on the worksheet. For example, here are several macro labels that enter formulas:

write
formulas
just as you
would
values

```
'@now~

'10+A5~

'+B7*(10^2)~
```

A macro can enter any formula at all, just as long as you remember to make the macro itself a label entry. In the case where you're storing a formula, which 1-2-3 would ordinarily store as a value, you must force 1-2-3 to store the formula as a label by typing a label prefix character before you type the macro itself.

You can also enter only part of a formula. If you're like most people, you use the @sum function frequently. Even though you may want to specify a different range each time you use it, you can still save keystrokes by storing part of the formula in a macro:

```
'@sum(
```

This macro will type @sum and an open parenthesis, then terminate with the partially typed formula in the control panel. You can then either point or enter a range specification and type a close parenthesis to complete the formula.

Optional Exercise

sometimes
the best
way to see
why you
should do
something
in a macro
is to do the
opposite

What would happen if you were to remove the extra label prefix character? In the next step, you will return the cell pointer to the macro you just wrote and remove the additional label prefix to see the effect it has on 1-2-3 when you activate the macro.

Move: To cell B7

Press: the Edit key (the F2 Function key)

Press: Home

Press: the Delete key

Press: Return

There is no longer a label prefix showing on the worksheet.

Figure 2-40

Even though you have changed the content of the macro, you need not revise the named range you assigned to it. That named range will apply to any macro entered in this cell. Watch and listen carefully as you execute the macro.

Move: To cell F10

Depress: Macro

Type: C

Release: Macro

1-2-3 should have beeped and reverted to Edit mode, indicating it could not accept the entry into a cell. You can either press Home and type the missing label prefix or press Escape to cancel the entry (do one or the other now). Now you'll return to the macro cell and put the missing label prefix back into the macro label.

Move: To cell B7

Press: The Edit key

Press: Home

Type: '

Press: Return

Summary

Wrap Up

- / Range Erase the entries in your scratch column, column F.

- Use the / File Save command to save your worksheet so you can use it again later. Use the name EX2, for exercise number two.

Summary

You learned to write macros that enter values or formulas on the worksheet as well as macros that enter labels beginning with a number.

There are three points to keep in mind from this section:

macros are always labels

Regardless of what data a macro may enter, the macro itself must always be a label.

If, after you've begun typing a macro, the mode indicator displays the word VALUE, press the Edit key, press the Home key, and type an apostrophe to convert the entry to a label. You can avoid that problem. When you begin typing a macro label that will enter a value or a formula, type a label prefix as the first character of that label.

If the macro must type a label that begins with a number (such as "10 Elm Street"), then the macro label should begin with *two* label prefixes (you'll see both label prefixes if you look at the macro label in the control panel, but only one such label will be visible on the worksheet).

more practice questions

Experiment with some macros that will help you practice these skills. Try writing macros that enter the following:

- The value "50"

- The label "50"

- The label "Fifty"

- The label "50 gallons"

and answers

Here are the macro labels in their entirety. The leading label prefix you'd see in the control panel won't appear on the worksheet (the two views of each label appear in the table below). If an entry has two label-prefixes, the second will appear on the worksheet.

Table 2.2. Macro Labels

Question Number:	What you'll see in the Control Panel:	What you'll see on the Worksheet:
1.	'50~	50~
2.	"50~	'50~
3.	'Fifty~	Fifty~
4.	"50 gallons~	'50 gallons~

Although the macros shown above represent their appearance in the control panel, unless otherwise noted, the macros you'll see throughout the book are represented as they appear on the worksheet. When you look at a macro label in the control panel, just as with any other label, you'll see a leading label prefix that won't appear when you view the same label on the worksheet.

In the next section, you'll learn to write macros that execute 1-2-3 commands.

Type 3: Macros That Enter 1-2-3 Commands

In this section, you will learn to write macros that enter commands. You've already learned how to write macros that enter data (labels, values, and formulas) on the worksheet; now you'll learn to create macros that enter commands. Regardless of which kind of macro you write, the steps you'll use are the same.

formatting
a range
under
macro
control

The first macro you'll write will automate the process of formatting a range. First, enter the value 150 in cell F1 (do that now). Now you'll model the operation you're going to automate.

Step 1: Model the Operation

Note: As you execute the commands that follow, keep a written record of your keystrokes on a pad of paper. When you read the upcoming instruction to enter the formatting commands, do so by pressing the first letter of each command (rather than pointing at the command and pressing Return).

Move: To cell F1

Select: / Range Format Currency

Press: Return Return

Your keystroke record should look different than the ones you wrote earlier. Those keystroke records looked exactly like words and numbers with a few tildes appended to them. In this case, your keystroke record won't resemble any words. Keep in mind that although you selected the commands Range Format Currency, you pressed only the keys R, F, and C to do that. *It is the keys you actually pressed—not the commands those keys selected for you*—that you should record.

Your keystroke record should look like this: /rfc~~

You now know how to enter the commands interactively, and you have an accurate keystroke record to use as the basis for a macro. Before you reproduce your keystroke record as a macro label, ask yourself what will happen if you begin that label by typing the first character of your keystroke record, the slash.

like other macros, these are label entries

When 1-2-3 is in Ready mode, if you press the slash key you will display a menu. That isn't what you want to do here; you want to write a macro label. The solution, one you used earlier, is to enter a label prefix as the first character of the macro label.

Step 2: Write the Macro

Move: To cell B3

Type: '/rfc~~

Press: Return

Step 3: Name the Macro

Remember that macros must be assigned a special range name consisting of two characters—a backslash (don't confuse that with a slash) followed by a single letter. In previous exercises, you used such range names as \A, \B, and \C. In this exercise, create a range name using whatever the next letter of the alphabet is in your list (for the sake of example, we'll assume that's \D).

Position the cell pointer in the same cell where you entered the macro label.

Select: / Range Name Create

Type: \D

Press: Return Return

You've modeled, written, and named the macro. You're now ready to activate it.

Move: To cell F2

Enter: 150

Note: Watch cell F2 as you activate the macro.

Depress: Macro (Alt)

Type: D

Release: Macro (Alt)

asterisks
indicate that
the column
is too
narrow

Now move the cell pointer elsewhere on the worksheet, enter a value, and activate the macro to format that value. If you ever see asterisks across the cell after activating the macro, the width of the column is insufficient to display the formatted value (1-2-3 displays asterisks instead of truncating values). Use the / Worksheet Column Set-Width command to increase the width of the column until you can see the formatted value on the worksheet.

What To Do If the Macro Did Not Work

If your macro did not work properly, first check to see that the keystrokes in the macro label consist of /rfc~~. If they do and the macro still doesn't work, refer to instructions on pages 40 and 41.

Applications

You are now in a position to automate any simple series of commands you use frequently, including:

- Setting the cells to other formats (for example, the macro label for fixed format with two decimal places is /rff~~).

- Reprinting a worksheet (if you've already specified a range to be printed, the macro label is /ppagpq).

- Resaving a file that's already on the disk (/fs~r).

exercise

For practice, try writing a macro that changes the width of a column to 35 spaces. Remember the process:

1. Perform the operation manually, and accurately record the keystrokes you use.

2. Transcribe the keystroke record into a macro label.

3. Assign a special range name to the cell containing the macro label.

Solution. The macro that would set the current column width to 35 would look like this on the worksheet: /wcs35~

Summary

Wrap-up. Before proceeding, do two things: *(1)* Erase the entries you made in column F with the / Range Erase command. *(2)* Save the worksheet with the / File Save command. Use the name EX3 to represent exercise number three.

To summarize, in this section, you learned to store commands as a macro label. In particular, you learned that when you write a macro that begins with a series of commands, you must precede it with a label prefix. If you fail to do so, intead of writing a macro label, 1-2-3 will immediately execute the commands.

In the next section, you will learn how to:

- Write labels consisting of more than one line.

- Combine different kinds of macros.

Two Ways to Revise Macros

Now that you know how to write a wide variety of macros, you should also know that you may not have to—the macros you have already written may do just fine if you change them a bit.

For example, if you've written a macro to change the width of a column to 35 spaces (/wcs35~) and you need a macro to change the width of a column to 45 spaces (/wcs45~), notice that there's only one character difference between the two macros. Similarly, if you have a macro to format a range as Fixed with two decimal places (/rff~~) and you want a macro to format a range as Comma with two decimal places (/rf,~~), the two macros are identical with the exception of one character.

Since macros are labels, you can edit them just as you can any other label on your worksheet. There are two ways we commonly revise macros.

you can edit
a macro just
as you can
any other
label

1. If you want to the replace the current macro with another similar macro, place the cell pointer on the cell containing the macro label you want to change, press the Edit key, and revise it. Press Return when you are done. For example, the macro to set the current column-width to 30, /wcs30~, can become a macro to reset the current column-width to its default setting, /wcr. After you've changed the macro, you do not need to assign it another range name. The range name you originally assigned remains intact.

you can also
copy that
label and
revise it—
but
remember
to name the
copy

2. If you want to leave the current macro intact and you need another macro similar to the one you already have, use the / Copy command to create a copy of the current macro. Make sure to leave at least one blank space beneath each macro. Then place the cell pointer on the new label, press the Edit key, and revise the label. After you've finished editing, press Return. You must now assign a new range name to the new label (the old range name remains with the old label). With the cell pointer on the new label (or on the first label of the new macro if the macro you copied is a multiple-line macro), enter / Range Name Create, enter a new macro name (such as \B) and press Return twice.

Multiple-Line Macros

Objectives:

- To learn to write macros that consist of more than one line.
- To learn to combine existing macros.
- To learn to stop a macro.

write
macros that
mix the
ability to
enter
commands,
enter text,
and enter
values

You've already written macros that perform a variety of useful functions. In this lesson, you'll learn how to create macros that mix each of the types you've covered so far. The first example will encompass the sequence of (1) entering a value on the worksheet and (2) formatting the cell containing that value as Currency with two decimal places.

Step 1: Model the Operation

Begin with a blank worksheet. Move your cell pointer to column F and perform the following operations. As you do, record your keystrokes on a separate piece of paper.

Type: 500

Press: Return

Press: / Range Format Currency

Press: Return Return

Now review your keystroke record. Using tildes to represent the Return key, the keystroke record should look something like this:

Figure 2-41

The handwritten content shows "500~/rfc~~"

writing the macro

Step 2: Write the Macro

In cell B3, write a macro label containing the keystrokes for the first part of the operation (entering the value 500 on the worksheet). Remember to begin the macro label with a label prefix.

Here's how the macro should look on the worksheet:

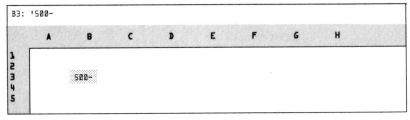

Figure 2-42

In the next step, you'll assign a range name to the cell containing the macro label.

naming the macro

Move: To cell B3

Select: / Range Name Create

Type: \A

Press: Return Return

To verify that the macro works, move the cell pointer to column F and execute the following commands:

Depress: Macro

Type: A

Release: Macro

Note: If the macro did not work, repeat the preceding steps. For more help, refer to the section, "What To Do If the Macro Did Not Work" on page 40.

adding
another line
to the
macro
You now have a single line macro that enters the value 500 on the worksheet. As you can see from your keystroke record, that's only part of the operation you want to perform. In the next step, you'll complete the macro on the line directly beneath the first macro label. Unlike your previous instructions, this time you should not leave a blank cell between the two macro labels.

Move: To cell B4

Type: '/rfc~~

Press: Return

Here's how the macro should now look on the worksheet:

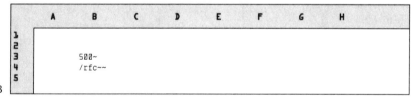

Figure 2-43

Now move your cell pointer back to column F and position it in an empty cell. As you execute the following operation, watch the screen carefully.

Depress: Macro

Type: A

Release: Macro

Although the macro carried out its two operations quickly (just how quickly depends on the speed of your computer), you may have been able to distinguish them:

1. The value 500 appeared in a cell.

2. The value was formatted as Currency with two decimal places.

How Multi-Line Macros Work

You've just written and used a multiple-line macro. Whether a macro has one or more lines, it operates according to several principles common to all macros. Here they are.

macros start reading the named cell . . .

(1.) 1-2-3 always begins reading a macro in the cell named by the special range name. Notice that the range to be named need only encompass the first cell of the macro. You don't have to extend that named range to include all the labels in the macro.

In the exercise you just completed, the macro range name was assigned to cell B3, which contained the macro label 500~. When activated, the macro's first action was to enter those keystrokes on the worksheet. The reason that the macro entered the keystrokes in the same order you did (that is, 500~ and not ~005), is because 1-2-3 reads macro labels from left to right, just as we read.

. . . and proceed with the one directly beneath . . .

(2.) When 1-2-3 finishes reading the contents of one cell of a macro, it immediately looks to the cell directly below (one row down in the same column). In the exercise, 1-2-3 read the first cell in the macro containing the label 500~. When it finished, 1-2-3 continued reading keystrokes in the cell directly below. The cell below contained the instructions "/rfc~~".

. . . until reaching a blank cell.

(3.) When 1-2-3 encounters a blank cell while reading a macro, it terminates the macro and returns to interactive mode. After reading the contents of cell B4 (containing the macro label "/rfc~~"), 1-2-3 continued reading in cell B5. Since cell B5 is blank, the macro ended.

Multi-Line Macros as Newspapers

1-2-3 reads macros like you read newspaper columns

Here's another way to understand multiple-line macros. Think of your worksheet as a newspaper—the multiple-line macro is like a newspaper article and the uppermost label in the macro (the one that bears the special range name) is the start of that article. The macro, like a newspaper article, must be written in one column. When you activate the macro, 1-2-3 begins reading the macro at the top and, like a newspaper reader, reads from left to right. When it reads to the right side of the column, it drops to the next row down in the same column and continues reading (it does not read across columns). When 1-2-3 encounters a blank cell (signalling the end of the story), it stops reading and the macro ends.

Flow of Control

The concept you are learning about is sometimes referred to as "flow of control." While the macro is running, you might say 1-2-3 is being controlled by a macro rather than by the keyboard.

where the flow starts . . .

When you press the Macro key and type a letter (such as A), 1-2-3 looks up the location of the cell with the two character range name (such as \A) that includes that letter. It transfers control from the keyboard (which is what you normally use to control 1-2-3) to the macro, beginning with the first visible character in that cell (in this case, the "5" in "500~"). After 1-2-3 has read and carried out that keystroke, control passes to the next character (the first "0" in "500~") and so forth. When the last character in the first cell has been read (in this case, the tilde following "500"), control passes to the first character in the cell directly below. In aggregate, we have just described the flow of control.

. . . and where it stops.

If the macro reads a blank cell, the macro loses control of 1-2-3. Control returns to the keyboard so that 1-2-3 can be used interactively again. Interestingly, if 1-2-3 reads a cell containing a value, or a formula that returns a value, the macro responds in the same way as it does to a blank cell—the macro ends—because a macro can read only label entries.

it doesn't matter how many lines there are in a macro

Now that you know how to write a macro with several lines in it, you can also write a macro with several hundred lines in it. The principles by which you write them (and by which 1-2-3 reads them) are the same.

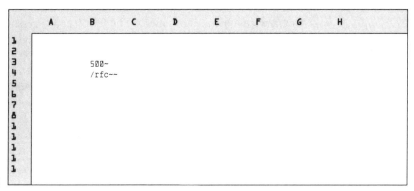

Figure 2-44

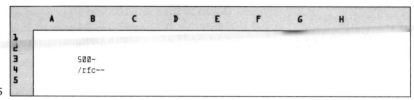

Figure 2-45

Summary

1. Multi-line macros read from left to right across a single cell, then to the cell directly beneath them.

2. The macro range name still has to refer to only the very first cell of the macro.

3. When 1-2-3 reads a blank cell while executing a macro, macro control ends and control returns to the keyboard. A cell that returns a value entry has the same effect as a blank cell.

Letting 1-2-3 Write Your Macros

Now that you understand how macros work, let's look at a way to reduce the effort needed to write them: the Learn command. Learn invokes a mode in which 1-2-3 automatically records as a macro any key you type or press. So, if you turn on Learn mode, press the Downarrow key three times, and turn off Learn mode, you'll have a macro consisting of the following: {D}{D}{D}[9]

If you're using Release 2 or 2.01, Learn is available as an add-in (as part of the Value Pack, from Lotus Development); in Release 2.2 it's part of 1-2-3 itself. If you're using the add-in version, refer to the documentation for installation instructions, and install and attach the add-in LEARN.ADN.

Begin with a blank worksheet. The first step is preparatory. You must specify a range within which 1-2-3 will record the keystrokes you type at the keyboard. Select / Worksheet Learn. The three options available include Range, to specify a range within which to record keystrokes; Cancel, to cancel a range you earlier specified with Range; and Erase, to erase anything within the currently specified Learn range. Select Range, move the cell pointer to cell B1, type a period to anchor the cell pointer, press End Down to specify the entire column, and press Return.

---

[9] In the next chapter we'll cover in detail the macro representation for various keys such as Downarrow and Escape. You can, nonetheless, use Learn to write them for you for now.

If you fail to define a Learn range and you press the Learn key, 1-2-3 will issue the error message "Learn range has not been defined." If you fill the Learn range, 1-2-3 will issue the error message "Learn range full" and will fail to record the last two keystrokes you've entered.

Now activate Learn mode and begin recording keystrokes: Press the Learn key (Alt-F5). Note the Learn indicator at the bottom center of your screen. As long as you see that indicator, 1-2-3 will record your keystrokes in the Learn range. Select / Worksheet Column Set-Width, type 15, and press Return. Press Learn (Alt-F5) again to turn off Learn mode, and note that the Learn indicator disappears.

1-2-3 shows a Calc indicator at the bottom of the screen, even though you did not set the / Worksheet Global Recalculation command to Manual. Press Return. The keystrokes you just recorded will appear on the screen, and the Calc indicator will disappear. The macro label that appears on cell B1 is /wcs15~. To run this macro, you need to assign to it a range name. Select / Range Name Create, enter \a, and specify cell B1. Now you can run this macro as you would any other: Move the cell pointer one column to the right, press the Macro key (Alt) and type A.

If you turn on Learn mode again, 1-2-3 will record beginning in cell B2 the next keystrokes you enter. If you intend the second set of keystrokes to be a part of the ones above, that's fine, as you will have created a multi-line macro.

However, if that's not what you wish, you can do one of two things. Option one: Select / Worksheet Learn Range, type the period key twice to view the top of the existing Learn range, press the Downarrow key twice to shorten the range, and press Return. When you next use Learn mode, the first line of the resulting macro will appear in cell B3. Then, when you later run the macro you named \a, the intervening blank cell will prevent 1-2-3 from running both macros.

Option two: Leave the Learn range alone, record your macro, and later use the Move command to move the resulting macro down one cell. That way you'll get a blank cell between the two macros and you won't have to fiddle with the Learn range specification.

Learn is relatively inefficient in its use of the cells it fills with macro labels. For example, if you press the Downarrow key four times with Learn mode on, it'll record each keystroke in four successive cells. Each command sequence, such as / Worksheet Column Set-Width 15, will appear in one cell. If any single command sequence is too lengthy, Learn will break it across two or more cells.

As you use Learn mode with command sequences, Learn will record every keystroke you use. For that reason, use the first letters of each command. To illustrate the problem of instead using the arrow keys to highlight commands you want to select, consider the following examples. If you press the slash key and select the Worksheet command by pressing Return, Learn will record /~, not /w.

Similarly, If you resave the current worksheet by pressing the slash key, pressing Rightarrow four times and pressing Return (to select File), pressing Rightarrow once and pressing Return (to select Save), pressing Return (to accept the current filename), pressing Rightarrow once and pressing Return (to Select Replace), Learn will record /{R}{R}{R}{R}~{R}~~{R}~.

If you performed the same operation using the first letters of the commands, you'd press slash, type fs, press Return, and type r. Learn would record the more succinct, readable macro /fs~r. And, as in other areas of your work, macros that are more succinct and more readable are preferable to those that are not.

While you can avoid the preceding problem easily enough, a problem you may be unable to avoid is making an occasional error while in Learn mode. For example, suppose that you selected an incorrect command, then press Escape to cancel it and select the correct command. Learn will record all the keys you pressed, including the Escape key.

While it won't hurt to leave the macro as Learn has written it, each time you run the macro, that macro too will select the wrong command, press the Escape key, and then select the right command. The first two operations are unnecessary. You can use the Edit key to modify the macro to eliminate the characters representing the Escape keystroke, {ESC}, and those representing the wrong command.

Learn mode is a helpful tool for recording macros any time you're unsure of the keystrokes that go into a macro. Once you learn those keystrokes, you may prefer to write the macros yourself. Not only is it quicker, but you can control how many keystrokes you record on each line. Learn makes that decision for you. Once made, it is not easy to change. Note: A technique for doing just that appears in the chapter entitled Macro Libraries, under the subhead *Macro Library Manager Tips*.

How To Build on Existing Macros

save time by retro-fitting existing macros to serve new purposes

One way to build longer macros is to write them from scratch. Another way is to reuse all or part of macros you've already written.

We've already shown you how to copy existing macros and edit them, now let's look at how you can combine existing macros to form longer, more capable ones.

Suppose your worksheet looks like the one shown below:

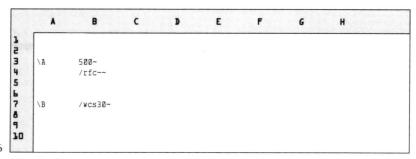

Figure 2-46

Use the / Copy command to copy the macro label in cell B7 to cell B5. The revised worksheet looks like this:

```
          A         B         C         D         E         F         G         H
   1
   2
   3    \A        500~
   4              /rfc~~
   5              /wcs30~
   6
   7    \B        /wcs30~
   8
   9
   10
```

Figure 2-47

Now, activate the newly lengthened macro by pressing Macro A and observe the result.

Points To Remember:

1. Your macro must still consist of an unbroken column of macro entries beginning with the cell named with the special range name.

2. You should **not** need to assign a new range name to the newly lengthened macro. 1-2-3 will read the new label as part of the macro because the new label is in the cell directly beneath the last existing entry.

3. After copying the macro code to its new location, you may wish to use the Edit key to modify it to precisely suit the needs of the new macro (in the example above, you might want to change the copied label /wcs30~ to /wcs15~).

Adding Style to Your Macros

Up until now we've dealt with the things that you *must* do when writing a macro. Now let's talk about something that's entirely discretionary: style. For many people, style is a matter of personal preference and convenience. However, for a growing number of people, choice of style is dictated by their need to make the macro as easy as possible to understand and to revise.

Macro Labels Can Be Any Length

You know that a cell can store a label longer than that cell's width. Suppose there is a label 18 characters long in cell A1. Since cell A1 is only nine spaces wide, 9 characters spill over to the right. If cell B1 is empty and 9 spaces wide, those 9 characters will appear to fill cell B1 as well. Appearances aside, the long label is entirely stored in cell A1, as you can see if you move the cell pointer to cell A1 and look at the cell entry in the control panel.

long macro labels are still stored in the cell in which they were entered

Macro labels can also be wider than the cell in which they are stored. Although they may appear to overwrite a blank cell to their right, the macro label is still stored entirely in the left-most cell.

Regardless of the length of a macro label, 1-2-3 will read the entire label if it is stored in a cell being read as a macro. However, 1-2-3 will not read macro labels that are actually stored in the cell to the right. Successive labels in a single macro must be stored in successive cells in the same column (that is, they proceed down the column, not across the row).

The limit on the length of any one macro label is 1-2-3's limit of 240 characters per cell. However, now that you know how to write multiple line macros, you can write that same macro in successive cells down a column instead of writing it within one cell.

Let's examine our options for writing the macro: one label or several. The screen below shows a single macro label. If the macro range name is assigned to cell B3, when you activate this macro, it will enter the value "500" and format the entry as currency.

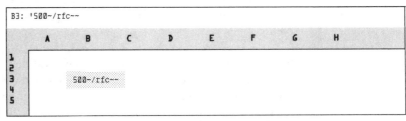

Figure 2-48

The screen below shows the same macro written in two successive cells in the same column. If the range name is assigned to cell B3, when you activate this macro, it will do the same thing as the previous macro.

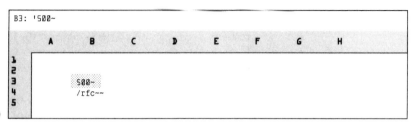

```
B3: '500~

        A       B       C       D       E       F       G       H
   1
   2
   3                   500~
   4                   /rfc~~
   5
```

Figure 2-49

How long should a macro label be before you divide it? That's a matter dictated by style and by a few practical considerations. Let's take the practical considerations first, style afterward.

When you are writing keystroke macros, as we have exclusively so far in this book, you can divide a macro label into two labels at any point. (That is not true with many of the customizing macros you'll write later. We'll discuss those limits in the Advanced Commands section of the book). In other words, if I have a macro that enters a name on the worksheet, any of the following forms will produce the same result:

```
        A       B       C       D       E       F       G       H
   1
   2
   3    \A      Chris~
   4
   5    \B      Chr
   6            is~
   7
   8    \C      C
   9            h
  10            r
  11            i
  12            s
  13            ~
  14
  15
```

Figure 2-50

generally, I keep each macro label short

You may already know that 1-2-3 places a limit of 240 characters per cell (if the entry is a label, that's 239 characters plus the label prefix). While that limit means it's possible to enter lengthy macro labels into a single cell, long macro labels are:

- Difficult to understand.

- Difficult to correct when they contain errors.

- Difficult to revise to encompass new functions.

For those reasons, we recommend that you limit the length of each line of macro code so that it remains entirely visible when you view it on the worksheet. You may further wish to restrict the contents of each label to one group of logical activity.

how to
divide a
macro into
separate
lines

For example, the instructions to print a worksheet might constitute one such group. The 1-2-3 commands to print a worksheet are / Print Printer Range A1..H100 <Return> Align Go Page-Advance Quit. The corresponding macro is /pprA1..H100~agpq. That series of instructions represents one discrete activity (printing a report) and is a good candidate to compose a single macro label. If the macro carried out other instructions following that, you would place them in cells beneath.

Here are two ways to lay out the same macro. They both function identically. Which seems easier to understand?

Below is a macro written in compact form:

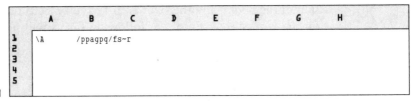

Figure 2-51

The same macro, divided into logical groups:

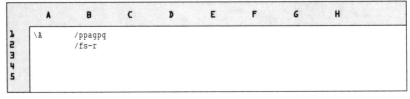

Figure 2-52

Macro Documentation

Keeping your macro labels relatively short is one step you can take to make your macros more managable, but there are others. Let's consider a few other needs:

- If you don't use your macro for a while, how will you remember the names you assigned to the first cell of each macro? If you don't know those names, you cannot activate the macros.

- Why should others in your organization with needs similar to yours write all their macros from scratch? The time you've invested developing your worksheets and macros would go further if others could use them. In order to do so, they'll have to understand your worksheets and macros so they can revise them.

- If you move on to another job, how will the person who replaces you be able to use your macros? What will happen when needs change and that person must modify your macros?

These questions suggest that you should strive to make your worksheets and macros as easy as possible to understand. Let's look at some ways to do that. Here's a worksheet containing several macros you've written in previous exercises:

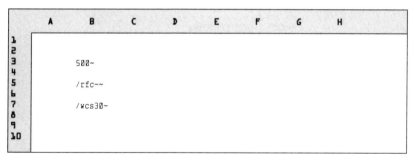

Figure 2-53

needs to
fulfill

To make these macros easier to understand, we need to give them some structure. Our tasks are threefold:

To document the range name assigned to each macro.

To briefly explain the function of each macro.

To provide a well organized environment in which to store macros on the worksheet.

To begin, you'll enter labels to identify the purpose to which you will dedicate each column. In the instructions that follow, when you read the prompt ENTER:, enter the text that follows the prompt into the current cell on the worksheet (the current cell is the cell where the cell pointer currently resides).

Move: To cell A1

Enter: NAME

Move: To cell B1

Enter: MACRO

Move: To cell F1

Enter: COMMENT

Move: To cell A2

Enter: \-

Enter: / Copy

Press: Return

Move: To cell B2

Press: . (the period key)

Press: Rightarrow Rightarrow

Press: Return

The worksheet should now look like this:

headers for
your
macro-
writing
columns

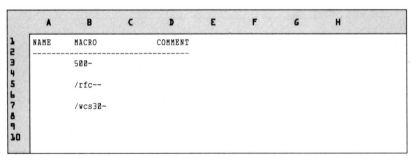

Figure 2-54

So far, so good. You've got three columns, the middle of which has the macro labels in it. Now you'll document the range names assigned to each macro. As you type the following three entries, be sure to precede each of them with a label prefix. If you do not, the backslash, which is intended to be part of each label, will instead function as a label prefix, causing the rest of the label to repeat across the cell.

how to
document
your range
names

Move: To cell A3

Enter: '\a

Move: To cell A5

Enter: '\b

Move: To cell A7

Enter: '\c

The worksheet should now look like this:

	A	B	C	D	E	F	G	H
1	NAME	MACRO		COMMENT				
2	--------------------------------							
3	\A	500~						
4								
5	\B	/rfc~~						
6								
7	\C	/wcs30~						
8								
9								
10								

Figure 2-55

Now you've documented the range names assigned to each macro cell. If in any of the cells in which you've just made entries, you see a repeating letter (for example, aaaaaaaaa) instead of a backslash and a letter (for example, \a), then you need to edit that cell and insert an apostrophe to the left of the label. (If the backslash isn't preceded by an apostrophe, the backslash will act as a label prefix. The backslash label prefix causes the label that follows it to repeat.)

adding
comments
to each line
of your
macro

In the next step, you'll provide brief comments to explain each macro.

Move: To cell F3

Enter: Enter a number

Move: To cell F5

Enter: Format a range

Move: To cell F7

Enter: Set column to 30 spaces

The worksheet should now look like this:

	A	B	C	D	E	F	G	H
1	NAME	MACRO			COMMENT			
2	----	-----	-----	-----	------	-----		
3	\A	500~			Enter a value			
4								
5	\B	/rfc~~			Format a cell			
6								
7	\C	/wcs30~			Set column to 30 spaces			
8								
9								
10								

Figure 2-56

how much is enough?

How much documentation is enough? That depends on you and the business in which you work. The more complex the macros and the more people who need to understand them, the more thorough your documentation should be.

Regardless of your situation, we recommend that you at least document your range names. Beyond that, you can choose among omitting further documentation, including only a descriptive title for each macro, documenting only the more complex lines, or documenting every line in the macro. As you write more macros, consider the needs outlined earlier and formulate a style that works for you.

A Few Documentation Guidelines

the labels in column A don't name the ranges for you

Column A displays the range name assigned to each macro. Keep in mind that the entries in column A do no more than that. It's common to mistakenly believe that because you have entered the label identifying the range name, you have also assigned the range name. Remember that when you write another macro, you should not only enter a label to identify the range name, you must still assign that range name to the macro using the / Range Name Create commands.

Column B displays the macro labels, also known as macro code. Since you've already run these macros, you know that this column contains the only labels needed to run the macro. The labels in columns A and F only document the macros in column B.

Column C contains descriptive comments about each line of the macro. You may not need to describe each line of every macro, but at least part of every macro should be accompanied by comments.

Use the / File Save command to save this file to disk. Now document any other macros you may have written in this fashion.

respond to the situation at hand

Keep in mind that we're not prescribing this structure for every macro. If you're going to write and dispose of a macro in a matter of minutes, you don't need any structure. At a minimum, we recommend that you

document the range name you've assigned to the first cell of the macro.
Adding the comments in the right hand column won't take much longer,
and they'll go a long way toward improving the usefulness of your
macros. Don't be concerned if your macros occupy so much of the screen
that you cannot see both the macro and the comment on the screen together. Even if people have to flip between two screens to read the macro,
as long as there is some documentation, they'll figure things out. Without
documentation, they may not.

Assigning Range Names to Macros the Quick Way

The three part macro structure also makes it easier for you to assign range
names to macros. Here's the worksheet you've just prepared:

```
        A       B       C       D       E       F       G       H
   1  NAME    MACRO           COMMENT
   2  ------------------------------------
   3  \A      500~            Enter a value
   4
   5  \B      /rfc~~          Format a cell
   6
   7  \C      /wcs30~         Set column to 30 spaces
   8
   9
  10
```

Figure 2-57

caution
about
/ Range
Name Reset
command

Before you take the next step, we want to caution you about the next
command. The / Range Name Reset command will remove all range
names from the current worksheet. Since macro applications and the
spreadsheets that accompany them are likely to incorporate many range
names, that command could easily remove a lot of your work.

So, before you use it, let's take a precautionary step. Move the cell
pointer to a blank section of the worksheet and select / Range Name
Table, indicate a cell on the worksheet and press Return. 1-2-3 will enter
on the worksheet a table of range names and the range specifications to
which they refer. If you discover subsequently that you've eliminated
range names in error, you can use the table as a guide to restore them.

Now you can delete the range names in this file by selecting / Range
Name Reset. To verify that the range names are gone:

Press: Goto (F5 on most computers)

Press: Name (F3 on most computers)

If you have any range names, this operation will display a menu of all or some of them in the control panel. Verifying that they have indeed been removed, you should see no names there now.

Press: Escape

naming all
your macro
ranges in
one step

Let's imagine that you have created this worksheet anew and need to assign range names to the macros it contains.

Move: To cell A3

Press: /

Select: Range Name Labels Right

Press: Downarrow Downarrow Downarrow Downarrow

Note: You should have highlighted the range A3..A7

Press: Return

Now, check for those range names once again:

Press: Goto (F5 on most computers)

Press: Name (F3 on most computers)

You should see displayed in the control panel the three range names \A, \B, \C. The Range Name Labels command used the labels on the worksheet to define the range names.

Select: \B

The cell pointer should have moved to cell B5, which is the location of the second macro label and the cell to which the range name \B refers. Let's spend a moment reviewing how this command works. You used the menu choices Range Name (when you used the command Range Name Create) to assign a range name. Range Name Labels Right also assigns range names, but it operates a little differently. The option Labels designates that you wish to use one or more labels on the worksheet to specify the range name(s) you are going to assign (so if the label is the word Sample, that becomes the name of the range). The label or labels you use must be located in a single range (as are the labels in the range A3..A7).

Your next choice is to choose Right, Left, Up, or Down. 1-2-3 can assign the range names created from labels to any of the cells adjacent to those labels. For example, if you have a label in cell B2, you can use that label as a range name for cell A2 (choose Left), cell B1 (Up), cell C2 (Right), or cell B3 (Down). A moment ago, when you selected Range Name Labels Right and indicated the range A3..A7, 1-2-3 assigned a range name to each cell in column B directly to the right of each label in the range A3..A7. Since there are labels in cells A3, A5, and A7; the range names were assigned to cells B3, B5, and B7.

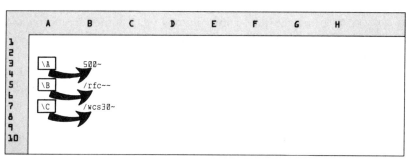

Figure 2-58

caution about the Range Name Labels command

The Range Name Labels command is a powerful addition to your macro-writing skills, but its use subjects you to a common error. Many people think that because they have labels on the worksheet that look like range names, they automatically have range names. In other words, they enter the label \A on the worksheet, and think that they have also created the range name \A, when in fact they did not create the range name. Remember, only the / Range Name command can create a range name. Whether you use Range Name Create or Range Name Labels is immaterial, but you must use one or the other in order to create a macro range name.

There is one other characteristic of the / Range Name Labels command you should know about. If you already have named a range with one of the names included in the column of entries you are about to use with the / Range Name Labels command, the / Range Name Labels command will replace the old named range with the new one.

Where To Place Your Macros on the Worksheet

Where's the best place to store your macros on the worksheet? 1-2-3 Release 2 and subsequent releases use a form of memory management (known as sparse matrix memory) that largely removes memory as a factor in the decision. Whether you place your macros five columns away from your data or one hundred and five columns away, you will use about the same amount of memory (that was not the case in earlier releases of 1-2-3).

One factor that should affect your decision is integrity. Suppose you have a budget spreadsheet on one part of the worksheet. You regularly insert and delete rows of the spreadsheet using the / Worksheet Insert Row and / Worksheet Delete Row commands. Even though your macros may be quite a few columns away, if they are located on the same rows as that spreadsheet, you are inviting trouble. If you delete a row of the spreadsheet and a macro label is also on that row, you'll lose that macro label. If, instead, you insert a row, you'll insert a blank cell in the midst of your macro. When you next activate it, the macro will end prematurely when it reads that blank cell.

You should also be cautious about locating your macros in columns that also contain data. If you use the / Worksheet Delete Column command, you might unintentionally delete your entire macro.

Avoid placing macros on rows you intend to modify with the /Worksheet Insert Row or / Worksheet Delete Row command. If you intend to use these commands in your spreadsheet, the best place for your macros may be beneath your data.

The same caution applies to placing macros in columns you intend to modify with the / Worksheet Delete Column command. While inserting a new column is less serious, it can still cause problems in some macros. If you intend to use these commands with your worksheet, the best place for your macros may be off to the right or left of your spreadsheet data.

What if you're unable to predict how you will use your spreadsheet? Or what if you're going to both delete rows and columns? Then the best place for your macros may be on a diagonal to your data. For example, if your data is in the range A1..M50, you might begin writing your macros in the range Z100..AB150, where the two ranges share neither columns nor rows.

If you've placed your macros somewhere far off on the worksheet and you forget where you placed them, press Goto Name End and Return. When you press Goto (F5), Name (F3), and End, 1-2-3 moves the menu pointer to the last position in the list of range names. Since the character with which macro range names begin, the backslash, has a relatively high LICS[10] number (92), macro range names are often last on the list. You can use that knowledge to locate the macros on any worksheet you review.

---

[10] Lotus International Character Set. LICS is a set of codes and corresponding characters 1-2-3 uses to create the characters you see on the screen. We'll discuss LICS in more detail in Chapter 10.

How To Reduce the Screen Hopping

how to end the hop scotch around the worksheet

We've just introduced two topics that, while helpful, can also complicate your work. First, we suggested you write macros across three columns (with the columns consisting respectively of the range name documentation, macro code, and macro documentation). That structure demands the full width of your screen, so you're likely to need to switch screens to view your data. Second, we advised that you keep your macros physically separate from the worksheet data on which they operate; which again means you'll be changing screens to view your data.

Since most people model some of the operation they want to automate, write some of it, test that part, and then return to model more of the operation, they spend a lot of time hopping from one section of the worksheet to another. That creates two problems: It can be difficult to remember where everything is and all that hopping around can be annoying. Here are two techniques to end all that screen hopping, or at least reduce it significantly.

Speeding Up Screen Switching with Range Names

You can use range names to vastly speed up the hopping around that comes with writing a macro. To begin, move the cell pointer to the top left corner of your macro writing area, then follow these instructions:

Select: / Range Name Create

Type: Macros

Press: Return Return

coupled with range names, the Goto key can whisk you between macros and test area

Now move to the place where you are modeling and testing your macro.

Select: / Range Name Create

Type: Test

Press: Return Return

Press: Goto (F5)

Press: Name (F3)

Select: Macros

You just used the Goto function key to move rapidly from your testing area to your macro-writing area. Use the same procedure and substitute the name Test when you wish to move the cell pointer back to your spreadsheet. If, during the course of developing an application, you accumulate so many range names that you have difficulty scrolling through them, press the Name key twice instead of once in the preceding procedure. You will see a full screen menu of range names from which you will be able to more easily select the proper range name.

There are a few other tricks you can use to further speed the process. You can assign a single letter range name that is a mnemonic for the area of the worksheet to which it refers. For example, instead of assigning the top left cell in the macro-writing area the name Macros, name it M. Then you can press Goto Name, type m, and press Return.

You can also create range names that will appear in the first or last position in the range name menu. Since the first range name is the default selection on the menu, you can move the cell pointer there by pressing Goto Name and pressing Return. To move the cell pointer to the last name, press Goto Name End and press Return.

place range names you often use in the first or last position in 1-2-3's range name menu

It's easy to control which names appear in those positions once you know how 1-2-3 orders the names that appear in a menu of range names. 1-2-3 assigns a numeric code to each of the characters on the worksheet[11] Menus of range names (and menus of file names) appear in ascending order by the LICS code number of each item in the menu, so the characters with the highest code numbers appear at the end of the list. The exclamation mark is the visible character with the lowest code number, so if you begin a range name with an exclamation mark, it'll be listed before range names that begin with some other character. The code for a blank space is even lower, so if you begin a range name with a blank space, it also stands a good chance of being listed first on the range name menu.

If you want a range name to appear at the end of the range name menu, try beginning that range name with a split vertical bar (¦), a character with one of the highest codes of all standard keyboard characters. If you create such a range name, and your other range names begin with a backslash or a letter, then the keystrokes Goto End Return will automatically select that range name and transport you to that range.

---

[11] To ascertain the code number for any character, use the @code function. For example, if you enter an exclamation mark in cell B2, and @code(B2) in cell A2, you'll see the LICS code for an exclamation mark (it's 33).

Eliminating the Screen Switching with Worksheet Windows

If you have but two areas you need to move between, you can eliminate the screen hopping altogether by splitting the screen and using the Window key to move between the two windows.

Place the cell pointer at the top left corner of your macro-writing area. Now, move it down 10 rows in the current column.

Select: / Worksheet Window Horizontal

Select: / Worksheet Window Unsync

We'll explain the Unsync command in a moment. For now, note that the cell pointer resides in the upper window.

Press: The Window key (F6 on most computers)

to change windows, press the F6 key

Note that the cell pointer now resides in the lower window. Move the cell pointer to the place on the worksheet where you are modeling and testing your macro. You can now model and test your macro in the lower window. When you are ready to write the macro, press the Window key (F6). With the cell pointer in the top window, you can write your macro while still observing the worksheet in the lower window.

Whenever you press the Window key, the cell pointer will return to the cell it last occupied in the other window. When you are ready to rejoin the two portions of the display, select / Worksheet Window Clear. If you again split the worksheet display with / Worksheet Window Horizontal, you do not need to reselect / Worksheet Window Unsync. The latter command establishes a setting that this worksheet retains until you reverse it with / Worksheet Window Sync.

The setting established by the / Worksheet Window Sync command is the default setting whenever you begin a new worksheet. Whenever the worksheet is set in this manner, and you scroll the display in one window of a split-screen display, the display in the other window will scroll, too. However, if you select / Worksheet Window Unsync and do the same thing while the current window scrolls, the other window remains motionless.

you can also freeze the column headers on the screen

If you are writing macros longer than 10 lines and you want to be able to see the column headings in your macro writing area, there's another command that can help you. With the display split, move into the upper window where you are writing macros. Move the cell pointer to the row on which the headings Name, Macro, and Comment appear. Position the display so that those are the topmost lines on the worksheet display. If you engaged the Scroll Lock to do that disengage it before carrying out the instructions below.

Press: Downarrow Downarrow

Select: / Worksheet Titles Horizontal

Press: Uparrow

You should hear a beep and 1-2-3 should prevent you from moving the cell pointer upward. Now depress and hold the Downarrow key until the screen scrolls downward. Note that the column headings remain in place. You will be able to see them above the macro-writing columns no matter how far down these columns your macros extend. If you wish to remove them, select / Worksheet Titles Clear.

If, while building a formula, you ever need to point to a cell entry that is inside a range you have locked with the / Worksheet Titles command, 1-2-3 will allow it. In so doing, 1-2-3 will create a duplicate of the locked range on the screen and allow you to move through it with the cell pointer. However, 1-2-3 will sometimes leave that duplicate on the screen when you're done. You can eliminate such duplicate images by moving the cell pointer off the current screen and then returning it: press the Pagedown key, then press the Pageup key to redisplay the original screen.

Testing Your Macros

You now know how to write macros of considerable length. If you're experimenting liberally on your own and finding that after you've written a long macro you spend a significant amount of time correcting flaws in it, there are a several things that can help you.

your primary challenge is to find the problem—fixing it is often easy

Test in Small Pieces. The primary challenge lies in identifying problems. Once you've done that, fixing them is usually a relatively simple matter of changing a character or two in the macro. Therefore, we suggest that you begin by writing smaller pieces of that macro, then testing and debugging (removing problems from) each new piece before proceeding. Since you'll be testing smaller amounts of new macro instructions each time than if you tested the entire macro at once, you'll find it easier to pinpoint any problems that occur.

Next we'll introduce you to two general testing techniques—one to stop a macro in mid-execution when you've observed a problem; another to temporarily suspend its execution (so you can assess its progress) and later restart it.

Stopping A Macro.

In the process of testing a macro, you may need to stop it before it runs its course. You already know that when a macro reads a blank cell, macro control ends and control reverts to the keyboard (in other words, to you). You can force that to happen by pressing the Break key sequence.

use the Break key to interrupt a macro

On most computers, pressing the Break sequence involves two separate keys—the Control key (marked Ctrl) and the Break key. The position and appearance of the Break key depend on the computer on which you are running 1-2-3; it most often has the word Break emblazoned on the front of the key (not the top), and is located at the farthest right position of the top row of the keyboard. To use the Break key sequence, hold down the Control key, briefly press the Break key, and release the Control key.

When you do that, macro control will terminate and control will return to the keyboard, but 1-2-3 will be in Error mode. Press the Escape key to clear the error. There are other ways of stopping macros prior to their conclusion; those methods involve more advanced techniques that we'll introduce later.

Temporarily Interrupting a Macro.

If your macros grow long, and you have an error in the macro, you may have difficulty identifying the source of the trouble. If you see the error as it occurs, you can press the Break key to interrupt the macro. However, you may not always be able to identify an error while the macro is running at full speed. There are three additional techniques that can help you.

how to step through a macro

(1.) 1-2-3 offers a way for you to activate a macro one keystroke at a time, or to temporarily interrupt the macro at any point. Before you activate the macro, depress and hold down the Alt key, then press the F2 function key (normally, the Edit key). Notice that the Step indicator appears at the bottom of your screen.

Now depress and hold down the Macro key (the Alt key on most computers), type the letter of your macro, and release the Macro key. Nothing—or almost nothing—should happen. Although the macro will not have begun carrying out its keystroke instructions, notice that the Step indicator at the bottom of the screen has changed to SST (for Single STep) and is flashing. In Release 2.2, the Step indicator will instead disappear and the first line of the macro will appear in the bottom left corner of the screen, with the first instruction highlighted.

Press the Return key once and the macro will read the first keystroke instruction. In Release 2.2, note also that the highlight advances to show you the *next* macro instruction that 1-2-3 will read. If your macro malfunctions, the highlight will help you pin down the instruction involved. Press Return once more and 1-2-3 will read the next instruction. Continue pressing the Return key until the macro finishes. The step indicator will again appear at the bottom of the screen.

use the
Return key
to advance
the macro

You can press most any key on the keyboard to advance the macro instead of the Return key, but we recommend you use the Return key to avoid problems that can arise if you use some other key. If you inadvertently hold the Return key down after the macro ends, it'll have no effect in most cases.

However, if you use an alpha-numeric key (such as the space bar), and the macro ends with the worksheet in Ready mode, 1-2-3 will respond by typing the character associated with that key. If you then move the cell pointer or press Return, 1-2-3 will enter those characters in the current cell. If that cell had contained data, the spaces will overwrite that data. Had you used the Return key instead of the space bar and made the same mistake, however, the additional Return keystrokes would have had no effect on your worksheet. Use the Return key, it's safer.

use the
Break key
to interrupt
the macro
in Step
mode

If you discover an error in your macro while using Step mode, press the Break key to terminate the macro. Correct the macro label containing the error and run the macro once again to be sure the problem is solved, and that no others occur in macro labels that follow.

As long as you see the Step indicator at the bottom of the screen, any macro you activate will respond in single step mode. The Step key works like a light switch—once you turn it on, it stays that way until you turn it off. When you no longer want your macros to operate in single step mode, press Alt F2 once more, the Step indicator will disappear, and your macros will run uninterrupted.

hold down
the Return
key to
suspend
Step mode
until you
want to
stop the
macro

(2.) You can use a variation of that technique to interrupt the macro while it is running. Suppose you suspect that you have a problem toward the end of a long macro. Press the Step key to turn on Step mode. Now activate the macro and hold down the Return key. The macro will run at or near normal speed. When 1-2-3 is about to read the part of the macro you suspect, release the Return key. The macro will immediately suspend operation. You can now revert to stepping through the macro as we described earlier.

Finally, when you've identified and corrected any errors, press the Step key once more (Alt F2) to turn off Step mode. Check the Status line at the bottom of the screen to make sure the Step indicator has disappeared, which confirms that Step mode has been cancelled.

(3.) If you are using an IBM compatible computer, there's another way that you can interrupt a macro. You don't need to be in Step mode to use this technique.

freezing a macro at any time

While running a macro, if you depress the Control key, briefly press the Num Lock key, and then release the Control key, the macro will freeze. When you subsequently press any key on the keyboard, the macro will continue.

If after trying these testing techniques you're still unable to discover the trouble with the macro, refer to Chapter 8, Debugging Your Macros. While this section is intended to equip you with some general testing methods that'll help you catch many errors, the chapter on debugging contains a more rigorous and specialized series of diagnostic tests and prescriptive actions to help you.

Summary

Macros and macro-driven applications are more than mere conveniences, they are an asset resulting from the investment of your time, your microcomputer skills, and your knowledge of the subject matter of your application. The rationale for that investment is increased productivity, and you can increase that productivity further by incorporating good structure and documentation into your macros. Such practices will make it easier for others to understand and correctly use your application. Further, developers of new applications can reuse parts of your application rather than starting from scratch.

Saving time is the raison d'etre for most macros. You can save even more time while you're developing them if you adopt a structured development, testing, and debugging process.

3

Using
Special
Key Names

You've already seen that, lacking any direct way to represent the Return key in a macro, you must symbolize it with the tilde (~). You may have noticed that there are other keys on the keyboard that pose a similar problem. Among those keys are the Home key, the Edit function key, and the Rightarrow key. We call such non-alphanumeric keys special keys, and you represent them in a macro with a symbol (such as the tilde) or with something known as a key name.

{Home}, {edit}, and {right}, are the key names used to represent the Home, Edit, and Rightarrow keys. Most special key names are single words enclosed in braces. Tables 3-1 through 3-4 show the full complement of key names used in Releases 2.01 through 2.2[12]

---

[12] We've covered one subgroup of special key names, those you use to call up Add-ins and 1-2-3's Add-in Manager, in a later chapter. Turn to Chapter 16, Add-ins, for instructions on how to automate the Alt-7, Alt-F8, Alt-F9, and Alt-F10 keystrokes used to access Add-ins and the 1-2-3 Add-in Manager.

Table 3.1. Function Keys

Function Key	Key Name
F1	{ help } ★
F2	{ edit }
F3	{ name }
F4	{ abs }
F5	{ goto }
F6	{ window }
F7	{ query }
F8	{ table }
F9	{ calc }
F10	{ graph }

★In 1-2-3 Releases 2.01 and lower, the Help (F1) function key can not be represented in a macro. It is available, however, in Release 2.2 and higher releases.

Table 3.2. Directional Keys

Directional Key	Key Name
Tab	{ bigright }
Backtab	{ bigleft }
Home	{ home }
End	{ end }
PgUp	{ pgup }
PgDn	{ pgdn }
Uparrrow	{u} or {up}
Downarrow	{d} or {down}
Leftarrow	{l} or {left}
Rightarrow	{r} or {right}

Table 3.3. Editing Keys

Editing Key	Key Name
Esc	{esc} or {escape}
Backspace	{bs} or {backspace}
Ins	{insert} or {ins}★
Del	{del} or {delete}

★Release 2.2 and higher releases will recognize either {insert} or {ins} as the Insert key. Release 2.01 and lower releases do not recognize {ins}.

Table 3.4. Miscellaneous Keys

Miscellaneous Key	Key Name
Return	~
Tilde	{~}
Left brace	{{}
Right brace	{}}
Menu slash	{menu}, /, or <

Notes:

1. You can use a macro to display 1-2-3's menu in any of three ways: using the slash key (/), the {menu} key name, or the < key. All of the following macros produce the same result:

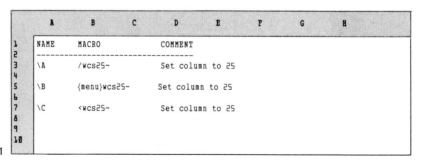

	A	B	C	D	E	F	G	H
1	NAME	MACRO		COMMENT				
2	----	-----		------				
3	\A	/wcs25~		Set column to 25				
4								
5	\B	{menu}wcs25~		Set column to 25				
6								
7	\C	<wcs25~		Set column to 25				
8								
9								
10								

Figure 3-1

Because {menu} is a key name, you may use it only in a macro, but you may use the less-than sign (<) to invoke 1-2-3's menu from the keyboard, just as you can use the slash (/) key.

2. While there is no key name for the Ctrl-Break key sequence, Release 2.2 incorporates an advanced macro command that does some of what Ctrl-Break does. Refer to the listing for the {break} command in the chapter on Allowing Keyboard Interaction for a description.

Note also that some keys on an IBM compatible keyboard are entirely unavailable from within a macro: the Ctrl key, the Alt key, and the three "Lock" keys (Num Lock, Scroll Lock, and Caps Lock).

don't split
key names

Unlike the contents of macros you've learned about thus far, you cannot split a key name between two lines, so this macro won't work:

Figure 3-2

```
        A         B         C         D      E      F      G      H
  1  NAME      MACRO               COMMENT
  2  --------------------------------------
  3  \A        {rig
  4            ht}
  5
```

Let's write a simple macro using some of these key names. Reproduce the macro shown below.

a simple
pointer-
movement
macro

```
        A         B         C         D      E      F      G      H
  1  NAME      MACRO               COMMENT
  2  --------------------------------------
  3  \A        {right}{down}
  4            {left}{up}
  5
```

Figure 3-3

Once you've entered the macro labels as shown, assign the macro a special range name as follows:

Enter: / Range Name Create

Type: \a

Press: Return Return

Now, move the cell pointer to cell C10, watch the screen closely, and activate the macro:

Depress: Macro

Type: A

Release: Macro

That's a simple macro using key names. Now, for a bit of amusement, try this:

Depress: Macro (and hold it down)

Depress: A (and hold it down)

If your computer begins to beep, release the A key briefly, then depress it again. You should see the macro move the cell pointer so quickly that it resembles a checkerboard square.

In a moment, we'll begin exploring some of the many ways to use key names in macros. First, however, there are several things to keep in mind when using key names.

{ } looks like (), but don't confuse them

(1.) Depending on the resolution of your screen, the braces { } which enclose these key names may appear to be parentheses (). Regardless of their similar appearance, the two are not interchangable. If you use parentheses to enclose key names, 1-2-3 will not interpret them properly when it reads them.

(2.) When you use a key name in a macro, be sure that you spell it correctly, and beware that proper macro spelling sometimes deviates from proper English spelling. Here are some examples:

you must spell key names correctly

- The key name for the Goto key, { goto }, does not have a space between the words "go" and "to".

- The key names for the PageUp and PageDown keys are spelled the same as the names of those keys as they appear on key tops of IBM compatible keyboards: { PgUp } and { PgDn }. Since upper and lower case are insignificant you could also properly write them as { pgup } and { pgdn }. (Variations in upper and lower case are largely a matter of style in macros; we'll address that point later.)

Because 1-2-3 can interpret only the precise form of a key name, you may find your macros occasionally running into problems caused by your typographical errors. For example, one common typing error is transposing letters: typing { letf } instead of { left }. Let's intentionally introduce that error into the macro you last used to see you how 1-2-3 responds to it. Modify the macro as shown below.

```
        A        B         C       D      E      F      G      H
1    NAME     MACRO            COMMENT
2    ----------------------------------
3    \A       {right}{down}
4             {letf}{up}
5
```

Figure 3-4

Note the current position of the cell pointer and activate the macro once more. You should see the cell pointer quickly move one cell to the right, one cell down, then the computer will beep and 1-2-3 will display an error indicator in the top right corner of the screen. Look at the lower left corner of the screen and you'll see the following message:

```
Unrecognized key/range name {...} (B4)
```

1-2-3 identifies the cell in which the improperly spelled key name resides—B4, in this case. If you keep each label in your macro reasonably short, when 1-2-3 indicates such an error has occurred, you'll be able to easily identify the key name at fault.

Press the Escape key to clear the error and correct the macro.

(3.) Avoid confusing the key name for the Return key (the tilde) with the key name for the tilde itself (the tilde enclosed in braces, { ~ }). When you want to represent the Return key in a macro, use the tilde alone. For those infrequent times when you need to represent the tilde in a macro (such as when you want a macro to type a tilde), use the tilde enclosed in braces. To recap:

When you want to represent the Return key: ~

When you want to represent the tilde: { ~ }

(4.) You know that you can use the Rightarrow, Leftarrow, End, and Home keys to move the menu pointer to a menu item you wish to select. Now that you know how to activate those keys under the control of a macro using the { right }, { left }, { end } or { home } key names, you can do the same thing in a macro, but we recommend that you don't.

New releases of 1-2-3 often incorporate new menu items that affect the positions of existing menu choices. For example, 1-2-3 Release 2.0 added the System command to the main menu. If you'd written a macro in Release 1A that selected the Quit command by moving the menu pointer eight items to the right ({ right 8 }), when you ran that macro in Release 2.0, 2.01, or 2.2 it would instead select the System command.

If your macros continue making menu selections via the first letter of each menu item you wish to choose, you'll avoid this compatibility problem.

Compatibility

There's a bit more to be said about macro compatibility among releases 2, 2.01, 2.2 and higher releases of 1-2-3. Of the preceding lists of key names, two work only in Release 2.2 or a higher release of 1-2-3 — { ins } and { help }. If you are developing macros for use by people using either Release 2.2 or Release 2.01, you'll need to avoid using the key names that work only in the higher releases.

{ Ins } is merely one of two key names you can use to represent the Ins key in a macro ({ insert } is the other), so your macros don't lose use of the Ins key if you write them to be compatible with lower releases of 1-2-3. However, { help } is the only way you can access 1-2-3's Help facility from within a macro. If you must write macros that remain compatible with Releases 2 or 2.01, you don't have an alternative way to access 1-2-3's Help facility. Instead, you can write your own Help facility. The Advanced Techniques section of this book explains several ways to do it.

We'll discuss cross-release compatibility in more depth in the chapter on Application Design. In the intervening chapters, we'll simply tell you when a key name, macro command, or other feature works only in a particular release and let you decide whether or not to use it.

Sample Macro for Goto

Earlier we discussed ways to simplify the development of macros. Among those methods was the recommendation that you name the top left cell of the screen on which you are writing your macro and the top left cell of the screen on which you are testing it, then use the Goto–Name key sequence to assist you in navigating between the two locations.

One limitation to the aforementioned technique is that the area in which you are testing the macro can move about as you develop the worksheet. To effectively use the Goto key under that circumstance, you'd have to continually use the / Range Name Create command to assign new range names. That would be too tedious to qualify as a handy tool. Using key names can automate the entire operation and solve the problem of the moving testing area all at once.

Here's a macro named \A that'll mark the location in which you're currently testing your macro and then move the cell pointer to your macro-writing area. When you're ready to return to your work area, use the macro named \B. Prior to using the macro, use the / Range Name Create command to assign the name Macros to the top left cell of your macro writing area.

	A	B	C	D	E	F	G	H
1	NAME	MACRO		COMMENT				
2	------	------	------	------	------	------		
3	\A	/rncTEST~~		Create range name				
4		/rndTEST~		Delete range name				
5		/rncTEST~~		Recreate range name				
6		{goto}MACROS~		Goto macro area				
7								
8	\B	{goto}TEST~		Go back to Test area				
9								
10								

Figure 3-5

The first two lines of the macro are safeties—they accommodate both the possibility that the range name already exists and the possibility that it does not.

If the range name Test does exist, the first line will simply recreate it in its existing position, the second line will delete it, and the third line will create it again at the the cell pointer location. Line 1 is useless in that case, but consider what would happen if the range name did *not* exist when you activated the macro. If line 2 tried to delete a nonexistent range name, the macro would end in an error. Instead, the first line will create the range name at the cell pointer's current position. The second line will delete it and the third line will create it once again.

In either case, line 4 will transport the cell pointer to the named range Macros.

Part of our earlier discussion told you how to create range names that will show up either first or last when 1-2-3 displays those range names in the control panel (such as when you press Goto Name). Another character you can begin a range name with to assure it will appear at the end of a list of range names is a tilde. However, if you do this and intend to use that range name in a macro, it could pose a problem. When 1-2-3 reads the tilde, it interprets it as the Return key. To force 1-2-3 to regard the tilde as just another character to be typed, enclose the tilde in braces: {~}.

In the following macro, suppose you want the range name Macros to appear last in the list of range names 1-2-3 displays. You could rename the range ~Macros. However, if you do, you must represent that range name as {~}Macros (not simply ~Macros) in the macro itself.

```
         A          B          C          D          E          F          G          H
1   NAME       MACRO                 COMMENT
2   ----------------------------------------
3   \A         /rncTEST~~            Create range name
4              /rndTEST~             Delete range name
5              /rncTEST~~            Recreate range name
6              {goto}{~}MACROS~      Goto macro area
7
8   \B         {goto}TEST~           Go back to Test area
9
10
```

Figure 3-6

If you don't enclose with braces the tilde that begins the name ~Macros, when 1-2-3 reads the fourth line of the macro, it will press the Goto key, press Return (cancelling the Goto operation with no change in cell pointer position), then type the word Macros and enter it into the current cell. Placing the tilde within braces allows 1-2-3 to read that tilde as part of the range name, and not treat it as the Return key.

Applying Key Names To Write Formulas That Point

Using key names to represent any of the directional keystrokes in 1-2-3 greatly enhances the utility of macros for writing formulas. When we first showed you how to write formulas with macros, those formulas could only contain values and cell addresses. For example, you could write macros that contained formulas like: '12+10~ or '+A2+(A3*10)~.

However, there are times when it's useful to have a macro enter a formula by pointing to the cells. For example, suppose you have a check register that looks like this:

```
         A     B     C              D       E       F        G
    1  DATE  CK#   DESCRIPTION     DEBIT   CREDIT  BALANCE
    2  ----------------------------------------------------------
    3              Balance Forward                 550.54
    4
    5  11/22  422  Lex's Hardware   35.32          515.22
    6              Wheelbarrow
    7  11/25  423  Sotheby's       300.00          215.22
    8              Future heirloom
    9  11/26       Deposit                 815.00  1030.22
   10              Tax refund
   11
   12
   13
   14
   15
```

Figure 3-7

When you make a new entry and need to calculate a new balance, you could copy the previous new balance to the current line (such as from cell F9 to cell F11), or you could store the formula in a macro and have the macro enter the formula for you. If you had to write the formula with cell addresses in the macro, it wouldn't work because those cell addresses must change with every successive entry. Why not build the ability into the macro to accommodate the changes in cell addresses? Here's how to do it.

The formula that calculates each balance adds the contents of the cell located two cells above (the prior balance), then subtracts the contents of the cell located two cells to the left (the debit column), then adds the contents of the cell located one cell to the left (the credit column).

it's important that the model be consistent

Note that we set up the check register so that each entry occupies two rows. In that way, each new balance formula can reference the cell two cells above it for the prior balance, two cells to its left for any debit, and one cell to its left for any credit. Were you to vary the position of each entry, you'd have to write a much more complex macro to calculate each new balance.

Here's a macro that will enter that formula into any line of the check register.

```
         A       B          C      D       E         F     G     H
    1  NAME    MACRO               COMMENT
    2  ----------------------------------------------------------------
    3  \A      +{up}{up}           Add prior balance
    4          -{left}{left}       Subtract debit
    5          +{left}~            Add credit
```

Figure 3-8

using the
short forms
of key
names

You may recall from the table of key names that you can abbreviate each of the directional arrow keys. Here's an abbreviated form of the macro presented above. When you enter it, be sure to represent the Leftarrow key with an L, not the numeral one (1).

```
        A        B        C        D        E        F        G        H
1   NAME     MACRO              COMMENT
2   ------------------------------------
3   \A       +{u}{u}            Add prior balance
4            -{l}{l}            Subtract debit
5            +{l}~              Add credit
```

Figure 3-9

In all fairness, you should know there's yet another way to approach the task we've just outlined. You could write the proper formula once and enter it into a cell in your macro writing area.

The result in the macro-writing area will probably be zero. When you copy the formula into the proper cell in the check register, however, it'll reference the prior balance, debit, and credit cells and return the new balance.

First, assign the range name Formula to a cell in your macro writing area. Enter the formula in your check register once to test it, then copy that formula to the cell named Formula. Erase the original entry in the check register. The following macro will do the work for you:

```
        H        I        J        K        L        M        N
1   NAME     MACRO              COMMENT
2   ------------------------------------
3   \A       /cFORMULA~~        Enter new balance
4
5   FORMULA         0           Stores formula
```

Figure 3-10

Before using this macro, you should place the cell pointer on the cell in the check register where you want the new balance to appear. The / Copy command in the first line of the macro will copy the contents of the named range Formula to the current location of the cell pointer. Note there is no address provided prior to the second tilde. The absence of that address means that 1-2-3 will use the current location of the cell pointer as the destination of the copy command.

when
formulas
should
NOT be
labels

In this case, the formula stored in the range named Formula has been entered as a valid formula, not as a label. If we wanted the macro to read the cell containing that formula, we'd have entered the formula as a label. However, this macro only reads the entry in cell I3. That entry contains the command to copy the cell named Formula. There is no need for the formula to be a label; in fact, if it were entered as a label in this case, the operation wouldn't work.

use / Range
Name
Labels to
name all
macro
ranges

Two more notes about this macro. Notice the name "formula" in cell H5. The formula is in the cell to its right, I5. With the label Formula in column H, you can use that label as a range name for the cell to its right, just as you learned to do earlier with macro names. When you want to assign the macro name in cell H3 to cell I3, you'd select / Range Name Labels Right. In this case, when 1-2-3 prompts you to "Enter label range:," extend the cell pointer down the column to include H3..H5. 1-2-3 will use both labels in column H as names for the cells to their right.

separating
variables
from your
macro

Although you probably wouldn't want to vary the formula in this macro, an advantage of placing the formula in its own cell is that if you needed to change it, you can do so easily without touching the rest of the macro. Because the formula has been separated from the macro and can be varied without varying the macro itself, you can think of the formula as a variable. Keep that design concept in mind. It's common to need to change macros. Breaking parts of them into separate variables like this can save time and help to ensure you won't inadvertently introduce problems into other areas of the macro at the same time.

Saving Time When You Write Macros

key names
can save
you time
when you
write
macros

Macros are time savers when you use them, but there are a number of ways you can save time when you develop them. Here are three tips for saving time when you use the key names:

- Use the briefest form of each key name.

- Use a number to repeat key names.

- Create your own synonyms for key names.

Use the Briefest Form 1-2-3 Offers

As the list of key names shows, 1-2-3 allows you to represent several keys in more than one way. The Escape, Backspace, Uparrow, Rightarrow, Downarrow, Leftarrow, and Delete keys all have more than one key name to represent them (in Release 2.2, the Insert key also falls into that category). To save typing time, we recommend that you adopt the briefest form available. For example, use {r} instead of {right} and {esc} instead of {escape}.

The only time you should avoid using such brief forms is when you feel that they would confuse those who have to read and modify your work. Or, in the case of Release 2.2's {ins} key name, avoid using it if you wish the macros you write to work in lower releases of 1-2-3.

Use a Number To Repeat Key Names

In Release 2.0 and all subsequent releases of 1-2-3, you have the option to designate any number of repetitions of a keystroke represented by a key name.

For example, should you want 1-2-3 to move the cell pointer four cells to the left during macro execution, you can do so without writing four {left} commands. Instead, before you type the closing brace on the command, type a space followed by a value representing the number of repetitions you desire. Here's an example: {left 4}.

Here are some special cases to know about:

- You cannot use this technique to repeat the Return key. You must represent the Return key with a tilde, and a tilde will not accept an argument.

- Both {left} and {left 1} have the same effect.

- You can provide a range name to substitute for the numeric argument. So {left REPEAT} has the same effect as {left 6} if the cell named Repeat contains the value 6. If the referenced cell contains a zero, is empty, or contains a string when 1-2-3 reads the key name in a macro, the key name will have no effect. If the value in the referenced cell contains a fractional (perhaps it was calculated), only the integer portion of the number will be significant: {left 6.99999} and {left 6} have the same effect.

We recently presented the following macro. It writes a formula in the current cell using abbreviated versions of the {up} and {left} directional commands.

	A	B	C	D	E	F	G	H
1	NAME	MACRO		COMMENT				
2	----------------------------------							
3	\A	+{u}{u}		Add prior balance				
4		-{l}{l}		Subtract debit				
5		+{l}~		Add credit				

Figure 3-11

Notice that the macro contains two {u} commands in cell A3 and two {l} commands in cell A4. Here's an example of how you can use numer-

ic arguments to eliminate those duplications and shorte
further:

keep a space
between the
key name
and the
number that
follows

Figure 3-12

```
         A      B       C      D      E      F      G      H

   1 │ NAME    MACRO           COMMENT
   2 │ ----------------------------------
   3 │ \A      +{u 2}          Add prior balance
   4 │         -{l 2}          Subtract debit
   5 │         +{l}~           Add credit
```

Application

Try writing a macro to perform the following operations automatically.

a macro to
set up
worksheet
headers

Suppose you frequently prepare budgets, price projections, and other time-series oriented reports. Write a macro that automatically enters the name of each of the twelve months of the year across the top of twelve contiguous columns. Remember to use the three steps for writing a macro:

- Model the operation.

- Write the macro.

- Name the macro.

plan the
macro by
doing it

Step 1: Model the Operation

Assuming that you'll be placing entries in columns A through H later, begin your month name entries in column J. Place your cell pointer in cell J2 before beginning. As you perform the operation manually, keep a written record of your keystrokes. Begin by typing the label "January", move right one cell, type "February", move right one cell, and so forth until you reach December. Now return the cell pointer to cell J2 by pressing the Leftarrow key repeatedly.

Step 2: Write the Macro

Use the / Range Erase command to erase your entries. Beginning in cell B3, enter the macro on the worksheet. Represent the pointer movement commands with the key name { right } .

you can
only use a
numeric
argument
for
continuous
repeats

Although you used the {right} command more than once, because you intermingled it with label entries, you used it no more than once each time. Accordingly, you shouldn't use a numeric argument to indicate repetition of the Rightarrow keystroke. However, when you returned the cell pointer to cell J2, you used the Leftarrow key repeatedly, without any intervening keystrokes. Represent those repetitions with a number as part of the {left} command (remember to leave a space between the key name and the number: {left # }).

Refer to the
solution
directly
following
step 3
should you
wish to
confirm the
correctness
of your
macro.

Step 3: Name the Macro

Use the / Range Name Create command to assign a range name to the first cell of the macro. Remember to use a range name consisting of only two characters—the first a backslash, the second any single letter.

Solution to the macro:

	A	B	C	D	E	F	G	H
1	NAME	MACRO		COMMENT				
2	----	-----	----	----	----	----	----	----
3	\A	January{r}		Enter months and move right				
4		February{r}						
5		March{r}						
6		April{r}						
7		May{r}						
8		June{r}						
9		July{r}						
10		August{r}						
11		September{r}						
12		October{r}						
13		November{r}						
14		December						
15		{left 11}		Move left 11 times				
16								
17								
18								
19								
20								

Figure 3-13

Note: The last line of the macro, {left 11}, breaks with the convention of using the single-letter representation for key names. The reason for that is that the single-letter form, {l 11}, is confusing; it looks like either three lower case L's or three numeral ones. In any case, when your normal macro-writing convention leads to such problems, make an exception to it.

Create Your Own Synonyms for Key Names

If you find you are repeatedly using key names for which 1-2-3 offers no shortened form, you can create your own shortened form. For example, there is no abbreviated form of the key name for the tab key, {bigright}. If you found yourself using {bigright} frequently, you could create a new key name, {t}, to use in its stead. You might think of that as creating a synonym.

Let's suppose you want to replace the command {bigright} with {t} in the following macro:

```
        A        B         C       D       E        F       G       H
  1  NAME     MACRO                      COMMENT
  2  -----------------------------------------------
  3  \A       Subtotal{bigright}         Enter labels
  4           Total{bigright}
  5           Grandtotal{bigright}
  6
  7
  8
  9
 10
```

Figure 3-14

Here's how to do it:

1. Move your cell pointer to cell A7. That leaves at least one blank cell beneath your macro.

2. Enter the label "t" there (note: that is not \t, it's just t). Now enter the following commands:

Select: / Range Name Labels Right

Press: Return

Move: To cell B7

Enter: {bigright}

Note: You must leave a blank cell directly beneath this entry as well as directly above it.

3. Now when you write a macro on this worksheet and want to include the tab key, you can simply use the command {t} instead of {bigright}. {t} will work in any macro on this worksheet.

you can
shorten the
key name to
any other
string of
characters

You don't have to assign a single letter range name; you can use something a bit more descriptive if you prefer. In the example above, you could have used the name "tab" instead of "t". Then, when you wrote the macro, you would have used the command {tab} instead of {t}. However, if you change the name in B7 after using the / Range Name Labels command to assign the range name to cell B7, you should do two things:

- Use the / Range Name Delete command to delete the old name (in this case, select / Range Name Delete and enter T).

- Assign the new range name to cell B7. To do so, position the cell pointer on the new label in cell A7, select / Range Name Labels Right, and press Return.

Here are two forms of the same macro:

	A	B	C	D	E	F	G	H
1	NAME	MACRO			COMMENT			
2	---							
3	\A	Subtotal{T}			Enter labels			
4		Total{T}						
5		Grandtotal{T}						
6								
7	T	{bigright}			Synonym			
8								
9								
10								

Figure 3-15

	A	B	C	D	E	F	G	H
1	NAME	MACRO			COMMENT			
2	---							
3	\A	Subtotal{TAB}			Enter labels			
4		Total{TAB}						
5		Grandtotal{TAB}						
6								
7	TAB	{bigright}			Synonym			
8								
9								
10								

Figure 3-16

you can also
shorten any
mix of
entries or
commands
with a
synonym

Regardless of the range name you assign to cell B7, when you want to include the synonym command in the main macro, you will always enclose in braces the range name you assigned.

You can also apply this technique to shorten any series of macro entries, including a series of key names, a long label, or a series of commands. Here is an example.

```
        A        B       C      D      E       F     G      H
   1 | NAME     MACRO                  COMMENT
   2 | ------------------------------------------------
   3 | \A       Subtotal{NEXT}         Enter labels
   4 |          Total{NEXT}
   5 |          Grandtotal{NEXT}
   6 |
   7 | NEXT     {bigright}{down 5}     Synonym
   8 |
   9 |
  10 |
```

Figure 3-17

Example

put your
skills to
work now

You've now acquired a very versatile set of skills. Even though the number of pages remaining in this book testify that there's much to be learned, you should also realize that you can do a lot of useful work right now.

For example, here's a macro that creates running totals. Assume you have the worksheet shown below:

a macro to
create
running
totals

```
        A          B         C          D        E      F
   1 |            This period  Cumulative  Working
   2 |            -------------------------------------
   3 | Marketing                 250        250
   4 | Sales                     300        300
   5 | Production                225        225
   6 | Purchasing                200        200
   7 |
   8 |
   9 |
  10 |
```

Figure 3-18

The range B3..B6 is empty now, but that will hold value entries made by you when you next post the worksheet. Those in column C are also values, although they were entered by a macro, not by you. The entries in column C are the cumulative totals to date.

Each entry in column D is a formula that adds the contents of the two cells directly to its left. For example, the entry in cell D3 is @sum(B3..C3). Since, at this point, the referenced cells in column B are empty, the formulas in column D return the same value as the cells to their left in column C.

Now enter the data shown in cells B3..B6 below and watch the formulas update themselves in column D.

	A	B	C	D	E	F
1		This period	Cumulative	Working		
2		--------	----------	-------		
3	Marketing	50	250	300		
4	Sales	75	300	375		
5	Production	35	225	260		
6	Purchasing	45	200	245		
7						
8						
9						
10						

Figure 3-19

Column D now reflects the new working totals. Column C contains cumulative totals as of the last period; it doesn't yet reflect the cumulative totals incorporating this period.

You'll need to erase the entries in column B when you're ready to post the next period's data to the model. However, in the worksheet's present form, as soon as you erase the current posting from column B, the cumulative total in column D will shrink accordingly. If that happens, you won't be able to accumulate your totals from period to period.

the / Range Values command not only copies—it converts formulas to values

Our strategy is to update the entries in column C to reflect the new working totals in column D before removing the periodic entries in column B. Since the entries in column C are values (not formulas), once they've been updated, it won't matter if you erase the entries in column B. The entries in column D will reflect the change, but those in column C will remain constant.

To update the cumulative totals in column C, we'll use the / Range Values command. That command copies the contents of one range to another, converting any formulas to values in the process. The keystrokes to invoke that command appear in line 1 of the macro shown below.

	R	S	T	U	V
1	NAME	MACRO	COMMENT		
2		--------	-------		
3	\A	/rv	Copy values from		
4		.{end}{down}~	working column to		
5		{left}~	cumulative column		

Figure 3-20

Before using the macro, you must move the cell pointer to cell D3, the first cell of the Working Totals column. After line 1 selects the / Range Value command, 1-2-3 will prompt for the range from which to copy. Line 2 anchors the cell pointer, expands it down the range of entries in column D, and presses Return to enter the Copy From range. 1-2-3 will then prompt for the range to copy to. Line 3 moves the cell pointer left one cell to the top of column C and presses Return to enter the Copy To range. 1-2-3 will then copy the entries in column D into column C as values.

With column C updated with the most recent cumulative total, you are free to erase the entries in column B and enter new data from the next period.

```
        A           B            C            D          E          F
    1               This period  Cumulative   Working
    2               ------------------------------------------
    3   Marketing                    300         300
    4   Sales                        375         375
    5   Production                   260         260
    6   Purchasing                   245         245
    7
    8
    9
   10
```

Figure 3-21

placing the
cell pointer
at the start
of a macro

One of the most useful additions you can make to any macro is to eliminate the need for the operator to position the cell pointer prior to using the macro. You can do that in this macro with two steps.

- Assign a new range name on the worksheet. Move to cell D3. Press slash and select Range Name Create, type Start, and press Return twice.

- Modify the macro. Use the / Move commmand to move the entire macro down one row. Add the new label shown below. Since 1-2-3 moved the the macro range name \A along with the label '/rv, you should reassign the macro range name to cell S3 (otherwise, the macro will begin on line 2). The easiest way is to position the cell pointer on cell R3, press slash, select Range Name Labels Right, and press Return twice.

```
        R       S                    T              U      V
    1   NAME    MACRO                COMMENT
    2   ---------------------------------------
    3   \A      {goto}START~         Position cell pointer
    4           /rv                  Copy values from
    5           .{end}{down}~          working column to
    6           {left}~               cumulative column
    7
    8
    9
   10
```

Figure 3-22

You might also add an operation that, after the cumulative total has been transferred to the Cumulative column, will erase the entries in the "This period" column. If those entries remain on the worksheet and in the next period you don't have an entry to post for one line item and you mistakenly leave the old entry intact, your totals will be wrong. Erasing all the entries first will eliminate that risk.

Here's the revised macro.

Figure 3-23

	R	S	T	U	V
1	NAME	MACRO	COMMENT		
2	------	-----------	-----------		
3	\A	{goto}START~	Position cell pointer		
4		/rv	Copy values from		
5		.{end}{down}~	working column to		
6		{left}~	cumulative column		
7		{left 2}	Move to top of This Period		
8		/re{down 4}~	Erase entries		
9					
10					

Summary

what's next   In this chapter, you learned to use a variety of key names to represent function keys, pointer movement keys and editing keys, as well as a number of time-saving ways to use them. In the next chapter, you'll learn another command that you will enclose in braces—but there the similarity to key names ends. This new command will greatly extend the power and flexibility of your macros.

4

The { ? } Interactive Command

making macros more flexible will save you time

The macros you've learned to write thus far are powerful, yet somewhat inflexible. For example, suppose you've written a macro to set the width of a column to 35 spaces. On occasion, you might want to set the number of spaces to 25 or 40. Yet, you can't do that unless you first rewrite your macro or create another one.

Rewriting a macro is appropriate when you want to change that macro permanently. However, the situation cited above might require you to change your macros every time you use them. That's a poor solution.

Instead, what if you could make the macro flexible enough to enable you to opt for a different column width each time? You can do just that with 1-2-3's interactive macro command, { ? }.

The { ? } command lets the user supply the keystrokes

Like the special key indicators, the interactive command is enclosed in braces. Unlike special key indicators, it doesn't supply the specific keystroke. Instead, the braces enclose a question mark—{ ? }—as if to ask *you* to supply the keystroke(s). When 1-2-3 reads an interactive command in a macro, control temporarily returns to the keyboard, and the macro pauses. You can supply as many keystrokes as you like, until you press the Return key, whereupon control reverts to the macro once more.

Let's look at some examples:

	A	B	C	D	E	F	G	H
1	NAME	MACRO		COMMENT				
2								
3	\A	/wcs{?}~		Set any column width				
4								
5	\B	/c{?}~F1~		Copy any cell to cell F1				
6								
7	\C	/rf{?}~~		Select any range format				
8								
9	\D	/ppcrr{?}~agpq		Print any range				
10								

Figure 4-1

The { ? } Interactive Command and the Return Key

The second macro above (named \B) automates the / Copy command. In the explanation that follows, we'll discuss the / Copy command in detail, so try using the / Copy command interactively for a moment, just to make sure you follow each step in the macro before you continue reading. Keystroke by keystroke, here's how that macro reads (we've numbered the steps for clarity):

1. /   Display the 1-2-3 menu.

2. c   Select the copy command.

3. {?} Allow the user to specify a cell address in response to the prompt "copy FROM".

4.   When the user presses the Return key, continue reading the macro.

5. ~   Return to complete the "copy FROM" range specification.

6. F1 The "copy TO" address.

7. ~   Return to complete the "copy TO" range specification.

analyzing the macro

Step 1 displays the 1-2-3 command menu; step 2 selects the Copy command from that menu. 1-2-3 prompts for the "copy FROM" range. In step 3, the interactive command gives control to the user to supply the "copy FROM" address specification.

In order to complete that specification, 1-2-3 requires that the Return key be pressed. However, when the user enters a range specification and presses the Return key, 1-2-3 interprets that Return keystroke to mean that the interactive pause is over; the macro should resume control and continue reading keystrokes.

The Copy command never receives the Return keystroke that the user intended to use to enter the "copy FROM" range. That leaves 1-2-3 waiting for a Return keystroke to complete the "copy FROM" step of the Copy command. That's why the next character in the macro is a tilde. In step 4, a tilde (which represents the Return key) enters the "copy FROM" specification provided by the user during the interactive command's pause.

That's a key point about the interactive command. When the user presses the Return key, the interactive command "steals" that keystroke and uses it as an instruction to continue reading the macro. If the operation the user was engaged in at that moment required a Return as the next keystroke, then you must include a tilde as the next keystroke in the macro to provide that Return keystroke.

That's a bit complicated, so if you're having trouble following our reasoning, try the following exercise.

1. Edit the \B macro and remove the tilde that directly follows the interactive command. The macro should now look like the one below:

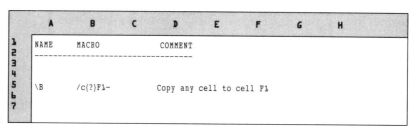

Figure 4-2

2. Press the Step key (Alt F2 on most computers); you should see the STEP indicator come on at the bottom of your screen.

3. Activate the macro by depressing the Macro key, typing A and releasing the Macro key. The STEP indicator will change to SST and flash. In Release 2.2 and higher releases, 1-2-3 will instead display the current line of the macro at the bottom of the screen with a highlight on the *next* instruction to be read.

4. We normally recommend that you use the Return key to step through a macro in Step mode. However, because we want to make a point about the Return key, we'll use the space bar this time.

Press the space bar once to get started. Now press it once for each key-stroke in the macro and watch what happens in the control panel. When the macro reads the pause command, type the cell address G15 and press the Return key. Resume pressing the space bar and watch the control panel. Notice that even though you pressed the Return key after typing the cell address, 1-2-3 did not enter the "copy FROM" range. Instead, that range remained in the control panel and 1-2-3 appended the cell address F1 to the cell address you typed, creating the entry G15F1. How-ever, F1 was intended to be the "copy TO" range. When the macro reads the tilde that follows the F1, 1-2-3 will generate an error because it won't recognize the entry G15F1 as either a cell address or range name. The solution is to add back the tilde following the interactive command.

try some variations on your own

Now, try writing some macros using the interactive command. As we have done in the examples above, you might try including the interactive command in some of the macros you wrote earlier.

Data Entry with the { ? } Interactive Command

So far, we've showed you how to use the interactive command to com-plete choices in the process of issuing a 1-2-3 command (such as the / Copy command). You can also use the interactive command to facilitate entering data.

We'll show you how you might use the interactive command to enter data into the check register shown earlier. Here's the check register tem-plate again:

	A	B	C	D	E	F	G
1	DATE	CK#	DESCRIPTION	DEBIT	CREDIT	BALANCE	
2	---------	---------	---------	---------	---------	---------	
3			Balance Forward			550.54	
4							
5	11/22	422	Lex's Hardware	35.32		515.22	
6			Wheelbarrow				
7	11/25	423	Sotheby's	300.00		215.22	
8			Future heirloom				
9	11/26		Deposit		815.00	1030.22	
10			Tax refund				
11							
12							
13							
14							
15							

Figure 4-3

Here's a macro you can use to post each entry in the ledger. Note that the macro must pause at each column even if the user doesn't have any data to enter. The user must press the Return key in order to make the macro move the cell pointer leftward between entries. The macro requires that you position the cell pointer in the Date column before you activate it. After each row, it returns the cell pointer to the next row in the Date column.

	A	B	C	D	E	F	G	H
1	NAME	MACRO		COMMENT				
2	----	------	--	------	----			
3	\A	{?}{r}		Enter date, go right				
4		{?}{r}		Enter check #, go right				
5		{?}{r}		Enter description, go right				
6		{?}{r}		Enter debit, if any				
7		{?}{r}		Enter credit, if any				
8		+{u 2}		Write formula for balance				
9		-{l 2}						
10		+{l}						
11		{l 5}{d}		To start of next row				
12								
13								
14								
15								

Figure 4-4

cautions for
this macro

Once again, the interactive commands contained within this macro require the user to act in a predictable, consistent manner. After each entry, the user must press the Return key. The macro will respond by moving the cell pointer one cell to the right and pausing for more data or, when the cell pointer reaches the Balance column, by entering a formula, moving down one cell, and moving left five cells.

However, consider another scenario that's not entirely unlikely. Suppose instead of pressing the Return key after entering a debit, the user mistakenly presses the Rightarrow key to move to the Credit column. Although the cell pointer is now in the Credit column, the macro is still reading the instruction intended for the Debit column. Consider what will happen when the cell pointer gets to the Balance column. Instead of calculating a new balance there, the macro will continue to pause. If you then press Return, the macro would move the cell pointer one cell to the right of the Balance column, and enter the formula there to calculate a balance, a formula whose references would in each case be one cell to the right of the cells intended. The cell pointer would then move leftward only to the CK# column, not the Date column. That's further evidence of the need for more instruction, and of a weakness with these kinds of macros.

a tilde
doesn't
always
follow the
{?}
command

Although we earlier made a point of the important role that a tilde can play following an interactive command, the preceding macro is a good example of a situation where no tilde needs to follow that command at all. Whether you should use a tilde is a matter of circumstances. You can easily determine whether or not to use one by manually entering the keystrokes associated with the operation you're trying to automate with a macro. Watch as you do, and if you must press the Return key at the point at which you want to include an interactive command, you need a tilde following the command.

Macro Testing with the {?} Interactive Command

Earlier, we introduced you to several techniques (including the use of Step mode, the Break key, and the Control-NumLock key) to help you test your macros. You can use the interactive command in much the same way. For example, suppose you are writing a long macro, and you've mentally divided the macro into several steps. At the conclusion of each step, you'd like to ascertain if everything has functioned correctly up to that point. You insert interactive commands at the end of each step of the macro to create a series of check points.

{?}
commands
can act as
milestones
for you to
check
during
macro
testing

When you activate the macro, it pauses when it reaches the first interactive command. You can verify that the macro has worked as intended so far. If it has, press Return and the macro will proceed to the next interactive command. If it hasn't, press the Break key to end the macro so you can diagnose and correct the problem. If there is a problem, you won't have to search through the entire macro for the cause, you'll only have to investigate the portion of it that's run so far.

You can also use Step mode in concert with the interactive command for even more help. Suppose the macro reaches an interactive pause and you want to carefully examine each keystroke of its next phase. Press Alt-F2 to activate Step mode, then press Return for the macro to proceed. Continue to press Return to step the macro through subsequent keystrokes. At any point that you want 1-2-3 to resume reading the macro at its normal speed, press Alt-F2 again to cancel Step mode.

You may want to place a telltale mark (such as the letters CP for Check Point) in the Comment column next to each interactive command you've inserted to help you check the macro. Once you're satisfied the macro works properly, you must remove all such interactive commands. The telltale mark will help you identify the interactive commands to take out and, just as importantly, it'll help you avoid removing interactive commands that were not meant as debugging aids.

Applications

Experiment with the interactive command in the sample macro that follows. You can modify the example application to provide pauses where the macro selects the type of format and where it specifies the number of spaces to widen the column to. When you do, make sure to preserve the tildes that terminate each line.

```
        A        B        C        D        E        F        G        H
  1   NAME     MACRO             COMMENT
  2   ----------------------------------
  3   \A       {?}~              Pause for a value
  4            /rf{c}~~          Format the value
  5            /wcs{25}~         Adjust width of column
```

Figure 4-5

Summary

Here's a summary of the interactive command:

1. The interactive command can allow the user of a macro to make a choice in the course of the macro, allow the user to enter data, or stop the macro at key points to allow you to check for errors.

2. The interactive command consists of a question mark surrounded by a pair of braces: { ? }.

3. When read in a macro, the interactive command temporarily suspends macro control and returns control to the keyboard (allowing you to enter keystrokes from the keyboard).

4. During an interactive pause in a macro, as soon as you press the Return key, control reverts back to the macro.

5. The Return key that the user presses during a interactive command has no effect on the 1-2-3 operation the macro is automating. If that operation requires that the Return key be pressed, you must include that Return keystroke in the form of a tilde as the next keystroke in the macro.

6. Since the interactive command results in a pause in macro execution when the macro reads it, you'll probably hear people refer to it informally as the pause command. The pause command and the interactive command are one and the same: {?}.

Next

If you skipped the Quick course that preceded the Detailed course, return there and review the host of keystroke macros it includes.

So far, your macros have been restricted to the worksheet on which they were created. In the next section, you will learn how to store macros so they can be used on any worksheet.

5

Macro Libraries

You already know how to combine macros by copying or moving them from one part of a worksheet to another. You may have wondered, however, if similar time-saving techniques exist to help move macros between worksheets. They do. They're called macro libraries.

In Release 2 or 2.01, a macro library is a worksheet file dedicated to storing macros. Used in concert with 1-2-3's File Combine commands, a macro library removes the need to recreate frequently used macros in each new worksheet. Instead, you can copy those macros into your new worksheet from the macro library worksheet.

The Release 2.2 macro library is both similar to and different from the macro libraries in Release 2 and 2.01. It performs the same functions and more, yet its design is somewhat different. Because how you operate a 2.2 macro library differs substantially from macro libraries in earlier releases of 1-2-3, we'll cover that separately, after discussing Release 2 and 2.01.

Release 2 and 2.01 Macro Libraries

preparing a
macro
library

Prepare the worksheet depicted below, select the / File Save command, and enter the name Maclib.

```
         A       B       C       D       E       F       G       H
    1  NAME    MACRO                                   COMMENT
    2  ----------------------------------------------------------------
    3  \A      /rf{?}~~
    4
    5  \B      AAA Financial Services, Inc.~
    6
    7  \C      /wcs{?}~
```

Figure 5-1

Now select / Worksheet Erase Yes to clear the worksheet.

Imagine that you are creating a new application. Before beginning, you will want to set up some macros that will help in the process of building the application.

Move: To cell I3

Select: / File Combine Copy Entire-file

Enter: MACLIB

1-2-3 copied the contents of the Maclib file onto the current worksheet. Note that the macros are entered in column J beginning with cell J3. In the Maclib file those macros were entered in column B beginning in cell B3 (refer to the illustration of the Maclib worksheet).

how to
choose the
position of
the
incoming
macros

1-2-3 used the position of the cell pointer at the time you executed / File Combine to position the contents of the top left cell in the incoming file. By positioning the cell pointer on the worksheet prior to executing the / File Combine command, you can choose the worksheet location where the incoming macros will be stored.

Although you can copy data (such as a macro label) between files, you can't transfer range names. Whether or not the macros had been assigned a special range name in the Maclib file, you will have to assign them range names when you complete the / File Combine operation. Since your Maclib file contained not only the macro labels, but the range name labels in the column to the left of the macros, your job is easy.

Move: To cell I3

Select: / Range Name Labels Right

Press: Downarrow Downarrow Downarrow Downarrow

Press: Return

The range names have been created and properly assigned. Verify that with the following steps.

Press: Goto (F5 on most computers)

Press: Name (F3 on most computers)

Note: Highlight one of the macro range names and press Return.

The cell pointer should move to the macro label corresponding to the range name you selected.

Here are a few other points you should know about using / Range Name Labels Right:

quickly
assigning
range
names to
combined
macros

(1.) Before beginning the / Range Name Labels Right command, move the cell pointer to the cell containing the topmost macro name in the column. When 1-2-3 prompts you for the range containing the labels, press the PageDown key as many times as you need to cover the entire range quickly.

(2.) Even if your list of macro names is brief, when 1-2-3 prompts you for the range containing the labels, you can quickly cover that range by pressing PageDown once. As long as the cells in the range you've highlighted are all blank, don't worry about reducing the size of the range if pressing the PageDown key displays a range that stretches somewhat beneath the lowermost macro label. When you indicate a range of labels that includes blank cells, 1-2-3 disregards those blank cells when it assigns names to the cells to the right.

With the range names assigned, you can execute these macros at your leisure. Try several now, on your own.

An Organized Macro Library

You saw that you can combine an entire file containing macros into the current worksheet. As your prowess with macros increases, you'll write macros to help you with a variety of tasks. Many of those macros will be worth keeping in a macro library.

As your macro library grows and diversifies, you'll find that you'll need only a small portion of the macros in the library in any one worksheet. Wouldn't it be nice if you could selectively choose just the macros that you need? For example, what if you could organize your macros into libraries that are particularly well suited for such things as:

- Financial applications

- Worksheet consolidations

- Database work

- Graphics

You can do this in either of two ways: create a separate macro library worksheet for each kind of macro you wish to store, or segment your current macro library by function. We'll now review how to implement each of these approaches.

Create Separate Macro Library Worksheets

Here's how to create several macro libraries in order to store different kinds of macros in each library.

When you use the File Save command to save each worksheet, assign a special worksheet name.

use file names that represent the kind of work the library is for

Type in a worksheet name representative of the function of that macro library. Names such as Finance (financial macros), Consolid (consolidation macros), Database (database macros), and Graphics (graphics macros) are excellent ones. Use up to eight characters for each file name. We suggest you use close to the full complement in order to provide a clear description of the purpose of each macro library. If you use fewer letters and later have to hesitate while you recall the meaning of your abbreviations, you've done yourself a disservice.

assign the file an extension that suggests it is a macro library

After typing the filename, type a period key and a three letter filename extension, such as .LIB for library. We suggest you avoid using .MLB (for Macro Library) for two reasons. Both 1-2-3 Release 2.2 and Symphony use that extension for their macro libraries, and in each case those file formats differ from the worksheet-based libraries we'are discussing here. Since those programs' macro library managers will consider any file with the .MLB extension as a valid macro library, that could lead to trouble later. Even if you don't use one of those programs later, you might end up working on a network with someone who does. Whichever extension name suits you, use the same one for each macro library file you create.

When you assign this special filename extension to the worksheet, you effectively segregate it from the other worksheets when you later combine or retrieve files. 1-2-3's / File Retrieve and / File Combine commands normally search for files with extensions that begin with the letters WK (typically, the full extension is WKS, or WK1). If you assign a different extension to a worksheet, 1-2-3 will not display that worksheet as an option when you select the File Retrieve or File Combine command.

to retrieve a
macro
library file

Conversely, when you do want to retrieve a macro library worksheet, you can arrange it so that 1-2-3 will show only your macro library files.

To use a particular library, position the cell pointer on a blank area on your worksheet and enter the / File Combine Copy Entire-File command. When 1-2-3 displays the files for you to combine, press the Escape key once and the default filename specification,—*.wk?—will disappear. In its place, type an asterisk, a period, and the filename extension you assigned to the macro libraries. For example: *.lib (upper or lower case make no difference). Press Return and you will see a menu of the macro library files. If you then press the Name function key (F3), 1-2-3 will display all your macro library files in full screen mode. (If you are using a hard disk and have subdirectories subordinate to the one you are currently logged to, you will see the names of those subdirectories following the macro library file names). Highlight the file you want to combine and press the Return key.

how to
resave a
macro
library file

When you want to add macros to your library file, you must follow a similar method to retrieve the file. Select / File Retrieve, press the Escape key, enter the macro library file specification *.lib, highlight the macro you want, and press Return.

When you finish editing the file and wish to save it again, select / File Save. 1-2-3 will beep and add the extension WK1 to the file. Press the space bar once, press the backspace until the extension is erased, type the proper file extension for the macro library, and press the Return key, then select Replace (or Backup in Release 2.2).

Segment Your Macro Library

keeping the
macros in
one file is
better for
floppy disk
systems

Your second option is to segment your macro library file into functional units. Rather than separate each kind of macro into a different library file, keep them together in one file—but organize the macros into groups. This is a good strategy if you use a floppy disk based system, whereon the fewer files you need to keep track of, the better. You will also use slightly less disk space if you store the same macros in one file.

Begin by deciding how you will segment your macros. Let's suppose you want one group for use with graphics, one group for use with database applications, and one group to act as general worksheet utilities. Enter all the macros of a certain kind in a single column. Use the standard three-column format (names in the first column, macros in the second, and comments in the third) you learned earlier. Leave the usual single blank cell following each macro. After the last macro of a group, leave several blank cells before beginning the first macro of the next group.

assign range names that are easy to recall

Assign a range name to each group of macros. For each group, include in the named range all three columns (names, macros, and comments) of all the macros in that group (one range name per group). The range name does not need to be a special, two-character macro range name. Unlike naming files, you can use up to fifteen characters to name a range. Any characters—including spaces—are acceptable. It's imperative that you assign range names to these groups that you can readily recall because later, when you are ready to use the / File Combine command to read your macros into your worksheet, you'll have to supply the range name for the group of macros you want. 1-2-3 can not prompt you with the available range names (although, below, we'll describe a way to view a list of them).

For example, let's suppose that one of the range names you assign to a group of macros is Database. After you have used the File Save command to save the file to disk, use the / Worksheet Erase Yes command to clear the worksheet. Move the cell pointer to wherever on the worksheet you want your macros to reside.

File Combine enables you to select a named range from a file

Select / File Combine Named/Specified-Range, enter Database, then select the name of the file in which your macros reside. 1-2-3 will copy just the names, macros, and comments stored in the named range Database in the macro library. If it suits you, you may move the cell pointer farther down the worksheet and repeat the operation, this time requesting a different group of macros by specifying a different range name following the Named/Specified-Range command.

If you are prone to forgetting the names of the ranges you used to segment your macro library, you can give yourself some help in either of two ways.

shortcuts to simplify the job

- Simply select the Entire-File option (rather than Named/Specified-Range) and you will combine the entire file of macros. Then use the / Range Erase command or the / Worksheet Delete Row command to eliminate the macros you don't want.

- Store a table of the range names in your macro library file in such a way that you can easily request them when you are retrieving your macros.

After you've finished assigning your range names in the macro library file (but before you have saved the file), move the cell pointer to a blank area of the worksheet (you'll need two columns for this technique). Select / Range Name Table and indicate the top left cell of the blank range on the worksheet. 1-2-3 will enter a table consisting of the range names and the ranges to which they refer. With your cell pointer at the top of the column of range names, enter the / Range Name Create command, type Names, and press Return. Indicate the column of the table that contains just the names (there's no need to include the cell addresses to their right). Now use the / File Save command to save the file.

Enter the / Worksheet Erase Yes command to clear the worksheet. Now move your cell pointer to where you wish to enter your macros on this new worksheet. Imagine that you're about to combine one of the segments of your macro library and you have forgotten the name of that segment. Instead of retrieving the entire file, enter the command / File Combine Copy Named/Specified-Range, enter Names, and select the name of the file containing your macro library. Next you'll see the list of range names from your macro library on your worksheet. Identify the name you want, repeat the File Combine commands but substitute the range name for the macros you want, and you're done.

Formula Libraries

You might also apply the library concept to formulas. A formula library would contain useful but complex formulas such as a formula that converts numbers into words. Formulas aren't our focus in this book, but there's no reason not to extend your use of macro libraries to formulas as well.

Release 2.2 Macro Libraries [14]

Release 2.2 macro libraries are a big step up over those in Release 2 or 2.01. Release 2.2 macro libraries can produce the same results you can achieve with the macro libraries we've just covered, and much more.

The advantage a Release 2.2 macro library has over a traditional worksheet file is that you can keep it in RAM along with your current worksheet. You can't do that in either Release 2 or 2.01. Since the macro library can reside in RAM, you can control a worksheet with macros, yet store those macros off that worksheet.

That scheme also means you can design worksheets with no regard for where macros reside, and while you use those worksheets, you have no concern about accidentally overwriting or deleting macros. Commands that affect range names, such as Range Name Reset, have no effect on the range names of macros residing in a library. A macro can retrieve a worksheet, modify it, save it, retrieve a second worksheet, modify that, save the second worksheet, retrieve a third worksheet, and so forth. In other

---

[14] Release 3 uses yet another scheme for its macro libraries. It can load many worksheet files at the same time, so it simply stores the macros in one of the worksheet files.

words, in Release 2.2 macros and worksheets can be independent of one another.

The 2.2 macro library is structured like a worksheet file, but it's smaller. It can contain the equivalent of 16,376 cells, arrayed in any configuration of columns and rows you wish. Although a library has cells, it has no cell coordinates (that is, addresses such as A1 and C7), so you make all references to it through range names. If you forget the range names assigned to different parts of the macro library, you can request a list of them.

As the size specification suggests, macro libraries can hold fewer macros than can a full worksheet. However, you can develop as many macro libraries as you like and store each library on disk. When you need a given library, you load it into RAM just as you would a worksheet. You can keep up to ten libraries in memory (that is, libraries whose macros are available for use) at once.

You cannot directly view the macro library's contents. Instead, you create your macros on the current worksheet, debug them, then move them to the macro library. Once they are stored there, you run them by referring to their range name in the same way you run a macro stored on the current worksheet. Whether you use the Alt-letter approach or the Run key, the keystrokes you use to run a macro are the same ones you'd use if the macro were on the current worksheet.

If you need to modify a macro stored in the macro library, you copy it from there onto the current worksheet, edit it, and move it back to the macro library under the same range name. When you move it back, it overwrites the original macro stored under that name.

While you cannot directly view macros once they reside in a macro library, you can, if you wish, view any such macro one line at a time. Turn on Step mode by pressing Alt-F2, activate the macro you wish to view, and press Return. You'll see the first line of the macro appear in the lower left corner of your screen. Step mode works as it does for macros stored on the worksheet. A highlight will show you the next macro command that will be read. When 1-2-3 finishes reading the first line, if there is a second line to the macro, that will appear in the place of the first line in your screen's lower left corner.

Release 2.2's macro library feature is implemented as an add-in program called the Macro Library Manager. You control each of the aforementioned operations via the add-in's menus. Before you can use that menu, you must attach the Macro Library Manager (MLM) add-in, just as you would any other add-in.

You can do that in one of two ways. You can configure 1-2-3 to attach the MLM automatically when you load 1-2-3, so the MLM is always available, or attach it only when you need it. We recommend you choose the former scheme, so you'll always have this versatile tool available. The memory required for the library manager itself is a little more than 13 K. If you can't spare even that much RAM, attach the MLM only when you need it and detach it when you don't. Like most other add-ins, when you detach it, 1-2-3 immediately reclaims the memory the add-in formerly occupied.

Two Methods of Attaching the Macro Library Manager

To configure 1-2-3 to automatically attach the MLM each time you load 1-2-3:

On a hard disk: Change to the subdirectory containing the 1-2-3 program files. If those files are in the subdirectory c:\123, from the DOS prompt, type "cd\123" and press Return. Type "dir *.adn" and press Return. You should see the file MACROMGR.ADN listed. If you don't, place the original 1-2-3 disk marked "Install" in your floppy disk drive and copy the MACROMGR.ADN file from it into the subdirectory containing your 1-2-3 program files.

Load 1-2-3. Select / Worksheet Global Default Other Add-In Set. Look at the bottom left corner of the Default Settings sheet on your screen. There you'll see a list of eight numbers. Select from the menu the lowest number that has no text listed immediately to its right. If you haven't installed any other add-ins, that will be number 1.

1-2-3 will now display a menu at the top of the screen of the available add-in files in the current subdirectory. If the current subdirectory is not the one containing your 1-2-3 files, enter the name of that subdirectory and press Return. Highlight the file named MACROMGR.ADN and press Return. Choose either to assign the MLM to the Alt-F7, Alt-F8, Alt-F9, Alt-F10 key, or to no key at all. If you haven't assigned any add-in to the Alt-F10 key, we suggest you select 10 from the menu to do so.

Now select No, or else 1-2-3 will show you the MLM menu each time you start up. While that option may be useful with other add-ins, there's no need for it here. Select Quit Update Quit and you're done.

To attach the MLM to 1-2-3 only when you need it:

On a hard disk: Change to the subdirectory containing the 1-2-3 program files. If those files are in the subdirectory c:\123, from the DOS prompt, type "cd\123" and press Return. Type "dir *.adn" and press Return. You should see the file MACROMGR.ADN listed. If you don't, return to your original 1-2-3 disks and copy the MACROMGR.ADN file from one of them into the subdirectory containing your 1-2-3 program files.

Load 1-2-3. Select / Add-In Attach. 1-2-3 will now display a menu at the top of the screen of the available add-in files in the current subdirectory. If the current subdirectory is not the one containing your 1-2-3 files, enter the name of that subdirectory and press Return. Highlight the file named MACROMGR.ADN and press Return. Choose either to assign the MLM to the Alt-F7, Alt-F8, Alt-F9, Alt-F10 key, or to no key at all. If you haven't assigned any add-in to the Alt-F10 key, we suggest you select 10 from the menu to do so. Select Quit and you're done.

On a floppy-disk system: With 1-2-3 running, place in drive B: the 1-2-3 disk marked Install or any disk to which you have copied the file MACROMGR.ADN. Select / Add-In Attach, press Escape twice, enter B: (or the name of the drive where you have placed the disk containing the MACROMGR.ADN file) and press Return. Highlight the file named MACROMGR.ADN and press Return. Choose either to assign the MLM to the Alt-F7, Alt-F8, Alt-F9, Alt-F10 key, or to no key at all. If you haven't assigned any add-in to the Alt-F10 key, we suggest you select 10 from the menu to do so. Select Quit and you're done.

A Quick Tutorial

Attach the Macro Library Manager through one of the aforementioned methods. The following instructions will give you a feel for how the MLM works. After you keystroke through them, we'll acquaint you with the full range of capabilities and limitations of each command.

1. Write, name, and test macros on the worksheet. The first step to creating a macro library is to create on the worksheet the macros that will go in it. You write them, name them, and test them just as you would macros that you intend to keep on the worksheet. Here are two macros, one to increase the width of a column and the other to format a cell as Currency. On a blank worksheet, enter the following:

In cell A1, enter: '\A

In cell B1, enter: '/wcs25~

In cell A3, enter: '\B

In cell B3, enter: '/rfc~~

To assign range names to the macros, place the cell pointer on cell A1, select / Range Name Labels Right, press the Downarrow key twice to select the range A1..A3, and press Return.

Now test the macros. Press and hold down the Macro key (Alt) and type A. The macro should increase the width of column A to 25. Move to cell D1 and enter 100. Press the Macro key (Alt) and type B. The macro should format the cell as Currency with two decimal places.

2. Save the macro in a macro library. Display the Macro Library Manager menu by pressing whichever of the Alt-Function key assignments you selected when you attached the MLM to 1-2-3. If you followed our suggestion, that was Alt-F10. (If you selected the No-Key option, select / Add-In Invoke, then highlight MACROMGR and press Return.) With the MLM menu in the control panel, if you wish, move the menu pointer to each menu selection and read the description that appears beneath it. We'll use each of the selections during this tutorial. For now, select Save.

The MLM prompts for the name of the macro library to save and, if any macro library files reside in the current data directory, it shows you those files. Enter Tutor. Then press the Backspace key to unanchor the pointer, press Home to move to cell A1, type a period to re-anchor the pointer, indicate the range A1..B3, and press Return. Select No to save the library file without a password. The MLM saves the entries within A1..B3 in a library file named TUTOR.MLB and erases those entries from the worksheet.

You can now use the macros anywhere within this worksheet, or in any another worksheet. Press the Pagedown key and move into column B. Press the Macro key (Alt) and type A. Press the Goto and Name function keys and note that no range names appear there. That's because the named ranges now reside in the macro library named Tutor, not in the current worksheet, and you cannot move the cell pointer into a macro library. Press Escape to cancel the operation. However, if you press the Run key (Alt-F3), you will see the macro names available for you to run. Press Escape twice to cancel that operation.

Now select / Worksheet Erase Yes to erase the current worksheet. In cell A1 of the new worksheet, enter 255.32; then press the Macro key (Alt) and type B. Note that the macro remains active, despite the fact that you cleared memory and you're no longer using the worksheet it was created in.

Suppose you want to revise one of the macros in the macro library, or add another macro. Display the Macro Library Manager menu (press Alt-F10 or whatever Alt-key you assigned to it) and highlight Edit. As the description line of the menu says, Edit copies the contents of a macro library back to the worksheet, where you can work on it. Select Edit and specify the macro library file TUTOR.MLB.

You'll next see the choices Ignore and Overwrite. Press Control-Break to cancel the operation in progress while we explain the choices you face now. We'll resume the operation in a moment.

When you use the Edit command, the MLM not only copies the macros back to the worksheet, it also creates within the worksheet the range names that go with those macros. If you select Ignore, in the event any incoming range name already exists within this worksheet, the MLM will let the worksheet-based range name stand and copy the macro into the worksheet without creating its associated range name. Selecting Overwrite does the opposite: it grants precedence to the range names of the incoming macros. In any case, if there's duplication between a range name in the incoming macro(s) and one on the worksheet, one of the two will be invalidated. However, 1-2-3 can neither tell you whether one has been eliminated nor, in the event that happens, which one it was.

For those reasons, we recommend that you avoid any potential for conflict between incoming range names and those in your worksheet. Before you use the Edit command, save your worksheet, select / Worksheet Erase Yes to begin with a fresh worksheet, and import your macros into that. Do what you need to do with them, save them back to a macro library file, and retrieve your saved worksheet to pick up where you left off.

There are times when you'll want to import those macros into an existing worksheet, so let's review the consequences of using either Ignore or Overwrite. You might choose Ignore if you're importing macros into a complex worksheet containing many range names. With such a worksheet, if you select Overwrite, and the incoming macros remove some range names from the worksheet, it may be difficult to identify the range names affected, to remember the location to which they were originally assigned, and the reason you assigned them. That may lead to problems in the worksheet later on.

Consider that if you do lose some of the macros' range names, the associated macros won't work in the worksheet. Further, if one or more macro range names have been eliminated and you don't discover that fact, then you re-save your macros to a library, you won't find out that some of them no longer work until you try to use those macros.

Either way, if you choose to use the MLM's Edit command with an existing worksheet, you must exercise great caution.

Now, complete the Edit command sequence: Display the Macro Library Manager menu (press Alt-F10 or whatever Alt-key you assigned to it), select Edit, specify the macro library file TUTOR.MLB, and select Ignore. Now point to cell C1 and press Return. The MLM copies to the worksheet the macros you earlier moved to the library. Since it is copying those macros, they still exist in the macro library file. Now, edit the macro in cell D1 to read /wcs{?}~. Try out the new macro to make sure it works.

Note that even though you wished to revise just one of the two macros, you had to copy the entire macro library to the worksheet. Similarly, you must resave both macros to the macro library file, even though you changed just one of them. That's because when you use the Save command, you'll be writing over the old copy of the macro library file, so you must save all the macros you wish to be in the new file.

Display the MLM menu by pressing Alt-F10 (or whatever Alt key you assigned), select Save, specify TUTOR, select Yes to overwrite the existing file, if necessary, unanchor the pointer by pressing the Backspace key, and specify the range C1..D3. Note that if you had wanted to add a macro to the library, you'd have entered it beginning on row 5, and would have included the range containing it in the specification you just entered. So instead of C1..D3, that specification might have been C1..D5. Select No to decline to assign a password to the library file.

Macro library files are stored on the disk, just as are worksheets. Also like worksheets, they don't become active until loaded into memory. When you use the Save command to create a new library, the MLM not only saves the library to disk, it puts the library in memory.

With the macro library file saved, select / Quit Yes Yes to exit 1-2-3 without saving the current worksheet. That also removes from memory any macro libraries that were in memory, but leaves them stored on the disk.

Let's assume you're going to start a new session. Load 1-2-3. If you didn't install the Macro Library Manager to attach itself automatically, attach it now using the / Add-In Attach command. No macro libraries reside in memory now, so you can't yet use a macro stored in a library. To place a library into memory, display the MLM menu, select Load, and specify the macro library file TUTOR.MLB. If TUTOR.MLB doesn't show up in the control panel as an available file, you were probably logged to a different directory when you saved it. Specify the name of that directory (such as C:\123\finance\) and press Return. If you specified the correct directory, you'll see the name TUTOR.MLB. After selecting the file, select Quit to return to Ready mode.

Suppose it has been a while since you last used these macros and while you remember what macros are in the file, you've forgotten their range names. First, you can use the Run key (Alt-F3) to see the available range names. However, if the worksheet or other macro libraries also have range names, you may not be able to identify the ones for this particular library. Press Name (F3) for a full-screen list of range names. Note that the third line of the screen lists, for the currently highlighted range name, the name and either the worksheet range or the macro library file associated with that name.

If you need to know every one of the range names in a given library, you can place such a list on the worksheet. Display the Macro Library Manager and select Name-List. You must select the macro library file you wish to obtain a list of names from, but the MLM will present to you only macro libraries currently in memory. Any residing on the disk but not in memory won't appear on the menu. Select TUTOR.MLB and specify the top left corner of the range on the worksheet where the list of names should appear.

If the names themselves are insufficient, that is, if you need to see the macros, too, use the Edit command. If you are using the Edit command only to view the macros but not to modify them, you need not resave those macros. Remember that the Edit command copies the macros from the library file to the worksheet, so the library file remains. Also, this is a place to use the Edit command's Ignore option, since you're just browsing the macros and don't need to use them in the worksheet.

When you earlier used the Load command, you may recall that after you selected the library file TUTOR.MLB, the menu returned. That means that if you had another macro library file, you could then have selected Load and selected it, too. Up to ten macro libraries can reside in memory at once. However, there are consequences with respect to available memory that you'll want to consider. A thorough explanation of that subject appears later in this section. For now, suffice it to say that there will come times when you'll want to remove a macro library from memory without exiting 1-2-3. To do that, select the Remove command from the MLM menu. You'll then see a menu of just the macro library files in memory. Highlight the one you wish to remove and press Return.

So ends our quick tour. You can now use the Macro Library Manager, but there's a lot more that you may want to know about it. Following is a more detailed review of each MLM menu item, followed by a series of tips for using the MLM effectively.

The Macro Library Manager Menu

A good way to understand the fundamentals of the Macro Library Manager is to review the selections on its main menu. Press Alt-F10 to view the MLM menu. The selections include Load, Save, Edit, Remove, Name-List, and Quit. Here's a summary of each command.

Load: You can use only those macros that reside in a macro library file that's been loaded into memory. As soon as you remove a library from memory, the macros it contains become unavailable for use. You can load more than one macro library into memory, as long as there remains enough free memory to load it. Select Load when you want to use a macro library that you've previously saved to disk. 1-2-3 will display a menu of the macro library files stored in the current directory (that is, the directory that 1-2-3's File Directory command shows as its current setting). If that's not the location of the macro library you now want to use, press Escape, specify a new directory, and press Return. Because the MLM logs onto the same directory as does 1-2-3, it's a good idea to store your macro library files in the same directory as your data files. However, if you already store your worksheets in more than one subdirectory on a hard disk, you might also create a special subdirectory just for macro libraries.

Save: Select Save when you want to save in a macro library one or more macros that you've written on the current worksheet. Make sure the macros have been assigned range names, and that they have been debugged. After selecting Save, specify the name you wish the macro library file to assume, or specify an existing macro library that you wish to overwrite. The MLM assigns to macro library files the extension MLB. Although you can override that by specifying an extension of your own, it's usually best to let the MLM assign the extension. If you assign a different extension, when you next try to retrieve the library, you'll have to specify the extension or the file won't appear on the MLM's menu.

Next, specify the worksheet range containing the macro(s) you want to save. If you want to password-protect the macro library file, select Yes and enter the password. If not, select No. Note that passwords are case sensitive. If you assign one, you must enter the password later using the same case you used when you assigned the password. Be aware that if you assign a password and later forget it, you will be unable to retrieve your macros. We recommend you weigh carefully against this risk any advantages to be gained from using a password. After saving macros in a macro library the MLM will erase the macros from the current worksheet and delete from the worksheet the range names assigned to them. Both macros and range names transfer to the newly created macro library, and that library is stored both in memory (so the macros it contains are active) and on disk. You cannot save within a library file any formulas containing links to external files. If you specify a range containing such formulas, 1-2-3 will issue an error message.

Edit: Select Edit when you want to copy the macros from a macro library onto the current worksheet. The macro library must already be in memory. That is, you must either have used the Save command to create it during this session, or have used the Load command to load it from the disk into memory. After selecting Edit, the MLM will display a menu of any macro libraries in memory. Select the one whose contents you want to copy onto your worksheet. Next, in the event any of the range names in the selected library duplicate range names in the current worksheet, choose whether to let the incoming range names overwrite the existing ones (select Overwrite) or let the worksheet's current range names remain assigned to their current ranges (select Ignore). Finally, select the top left corner of the range where the macros in the selected library will reside in the current worksheet.

Remove: Select Remove to remove a macro library from memory. After you do, the range names you once used to activate the macros in that library will no longer perform that task. To reactivate the macros, use the MLM's Load command. You'll recover some memory for each macro library you remove from memory. How much you recover depends on how much memory that library occupied. You can check that figure by using the / Worksheet Status command and noting the first figure to the right of the Conventional memory prompt. Do so before and after you use the Remove command, then subtract the second amount you recorded from the first. When you select the Remove command, the MLM will display a menu of only those macro libraries in memory. If there are none, the MLM will put 1-2-3 into error mode and display the message "No macro libraries in memory".

Name-List: Select Name-List to display on the current worksheet a list of range names in any of the active macro libraries. Use this command when you've forgotten the range names you use to activate a given macro library's macros, or when you want to prevent range name conflicts with a worksheet currently in memory.

Quit: Return to 1-2-3's ready mode.

Macro Library Manager Tips

The following tips should help you exploit the capabilities and circumvent some of the limitations of the Macro Library Manager.

Minimizing Memory Use: The MLM uses exclusively conventional memory. It cannot use expanded memory. That can significantly limit your work, but you can minimize that effect with the proper approach.

First, let's understand the limitation. You can have considerably less conventional memory than expanded memory. However, access to the megabytes of expanded memory you can install depends on the availability of conventional memory. The possibility exists that a worksheet and a macro library might use up all your conventional memory, leaving you with lots of available expanded memory that you can't use.

Since macro libraries exclusively use conventional memory, avoid loading more macro libraries into memory at once than you plan to use. Use the / Worksheet Status command to keep track of how much conventional memory you have left (it's the first of the two kinds of memory listed on the settings sheet you'll see) after loading each macro library. If you deplete available conventional memory, use the Remove command to remove any libraries you aren't using and you'll regain immediately the memory those libraries occupied. How much memory depends on the size of the libraries involved. Use the / Worksheet Status command to keep track of how much memory you regain. If you are really pressed for memory, use the / Add-In Detach command to remove the MLM itself. You'll see it on the Add-In Detach command's menu as a file named MACROMGR. That step will net you a little more than 13 K of conventional memory.

Unlike 1-2-3 Release 2 and higher releases of 1-2-3, the MLM does not use a sparse matrix memory allocation scheme. That means that every empty cell within the range saved to a macro library will occupy memory. To conserve the conventional memory the library uses, keep all macros that are stored in the library as close to one another as possible. The time you can effect that optimization is when you create your macros on the worksheet. Minimize the number of cells contained in the range you intend to save to the macro library. A range containing many empty cells will unnecessarily encumber conventional memory. For a suggestion on consolidating an existing macro, particularly one created with Learn mode, see the next tip.

It's somewhat more efficient to have in memory one macro library file containing all the macros that you'll use, versus having several macro library files in memory with the same macros distributed among them. For example, in a test using two macros, those macros occupied 25% more memory when they were stored in two different macro libraries, compared to the same macros stored in a single library. To learn how to combine macros from two libraries into one, see the second tip following.

Consolidating Macro Labels Into Fewer Cells: If you've used Learn mode to create a macro, especially if that macro enters data or uses any of the special keys, such as the Goto key or the Escape key, it's likely that the macro will be stored in many more cells than are needed.

There may be a way to consolidate the macro labels into fewer cells a little more quickly than performing the entire operation manually. Select the / Range Justify command, and specify the number of rows to include as many macro labels in a single column as you wish to consolidate; next, expand the cell pointer across as many columns as you wish the labels to be wide, and press Return.

The labels will be drawn upward into fewer cells, but spaces will have been inserted between any entries that formerly resided in different cells. You may remove those spaces manually, or you might wish to use the /

Range Search command. Specify the range containing the new labels as the range to search. In response to the prompt "Enter string to search for", press the space bar and press Return, select Both Replace, and press Return. In the control panel, 1-2-3 will show you the first space it encounters and let you choose to replace it or not. If you wish to remove it, select Replace; if not, select Next. Do not select All, as there may be blank spaces in the macro label that you want to preserve, such as those in macro statements incorporating advanced macro commands. [15]

Adding Macros To A Macro Library: Once you've saved one or more macros to a macro library with the MLM's Save command, you can't add any more macros to the file. If you try to save again, you'll overwrite the existing macro library. However, you can easily work around that limitation. Use the Edit command to copy the macros from the library back to the worksheet, then use 1-2-3's Move command to move any macros you wish to add to the library, to the range directly beneath the range now occupied by the macros from the library. With the macros stored in one column, display the MLM's menu, select Save, specify the same macro library from which you copied the macros, select Yes to overwrite its current contents, specify the range containing both old and new macros, and choose whether or not to password-protect the file. MLM will store all the macros in that range in the macro library.

If You Forget What Macros Are In A Given Library: Use the MLM's Edit command to copy the macros from the macro library into the current worksheet. Once you've refreshed your memory, erase the macros from the worksheet. The macros still exist in the macro library, so you don't need to resave them. If you forget only the range names of those macros, press Run (Alt-F3) Name (F3). 1-2-3 will display a full-screen list of all range names both in the worksheet and in all macro libraries currently loaded. Press Escape twice when you're finished viewing the list. If you're mainly concerned with one particular macro library, or if there are so many range names that you need to manipulate them in the worksheet, select the MLM's Name-List command instead of Edit. It will populate the worksheet with a list of all the range names in the macro library you select.

If you don't know what macro library file a given range name is stored within: Turn on Step (press Alt-F2), press Run (Alt-F3), and look in the lower left corner of the screen. The macro library filename will appear there. If

---

[15] When you finish, beware that the Replace command will retain the space character you earlier specified at the "Enter string to search for:" prompt, although its presence is hard to notice. If you later specify a search for the character # and fail to delete the space, you'll unwittingly search for a space followed by a #, not the # alone. To remove that space now, select / Range Search, specify the current cell, press the Backspace key to remove the space character, and select Both Find.

the library isn't password-protected, the particular line of macro code bearing the range name in question will appear directly to its right.

Macro Library Manager And Range Names: You can refer to items stored in a macro library only by their range name. That means that before you move a macro from the worksheet into a macro library, you must be sure that all references it contains identify the object of that reference with a range name. If a macro you move to a macro library contains a reference consisting of cell coordinates—that is, things such as A1 or C7—when the macro runs that reference will always be to the cell that is identified by those coordinates on whichever worksheet is the current worksheet at the time. This may cause unintended results in your macro.

There's another situation where the reference will resolve in favor of the worksheet. Suppose a macro stored in a macro library contains a reference to a range named Stock_price, that Stock_price is a named range also stored in that macro library, and that that macro library currently resides in memory. Further suppose that you retrieve a worksheet, Stocks, that also has a range named Stock_price. If you run the macro while the worksheet Stocks is in memory, the macro will ignore the contents of the Stock_price range stored in the macro library, and instead refer to the contents of the range stored in the worksheet.

One way to avoid that problem is to assign special names to ranges that you intend to store in a macro library. Our recommendation is to always enclose the standard range name in a pair of square brackets. So, if you would normally name a range Price, if you intend to store it in a macro library, you should name it [Price]. The brackets present a convenient visual cue that the range is one of those stored in a macro library.

When you use the MLM's Save command to move a macro from the worksheet to a macro library, the range name goes with the macro, and that range name has been deleted on the worksheet. Like any other deleted range name, you will no longer see those range names on the menu of range names that appears when you press the Goto and Name function keys. Nor will formulas that once referred to those range names reflect that range name any longer. If you reexamine them, you'll see 1-2-3 has substituted the cell addresses for the same worksheet range. However, as long as that macro library remains in memory, the range name will appear on 1-2-3's Run-key range-name menu. That'll let you use the Run key to activate the macro. If you subsequently name a worksheet range with that name, two copies of the same range name will appear on the Run-key menu. The worksheet-based range name always appears before the library-based range name on that menu.

If you have used a backslash-letter combination to name a macro you have stored in a macro library, and you subsequently assign that name to another macro that resides on the worksheet, when you next press Alt and that letter, 1-2-3 will run the macro stored on the worksheet, not the one in the library. You can, however, still press the Run key, select the second instance of that range name on the menu, and the macro library-based macro will run.

Using a formula reference, you cannot reference the contents of a named range stored in a macro library as you can a named range stored on the worksheet. For example, if the value 100 is in cell A1 on the worksheet, and you've assigned the range name Start to cell A1, if you enter the formula + START into cell C2, then cell C2 will return the value 100. That sort of reference will not work if the named range resides in a macro library. There are ways to reference entries in a macro library, but they involve use of the advanced macro commands, such as { let } , that you'll learn about later.

The / Range Name Reset command affects only those range names stored in the current worksheet. It will not cancel range names stored in macro libraries. Similarly, when you retrieve a worksheet file, only the range names stored in the preceding worksheet vanish. Range names stored in macro libraries that are themselves stored in memory remain extant.

Macro Security: Macro libraries are an excellent way to protect your macro code from anyone else's eyes. When you use the MLM's Save command, you have the option to assign a password of up to 80 characters to the macro library you are creating. Password protection doesn't restrict use of the macros, it restricts access to the macro code. So if you assign a password, anyone can still load the library file into memory and use the macros it contains, but only someone who knows the password can use the Edit command to copy that library's contents onto the worksheet. As you might expect, if you invoke Step mode and activate a macro from a password-protected library, you'll see that Step will not display the contents of the macro as it steps through the macro commands.

There are several other things that you can't do to view a library file, whether or not that file has been password-protected. You can't use 1-2-3's File Combine command to combine any part of a macro library into a worksheet. If on the worksheet you enter a reference to a range name stored in an active macro library, you will not see the contents of that range, so it's impossible to view a macro through a range name reference. Finally, our attempts to use the Norton Utilities and to use Lotus Magellan to view the macro library file showed that neither would display the contents of macros contained within a macro library, whether or not the file was password-protected.

There is, however, a way to see some of the contents of a password-protected macro library file without knowing the password. The method involves the use of the advanced macro command {let}, a command you'll learn about in the section on macro programming. For a description of this technique, see the chapter entitled Manipulating Data and refer within it to the coverage of the {let} command.

The MLM does not require the password before it will provide a list of range names from the library file, nor does the password prevent anyone from overwriting the macro library with another library of the same name. If you do use a password, we strongly recommend that you write it down as part of the documentation for that macro library. Failing that, here's a strategy you might use:

1. Use mnemonic passwords, or ones you can associate to something meaningful. For example, the middle three letters of your middle name. Avoid totally nonsensical passwords.

2. Use as few passwords as possible. You may be able to use the same password on every macro library you decide to protect.

Last, remember that passwords are case sensitive. If you assign the password LetMeIn, then only that precise combination of upper and lower case characters will retrieve it.

Automatically Loading Macro Libraries: You can have a macro library load itself into memory at the time you load 1-2-3. We'll explain how in the next chapter.

Summary

You've seen how to construct a macro library and copy those macros from one worksheet to another. You can now begin keeping your own favorite macros in a library and gain access to them at any time.

In the next chapter, you'll learn how to automate some of the work you do with macros, including entering data, loading worksheets or macro libraries into memory, and activating macros that reside in either location.

6

Macro Automation Features

You've seen how macros enable you to automate a wide spectrum of operations that you'd otherwise perform interactively with 1-2-3. In this section, we'll present some related 1-2-3 features that work in conjunction with macros to further automate your worksheets:

- Automated data entry
- Auto-start macros
- Auto-load worksheets
- Auto-load macro libraries

Automated Data Entry

the only
1-2-3
command
meant for
macros

1-2-3 contains a command that seems as if it was intended exclusively for use with macros, / Range Input. Range Input allows you to restrict cell-pointer movement to certain cells on the worksheet. Those cells need not be contiguous; they can be spread over the entire worksheet.

When you select the / Range Input command, although the mode indicator will display Ready and there will be no unusual messages posted on the screen, 1-2-3 will restrict the control usually granted to the keyboard in several ways.

how Range
Input
changes
what the
user can do
on the
worksheet

1. You will be able to move the cell pointer only to unprotected cells within a range you have specified. The exception occurs when you point to build formulas, when it will still be possible to point to other cells.

2. You will be restricted to entering labels, values, or formulas and to editing existing entries.

3. You will be unable to display 1-2-3's menu. If you press the slash key, 1-2-3 will treat it as any other typed character. Just three function keys remain active (the Help key will display a help screen for the Range Input command, the Edit key will allow editing in the current cell, and the Abs key—F4 on most computers—works normally).

preparing to
use Range
Input

Here's how to use / Range Input. First, decide which range will contain the cells you'd like to enable someone to move to, enter data into, or edit.

If you are at all uncertain about the protection status of the cells in that range (i.e., which of them have been unprotected with the / Range Unprotect command), use the / Range Protect command to protect the entire range. As long as you do not enable global worksheet protection with the / Worksheet Global Protection Enable command, you'll still be able to edit any of these cells.

Now, use the / Range Unprotect command to unprotect each cell within the range that you want to allow someone to move the cell pointer to, enter data into, or edit. After using the / Range Unprotect command, if you move to one of the unprotected cells and look in the control panel, you should see a U (for Unprotected) just to the right of the cell address that appears there.

Range Input
will move
the screen
and the cell
pointer

Now select / Range Input and designate the range that contains all of the unprotected cells. The cell pointer will jump to one of those cells and the screen will reposition itself so that the top left corner of the entire range is in the top left corner of the screen. 1-2-3 will position the screen that way even if the top left corner of the range was on the screen at the time you selected / Range Input.

If you press a directional arrow (such as the Rightarrow key), the cell pointer will move to the next unprotected cell in the range. If you press the Return key without having entered any data beforehand, the Range Input command will restore control to the keyboard, and the cell pointer and screen will return to the positions they occupied prior to your use of the command.

Automatic Macro Activation

you can
assign a
range name
that causes
1-2-3 to
start a
macro by
itself

Up until this point, in order to use a macro you had to activate it yourself. However, there's a way to have 1-2-3 start the macro for you. You can assign a unique range name to a macro that will cause 1-2-3 to automatically activate that macro when you retrieve the worksheet containing it from disk. Here's how to do it.

In this example, we'll create a macro that we want 1-2-3 to automatically activate and assign to it a special range name. Before beginning, clear the worksheet by selecting / Worksheet Erase Yes. As you enter the macro shown below, make sure to enter a label prefix character manually before you type the labels in cells B5, B6, or B7. The first character following the label prefix character should be a caret (^).

	A	B	C	D	E	F	G	H
1	NAME	MACRO						
2	-----	------------------------------						
3		{goto}J1~{goto}J9~						
4		/wcs72~						
5		^Automatic{d}						
6		^Macro{d}						
7		^Activation!						
8		{u 2}{d 2}						
9		{u 2}{d 2}						
10		{u 2}{d 2}						
11		{u 2}{d 2}						
12		{u 2}{d 2}						
13		{u 2}{d 2}						
14		{u 2}{d 2}						
15		{u 2}{d 2}						
16		/re.{u 2}~						
17		/wcr						
18								
19								
20								

Figure 6-1

an auto-
execute
macro is the
only macro
with the
name \Ø

In the next step, you're going to use the only exception to a rule we introduced earlier. We told you that all macro range names consist of two characters, a backslash followed by a single letter.[16] You distinguish an auto-execute macro by assigning to it the name \Ø (that's a backslash followed by a zero, not the letter "O").

In the following steps, wherever you see the numeral zero (it looks like an oblong "O" but with a strikethrough, like this: Ø), be sure to enter a zero. Don't confuse it with the letter "O"; those characters are not interchangable. Now follow these instructions:

---

[16] In Release 2.2, macro names need not assume the backslash-letter combination because you can use the Run key (Alt-F3) to run a macro the first line of which has been assigned any range name at all.

Move: To cell A3

Enter: '\∅

Select: / Range Name Labels Right

Press: Return Return

Press: Tab

In Release 2.2, a global setting allows you to disable the worksheet's ability to run an autoexecute macro. You might use that if you wanted to edit a worksheet containing an autoexecute macro that begins with the {breakoff} command and that doesn't otherwise allow you interactive access to the worksheet. It would ordinarily be impossible to break out of such a macro to modify the worksheet. However, you can disable such a macro before it ever starts running. In order for an autoexecute macro to work, the / Worksheet Global Default Autoexec setting in the worksheet containing it must be set to Yes. That's the setting 1-2-3 has when you receive it. So, for this exercise, if you haven't changed the setting, leave it be. However, if you have changed the setting, or if an autoexecute macro isn't working and you don't know why, select / Worksheet Global Default and look at the settings sheet that displays. If the setting to the right of the prompt "Autoexecute macros:" says "Yes", select Quit. If not, select either Autoexec Yes Quit (to change the setting for the current session only) or Autoexec Yes Update Quit (to change it until such time as you change it back).

Select: / File Save

Enter: Test

Select: / Worksheet Erase Yes

trying out
an auto-
execute
macro

Now you've got the macro named and the worksheet containing it saved. In the next step, you'll retrieve that file from disk. As you do, watch the screen carefully.

Select: / File Retrieve

Enter: Test

1-2-3 should have activated the macro automatically as soon as you retrieved the file from disk. If it didn't, review the preceding instructions to discover the problem.

you can
assign more
than one
name to a
macro

If you try to reactivate the macro by depressing the Macro key and typing a 0, you'll see that an auto execute macro can't be reactivated with the Macro key. Although if you are using Release 2.2, you can use the Run key to activate the macro, there's another method that works in all releases of 1-2-3 without retrieving the file from disk again. You can assign to any cell of the worksheet more than one range name. You've already assigned the name \0 to the first cell of the macro. You can also assign a conventional macro range name (such as \A) to that cell. This time, use the / Range Name Create command to assign the range name instead of the / Range Name Labels command. After you do, you can reactivate the macro at any time by depressing the Macro key and typing the letter used in the conventional macro name (such as A).

Since there is just one range name (\0) to assign to an auto-execute macro, each worksheet can contain just one such macro. However, once you've assigned that name to a macro, you can reassign it to any other macro whenever you wish. Like other changes to a worksheet, in order to preserve this one, be sure to save your worksheet to disk afterward.

Automatic Worksheet Loading

let 1-2-3
load a
worksheet
for you

At the time you load 1-2-3, it can automatically load a worksheet from the disk without further intervention. This feature is helpful if:

- You almost always work with the same worksheet each time you begin working with 1-2-3.

- You have a customized application that uses a menu on one worksheet as a gateway to a host of other applications.

- You have a simple routine, such as one to allow you to change directories, that you wish to use before doing any other work with 1-2-3.

In Release 2.2, each time you load 1-2-3, you can designate a different worksheet file to be automatically retrieved. That's helpful if you know in advance of loading 1-2-3 which worksheet file you want loaded, even if that's a different file each time.

Used in concert with an auto-execute macro, this is a particularly powerful feature. Here's how it works.

Prepare the worksheet you wish 1-2-3 to retrieve automatically (in this case, we'll use the worksheet with the auto-execute macro from the previous section).

name the
file Auto123
and 1-2-3
will load it
for you

Select: / File Save

Enter: Auto123

If you are using a floppy-disk based system, before you next boot 1-2-3, place the disk containing the Auto123 file into the drive you have designated as the default directory.[17] When you next load 1-2-3, the program will load the file into memory automatically. If you are using a floppy-disk based system and you use drive B as your default data directory, in the past when you loaded 1-2-3 you may have noticed the B drive light come on briefly. Now you know that 1-2-3 was looking for a file called Auto123.

specify
a worksheet
when you
load 1-2-3

In Release 2.2, you can instruct 1-2-3 to automatically retrieve any worksheet file upon startup. Instead of entering 123, enter 123 -w*Name*, where *Name* is the name of the worksheet file you wish to load. For example, if you want to load a worksheet named Tax.wk1, enter 123 -wtax. You need not enter the filename extension. If you are also specifying a custom driver set as part of your command, it doesn't matter whether you specify the auto-load worksheet before or after the name of the custom driver set.

If you are using a batch file to load 1-2-3, you can still take advantage of Release 2.2's command-line autoload feature. Suppose you use DOS's Edlin editor to edit the file. With Edlin and the batch file in the same directory, enter *edlin 1.bat*, where 1.bat is the name of the batch file you use to load 1-2-3. Your screen may now look like this:

```
C:edlin 1.bat
End of input file
*
```

Now type an L and press Return, and Edlin will list the file. Let's suppose your screen now looks like this:

```
C:edlin 1.bat
End of input file
*l
        1:*cd\123
        2: 123
        3: cd\
*
```

[17] The default data directory is the directory where 1-2-3 will store files and retrieve files unless otherwise instructed. You set the default directory with the command / Worksheet Global Default Directory. If you are working on a floppy disk system, you should then remove the write protect tab from your 1-2-3 System disk and reinsert the disk into the drive. Select Update to store your changes on the disk. If you are using a floppy system, replace the write protect tab on the 1-2-3 System disk.

Type 2, press Return, and press F3 to redisplay the current line. Type a space, then type %1 and press Return. Now type L and press Return. You should now see the following listing.

```
1:*cd\123
2: 123 %1
3: cd\
```
*

Then type E and press Return. The %1 you appended to line 2 of the batch file modifies the way that line will read when the batch file executes. If when you run the batch file you enter another word following the name of the batch file, DOS will substitute that word for the %1 when it reads line 2 of the batch file.

When you want 1-2-3 to load a specific worksheet automatically, instead of merely typing 1 to load 1-2-3, type 1 -wName, where Name is the name of the worksheet you wish to load. If you don't care to have 1-2-3 auto-load a worksheet, simply enter 1. Either command will work.

Automatically Loading Macro Libraries in Release 2.2

You can arrange things so that when you start 1-2-3 Release 2.2, a macro library will automatically load into memory. Further, you can have a macro in that library automatically execute itself. Here's how.

First, we'll assume that you've set 1-2-3 to automatically attach the Macro Library Manager add-in. If you haven't, refer to the instructions in chapter 2 for doing so. Now create one or more macros and save them in a macro library, assigning to that library the name Autoload.mlb. When you next load 1-2-3, provided you have saved the macro library file in 1-2-3's default data directory, the Macro Library Manager will automatically load Autoload.mlb into memory. You can verify that, after loading 1-2-3, by activating one of the macros you earlier stored in Autoload.mlb.

have 1-2-3 load a macro library and run a macro

You can further have Autoload.mlb automatically execute a macro. Store in Autoload.mlb a macro to which you have assigned the range name \0 and save Autoload.mlb. To make the autoexecute macro work, you need one other component. Autoexecute macros work only at the time a worksheet loads into memory. They won't work if only a macro library loads into memory.

For that reason, you need also a worksheet named Auto123.wk1 stored in the default data directory. It matters not what's on the worksheet, it can even be empty, with one exception. If it contains an autoexecute macro of it's own, then the worksheet-based macro will take priority over the one in the macro library.

After making each of the preceding arrangements, when you start 1-2-3, the following sequence will take place:

A. The macro library manager will automatically attach itself.

B. The macro library Autoload.mlb will automatically load.

C. The worksheet Auto123.wk1 will automatically load into memory.

D. The autoexecute macro named \0 will automatically activate.

Here's a recap of the steps you must take to have an autoexecute macro work from a macro library.

three steps
for
autoexecute
macros in
macro
libraries

1. Use the / Worksheet Global Default Other Add-In Set command to specify that 1-2-3 should automatically attach the Macro Library Manager whenever you load 1-2-3.

2. Create an autoexecute macro (with the name \0) and save it in a macro library named Autoload.mlb.

3. Create a worksheet named Auto123.wk1. Before you save the worksheet, make sure the / Worksheet Global Default Autoexecute command is set to Yes. If it was set to No, select Yes Update Quit to change it. Make sure, too, that you have not placed any other autoexecute macro on this worksheet. Save the worksheet to disk in whichever data directory is the default when you load 1-2-3.

Summary

In this chapter, you've taken a significant step forward in your ability to automate the work you do through macros. In the next chapter, you'll advance yet another step by, among other things, learning to write macros that automatically repeat themselves, a step you'll find particularly useful as you write data-entry macros.

7

A Prologue
to More Advanced Macros

In this section, you'll learn about two advanced macro commands, {branch} and {quit}, that will enable you to increase the power of your macros significantly. Later, when you learn about the rest of the advanced macro commands, you'll learn more about these powerful commands. We'll then introduce you to a host of powerful new macros that they enable you to write. For now, let's put them to work with the macros you're already writing. At the same time, you'll learn more about how to use range names in your macros.

An Introduction to Loops

Your objective is to learn to write macros that automatically repeat themselves.

The macros you've written so far have been limited in one crucial way—they're unable to repeat themselves. Here's an example to illustrate the problem. The following data-entry macro pauses to allow the user to enter data, then moves the cell pointer downward one cell to eliminate the need for you to press the Downarrow key after making each entry. A common way to use this macro is to disable the directional arrow keys by pressing the NumLock key, activate this macro, and use the numeric keypad to enter values.

	A	B	C	D	E	F	G	H
1	NAME	MACRO		COMMENT				
2	----------------------------							
3	\A	{?}		Pause for data				
4		{d}		Move down to next cell				
5								

Figure 7-1

However, as it's currently written, the macro is impractical. After it pauses and moves the cell pointer down once, it ends. You'll have to reactivate it after making each entry. The macro would be a lot more useful if you could have it automatically repeat itself; that is, pause for data entry, move down one cell, and then pause for data entry once more.

the
{branch}
command
can make
1-2-3 repeat
a macro

You can, using the {branch} command. {Branch} does not appear on a 1-2-3 command menu, so unlike commands such as / Move, you cannot invoke {branch} from the keyboard; it works only in the context of a macro. It's one of a group of advanced macro commands that we'll explain in detail in the next chapter. Here we'll discuss just enough to show you how to use it to make a macro repeat itself.

1-2-3 normally reads each cell in a macro until it reaches the last cell, whereupon it stops. {Branch} can redirect a macro's flow of control[18] from the last cell of the macro back to its first cell, whereupon 1-2-3 simply begins reading the macro all over again.

Suppose we once again consider the data entry macro shown above. That macro occupies cells B3 and B4; imagine that we have added a {branch} command in cell B5 (don't do it yet—we have yet to explain how). When you activate the macro, 1-2-3 will begin reading in cell B3, then read the label in cell B4, and then read the {branch} command in cell B5. Every time 1-2-3 reads the {branch} command, it will start reading at cell B3 once more. Over and over, 1-2-3 reads the macro in one continuous loop.

the
{branch}
command
specifies the
location of
the first cell
of the macro

To put that scenario into practice, the {branch} command must specify the location of the first cell of the macro. The location reference, in the form of a cell address or a range name, tells 1-2-3 where to continue reading in order to repeat the macro. In our example, the first cell of the macro is in cell B3, so you would write the {branch} command as {branch B3}. When a macro reads {branch B3}, it will discontinue reading keystrokes in the current location and continue reading them in cell B3.

Here's how the modified data entry macro might look:

[18] In an earlier chapter you learned about macro flow of control. To recap, 1-2-3 begins reading macro keystrokes in the cell that bears the macro range name. The macro reads from left to right across that cell, then macro control drops to the cell directly beneath. If the cell below contains a label, 1-2-3 reads it in the same manner (left to right) and control drops to the next cell beneath that. When the macro encounters a cell that doesn't contain a label (one that is empty or contains a value or formula), macro control terminates and control returns to the keyboard.

```
        A        B        C        D        E        F        G        H

 1    NAME     MACRO              COMMENT
 2    --------------------------------------------------
 3    \A       {?}                Pause for data
 4             {d}                Move down to next cell
 5             {branch B3}        Repeat macro
```

Figure 7-2

When you write this new macro command, be sure to use braces { } to enclose it, as you do the special key indicators (such as {down}). If you substitute parentheses ( ) or brackets [ ] for the braces { }, the macro will not read the command properly. If you had already written the macro in cells B3 and B4 and had assigned a macro range name to cell B3, you do not need to assign a new range name when you add the command in cell B5. However, if this is the first time you've written the entire macro, remember to assign a valid macro name (such as \A) to cell B3.

how 1-2-3 reads the data entry macro

When you activate the macro, 1-2-3 will read the interactive command in cell B3 and immediately pause. You should type an entry and press the Return key. 1-2-3 will read the command in cell B4, move the cell pointer down one cell, read the command in cell B5, and branch to continue reading in cell B3 once again. At this point the macro will repeat itself.

stopping the macro

This macro has no way of stopping itself. When you finish using it, you should press the Break key (Control-Break on most computers) to stop it. There are ways to make the macro terminate itself using other advanced commands; we'll discuss them in the next chapter.

If you want this macro to move the cell pointer in any direction besides down, just substitute the command {u}, {l}, or {r} for the command {d} in cell B4.

Using Range Names

range names are a better way of specifying locations in macros

The cell address contained in the {branch} command is a way of specifying the location where 1-2-3 should continue reading the macro. However, as you already know, a cell address is just one way to specify a worksheet location. You can also use a range name, and, in this case, a range name is preferable. We'll explain the reason in a moment. First, let's see how to do it.

Suppose you want a macro to loop back to its starting point after reading its last line. Since you know that the first cell of your macro has a certain range name assigned to it, you can use that range name instead of the cell address in the {branch} command. For example, {branch \A} instead of {branch B3}. Here's how the macro would look on the worksheet:

	A	B	C	D	E	F	G	H
1	NAME	MACRO		COMMENT				
2	----------------------------------							
3	\A	{?}		Pause for data				
4		{d}		Move down to next cell				
5		{branch \A}		Repeat macro				

Figure 7-3

To see why a range name is a better way for you to specify a location in a macro than is a cell address, let's use a cell address in the macro again and examine the consequences as we do some work on the worksheet containing the macro.

Imagine that you have a worksheet containing a macro in columns A through D and a budget in columns H though J (views of the worksheet appear below).

The macro is in columns A through D:

	A	B	C	D	E	F	G	H
1	NAME	MACRO		COMMENT				
2	----------------------------------							
3	\A	{?}		Pause for data				
4		{d}		Move down to next cell				
5		{branch B3}		Repeat macro				

Figure 7-4

The budget is in columns H through J:

	H	I	J	K	L
1	Meals	154.56			
2	Lodging	450.95			
3	Travel	657.71			

Figure 7-5

Suppose that you have to add a new account in which to record budgeted entertainment expenses. To insert a new row for the new account, you move your cell pointer to row 1, select / Worksheet Insert Row, and press Return. A new row appears on the worksheet, as shown below. In the new row you fill in the new expense line item.

after you insert a new row, the data and the macro have been moved down one row

	H	I	J	K	L
1	Entertainment				
2	Meals	154.56			
3	Lodging	450.95			
4	Travel	657.71			

Figure 7-6

if you don't change the cell address in the macro, the macro will no longer work properly

If you now display the area of the worksheet containing your macros, you'll discover it's changed as well. Note that the newly inserted row has moved everything down one row.

Figure 7-7

	A	B	C	D	E	F	G	H
1								
2	NAME	MACRO		COMMENT				
3	------------------------------------							
4	\A	{?}		Pause for data				
5		{d}		Move down to next cell				
6		{branch B3}		Repeat macro				

Consider what will happen if you activate this macro now. The flow of control begins reading in cell B4 with the pause command, then moves to cell B5 (which moves the cell pointer down one row), and finally to cell B6 (the {branch} command). The {branch} command still contains the location "B3", but note that the first cell of the macro now resides in cell B4. Cell B3 contains a repeating label-prefix and a dash (\-). When 1-2-3 reads the {branch} command, this macro will run into problems.

In order to set things right, you'll need to change the cell address in the {branch} command, as you will have to each time you make such a change to your worksheet. That's inconvenient. Further, considering the likelihood of such changes, writing your macros that way makes your worksheets less reliable.

There's a better way. Remember that, instead of specifying a cell address in the {branch} command, you could use a range name. If the {branch} command were written {branch \A}, this macro would require no revisions in the event rows were inserted above it.

when a named range moves, so does the range name assigned to it

Here's why. When a named range moves, the range name moves with it. If you insert a new row above the macro, not only will the range containing the first macro label move, the range name will move with it. As a result, you won't need to rewrite the range name in the {branch} command because that name has already changed to refer to the new location of the first cell of the macro.

You can easily demonstrate this capability with the following exercise.

1. Create a range name on the worksheet.

2. Move the cell pointer to another cell, press the Goto key, and enter the name of the range. The cell pointer should move to that named range.

3. Now insert a new row above the named range. Move the cell pointer to a different cell, press the Goto key, and enter the name of the range once again.

The cell pointer will move to the new location of the range, one cell beneath its former position.

Style Guidelines for Range Names in Macros

uncreated range names in macros cause errors

We've introduced you to the value of using range names in the course of writing macros. As evidence of that value, in the chapters that follow, you'll be seeing many more range names in macros.

As you use them in your own macros there's one thing you'll have to be cautious of. You'll probably find yourself writing in macros names that you haven't yet assigned to ranges. That's O.K., but you must be sure that you create those range names before you use the macro that contains them. If you fail to create the names and you activate the macro, the macro will end in an error when 1-2-3 reads the first unassigned name.

write range names in capital letters

In light of that possibility, before you activate a newly written macro, it helps to make sure you've assigned all the range names it includes. The first step of that process usually involves identifying those range names by scanning through the macro. You can more easily identify the range names if you can make them stand out from the rest of the macro. You can achieve that when you write the macro, if you capitalize range names and write other parts of the macro in lower case. You could easily do the reverse, but since there are fewer range names than other parts of the macro, it's simpler to capitalize the range names than to capitalize the rest of the macro.

In the data entry macro we used earlier (which appears below), the range name assigned to cell B3 is \A. Note how we've capitalized that name in the {branch} command.

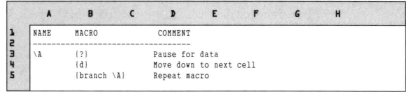

Figure 7-8

range names are useful anywhere you'd specify a cell address in a macro

If you've been using Learn mode to record macros, you may now wish to make a change in those macros. Learn mode automatically capitalizes all keynames, such as {ESC}, in the recorded macro labels. We've just advised you to capitalize range names in a macro to make them stand out. Those names won't stand out if all key names are also capitalized.

We should note that Learn mode won't write any range names into a macro label it creates. However, it's common to use Learn mode to record the keystroke portion of a macro, then edit it to add commands such as {branch} that can contain range names.

The uppercase keynames generated by Learn are easy enough to fix. Before you add any other macro commands to the recorded macros, in a cell in an empty column to the right of the existing macro and on the same row as that macro, enter the formula @lower(B1), where B1 is the top-most cell in the macro containing uppercase keynames. Copy the formula as far down the column as the macro extends in its column. Erase any ERR values returned where the @lower formula references within the macro column a blank cell or a cell containing a value. Place the cell point-er on cell B1, select / Range Value, specify the cells containing the @low-er formula as the copy FROM range, and specify the column containing the recorded macros as the copy TO range.

The Range Value command not only copies from one location to another, it transforms the copied formulas into the values those formulas return. In this case, it'll change the copied data from @lower formulas into macro labels. Erase the @lower formulas and you're done.

There are any number of other ways in which you can use range names in macros. Range names can be used effectively anywhere you might oth-erwise use a cell address. For example, consider the following macro:

	A	B	C	D	E	F	G	H
1	NAME	MACRO		COMMENT				
2	-----	-----------	-----------	-----				
3	\A	/cA10~R32~		Copy				
4		/ppcr		Clear print range				
5		rR1..R50~		Set new print range				
6		agpq		Print				

Figure 7-9

In that macro, we used cell addresses (in line 1) to provide the range to copy from and the range to copy to and (in line 3) to supply the print range. In the following macro, those ranges are supplied through range names.

	A	B	C	D	E	F	G	H
1	NAME	MACRO			COMMENT			
2	-----	-------------	-------------	-----------				
3	\A	/cENTRY~INTEREST_RATE~			Copy			
4		/ppcr			Clear print range			
5		rMORTGAGE_AMORT~			Set new print range			
6		agpq			Print			

Figure 7-10

By now we trust that you've noticed that the purposes of most macros are a bit obscure. While range names can't entirely solve that problem, notice how much they improve things in the macro shown above.

So, in addition to the higher level of reliability that range names confer on your macros, they'll also help you understand those macros more easily. Those benefits—reliability and clarity—are the reasons we recommend that you use range names instead of cell addresses in your macros.

Another Sample Loop

a macro to set the width of as many columns as you want

Here's another simple macro using the {branch} command. Release 2.01 and lower releases can set the width of a single column or all columns, but lacks the ability to do so for a range of columns[19]. You can write a macro to increase the speed with which you can set the width of any number of contiguous columns. (Later you'll see a more sophisticated version of this macro.) This macro allows you to set the width of the column in which the cell pointer resides, then it moves one column to the right and repeats itself. The macro will continue that process until you press the Control-Break key sequence to end the macro.

	A	B	C	D	E	F	G	H
1	NAME	MACRO		COMMENT				
2	----	-----		-------				
3	\B	/wcs{?}~		Set column width				
4		{r}		Move right one cell				
5		{branch \B}		Loop				
6								
7								
8								

Figure 7-11

In the next section, you'll learn another advanced command, {quit}. Like {branch}, its function is to modify the normal flow of control of a macro, but instead of repeating them, {quit} terminates them.

Terminating a Macro with a Command

You already know two ways to terminate a macro. In this section you'll learn another way—one that uses another of 1-2-3's advanced macro commands. The two ways you already know are:

---

[19] Release 2.2 performs this function using the / Worksheet Column Column-Range command. Nevertheless, even if you're using Release 2.2, try writing the macro anyway. Doing so will help you learn to use the {branch} command.

a blank cell
or pressing
the Break
key to end a
macro

- Leave a blank cell at the bottom of the macro. When 1-2-3 reads the blank cell after executing the macro above, macro control terminates and control returns to the keyboard.

- Press the Break key (Control-Break on most computers) to manually terminate a macro at any time.

You might think of a blank space at the end of a macro as an implicit way of ending a macro. When a macro encounters a blank cell it terminates for lack of further instructions. In many cases, that method is sufficient. However, it introduces the risk that you, or someone else, will later inadvertently place unrelated labels just below the macro. If that happens, when 1-2-3 next reads the macro, it will read those labels as macro instructions even though they were not intended as such.

{quit}
makes sure
the macro
stops where
you intend

You can avoid that risk by placing an explicit terminator—the {quit} command—at the end of the macro. When 1-2-3 reads {quit}, macro control terminates and control returns to the keyboard, even if the cell just below contains another label. The {quit} command is complete in and of itself. Unlike the {branch} command, which needs an argument, you need add nothing to {quit}.

Sample Applications of {quit}

Here's a simple example of the {quit} command at work.

	A	B	C	D	E	F	G	H
1	NAME	MACRO		COMMENT				
2	----------------------------------							
3	\C	500~		Enter a value				
4		/rfc~~		Format as currency				
5		/wcs15~		Set column to 15 spaces				
6		{quit}		End				

Figure 7-12

Even if you place a label entry in cell B7, the macro will not continue reading beyond the {quit} command in cell B6.

sample
macro that
converts
formulas to
values

Here's another macro that uses the {quit} command. This macro also incorporates 1-2-3's / Range Value command (in lines one through three). As you saw in the discussion of Learn mode presented earlier in this chapter, that command copies any range and in the process converts any formulas it contains into values. Line four contains the {quit} command to end the macro.

```
         A          B          C        D        E        F        G        H
    1  NAME      MACRO               COMMENT
    2  ------------------------------------------
    3  \A        /rv                 Copy formulas as values
    4            .{end}{d}~          Set range to copy from
    5            {left}~             Range to copy to
    6            {quit}              End the macro
    7
    8
    9
   10
```

Figure 7-13

Next

In this chapter, you learned two of 1-2-3's advanced macro commands. You'll later learn the rest of those commands. Now it's time to review some of the most common macro–writing problems and how to fix them.

8

Debugging Your Macros

Most macro problems result from simple typographical errors: transposed characters, misspelled range names, and the like. You can spot most of those errors by scanning your macro visually. However, occasionally you'll encounter one or more seemingly insoluble problems in your macros. If now is one of those times, read this section to learn how to identify those errors and correct them. If your macros are humming along like well-oiled engines we recommend that you:

- Skip to the next section, if you're writing macros only for yourself. Return here later if you encounter a problem you can't otherwise resolve.

- Review this section now to gain a general sense of what can go wrong if you're called on to help others debug their macros and want to better prepare yourself for that role. You can then refer back to this material for specific help when you're confronted with a tough problem.

mistakes will happen— just learn to fix them

The first thing you should know about those mistakes is that they are bound to happen. Macros require a high degree of precision. In a macro consisting of thousands of keystrokes, if just one is erroneous, the macro will probably malfunction. While you might conclude that you should be very concerned about making mistakes, that isn't so.

The fact is, everyone makes mistakes while writing macros. You should exercise reasonable caution, but the only thing that seems to help reduce the incidence of mistakes is learning how to identify and correct them. As you write more macros, you will make fewer errors.

We earlier outlined some of the fundamental errors and prescribed some techniques to fix them. In this segment, we'll summarize those techniques and extend them.

Debugging consists of two steps—testing to identify the cause of problems and correcting them. Testing is the more challenging of the two activities; once you've identified the source of a problem, correcting it is usually relatively simple. The difficulty inherent in testing leads some people to attempt to correct a problem without testing for its cause. In other words, they guess at the source of a problem and try solutions that they think might work.

That strategy may work well for short, simple macros. However, since it can lead you to fix parts of a macro that aren't broken, in a larger macro that's a fine way to turn a small problem into a big one. So if you don't know what the problem is, devise some tests to find out. Here's how.

(1.) Run the macro and carefully observe the results. Each result, or effect, that you observe can be traced to some cause. For example, suppose you've run a macro and after its termination there is an entry on the edit line of the control panel and 1-2-3's mode indicator says LABEL. Think about what could have caused that to happen.

You will note that the macro typed an entry, but somehow that entry did not transfer to the worksheet. The way most entries are transferred from the edit line to a cell is through pressing the Return key when the entry is complete. 1-2-3 uses the tilde to represent the Return key in a macro, so in this case you would examine your macro to see if a tilde is missing at the end.

(2.) Insert interactive commands ({?}) in the macro. Position them to force the macro to pause at various milestones. For example, if you are performing a complex file consolidation operation, place a pause after the commands to combine each file. Use that pause to check the worksheet for any problems. (However, if you move the cell pointer in doing so, note first its location and return it to that location before allowing the macro to proceed.)

Using interactive commands that way allows you to verify each result the macro is designed to achieve as soon as it is supposed to have achieved it. Since one problem in a macro can beget others, if you can nip the problem in the bud, you won't waste time trying to rectify secondary problems instead of dealing with the real trouble.

---

if you don't know what's broken, you can't fix it

{?} commands can help you test a macro

step mode is
1-2-3's
built in
macro
testing tool

(3.) Step your way through the macro. There are two methods for stepping through a macro; we'll refer to them as automated single step and manual single step.

Automated Single Step. You can observe the effect of each keystroke the macro contains by using 1-2-3's macro Single Step mode. In this mode, 1-2-3 will read only one keystroke of the macro at a time. To use Single Step mode, with a valid macro on the current worksheet, follow these directions:

Depress: Macro (Alt on most computers)
Press: F2 (normally known as the Edit key)[20]
Release: Macro

1-2-3 responds by turning on Single Step mode and displaying the STEP indicator at the bottom of the screen. When you next activate a macro, you will see the indicator at the bottom of your screen change to SST (for Single Step) but nothing else will appear to have happened. You must now press a keystroke for the macro to begin. Each time you press another key on the keyboard (we recommend you use the Return key), 1-2-3 will read the next instruction in the macro label.

In Release 2.2, you'll see the macro label that 1-2-3 is now reading, with a highlight on the *next* instruction to be read. Each time you press a key, the highlight will advance to show the next instruction 1-2-3 will read.

Step mode works like a light switch; it's either on or off. While Step mode is on, any macro you run will operate in Single Step mode. After you turn it off, macros revert to their normal method of operation. To turn Step mode off, repeat the same keystrokes you used to turn it on (press Macro and F2) and watch the Step indicator at the bottom of your screen disappear. Remember: as long as the Step indicator displays at the bottom of your screen, *any* macro you activate will proceed in Single Step mode.

step mode
often can't
show you
which 1-2-3
commands
the macro is
reading . . .

Unfortunately, if you are using a Release of 1-2-3 designated by a number lower than 2.2,[21] while you may see the effect of each keystroke when you walk through a macro in Single Step mode, it will often be impossible for you to see which commands the macro is selecting. For example, if at one point in the macro, 1-2-3 has read the keystroke /, you will see the main command menu displayed in the control panel. If the next keytroke is *p* (to select the Print command), the Print menu will replace the main menu in the control panel. However, except by observing

---

[20] If you used this feature in Release 1A, note that it is no longer activated with the Alt F1 key.

[21] In Release 2.2, single step mode highlights at the bottom of the screen the next keystroke or instruction that the macro will read.

which menu replaced the main menu, you won't have any way of knowing which command your macro selected. As a result, if you're confused about what your macro is doing, Single Step mode may not help. Instead, use the following technique.

Manual Single Step. Manual single step involves replicating the macro's action by using 1-2-3's interactive mode to key in the keystrokes that the macro contains. First, print a hard copy of the macro label(s) to use as a guide. Position the cell pointer to its intended starting location and, following the printed macro instructions exactly, key them in and observe the results. Using this method, you will more easily identify the menu choice selected by each keystroke. You should realize that manually single stepping through a macro is no different than the modeling technique introduced earlier. Use modeling before you write a macro to define the keystrokes the macro should contain; use Single Step after you write the macro to uncover errors made in transcribing the macro keystrokes from your model.

. . . but you can see the commands if you key them in yourself

Prescriptions for Common Macro Problems

Following is a list of several problems that commonly occur in macros. Accompanying each problem is a prescription to help you correct it.

1-2-3 Beeps and the Macro Does Not Run

Symptom. When you press the Macro key and a letter to activate a macro, the computer beeps. Nothing else happens.

Diagnosis. When you press the Macro key and a letter, 1-2-3 looks for a range name consisting of a backslash and that letter. If that range name doesn't exist, 1-2-3 will beep. In effect, it is saying "I don't find that range name."

the range name must be a backslash and a single letter

Prescription. In most cases, you can use the / Range Name Create command to verify that the range name is missing. Enter that command and when you see in the control panel the prompt "Enter name:", look on the line below. If you have any range names in this worksheet, they will appear there. If you have more than five of them, press the Name key (F3) to see them all simultaneously. If you don't see the range name you're seeking, read the second paragraph below.

If you do see it, it is for some reason invalid. That may be because the range name contains a space you cannot easily see (such as before or after the visible characters) or because you've used the Move command to move something onto the cell to which it refers.[22] In any case, press Control-Break to cancel the current operation, use the / Range Name Delete command to remove the name, and follow the instruction in the next paragraph to properly create a new, valid name.

Remember that the macro range name must consist of exactly two characters, the backslash (\ ) followed by a single letter. If the name looks similar, such as a slash (/) followed by a single letter, that won't do. To create the range name, with the prompt "Enter name:" still showing in the control panel, type the name you wish to assign (such as \A), press Return, and indicate the first cell of the macro. If you previously assigned an incorrect range name, also use the / Range Name Delete command to remove the incorrect name.

The Macro Doesn't Run; 1-2-3 Doesn't Beep

Symptom. When you press the Macro key and a letter to activate the macro, nothing happens. 1-2-3 does not beep.

Diagnosis. As long as 1-2-3 doesn't beep when you try to activate the macro, then the range name has been properly assigned to somewhere on the worksheet.[23] The problem is one of four things: 1-2-3 is in Step mode, the range name is not assigned to a cell containing a label, you tried to activate an auto-execute macro from the keyboard (with Alt-∅), or the macro did work but you didn't observe it.

Prescription. Check to see if 1-2-3 is in Step mode by looking at the status line at the bottom of the screen. Do you see the STEP indicator or a flashing indicator containing the letters SST (for Single STep)? If so, 1-2-3 is in Step mode. To cancel Step mode depress and hold down the Alt key, press the F2 function key, and release the Alt key. If you are in the midst of running a macro, press Return to have it resume normal operating speed.

---

[22] There are several ways in which a previously valid range name can be rendered invalid. For a more detailed discussion of such problems and how to avoid them, refer to the heading "Underlying Problems With Range Names" toward the end of this chapter.

[23] If you're using Release 2.2, keep in mind that if the / Worksheet Global Default Other Beep command has been set to No, you won't hear a beep even if the range name hasn't been properly assigned. If you find one of your more common errors is forgetting to assign range names, leaving that command set to Yes will make the error easier to identify. If you select Yes, next select Update to preserve the new setting for future 1-2-3 sessions.

the cell to which the name was assigned may not contain a macro

If 1-2-3 is not in Step mode, check to see if the cell to which the range name has been assigned does not contain a label (it's either empty or contains a value or formula). 1-2-3 cannot read any of those as a macro instruction. To identify the cell in question, press Goto and Name. Select the range name representing the macro in question. The cell pointer will highlight the cell to which the name is assigned (or, if you've opted to include the entire macro label in the named range, the cell pointer will highlight the top left cell in that range—which should still be the first macro label). If that's not the cell containing the first line of the macro, select / Range Name Delete to eliminate the range name, move the cell pointer to the proper cell, select / Range Name Create, enter the proper name (a backslash followed by a single letter), and indicate the cell containing the first line of the macro.

If neither of those prove to be the trouble, did you try to activate an auto-execute macro (if so, you pressed Alt-0)? Auto-execute macros carry the range name \0 (remember, that's a zero, not a capitalized letter "O"). You cannot activate such a macro by pressing Alt and typing 0. However, you can assign to the macro a second range name, a conventional macro name that you can activate from the keyboard. Then it will carry two range names; one that will cause it to activate automatically when you retrieve the file containing it, and one that you can use to activate it from the keyboard. If you are using release 2.2, another way to run the macro is with the Run (Alt-F3) key. Press the Run key and select the range name \0.

The final possibility is that the macro did activate, and you simply did not see it. That could easily happen if it modified the worksheet only in an area other than the one you were viewing when you activated it. First use the Goto key to locate the macro, then read it. Write down the keystrokes on a separate piece of paper, return the cell pointer to its location the last time you tried activating the macro, and manually key in those keystrokes. See if the macro did what it was supposed to have done.

The Macro-Name Letter Appears in the Control Panel or on the Worksheet

Symptom. After trying to execute the macro, you see a letter repeated in the control panel or in a cell on the worksheet. The letter is the same one you used, with the Macro key, to activate the macro.

Diagnosis. You made a simple error. Instead of holding down the Macro key and typing the letter used in the macro name, you did one of two things:

if you hold down the letter key, you'll end up with letters written in the control panel or on the worksheet

- You held down the backslash key and typed the letter. That won't activate a macro, but it could enter a label on the worksheet. When you precede any label with a backslash, that label repeats across the cell containing it.

- You may have released the Alt key before typing the character, and then activated your keyboard's auto-repeat function by holding down that character, thereby typing the letter several times.

Prescription. If the letter is still in the control panel, press Escape to clear it. If it's on the worksheet, use the / Range Erase command to erase the entry. In either case, using care not to repeat the mistake, activate the macro once more.

Characters Appear in the Control Panel Instead of on the Worksheet

Symptom. A macro that's meant to type a label types that label into the control panel's edit line, but never enters that label onto the worksheet.

Diagnosis. Just as you often press the Return key at the end of typing a label to enter that label on the worksheet, many macros that are supposed to type labels should include a tilde as the means for transferring that typed label from the control panel to the worksheet.[24] In a macro that's supposed to enter a label, if you forget the tilde afterward (and don't otherwise provide a way to enter the label on the worksheet), the macro will type the label but leave it in the control panel. In the example below, suppose the cell pointer is in cell E5. After activating macro \A, here's what you'd see.

the macro types a label but doesn't enter it on the worksheet

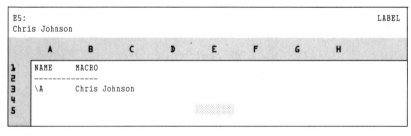

Figure 8-1

---

[24] It's also possible to enter a label with one of the directional keys, such as the Downarrow key. Just as you can press one of those keys after typing a label, so you can include the key name for that key in a macro to enter the label.

don't retype the whole entry—use the Edit key to add a tilde

Note that the macro faithfully typed the keystrokes stored in the macro label (you can see them in the control panel to the right of the address of cell E5). However, since the stored keystrokes do not include a tilde at the end, 1-2-3 has not entered what it typed on the worksheet. When the macro finishes, it leaves those typed characters in the control panel. Accordingly, the mode indicator shows that 1-2-3 is in Label mode. Were you to execute from the keyboard the keystrokes contained in the macro, but refrain from pressing Return at their conclusion, you'd see the same thing.

Prescription. To correct the problem, position the cell pointer on the cell containing the incorrect macro label, press the Edit key, type a tilde (so that the tilde appears to the right of the existing entry), and press the Return key.

when you want to omit the tilde

We should point out that's its perfectly O.K. to omit the tilde intentionally. For example, suppose that when you create worksheets, you frequently type the lengthy name of your company, Hieronomous Consolidated Industries, Inc. You realize that a macro would save you typing time, so you create one to enter your company's name. Thinking back, you realize that you most often type that name in the middle of sentences rather than all by itself. If you place a tilde at the end of the macro, it will type your company's name and enter it on the worksheet; but that isn't what you want. You want the macro to type your company's name and then leave you in Label mode so you can keep typing until you finish the sentence. So omit the tilde at the end of the macro and you will be able to keep typing.

Macro with the tilde . . .

	A	B	C	D	E	F	G	H
1	NAME	MACRO						
2	--------------							
3	\A	Hieronomous Consolidated Industries, Inc.~						
4								
5								

Figure 8-2

. . .And without the tilde.

	A	B	C	D	E	F	G	H
1	NAME	MACRO						
2	--------------							
3	\A	Hieronomous Consolidated Industries, Inc.						
4								
5								

Figure 8-3

Embedded Spaces in a Macro

Symptom. The macro doesn't do what it's supposed to. However, when you test the macro by keying in the same commands manually, everything works fine.

Diagnosis. There may be spaces embedded in the macro. Such spaces are created when you inadvertantly press the space bar while writing a macro label, and they most often occur at the end of the label, where you cannot see them.

Prescription. Test the macro labels for the presence of spaces and remove them.

spaces embedded in a macro, though invisible, can totally change the way the macro works

Before we discuss the prescription fully, this tricky problem bears a little more examination. Let's look at an example of the effect of an embedded space on a macro that formats a cell and enters a value into it. On a blank worksheet, enter and name the macro shown below:

	A	B	C	D	E	F	G	H
1	NAME	MACRO		COMMENT				
2	----	-----	----	-------				
3	\D	100~		Value entry				
4		/rfc~~		Format as currency				
5								

Figure 8-4

Move the cell pointer to cell C6 and activate the macro. The entry $100.00 should appear in cell C6. In the next step, you'll embed a space in the macro. Move the cell pointer to cell B3, press the Edit key, press the space bar once, and press Return. Although it isn't visible, you've just entered a space at the end of the label '100~. Move to cell C7 and activate the macro once more. The entry /rfc should appear in cell C7.

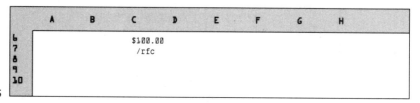

	A	B	C	D	E	F	G	H
6			$100.00					
7			/rfc					
8								
9								
10								

Figure 8-5

The difference in the results you attained is due to the space character you added to the macro. We'll review the macro keystroke by keystroke to determine what went wrong the second time.

The first six keystrokes are the same in the second macro as they are in the first, and they have the same effect—they enter the value 100 in the current cell. However, the next keystroke is the hidden space character. When 1-2-3 reads the hidden space character, it types a space and places itself into Label mode. Since there is not a tilde directly following, 1-2-3 stays in Label mode and continues typing characters. Those characters are /rfc. In the first macro, 1-2-3 was in Ready mode when it read these characters, so the characters were read as commands, not as a continuation of a label already in progress.

spaces are
usually
located at
the end of a
macro label

In the second macro, the next keystroke is a tilde, so the macro presses the Return key, thereby entering onto the worksheet the label it had been typing. That label now consists of a space followed by the characters /rfc. The last keystroke of the macro, another tilde, causes 1-2-3 to press the Return key once again. This time 1-2-3 is already in Ready mode, so the space has no effect.

Those spaces are usually located at the very end of a macro label. Because they are invisible, it looks like there is no space there. Position the cell pointer on the first macro label, press Edit, and look in the control panel. The flashing cursor should be directly to the right of the last character in the macro label. If there is a space between that character and the cursor, that's a space. Continue testing label entries until you locate a space. When you do, press the Backspace key to remove it, then press Return to enter the revised macro label back on the worksheet. Retest your macro.

Assumptions in Macros

Before we leave the subject of problems in macros, let's consider one of the most subtle potential sources of those problems: the assumptions you make about the worksheet conditions under which your macros will operate.

Consider the following data entry macro. It enables someone to post a large budget spreadsheet.

	A	B	C	D	E	F	G	H
1	NAME	MACRO		COMMENT				
2								
3	\E	{?}{r}{?}{r}{?}{r}						
4		{?}{r}{?}{r}{?}{r}						
5		{?}{r}{?}{r}{?}{r}						
6		{?}{r}{?}{r}{?}{r}						
7		{?}{r}{?}{r}{?}{r}						
8		{?}{r}{?}{r}{?}{r}						
9		{?}{r}{?}{r}						
10		@sum({1}.{1 3})~						
11		{1 20}{d}						
12								
13								
14								
15								

Figure 8-6

This application calls for data to be entered across twenty columns (instead of the six we saw in an earlier worksheet). Following the {120} command on line 11 it will take several moments to return the cell pointer across twenty cells, one cell at time.

That delay might make you consider an alternative method of returning the cell pointer to the beginning of the next row. Suppose the cell pointer was in column A when you activated this macro. If after entering all the data, you were to press the End key and then Leftarrow, the cell pointer would travel across all twenty cells much more rapidly and stop in column A. In fact, on an IBM PC equipped with a monochrome display adapter, the End–Leftarrow method is four seconds faster than moving one cell at a time.

sometimes a faster method may not be better

However, the success of that second method depends on conditions the macro, as written, can't guarantee. End Leftarrow will move the cell pointer across all the cells in the row until it reaches the first column, only if either all the intervening cells are full or they are empty. If most of them contain entries and one or two are empty, the cell pointer will stop on the last entry before the blank cell.

What guarantee do you have that all the cells will contain entries on each row? If you're the only one who uses the macro, you can make sure you enter something into every cell, even if it's a zero. But if someone else uses it, they may overlook that need.

If you are writing a macro for someone else to use, it may be better to use a technique that's a little slower but more reliable (such as {1 20}) than to gamble on something faster but less sure (such as {end}{1}).

saving your
worksheet
is like
having an
Undo
command if
the macro
causes
problems

The real challenge, however, isn't following such straightforward advice as we just offered, it's detecting when you've made an assumption
that may, under slightly different worksheet conditions, lead to trouble.
Given the variety of situations you'll encounter, that's difficult to know.
You'll learn to avoid most such assumptions with time, but even then
you'll be subject to those mistakes occasionally. You can minimize the effect of those errors if you save your worksheet prior to running new (or
newly revised) macros. The technique gives you, in essence, an Undo
command. If you overlook a problem and the macro you run destroys
your work, retrieve the worksheet from the disk and you'll have reversed
the damage.

Underlying Problems with Range Names

Because macros depend on range names, you should know how to handle
the three most common problems with them. Here we'll describe the
underlying causes of problems with range names, problems that not only
could be the cause of some of the problems diagnosed earlier in this chapter, but could impair other 1-2-3 operations that depend on named ranges
as well. Those range-name related problems arise from inadvertently
deleting, associating, and transferring range names. Let's review how to
avoid each of those situations.

How To Avoid Inadvertently Deleting a Range Name

If you name a range that is larger than one cell, you must specify that
range by identifying two cells in that range, either the top left and bottom
right cells or the top right and bottom left cells. However, regardless of
which two cells you use to specify the range, 1-2-3 will remember the
range by storing the top left and bottom right cells. Those cells are
known as the range's anchor cells. If you should ever do either of the following things to either of those cells, 1-2-3 will invalidate that range
name:

things that
will invali-
date a
range name

- Use the / Move command to move anything into either cell.

- Use either the / Worksheet Delete Column or / Worksheet Delete
  Row command to delete a column or row containing either cell.
  Release 3 is an exception to this rule. Release 3 was designed to

shrink the named range by the number of columns or rows deleted from the range—even if those columns or rows include an anchor cell. If the columns or rows deleted entirely contain the named range, then the range name will be deleted.

In either case, the range name will be invalidated. Curiously, if you press the Goto key followed by the Name key (F5 and F3, respectively, on most computers), you will still see that range name in the menu at the top of the screen. If you then try to select it, 1-2-3 will beep and issue an error message. In this area, too, Release 3 was designed to work a bit differently. If in Release 3 you delete a range name by deleting of all its rows or columns, the range name will disappear from the range name menu.

How To Avoid Inadvertently Transferring a Range Name

range names can be moved without your knowledge

If you use the / Move command to move the contents of a cell that has been assigned a range name, the range name will move, too. If you want to move the contents of a cell that is a named range, but you want to leave the range name in its present location, use the / Copy command instead. Copy the macro label to a new location, then copy a blank unformatted cell to the original location to erase the original label. The named range will remain intact in its original location.

How To Avoid Inadvertently Associating Named Ranges

The conventional way to redefine the boundaries of a named range is to enter the / Range Name Create command, select the name of the range, and use the directional keys to expand or contract the boundaries of that range. If you look in the control panel while you are pressing the directional keys, you'll see that 1-2-3 is changing the cell addresses of the anchor cells that define that range. So another way to think about this change to the boundaries of a named range is that you've just changed the specifications of that range's anchor cells.

range names can be associated without your knowledge

Another, and often inadvertent, way to redefine the boundaries of a named range is to use the / Move command to move one of that range's anchor cells. The cell address of the destination of that Move command becomes the new address of the named range's anchor cell.

When more than one named range shares the same anchor cell, we say that those two range names are associated with one another. For example, if two named ranges' lower right corners are the cell F5, then those two named ranges are said to be associated. For example, a named range defined as A1..F5 and a named range defined as C3..F5 are associated. That means two ranges can be associated even if they share only one anchor cell. If you use the / Move command to move the contents of the shared anchor cell—1-2-3 will modify both ranges by using the new location of the anchor cell to define whichever boundary of the range that anchor cell originally defined.

A more troublesome circumstance occurs when more than one range name shares both anchor cells. In other words, more than one range name refers to the same range. That's not an uncommon occurrence when you assign and subsequently redefine a named range on a worksheet containing other named ranges. When it happens, the range names' identities effectively merge. Thus, if you have two names assigned to the same range and you use / Range Name Create to change the boundaries of one of the named ranges, the boundaries of the other one will change as well. The implication is that macros using the keystrokes /rnc to repeatedly change the boundaries of a range name may end up changing more range names than the you intended. This problem can have repercussions beyond your macro: formulas that contained references to the range in question may now refer to new ranges.

Fortunately, there's a simple preventative procedure for the problem. If your macro uses the / Range Name Create command to repeatedly change the boundaries of a range name, and you believe that range names could become associated, have the macro delete the range name and then create it anew instead of using the Range Name Create command and the pointer movement keys to revise the range. Even if two range names become associated, when you next redefine one of them, the other will remain where it was. Note that in Release 3, the program obviates the problem. If you redefine one range name and another range name shares the same range, only the range name you explicitly redefine will change.

Next

Now that you've learned to correct the most common macro-writing problems, it's time to return to the subject of making those macros more powerful. Earlier we showed you how to use the {?} interactive macro command to allow you to modify a macro while it is running. Now we'll introduce you to a group of techniques through which macros can modify themselves.

9

Dynamic Code: Self-Modifying Macros

In Chapter 2 we showed you how to edit your macros. Although the technique we showed you there enables you to use one macro to do several jobs, because you have to change the macro every time you want to change the job it performs, it's best suited for applications that seldom change. We also discussed varying your macros by using the {?} interactive command, but that command has some limits as well. If you use an interactive command, the macro will pause each time to allow you to change some part of the procedure it controls, whereas you might not need to change the macro each time it runs.

self-modifying macros, or dynamic code, enable a macro to change itself

In this chapter, we'll tell you how to include in a macro something known as a variable. A variable enables a macro that contains it to modify itself. A variable is anything that changes, and there are numerous ways these handy tools will make your macros more useful. We'll discuss variables throughout the rest of the book; the two variable techniques we'll cover here are blank cells and string formulas.

Since the effect of each of these techniques is that the macro can modify itself, macros incorporating them are sometimes called self-modifying macros, or the macro instructions themselves are referred to as dynamic code.

Creating Variables Through Blank Spaces

Suppose you have a macro (such as the one below) that prints a range from your worksheet.

Figure 9-1

	A	B	C	D	E	F	G	H
1	NAME	MACRO		COMMENT				
2	------	-----------	-----	--------				
3	\P	/ppcrrA1..F30		Cancel/reassign print range				
4		~agpq		Print, advance page				
5								

Line 1 contains the keystrokes to clear a prior print range and set a new one: / Print Printer Clear Range Range A1..F30. Line two begins with a tilde to enter the new print range and follows with the keystrokes for Align Go Page Quit.

We've rewritten the macro and reproduced it below. Note that we've extended it over three lines.

enter the
macro code
you want to
change on
its own line

Figure 9-2

	A	B	C	D	E	F	G	H
1	NAME	MACRO		COMMENT				
2	------	------------	-----	--------				
3	\P	/ppcrr		Cancel print range				
4		A1..F30		New Range				
5		~agpq		Print, advance page				

The first line of the macro contains the keytrokes for / Print Printer Clear Range (to clear the current print range) Range (to set a new print range). The second line contains the print range specification. The third line contains a tilde (to enter the new print range from the previous line) and the keystrokes for Align Go Page Quit.

With the print range specification on its own line, that range is much easier to change than if it's imbedded in other keystrokes. You can replace the range in line 2 with another range by entering the new range in the cell in which line 2 resides:

	A	B	C	D	E	F	G	H
1	NAME	MACRO		COMMENT				
2	------	------------	-----	--------				
3	\P	/ppcrr		Cancel print range				
4		K45..Q131		New Range				
5		~agpq		Print, advance page				

Figure 9-3

Creating Variables Through String Manipulation

You can also arrange for the worksheet to provide input to the macro. Rather than changing the macro directly by rewriting one of its lines, you need only change a cell elsewhere on the worksheet to produce a corresponding change in the macro.

a person can change a macro without knowing anything about that macro

For example, you could enter a value in a cell that would determine how wide a macro would make columns whose widths it was changing. This technique is particularly effective if you want someone to make the change to the macro without that person ever seeing the macro itself. The cell entry you change can be anywhere else on the worksheet; you can even place it on a screen with instructions for the macro's user to follow. The person need know nothing about how to write or modify a macro. All he has to do is enter something into a cell on the worksheet.

This technique requires you to use string formulas to change one or more lines of the macro. These formulas can manipulate strings in any of the following ways:

1. Make a string appear in the current cell by referencing a string stored in another location, just as you can do with a value.

2. Concatenate (or combine) two strings. For example, if cell A1 contains the string "Tom" and cell A2 contains the string "Cat", then if in cell A3 you enter the formula +A1&A2, cell A3 will return the string "TomCat".

3. Extract substrings from within existing strings. You can use the @LEFT, @MID, and @RIGHT functions to extract any portion of an existing string. With the string "TomCat" appearing in cell A3, the formula @LEFT(A3;2) would return the string "To".

you can substitute a string formula for a macro label

Labels are strings. Macros, being labels, are also strings, so it follows that you can substitute a string formula for a macro label. As long as the string formula returns a string of valid macro instructions, 1-2-3 treats it exactly as if it were a macro label.

We'll explore the power of string formulas in macros by considering the formatting macro /rfc~~. We've already discussed how you can supply input to that macro by rewriting it with the interactive command: /rf{?}~~. Now we'll see how you can use the worksheet to supply that input by writing the macro instruction as a string formula.

Writing the String Formula

Here's how to do it. Instead of writing a macro label, enter a string formula as one line of the macro. In this case, the string formula will concatenate a string (derived from a label located elsewhere on the worksheet) with macro instructions (contained in the string formula itself) to form a single, complete macro label.

Consider the following string formula that might be used as a macro:

```
+"/rf"&D10&"~~"
```

On a blank worksheet, enter this formula in cell A1. Unlike other times you've used formulas in macros, this time you should not enter a label prefix before the formula. When you finish, the formula will return the value ERR; in a moment, you'll change the worksheet to make the formula useful. For now, use the / Range Name Create command to assign the name \A to cell A1. For the moment, keep your cell pointer in cell A1 so you can see the formula in the control panel while we describe it piece by piece. The string formula consists of three parts:

a string formula that offers you different range formats

```
+"/rf"
```

The formula begins with a plus sign followed by the string **/rf** enclosed in quotation marks (all strings contained in formulas must be enclosed in quotation marks). /rf will execute the commands / Range Format when 1-2-3 reads them in a macro.

```
&D10
```

The second part of the formula begins with an ampersand to concatenate (join) the string contained in the first part of the formula to the string that will be produced by the cell reference to D10. D10 will contain a character that will select the type of format (such as a **c** for currency format or a **d** for date format). When D10 does contain such a character, the concatenated string might be /rfc, /rfd, or /rf followed by any other character representing a range format option in 1-2-3.

```
&"~~"
```

The last portion of the formula begins with an ampersand to concatenate the string formed by this portion of the formula with the string formed by the first two parts of the formula. The string in this portion of the formula consists of two tildes and, like all strings in formulas, the tildes are enclosed in quotation marks. When 1-2-3 reads them in a macro, those tildes will (1) confirm the type of cell format and (2) accept the default range (the current cell) to be formatted. If cell D10 contains a c, the complete concatenated string produced by the formula would be /rfc~~; if D10 contains a d, the string would be /rfd~~.

with one character, you can change the type of range format the macro will supply

Now, move your cell pointer to cell D10 and enter a character that represents one of the Range Format options. We suggest you begin with the letter c. Notice that as soon as you complete that entry, cell A1 will return a valid string incorporating the character you entered.

Now move the cell pointer to an empty cell elsewhere on the worksheet, enter a value into it, and press Macro-A to activate the macro. If the cell you formatted shows asterisks now, use the / Worksheet Column Set-Width command to increase its width.

Change the character in cell D10 to one of the other characters representing a range format option. For a list of those options, select the / Range Format command and note the first letter of the option that you want to enter in cell D10. As you change the entry in cell D10, watch cell A1 change. Move to another cell, enter a value, and invoke the macro to format the cell.

Numbers in Macro String Formulas

a macro to set variable column widths

In our last example, the string formula referenced a cell that contained a label to supply the range format selection. In other macros, however, you may want to reference a cell containing a value. For example, suppose you've written the following macro to set the width of a column: /wcs25~. The macro will invoke the 1-2-3 commands / Worksheet Column Set-Width, enter 25, and press Return.

Because you'll want to set different columns to different widths, you decide to incorporate into the macro a string reference that will supply the number of spaces wide a given column should be. That way, you can easily modify the macro to replace 25 with other numbers.

Your string formula looks like this: +"/wcs"&F10&"~"

a string formula cannot combine a value and a string . . .

In this case, cell F10 should contain the entry that you will change when you want to change the width setting in the macro. Since the Worksheet Column Set-Width command requires a number, cell F10 must contain a number. However, because the formula you've written is a string formula, the reference to cell F10 within that formula must return a string entry, not a value. If the reference returns a value entry, 1-2-3 will be unable to combine it with the two strings embedded in the formula, and the entire formula will return the value ERR.

You could always enter a number in cell F10 as a label (that is, a number preceded by a label-prefix character), but that's awkward and un-reliable. If you or whoever uses your macro forgets to enter the label pre-fix, the string formula will return ERR. Since ERR is a form of value en-try, 1-2-3 won't be able to read it as a macro. [25]

... unless you use the @string function

There is a simple solution. Modify the string formula so that it can ref-erence a value and convert the resulting reference into a string. That's the purpose of 1-2-3's @string function. @String takes two arguments: the entry you wish to convert, and the number of decimal places you want the resulting string entry to show (that's zero, in this case). Here's how you'd apply it:

```
+"/wcs"&@string(F10;0)&"~"
```

When you supply the cell reference F10 as the argument to the @string function, 1-2-3 will convert the resulting reference into a string. Let's break that formula down:

`+"/wcs"` The string formula begins with a plus sign just as most for-mulas containing references do. The first string, /wcs, is contained within quotes.

`&@string(F10;0)` The ampersand concatenates the preceding string to the string contained in this expression. Since you expect that there will be a value in cell F10, you must use the @string function to convert the reference into a string. Otherwise, you wouldn't be able to concatentate that reference to the preceding string, because 1-2-3 cannot join a string and a value. The second argument, zero, means that you want the number reproduced with no decimal places showing (that's a required argument—even if you want no decimal places, you must indi-cate as much).

`&"~"` The ampersand concatenates the third string (contained in this expression) to the one that preceded it. The third string appears in quotes—it's a tilde.

If cell F10 contains the value 10, what you'll see on your screen (and what the 1-2-3 reads as a macro) is /wcs10~. Were you to change the con-tents of cell F10 to the value 15, you'd see /wcs15~. Enter the formula into a cell, use the / Range Name Create command to assign to it a valid macro name, enter a value in cell F10, and activate the macro. To see the flexibility this kind of macro offers, now change the value and activate the macro once more.

---

[25] When a string formula returns the value ERR and a macro attempts to read it, the macro will terminate just as if it had come to a blank cell. 1-2-3 regards ERR as a numeric value, and because macros can't read numeric values, 1-2-3 will terminate the macro just as if it had encountered a blank cell. No error condi-tion will result; the macro will merely end.

String Formula Limitations

string formulas can make macros harder to document and debug

As you've just seen, string formulas are powerful and flexible, but they do have one large drawback—macros containing them are difficult to document and can be troublesome to debug. Let's take the documentation problem first.

One common way to document macros is to print the three columns—Name, Macro, and Comment. However, the printout will reveal only the current result returned by the string formula, not the underlying formula itself. Under other circumstances, that formula might read very differently as it responds to changes in the cells it references. Your documentation won't reveal the potential for those changes; the formula will look like any other line of the macro.

When you view the macro on your screen, you won't even know that the line in question is generated by a string formula. Unless you place the cell pointer directly on the cell containing the string formula and look in the control panel, that line will appear to be a conventional label. Because you can be misled by the effect of such lines in your macros, the string formulas that produce them can make it difficult to test and debug your macros.

put the formula in the comment column . . .

There is, however, something you can do to lessen the problem. Move to the cell you've reserved for comments to the right of the cell containing the string formula. Use the / Worksheet Column Set-Width command to increase its width as much as possible without pushing off the screen the two columns to its left (which contain the range names and macros). Enter the string formula in the Comment cell located directly to the right of the cell in which you would ordinarily enter the macro. Select / Range Format Text, indicate the cell in the Comment column, and press Return. You should now see the string formula, not its result, in the Comment column. Move the cell pointer one cell to the left, into the Macro column. Enter a cell reference to the Comment cell to the right. If the macro cell is B3, then B3 should contain the formula +C3. You should now see the result of the formula in the Macro column, and the formula itself in the Comment column. The formula in the Comment column now documents the macro to its left.

. . . use /Range Format Text to show the formula itself . . .

In the example shown below, the string formula is in cell C3. That cell has also been formatted as Text. Cell B3, the macro code, contains the formula +C3. Cell B3 has not been formatted.

	A	B	C	D	E
1	NAME	MACRO	COMMENT		
2	----------------------------------				
3	\A	/wcs25~	+"/wcs"&@STRING(D10,0)&"~"		
4					
5					

Figure 9-4

. . .and put
a cell
reference to
it in the
macro
column.

You might enter the same formula into cell B3 as in cell C3, but it's better to use a cell reference in cell B3. If you use two separate formulas, you might edit the formula in cell B3 and forget to change the documentation in cell C3. When you use a cell reference, you can make all your formula changes in cell C3, and cell B3 will automatically change to reflect those changes.

If your string formula in the Comment column is longer than the width of that column, you will see only the leftmost portion of the formula that can be displayed within the column. Unlike labels, formulas that have been formatted as Text will not overwrite the cell to their right. Although this curtails the effectiveness of this technique for long string formulas, that limit will affect only your printed documentation. It shouldn't hinder your visual scanning since you can easily see the entire formula in the control panel.

When we cover the advanced macro commands, we'll introduce you to another method for modifying macros that offers more control and is thus appropriate for use with the more complex macros you'll write with those commands. For now, use string formulas as one way to vary your macros. However, because those formulas make it more difficult to debug your macros—and for others to revise them—we recommend you make an extra effort to document your work clearly.

Next

In the next section, you'll learn to use the advanced macro commands to write macros that customize 1-2-3 to your particular requirements.

Section III

Macro Programming

10

Introduction to Macro Programming

Overview

This chapter will:

- Introduce you to each of the advanced macro commands, in preparation for learning how to employ those commands in customized macros.

- Provide a detailed reference to the functioning of the advanced macro commands for use as you develop customized macros.

- Introduce you to command-enhancement macros. These types of macros can enhance 1-2-3's interactive commands or its macro commands by making those commands more powerful, simpler, or briefer.

We recommend that you use this chapter in either of two ways:

- To continue your tutorial on macros, read this section to learn how to use each of the advanced macro commands. If you're reading this for the first time, feel free to skim the more detailed aspects of each command explanation. Those details will be useful to you later, once you're writing more sophisticated macros.

- If you're already acquainted with the advanced macro commands and just need a review of a given command's syntax, refer to the Reference card that came with this book. If you need more information than the card can supply, use the following table to locate in this section the command you have a question about, and turn directly to that command's explanation.

Table 10.1 Commands

Command	Page
{ }	238
{?}	235
{App1}-{App4}	328
{Beep}	192
{Blank}	276
{Bordersoff}	194
{Borderson}	194
{Branch}	246
{Break}	211
{Breakoff}	212
{Breakon}	213
{Close}	298
{Contents}	277
{Define}	247
{Dispatch}	250
{Filesize}	301
{For}	252
{Forbreak}	256
{Frameoff}	195
{Frameon}	196
{Get}	214
{Getlabel}	216
{Getnumber}	219
{Getpos}	302
{Graphoff}	197
{Graphon}	198
{If}	258
{Ifkey}	263
{Indicate}	199

(Continued)

Table 10.1 Commands *(continued)*

Command	Page
{ Let }	281
{ Look }	223
{ Menubranch }	226
{ Menucall }	230
{ Onerror }	265
{ Open }	304
{ Paneloff }	201
{ Panelon }	203
{ Put }	284
{ Quit }	267
{ Read }	308
{ Readln }	315
{ Recalc }	287
{ Recalccol }	289
{ Restart }	268
{ Return }	270
{ Setpos }	319
{ System }	271
{ Wait }	233
{ Windowsoff }	204
{ Windowson }	206
{ Write }	320
{ Writeln }	324

Benefits

In the last chapter, we introduced you to the advanced macro commands through the { branch } and { quit } commands; you'll see more of those and other advanced macro commands in this chapter. Before introducing other advanced macro commands, let's review why you might want to use them.

turbo power for your macros

Think of the advanced macro commands relative to keystroke macros as you would a turbocharged engine relative to a normally aspirated one. Keystroke macros can run without the advanced macro commands, but the advanced commands add tremendous boost. The advanced macro commands can do such things as:

- Provide a means for you and your macro to communicate. You can write menus that look and work just like 1-2-3's menus—but they are menus you've written, and through them you can activate your own macros. Your macros can prompt you for information specific to your application. For example, you might write a prompt that says "Enter December's travel expense:". They can also change the indicator in the top right corner of the screen, and in Release 2.2, turn off 1-2-3's inverted "L" frame to allow you to customize the appearance of the display.

- Make decisions for you. Your macros can detect and trap errors. Suppose you come to a point where the macro is supposed to print a report but the printer is switched off. The macro can inform you of the problem, wait for you to correct it, and try again. It can test worksheet conditions and select the most appropriate steps to take. For example, if the macro is processing a list of values and comes to the end of the list, it can stop automatically.

- Create entirely new macro commands to extend the language to suit your needs. For example, 1-2-3 Release 2.01 (and lower releases) can't set the width of several columns with one command; it can either set the width of one column, or change the default width of all columns. You can use the advanced macro commands to create a command through which you can set the width of several columns.

Syntax

The remainder of this section is largely devoted to an encyclopedic list of advanced macro commands. Part of each entry in that list explains the way in which you write each command—otherwise known as that command's syntax.

Advanced macro command syntax has a lot in common with the syntax for special key names. Consider the key name {right} and the advanced macro keyword {branch \A}.

1. Both begin and end with a brace character.

2. Most key names and advanced macro commands contain a keyword that stays the same no matter what form the command takes. The word *branch* in {branch} is such a keyword.

arguments
specialize
the way a
given
command
works

3. You can include a space and a value in a special key name to designate the number of times to repeat the keystroke. For example, { right 6 }. Used in that way, the 6 is known as an argument. Arguments modify the manner in which a special key indicator works. Since the argument can vary (in this case, it could be any value from 1 through 255), it's also called a variable.

You can use arguments with some of the advanced macro commands, too. Like the 6 in the example above, arguments used with advanced macro commands specialize the action of the commands with which you use them. However, the arguments for the advanced macro commands are more diverse than those you can use with special key indicators. For example, some arguments are values and some are strings, some commands accept only single arguments, some accept multiple arguments, while others accept no arguments at all. As we introduce you to each command in the sections that follow, we'll explain the arguments with which it can be used.

write
commands
on a single
line

Advanced macro commands are also like special key indicators in that you can't divide them across lines in a macro. Even if a blank space appears in an advanced macro command, that command must appear entirely on a single line in order for 1-2-3 to read it.

A Warning About Certain Range Names

don't
duplicate a
command
keyword
with a range
name

Since you'll begin using the advanced macro commands as you use this chapter, you now need to avoid using range names that duplicate the keywords used in any of those commands. For example, one of the advanced macro commands is {branch}, so you should refrain from assigning the name *branch* to any range.

If you do assign a range name that duplicates the keyword used in an advanced macro command, you'll automatically invalidate that command. If you include in a macro an advanced command that you have invalidated in that manner, when 1-2-3 reads the command the macro will malfunction.

Specifically, instead of reading the command normally, 1-2-3 will transfer macro control to the range bearing the name of the command in question. From there, what happens will depend on circumstances—but it certainly won't be what you intended when you wrote the macro.

Consult the list of advanced macro commands that appears at the front of this chapter to see which names to avoid.

how to fix an existing worksheet

If you are adding macros to an existing worksheet, you may have already assigned range names that duplicate advanced macro command keywords. Follow these steps to identify and change any such range names. [26]

Retrieve the worksheet containing the names in question and press the Goto key, then twice press the Name key. 1-2-3 will display a full screen menu of range names in alphabetical order. Scan the list, compare it with the list of advanced macro commands at the beginning of this chapter, and write down any range names that you must change.

Begin with the first range name on your list. Write beside it the name you wish to change the existing name to. Select / Range Name Create, type the new name and press Return, then enter the old name and press Return. Now select / Range Name Delete, type the old name and press Return.

Using this method guarantees that any ranges that were associated through an old range name will remain associated through the new range name that replaces it. [27]

don't duplicate a key name with a macro range name

There's another group of names you should now avoid using to name certain kinds of ranges. Our warning to you is a little in advance of you understanding how you might use those names, but you need the warning now, so you don't create trouble now that you'll later have to fix.

Specifically, avoid using key names (such as the name right, which is used in the key name {right}) as range names for macro routines. You can use such names for ranges in a spreadsheet or database, such as to name a range containing a formula you want to refer to, but you must not name a macro routine with such a name.

If you ignore this suggestion, when you begin using the advanced-macro subroutine command, { }, covered in the forthcoming chapter on Controlling Program Flow, you won't be able to run as a subroutine any

---

[26] The steps that follow in the text are useful also when you upgrade to a new release of 1-2-3. First, check to see if new macro commands have been added. If they have and if you intend to use any of those new commands, you can use those steps to check your worksheets for range names that duplicate the new commands, and change them.

[27] When we say that two or more ranges are associated, we're referring to a technique that uses a single range name to link many range settings. After defining the range name and using it to establish one or more settings, if you then redefine the range name, all of the associated range settings change automatically. For example, suppose you used the range name Data to define a / Data Query Input range and then used that same name as the database range argument in a slew of database statistical functions. Further suppose that after establishing those settings you added records to the database. Redefining all those ranges is simply a matter of redefining the range name Data; 1-2-3 will automatically make the changes to all the associated settings and to the formulas.

macro routine that bears a key name. The command you'd use to run that routine as a subroutine, {right}, would exactly duplicate the key name, and 1-2-3 would interpret the command as a key name, not as a subroutine. [28]

Command Components

What goes into an advanced macro command? Some, like the {quit} command, are simple. Other, more powerful commands are somewhat complex. Before we introduce any more advanced macro commands, let's take a moment to review each of their components—keywords, arguments, and separators—in more detail.

Keywords

Like the special key names (such as {edit}), all advanced macro commands begin and end with braces. Don't confuse braces { } with brackets [ ] or parentheses ( ). You can't use them interchangeably in macros.

In the advanced macro commands, the keyword is typically the first word following the opening brace. For example, in the {quit} command, the keyword is *quit*. Unlike arguments, which vary, keywords are literals; you cannot change them.

don't use
keywords
as range
names

Again, don't assign any range names that duplicate the keyword used by an advanced macro command. For example, avoid assigning to a range the name wait, since wait is the keyword for the command {wait} (see the keyword list that follows under the heading "Organization of the Commands").

Arguments

Some advanced macro commands either can, or must, contain one or more arguments. Arguments specialize the action of the command of which they are a part. For example, in the command {branch A12}, the

[28] If you upgrade to a new release of 1-2-3, the recommendation we earlier made about checking for new macro commands applies also to checking for new key names. Check for any new key names, and if you've used them to name a macro routine, change the name of the routine. For example, Release 2.2 added the key name {help}, so if you've upgraded to Release 2.2, rename any routines named Help to something else, such as Helper.

cell address A12 is an argument that specializes how 1-2-3 will respond to the {branch} command—it will branch to cell A12.

Arguments are also variables. In the previous example, we could have used any other cell address besides A12, or we could have used a range name.

While some commands take one argument, others take more than one argument, still others take none at all.

four kinds of arguments

The contents of an argument consist of one of four things:

(*1*) A numeric value or numeric formula. In the syntax descriptions that follow, numeric arguments are represented as [number]. You can substitute a cell reference (in the form of a cell address or range name) for a numeric argument. In that case, the referenced cell should contain the appropriate value, or a formula that returns that value.

(*2*) A string value or string valued formula. In the syntax descriptions that follow, string valued arguments are represented either as [string] or ["string"]. In most cases, you can substitute a cell reference (in the form of a cell address or range name) for a string argument. If you do, the referenced cell should contain the appropriate string, or a formula that returns that string value.

In Releases 2.2 and 3, any macro command will accept range names or formulas as arguments. In previous releases, some but not all macro commands accepted range names or formulas as arguments. Because of that, whenever you supply a string directly as an argument, as opposed to when you use a cell reference or a string formula to supply the argument, we recommend that you enclose that string in quotation marks.

Doing so will guarantee that 1-2-3 will interpret the string as a string, and not construe it as a range name. If you ever assign the string as a range name that you've used as an argument in an advanced macro command, unless the string is enclosed in quotation marks, 1-2-3 will construe the string as a reference to that range. So, if you've used the command {open "FILE1.PRN";m} in your macro (to open in modify mode a file called File1.prn) and you later assign to a range the name *M*, when you next run this macro, it will malfunction. 1-2-3 will construe the argument *m* as a reference to the range of the same name. To avoid this, enclose the *m* in quotation marks: {open "FILE1.PRN";"m"}. If you use 1-2-3 Release 2 or 2.01 now, enclosing literal strings in quotation marks is an investment in compatibility. If you pass your macros to someone using a later release, or you later upgrade, your macros won't require modification.

Numbers used as arguments don't require quotation marks. Even if you use a number as a range name, 1-2-3 will interpret it correctly. It is generally a bad idea to name a range with a number, because you can't use the number to refer to the range. 1-2-3 will interpret such a reference as a number. [29]

(3) A location on the worksheet. In the syntax descriptions that follow, location arguments are represented as [location]. You can represent them through a cell address or range name.

(4) A logical expression or other formula evaluating to either zero or one, or the values zero or one. In the syntax descriptions that follow, logical arguments are represented as [logical]. You can substitute a cell reference (in the form of a cell address or range name) for a logical argument. In that case, the referenced cell should contain either the value zero or one, or a formula that returns either of those values.

when you must use quotation marks

As noted above, when a listing displays a string valued argument enclosed in quotation marks, you must include those quotation marks when you write the command. There are three other circumstances under which 1-2-3 may require you to enclose an argument in quotes. If an argument meets any of the following criteria, enclose that argument with quotation marks.

1. The argument is a string or a range name containing a colon (:), a comma (,), or a semicolon (;). Those characters normally act as argument separators. Quotation marks prevent 1-2-3 from erroneously interpreting these characters as argument separators when they are meant to be part of the argument itself.

2. The argument is a string duplicating a range name. Quotation marks prevent 1-2-3 from interpreting the string as a range name when it's not meant that way. We recommend that you always enclose literal text (that is, text other than a range name) in quotation marks. Otherwise, each time you create a new range name you will have to make sure it doesn't duplicate an existing string argument. If it does, you'll have to put quotation marks around the argument. That's an unreliable way of working. Use quotation marks around literal text when you write the argument and you'll avoid such concerns.

3. The argument is a formula that you wish to treat as a label.

---

[29] This discussion begs the question of order of precedence in parsing macros. 1-2-3 will always interpret numbers as numbers, cell addresses as cell addresses, and key names as key names—even if a range name duplicates them. Macro keywords are another story. If a range name duplicates a macro keyword, 1-2-3 will interpret any such reference as a range name (resulting in a subroutine call), not as an advanced macro command.

We'll detail the number and type of arguments for each command in the section that follows. Keep in mind that you will have to add quotation marks to an argument if it meets any of the preceding three conditions. The exception is that we'll use them where an argument contains literal text.

using range names

There are two ways in which you may refer to a worksheet location in an advanced macro command—through a cell address or a range name. In a number of instances, the only acceptable reference is to a single cell, rather than to a multi-celled range. One example of that occurs when you use a reference to supply the logical formula in an {if} command. The reference to the worksheet location must be to a single cell, such as D1, not to a multi-celled range such as D1..D5.

In those cases, if you use a range name, the range to which that name refers must consist of only a single cell.

Separators

Advanced macro commands sometimes require blank spaces in certain places. In the case of the command {branch \A}, there must be a space between "branch" and "\A." Those spaces appear in the listings that follow.

argument separators

Where a macro command takes more than one argument, those arguments must be separated by one of several punctuation marks. However, although one form of punctuation is always a valid separator, the others are valid only under certain conditions.

The semicolon is always a valid argument separator. The comma or the period may also act as an argument separator, but only if the / Worksheet Global Default Other International Punctuation command has been set properly. Use the / Worksheet Global Default Other International Punctuation command to make the comma and semicolon valid and the period invalid (selections A or E), the period and semicolon valid and the comma invalid (selections B or F), or only the semicolon valid (selections C, D, G or H). The default choice with which 1-2-3 is shipped in the United States is selection A, so in its default configuration, both the semicolon and comma are valid argument separators.

use semicolons as argument separators to make your macro the most portable

Requisite spaces and punctuation, collectively called separators, are described in the listing for each command. We will always use the semicolon as the separator punctuation mark and we recommend that you follow suit. The / Worksheet Global Default Other International Punctuation settings are stored with 1-2-3, not with the worksheet file. If you use commas or periods as argument separators in a macro and then give the worksheet file containing that macro to someone whose copy of 1-2-3 contains different Default International Punctuation settings, the macro won't work. Using the semicolon as an argument separator guarantees your macros will work regardless of the status of the Default International Punctuation settings.

Form of the Command Definitions

Since the arguments possible with each command can vary so widely, we'll begin the explanation of each command with an explicit description of its possibilities. If you've already learned the commands and are using this section to remind you how to write a particular command, you'll probably only need to consult that definition. If you're reading about these commands for the first time, a detailed description of the arguments and uses of the command follow.

Here's an overview of the structure we'll use to explain each command to you.

Purpose: Briefly defines the primary purpose of the command.

Format: Describes the syntax of the command. Square brackets [ ] enclose arguments; omit the square brackets when you write the command. Arguments that appear in regular type are mandatory. If those arguments are optional, they'll appear in italics. A one word descriptor appears within the brackets to represent each argument. A brief explanation of the allowable forms of the argument follows each format diagram.

Sample: To clarify the syntax described above, the sample demonstrates how you might write the command. (For a more complete example of the command in a functioning macro, see the Example section that follows.)

Complements: A list of other advanced macro commands, if any, that either must be or are normally used in association with this command. If you see a command listed here and you don't know how to use it, refer to that command's listing.

See also: Lists macro commands that implement related functions. If you've come to this macro command because you want to do something and don't know what command to use to do it, you may find additional helpful information listed under the commands that appear here.

Compatibility: Appears in the listings of commands that work only in Releases 2.2 and 3 of 1-2-3. This notation won't appear in listings for commands that work in Releases 2, 2.01, 2.2, and 3.

Release 1A Equivalent: If a command equivalent to this one exists in 1-2-3 Release 1A, the Release 1A command will be listed here.

Release 1A Format: Describes the syntax of the Release 1A command in the same manner as the format description above.

Description: A statement of common uses for the command, the context in which it's used, and a list of any factors that affect your use of it. Here's where you'll find the most detailed explanation of each command. If the command has a Release 1A equivalent and that Release 1A equivalent has any capabilities not available in the newer version of the command, this section will separately describe the Release 1A command's capabilities.

Example: A sample of the command within the context of a macro. There may be multiple examples imbedded in the Description section of each command's listing.

Command Definitions

Organization of the Commands

We've grouped the following definitions of each of the advanced macro commands according to their function. A list of each group's name and the commands within that group appear below. The commands within each group appear in alphabetical order.

If you know what you want to get done but don't know which command to use to do it, you can locate it by following these steps:

how to find the command you want to learn about

- Scan the group headings listed in the table of Command Groups below. They describe the general function of each group of commands and can help you identify the group into which the command you need may fall.

- The section immediately following the table provides, by command group, an overview of the purpose of each command.[30] Locate the heading of the group you chose and by reading about the commands it contains, try to identify the command(s) within that section that will help you.

• Refer in the next six chapters to the descriptions of each command for information about the specific capabilities, limitations, and syntax of each command (those descriptions follow the grouping scheme shown in the table below). If, after reading the description, you feel the command isn't the one you're seeking, consult the heading "See also:" near the top of that command's listing. There you'll find a list of related commands that may include the command you're seeking. You can find the page number for that command at the beginning of this chapter.

Table 10.2 Command Groups

Group	Commands
Controlling the Screen	{Beep}, {Bordersoff}, {Borderson}, {Frameoff}, {Frameon}, {Graphoff}, {Graphon}, {Indicate}, {Paneloff}, {Panelon}, {Windowsoff}, {Windowson}
Allowing keyboard interaction	{Break}, {Breakoff}, {Breakon}, {Get}, {Getlabel}, {Getnumber}, {Look}, {Menubranch}, {Menucall}, {Wait}, {?}
Controlling program flow	{}, {Branch}, {Define}, {Dispatch}, {For}, {Forbreak}, {If}, {Ifkey}, {Onerror}, {Quit}, {Restart}, {Return}, {System}
Manipulating data	{Blank}, {Contents}, {Let}, {Put}, {Recalc}, {Recalccol}

(Continued)

---

[30] Individual overviews appear again at the beginning of the chapter covering the commands referred to in that overview (chapters 11-16 cover those commands). The information appears twice to enable you to read those chapters serially, where you'll appreciate such introductions as you begin to read about a new command group, or randomly, where you'll use the overview here to jump directly to the command you need help with.

Table 10.2 Command Groups *(Continued)*

Group	Commands
Working with files	{Close}, {Filesize}, {Getpos}, {Open}, {Read}, {Readln}, {Setpos}, {Write}, {Writeln}
Accessing Add-ins	{App1}, {App2}, {App3}, {App4}

Controlling the Screen: Command Overview

controlling the screen

These commands enable you to control the appearance of the screen: change 1-2-3's mode indicator ({indicate}), freeze the worksheet portion of the screen ({windowsoff}), freeze and optionally clear the control panel and status line portions of the screen ({paneloff}), restore normal functioning to both those screen segments ({windowson} and {panelon}), eliminate the inverted "L" row and column frame ({bordersoff} and {frameoff}) and restore it ({borderson} and {frameon}), make a given graph's settings current without displaying that graph or display a graph while a macro continues running ({graphon}) and clear the graph ({graphoff}).

We've also included a command that enables you to sound the computer's speaker ({beep}). While it has no direct effect on the screen, it can draw the user's attention to the screen.

Allowing Keyboard Interaction: Command Overview

allowing keyboard interaction

These commands enable you to interact with the user of the macro: to gather data from the user ({get}, {look}, {getlabel}, and {getnumber}), pause for a specified period of time ({wait}), obtain decisions from the user ({menubranch} and {menucall}), prevent the user from interrupting the macro ({breakoff}), restore that ability ({breakon}), cancel a 1-2-3 command sequence or cell entry in process and return 1-2-3 to Ready mode without interrupting macro control ({break}), and temporarily suspend macro control and return control of the application to the user ({?}).

Controlling Program Flow: Command Overview

controlling program flow

The commands in this chapter will enable you to control the flow of the macro: to continue reading the macro in a new location ({branch}), continue reading the macro in a new location specified in a third location ({dispatch}), temporarily transfer control to a subroutine location ({ }), resume reading in a location from which you called a subroutine ({return}), clear the subroutine stack ({restart}), transfer control to DOS and optionally start a DOS program or batch file {system}, test a condition and use the result to select one of two locations in which to resume reading macro instructions ({if}), redirect control in the event of an error ({onerror}), create a counter-controlled loop ({for}), cancel a counter controlled loop ({forbreak}), temporarily return control to the keyboard ({?}), and terminate the macro and unconditionally return control to the keyboard ({quit}).

Manipulating Data: Command Overview

manipulat-
ing data

The following commands enable macros to manipulate data on the worksheet. They fall into three groups: those that enter data into cells ({contents}, {let}, and {put}); those that erase data from cells ({blank}); and those that recalculate portions of the worksheet ({recalc}, {recalccol}).

entering
data into
cells

{Let}, {contents}, and {put} differ in the way in which they enter data onto the worksheet:

- {Let} is the most commonly used of the three; it transfers a value or label into any cell you designate.

- {Contents} translates a formatted value into a label and enters it into any cell you designate. Numbers may be assigned any of 1-2-3's range formats.

- {Put} allows you to build a table of values or labels or insert data into an existing table.

removing
data
recalcu-
lating
ranges

{Blank} erases data from a single cell or a range of cells. {Recalc} and {recalccol} both selectively recalculate ranges on the worksheet during a macro, but do so in a different manner:

- {Recalc} selectively recalculates ranges on the worksheet in a row-wise manner.

- {Recalccol} selectively recalculates ranges in a columnwise fashion.

File Manipulation: Command Overview

The following commands enable macros to manipulate files: to open them ({open}), assess their size ({filesize}), write data into them ({write} and {writeln}), read data from them ({read} and {readln}), and close them ({close}). Collectively, the commands are sometimes referred to as the macro file input/output commands (or, more simply, the macro file i/o commands) because they manage the process of moving data in and out of files. Most of these commands work only with ASCII files, but several ({open}, {filesize}, and {close}) work equally well with worksheet files and other types of files.

Accessing Add-ins: Command Overview

Release 2 of 1-2-3 introduced the capability to serve as a host for separate programs, called add-ins, that work as part of 1-2-3. Add-ins comprise as diverse a group of programs as does software in general; word processors, databases, and goal-seeking programs are just several of many categories of add-in software on the market. Release 2.2 comes with two add-in programs: Macro Library Manager, which lets you store macros off the worksheet, and Allways, a desktop publishing program for worksheets.

Add-ins make good application adjuncts for three reasons: they can add considerable functionality to 1-2-3, they can be controlled by macros in most cases, [31] and the memory they occupy can be retrieved at any time by detaching them from 1-2-3.

In order to transfer macro control from the worksheet to an add-in, you must first load 1-2-3 with the Add-In Manager (a program you receive with any add-in; in Release 2.2, it's included in 1-2-3 so you need not load it separately). Provided the add-in was written to support 1-2-3 macros, you can then use a macro to:

- Display the add-in manager menu and either attach an add-in to 1-2-3, assign the add-in to an Alt-function key, invoke the add-in, or detach the add-in from 1-2-3.

---

[31] Check with the developer of any add-in you are considering about that add-in's support for macros. Many add-ins can be controlled by a macro residing on the worksheet in exactly the same manner as you can control 1-2-3 with such a macro. Some add-ins can be controlled with macros, but with some reservations. For example, you might be able to use a macro to invoke the add-in and perform some operation as long as you are in 1-2-3 when you initiate that operation, yet you would not be able to activate a macro if you are already inside the add-in when you wish to do so. Such variations are at the discretion of the add-in's developer, thus the need to evaluate each add-in individually.

- Operate the add-in in the same manner in which macros can operate 1-2-3: by passing to the add-in keystrokes to enter data, navigate through the application, or execute commands.

- Customize the add-in through advanced macro commands such as {menubranch}, {if}, and {getlabel}.

Since you can have more than one add-in attached to 1-2-3 at a time, you can transfer control between all the attached add-ins and 1-2-3 at will.

The key names {app1} through {app4} are the keys to controlling add-ins. The number included in the key name refers to each of the four Alt-function keys by which you access the add-in manager or add-ins themselves. Although {app1}, {app2}, {app3}, and {app4} are key names—not advanced macro commands—the subject of controlling add-ins via macros is an advanced topic, so we've chosen to cover these key names in the chapter directly following the chapters on the advanced macro commands (see chapter 16).

11

Controlling the Screen

Overview and Introduction to New Concepts

scope

The commands discussed here will enable you to control the appearance of the screen—change 1-2-3's mode indicator ({indicate}), freeze the worksheet portion of the screen ({windowsoff}), freeze and optionally clear the control panel and status line portions of the screen ({paneloff}), restore normal functioning to both those screen segments ({windowson} and {panelon}), eliminate the inverted "L" row and column frame ({frameoff} and {bordersoff}) and restore it ({frameon} and {borderson}), make a given graph's settings current without displaying that graph or display a graph while a macro continues running ({graphon}) and clear the graph ({graphoff}).

We've also included a command that allows you to sound the computer's speaker ({beep}). Although it has no direct effect on the screen, it can draw the user's attention to the screen.

{Beep}

Purpose: Use {beep} to provide auditory feedback to the user of a macro.

Format: {beep [tone]}

192

Where [tone] is an integer between 0 and 3. [Tone] may be a number, a formula, a cell address, or a range name describing a single cell.

Sample: { beep }

Complements: None.

Description: Although { beep } doesn't affect the screen, like the rest of the commands in this chapter, it provides a tool through which the application can communicate with its user.

{ Beep } momentarily sounds one of 1-2-3's four standard tones on the computer's speaker,[32] and is most often used to signify that some significant event, such as an error, has occurred. You might also use it to alert the user that a prompt has appeared on the screen, or to indicate the continued operation of a lengthy procedure that doesn't otherwise inform the user of its progress.

Because the { beep } command looks so much like a key name (such as { right }), a common misunderstanding is that { beep }'s optional numeric argument repeats that command; it does not. The numeric argument allows you to select one of four tones to sound. If you wish to sound repeated tones, you must include multiple { beep } commands in the macro.

tone
argument

Typically, integers between 0 and 3 are used for the tone argument. However, only the integer portion of that number matters: 1.9 sounds the same tone as 1.

If the number of the tone argument falls outside the 0–3 range, the tone will be determined by the remainder obtained by dividing the number by four. For example, 41 divided by 4 is 10 with a remainder of 1, so the tone sounded by { beep 41 } and { beep 1 } are the same.

tone
selection

Used without its optional numeric argument, { beep } sounds the same tone you hear when you attempt to move the cell pointer past the end of the worksheet. That is also the tone produced by { beep 1 }. The tone of the computer's speaker ascends with the value of the { beep } command's argument; 0 is the lowest, 3 the highest.

Example:

Figure 11-1

	A	B	C	D	E	F	G	H
1	NAME	MACRO				COMMENT		
2	------	-------	---	---	---	--------	---	---
3	PRINT	/ppagpq				Print report		
4		{goto}DONE_SCREEN~				Display "done" message		
5		{beep 3}{beep 3}				Beep twice		

---

[32] In Release 2.2, for { beep } to sound a tone, you must also have the / Worksheet Global Default Other Beep command set to Yes.

You may also use a named range in place of the argument.

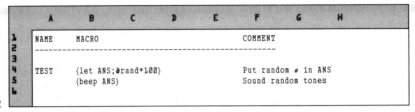

Figure 11-2

{Bordersoff}

Purpose: {Bordersoff} suppresses display of the inverted "L" worksheet frame.

Format: {bordersoff}

Sample: {bordersoff}

Complements: {borderson}, {frameon}

See also: {frameoff}, {paneloff}, {indicate}

Compatibility: Releases 2.2 and 3

Description: {Bordersoff} suppresses display of the inverted "L" worksheet frame until the macro either reads a {borderson} command or terminates. {Bordersoff} and {frameoff} function identically. {Bordersoff} exists to maintain compatibility with 1-2-3 Release 2J, which is the dominant release of 1-2-3 in use in Japan. If you expect your macros to be run on Release 2J, use {bordersoff} instead of {frameoff}.

For details on the {bordersoff} command, see the entry for {frameoff}.

{Borderson}

Purpose: {Borderson} redisplays the worksheet border after that border has been suppressed with {bordersoff} command.

Format: {borderson}

Sample: {borderson}

Complements: {bordersoff}

See also: {frameon}, {panelon}, {indicate}

Compatibility: Releases 2.2 and 3

Description: {Borderson} redisplays the inverted "L" worksheet frame after a macro has read a {bordersoff} command. {Borderson} and {frameon} function identically. {Borderson} does have one indispensable role. Since it is the only command for this function that exists in 1-2-3 Release 2J, which is the dominant release of 1-2-3 in use in Japan, if you expect your macros to be run on Release 2J, use {borderson} instead of {frameon}.

For details on the {borderson} command, see the entry for {frameon}.

{Frameoff}

Purpose: {Frameoff} suppresses display of the inverted "L" worksheet frame.

Format: {frameoff}

Sample: {frameoff}

Complements: {frameon}

See also: {bordersoff}, {paneloff}, {indicate}

Compatibility: Releases 2.2 and 3

Description: {Frameoff} suppresses display of the inverted "L" worksheet frame until the macro either reads a {frameon} command or terminates.

This command is useful primarily in turn-key applications. By turning off the worksheet frame, you make an environment less like the familiar 1-2-3 worksheet. That gives you the opportunity to create a visual environment that users will associate more closely with your application.

You can achieve a greater effect by using this command in concert with two other commands, {paneloff} and {indicate}. {Paneloff} lets you freeze the display of the control panel (and, in Release 2.2, clear it).

{Indicate} lets you eliminate the mode indicator or change it to an indicator of your choice.

{Frameoff} functions identically to {bordersoff}, with one exception. {Bordersoff} is the only command that performs this function in Release 2J, the dominant release of 1-2-3 in use in Japan. If you expect your macros to be run on Release 2J, use {bordersoff} instead of {frameoff}.

Example:

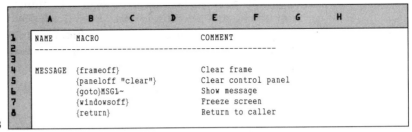

```
        A       B        C      D       E       F      G      H
  1  NAME    MACRO                    COMMENT
  2
  3  ------------------------------------------------------------
  4  MESSAGE {frameoff}              Clear frame
  5          {paneloff "clear"}      Clear control panel
  6          {goto}MSG1~             Show message
  7          {windowsoff}            Freeze screen
  8          {return}                Return to caller
```

Figure 11-3

{ Frameon }

Purpose: {Frameon} redisplays the worksheet frame after that frame has been suppressed with {frameoff} command.

Format: {frameon}

Sample: {frameon}

Complements: {frameoff}

See also: {borderson}, {panelon}, {indicate}

Compatibility: Releases 2.2 and 3

Description: {Frameon} redisplays the inverted "L" worksheet frame after a macro has read a {frameoff} command. {Frameon} and {borderson} function identically.

If you want to redisplay the frame only when the macro finishes, you need not use the {frameon} command. If the worksheet frame has been suppressed by the {frameoff} command, 1-2-3 will automatically redisplay that frame when the macro terminates.

Use the {panelon} command to redisplay the control panel and the {indicate} command to redisplay the mode indicator.

{Frameon} functions identically to {borderson}, with one exception. {Borderson} is the only command that performs this function in

Release 2J, the dominant release of 1-2-3 in use in Japan. If you expect your macros to be run on Release 2J, use {borderson} instead of {frame-on}.

```
        A        B         C      D      E         F       G       H
  1   NAME     MACRO                    COMMENT
  2   ----------------------------------------------------
  3   REFRSH   {frameon}                Clear frame
  4            {goto}DATA~              Position cell pointer
  5            {panelon}                Unfreeze control panel
  6            {windowson}              Unfreeze worksheet screen
  7            {return}                 Return to caller
```

Figure 11-4

{Graphoff}

Purpose: {Graphoff} clears from the screen a graph displayed using the {graphon} command.

Format: {Graphoff}

Sample: {graphoff}

Complements: {graphon}

Compatibility: Releases 2.2 and 3

Description: With a graph displayed on the screen that was selected using the {graphon} command, use {graphoff} to redisplay the worksheet.

{Graphoff} will not affect a graph that was displayed using the {graph} key name, the Graph View command, or the Graph Name Use command. A graph displayed using any of those methods suspends a macro. It requires that the user press a keystroke in order to clear it from the screen and cause the macro to resume operation.

Example:

```
        A        B         C      D      E         F       G       H
  1   NAME     MACRO                    COMMENT
  2   ----------------------------------------------------
  3   GRF_CLR  {goto}DATA~              Position cell pointer
  4            {graphoff}               Clear graph display
  5            {ON}                     Unfreeze screen
  6            {return}                 Return to caller
```

Figure 11-5

{Graphon}

Purpose: {Graphon} can redisplay the most recently displayed graph, display any named graph, or make current a given named graph's settings without displaying the graph.

Format: {Graphon ["name_of_graph"],["nodisplay"]}
Where ["name_of_graph"] is the name of a named graph and nodisplay is the string nodisplay in quotation marks. You may use in place of either or both strings a cell address, range name, or formula that evaluates to that string.

Sample: {graphon QTR_1;"nodisplay"}

Complements: {graphoff}

Description: {Graphon} is the only way to make a given graph's settings current without displaying that graph. Displaying a graph with the {graphon} command is also the only way to have 1-2-3 continue reading a macro while a graph displays. Because the {graphon} command allows the macro to continue running while the graph displays on the screen, using that command to display a graph is also a key to controlling when the graph display will be replaced by another graph or by the worksheet (see the {graphoff} command).

If while in a macro you select a graph using the {graph} key name, the Graph View or the Graph Name Use command, the macro will suspend its operation while the graph is in view. To restore the worksheet display and cause the macro to resume operation, the user must press a key.

If you want to have a macro continue reading while a graph displays, use {graphon} to display the current graph or {graphon ["name_of_graph"]} to display a named graph of your choice. Either will let the macro continue running while the graph is on the screen. The graph will remain on the screen until one of several things happens: until the macro reads another {graphon} command, until the macro reads a {graphoff} command, or until the macro reads a command that requires it to display something in the control panel, such as a custom prompt command, custom menu command, or an {indicate} command.

If you want to change a graph's settings without displaying that graph to the user, use {graphon ["name_of_graph"];"nodisplay"}, where ["name_of_graph"] is the name of a graph stored earlier with the Graph Name Create command.

Example:

```
         A        B        C        D        E        F        G        H
    1  NAME     MACRO                    COMMENT
    2  ---------------------------------------------------
    3  HIDE     {graphon "SALES_COMP"}   Display graph
    4           {SORT}~                  Sort database
    5           {return}                 Return to caller
    6
```

Figure 11-6

{ Indicate }

Purpose: { Indicate } changes 1-2-3's mode indicator.

Format: { indicate ["ind"] }
Where ["ind"] is a string up to 5 characters long. In Release 2.2, ["ind"] can be a string up to 80 characters long and can consist of a cell address, range name reference, or a string formula.

Sample: { indicate "ENTRY" }

Complements: None.

Description: 1-2-3's mode indicator appears in the top right corner of the control panel (it often displays the word Ready). Depending on how you use it, the { indicate } command either changes the mode indicator to any string of up to five characters in length (in Release 2.2, up to 240 characters in length, though usually limited to 80 characters, depending on the display adapter you're using), removes the mode indicator entirely, or restores the mode indicator to 1-2-3's control.

uses

{ Indicate } is most often used to provide the user with a context for the operation currently underway. For example, when you point to a cell while writing a formula, 1-2-3 changes the mode indicator to Point. You can provide that same kind of feedback to users of macros that you write. For example, during a data-entry operation you might want to change the indicator to the word Entry. You must issue another { indicate } command each time you wish to change the mode indicator's prompt from one string to another.

{ Indicate } is the only command through which a macro can post a message in 1-2-3's control panel without awaiting user input of some kind. That is, it is the only command with which you can post a message and have the macro continue processing.

longevity

Unlike the action of most other macro commands, { indicate } remains in effect after the macro has relinquished control to 1-2-3. For example, if you change the mode indicator to Enter, after the macro terminates, the mode indicator will continue to display Enter, irrespective of the mode in which 1-2-3 is operating. Even if 1-2-3 encounters an error, if you've used {indicate} to set the mode indicator, you won't see the flashing Error indicator 1-2-3 would otherwise display. (However, the error message that normally appears at the bottom of the screen when an error occurs still displays.) {Indicate} differs from {paneloff} in this way. Errors override {paneloff}.

You can return control of the mode indicator to 1-2-3 either by saving and retrieving the file, or by issuing the {indicate} command with no argument: {indicate}.

where to include it in a macro

- If you've written an auto-execute macro and want to maintain control over the mode indicator from the time the file is retrieved, the {indicate} command should be one of the first commands you invoke.

to reset the indictator

- If you want your macro to reset the mode indicator to its default state, use the {indicate} command without any arguments: {indicate}.

to remove the indicator

- If you want to remove the mode indicator entirely, specify a blank string: {indicate ""}.

The mode indicator resides on the top line of the screen whereas prompts generated by commands such as {getlabel} reside on the second line. Therefore, even if in Release 2.2 you use the full width of the screen as your indicator, that indicator won't conflict with prompts generated by other kinds of commands. It will, however, overwrite the cell contents display on the top line of the control panel.

precedence

If you invoke the {paneloff "clear"} command, and subsequently use the {indicate} command, {indicate} will still superimpose its prompt on the control panel.

errors

In Release 2.01 and 3, you must be careful to enclose in quotation marks literal strings used as arguments. Words commonly used to indicate messages, such words as Enter and Stop, are also among the most common names for ranges. If you specify a string as an indicate message that duplicates the name of a single-cell range and you fail to enclose that string in quotation marks, 1-2-3 will do one of two things. If the range contains a label, 1-2-3 will display that label in the indicator. If is empty or contains a value, the macro will terminate and 1-2-3 will issue the error message "Macro: Invalid string value in INDICATE" (followed by the cell address of the {indicate} command. That latter error cannot be trapped with {onerror}.

If the named range consists of more than one cell, the macro will treat the string as if it had had quotation marks around it.

In Release 2 or 2.01, if you include more than five characters in the {indicate} command's argument, when 1-2-3 reads the command it will post just the first five of those characters in the indicator but will not issue an error. Example:

	A	B	C	D	E	F	G
1	NAME	MACRO				COMMENT	
2	----	-----				-------	
3	ENTRY	{indicate "-1-"}				Change mode indicator	
4		{getnumber "Enter 1st number. ";FIRST}				Get first entry	
5		{indicate "-2-"}				Change mode indicator	
6		{getnumber "Enter 2nd number. ";SECOND}				Get second entry	

Figure 11-7

centering a prompt

In Release 2.2, to center an indicate string in the control panel, first name one cell String and another Len. In the cell named String, enter the string you wish the prompt to consist of. In the cell named Len, enter the formula @round((80-@length(STRING))/2;0). Now enter the macro as follows: {indicate @repeat(" ";LEN)&STRING&@repeat(" ";LEN)}

To post a different message in the control panel, change the string in the cell named String. If you are using a display adapter that displays some width other than 80 columns, substitute that width for 80 in the formula stored in Len.

{Paneloff}

Purpose: {Paneloff} freezes the control panel (consisting of the top three lines of the screen) and the status line (the bottom line of the screen).

Format: {paneloff ["clear"]} where "clear" is an optional string contained in quotation marks, or a cell address, range name, or string formula that evaluates to that string.

Sample: {paneloff}

Complements: {panelon}

See also: {windowsoff}, {bordersoff}, {frameoff}

Description: While a macro is running, {paneloff} prevents 1-2-3 from updating both the status line (the bottom line of the screen) and the control panel (the top three lines of the screen). In Release 2 or 2.01, {paneloff} can not clear those areas of the screen; it reduces distraction by freezing in place whatever is there at the time 1-2-3 reads the {paneloff} command in a macro. In Release 2.2, you may use the optional argument "clear" in the {paneloff} command to also erase the contents of the control panel. In either case, {panelon} will cause 1-2-3 to once again continuously refresh the control panel.

{Paneloff} is useful when the macro makes a lot of command-menu selections, which would otherwise cause the control panel to flash. The command will also help speed up the macro. If 1-2-3 doesn't have to update the control panel, it can process the macro more quickly (the {windowsoff} command will speed it up a great deal more).

exceptions

Macro commands that ordinarily display something in the control panel are unaffected by {paneloff}. For example, if the macro reads the command {getlabel "Enter your name: ";NAME1} after reading a {paneloff} command, you will still see the prompt "Enter your name: " in the control panel, and that prompt will still disappear after you respond to it.

If an entry is in the edit line of the control panel (such as occurs when you are typing an entry or editing one)[33] at the time that 1-2-3 reads the {paneloff} command, 1-2-3 will cease to display that entry on the edit line. Although invisible, the entry itself will remain in the edit line unless otherwise removed.

clearing the
control
panel

Although in Release 2.2 you can clear the control panel, in Release 2 or 2.01, {paneloff} preserves the control panel's current contents. For that reason, in Release 2 or 2.01 you may wish to minimize the control panel's contents directly before you use {paneloff}. Although there isn't much you can do about the content of the status line at the bottom of the screen, you can reduce the content of the control panel.

Just prior to using the {paneloff} command, place the cell pointer in a blank cell which has not been formatted with the / Range Format command, has not been unprotected with the / Range Unprotect command, and does not reside in a column the width of which has been changed with the / Worksheet Column Set-Width command. If a cell has an entry in it, has been range formatted, has been unprotected (with the / Range Unprotect command), or has had the width of the column in which it resides modified (with the / Worksheet Column Set-Width command), 1-2-3 will post something to the right of the cell address in the control panel when the cell pointer resides in that cell. By placing the cell pointer

---

[33] The edit line of the control panel resides on the second line of the screen. When you type an entry (but before you press Return to place it on the worksheet) or edit an entry, 1-2-3 will display that entry on the edit line.

in a cell that contains none of those attributes, you'll leave the the control panel as empty as possible when you freeze it with {paneloff}.

posting
messages

You might also post a message with the {paneloff} command. Position the cell pointer on a cell containing a label you want to display in the control panel while your next routine is running. Then issue the {paneloff} command and run the routine. The label will remain in the control panel, acting as a message. For better effect, you might center the message in the control panel by putting as many spaces to the left of your text in that label as are needed to center it.

longevity

Unlike the {indicate} command, the effect of {paneloff} terminates as soon as the macro does. That means that if you retrieve another worksheet file you must reinvoke the {paneloff} command if you wish to continue to suppress updating of the control panel. The same holds true if you trap an error with the {onerror} command. Since an error will reset the status of the control panel, you must include another {paneloff} command in the routine to which the {onerror} command branches. {Paneloff} differs from {indicate} in this regard. {Indicate} will override the error indicator. Example:

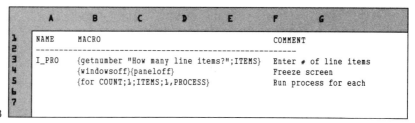

Figure 11-8

{Panelon}

Purpose: The {panelon} command reverses the effect of the {paneloff} command; it reenables 1-2-3 to update the contents of the control panel and the bottom line of the screen.

Format: {panelon}

Sample: {panelon}

Complements: {paneloff}

See also: {windowson}, {borderson}, {frameon}

Description: {Panelon} reverses the effect of {paneloff}, allowing the control panel and status line to be refreshed continuously during a macro.

Unlike the {indicate} command, {paneloff} has no effect after a macro ends, so you need not issue a {panelon} command at the end of a macro to restore the control panel; it's implicit in the act of terminating macro control. Use {panelon} only when you want 1-2-3 to resume continuously updating the control panel while the macro is still running.

Example:

```
           A         B         C         D         E         F         G         H
   1   NAME      MACRO                                 COMMENT
   2   --------------------------------------------------------
   3   I_PRO     {windowsoff}{paneloff}                Freeze screen
   4             {for COUNT;1;ITEMS;1;PROCESS}         Run once for each item
   5             {panelon}{windowson}                  Restore screen
```

Figure 11-9

{Windowsoff}

Purpose: Use {windowsoff} to freeze the worksheet portion of the screen during macro processing.

Format: {windowsoff}

Sample: {windowsoff}

Complements: {windowson}

See also: {paneloff}, {bordersoff}, {frameoff}

Description: {Windowsoff} prevents the worksheet portion of the screen (lines 4 through 24 on an 80 by 25 display) from being updated while a macro is running. In Release 2.2, it also restores the suppression of settings sheets.

Use {windowsoff} to:

• Suppress screen activity that the user has no need to view.

• Increase the speed of macros that generate a lot of screen activity (by freeing 1-2-3 from the job of updating the screen, you enable it to process macro instructions more quickly).

- Restore the suppression of settings sheets during a macro in Release 2.2, after you've used the { windowson } command to force 1-2-3 to display settings sheets.

does not
clear the
screen

Just as { paneloff } does not clear the control panel, { windowsoff } does not clear the screen before freezing it, so you might want to first move the screen to display something you want the user to see while { windowsoff } is in effect. For example, if it will be a while before you resume updating the screen, you might display a screen containing a message telling the user approximately how long the operation will take.

longevity

{ Windowsoff } remains in effect until the macro ends or until 1-2-3 reads a { windowson } command.

Release 2.2 contains settings sheets for some operations. Those settings sheets are there only to allow you to easily check current settings and they take some time to display. That means that during macro execution, you normally have no use for them and, were they to display, they'd lengthen the time it takes for the macro to run. That's why Release 2.2 by default suppresses those settings sheets from displaying during a macro. However, you can use the { windowson } command to force them to display (see the discussion of "forcing settings sheets to display" under that command). When you have used a { windowson } command to force settings sheets to display during a macro, the next time that macro reads a { windowsoff } command, the { windowsoff } command will force 1-2-3 to again suppress settings sheets for the balance of the macro.

In some cases, { windowson } and { windowsoff } affect the screen and settings sheets simultaneously, so you may have to use them carefully to obtain the precise effect you want. To understand how these commands work, imagine for a moment that there's an invisible cell in your computer's memory that we'll call a flag. The current value stored in flag controls whether Release 2.2 macros display movement on the worksheet and whether they display settings sheets.

suppressing
display of
settings
sheets

The { windowsoff } and { windowson } commands control the current value of the flag. At any time, the flag can be set to just one value of three possible values. The possible values are zero, one, or two. { Windowson } always increments the flag by one up to a maximum value of two, after which { windowson } has no further effect. { Windowsoff } always sets the flag to zero.

The following table shows the effect on Release 2.2 macros of each value for flag:

If flag = 0: Display neither cell pointer movements nor settings sheets.

If flag = 1: Display cell pointer movements but not settings sheets.

If flag = 2: Display both cell pointer movements and settings sheets.

1-2-3's default value for the flag is one. That means that if you do nothing to change the flag, your macros will display cell pointer movements but not settings sheets. However, if you include in your macro a single {windowson} command, the value of the flag will increase to two and your macros will display both cell pointer movements and settings sheets. If you then include a {windowsoff} command, the flag is set to zero and your macros will display neither cell pointer movements nor settings sheets. If you want to again display both cell pointer movements and settings sheets, you must include two {windowson} commands to increment the value of the flag to two.

Let's suppose the value of the flag is two and you want to return it to one, so 1-2-3 will display cell pointer movements but not settings sheets. You should use a {windowsoff} command followed by a {windowson} command. The {windowsoff} command sets the value of the flag to zero and the {windowson} command increments it to one.

Note two things. First, you can reduce the value of the flag only to zero. If the value stored in the flag is two, to set it to one, you must first reduce it to zero and then increment it to one. Second, since {windowson} is an advanced macro command and not a key name, the form {windowson 2} will not work. You must write out each of the two commands in full: {windowson} {windowson}.

common error

Note that the string "windows" in the {windowsoff} command ends with an "s". The most common syntax error is to forget that "s". As is true of all advanced macro command key words, there are no spaces in the key word: Windowsoff is one key word.

Example:

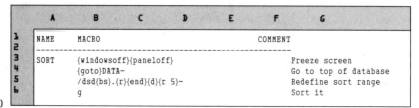

	A	B	C	D	E	F	G
1	NAME	MACRO				COMMENT	
2	--------	--					
3	SORT	{windowsoff}{paneloff}				Freeze screen	
4		{goto}DATA~				Go to top of database	
5		/dsd{bs}.{r}{end}{d}{r 5}~				Redefine sort range	
6		g				Sort it	

Figure 11-10

{Windowson}

Purpose: Use {windowson} to reenable 1-2-3 to update the worksheet portion of the screen during a macro after you have used {windowsoff} to suppress that capability. In Release 2.2, it can be used to force 1-2-3 to display settings sheets during a macro.

Format: { windowson }

Sample: { windowson }

Complements: { windowsoff }

See also: { panelon }

Description: { Windowson } reverses the effect of { windowsoff }, allowing 1-2-3 to continuously refresh the screen display during a macro. { Windowsoff } has no effect after a macro ends, so you need not issue a { windowson } command at the end of a macro; 1-2-3 will automatically resume continuously updating the control panel. Use { windowson } only when you want 1-2-3 to resume continuously updating the worksheet screen while the macro is still running.

forcing
settings
sheets to
display

Release 2.2 contains settings sheets for some operations. Those settings sheets are there only to allow you to easily check current settings and they take some time to display. That means that during macro execution, you normally have no use for them and, were they to display, they'd lengthen the time it takes for the macro to run. That's why Release 2.2 by default suppresses those settings sheets from displaying during a macro.

However, there are times when you want a settings sheet to display during a macro. For example, you might want to do so to debug your macro or to allow a user to make a choice from the settings sheet. You use the { windowson } command to force 1-2-3 to display settings sheets. Depending on circumstances, you either issue that command once or twice in order to obtain that effect. To understand how to use the command properly, imagine for a moment that there is an invisible cell in your computer's memory that we'll call a flag. The current value stored in the flag controls whether Release 2.2 macros display movement on the worksheet and whether they display settings sheets.

suppressing
display of
settings
sheets

The { windowsoff } and { windowson } commands control the current value of the flag. At any time, the flag can be set to just one value of three possible values. The possible values are zero, one, or two. { Windowson } always increments the flag by one up to a maximum value of two, after which { windowson } has no further effect. { Windowsoff } always sets the flag to zero.

The following table shows the effect on Release 2.2 macros of each value for flag:

If flag = 0: Display neither cell pointer movements nor settings sheets.

If flag = 1: Display cell pointer movements but not settings sheets.

If flag = 2: Display both cell pointer movements and settings sheets.

1-2-3's default value for the flag is one. That means that if you do nothing to change the flag, your macros will display any cell pointer movements but not settings sheets. However, if you include in your macro a single {windowson} command, the value of the flag will increase to two and your macros will display both cell pointer movements and settings sheets. If you then include a {windowsoff} command, the flag is set to zero and your macros will display neither cell pointer movements nor settings sheets. If you want to again display both cell pointer movements and settings sheets, you must include two {windowson} commands to increment the value of the flag to two.

Let's suppose the value of the flag is two and you want to return it to one, so 1-2-3 will display cell pointer movements but not settings sheets. You should use a {windowsoff} command followed by a {windowson} command. The {windowsoff} command sets the value of the flag to zero and the {windowson} command increments it to one.

Note two things. First, you can reduce the value of the flag only to zero. If the value stored in flag is two, to set it to one, you must first reduce it to zero and then increment it to one. Second, since {windowson} is an advanced macro command and not a key name, the form {windowson 2} will not work. You must write out each of the two commands in full: {windowson}{windowson}.

common error

Note that the string "windows" in the {windowson} command ends with an 's'. The most common syntax error is to forget that "s". As is true of all advanced macro command key words, there are no spaces in the key word: Windowson is one key word.

Example:

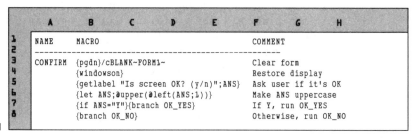

	A	B	C	D	E	F	G	H
1	NAME	MACRO				COMMENT		
2								
3	CONFIRM	{pgdn}/cBLANK~FORM1~				Clear form		
4		{windowson}				Restore display		
5		{getlabel "Is screen OK? (y/n)";ANS}			Ask user if it's OK		
6		{let ANS;@upper(@left(ANS;1))}			Make ANS uppercase		
7		{if ANS="Y"}{branch OK_YES}			If Y, run OK_YES		
8		{branch OK_NO}				Otherwise, run OK_NO		

Figure 11-11

12

Allowing Keyboard Interaction

Overview and Introduction to New Concepts

scope

These commands enable you to interact with the user of the macro: to gather data from the user ({get}, {look}, {getlabel}, and {getnumber}), pause for a specified period of time ({wait}), obtain decisions from the user ({menubranch} and {menucall}), prevent the user from interrupting the macro ({breakoff}), restore that ability ({breakon}), cancel a 1-2-3 command sequence or cell entry in process and return 1-2-3 to Ready mode without interrupting macro control ({break}), and temporarily suspend macro control and return control of the application to the user ({?}).

don't
overlook
/ Range
Input

Although it's not listed here because it's not an advanced macro command, the / Range Input command (available on 1-2-3's command menu) is one of the most powerful methods for managing keyboard interaction. It enables you to restrict the cell pointer to unprotected cells within a given range. While Range Input is in effect, the user can move the cell pointer between these cells, enter labels, formulas, or values, and edit those entries. However, 1-2-3 will prevent the user from accessing the command menu or from moving to cells other than the unprotected cells within the specified range. You can find a description of the / Range Input command on page 145.

keyboard buffer

Some of these commands obtain data through the keyboard buffer. The keyboard buffer is an area of your computer's memory set aside to store keystrokes entered at the keyboard that have not yet been processed by the application.

Although you can't see the keyboard buffer, you can observe its work. If you're working on a large worksheet and select / File Save to save the file, while 1-2-3 is writing the file to disk, you'll see the Wait indicator flashing in the top right corner of the screen. If you type several numbers and press Return while 1-2-3 is saving the file, you won't see those characters in the edit line or entered in the current cell. Those keystrokes are being held in the keyboard buffer until 1-2-3 is ready to process them.

Once 1-2-3 has finished saving the file, it will retrieve those keystrokes from the keyboard buffer and process them. You'll know when that happens because you'll see the numbers appear in the current cell.

1-2-3 uses the keyboard buffer as it's been defined by DOS, which means that unless you're using some other program to change the size of the keyboard buffer (there are utilities that will increase its capacity), it can store 15 characters at a time. That means that if you type ahead more than 15 characters, 1-2-3 will beep and discard those additional characters.

{menucall} and subroutine calls

The {menucall} command is one of two commands that enables you to create custom menus. It differs from the other custom menu command in the manner in which it transfers control to the routines that execute in response to menu choices. Specifically, it calls a subroutine when the user selects one of its choices. A subroutine is a special way of changing the flow of control of a macro.

When a subroutine call is made by a macro command, 1-2-3 notes the current location of the command that made the call. Macro control then moves to the location specified in the subroutine call and the macro resumes reading in the new location. The macro continues reading in the new location either until the routine ends or the macro reads a {return} command, at which time control will return from the subroutine to the command directly following the one that made the subroutine call. [34]

While a subroutine is running, it can make a subroutine call to transfer control to yet another subroutine. Each time a macro makes a subroutine call, 1-2-3 increments the subroutine chain by one. If there is one subrou-

---

[34] Actually, this is an incomplete list, but this is a complex topic we'll deal with completely in the relevant command descriptions that follow. Please refer to the descriptions of subroutines in the listing for {menucall} (and the listing for the { } command in Chapter 13) for a complete list of the factors affecting a subroutine's ability to return control to its caller.

tine call, the subroutine chain is nested one level deep. If the subroutine makes another subroutine call, the chain is nested two levels deep. Each time the macro returns control from a subroutine to the routine that called it, 1-2-3 decrements the subroutine chain by one nesting level. 1-2-3 can nest a maximum of 31 levels in the subroutine chain.

commands
that call
subroutines

In this group, {menucall} is the only command that calls subroutines. The {} (subroutine) and {for} commands, which belong to the Controlling Program Flow group of commands, also call subroutines.

break

The way to interrupt a macro is to use the Break key sequence. It's called a key sequence because, on most computers, the Break key comprises two keystrokes: holding down the Ctrl key and pressing the key with Break written across its front (usually located near the top right of the keyboard). Don't confuse this description of the Break key sequence with Release 2.2's {break} macro command; they differ. See the description of that command in this section for details.

{Break}

Purpose: Use {break} to cancel a cell entry or 1-2-3 menu sequence in process, without interrupting the macro.

Format: {break}

Sample: {break}

Complements: None

Compatibility: Release 2.2 and 3

Description: While a macro is underway, the {break} command will return 1-2-3 to Ready mode under two circumstances. They are, first, if a cell entry is underway—that is, it appears on the edit line but not yet in the cell itself—and, second, if 1-2-3 is in the midst of a menu sequence. In either case, the macro will remain in control of the worksheet.

When you use 1-2-3 interactively (not under macro control), the Control-Break key combination (also known as the Break key sequence) performs the same function as the {break} key does while a macro is running. So, if you use 1-2-3 interactively to type something into the edit line, then press the Break key sequence, 1-2-3 will cancel the entry and return to Ready mode. Likewise, if you use 1-2-3 interactively to select a command sequence, such as \ Print Printer Options, and then press the Break key sequence, 1-2-3 will cancel that command sequence and return to Ready mode.

compared to the Break key

However, the Break key sequence does something the {break} command does not do: it terminates a macro. When you use the {break} command, although any cell entry or command sequence in progress will be cancelled, the macro itself will continue to run.

{Breakoff} has no effect on the function of the {break} command. {Breakoff} affects only the Break key sequence.

as a safety

You might use {break} to ensure that 1-2-3 is in Ready mode when the macro begins. If you're uncertain as to what mode 1-2-3 will be in when the user invokes your macro, and you want to guarantee that 1-2-3 will be in Ready mode from the outset of the macro, simply begin that macro with the {break} command.

Sample Macro:

Figure 12-1

{Breakoff}

Purpose: Use {breakoff} to disable the Break key (Ctrl-Break).

Format: {breakoff}

Sample: {breakoff}

Complements: {breakon}

Description: {Breakoff} prevents users from terminating your macro with the Break key sequence (Ctrl-Break). For that reason, {breakoff} is particularly useful for securing applications against abuse. You can use {breakoff} in conjunction with a prompt (see {getlabel}) to implement an effective password system. (Also see the reference below about one lapse in the security of such a system.)

{Breakoff} has no effect on the function of the {break} command. {Breakoff} affects only the Break key sequence.

cautions: when to put it into a macro

As you develop and test your macros, {breakoff} should be nearly the last—if not the very last—command you add to your macro before its completion. Once you add the {breakoff} command, if the macro errs, even you will be unable to stop it. For that reason, we recommend that you test and debug all other portions of the macro before you add the {breakoff} command. While it's a good idea to save the worksheet before running any macro for the first time, it's imperative that you do so before testing a macro that contains {breakoff}.

longevity and limits

When macro execution comes to a halt, 1-2-3 restores the function of Ctrl-Break. Thus, if you want to continuously disable the Break key, you must use {breakoff} every time you activate a new macro. If you are merely transferring control from one location to another with a command such as {branch} or {menubranch}, {breakoff} remains in effect. {Breakoff} also remains in effect during an interactive pause in a macro (initiated with the {?} command).

when it won't protect macros

In Release 2.2, you can use the / Worksheet Global Default Autoexec command to set whether 1-2-3 will run auto-execute macros. Suppose you have included the {breakoff} command in an auto-execute macro to protect it from prying eyes. If that macro is used with a copy of 1-2-3 on which auto-execute macros have been disabled, the macro will never begin running, and the user will have full access to your macros.

There's yet another way to defeat an auto-execute macro thus protected in Release 2.2. Configure the Macro Library Manager to attach itself to 1-2-3 automatically on start up and place into an autoload macro library file a macro named Breakoff. If the macro consists of nothing more than a null command ({ }), it will disable the {breakoff} command without otherwise altering the auto-execute macro on the worksheet. That makes this technique a good debugging tool.

The moral of these examples is that while {breakoff} is generally a useful tool, it can't protect your macros from well-informed users.

Sample Macro: A password security system.

Figure 12-2

	A	B	C	D	E	F	G
1	NAME	MACRO				COMMENT	
2	----	-----					
3	PASSW	{goto}PASSWD_SCREEN~				Display password screen	
4		{breakoff}				Disable Break key	
5		{getlabel "Enter Password:";ANS}				Ask for password	
6		{if @upper(ANS)=@upper(PW)}{branch GO}				If match, GO	
7		{branch STOP}				If not, STOP	

{Breakon}

Purpose: Use {breakon} to reenable Break (Ctrl-Break) after it has been disabled with {breakoff}.

Format: {breakon}

Sample: {breakon}

Complements: {breakoff}

Description: The sole purpose of {breakon} is to restore the function of the Ctrl-Break key sequence after it has been disabled by the {breakoff} command.

Since 1-2-3 restores the function of the Break key after a macro ends, you do not need to use {breakon} to do that job at the end of a macro.

If a macro reads {breakon} while the Ctrl-Break key sequence is in effect, {breakon} will have no effect.

```
        A       B       C     D     E     F       G       H
1   NAME    MACRO                            COMMENT
2   -------------------------------------------------
3   GO      {breakon}                        Restore Break
4           {goto}INTRO_SCREEN~              Display Intro screen
5           {branch CONTINUE}                Continue the macro
```

Figure 12-3

{Get}

Purpose: Use {get} to capture a keystroke from the user.

Format: {get [location]}
Where [location] is the name or address of the range to store the keystroke. [Location] may be a cell address, a range address, range name, or in Release 2.2, a formula.

Sample: {get ANS} {if @upper(ANS) = "N"} {branch STOP} {branch CONTINUE}

Complements: None

See also: {Getlabel}, {Getnumber}, {Look}.

Description: Use the {get} command to fetch a keystroke from the keyboard buffer and enter it into a worksheet cell.

uses

{Get} is particularly useful in the following three applications:

- Posting a message to the user with the instruction to press any key. Since {get} will interrupt macro processing until such a keystroke has been entered, it will leave the message on the screen until the user presses the key to continue.

- Creating a full-screen menu. Such menus can include more than eight choices (the limit of the {menubranch} and {menucall} commands).

- Capturing and filtering each keystroke that a user types to maintain macro control at all times.

The {get} command moves a single keystroke from the keyboard buffer to a worksheet cell and enters it there as a label. The keystroke is stored in the range designated in the sole argument to the {get} command. If there are no keystrokes in the keyboard buffer, the {get} command will suspend macro processing until the user provides one (it will not however, provide a prompt to the user regarding what it is waiting for).

screen
updating

{Get}'s results are not posted to the screen automatically. If you wish to update the screen after a {get}, include a tilde (~) in the macro just after the {get} command. However, whether you force 1-2-3 to update the screen or not, 1-2-3 will respond to the presence of the captured, though invisible, keystroke if you test for it just after the {get} command.

For example, if the command following the {get} command tests the value of the cell designated in the {get} command, 1-2-3 will use the value that would appear in the cell had the screen been updated.

Example 1:

	A	B	C	D	E	F	G	H
1	NAME	MACRO				COMMENT		
2	--							
3	MSG	{goto}MSG_SCREEN~				Display message screen		
4		{get ANS}{branch CONTINUE}				Pause for key, continue		
5								

Figure 12-4

Example 2:

	A	B	C	D	E	F	G	H
1	NAME	MACRO				COMMENT		
2	--							
3	MENU	{goto}MENU_SCREEN~				Display menu screen		
4		{get ANS}				Pause for a keystroke		
5		{let ANS;@upper(ANS)}				Convert to upper		
6		{if ANS="A"}{branch MACRO_A}				Test keystrokes		
7		{if ANS="B"}{branch MACRO_B}						
8		{if ANS="C"}{branch MACRO_C}						
9		{if ANS="D"}{branch MACRO_D}						
10		{branch INVALID_ENTRY}				Correct entry error		

Figure 12-5

Example 3:

```
       A         B         C         D       E       F       G       H
   1  NAME      MACRO                                    COMMENT
   2  -----------------------------------------------------------------
   3  LOOP      {get ANS}                                Pause for a keystroke
   4            {if ANS="{CALC}"}{branch STOP}           If CALC,
   5            {ANS}                                    Else, send to 1-2-3
   6            {branch LOOP}                            Do it again
   7
```

Figure 12-6

{ Getlabel }

Purpose: Use { getlabel } to prompt the user and store that user's input as a label in a worksheet cell.

Sample: { getlabel "Enter your city:";CITY }

Format: { getlabel ["prompt"];*[location]* }
Where ["prompt"] is an optional string, and [location] is the cell in which to store the user's response. [Location] may be a cell address, a range address, or a range name. In Release 2.2, both the prompt string and the location may be formulas.

Complements: None

See also: { get }, { getnumber }

Release 1A Equivalent: /xl

Release 1A Format: /xl[prompt]~[location]~
Where [prompt] is an optional string and [location] is an optional location on the worksheet.

Description: { Getlabel } pauses for user input. If you have supplied the optional prompt string, it also displays a one line prompt at the top of the screen. The user may type a response of up to 80 characters in length; in any event, the user must press the Return key before the macro will proceed. If the user types a response before pressing Return, 1-2-3 will store that entry in a worksheet cell as a label. If the user doesn't enter anything before pressing Return, 1-2-3 will enter just an apostrophe (left-alignment label prefix) in the designated cell.

uses

{Getlabel} is particularly useful for controlling the data type of the cell entry that results from user input. For example, if you are entering zip codes, {getlabel} frees you from entering a label prefix before each entry.

[location]
argument

1-2-3 uses the mandatory [location] argument to determine the cell in which to store the entry. You can supply a range with either a cell address or a range name. If that range consists of more than one cell, 1-2-3 will store the entry in the top left cell of the range. The range can be a cell address, a range address, a single-cell named range, or a multi-cell named range. In the case of a multi-cell range, 1-2-3 places the entry in the upper-left cell in the range, even if you have specified that range in reverse order (1-2-3 will use cell A1 to store the entry whether the range was specified as A1..D4 or D4..A1).

effects on
display in
the control
panel

There are 74 characters available in the control panel to display both the prompt and the user's input. For example, if your prompt is 70 characters long, just 4 characters will remain for the user's response to display. If the user's typing fills the portion of the control panel allocated to display user input (in the previous example, 4 characters) the input text will scroll to the left as the user types. If you allocate too few characters for user input to display (in our tests, that was three or fewer), 1-2-3 may refuse to accept all of the user input.

quotation
marks
around
prompt
string

The quotation marks around the prompt string are optional, but strongly recommended.

In Release 2.2, enclosing the prompt string in quotation marks prevents that string as ever being construed as a range name. Because in Release 2.2 or Release 3 you can include a range name in a {getlabel} command as a way of specifying a prompt string stored in the named range, if you ever named a range with the same name as your prompt string, which is feasible, you'd inadvertently change the way that particular {getlabel} command works. Even if you don't use either of those releases today, because it's possible that your macro will at some later time be run under one of those releases, it's wise to use quotation marks to head off any problems.

In any release of 1-2-3, if you plan to include characters in the prompt string that could be interpreted as having some other meaning, you must enclose the entire prompt string in quotation marks. In addition, some characters are not permitted in the prompt string. For example, if you want to include a colon at the end of your prompt string, you should enclose the entire string in quotation marks—{getlabel "Enter customer name: ";E1}.

prompt tips

As shown in the previous example, it's useful to include a blank space at the end of the prompt string. When the prompt displays in the control panel, the cursor will be separated from the prompt by a blank space.

That space will also separate the prompt from the user's response. When the user types a response to the prompt, it'll be easier to read.

However, be careful of misplacing spaces in the {getlabel} command. For example, if you use quotation marks to enclose the prompt string, place the blank space inside them (it is actually part of the prompt string). If it goes outside the closing quotation mark—{getlabel "Enter:" ;E1}, — when 1-2-3 reads the command in a macro, you'll get a syntax error. If you place the blank space after the semicolon that separates the range from the prompt—{getlabel "Enter:"; E1}—1-2-3 won't be able to read the range and you'll receive the error message Invalid range in GETLABEL.

versus /xl command

{Getlabel} differs from a similar command, /xl, in several ways.

- Range Argument: {Getlabel} requires a range to be specified whereas /xl allows you to omit the range argument if you wish 1-2-3 to enter the input in the current cell. In Release 2 or 2.01, you can create the same effect using {getlabel}, but it requires more coding. In Release 2.2, the method is simpler, because you can use the formula @cellpointer("address") as the range argument.

- Prompt and Response Length: The /xl prompt line can be a maximum of 39 characters long versus 72 characters for the {getlabel} command. The user entry that {getlabel} accepts is limited to 80 characters whereas the /xl command will accept 239 characters.

- Error Trapping: If the user presses the Escape key in response to a prompt generated with the /xl command, the macro will terminate. The Escape keystroke in response to a {getlabel} prompt has the same effect as pressing Return without typing anything (1-2-3 stores a null string in the designated location).

- Screen: While /xl causes 1-2-3's menu to momentarily display in the control panel (causing a flashing effect in the control panel), {getlabel} does not.

- Prompt: Both prompts can contain characters that normally act as separators; with {getlabel} you must then enclose the prompt string in quotation marks. A {getlabel} prompt enclosed in quotation marks can also contain a tilde; an /xl prompt cannot.

Example: Traveling data entry macro.

```
        A          B           C          D         E         F        G
1    NAME       MACRO                                       COMMENT
2    ---------------------------------------------------------------
3    \A         {getlabel "Enter first item:";ENTRY}        Get entry
4               {ENTER}                                      Call entry routine
5               {gotlabel "Enter second item:";ENTRY}       Get next entry
6               {ENTER}                                      Call entry routine
7    .          {quit}                                       End
8
9
10   ENTER      +ENTRY{calc}{home}'~                         Enter into cell
11              {d 2}                                        Move down 2 cells
12              {return}                                     Return to main routine
13
14
15
16.  ENTRY                                                   Store entry
```

Figure 12-7

note about
preceding
macro

The preceding macro allows you to easily enter data in the current cell, move to another cell, and enter data there. However, the line +ENTRY{calc}{home}'~ is only appropriate for use with the {getlabel} command, not the {getnumber} command. (See the Advanced Techniques topic "Data Entry" for more information.)

Example: Password macro.

```
        A          B           C          D         E         F        G
1    NAME       MACRO                                       COMMENT
2    ---------------------------------------------------------------
3    PSSWD      {goto}PSSWD_SCREEN~                          Password screen
4               {breakoff}                                   Disable Break
5               {getlabel "Enter Password: ";ANS}           Get password
6               {if @upper(ANS)=@upper(PW)}{branch GO}       Test;if match, GO
7               {branch STOP}                                If not, STOP
8
```

Figure 12-8

{Getnumber}

Purpose: Use Getnumber to prompt the user for number input, to be stored in a worksheet cell.

Format: {getnumber ["prompt"];[location]}

Where ["prompt"] is an optional string, and [location] is a cell on the worksheet. [location] may be a cell address, a range address, or a range name. In Release 2.2, both the prompt string and the location may be formulas.

Sample: { getnumber "Enter number of branch offices:";OFFICES }

Complements: None

See also: { get }, { getlabel }

Release 1A equivalent: /xn

Release 1A Format: /xn["prompt"]~[location]~
    Where ["prompt"] is an optional string and [location] is an optional location.

Description: { Getnumber } is most often used for form-type data entry. It allows you to prompt a user for data and specify the cell where 1-2-3 will enter it on the worksheet.

    { Getnumber } pauses for user input. If you have supplied the optional prompt string, it also displays a one-line prompt at the top of the screen. The user may type a response of up to 80 characters in length; in any event, the user must press Return before the macro will proceed.

storing
entries

If the user typed anything before pressing Return, 1-2-3 will store that entry in a worksheet cell as a value. If the user doesn't enter anything in that cell before pressing Return, enters a label, or presses the Escape key, 1-2-3 will enter the value ERR in the designated cell.

    Since { getnumber } won't screen out erroneous entries (either values you don't want entered or label entries), if you're concerned about that, you should write a routine to test the entry directly following a { getnumber } command (see the chapter on Managing User Input in the Advanced Techniques section).

    [location] 1-2-3 uses the mandatory [location] argument to determine the cell in which to store the entry. You can supply a range with either a cell address, a range name, or in Release 2.2, a formula. If that range consists of more than one cell, 1-2-3 will store the entry in the top left cell of the range. The range can be a cell address, a range address, a one cell named range, or a multi-cell named range. In the case of a multi-cell range, 1-2-3 places the entry in the upper-left cell in the range, even if you have specified that range in reverse order (1-2-3 will use cell A1 to store the entry whether the range was specified as A1..D4 or D4..A1).

effects on
displaying
prompts
and user
entries

There are 74 characters available in the control panel to display both the prompt and the user's input. For example, if your prompt is 70 characters long, just 4 characters will remain for the user's response to display. If the user's typing fills the portion of the control panel allocated to display user input (in the previous example, 4 characters) the input text will scroll to the right as the user types. If you allocate too few characters for user input to display (in our tests, that was three or fewer), 1-2-3 may refuse to accept all of the user input.

optional
quotation
marks
around
prompt

The quotation marks around the prompt string are optional. If you plan to include characters in the prompt string that would otherwise be interpreted as part of the {getnumber} command, you must enclose the entire prompt string in quotation marks. For example, if you want to include a colon at the end of your prompt string, you should enclose the entire string in quotation marks—{getnumber "Enter May sales:";E1} Without them, 1-2-3 will generate an error when it reads the macro command.

prompt tips

It's useful to include a blank space at the end of the prompt string. When the prompt displays in the control panel, the cursor will be separated from the prompt by that a blank space. That space will also separate the prompt from the user's response. When the user types a response to the prompt, it'll be easier to read.

However, be careful of misplacing spaces in the {getnumber} command. For example, if you use quotation marks to enclose the prompt string, place the blank space inside them (it is actually part of the prompt string). If it goes outside the closing quotation mark— {getnumber "Enter:" ;E1}—when 1-2-3 reads the command in a macro, you'll get a syntax error message. If you place the blank space after the semicolon that separates the range from the prompt—{getnumber "Entry:"; E1}—1-2-3 will be unable to read the range and you'll receive the error message Invalid range in GETNUMBER.

versus /xn
command

{Getnumber} differs from a similar command, /xn, in several ways.

- Range Argument: {Getnumber} requires a range to be specified whereas /xn allows you to omit the range argument if you wish 1-2-3 to enter the input in the current cell. In Release 2 or 2.01, you can create the same effect using {getnumber}, but it requires more coding. In Release 2.2, the method is simpler, because you can use the formula @cellpointer("address") as the range argument. That formula will always evaluate to the address of the current cell.

- Prompt and Response Length: The /xn prompt line can be a maximum of 39 characters long versus 72 characters for the {getnumber} command. The user entry that {getnumber} accepts is limited to 80 characters whereas the /xn command will accept 239 characters.

- Error Trapping: /xn will handle inappropriate data-type errors automatically; {getnumber} will not. If the user presses the Escape key or enters a label in response to a prompt generated with the /xn command, 1-2-3 will beep, show ERR in the mode indicator, and display the error message "Invalid number input" in the lower left corner of the screen. The user can then press Escape or Return; the error will clear and the /xn prompt will reappear. If the user presses Escape or enters a label in response to a prompt generated with the {getnumber} command, 1-2-3 will enter the value ERR in the designated cell. To trap the error, the macro will then have to test that cell and run an error-trapping routine.

- Screen: While /xn causes 1-2-3's menu to momentarily display in the control panel (causing a flashing effect in the control panel), {getnumber} doesn't.

- Prompt: Both prompts can contain characters that normally act as separators; with {getnumber} you must then enclose the prompt string in quotation marks. A {getnumber} prompt enclosed in quotation marks can also contain a tilde; an /xn prompt can't.

Example: Traveling data entry macro.

```
        A        B            C          D        E        F         G          H
 1   NAME     MACRO                                         COMMENT
 2   ---------------------------------------------------------------------------
 3   \A       {getnumber "Enter first number:";ENTRY}       Get entry
 4            {ENTER}                                        Call entry routine
 5            {getnumber "Enter second number:";ENTRY}       Get next entry
 6            {ENTER}                                        Call entry routine
 7            {quit}                                         End
 8
 9   ENTER    {if @iserr(ENTRY)}{branch FIX}                Test entry
10            +ENTRY{calc}~                                  Enter into cell
11            {d 2}                                          Move down 2 cells
12            {return}                                       Return to main routine
13
14   FIX      {getnumber "Enter a valid number:";ENTRY}  Reprompt
15            {branch ENTER}                                 Test again
16
17   ENTRY                                                   Store entry
18
19
20
```

Figure 12-9

note about
the
preceding
macro

The preceding macro allows you to easily enter data in the current cell, move to another cell, and enter data there. However, the line +ENTRY{calc}~ is appropriate for use only with the {getnumber} command, not the {getlabel} command. (See the Advanced Techniques topic "Data Entry" for more information.)

{ Look }

Purpose: Use Look to capture a keystroke from the user.

Format: { look [location] }
Where [location] is the location to store the keytroke. [Location] may be a cell address, a range address, a range name, or in Release 2.2, a formula.

Sample: { look ANS } { if @length(ANS) > 0 } { get ANS }

Complements: None

See also: { get }, { getlabel }, { getnumber }

Description: { Look } examines the keyboard buffer for a keystroke. If it finds a keystroke stored there, it stores that keystroke in the location specified by the range argument as a label entry. If the keyboard buffer contains more than one keystroke, { look } will store only the first of those keystrokes. Thus, if the macro contains the command { look E1 } and the Return keystroke is the keystroke stored in the buffer, then after the macro finishes and the worksheet has been updated, a tilde will appear in cell E1.

the status of the keyboard buffer

{ Look } will not cause the macro to pause if no keystroke is waiting in the buffer, unlike { get }, which will. If the buffer is empty, { look } will enter a null string (consisting of an apostrophe label-prefix character in the designated cell. To test to see if there has been no keystroke, first, before the { look } command, use the { blank } command to clear the cell you will be testing. Second, test for a null string, as in { if CHAR = "" }, or for the opposite condition, as in { if CHAR < > "" }.

{ Look } does not clear the keystroke from the buffer, unlike { get }, which does. You might say that { look } *copies* the keystroke from the buffer to the worksheet (so the keystroke resides in both places) while { get } *moves* it. Following the { look } command, 1-2-3 will send any keystrokes in the buffer to the next command that requests them— whether that be { get }, { getlabel }, { getnumber }, or, in Ready mode, the edit line for entry into the current worksheet cell.

clear the buffer

Although { look }'s characteristic of leaving the keystroke in the buffer has uses, it can also cause trouble if improperly handled. For instance, suppose you've used { look } to store a keystroke in a cell called Char, and then tested that cell to see if there is one specific character there that you are waiting for. If the character is not the one you want, you repeat the previous routine, including the { look } command. Your intent is to set up a loop that will repeat until the application detects the character you want, then the application will either quit or branch to another routine.

Unless the very first character that {look} traps is the right character, the aforementioned routine will not work. Here's what will happen. {Look} will trap the first character and, if it's not the right character, the macro will detect that and repeat the loop. However, no matter what keystroke you type thereafter, the first keystroke you typed will remain in the keyboard buffer, so each time the macro reads the {look} command, it will reenter the same character in the cell you are testing, then test against that same incorrect keystroke and put itself in an endless loop.

The solution to this problem is to use a command that will clear the keyboard buffer if the keystroke stored there is incorrect. The easiest way to do that is to use a {get} command because {get} will clear the buffer of the erroneous character so {look} won't store it on the worksheet again with the next loop of the macro.

where to
place {get}

However, the proper placement of {get} in your macro is important. It should follow only conditional statements that test for characters. If {get} sits in the main routine and the user doesn't type a character, the {get} command will force the macro to pause. Avoiding such a pause is the reason you'd use {look} in the first place, so restrict {get} to following a conditional command that can bypass it if there's been no character typed at all.

Even after {look} has detected the correct keystroke, it's often important to use a {get} command to clear the keyboard buffer of that keystroke. {Look} will copy it to the cell you are going to test, but remember that the keystroke also remains in the keyboard buffer, waiting to be passed to the next operation that will accept such a keystroke. After you've stored the keystroke and tested it, it's rare that the keystroke remaining in the buffer has any further use, and it could easily cause problems if you let it remain in the buffer. For example, if you have a custom menu following a {look} command, that keystroke in the buffer will be passed to the menu, just as if the user had pressed the keystroke in response to the menu. If the menu contains a choice that corresponds with the character, the keystroke will select that option. If not, the menu will reject the character like any other character that doesn't correspond to one of the menu's choices.

where to
place
{look}

You must also properly place the {look} command within the macro. 1-2-3 checks the keyboard buffer at the time the macro reads the {look} command, so you should position that command in the macro where it will be read only after the user has had a chance to enter a keystroke. For that reason, you wouldn't use {look} as the first command in a macro. Note that {look} and {get} can use the same cell to store their respective outputs.

stores
entries from
the
keyboard
only

screen
updating

The {look} command responds only to characters entered by the user through the keyboard; it will not record characters typed by the macro. Characters typed by the macro will appear on the worksheet just as characters entered from the keyboard do. But, since characters entered by the macro do not pass through DOS's keyboard buffer, which is what {look} reads, {look} cannot capture them.

{Look} is among the commands that do not update the worksheet automatically. Therefore, you will not see the keystroke appear in the designated cell as a character until you force 1-2-3 to update the worksheet by some other means. Nonetheless, the label is immediately available to any commands that may require it. For example, if you use the {look} command to store a keystroke in cell E1 in one line of a macro and in the next line test for its presence, {look} will update the cell immediately and the test will respond to the presence of the keystroke.

You can force 1-2-3 to update the screen by including a tilde or cell pointer movement command after the {look} command. Any movement of the cell pointer after the macro has ended will also update the worksheet.

Example:

	A	B	C	D	E	F	G	H
1	NAME	MACRO					COMMENT	
2	-----	---					------	
3	KEYCH	{look KEY}{if #not#KEY=""}{TEST}					Check keystroke buffer	
4		{return}					If empty, return	
5								
6	TEST	{get KEY}					Clear keystroke buffer	
7		{if KEY="{ESC}"}{restart}{branch HALT}					If key= ESC, run HALT	
8		{return}					Run previous routine	
9								
10								

Figure 12-10

In the example that follows, the macro displays a message on the screen and proceeds to print a report. The message instructs the user to press a key to indicate whether he'd like to next print another copy of the report (option A), print a different report (option B), or continue with some other work the macro performs (no entry at all). The {look} command follows the commands to print the report. While the report's been printing, the user has had a chance to make a choice. The keystroke he pressed, if any, now waits in the keyboard buffer.

In row 6, the first command following {look} checks to see if no keystroke was typed at all. If so, the macro branches to a routine called Morework. Note the absence of a {get} command following the {if} command on this line, in contrast to rows 7 and 8. The reason there should be no {get} command on this line is that it tests for a null string, which indicates that no character was typed. If 1-2-3 reads a {get} in that case, the macro will halt while {get} forces it to wait for a keystroke that won't be forthcoming.

In the last row, a {get} command captures any keystroke other than A or B, and branches to a routine called Other to handle any other keystrokes. This row is important for two reasons. If the user types any character other than the ones requested, the routine Other will tell him of his error. Just as important, the {get} command on this line will dispose of the keystroke sitting in the keyboard buffer. Without that command, that keystroke would emerge from the buffer at the next opportunity, such as when the next custom menu displays. The result would almost certainly be other than what you'd wish for.

	A	B	C	D	E	F
1	NAME	MACRO			COMMENT	
2		--			-----	
3	PRINT	{goto}MSG1~			Show message	
4		/ppcrrREPORT~agpq			Print report	
5		{look CHAR}			Check for character	
6		{if CHAR=""}{branch MOREWORK}			If none...	
7		{if @upper(CHAR)="A"}{get CHAR}{branch A}			If "A"...	
8		{if @upper(CHAR)="B"}{get CHAR}{branch B}			If "B"...	
9		{get CHAR}{branch OTHER}			If other character	
10						

Figure 12-11

{Menubranch}

Purpose: Use {menubranch} to branch to a custom menu.

Format: {menubranch [location]}
   Where [location] is the upper left cell of a range encompassing menu items and associated prompts. [Location] may be a cell address, a range address, a range name, or in Release 2.2, a formula.

Sample: {menubranch PMENU}

Complements: None

See also: {menucall}, {branch}

Release 1A Equivalent: /xm

Release 1A Format: /xm[location]~
   Where [location] is a cell address or range name referring to the top left menu choice in a range containing one or more menu choices.

Description: Use the {menubranch} command to display a custom menu in the control panel and interrupt processing of the macro until the user selects an option from the menu.

[location]

[location] is the upper left cell in a range containing label entries representing menu choices and their associated explanation lines. At a minimum, the cell designated in [location] must include a label entry. Label entries representing additional menu option(s) and explanation line(s) are optional.

menu
options

The labels you wish to represent menu options should be entered in consecutive cells to the right of the cell designated in range. 1-2-3 will represent up to eight consecutive entries as menu choices in the control panel when it reads the {menubranch} command in a macro. If you make any more entries than that, 1-2-3 will ignore them. If an empty cell appears to the right of one of these label entries, the label directly to the left of the empty cell will be the last menu item displayed. For example, in the menu shown below if cell C5 were blank, the item in cell D5 would no longer appear on the menu.

	A	B	C	D	E	F
1	NAME	MACRO		COMMENT		
2	-------	------------	------------	--------		
3	\M	{menubranch MEN1}		Display Menu		
4						
5	MEN1	Post	Clear	Exit		
6		Post entries	Clear entries	Exit to DOS		
7		{branch POST}	{branch CLEAR}	/qy		
8						
9						
10						

Figure 12-12

total
characters
in menu

Aside from the constraint of eight menu choices, 1-2-3 also imposes a constraint on the amount of characters that may, in aggregate, appear in any list of menu items. The control panel can accommodate a total of 80 characters, and if your menu consists of only one menu item, you may use all 80 characters. However, in multiple choice menus, 1-2-3 will add two blank characters to the right of each item except for the rightmost item on the menu. So a menu with two items can have at most 78 characters total (or an average of 39 per item), a menu with 4 items can have at most 74 characters total (or an average of 18.5 per item), and so on. Where ITEMS equals the number of items on the menu, the formula 80-(2*(ITEMS-1)) calculates the total number of characters you can use in all of the items on that menu.

explana-
tions

You may also enter labels in the cells beneath each of the labels representing menu options. When 1-2-3 displays the menu, it will use each of the lower entries as explanation lines for the menu choice entered in the cell above it. When the menu pointer highlights a given menu choice, the associated explanation label will appear in the control panel. For example, if 1-2-3 read the {menubranch} command depicted in the last macro, the menu pointer would by default highlight the choice Post and the explanation line would read Post entries. If you moved the menu pointer to highlight the choice Clear, the explanation line would read Clear entries.

Menu choices and explanation lines must all be label entries. If you enter a value instead of a label as one of the menu choices, 1-2-3 will treat that value entry as if it were a blank cell defining the end of the menu options. That is also true if you use a value entry as an explanation line for a menu choice. 1-2-3 will regard it as a blank cell and display only those menu items that appear to the left of it. If you use a value entry for either the leftmost menu item or that menu item's explanation line, when 1-2-3 reads the {menubranch} command, it will issue the error message Invalid use of Menu macro command.

function

When 1-2-3 displays the menu in the control panel, it will automatically capitalize the first letter of each menu option and each explanation line.

The menu will function like a 1-2-3 menu: The user may select an option by positioning the menu pointer and pressing the Return key or typing the first character of an option. If the macro contains more than one choice that begins with the same character and the user uses that character to select a choice, the option located farthest to the left will be selected.

control
flow

While the menu displays in the control panel, the flow of control remains stopped at the {menubranch} command. When the user selects a menu option, the flow of control jumps to the cell located two cells below the cell containing the label representing the selected menu choice. In the example below, if the user selected Clear from the menu, control would move from cell B3 to cell C7.

	A	B	C	D	E	F
1	NAME	MACRO		COMMENT		
2		--				
3	\M	{menubranch MEN1}		Display menu		
4						
5	MEN1	Post	Clear	Menu options		
6		Post entries	Clear entries	Explanation lines		
7		{branch POST}	{branch CLEAR}	Macro instructions		
8						
9						
10						

Figure 12-13

where to
write
routines
that support
menu items

Since, if you select Clear, control will move from B3 to cell C7, C7 is where you should write the macro instruction you want carried out when someone selects the menu item Clear. We strongly recommend that, instead of writing an entire macro there, you place a {branch} command there to redirect control to a macro residing in column B. Otherwise, you'll be writing macros in as many columns as there are menu items in your menu and, since they'll be written side by side, those macros will be difficult to read and impossible to document.

escape key

If the user presses the Escape key while the menu displays, control will continue beyond the {menubranch} command to the next label in the macro. If there is a blank cell immediately below the cell containing the {menubranch} command, macro control will end. If there is anything else on the same line but to the right of the {menubranch} command (or, if there is nothing to its right, in the cell directly below), 1-2-3 will read that as a macro.

In the example below, if the person using the menu presses the Escape key, the macro will read the {branch \M} command and loop back to the {menubranch} command—in effect, disabling the Escape key. If the user selects a menu choice, control will jump directly from the {menubranch MEN1} command to the selected routine and never encounter the command {branch \M}.

	A	B	C	D	E	F
1	NAME	MACRO		COMMENT		
2	-------	--				
3	\M	{menubranch MEN1}{branch \M}		Display menu		
4						
5	MEN1	Post	Clear	Menu options		
6		Post entries	Clear entries	Explanation lines		
7		{branch POST}	{branch CLEAR}	Macro instructions		
8						
9						
10						

Figure 12-14

the range needs to refer only to the top left cell in the menu range

A common misunderstanding relating to the use of the {menubranch} command is that the range specified in that command's argument must include the cells containing all the menu options and their associated explanations. In fact, that range need include only the cell that contains the leftmost menu choice, (cell B5, above) although either range specification will work.

{menubranch} vs. /xm

The {menubranch} and /xm commands function almost identically.

Values As Entries. You can use value entries to represent either menu options or explanations if you use the /xm command, but values can't fulfill either role if you use the {menubranch} command. [35]

For example, using /xm, you might include the menu choice Today. In the explanation line corresponding to that choice, you could enter the

---

[35] In Release 3, {menubranch} has been changed to accept value entries to represent either menu options or explanations.

@NOW function and format it as a date. If you display that menu and highlight the choice labelled Today, you'll see the current date in the explanation line.

{ Menucall }

Purpose: Use { menucall } to call a custom 1-2-3 style menu as a subroutine.

Format: { menucall [location] }
Where [location] is the upper left corner of the menu items and prompts. [Location] may be a cell address, a range address, a range name or in Release 2.2, a formula.

Sample: { menucall PMENU }

Complements: { Return }

See also: { Menubranch }

Description: { Menucall }, like { menubranch }, displays a custom menu in the control panel. The two commands differ in the way they transfer control to other macros when a user selects a menu choice. Unlike { menubranch }, { menucall } only temporarily transfers control to another location after the user makes a menu choice. When the selected routine finishes, 1-2-3 returns control to the command directly following the { menucall } command. In other words, { menucall } treats the other macro commands as a subroutine.

[location]

[Location] is the upper left cell in a range containing label entries representing menu choices and their associated explanation lines. At a minimum, the cell designated in [location] must include a label entry. Label entries representing additional menu option(s) and explanation line(s) are optional.

A common misunderstanding relating to the use of the { menucall } command is that the range specified in [location] must include all the menu options and their associated explanations. In fact, it need only include the cell which contains the leftmost menu choice, although either range specification will work.

menu options

The labels you wish to represent menu options should be entered in consecutive cells to the right of the cell designated in range. 1-2-3 will represent up to eight consecutive entries as menu choices in the control panel when it reads the { menucall } command in a macro. If you enter any more entries than that, 1-2-3 will ignore them. If an empty cell appears to the right of one of these label entries, the label directly to the left of the empty cell will be the last menu item displayed. For example, in the menu shown below, if cell C6 were blank, the item in cell D6 would no longer appear on the menu.

	A	B	C		D	E	F
1	NAME	MACRO					
2	-------	-------	-------	-------	-------		
3	\M	{menucall MEN1}					
4		{branch REPORTS}					
5							
6	MEN1	Post	Clear		Edit		
7		Post entries	Clear entries		Edit an Entry		
8		{branch POST}	{branch CLEAR}		{branch EDITOR}		
9							
10							

Figure 12-15

explanation
line

You may also enter labels in the cells beneath each of the labels representing menu options. When 1-2-3 displays the menu, it will use each of the lower entries as explanation lines for the menu choice entered in the cell above it. When the menu pointer highlights a given menu choice, the associated explanation label will appear in the control panel. For example, if 1-2-3 read the {menucall} command depicted in the last macro, the menu pointer would by default highlight the choice Post and the explanation line would read Post entries. If you moved the menu pointer to highlight the choice Clear, the explanation line would read Clear entries.

Menu choices and explanation lines must all be label entries. If you enter a value instead of a label as one of the menu choices, 1-2-3 will treat that value entry as if it were a blank cell defining the end of the menu options. However, if you use a value entry as an explanation line for a menu choice, when 1-2-3 reads the {menucall} command, it will issue the error message Invalid use of Menu macro command.

When 1-2-3 displays the menu in the control panel, it will automatically capitalize the first letter of each menu option and each explanation line.

menu
function

The menu will function like a 1-2-3 menu: the user may select an option by positioning the menu pointer and pressing the Return key or typing the first character of an option. If the macro contains more than one choice that begins with the same character and the user types that character to select a choice, the option located farthest to the left will be selected.

control
flow

While the menu displays in the control panel, the control flow remains stopped at the {menucall} command. When the user selects a menu option, the control flow jumps to the cell located two cells beneath the cell containing the label representing the selected menu choice. In the following example, if the user selected Clear, control would move from cell B3 to C8. However, 1-2-3 treats the change in control as a call, not a branch (the {menubranch} command treats the change of control as a branch) So, in the following example, when either the Post or Clear routine ends, the macro will next read the instructions in cell B4 (or, if more instructions followed the {menucall} command in cell B3, the macro would resume with them).

	A	B	C	D	E	F
1	NAME	MACRO		COMMENT		
2	-----	------		-------		
3	\M	{menucall MEN1}		Display menu		
4		{branch REPORTS}		Reporting routine		
5						
6	MEN1	Post	Clear	Menu options		
7		Post entries	Clear entries	Explanation lines		
8		{branch POST}	{branch CLEAR}	Macro instructions		
9						
10						

Figure 12-16

calls vs. branches

In a branch, once the macro control flow has begun reading at a new location, it continues there unless further modified. In a call, control continues at the new location only until one of several things happens: the macro encounters a {return} statement, the macro encounters an empty cell or one containing a value, or until calls reach 31 levels deep.

If 1-2-3 reads a {return} command, an empty cell or one containing a value, control will return to the command directly following the {menucall} command. You might use that feature to cause the macro to redisplay the menu: Place the command {branch [location]} directly after the {menucall} command, where [location] is the cell containing the {menucall} command. If you do, make sure your menu has a Quit option to allow the user to get out of the loop you've created.

Note that if the macro encounters a {quit} command in the called subroutine, macro control will terminate completely—control will not return to the calling routine as it would if the macro encountered a {return} command.

where to write routines that support menu items

If in the example above someone selects Clear, control will have moved from B3 (containing the {menubranch} command) to cell C7, since C7 is where you should write the macro instruction you want carried out for the menu item Clear. We strongly recommend that you place a {branch} command there to redirect control to a macro residing in column B. Otherwise, you'll be writing macros in as many columns as there are menu items in your menu and, because they'll be written side by side, those macros will be impossible to document and very difficult to read.

nesting
limits

Each time the macro reads a {menucall} statement and calls a subroutine, the macro is said to be nested one more level deep. For example, after reading one {menucall} command, the macro is nested one level deep. If it reads four {menucall}s without returning control to any of the calling routines, then the macro is four nesting levels deep. If the macro makes 32 calls without returning control to the calling routine, 1-2-3 will issue the error message Too many nesting levels in macro calls.

Note that {menucall} is just one of several sources of subroutine calls. Any {} (subroutine) command generates a call, as does the {for} command.

escape key

If the user presses the Escape key while the menu displays, control will continue beyond the {menucall} command to the next label in the macro. Were you to use the {menubranch} command, you'd probably place a {branch} command there to cause the macro to reread the {menubranch} command and redisplay the menu.

However, the {menucall} command will always read the command that directly follows it after the subroutines it calls terminate. Since it is highly unlikely you want the macro to process the same command if a person presses Escape as you want processed at the end of the subroutines, you have to make a choice between them. The more important of the two is the command you use to continue processing after the subroutines terminate. That means that you should plan to subsequently offer the user the choice to return to this menu. Then, in the event the user does press Escape mistakenly, at least it will still be possible to return to this menu. The menu must contain an option the user can select to exit from the loop you've created with the {menucall} command.

{Wait}

Purpose: Use {wait} to cause 1-2-3 to wait until a specific date and time before reading the next command in the macro.

Format: {wait [time]}

Where [time] is a date and time serial number. [time] may be a number, a formula, a cell address, or a range name describing a single cell.

Sample: {wait @now + @time(0;0;5)}

Complements: None

See also: {?} (interactive command)

Description: {Wait} causes 1-2-3 to suspend reading the current macro until DOS's built in clock matches the date and time specified in the {wait} command. You can either use {wait} to pause until a given time (such as 11:30 p.m. on January 3, 1991) or for a certain length of time (such as 1 hour).

wait until a
certain time

To cause 1-2-3 to suspend reading the current macro until certain time you must first translate that time into 1-2-3's means for specifying it. For example, if you want to suspend the macro until 11:30 p.m. on January 3, 1991, you would use the command:

```
{wait @date(91;1;3)+@time(23;30;0)}
```

The command combines the @date and @time functions. The @date function uses the arguments year, month, day, so @date(91;1;3) translates to January 3, 1991. The @time function uses the arguments hours, minutes, seconds, so @time(23;30;0) is 11:30 p.m.

wait for a
certain
length of
time

If you want to suspend macro execution until some time later today, you could use either of two methods—either tell the macro to wait for a certain length of time, or tell it to wait until a certain time. To tell the macro to wait a certain length of time, use an argument that consists of the @now function added to a certain length of time. To wait ten minutes, use: {wait @now+@time(0;10;0)}. To wait five seconds use: {wait @now+@time(0;0;5)}.

uses

{Wait} is most often used to set the length of time a message will display to the user. For example, an error or information screen can be made to appear on the screen for three seconds, and then the macro can continue.

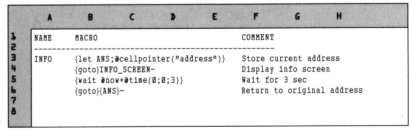

Figure 12-17

more uses

Another use for {wait} is to sequence macros to a certain time of day. For instance, a macro may combine information over a network from a file to be updated by another user prior to 8:00 pm.

```
      A        B              C      D     E     F     G
  1  NAME     MACRO                  COMMENT
  2  ------------------------------------------------
  3  JOIN     {wait TIME}            Wait until TIME
  4           {goto}JOIN_AREA~       Position cell pointer
  5           /fcce{file1}~          Combine file1
  6
  7  TIME                    8:01 PM Store time
  8
  9  file1    SALES.WK1              File to combine
 10           {return}               Return to main routine
 11
 12
```

Figure 12-18

Here's another example—this time specific to Release 2.2. Suppose you were using 1-2-3 on a network and this worksheet contained links to other worksheets. The other worksheets belonged to other users on the network, and you knew they would have been updated by the end of each day. The /fal command sequence used in the following macro, for / File Admin Link-Refresh, is what updates the worksheet.

```
      A        B              C      D     E     F     G
  1  NAME     MACRO                  COMMENT
  2  ------------------------------------------------
  3  JOIN     {wait TIME}            Wait until TIME
  4           /fal                   Update file links
  5           /fs~b                  Save and backup the file
  6
  7  TIME                    8:01 PM Store time
  8
```

Figure 12-19

{?} (interactive command)

Purpose: Use {?} to return control of the macro to the user temporarily.

Format: {?}

Sample: {?}

Complements: None

See also: {Get}, {getlabel}, {getnumber}

Description: Known either as the interactive command or the pause command, the {?} command does both. When 1-2-3 reads {?} in a macro, it temporarily interrupts the macro's processing (thus, the name "pause") and returns control to the keyboard (thus the name "interactive"). As soon as the user presses the Return key, the macro resumes control and continues reading with the next command.

uses

There are a number of ways you might use the {?} command. In simple macros, you can use it to allow the user to read a message. If you are testing a macro, insert {?} commands where you want the macro to pause so you can verify that the macro has performed properly (don't forget to remove them later). You can also use it to return control of 1-2-3 to the keyboard in the midst of a macro. You might want to allow the user to enter data, make menu selections, or move the cell pointer.

limits on
control

When you use the {?} to turn control of 1-2-3 back to the user, you do so unconditionally. You cannot prevent that user from doing things you don't want done; the macro has suspended all control.

{get} to
make a
macro
pause

For that reason, if all you want to do is have the macro pause while you read a message, use the {get} command instead. It does not permit simultaneous access to the interactive mode of 1-2-3. (A detailed description of {get} appears earlier in this chapter.) If you want to grant the person using the macro limited access to 1-2-3's interactive mode, see the section on Filtering Keystrokes in the Advanced Techniques chapter.

and the
Return key

You should also beware that the first time the user presses the Return key, the macro will continue processing where it left off. If the user has just done something that requires a Return keystroke to complete that operation, the macro must provide the Return in the form of a tilde directly following the {?}.

For example, if during an interactive pause in the macro, the user types some data and presses Return, the Return keystroke, which would normally enter the data in a cell, will not do so. Instead, it will trigger the macro to continue reading keystrokes. Since the typed data will still be in the control panel (with 1-2-3 in Edit mode) when the macro resumes, it falls to the macro to enter the data. Typically, you would include a tilde as the first character after the {?} command to do so. If you have to move the cell pointer next, you can omit the tilde and just follow the {?} command with the cell pointer movement command—it'll move the cell pointer and enter the data.

	A	B	C	D	E	F	G	H
1	NAME	MACRO			COMMENT			
2	------	------	------	------	------	------		
3	\A	{?}{r}			Data entry sequence			
4		{?}{r}						
5		{?}{r}						
6		{l 3}			Return to start of next row			
7		{d}						
8		{branch \A}			Repeat macro			
9								
10								

Figure 12-20

13

Controlling Program Flow

Overview and Introduction to New Concepts

scope
The commands in this chapter will enable you to control the flow of the macro: to continue reading the macro in a new location ({branch}), continue reading the macro in a new location specified in a third location ({dispatch}), temporarily transfer control to a subroutine location ({}), resume reading in a location from which you called a subroutine ({return}), clear the subroutine stack ({restart}), transfer control to DOS and optionally start a DOS program or batch file ({system}), test a condition and use the result to select one of two locations in which to resume reading macro instructions ({if}), redirect control in the event of an error ({onerror}), create a counter-controlled loop ({for}), cancel a counter controlled loop ({forbreak}), temporarily return control to the keyboard ({?}), and terminate the macro and unconditionally return control to the keyboard ({quit}).

subroutine calls
A subroutine is a special way of changing the flow of control of a macro. When a subroutine call is made by a macro command, 1-2-3 makes a note of the current location of the command that made the call. Macro control then moves to the location specified in the subroutine call and the macro resumes reading in the new location. The macro continues reading in the new location until either the routine ends or the macro reads a {return} command, at which time control will return from the

subroutine to the command directly following the one that made the subroutine call.

While a subroutine is running, it can make a subroutine call to transfer control to yet another subroutine. Each time a macro makes a subroutine call, 1-2-3 increments the subroutine nesting chain by one. If there is one subroutine call, the subroutine chain is nested one level deep. If that subroutine makes another subroutine call, the chain is nested two levels deep. Each time the macro returns control from a subroutine to the routine that called it, 1-2-3 decrements the subroutine chain by one nesting level. 1-2-3 can nest a maximum of 31 levels in the subroutine chain.

commands that call subroutines

In this group of commands, the { } and {for} commands call subroutines. {Menucall}, which belongs to the Allowing Keyboard Interaction group of commands, also calls subroutines.

{ } (subroutine call)

Purpose: Use { } to temporarily redirect macro flow of control from the current location to another location.

Format: {subroutine [*parameter1*];[*parameter2*];[*parameterN*]}
Where subroutine is a named range (not a cell address) to which control will be temporarily transferred and [parameter1] is an optional data element to be used by one of the commands in that location.

By default, each [parameter] is treated as a string. However, if the {define} command in the corresponding subroutine specifies that a [parameter] is to be a value (:v), it may be a number, a formula, a cell address, or a range name describing a single cell. Curiously, [parameter] need not evaluate to a number if it is a formula, a cell address, or a range name.

Sample: {WIDTH} or {WIDTH 30}

Complements: {return}

See also: {define}, {menucall}, {for}, {dispatch}, {branch}

Description: { } instructs 1-2-3 to temporarily discontinue reading macro instructions in the current cell and begin reading in the top left cell of the specified range. { } can also pass one or more labels or values (called parameters) to be used by macro commands in the new location.

subroutine
names

Like entire macros, subroutines are commonly referred to by the name of the cell containing their first instruction. However, you do not activate a macro with the first line of a subroutine; you transfer control of an already operating macro to that line, the subroutine name need not conform to the rules for naming macros.

You transfer control to a subroutine by including the name of that subroutine within curly braces in the macro. If cell B10 has been named Print, and the first line of a printing subroutine begins in cell B10, when 1-2-3 reads the command {PRINT} in a macro, it will transfer macro control to that subroutine.

The macro commands in the new location to which control has been redirected are known as a subroutine.

You cannot use key names, such as {right}, as subroutine range names. If you were to name a subroutine Right, you would be unable to invoke that subroutine. When 1-2-3 reads {right}, it will interpret it as the key name and not as a subroutine call. The relationship between subroutine names and key names is particularly important when running a macro in a new release of 1-2-3. For instance, Release 2.2 introduces the Help key name, so a macro that uses a subroutine named Help may run as intended in Releases 2 and 2.01, but in Releases 2.2 or 3 it will activate the online Help system of those products.

The simplest way around this problem is to become aware of the new key names in Release 3 (and there are many), and make sure that your macros do not use subroutines of the same name. This will greatly increase the chances of your macro running successfully in Release 2.2, Release 3, and future releases of 1-2-3. An additional strategy is to select subroutine names that will be unlikely to be assigned by Lotus as key names. For example, no existing macro keywords or key names contain the underscore character or have a numerical suffix. If you use such characters in association with the common-sensical nouns that often form range names, you should be safe. For example, don't use the word Form as a range name, use Form1. Form, a common enough noun, is one of those words that turns up as a macro keyword in Release 3. But Form1 doesn't, nor does Input_form.

subroutine
calls

A subroutine is a good place to store commonly used macro operations. Instead of repeating those operations within each macro, you can simply redirect control temporarily to the subroutine (that's known as "calling" a subroutine). When the subroutine finishes its work, it will return control to the macro that called it. Specifically, control will return to the command directly following the { } command in the calling macro. In that way, different macros can use the services of a single subroutine.

The sample macro below illustrates how a subroutine call affects the macro's control flow. We've numbered each line in the Comment column. This macro begins (1) with a copy command in the main routine, then (2) calls a subroutine named print, runs the subroutine (3) to print a report, (4) returns control to the main routine, and (5) finishes the main routine by saving a file. You should realize that any other macro could call the {print} routine.

```
       A        B          C      D       E      F       G      H
  1   NAME     MACRO              COMMENT
  2   -------------------------------------------
  3   \A       /INPUT1-FORM1-      1  main routine
  4            {PRINT2}            2  call subroutine
  5            /fsNEW-r            5  returned from subroutine
  6
  7
  8   PRINT2   /ppagpq             3  subroutine
  9            {return}            4  return to main routine
 10
```

Figure 13-1

example 1   Suppose you use the following data entry routine to fill in an onscreen form in several places in your macro:

```
{?}{r}
{?}{d}{r2}
{?}{d2}{r2}
```

Rather than writing this routine into your macro in each of the places you need to use it, you can make the routine into a subroutine and simply transfer control to it (or "call" it) when you need to use it. If you name the first cell in the data entry routine Entry, here's how that might work:

```
       A        B          C      D       E      F       G      H
  1   NAME     MACRO                      COMMENT
  2   -------------------------------------------
  3   \A       {goto}MESSAGE2-             Display message
  4            {ENTRY}                    Data entry
  5            /pprFORM-agpq              Print form
  6            {blank FORM}               Clear form
  7            {goto}MESSAGE2-            Display message
  8            {ENTRY}                    Data entry
  9            {menubranch MEN2}          Display menu
 10
```

Figure 13-2

example 2

Suppose you frequently use the command sequence {windows-off} {paneloff} to freeze the current contents of the display. Instead of writing the commands {windowsoff} {paneloff} repeatedly, you place them into a subroutine called Off. Likewise, you could store the complementary commands {windowson} {panelon} in a subroutine called On. When you use either Off or On in the macro, you'll enclose them in the subroutine command, { }, so they look like this, {OFF} and {ON}.

```
     A      B          C        D        E        F      G      H
 1  NAME    MACRO                        COMMENT
 2  --------------------------------------------
 3  \A      {goto}MESSAGE2~              Display message
 4          {OFF}                        Freeze display
 5          /dsg                         Sort list
 6          /cENTRY1~ENTRY2~             Copy entries
 7          {ON}                         Update screen
 8          {menubranch MEN2}            Display menu
 9
10  OFF     {windowsoff}{paneloff}       Freeze display
11          {return}                     Return to main routine
12
13  ON      {windowson}{panelon}         Thaw display
14          {return}                     Return to main routine
15
```

Figure 13-3

passing
parameters

A calling routine can send data to the subroutine it calls in order to specialize the way in which that subroutine works. The data it sends may be labels, values, or both, and are known collectively as parameters. The process of sending this data to a subroutine is known as passing parameters.

Suppose you want to use a subroutine to test whether a series of sales figures for different products are above or below budget. The budget figure you are testing for varies in each case, but the macro code you use to perform the test and record the result doesn't.

That's an ideal situation for a subroutine. You can write the macro instructions once, then use them with a different budget amount each time you test a sale. In this case, we'll plug in that budget amount by passing a parameter from the main routine to the subroutine.

In the following macro, the main routine (\A) uses a series of calls to a subroutine named Test to test each of the four entries in a column of sales figures. However, instead of simply calling the subroutine as {TEST}, each subroutine call also includes a number, such as {TEST 10}. The number 10 in {TEST 10} is a parameter. Directly following each subroutine call is the cell pointer movement key name {d}, which moves the cell pointer down to the next entry in the column.

	A	B	C	D	E	F	G	H
1	NAME	MACRO		COMMENT				
2	----	-----	----	----	----			
3	\A	{TEST 10}{d}						
4		{TEST 15}{d}						
5		{TEST 12}{d}						
6		{TEST 25}{d}						
7		{TEST 45}{d}						
8		{quit}						
9								
10								
11	TEST	{define BUDGET:v}						
12		{if @cellpointer("contents")>=BUDGET}{return}						
13		{r}						
14		Too low						
15		{l}						
16		{return}						
17								
18								
19	BUDGET							
20								

Figure 13-4

The subroutine named Test does the work of testing each entry.

The first command, {define}, stores the passed parameter in a cell named Budget as a value. (Without the :v at the end of the {define} command, the passed parameter would be stored as a label.)

The second line of the subroutine evaluates whether the current cell is greater or equal to the amount stored in the cell named Budget.

If so, the {if} statement is true and the macro reads the {return} command located to its right. The {return} command returns control to the main routine just after the command that called the subroutine. That next command is {down}, which moves the cell pointer to the next sales figure in the list. The command that follows is yet another subroutine call with another parameter.

But what happens if the entry being tested is less than the amount stored in the cell named Budget? The {if} command in the second line of the subroutine will evaluate to false. Rather than read the {return} command to its right, macro control will skip directly to the next line.

The macro moves the cell pointer one cell to the right, types the label "Too low", moves left again (and, in the process, enters the label on the worksheet), and returns control to the main routine.

For more information on the relationship between passing parameters and the {define} command, read the listing for the {define} command.

passing parameters— exceptional commands

By now, you may have assumed that any 1-2-3 command that uses a number for input could also take a range name in place of that number. While that's largely true, there are some exceptions, and those exceptions call for a slightly different approach to writing a subroutine.

You'll recall that so far, the way the subroutine uses the passed parameter has been to reference the cell in which the passed parameter is stored. If the command you want to use that parameter with won't accept such a reference as input, you'll need some other way to approach your subroutine. The change you need to make is a minor one.

Let's consider the Worksheet Column Set-Width command. Although this command uses a number to establish the width of the column, you can't substitute a range name for the number. A macro written as /wcs25~ works fine, but if you store the value 25 in a cell named SIZE, the macro /wcsSIZE~ will *not* work.

Subroutine That Does Not Work

	A	B	C	D	E	F	G	H
1	NAME	MACRO			COMMENT			
2	----------	---						
3	\A	{WIDTH 25}			Set column			
4		{r}			Move right			
5		{WIDTH 30}			Set column			
6								
7								
8	WIDTH	{define SIZE:v}			Store parameter			
9		/wcsSIZE~			Set column			
10		{return}			Return to routine			
11								
12								
13	SIZE				Store size setting			
14								
15								

Figure 13-5

The solution to this problem involves two changes from your normal approach to using passed parameters.

Suppose the parameter you pass to the subroutine shown above is 25. You know that you can't refer to the cell containing the number 25 when you use the Worksheet Column Set-Width command. However, if you pass the 25 as a label and store it in a named range, you can call that label as macro subroutine. Let's look at a properly written subroutine and then explain it step by step.

Subroutine That Works

```
        A        B        C       D       E       F       G       H
1    NAME     MACRO             COMMENT
2    ---------------------------------
3    \A       {WIDTH 25}        Set column 1
4             {r}               Move right
5             {WIDTH 30}        Set column 2
6
7
8    WIDTH    {define SIZE}     Store parameter
9             /wcs{SIZE}~       Set column
10            {return}          Return to routine
11
12
13   SIZE     25                Store size setting
14            {return}          Return to width routine
15
```

Figure 13-6

{WIDTH 25}: The first command in the macro calls the subroutine named Width and passes it the parameter 25.

{define SIZE}: The {define SIZE} command stores the parameter 25 in the cell named Size. Size is located near the bottom of the macro; it's shown in the example above as if it were still blank. Note that there is no :v argument in the {define} command. Without that argument, the parameter 25 will be stored as a label. We could've written {define SIZE:s}, but since string is the default, there's no need.

/wcs{SIZE}~: In the second line of the Width subroutine, notice that the word SIZE has been enclosed in braces: {SIZE}. That means that 1-2-3 will read Size a subroutine to the subroutine Width. When the macro reads /wcs, it will enter the command /Worksheet Column Set-Width. At this point, macro control moves to the cell named Size.

25: The macro reads the label 25 stored in the cell named Size, which provides the column width setting.

{return}: Next, the macro reads the {return} command. The {return} command returns control to the macro instruction directly following the last subroutine call made. That subroutine call was made in the macro line /wcs{SIZE} ~, and the next macro instruction is the tilde (~), which completes the Worksheet Column Set-Width command.

{ return } : 1-2-3 reads the next line of the macro, { return }. This command returns control to the main routine, \A.

{ right } : The next command in the main routine moves the cell pointer right one column.

{ WIDTH 30 } : This command calls the subroutine once again, this time to set the current column width to 30 spaces.

subroutine
chain

Each time a macro makes a subroutine call, 1-2-3 must make a note of where that call came from in order to return to that location when the subroutine ends.

As you saw in the previous example, you can call subroutines within subroutines. Each time you do, 1-2-3 adds the latest location of the subroutine call to the list of places it must remember. Collectively, that list of locations to which 1-2-3 must return control is known as the subroutine stack or the subroutine chain.

nesting
limits

Each time a macro calls a subroutine, the number of subroutines in the stack increases by one level. Each time a subroutine returns control to the calling routine, that stack decreases by one level. Another way to describe the status of the subroutine stack is to say that there are currently a certain number of levels of subroutines nested in the chain.

1-2-3 can accomodate 31 levels of subroutine calls before the stack fills to its capacity. If your macro encounters a 32nd subroutine call, it will terminate in an error and 1-2-3 will display the message **Too many nesting levels in macro calls**.

{ } without
arguments

You can also use the subroutine command without specifying the name of a subroutine: { }. Since there's no named subroutine to call, the command merely passes control to the next command in the macro. You may find that capability useful in certain self-modifying macros as an alternative to branching elsewhere.

You may see this use of the subroutine command referred to as the no op (for "no operation") command because it performs no operations.

other kinds
of
subroutines

{ } is not the only command that can call a subroutine, { menucall } (but not { menubranch }) and { for } also call subroutines. If you take care to include a { return } command at the end of each subroutine, it is not likely that you need to be concerned about exceeding the limit of 31 calls. Nonetheless, be aware that all three sources of subroutine calls—{ }, { menucall }, and { for }—increase the number of nesting levels in the subroutine chain.

call versus
branch

When 1-2-3 reads the { } (subroutine) command in a macro, it transfers control to the named subroutine. However, the transfer of control from the calling routine to the subroutine is conditional. As soon as the macro reads a { return } command or encounters a blank cell, control returns to the main routine at the command directly following the subroutine call.

When you use a {branch} command to transfer control to another routine, that transfer of control is unconditional. Unless you use some other means to transfer control back again, control will remain in the new location.

caution
regarding
loops

If you merely want to repeat a routine, use a {branch} command, not a subroutine command. A {branch} command redirects control to another location unconditionally, which is what you want in a loop. If you use a subroutine command within a loop to redirect control, you'll be incrementing the subroutine chain each time the macro repeats the loop.

If the loop repeats too many times, you'll exceed 1-2-3's maximum nesting limits (31 levels) and the macro will terminate in an error. Even if you don't exceed the maximum number of nesting levels before the loop ends, unless you also use the {restart} command, all those nesting levels remain in force. Any subsequent subroutine calls will add yet more nesting levels, increasing the possibility of an error.

{Branch}

Purpose: Use {branch} to redirect macro control flow from the current location to another location.

Format: {branch [range]}
Where [range] refers to the location of the macro commands to execute. [Range] may be a cell address, a range address, a range name, or in Release 2.2, a formula.

Sample: {branch NEXT}

Complements: None

See also: { }, {for}, {dispatch}, {onerror}, {menubranch}

Release 1A Equivalent: /xg

Release 1A Format: /xg[range]~
Where [range] is the name or address of the range containing the macro commands to execute.

Description: {Branch} instructs 1-2-3 to discontinue reading macro instructions in the current cell and resume reading in the top left cell of the specified range. {Branch} is equivalent to the GOTO command in the BASIC programming language.

versus subroutine calls

{Branch} redirects the macro control flow unconditionally. Once the control flow has been changed from one location to another, it will not return to the original location unless further instructed to do so—unlike a subroutine call (see the { } or {menucall} commands). Since 1-2-3 "forgets" the location from which it branches (it does not increment the subroutine nesting chain), you can make as many branches as you want—unlike subroutine calls, which are limited to 31 levels.

loops

{Branch} is the command through which you can implement a simple loop, that is, make the macro repeat itself. If you want to write a loop with a counter, either use the {for} command or use {branch} as part of a counter routine (see the sections on loops in Keystroke macros, and the section on loops and counters in the Advanced Techniques section).

Example 2

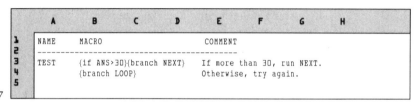

Figure 13-7

{branch} versus /xg

{Branch} and /xg work nearly identically. /xg differs in that it will accept the key name {name} in place of its [location] argument. When used in conjunction with an {?} interactive command (/xg{name}{?}~), it will display a menu of range names from which you may choose. When you make a selection, macro control will branch to the new location. This results in much the same effect as Release 2.2's Run command.

{Define}

Purpose: Use {define} to designate a range in which to store one or more subroutine parameters.

Format: {define [cell1]:[type1];[cellN];[typeN]}
Where [cell] represents the location in which to store the parameter and the optional [type] argument may be value (or simply v), or string (or simply s). If no type is specified, 1-2-3 assumes a string.
[Cell] may be a cell address, a range address, a range name, or in Release 2.2, a formula.

Sample: {define ANS:value}

Complements: { }

Description: When you call a subroutine (see the { } command), you have the option of passing parameters to that subroutine to specialize the way in which it works. A parameter could be a label or a value, and you can pass more than one parameter at a time.

The {define} command stores those parameters in worksheet cells so the subroutine can reference them. Since the calling routine will do the work of changing the parameters it passes, the subroutine need never be changed.

specifying parameters

When a parameter is a value, and that's frequently the case, you must specify it as a value in the {define} command. When you write the {define} command, you can do that by writing the entire word "value" or by writing only the first letter of that word.

1-2-3 evaluates only the first character of the {define} command's type argument. That means v has the same effect in that command as the word value (or any word beginning with the letter v, for that matter). Further, the case of that argument is insignificant. In this context, V, v, value, and VALUE are synonomous.

example 1: passing parameters to set column widths

For example, let's suppose you need to set columns to a variety of widths during your application. The commands to set column width are / Worksheet Column Set-Width followed by a value representing a number of spaces, and the Return key. If you wanted to set the column to 25 spaces wide, the macro would be /wcs25~. You could write one routine for each column-width setting, but that would involve a lot of rewriting of routines that are essentially the same. Instead, you could write just one subroutine to vary the width of a column and pass to that subroutine the appropriate width setting each time you use it.

If the column-setting subroutine is called Width, then the command {WIDTH 30} would call the Width subroutine and pass to it the parameter 30. The Width subroutine would then look like this:

Figure 13-8

The first command in the subroutine, {define}, stores the parameter (in this case, 30) as a label in a cell named Size. The next line of the macro uses that cell as a subroutine to supply the width setting to the /wcs command. Finally, the {return} command returns the flow of control to the calling routine.

Here's an example using two parameters. You might write a subroutine that tests whether the last entry was within a high-low range. If the upper and lower limits vary with each entry, you could write a different routine to handle each entry, but that would entail a great deal of repetitive work. Or, you could write one subroutine and each time you call that subroutine, pass the values of the upper and lower limits for that test. If the subroutine is called Test, then the command {TEST 50;100} would call the subroutine Test and pass it the parameters 50 and 100.

The first command in the subroutine Test should be the {define} command. The {define} command stores the parameters in the cells specified in the {define} arguments. The subroutine can then refer to these cells for input. For example, suppose you have cells named Upper and Lower. The {define} command to receive and store the parameters in the example above would be {define LOWER:v;UPPER:v}. In other words, store the first parameter, 50, as a value in the cell named Lower; and store the second parameter, 100, as a value in the cell named Upper.

The subroutine Test will refer to these two cells for the upper and lower limits it tests. That subroutine might look like this:

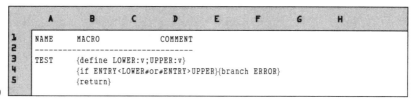

Figure 13-9

The first line of the subroutine stores the parameters passed from the calling routine. The second line uses the {if} command to test whether the cell named Entry contains an entry that is less than the value stored in Lower or greater than the value stored in Upper. If Entry is either less than Lower or greater than Upper, the statement is true. In that case, the macro will read the statement to the right of the {if} command and branch to a routine called Error. Otherwise, the macro will read the last line, {return} and the flow of control will revert to the calling routine.

There are other ways to pass parameters to a subroutine than the {define} command. {Define} only helps to pass parameters in the sense that it stores those parameters in cells that the subroutine subsequently references. Depending on the application you are developing, there may be other more convenient ways to store those parameters in the referenced cells. The unique strength of the {define} command is its ability to handle in just one command an entire slew of passed variables.

```
        A         B          C          D          E          F          G          H
1   NAME      MACRO                 COMMENT
2   ================================================
3   \A        {WIDTH 25}            Set column 1
4             {right}               Move right
5             {WIDTH 40}            Set column 2
6             {right}               Move right
7             {branch ENTRIES}      Begin data entry
8
9
10  WIDTH     {define SIZE}          Store paramater
11            /wcs{SIZE}~            Set column
12            {return}               Return to \A routine
13
14  SIZE                            Size setting
15            {return}               Return to width routine
```

Figure 13-10

{ Dispatch }

Purpose: Use Dispatch to indirectly branch to a macro at some other location.

Format: { dispatch [range] }
Where [range] is the name or address of range1. Range1 in turn contains a reference to range2. Range2 contains the macro commands to execute.

[Range] may be a cell address, a range address, or a range name. Additionally, [range] may be a formula that returns a cell address, range address, or range name. In Release 2 and 2.01, { dispatch } is the only macro command with this property.

Sample: { dispatch CHOICE }

Complements: None

See also: { Branch }, { }

Description: Dispatch transfers macro control from one routine to another by way of an intermediary range. This intermediary range contains the name or address of the range containing the actual macro commands to execute.

example

For example, suppose you want to offer your user a menu with more than eight choices. Rather than write a two level menu with the { menubranch } or { menucall } command, you decide to write the menu choices on the worksheet, along with a message instructing the user to choose a menu choice by highlighting the cell containing a menu letter and pressing Return. Here's how that menu screen might appear.

	A	B	C	D	E	F	G	H
1								
2								
3	To select a choice: Move the pointer to the letter							
4	representing that choice and press the Return key							
5								
6	A			Post monthly entries.				
7								
8	B			Produce reports.				
9								
10	C			Retrieve another file.				
11								
12								
13								
14								
15								

Figure 13-11

The macro code you might use to control that operation appears below.

	A	B	C	D	E	F	G	H
1	NAME	MACRO					COMMENT	
2	------	------					------	
3	\M	{goto}SCREEN_MENU~					Show menu	
4		{?}					Pause for user choice	
5		{let CHOICE;@cellpointer("contents")}					Store choice	
6		{dispatch CHOICE}					Branch thru CHOICE	
7								
8	CHOICE						Variable storage	
9								
10	A	{goto}SCREEN_ONE~					Routine A	
11		{quit}						
12	B	{goto}SCREEN_TWO~					Routine B	
13		{quit}						
14	C	{goto}SCREEN_THREE~					Routine C	
15		{quit}						

Figure 13-12

description
of the
macro
example

In the macro above, the first command displays the portion of the worksheet containing the menu; the second line uses the interactive command to temporarily return control to the user. The user is expected to read the menu, move the cell pointer to the letter beside a menu choice and press the Return key to select that choice.

If the user positions the cell pointer on one of the cells containing a menu letter and presses Return, the {dispatch} command will cause the macro to branch to the named location matching the menu letter.

In the macro, the cell named Choice stores a copy of the letter on which the cell pointer sat when the user pressed the Return key. The {dispatch} command transfers the macro control flow to the location named in Choice.

If when 1-2-3 reads the {dispatch} command, you receive the error message "Macro: Invalid string value in DISPATCH," in the {dispatch} command you've referred to a location that contains nothing. Place a reference to another location (either a range name or cell address) in that location and run the macro again. If you receive the error message "Macro: Invalid range in DISPATCH," you have referred to a named range that doesn't exist. Use the Range Name Create command to create the range name.

Note that the macro command {onerror} can trap neither of the above errors (for more information about the {onerror} command, see its listing in this chapter). For that reason, if you require macros that a user can't cause to crash, you shouldn't use the one shown above. Consider what would happen if the user pointed to any cell but one of those containing the menu letters—the {dispatch} command would generate an error and interrupt the macro. A similar macro that will not crash appears in the Advanced Techniques section.

errors related to {dispatch}

{For}

Purpose: Use {for} to implement a counter. It will run a macro subroutine any number of times you specified.

Format: {for [counter];[start];[stop];[step];[location]}
Where [counter] is a cell in which {for} will increment a value; [start] is the number at which to begin counting. [Stop] is the number at which to stop counting; [step] is the number by which to increment the counter with each repetition of the subroutine that begins at the location specified by [location]. [counter] may be a cell address, a range address, a range name, or in Release 2.2, a formula. Each of [start], [stop], and [step] may be a number, a formula, a cell address, or a range name describing a single cell. [location] may be a cell address, a range address, a range name, or in Release 2.2, a formula.

Sample: {for NUM;1;10;1;BELL}

Complements: None

See also: {forbreak}, {}, {branch}, {dispatch}

Description: {For} enables you to control the number of repetitions of a given subroutine. The {for} command passes control to a subroutine; when control returns, {for} increments a counter and compares it against a preset limit. If the counter value is less than the limit value, {for} passes control back to the subroutine and the process repeats. If the counter value is equal to or greater than the limit value, control passes from the {for} command to the next command in the macro (instead of the subroutine).

argument
meanings

The arguments to the {for} command define how the counter will work. The first of them, [counter], identifies the cell used to store the counter value; the second, [start], sets an initial value for that cell. Because {for} sets the initial value in (or "initializes") that cell, you won't have to zero the cell out before using the {for} command in order to prevent values previously stored there from throwing off the counter.

The third argument, [stop], establishes the stop value. Each time the subroutine called by {for} returns control to {for} and 1-2-3 increments the counter cell, 1-2-3 will also compare the stop value to the counter value. If the stop value is equal to or greater than the counter value, instead of running the subroutine again, the {for} command will relinquish macro control to the next command in the macro.

The fourth argument, [step], sets the amount by which to increment the counter each time macro control returns to the {for} command.

Finally, the fifth argument, [location], identifies the first cell of the subroutine that the {for} command will call.

argument
require-
ments

All the arguments that you supply through a cell reference or range name, except the last argument, may consist of only one cell apiece, although you may use either a cell address or range name to identify each of them. The last argument may consist of a range containing more than one cell, but, like other subroutine calls, that range need only consist of the first cell of the subroutine you wish to call.

what
number
should you
use to
initialize
counter?

The {for} command allows you to start counting with any value you wish. For example, if the second argument in the {for} command is a one, then the first value that the {for} command will assign to the counter cell is one. The difference between a start value of one and a start value of zero is significant. Given the same value for the upper limit argument, a counter that begins at value zero will process the loop once more than a counter that begins at value one. To make the number of loops equal the stop value (which is what most situations call for), use a one as your start value.

cautions
about the
subroutine
called by
{for}

Remember that, because {for} calls a subroutine, it's a good idea to end that subroutine with a {return} command to explicitly return control to the {for} command that called that subroutine.

Because {for} calls a subroutine, that call increases the subroutine chain by one. However, that subroutine also decrements the subroutine chain when it ends and returns control to the {for} command. So, {for} increases the subroutine chain only by one—regardless of how many times the {for} command repeats the subroutine it calls.

```
       A        B         C      D      E      F        G        H
 1  NAME    MACRO                                    COMMENT
 2  --------------------------------------------------------
 3  \A      {for COUNTER;1;LIMIT;1;WIDEN}            Set up counter
 4          {branch ENTRY}                           Do data entry
 5
 6  COUNTER                                          Store current count
 7
 8  LIMIT   5                                        Store limit value
 9
10  WIDEN   /wcs18~                                  Widen column
11          {r}                                      Move right
12          {return}                                 Return to \A
13
14
15
```

Figure 13-13

alternative
to the
{for}
command

If you find the {for} command a bit complex, you should know two things. First, in the chapter on Writing Your Own Commands you can read about a way to vastly simplify the {for} command. Second, you can also implement a counter controlled loop without the {for} command.

If for no other reason, you may want to read about an alternative to the {for} command to better understand how a {for}-controlled loop works. Refer now to the following screen showing the macro.

The macro begins by prompting the user for the number of times to repeat the operation and stores that value in a cell named Limit.

Line two assigns the value zero to the cell named Counter. Counter will be used to store the number of times the routine that begins on line 3 has been run. You store zero in Counter to remove the value left over from the last time you ran this routine.

The cell containing line three of the macro is named Loop1. This is the first cell of the routine the counter has been set up to control. Line three sets the width of the current column to 18. Line four moves the cell pointer one cell to the right, to a new column.

Line five increments by one the value of the cell named Counter. Line six compares Counter with Limit. If the formula Counter = Limit is true, then the macro has repeated the routine the proper number of times. When that formula is true, the macro will read the next statement on the same line—ending the loop. That next statement transfers control to a new location called Entry.

However, if Counter is less than Limit when the macro reads line six, the macro skips the remaining statement on the line (it will not read the {branch} command on line six). Instead, control immediately drops to the next line.

Line seven causes the macro to branch back to line three, named Loop. That begins another iteration of the routine that begins there.

Example: Counter controlled loop without {for} command.

```
        A         B        C        D        E        F        G        H
 1   NAME      MACRO                              COMMENT
 2   ------------------------------------------------   ------
 3   \A        {getnumber "How many times? ";LIMIT}   1 Request limit amount
 4             {let COUNTER;0}                         2 Zero out the counter
 5   LOOP      /wcs18~                                 3 Change column width
 6             {r}                                     4 Move right
 7             {let COUNTER;COUNTER+1}                 5 Increment counter by 1
 8             {if COUNTER=LIMIT}{branch ENTRY}        6 Test counter vs. limit
 9             {branch LOOP}                           7 Repeat from line 3
10
11
12   LIMIT                                        Store limit value
13
14
15
```

Figure 13-14

time is the cost of any loop

Perhaps the chief limitation of a {for} controlled loop—or any loop—is the time it takes for 1-2-3 to process the instructions in the loop. While loops provide a clearly structured programming tool, 1-2-3 reads them more slowly than it reads the same instructions written out repeatedly. Both of the following macros do the same thing, but the one with the loop will do it noticeably slower than the one without it. Where speed is of the essence—such as in screen-oriented operations—you may choose to write instructions out repeatedly in order to maximize their speed.

Example 1: Macro with instructions in a Loop.

```
        A         B        C        D        E        F        G        H
 1   NAME      MACRO                              COMMENT
 2   ------------------------------------------------
 3   \A        {for COUNTER;1;LIMIT;1;MOVER}      Call Mover routine
 4             {quit}                             Quit
 5
 6
 7   MOVER     {u 2}{d 2}                         Move pointer
 8             {return}                           Return to caller
 9
10
11   COUNTER                                      Store counter value
12   LIMIT             5                          Store limit value
13
14
15
```

Figure 13-15

Example 2: Macro with instructions not in a Loop.

	A	B	C	D	E	F	G	H
1	NAME	MACRO				COMMENT		
2	--							
3	\A	{u 2}{d 2}				Move pointer		
4		{u 2}{d 2}						
5		{u 2}{d 2}						
6		{u 2}{d 2}						
7		{u 2}{d 2}						
8		{quit}				Quit		
9								
10								

Figure 13-16

when not to use {for}

In particular, don't use the {for} command—or any other form of loop—when the routine you want to repeat consists only of a macro key name (for example, {r} or {pgdn}). Key names all accept numeric arguments that describe how many times 1-2-3 should repeat them when they're in a macro (e.g., {r 10}, {pgdn 2}), and they operate much faster than implementing the same scheme through a loop.

If you need to repeat a key name and want to be able to vary the number of times that 1-2-3 does so, use a range name as the key name argument ({r NUM}), then use a {let} or {getnumber} command to assign the contents of the range name. For example:

```
{let NUM;6}
{r NUM}
```

... or ...

```
{getnumber "Move to the right how many columns? ";NUM}
{r NUM}
```

{Forbreak}

Purpose: Use {forbreak} to prematurely end the execution of a {for} loop.

Format: {forbreak}

Sample: {if VALUE>MAX}{forbreak}{branch OVERMAX}

Complements: {for}

See also: {restart}, {return}

Description: {Forbreak} cancels a subroutine called by a {for} statement and returns control to the macro instruction that follows the {for} command immediately. If the macro reads a {forbreak} when no {for} loop is in effect, an irrecoverable error will occur accompanied by the error message Invalid FORBREAK.

{Forbreak} differs from a {return} command in a subroutine called by a {for} routine. {Return} only ends the current iteration of the {for} loop and returns control to the {for} statement, whereupon {for} will increment its counter and decide if it should rerun the subroutine. {Forbreak} terminates the current iteration of the subroutine, seizes control from the {for} command, and transfers control to the next macro instruction following the {for} statement.

Another related command, {restart}, does yet another thing. {Restart} severs all ties between the currently executing subroutine and the routine(s) that called it. If a macro encounters that in a {for} loop, 1-2-3 will clear the subroutine stack and continue reading in the current location. It will never return control to the main routine.

effect of
{restart}

Since {restart} will entirely cancel the subroutine nesting chain, including any subroutine calls made by {for} commands, any {restart} command will render any {forbreak} commands unnecessary.

To summarize, when 1-2-3 reads each of the following in a subroutine, here's what happens:

- {return} returns control to {for}

- {forbreak} returns control to the command directly following {for}

- {restart} leaves control in the current location, but changes the subroutine into a normal macro incapable of returning control elsewhere.

no effect
on {for}
subroutines

Because {for} increments the subroutine nesting chain by one, {forbreak} reduces it by one. For that reason, if you've nested {for} commands (one {for} statement calls a subroutine that uses yet another {for} statement to call a second subroutine), the {forbreak} command will cancel only the last {for} subroutine.

Higher-level subroutine calls (i.e., subroutine calls that precede the {for} subroutine call in the subroutine nesting chain) will remain unaffected by {forbreak}.

{Forbreak} is often used as an "escape hatch" from a {for} loop. To implement such an escape, place an {if} statement in the subroutine called by the {for} command. Structure the {if} statement so that one branch continues the subroutine while the other reads {forbreak} to break out of the loop.

restart during a {for} loop

If, during a {for} loop, an error occurs and is trapped by an {onerror} command, an implicit {restart} occurs, since the error cancels the entire subroutine chain, including any subroutines called by {for} commands.

{If}

Purpose: Use {if} to test a condition and direct program flow accordingly.

Format: {if [condition]}
Where [condition] is a numeric value. [condition] may be a number, a formula, a cell address, or a range name describing a single cell.

Sample: {if @cellpointer("row")<60}

Complements: None

See also: {branch}, {ifkey}

Release 1A Equivalent: /xi

Release 1A Format: /xi[condition]~
Where [condition] is a formula that returns a numeric result, any numeric value, or a reference to any cell containing a numeric value.

Description: The {if} command generally contains an expression that evaluates to zero or one. The expression is usually a logical condition containing at least one of 1-2-3's relational operators =, <, >, < =, or > =. If the condition is true, the conditional expression returns a one; if false, the expression returns a zero. Here's an example of a conditional expresssion: Test1 = Test2.

The {if} command will evaluate the expression and if it finds that expression to be false (that is, the expression returns a zero), it will modify the normal macro control flow by skipping over any remaining macro instructions on the same line, and jumping directly to the next line. If the condition is true (the expression returns a one), the macro will continue reading in normal fashion.

if, then, else. . .

{If} is most useful when you use it as part of an "if-then-else" construct. An "if-then-else" construct enables the macro to test an expression and *if* it's true, *then* perform one set of instructions; or *else* (if it's false), perform a different set of instructions.

Let's look at an example. This routine checks to see if a user has entered the letter Y and either runs the routine named Yes if the user did so, or runs the routine named No if the user entered any other letter or no letter at all.

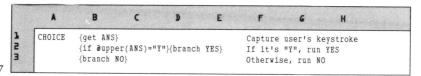

```
       A        B         C        D       E       F       G       H
  1  CHOICE  {get ANS}                              Capture user's keystroke
  2          {if @upper(ANS)="Y"}{branch YES}       If it's "Y", run YES
  3          {branch NO}                            Otherwise, run NO
```

Figure 13-17

a typical
application
of {if}

Line one of the macro captures a keystroke from the user and stores it in a cell named Ans. Line two contains two commands—an {if} command followed by a {branch} command. The {if} command checks to see if the keystroke, stored in Ans, is equal to a "Y". Since 1-2-3 discriminates between upper and lower case in conditional formulas, but you want to accept either "Y" or "y", this conditional formula first converts the string value in Ans to upper case: @upper(ANS). Whether the keystroke was upper or lower case, you can now test just for an upper case Y.

If the conditional formula is true, the macro will continue reading in normal fashion with the command {branch YES}. When it does, that command will transfer control directly to the routine named Yes, skipping the next line. If the conditional formula is false, the macro will skip any commands following the {if} command on the same line and transfer control directly to the line below. That line contains the command {branch NO}, which will transfer control to a routine named No.

In sum, the {if} command evaluates a condition and transfers control to one routine if the condition is true, or transfers control to another routine if the condition is false.

However, there's a potential for a problem with an if-then–else construct in a macro. Suppose that to the right of the {if} command you used some other command besides a {branch} command. For example, suppose you wanted the application to record the label "Yes" if the keystroke stored in Ans is a "Y", and the label "No" if the stored keystroke is anything else or no keystroke at all. Here's the macro.

```
       A        B         C        D       E       F       G       H
  1  CHOICE  {get ANS}                              Capture user's keystroke
  2          {if @upper(ANS)="Y"}Yes~                If it's "Y", enter Yes
  3          No~                                     Otherwise, enter No
```

Figure 13-18

potential
problem
with {if}
branching

If the condition is false, the macro works fine: it skips the instructions to the right of the {if} command, reads the instructions on the line below, and enters the label "No". However, if the condition is true, the macro won't perform as its writer seemingly intends: The condition is true, so the macro continues reading instructions on the same line and enters the label "Yes" in the current cell. However, it then continues reading on the next line, and enters the label "No" over the label "Yes" in the current cell. In other words, no matter what the condition is, the end result will be the label "No".

The only way an {if} command can properly perform its "if-then-else" mission is if its writer includes on the same line as the {if} command an instruction to transfer control elsewhere or an instruction that ends the macro. In short, if the instructions that follow the {if} command on the same line are read, they must prevent macro control from reaching the *next* line.

options and
alternatives

Earlier, we told you that {if} commands generally contain conditional expressions that return a zero if false or a one if true. It is actually the numeric values that determine how {if} will affect the macro, not the veracity of the formula. So, the command {if 1} has the same effect as an {if} command with a conditional expression that happens to be true, and {if 0} has the same effect as an {if} command containing a conditional expression that happens to be false.

Further, although you will not uncommonly see the value 1 used in an {if} command to allow the macro to continue reading instructions on the same line, any value other than zero will do the job. So, the values 1, 903, and − .00071 will cause the macro to continue reading instructions on the same line. However, only the value 0 will cause it to skip directly to the next line.

Like other commands that accept expressions, {if} will also accept values supplied by numeric formulas or formulas that reference cells elsewhere on the worksheet, such as {if 10-TEST}.

potential
problem
with the
conditional
formula

If you want a conditional formula in an {if} command to check to see if two cells are identical, you must know in advance whether you plan to test labels, or to test either values or two blank cells. The manner in which you write the testing formula depends on what pairs of entries you expect to test.

For example, if one cell is blank and the other contains a label, the statement {if CELL1 = CELL2} will improperly return a true result. Because the blank cell is valued as zero, 1-2-3 evaluates both entries as values, and since a label is also valued as zero, it finds the expression true. In this case, the formula {if @exact(CELL1;CELL2)} will work properly.

However, @exact is a string function and won't properly process values. If Cell1 and Cell2 contain the same value, or if they are both empty (equal to value zero), the formula {if @exact(CELL1;CELL2)} will improperly return a false result (since @exact can't process values, it returns ERR, and {if} responds to ERR as if it were a false result). Also keep in mind that if you use the @exact function, 1-2-3 will differentiate between upper and lower case letters ({if @exact(@upper(CELL1);@upper(CELL2))} will eliminate such distinctions).

In some instances, you may need to use neither of those tests. If Cell1 contains some entry that you want to compare to Cell2, you can instead place that entry right into the macro. For example, if you know that you want to test to see if Cell2 contains the entry "Y", {if @exact(CELL2;"Y")} will always work—no matter if Cell2 contains a label, a value, or is empty. If you want to make the same entry accept a lower case Y as well as its uppercase counterpart, use

```
{if @exact(@upper(CELL2);"Y")}
```

If you are testing an entry that was stored by a {getlabel} command, you can always use the simpler test {if @upper(ANS) = "Y"} [36]. This test won't fail because {getlabel} will always store something in the target cell (which we've called Ans here). As long as any label entry (even the sole label prefix that 1-2-3 will store if the user merely presses Return or Escape in response to a {getlabel} prompt) is in the tested cell, this simpler test will work.

All of these anomalies have nothing to do with the {if} command. They are instead the result of the manner in which 1-2-3 processes the conditional formula inside the {if} statement. You can see that by entering those formulas directly into cells on the worksheet and testing them. That is, in fact, the best way to test the validity of any conditional formula before you write that statement into a macro.

Release 2.0 versus Release 2.01 and later

1-2-3 Release 2.0 will sometimes process a given {if} statement differently than will later releases of 1-2-3. The {if} command works the same in both releases; the differences arise from the way that the conditional formula (in the {if} command) evaluates references to labels. Let's look at an example that could cause trouble if you run the macro with both Releases of 1-2-3, then rewrite it so that it works on either release.

Suppose you have written a macro that processes a list of labels stored in a column. With each loop of the macro, the cell pointer moves down one row and tests to see if the cell is blank. If it is, the macro terminates; if not, the macro processes the label it contains.

Example: A macro that will work in Release 2.0, but not in Release 2.01.

---

[36] Or use just {if ANS = "y"} if you know your application won't be run with a copy of 1-2-3 installed with the case-sensitive ASCII collating driver.

```
            A       B        C       D       E       F       G       H
      1  NAME     MACRO                                      COMMENT
      2  ------------------------------------------------------    --
      3  \A       /rncTEST~~
      4           {if TEST=0}{branch STOP}
      5           [...do some processing on Test...]
      6           /rndTEST~
      7           {d}
      8           {branch \A}
      9
     10
```

Figure 13-19

The key in this application is the manner in which the conditional formula tests for the presence/absence of a label each time it moves down another cell. The conditional formula shown above (in the {if} command) works fine in Release 2.0, because labels do not evaluate to zero. The routine continues to loop until the macro encounters a blank cell at the bottom of the list (or a cell containing a zero). However, in Release 2.01 and later, references to labels do evaluate to zero, so the preceding routine would stop upon encountering the first label.

What you need is a routine that works equally well in either Release 2.0 or later releases. Here is one such routine:

```
{if @cell("type";TEST)="b"}{branch STOP}
```

Actually, if you are moving the cell pointer through the list one cell at a time, you can omit the naming of the current cell to identify it as the cell to be tested; just use the @cellpointer function:

```
{if @cellpointer("type")="b"}{branch STOP}
```

{if} versus /xi

Although the formats you use to write {if} and /xi differ, there are no functional differences between the two commands.

```
            A       B        C       D       E       F       G       H
      1  NAME     MACRO                                      COMMENT
      2  ------------------------------------------------------------
      3  CHOICE   {get ANS}                                  Capture user's keystroke
      4           {let ANS;@upper(ANS)}                      Capitalize it
      5           {if ANS="Y"}{branch YES}                   If it's "Y", run Yes
      6           {branch NO}                                Otherwise, run No
      7
      8
      9
     10
```

Figure 13-20

{ Ifkey }

Purpose: Use {ifkey} to see if a given keyname is currently valid.

Format: {ifkey [keyname]}
Where [keyname] is the name of a 1-2-3 keystroke without the curly braces. [keyname] may be a string, a formula, a cell address, a range name describing a single cell, or in Release 2.2, a formula.

Sample: {ifkey APP4}

Complements: None

See also: {if}, {app}

Description: {Ifkey} checks to see if a key name (not an advanced macro command keyword) is currently valid. This command is useful if you're writing macros that use one or more 1-2-3 add-in programs and you wish to know if one of the add-in command keys is currently active.

testing add-in keys

Depending on how you've configured 1-2-3 Release 2 or 2.01 with the Add-in Manager program and add-ins, each of the Alt-F7 through Alt-F10 keys ({app1} through {app4}) are either active or not. If the Add-in Manager program was loaded with 1-2-3, the Alt-F10 key will be active; if an add-in has been attached to the Alt-F7, Alt-F8, or Alt-F9 keys, the key it was attached to will also be active. In Release 2.2, the Add-In Manager is part of 1-2-3 itself, and even without an add-in attached, the Alt-F10 key ({app4}) is always valid. Without an add-in attached to it, it calls up the same add-in manager menu you see after selecting / Add-In. Accordingly, if through a macro you'll want to test whether an add-in is attached to 1-2-3 or not, make a habit of attaching add-ins to the Alt-F7, Alt-F8, and Alt-F9 keys before using the Alt-F10 key. Since the Alt-F10 key is always valid, you can't as easily tell whether an add-in has been attached to it or not.

If any of these keys are inactive at the time the macro tries to read the particular key name that represents them ({app1}, {app2}, {app3}, or {app4}), 1-2-3 will sound a beep, just as it will when a macro tries to read any other keytroke that it doesn't recognize. When 1-2-3 reads a key name for an inactive Alt-function key, it treats it the same way it would if it read the keystrokes /B in a macro. The slash would invoke 1-2-3's command menu, but since that menu contains no choice beginning with a "B", 1-2-3 would simply beep.

Note that 1-2-3 will go into Error mode, so you can't handle such a problem with the {onerror} command. You must test for it first with {ifkey}.

testing 1-2-3 releases

Another use for {ifkey} is to assess whether the macro is being run with a copy of Release 2.2 or not. Use {ifkey help} to see if the key name {help} is valid. It is in Release 2.2, but not in Release 2 or 2.01.

{Ifkey} uses an unusual format: it evaluates only the word used within the braces of a key name. Suppose you wish to know if the Alt-F10 function key is active. The macro key name for Alt-F10 is {app4}, so your {ifkey} command should test only the string "app4": {ifkey APP4}.

Like {if} and the file manipulation commands, {ifkey} redirects control of the macro if the expression it contains is false (or otherwise evaluates to zero), but allows it to read in normal fashion if the expression is true (or otherwise evaluates to any nonzero number).

if-then-else construct

Typically, to the right of an {ifkey} command, you should write a macro instruction that will either direct control elsewhere or end the macro. If you do not, 1-2-3 will continue reading in normal fashion and read the instructions on the next line. In most cases, you will have placed commands on the next line that you only want read if the {ifkey} command evaluates to false, as in the example below.

Such a design is commonly referred to as an "if-then-else" construct because *if* the condition in {ifkey} is true, *then* the macro does one thing; *else* (if the condition is false), the macro does something else. (More discussion on designing "if-then-else" constructs appears in the listing for the {if} command under the topic "potential problems.")

Example:

	A	B	C	D	E	F	G	H
1	NAME	MACRO				COMMENT		
2	------	-------	-----	-----	-----	-------	-----	----
3	\A	{ifkey app4}{branch RUN}				If AddIn Mgr loaded, use it		
4		{let MSG1;"Add-in Mgr Not Loaded"}				Else, create message		
5		{let MSG2;"Press a key to continue"}						
6		{goto}MSG_SCRN~{get KEY}				Show message and pause		
7		{branch CONTINUE}				Continue processing...		
8								
9	KEY					Store keystroke		
10								
11	RUN	{app4}a4WORD~na				Attach word processor		
12		i4WORD~				Invoke WP		
13								
14								
15								

Figure 13-21

{ Onerror }

Purpose: Use {onerror} to specify a macro routine to be run in the event the macro encounters an error.

Format: {onerror [routine];[message]}
Where [routine] is a cell address, a range address, a range name, or in Release 2.2, a formula evaluating to the name of a macro routine; and where [message] is an optional cell address, a range address, a range name, or in Release 2.2, a formula evaluating to a location in which to store 1-2-3's error message.

Sample: {onerror RECOVER}

Complements: None

See also: {return}, {branch}, {}

Description: {Onerror} enables a macro to recover gracefully from many errors that would otherwise cause it to terminate in Error mode. Such errors include "Printer error," "File does not exist," and "Disk drive not ready." {Onerror} cannot trap macro syntax errors (see "untrappable errors," below).

The first argument supplies a location to which macro control will branch in the event of an error. The optional second argument designates a location in which to store 1-2-3's error message.

If you use the second argument, next you'll probably want to do one of two things, or both. You can include an instruction to display the designated location, to inform the user of the nature of the error, and to enable him to do something to correct it. You might also have the macro test the contents of that location, perform a table lookup on a table of error messages, and use the result to determine the proper error-handling routine to run. 1-2-3's on-line help contains a list of error messages upon which you can base such a table (see "writing the routine the error branches to", below).

{Onerror} not only prevents 1-2-3 from terminating macro control when one of the errors it can trap occurs, it suppresses 1-2-3's normal display of the error message at the bottom of the screen and the beep that normally accompanies such errors.

Consequently, you may wish to display the error message on the worksheet and use the {beep} command to alert the user of the problem before initiating corrective action.

untrappable
errors

{Onerror} cannot trap errors resulting from incorrectly written advanced macro commands. As long as you spell the macro command properly, if you otherwise incorrectly write an advanced macro command, you'll get an error message at the bottom of the screen that begins with "Macro:". For example, if you wrote a {branch} command in cell B3 and included in it an invalid named range, you'd get the error message "Macro: Invalid range in BRANCH (B3)". Other such errors include referencing a blank cell in a {dispatch} command and calling a nonexistent subroutine.

{Onerror} also can't trap errors arising from misspelled advanced macro commands or key names. For example, if you misspell the key name {goto} as {go to}, {onerror} can't trap the resulting error.

longevity

Once invoked, {onerror} remains in effect until the macro encounters an error and executes the {onerror} command's instructions, until another {onerror} command supercedes it, or until macro control ends. Each time 1-2-3 reads a new {onerror} command, 1-2-3 cancels the old {onerror} command's instructions and stores the new command's instructions.

effect on the
subroutine
chain

When 1-2-3 encounters an error and branches according to the instructions in the last {onerror} command, the subroutine chain is completely canceled, no matter how many levels of subroutines that chain may have contained. If the macro subsequently reads a {return} command, macro control will end—just as it will any time the macro reads a {return} when the subroutine chain is empty.

writing the
routine the
error
branches to

The routine you designate in the {onerror} command—the one the macro will branch to in the event of an error—should help you to correct the source of the trouble.

Such macros can either show the user the error message and expect the user to figure out the problem, or the macro can test for any of several likely error messages and specifically instruct the user how to correct the problem.

There are, however, too many error messages to test for them all, all the time. Instead, try to anticipate the kind of error that may occur given the current context (remember, you can issue a new {onerror} command with a different set of branching instructions at any point you deem appropriate). For example, a print macro might well encounter a "No print range specified" or "No printer driver loaded" error, but a file-save macro would not. A file save operation is more likely to be interrupted by a "Disk full" or "Invalid character in file name" error.

how much
is enough?

There is no single correct level of error trapping. You will have to decide how much error trapping is appropriate given the composition of the application's users, the sensitivity of the application to errors, and the time you have available to write the application.

```
         A        B          C       D       E       F       G          H
    1  NAME     MACRO                                          COMMENT
    2  ------------------------------------------------------------------
    3  PRINT    {onerror ERR1;ANS}                             Setup error trap
    4           /ppagpq                                        Print
    5           {return}                                       Return to caller
    6
    7  ANS                                                     Store Err message
    8
    9  ERR1     {if @mid(ANS;11;6)="driver"}{branch NO_DRV}    No Drvr, No Printer,
   10           {if @mid(ANS;0;7)="Printer"}{branch NO_PRN}   and No Print-Range
   11           {if @mid(ANS;9;5)="range"}{branch NO_RNG}     errors
   12
   13
   14
   15
```

Figure 13-22

{ Quit }

Purpose: Use { quit } to force the macro to stop.

Format: { quit }

Sample: { quit }

Complements: None

See also: { return }, { forbreak }, { restart }, { ? }

Release 1A Equivalent: /xq

Release 1A Format: /xq

Description: { Quit } stops the processing of the current macro and returns control of 1-2-3 to the keyboard. { Quit } returns control to the keyboard unconditionally—the macro won't resume control unless you re-activate it from the keyboard.

versus other ways of ending a macro

Because { quit } provides an explicit terminator to a macro, it eliminates the need to place a blank row between different macros. It's advisable to use the { quit } command wherever you want to end a macro. You can end the macro by leaving a blank cell below the last command of that macro, but if you later inadvertently enter a label there, the macro will read that label—whether or not it was intended as part of the macro.

{ Quit } supercedes any other conditional transfers in control, which may be in effect at the time. For example, if a macro reads the { quit } command in a subroutine, control won't return to the calling routine, the macro will end. { Quit } will return control only to the keyboard.

compared
to other
commands
that return
control
elsewhere

{ Quit } differs from a number of commands that cause conditional changes in control. For example, { ? } temporarily suspends macro processing and returns control to the keyboard—but only until the user presses the Return key—at which time the macro resumes control. { Return } returns control to the last calling routine. { Restart } clears the subroutine chain and allows the current routine to continue without any relationship to a higher level routine. { Forbreak } will interrupt a { for } loop and return control to the command directly following the { for } command in the macro.

when
{ return }
acts like
{ quit }

Under certain circumstances, { return } has the same effect as { quit }. If there is at least one level of subroutine in the subroutine chain, { return } will return control to the calling routine. However, if the subroutine chain is empty, { return } will return control to the keyboard, just as the { quit } command does.

{ quit }
versus /xq

{ Quit } and /xq work identically.

{ Restart }

Purpose: Use { restart } to prevent a subroutine from returning to the main routine when it's finished.

Format: { restart }

Sample: { restart }

Complements: None

See also: { }, { forbreak }, { return }, { quit }

nesting
limits

{ Restart } clears the subroutine nesting chain, thereby severing the relationship between a subroutine and its calling routine.

Each time a macro makes a subroutine call, 1-2-3 remembers where that call came from so as to return control to that location when the subroutine ends.

You can also call subroutines within subroutines. Each time you do, 1-2-3 adds the location of the latest subroutine call to the list of places it must remember. Collectively, that list of locations to which 1-2-3 must return control is known as the subroutine stack or the subroutine nesting chain.

Each time a macro calls a subroutine, the number of subroutines in the nesting chain increases by one. Each time a subroutine returns control to the calling routine, that chain decreases by one. { Restart } returns the nesting chain to level zero; that is, at the time that 1-2-3 reads the {restart} command in a macro, it immediately releases any nested subroutine calls. Consequently, {restart} converts any subroutine that contains it into a normal routine: control will not return to any calling routine when the subroutine ends.

other kinds
of
subroutines

{ } is not the only command that can call a subroutine. {Menucall} (but not {menubranch}) and {for} also call subroutines, and {restart} will also cancel the subroutine nesting chain invoked by any of these commands.

Example:

```
        A          B          C        D        E        F        G        H
1   NAME       MACRO                                  COMMENT
2   --------------------------------------------------------
3   \A         {getnumber "Enter value: ";ENTRY}      Prompt for entry
4              {TEST 100}                             Test entry
5              +ENTRY{calc}~                          Put entry on sheet
6              {d}                                    Move down one
7              {branch \A}                            Repeat macro
8
9   TEST       {define LIMIT:v}                       Store param. as value
10             {if ENTRY>LIMIT}{branch ERROR}         Perform test
11             {return}                               Return to caller
12
13  ERROR      {goto}ERRORMSG1~                       Explain problem
14             {wait @now+@time(0;0;20)}              Pause 20 seconds
15             {restart}                              Clear subrt stack
16             {goto}DATA_SCRN~                       Restore display
17             {branch \A}                            Begin again
18
19  ENTRY                                             Store entry
20  LIMIT                                             Store limit parameter
```

Figure 13-23

In the above example, the main routine prompts the user for an entry, and then the subroutine named Test checks it. If the entry is within bounds, the subroutine immediately returns control to the main routine. The main routine places an entry in the current cell on the worksheet, and prompts for the next entry.

However, if the entry is out of bounds the subroutine branches to a routine called Error. Even though subroutine Test has transferred control to Error, 1-2-3 still regards the entire operation as a subroutine initiated by line two of the macro \A. If the macro encounters a {return} command or a blank cell, control will immediately return to the command directly following the subroutine call in line 2 of macro \A.

When an error occurs, the routine called Error first displays an error message, waits for 20 seconds, and then executes the {restart} command. {Restart} resets the subroutine chain to zero, severing the current routine's relationship with the main routine. That means that the current routine no longer acts as a subroutine. Once 1-2-3 has read the {restart} command, if the routine were to end, control would no longer automatically return to the second line of the macro named \A.

With the subroutine link severed, the second to last line of the Error routine restores the data-entry screen and the last line of the transfers control to the beginning of the macro \A to prompt the user for another entry.

{Return}

Purpose: Use {return} to return control from a subroutine to the command following the one that called it.

Format: {return}

Sample: {return}

Complements: { }, {menucall}, or {for}

See also: {restart}, {forbreak}

Description: When a subroutine encounters a {return} command, control returns to the command directly following the one that called that subroutine, and the subroutine chain is decremented by one. (Refer to the { } entry for an explanation of the subroutine chain.)

If a macro reads a {return} command when the subroutine chain is empty, {return} will return control to the keyboard; the macro will end just as if a {quit} command had been read.

{Return} always returns control to the command directly following the most recent subroutine call, no matter if it was called by a { }, {menucall}, or {for} command. If the subroutine chain is three levels deep, the first {return} command will return control to the third calling routine. The next {return} will return control to the second calling routine. The final {return} will return control to the first calling routine. If the macro encounters another {return} command before another subroutine has been called, macro control will end immediately.

If a subroutine doesn't contain any explicit terminator such as a {quit} or {restart} command, when the macro reads the last line of that subroutine it performs an implicit {return}. That is, the subroutine returns control to the routine that called it. However, we recommend that you do end a subroutine with an explicit {return} command. Doing so makes the flow of control that much easier to read and, should you ever inad-

vertently place a label in the cell directly below the last line of the subroutine, it would have no affect on the macro.

Example:

	A	B	C	D	E	F	G	H
1	NAME	MACRO				COMMENT		
2	------	---						
3	\A	{WIDE}				Call subroutine		
4		{branch PRINT}				Branch to print		
5								
6	WIDE	/wcs35~				Widen column		
7		{r}				Move right one cell		
8		{return}				Return to caller		
9								
10								

Figure 13-24

{ System }

Purpose: Use {system} to suspend the worksheet session, exit to
DOS, and run some DOS program or batch file from DOS, and
return to the worksheet.

Format: {system "program"} where "program" is the name of a
DOS program, command, or batch file that can be run from the current directory, or a range name, cell address, or formula that evaluates
to such a name. The string that makes up "program" can also include
any parameters for that command, such as a file you wish to load with
that program (refer to Sample, below).

Sample: {system "dbase payables"}

Complements: None

Compatibility: Release 2.2 and 3

Description: The {system} command temporarily sets aside the
worksheet session, loads DOS, and loads any other program for
which sufficient memory remains. When the program, batch file, or
DOS command you've initiated finishes, if it fails to pass control to
some other process, the worksheet returns and control returns to the
command following {system}.

versus /
System

The {system} command differs from selecting / System from the
1-2-3 menu in that the latter merely loads DOS and presents the DOS
prompt, whereas the former passes control to some DOS-based pro-

gram, batch file, or command. If that program, batch file, or command is unavailable to accept control, if there is insuffecent memory available for it to run, or if it finishes running control returns 1-2-3 and the calling macro.

When you complete a DOS session that you invoked via the / System command, you must enter the command Exit to return to 1-2-3. If you use the {system} macro command, control returns to 1-2-3 and to the calling macro automatically as soon as the last called procedure finishes. So if you use {system} to run a batch file that contains three commands, as soon as those three commands have been carried out, control will automatically return to 1-2-3 and the calling macro. The exception would occur when the called batch file ends with a command to run yet another batch file. In that case, control passes to the second batch file and when the commands it contains have been executed, control automatically returns to 1-2-3.

uses

You can use {system} to dramatically extend the scope of your macros. With sufficient memory in your computer, your macro applications can now include dBase programs, sophisticated batch files, BASIC, PASCAL, and C programs. You might, for example, call dBase, run a dBase accounting program, save one of your accounting database files in comma delimited format, return to 1-2-3, use the / File Import Numbers command to import it onto the worksheet, and have the macro analyze the file.

You can also call a program that you intend to use interactively, such as a word processor. Memory will be the prime constraint you'll face in deciding which applications you can run in this mode. With a sufficient amount of extended memory, Release 3 will let you run almost anything. Release 2.2 is bound by the amount of conventional memory your computer has (up to 640K) minus what's needed for DOS, 1-2-3, and the worksheet in memory when you invoked {system}. If memory is an active constraint, try reducing to a minimum the size of the worksheet before invoking {system}.

Used in combination with the file manipulation commands, you can have the macro write the commands it needs into a DOS batch file, temporarily pass control to DOS and run the batch file, then return to macro control in 1-2-3.

writing the command

The {system} command requires an argument. You might use the command to call a DOS batch file named trans.bat ({system "trans"}) or run a dBase program named Payables.prg ({system "dbase payables"}).

In most cases the command will work with arguments that are not enclosed in quotation marks. However, you cannot outside of quotation marks specify a drive name, and using quotation marks keeps the command from conflicting with new or existing range names. If a range name exists that duplicates the name of the program specified in a {system} command, 1-2-3 will treat the name of the program as a reference to that range. Enclosing the argument in quotation marks prevents that possibility. Conversely, when you use a range name as an argument and store in that range a label supplying the name of a program you wish to run, you should not enclose that range name in quotation marks in the {system} command.

If you do use quotation marks, enclose within them the entire string beginning with the first word following the word system. So if you use a drive name, file name, and file extension as an argument, enclose the entire string within one pair of quotation marks.

Note that the program or batch file must reside somewhere from which you can run it. When you use the {system} command, it loads DOS and logs onto the same directory from which 1-2-3 was loaded. Neither the Global Default Directory nor the File Directory settings have any effect on the directory used by {system}.

If a program you want to run is in some directory other than the directory from which you loaded 1-2-3, you have several choices.

- Providing you are using a version of DOS that supports this feature, you can specify the program's subdirectory path in front of the program name, including, if you wish, the drive name. Remember in that case that you must enclose the entire argument in quotation marks.

finding the
program
you want to
run

- You might also decide to write a batch file to do that work and have the {system} command pass control to the batch file. In that case, the batch file would call the application or batch file in question. For example, if you use the macro command {system run}, a batch file named Run.bat stored in the current data directory might contain the following commands to change directories and run your word processor: cd \wp wp You don't need to supply the DOS command Exit at the end of such a batch file. As soon as its executed the last command in the file, it'll perform an implicit Exit and return control to 1-2-3 and the calling macro.

- In DOS, you can use the Path command to specify the location of any programs you want to run. Once you have registered those locations with the Path command, you can run those programs, without specifying their location, from any directory you might be logged to. Be cautious, though, of using a Path command to reset a path you already have set. If you overwrite settings you'd already specified for other purposes, you may later find you can't run other programs that depended on the first path setting. It's better to add the new path specification(s) to the ones you've already established. This is most commonly done from within an Autoexec.bat file, which is the batch file DOS will read automatically when you start or reboot your computer.

batch file tip

When you use the {system} command, when a called batch file ends, control automatically returns to 1-2-3. However, that doesn't mean you can't transfer control to other batch files or programs, first. You can exercise some of the same control over the program's flow that you can with macros inside 1-2-3. DOS's batch file language contains commands to let you test for the existence of a file (If Exist) or of an error level (If Errorlevel), and to branch to another location in the batch file (Goto). Should you use any of these commands, you might want one of your branches to contain an explicit return to 1-2-3. In that case, simply include the command Exit at that point in the batch file. The batch file will immediately terminate and return control to 1-2-3 and the calling macro. For more information about DOS's batch file language, refer to your DOS manual or to a text on using DOS.

Example:

```
        A         B           C       D       E       F       G       H
1   NAME      MACRO                                   COMMENT
2   ----------------------------------------------------------
3   FORMAT    {system "format a:"}                    Format disk in A:
4             {branch MAIN}
5
6   BACK      {system "backup c:\wk1\*.* a: /s/m"} Backup files to A:
7             {branch MAIN}
```

Figure 13-25

14

Manipulating Data

Overview and Introduction to New Concepts

scope of operation

The commands in this chapter enable macros to manipulate data on the worksheet. The commands fall into three groups: those that enter data into cells ({contents}, {let}, and {put}); those that erase data from cells ({blank}); and those that recalculate portions of the worksheet ({recalc}, {recalccol}).

entering data into cells

{Contents}, {let}, and {put} differ in the way in which they enter data onto the worksheet:

- {Let} is the most commonly used of the three; it transfers a value or label into any cell you designate.

- {Contents} translates a formatted value into a label and enters it into any cell you designate. Numbers may be assigned any of 1-2-3's cell formats.

- {Put} enables you to build a table of values or labels or insert data into an existing table.

erasing data

- {Blank} erases data from a single cell or a range of cells.

275

recalcu-
lating
ranges

{Recalc} and {recalccol} both selectively recalculate ranges on the worksheet during a macro, but do so in a different manner:

- {Recalc} selectively recalculates ranges on the worksheet in a row wise manner.

- {Recalccol} selectively recalculates ranges in a columnwise fashion.

{Blank}

Purpose: Use {blank} to erase a range on the worksheet.

Format: {blank [range]}
Where [range] is a cell address, a range address, a range name, or in Release 2.2, a formula.

Sample: {blank FORM1}

Complements: None.

Description: Like the / Range Erase command, {blank} erases a designated range on the worksheet. {Blank} differs from Range Erase in three ways:

- When a macro reads the / Range Erase command, 1-2-3 will keystroke through that command sequence and the menus on which each of the two commands reside will briefly appear in the control panel (the faster the computer on which you are running 1-2-3, the less noticeable that effect will be).

- The / Range Erase command must be invoked from Ready mode. The {blank} is much more flexible; it can be invoked in the middle of a menu, a formula, and so on.

- The / Range Erase command will immediately update the screen, whereas the {blank} command won't. If you want 1-2-3 to update the screen immediately after reading a {blank} command, place a tilde directly after {blank} in the macro. Otherwise, 1-2-3 will wait to update the screen until after the macro ends and you move the cell pointer or press Return, or until some other command forces a screen update.

advantage
in release
2.2

Because in Release 2.2 { blank } accepts a formula as an argument, you can easily write a macro to erase the current cell, wherever that may be: { blank @cellpointer("address") }. In earlier releases, you'd have to write an entire routine to do the same work . . .

```
        A       B       C       D       E       F       G       H
1   NAME    MACRO                                   COMMENT
2   --------------------------------------------------------------
3   \A      /rncHERE~~
4           /rndHERE~/rncHERE~~                     Name current cell
5           {blank HERE}                            Erase current cell
6           /rndHERE~                               Delete name
7
```

Figure 14-1

. . . or you'd have to write a string formula: +" { blank"& @cellpointer("address")&" } "

Example:

```
        A       B       C       D       E       F       G       H
1   NAME    MACRO                                   COMMENT
2   ------------------------------------------------------
3   \A      {blank FORM}                            Erase data entry form
4           {branch ENTRY}                          Begin data entry
5
```

Figure 14-2

{ Contents }

Purpose: Use { contents } to place a formatted number into a cell as a label.

Format: { contents [destination];[source];[width];[format] }
Where [destination] is a cell in which to store the label entry produced by the command; [source] is a cell from which to copy the appearance of an entry, [width] is the length of the resulting label; and [format] is a code representing the range format to impose on the resulting label if the source data is a value. [Width] and [format] are optional arguments. While you can specify [width] and not [format], you cannot specify [format] without specifying [width].

Each of [destination] and [source] may be a cell address, a range address, a range name, or in Release 2.2, a formula. Each of [width] and [format] may be a number, a formula, a cell address, or a range name describing a single cell.

Sample: { contents DEST1;SOURCE1;12;78 }

Complements: None

See also: { let }, { put }

Description: { Contents } copies the appearance of a given source cell and places that copy into a given destination cell as a label. You can modify copy appearance of the original cell by specifying a width other than that of the source cell and, if the source cell contains a value, you may also specify a different format. When the source cell contains a value, { contents } mimics the appearance of any of 1-2-3's Range Formats as part of the label it enters into the destination cell. If you specify no format code in the { contents } command, it will imitate the format display of the source cell.

{ Contents } always produces a left aligned label entry in the destination cell. If the entry in the source cell is a value, the { contents } command will convert it to a label. If the entry in the source cell is a label, only the portion of the label that displays within the current column will be copied to the destination cell; portions of the label that overwrite adjoining cells won't be copied to the destination cell. Therefore, if you want to copy the entire label, adjust the width of the column containing the source cell so that it accommodates the entire label to be copied.

result is truncated or consists of asterisks

If you specify a width smaller than that needed to accommodate a source value, 1-2-3 will display asterisks in the destination cell, just as it would anytime a cell width prevents a value from fully displaying. If you specify a width smaller than that needed to accommodate a source label, 1-2-3 will truncate the label it enters into the destination cell, leaving off characters farthest to the right in the original entry. Both these strictures apply even if you don't opt to format the resulting entry, but the width of the destination cell itself is inadequate to display within its limits the appearance of the original cell.

The foregoing problem affects labels in a curious way. If the destination is insufficiently wide, 1-2-3 will truncate the label to fit the cell and will not write over the cell to the right, even if that cell is empty. To copy a label with the { contents } command in this case, you must specify a width large enough to accommodate the whole label. Only then will 1-2-3 let the label write over the cell directly to the right of the destination cell.

Although the label in the destination cell will be left aligned, { contents } may pad it with blank spaces to make it appear as it did in the source cell. Therefore, suppose the source cell is 15 spaces wide and contains the centered label Hello. If you use the { contents } command to copy it to a destination cell, the destination cell will contain a left aligned label consisting of 5 blank spaces, the string Hello, and five more blank spaces. The actual width of the destination cell is irrelevant. If the source cell was still 15 spaces wide but the label it contained was right aligned, the label in the destination cell would consist of the string Hello followed by ten blank spaces.

create +/-
graphs

If, in the {contents} command, you specify the width of the resulting label, that label will assume the designated length, regardless of the width of the source cell. Designating a length for the destination label is useful for reducing the length of the destination label compared with the width of the source cell. It is also useful for generating cell displays that are wider than any cell on the worksheet. One application for which you might use that is to create +/− graphs on the worksheet. To do so, you'd specify the code for +/− format, 112.

Since values are right aligned on the worksheet, when {contents} reproduces a value as a label, it will display it one space to the left of the right border of that label.

If the source cell is empty, {contents} will enter an apostrophe label-prefix in the destination cell.

If the source cell is a label and you have supplied a format argument, 1-2-3 will ignore that format argument.

for changing a value entry into a label entry

If you want to convert a value entry into a label entry, you can make both the destination and source ranges the same. When you execute the {contents} command, the macro will change the entry in the source cell into a label with the designated formatting.

versus
{let}

At first glance, {contents} appears similar to the {let} command. However, the two commands differ in a number of ways. {Contents} always deposits a label in the destination cell, whereas {let} can deposit a label or a value. The source designated in the {contents} command must be a cell address, except in Release 2.2, where it may also be a formula that evaluates to a cell address. Unlike the {let} command, {contents} will not accept a value, string, or formula as a direct argument.

common
syntax error

The most common error made when writing the {contents} command is to transpose the destination and source arguments. Contrary to the order most people naturally assume, the destination argument must appear first, the source argument second.

format
codes

Use the following table to select the value you should use as the last argument of the {contents} command to produce the corresponding format.

0-15	Fixed, 0-15 decimal places
16-31	Scientific, 0-15 decimal places
32-47	Currency, 0-15 decimal places

48-63	Percent, 0-15 decimal places
64-79	Comma, 0-15 decimal places
112	+/−
113	General
114	DD-MM-YY (D1)
115	DD-MMM (D2)
116	MMM-YY (D3)
117	Literal
118	Hidden
119	HH:MM:SS AM/PM (T1)
120	HH:MM AM/PM (T2)
121	MM/DD/YY Full international date (D4)
122	MM/DD Partial international date (D5)
123	HH:MM:SS Full international time (T3)
124	HH:MM Partial international time (T4)
125	General
127	Current Worksheet Global format

format code notes

Format codes 113 and 125 both produce general format. Use either.

Format code 118 (for Hidden format) produces a label in the destination range consisting entirely of blank spaces.

optional date and time formats

Date format code 121 (full international date) defaults to MM/DD/YY. However, you can reconfigure 1-2-3 with the /Worksheet Global Default Other International Date command to display it differently. If you do, the {contents} command will respond to this code with either DD/MM/YY, DD.MM.YY, or YY-MM-DD, depending on how you have reconfigured it.

Date format code 122 (partial international date) defaults to MM/DD. Reconfigured, it can display as DD/MM, DD.MM, or MM-DD.

Time format code 123 (full international time) defaults to HH:MM:SS. Reconfigured, it can display as HH.MM.SS, HH,MM,SS, or HHhMMmSSs.

Time format code 124 (partial international time) defaults to HH:MM. Reconfigured, it can display as HH.MM, HH,MM, or HHhMMm.

Example:

```
        A        B        C        D        E        F        G        H
1  NAME     MACRO                                  COMMENT
2  ------------------------------------------------------------
3  DATE     {let TODAY;@now}                       Enter date serial no.
4           {contents DATE1;TODAY;10;114}~         Date stamp the sheet
5           {quit}                                 End of macro
```

Figure 14-3

A macro for Release 2.2 that enters today's date as a string in the current cell:

```
        A        B        C        D        E        F        G        H
1  NAME     MACRO                                  COMMENT
2  ------------------------------------------------------------
3  DATE     {let @cellpointer("address");@now}  Enter date
4           {contents @cellpointer("address");@cellpointer("address");10;114}
5           {quit}                                 End of macro
```

Figure 14-4

{ Let }

Purpose: Use {let} to place the value of a cell or expression into another cell.

Format: { let [destination];[value] }
Where [destination] is the cell in which to store data and [value] is the data to be placed in the cell. [destination] may be a cell address, a range address, a range name, or in Release 2.2, a formula. [value] may be a string, a number, a formula, a cell address, or a range name describing a single cell.

Sample: { let DATE;@now }

Complements: None

See also: { contents }, { put }

Description: Use {let} to store data in a cell. The data that {let} places in the destination cell may be either a value or a label.

{ Let } will accept either a source range or a source expression. The expression may consist of a string, a value, or a formula. If the source expression contains a formula, { let } will evaluate it and enter the result as a simple value in the destination cell.

potential problem with using {let}

{Let} will not force the worksheet to recalculate before evaluating a formula contained in the source expression. As a result, you must exercise caution in order to avoid obtaining invalid results with {let}. Consider the following macro.

Example:

	A	B	C	D	E	F	G	H
1	NAME	MACRO				COMMENT		
2	--							
3	\A	{let CELL1;CELL1*2}				Double Cell1		
4		{let DEST;CELL2}				Make Dest = Cell2		
5		~				Recalculate		
6								
7								

Figure 14-5

Let's assume that the range named Cell1 contains the value 1 and Cell2 contains a simple reference to Cell1: +CELL1.

This macro doubles the value in Cell1, then assigns to Dest the value of Cell2, which is derived from a cell reference to Cell1. It would appear that when the macro finishes, the value in Dest should equal the value in Cell1. However, that is not the case. The value in Dest will be the original value of Cell1, not its doubled value.

You might lay the blame for this problem on the worksheet having been in manual recalculation mode, but that isn't the cause. The result will be the same whether the worksheet is in manual or automatic recalculation mode. However, if you reached that conclusion, you are on the right track. Lack of recalculation is at fault.

The problem is not that the first {let} command didn't assign a new value to Cell1. It did. The problem is that the formula, a cell reference, in Cell2 didn't recalculate to retrieve that new value from Cell1.

There are two solutions to the problem. The first solution is to force the worksheet to recalculate the cell reference in Cell2, thereby ensuring that when the second {let} command assigns the value of Cell2 to Dest, that Cell2 will contain the most recent value in Cell1. The simplest way to do that is to include a tilde directly after the first {let} command, on row 3.

Example:

	A	B	C	D	E	F	G	H
1	NAME	MACRO				COMMENT		
2	--							
3	\A	{let CELL1;CELL1*2}~				Double Cell1		
4		{let DEST;CELL2}				Make Dest = Cell2		
5		~				Recalculate		
6								
7								

Figure 14-6

The second solution is to forego altogether the cell reference as a way of transferring data into Cell2, and use instead another {let} command to do the job. Using this approach, you no longer need the tilde on row 3, because this approach isn't dependent on the worksheet recalculating. The tilde on row 6 remains to force the screen to update, but you can instead do that by pressing Return or moving the cell pointer after the macro ends.

Example:

	A	B	C	D	E	F	G	H
1	NAME	MACRO				COMMENT		
2	--							
3	\A	{let CELL1;CELL1*2}				Double Cell1		
4		{let CELL2;CELL1}				Make Dest = Cell2		
5		{let DEST;CELL2}				Make Dest = Cell2		
6		~				Update screen		
7								

Figure 14-7

effect of multi-celled ranges as arguments

If you use a multiple cell range as the destination in a {let} command, 1-2-3 will enter the data into the top left cell in that range. If you use a multiple cell range as the source, 1-2-3 will treat the range identifier (be it cell addresses or a range name) as a string.

using numeric and string expressions in {let}

{Let} will accept expressions and store the result of such expressions in a cell. The statement {let TOTAL;4+5} enters the value 9 in the cell named Total. The statement {let GREETING;"Hi "&"John!"} produces the label Hi John! in a cell (although, most often you'd use a reference to another cell to supply at least part of each expression).

modifying existing entries

One of the most common ways to use {let} is to modify an existing entry—perhaps to increment a value or to add to an existing string. For example, if the cell named Counter contains the value 5, then {let COUNTER;COUNTER+1} will change that to 6. If the cell named Name contained the label John, then {let NAME1;+NAME1&"Jones"} will change that to John Jones. [37]

Example:

	A	B	C	D	E	F	G	H
1	NAME	MACRO				COMMENT		
2	--							
3	DATE	{let TODAY;@now}				Enter date serial no.		
4		{contents DATE1;TODAY;10;114}~				Date stamp the sheet		
5		{quit}				End of macro		

Figure 14-8

[37] Note that in the preceding {let} statement, the range name Name1 is the only such name that has a numeric suffix. The range names Counter, Greeting, and Total stand alone. The reason is that {Name} is a key name (for the F3 function key), and no range name should duplicate a key name. For more information, refer to the discussion of allowable range names near the beginning of chapter 10.

If you are using a macro library to store a proprietary macro, be aware that, using the {let} command, someone else may view the first line of that macro, and any other line to which you assigned a range name, even if you have password protected the macro library containing that formula. Suppose you have stored a macro, the first line of which you named \A, in a password protected macro library. If you enter on the worksheet the macro {let A1;\A} and run it, cell A1 will contain a copy of the contents of the macro code stored in the macro library cell named \A.

{Put}

Purpose: Use {put} to enter a value or string into a table on the worksheet.

Format: {put [destination];[col_offset];[row_offset];[value]}
Where [destination] is the range that contains the cell in which to store data; [col_offset] describes how many columns the cell is from the left extent of the range; [row_offset] describes how many rows the cell is from the top of the range; [value] is the data to be placed in the cell.
[Destination] may be a cell address, a range address, a range name, or in Release 2.2, a formula. Each of [col_offset] and [row_offset] may be a number, a formula, a cell address, or a range name describing a single cell. [Value] may be a string, a number, a formula, a cell address, or a range name describing a single cell.

Sample: {put TABLE1;1;1;@sum(SALES_APR)}

Complements: None

See also: {let}, {contents}

Description: {Put} enables you to build tables or modify them.
Using the row and column position of any cell within a given range, {put} enables you to enter data into that cell. That entry can be a label or value produced by a string, a value, a formula, or a reference to any cell on the worksheet.

The {put} command consists of four arguments, beginning with the table range into which you want to place the entry. The next two arguments consist of values that identify the row offset and the column offset of the destination cell. To calculate the row offset, beginning with zero, count the number of rows from the top of the table range to the row in which the destination cell resides. To calculate the column offset, beginning with zero, count the number of columns from the left side of the table to the column containing the destination cell. The final argument supplies the source data.

To provide more detail, let's develop an example. Suppose your table looks like the one below:

sample
worksheet
containing
a table
to post

Figure 14-9

argument 1:
table range

The table resides in cells A3..E6, so that forms the first argument in the {put} command: {put A3..E6;. If you assigned the range name TABLE1 to that range, the {put} command would begin {put TABLE1;.

arguments 2
and 3: row
and column
offsets

If you want to change the figure in cell D5 (June's sales of oranges), you'll next need to calculate the offset values for the row and column in which that cell resides. The table range is A3..E6, so you begin counting columns with column A. Since you begin counting with 0, column A is offset 0, column B is 1, C is 2, and D (which contains the destination cell) is offset 3. Likewise, row 3 is offset 0 because it's the top row in the range A3..E6. That makes row 5—which contains the destination cell—offset 2.

argument 4:
the source
of data

Thus far, the {put} command consists of {put TABLE1;3;2;. We next have to supply some source of data. Suppose the data you want is stored in a cell called Entry. As long as you are sure that the named range Entry will exist at the time you activate the macro containing this {put} command, you can use Entry as your final argument.

in final
form: the
completed
{put}
command

Here's the final {put} command: {put TABLE1;3;2;ENTRY}. If the named range Entry does not exist at the time you use this macro, 1-2-3 will instead enter the word ENTRY in cell D5.

keeping
range
names and
strings
separate

That suggests a caution when you want to enter strings into cells using the {put} command. If an existing range name duplicates the string you want to enter and you use that string alone as an argument, 1-2-3 will instead enter into the destination cell the contents of that range name. To circumvent the problem, enclose the string in quotation marks: {put TABLE1;3;2;"ENTRY"}. Even if there is a range name Entry, 1-2-3 will interpret this argument as a string. In fact, even if there is a named range called "Entry" (with quotation marks as part of the range name), 1-2-3 will interpret "Entry" as a string when the macro reads the {put} command.

If you ever enter a range name that refers to a range consisting of more than one cell, 1-2-3 will treat that range name as a string when it reads {put} in a macro.

One of the most powerful ways to use {put} is in combination with the @INDEX function. While {put} places a value into a table at any row/column offset, @index retrieves any value from a table at any row/column offset. Used together, you might build a summary table of a large spreadsheet by using @index to retrieve specific values and {put} to enter them into the summary table.

automatically building summary tables

```
{put TABLE2;1;4;@index(TABLE1;10;15)}
```

Using cell references to supply the offsets for each row and column you can entirely automate the building of such tables.

The tables you produce with {put} consist exclusively of static cell entries in the form of labels or values. They never consist of cell references or formulas. Consequently, there is no active link between the table you produce or modify with {put} and the data you used in the process. If the source data changes after you use the {put} command, the destination data will not change unless you rerun the macro containing the {put} command.

no active links between source and destination data

One advantage of the {put} command producing static entries is that the resulting table will not add to the recalculation burden of the worksheet.

You should be aware, however, when using the {put} command to be sure that all the data you reference has been recalculated since it was last changed. {Put} will not force recalculation of the worksheet. If the data you reference consists of unrecalculated formulas, the {put} command will use the values that existed when the worksheet was last recalculated.

no recalculation overhead potential for transferring out-of-date data

Example:

	A	B	C	D	E	F	G	H
1	NAME	MACRO				COMMENT		
2	----	----				----		
3	\A	{let ROW;1}				Set ROW to 1		
4		{let COL;1}				Set COL to 1		
5		{for CTR;1;5;1;RUN}				Create table to print		
6		{branch PRINT}				Branch to print it		
7								
8	RUN	{let VALUE;@index(DATA;COL;ROW)}				Assign value to VALUE		
9		{put TABLE1;COL;ROW;VALUE}				Place value in TABLE		
10		{let ROW;ROW+1}				Increment ROW		
11		{if @mod(ROW;5)=0}{let COL;COL+1}				Every 5 rows increment		
12		{return}				COL		
13						Repeat routine		
14								
15	CTR					Store CTR number		
16	ROW					Store ROW number		
17	COL					Store COL number		
18								

Figure 14-10

{Recalc}

Purpose: While worksheet recalculation has been set to Manual, or during the course of a macro, use {recalc} to perform a rowwise recalculation of a range of cells.

Format: {recalc [range];[condition];[iteration]}
Where [range] is the range to be recalculated, [condition] is a formula evaluating to zero or one, and [iteration] is a number.

[Range] may be a cell address, a range address, a range name, or in Release 2.2, a formula. Each of [condition] and [iteration] may be a number, a formula, a cell address, or a range name describing a single cell.

Sample: {recalc TEST_RANGE}

Complements: No macro commands, but you should have used the / Worksheet Global Recalculation Manual command.

See also: {recalccol}

Description: {Recalc} recalculates a range of cells on a row by row basis. {Recalc} is used primarily to force the recalculation of a selected portion of the worksheet when recalculation mode has been set to Manual. {Recalc} is also used to force 1-2-3 to update formulas that refer to cells that were modified by a macro. Because {recalc} does not recalculate the entire worksheet, it is usually able to perform a recalculation in less time than it would take were you to use the {calc} key.

If you are using string formulas in your macros, you may use {recalc} to selectively update them.

If you want only to update the screen after using one of the advanced macro commands, such as {let}, (which may change the worksheet), simply follow that command with a tilde in the macro.

cautions

Not only does {recalc} recalculate only a selected portion of the worksheet, it does not follow the natural order of recalculation. That imposes two limits that may cause you to obtain results other than those you expect.

The natural order of recalculation—1-2-3's default mode—automatically determines all cell dependencies and recalculates each cell in the proper order to resolve those dependencies correctly.

{Recalc} follows a row by row order of recalculation, irrespective of the dependencies of the cells within the specified range. For example, suppose you have an entry in cell A3 that refers to an entry in cell A1.

Another entry in cell A2 refers to the entry in cell A3. The worksheet has been set to / Worksheet Global Recalculation Manual. You enter the value 100 into cell A1. Here are the entries:

```
A1:  100
A2:  +A3
A3:  +A1
```

rowwise
recalcula-
tion

1-2-3 displays the CALC indicator at the bottom of the worksheet to indicate that it contains unrecalculated formulas. Suppose you activate the following macro:

```
{recalc A1..A3}
```

1-2-3 will recalculate the range A1..A3 in a row by row fashion, and cell A3 will display the value 100. However, cell A2 will still display a 0. That's because the {recalc} command recalculated cell A1 first (it contains no formula), then cell A2 (cell A2 refers to cell A3, which currently holds a 0; cell A2 will remain at 0), and then cell A3 (cell A3 refers to cell A1, which contains 100; cell A3 now returns the value 100).

If you activate the macro once again, cell A2 will return the value 100 because that's the current value of cell A3. However, if you entered new data in cell A1 just before to recalculating A1..A3, cell A2 would always be one step behind.

Now consider what would happen if cell A2 referenced cell A100. Cell A100 contains a reference to cell A1:

```
A1:    100
A2:    +A100
A3:    +A1
A100:  +A1
```

Now, no matter how many times you activate the macro, 1-2-3 won't properly update cell A2. Cell A2 refers to cell A100, and the command {recalc A1..A3} won't update cell A100. In this case, even though the cell you want to update (cell A2) is within the range being recalculated, 1-2-3 will not update that range.

Unfortunately, there is no one way to verify whether {recalc} is returning the result you expect; the testing techniques vary with the application you are testing. However, you might try saving your file, entering sample data, recalculating the entire worksheet with the {calc} key, and printing the results. Retrieve the original worksheet, reenter the data, use the {recalc} command to recalculate the range you've selected, print the report once more, and compare the two reports for discrepancies.

options

{Recalc} will optionally repeat the recalculation until a specified condition has been satisfied or until a specified number of iterations has been reached. Note that if you use both a condition and an iteration count, 1-2-3 will stop recalculating as soon as it satisfies either argument, not both.

For example, in the first of the preceding examples, you might specify that 1-2-3 should continue recalculating A1..A3 until A2 equals A1: {recalc A1..A3;A2=A1}. Since 1-2-3 can satisfy that condition in two iterations, specifying an iteration count higher than two—such as {recalc A1..A3;A2=A1;3}—would have no effect.

alternatives

Aside from using the {calc} key to recalculate the entire worksheet or using the {recalccol} command to recalculate a range in columnwise fashion, you should know that if you edit any cell with the Edit function key or if you copy data to any cell, 1-2-3 will recalculate just that cell. However, copying a range to itself, one of the techniques used to recalculate ranges in 1-2-3 Release 1A macro programming, is little better: it recalculates in a rowwise fashion as well.

Example:

	A	B	C	D	E	F	G	H
1	NAME	MACRO				COMMENT		
2	------	------	------	------	------	------		
3	\A	/riFORM1~				Accept data		
4		{recalc FORM1}				Update form range		
5		/ppcrrFORM1~agpq				Print form		
6		{quit}				End		
7								
8								
9								
10								

Figure 14-11

{Recalccol}

Purpose: Use {recalccol} to perform a columnwise recalculation of a range of cells.

Format: {recalccol [range];[condition];[iteration]}
Where [range] is the range to be recalculated, [condition] is a formula evaluating to zero or one, and [iteration] is a number.

[Range] may be a cell address, a range address, a range name, or in Release 2.2, a formula. Each of [condition] and [iteration] may be a number, a formula, a cell address, or a range name describing a single cell.

Sample: { recalccol TEST_RANGE }

Complements: No macro commands, but you should have used the / Worksheet Global Recalculation Manual command.

See also: { recalc }

Description: { Recalccol } recalculates a range of cells on a column by column basis. Because it does not recalculate the entire worksheet, it will usually be able to perform a recalculation in less time than it would take were you to use the { calc } key.

If you are using string formulas in your macros, you may use { recalc-col } to selectively update them.

If you only want to update the screen after using one of the advanced macro commands, such as { let }, (which may change the worksheet) simply follow that command with a tilde in the macro.

cautions   { Recalccol } does not follow the natural order of recalculation. It recalculates cells one column at a time, and only the cells within a specified range. Both those factors may cause you to obtain unexpected results.

If a given formula in the recalculated range references cells outside the range, those cells will not have been recalculated. That may mean you're getting invalid results even inside the recalculated range.

If through any chain of cell references, a formula in the recalculated range references cells located in columns to the right of itself, and any of those cells were updated by the current recalculation, then the formula will return an invalid result.

Unfortunately, there is no one way to verify whether { recalccol } is returning the result you expect; the testing techniques vary with the application. However, you might try saving your file, entering sample data, recalculating the entire worksheet with the { calc } key, and printing the results. Retrieve the original worksheet, reenter the data, use the { recalccol } command to recalculate the range you've selected, print the report once more, and compare the two reports for discrepancies.

options   { Recalccol } will optionally repeat the recalculation until a specified condition has been satisfied or until a specified number of iterations has been reached.

alternatives   Aside from using the { calc } key to recalculate the entire worksheet or using the { recalc } command to recaclulate a range in rowwise fashion, you should know that if you edit any cell with the { Edit } function key or if you copy data to any cell, 1-2-3 will recalculate just that cell. However, copying a range to itself, one of the techniques used to recalculate ranges in 1-2-3 Release 1A macro programming, is little better: it recalculates in a rowwise fashion.

common
syntax error

The sixth and seventh letters of the keyword in { recalccol } are the letter C. Because of the unorthodox spelling, it's common to mistakenly omit the seventh C. (When 1-2-3 reads the macro, if you've misspelled the keyword, the macro will terminate in an error).

It'll help you spell the command properly if you think of it as a contraction of the words Recalculate and Column: Recalc-Col.

```
        A       B       C     D     E       F       G       H
  1   NAME    MACRO                       COMMENT
  2   ------------------------------------------------------
  3   \A      /wgrm                       Manual recalc
  4           /riFORM1~                   User input
  5           {let INPUT;@sum(DATA)}      Fill in statistics
  6           {let INPUT2;@avg(DATA2)
  7           {recalccol FORM1}           Update worksheet
  8           {branch PRINT}              Next routine
  9
 10
```

Figure 14-12

15

File Manipulation

Overview and Introduction to New Concepts

scope of
operation

The commands in this chapter enable macros to manipulate files: to open them ({open}), assess their size ({filesize}), write data into them ({write} and {writeln}), read data from them ({read} and {readln}), and close them ({close}). Collectively, the commands are sometimes referred to as the macro file input/output commands (or, more simply, the file i/o commands) because they manage the process of moving data in and out of files. Most of these commands work only with ASCII files.

alternative:
use the
/ File
Import
Commands

Generally speaking, the file manipulation commands are more challenging to use than other macro commands. If you're new to macros and find these commands too difficult, try using 1-2-3's / File Import Text and / File Import Numbers commands instead. Those commands accomplish some of the same things. Of course, the file manipulation commands offer more control and for that reason, if you opt to skip them for the present, we recommend that you return to them when you've gained more experience with macros.

how do you
know if a
file is an
ASCII file?

If you're not sure whether a file is in ASCII format or not, you can use the DOS Type command to find out. When you use that command with the file in question, if it's an ASCII file you'll see (and be able to read) the contents of the file; if not, you'll see something unintelligible.

For example, a worksheet file is not an ASCII file. If you have a worksheet file named Budget.wk1, and at the DOS prompt you enter the command type budget.wk1, you won't see the current contents of the worksheet. Instead, you'll see a lot of gibberish. A PRN file is a text file. If you have a PRN file named Budget.prn, and at the DOS prompt you enter the command type budget.prn, you will see the contents of the file on your screen.

kinds of
ASCII files

ASCII files are primarily of two types: text files and sequential data files.

Text files contain text and might be produced with 1-2-3 or with a word processor. DOS batch files (that is, files with the extension .BAT) are ASCII text files.

Sequential data files contain data arranged in records, as data would be in a 1-2-3 database. Sequential data files might be produced by 1-2-3, a database program, or a BASIC program.

text file
structure

A text file is characterized by having just one unit of data per line of the file. That line might be a sentence from a word processing file, or a series of numbers from a spreadsheet. In either case, the file contains no delimiters (such as commas) intended to separate the data within each line.

For example, here's a typical text file:

```
Budget
September 1988
          January   February   March   Total
Expense      100        110      115     325
Income       200        200      220     620
Profit       100         90      105     295
```

You can import such a file on to the worksheet with the / File Import Text command. 1-2-3 will enter each line in a separate cell as a long label; you may then divide those long labels into more workable entries with the / Data Parse command.

The macro file manipulation commands enable you to more precisely control—down to the character—which parts of the file you read onto the worksheet. They also enable you to write back to the file without overwriting the entire file—something no interactive 1-2-3 command can do.

delimited
files

Here's the same file in another form, as a comma separated file (also known as a comma delimited file):

```
"Budget"
"September 1988"
"","January","February","March","Total"
"Expense",100,110,115,325
"Income",200,200,220,620
"Profit",100,90,105,295
```

A comma separated file divides the data each line contains into fields. Each field should reside in a separate cell on the worksheet. Fields enclosed by quotation marks will be imported as labels, the unenclosed numbers will be imported as values. If you import such a file with the / File Import Numbers command, 1-2-3 will automatically divide it into cells at each comma.

It's more difficult to use the macro file i/o commands to read a delimited file because the delimiters, which are disposed of automatically when you use the / File Import Numbers command to import the file, must be stripped off by the macro.

invisible characters in an ASCII file

Each line of an ASCII file terminates with two invisible characters: a carriage return and a linefeed. These characters will not display if you type the file in DOS; however, they each occupy one byte in the file.

Only three of these commands work reliably with non-ASCII files: {open}, {filesize}, and {close}.

non-ASCII file capabilities

In 1-2-3, you're familiar with three ways of identifying the locus of action. The cell pointer identifies the current cell. In edit mode, the flashing cursor identifies the current character. In a macro, we've discussed the concept of macro control moving from command to command through the macro. Another concept identifies the locus of action in an ASCII file you are working with: the byte pointer.

the byte pointer

Using the file manipulation commands, you can move through an ASCII file byte by byte, writing to or reading from the file as needed. The special kind of pointer that keeps track of your location is called the byte pointer. Although you can't see the byte pointer in the same way you can see the cell pointer, you can use one of the file manipulation commands to determine the current position of the byte pointer (see {getpos}).

Many of these commands ({setpos}, {read}, {readlin}, {write}, and {writeln}) reposition the byte pointer, but each does so in a different way: See each command's entry for a description of the manner in which it affects the byte pointer.

relating characters to byte positions

Any character's position in a file can be identified by its offset from the first byte of the file. The first byte is identified as offset 0, the second byte as offset 1, and so on.

Because some of the commands require that you know in advance the byte offset at which a given string begins and how many bytes long that string is, if you intend to use those commands you'll want a way to easily determine those things. Here's one way.

Use the / File Import Text command to import the ASCII file on to the worksheet. The contents of the ASCII file might look like this on the worksheet:

This is a test file consisting of two lines.

Use the / Worksheet Insert Row command to insert a blank row between each line of the resulting text:

```
This is a test file

consisting of two lines.
```

Move to the blank line between the two labels and type a label prefix character. Then type numbers in sequence from 0–9. When you reach 9, begin again with 0 and continue until there are two numbers beyond the end of the line. On the next blank line, begin typing in sequence where the last line left off and continue until there are two numbers beyond the last visible character:

```
This is a test file
01234567890123456789
consisting of two lines.
123456789012345678901234567890123456
```

Note that the location of the first character in the file is not identified as offset 1; it's offset 0. If you interpret the next zero as offset position 10, the third as offset position 20, and so forth, you can easily determine the position of each character in the file. Two positions are reserved for two invisible characters at the end of each line. Those characters are the carriage return and linefeed characters. In the preceding file, the carriage return and linefeed characters at the end of line one are located at offsets 19 and 20, respectively, and those characters at the end of line two are located at offsets 45 and 46.

For example, the character *a* in line one is located at offset 8. The carriage return character at the end of line one is located at offset 19. The *w* in the word *two* is located at offset 36.

in most cases, write file manipulation commands last on each line

The macro file manipulation commands affect the macro control flow in an unusual way. When using the file manipulation commands, you will normally either write each such command as the last command on the line on which it appears or else write it entirely alone on that line.

If any of these commands succeeds in their task—for example, the {open} command opens a file or the {read} command reads some part of one—macro control will jump directly to the next line of the macro. Any more commands on the same line will be ignored. Contrarily, if any of these commands fails, macro control will continue normally—it will read the next command on the same line of the macro.

Note that the {if} command, which also affects macro control flow, works in exactly the opposite manner: When the conditional statement in an {if} statement is true, the macro reads the command to the right—

versus when the file manipulation command fails, it skips the command to the right. Since you'll probably use many more {if} statements than file manipulation statements in your macros, the file manipulation commands will probably represent an anomaly to you. You might make a mental note that file manipulation commands are unusual in this respect.

Unusual though this scheme may be, there is a reason for it. Working with files external to the worksheet means you are dealing with a terrain that is considerably less predictable than the environment of a worksheet. That's particularly true if you do your work on a network, where other people have access to files that you may design your macro to use. For that reason, files you'd planned to use may prove to be gone, or have been modified. Such changes may cause problems for a macro.

File manipulation commands affect macro control in the way they do to make it easier for you to trap such problems. If 1-2-3 merely generated an error at that time of such an error, you'd have to trap the error with the {onerror} command, then run through a series of tests to see which command generated the error.

The file manipulation commands make the job easier for you. If any file manipulation command can't do its intended work, it'll fail. So, if the macro attempts to open a file that doesn't exist, the {open} command will fail, and direct macro control to read the next command on the *same* line instead of skipping directly to the next line. Knowing that, you could place an error trapping routine to the right of the {open} command:

place only error trapping commands to the right of a file manipulation command

sample

```
            A         B          C       D      E      F      G         H
    1  NAME      MACRO                                       COMMENT
    2  ------------------------------------------------------------------------
    3  \A        {open "TESTFILE.PRN";"r"}{branch NO_FILE}   Open or branch
    4            {readln LINE1}                              Read line 1
    5            {readln LINE2}                              Read line 2
    6            {return}                                    Return to caller
    7
    8
    9  NO_FILE   {let MSG1;"TESTFILE.PRN does not exist"}    Assign error message
   10            {goto}MSG1~                                 Show error message
   11            {wait @now+@time(0;0;5)}                    Pause 5 seconds
   12            {branch CHOICES}                            Present choices
   13
   14
   15
```

Figure 15-1

Due to this error trapping design, remember never to place any commands to the right of a file manipulation command, unless those commands are ones you want read in the event the file manipulation command fails. If you do place normal commands on the same line and to the right of a file manipulation command and the file manipulation command succeeds, the macro won't read the commands placed to their right.

Remember, if any of the file i/o commands fail, 1-2-3 won't generate an error, so {onerror} cannot take over. Instead, you must provide a command to handle that situation on the same line as the file management command you suspect may fail. Most often, the command will be a {branch} command to redirect control to another routine.

One further implication of the design of these commands is that if a command fails and no error trapping routine follows on the same line, control will continue with the next line in the normal manner.

Now that you know why these commands redirect macro control in this manner, you should also realize that they redirect control in a manner opposite to the scheme used by the {if} command.

file import
text limits

The 1-2-3 command / File Import Text can read no more than 239 characters per line.[38] If the line exceeds that, 1-2-3 will issue an error when you attempt to import the file containing it.

Since the {read} and {readln} commands both allow you to read only portions of a line from an ASCII file, you can use either command to read portions of a line that the File Import commands won't read. Using more than one such command, you can read an entire line that proved unreadable with / File Import Text. However, each portion must still be no more than 239 characters.

creating a
sample
ASCII file

If you'd like to create a sample ASCII file with which to experiment as you learn the file commands that follow, you can do so through the following operation. At the end of each file management command description, we'll include a brief exercise using this file.

On a blank worksheet, make sure columns A and B are each set to nine spaces wide. Now enter the following text in the cells designated below:

A1: This is a simple

A2: sample ASCII file.

Now select / Print File, type SAMPLE and press Return, select Range, indicate the range A1..B2, select Options Margin Left, enter 0, select Other Unformatted Quit Go Quit. To view the file you just created, move to cell A4, select / File Import Text and indicate the file Sample.prn.

If you insert a blank row between the two lines of the imported file, you can apply the same scale we described earlier to map the position of

---

[38] If you're writing macros that run in Release 3 as well as Release 2.x(2, 2.01, and 2.2) be aware that you must use this figure as your upper limit. Don't use Release 3's 511 characters-per-line limit if you expect the macro to run in Release 2.x.

each byte in Sample.prn. Remember to type an apostrophe label prefix and to include extra spaces for the invisible carriage return and line feed characters at the end of each line.

```
This is a simple
0123456789012345?8
sample ASCII file.
9012345678901234567&
```

restoring
the ASCII
file

Since you'll be modifying Sample.prn as you try the examples that use that file, you should know how to restore it to its original form afterward.   You can do one of several things:

1. Select the / File Erase Print command, specify Sample.prn, and select Yes to erase it. Then repeat the above commands.

2. Run the following macro, which will erase the old file and create a new one just like the old one:

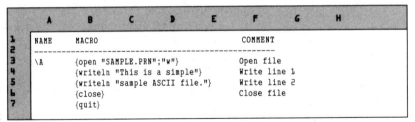

Figure 15-2

{ Close }

Purpose: In some circumstances, use { close } to terminate your work with a file previously opened with the { open } command.

Format: { close }

Sample: { close }

Complements: { open }

Description: Under certain circumstances, if you do not explicitly close an open file, you will lose some of the data you have written to that file. The { close } command is one way to close an open file.

1-2-3 can open only one ASCII file at a time. If you write to an open file with the {write} or {writeln} commands, 1-2-3 will leave the file open for more input unless one of the following things happens:

1. You open another file.

2. You invoke the / System command.

3. You retrieve another worksheet file.

4. You use the / Quit Yes command to leave 1-2-3.

5. You use the {close} command to close it.

If, after opening an ASCII file with {write} or {writeln} commands, the macro ends and none of the above events has occurred, the file will remain open, and you face two possible problems.

1. If you then try to use the / File Import Text command to import the text the file contains, depending on circumstances, one of two things will happen. If you have opened the file in write mode (such as with the command, {open "TEST.BAT";"w"}) you will import nothing. If you have opened the file in append mode (such as with the command, {open "TEST.BAT";"a"}) or in modify mode (such as with the command, {open "TEST.BAT";"m"}), you will get only the text written to the file prior to opening it this time. You will not get any text written to it since you opened it.

2. If you then shut your computer off or lose power without closing the file, depending on circumstances, one of two things will happen. If you have opened the file in write mode (such as with the command, {open "TEST.BAT";"w"}) you will lose the entire file. Your disk will show a file of that name, but it will contain nothing. If you have opened the file in append mode (such as with the command, {open "TEST.BAT";"a"}) or in modify mode (such as with the command, {open "TEST.BAT";"m"}), you will lose only the text written to the file prior to opening it this time. You will not lose text written to it before you opened it.

For these reasons, you may wish to avoid leaving a file in the open condition. It takes but one {close} command to close it, and just another {open} command to open it again later.

As pointed out above, the / File Retrieve command will close an open file. You might surmise that is because macro control ends when you retrieve another file, and conclude that when a macro terminates that any file it opened will be closed. Not so. The termination of macro control does not close a file. If the macro ends and the file is still open, you can activate another macro and continue to manipulate the same file without issuing another {open} command.

Although the / File Retrieve command will close an open file, File commands in general do not cause 1-2-3 to close open files. For instance, you can open a file, use the / File Combine command to consolidate another worksheet into the current worksheet, and afterward continue to manipulate the currently open file.

effect on the byte pointer

Once a file has been reopened in write, read, or modify mode,[39] 1-2-3 repositions the byte pointer to offset zero. Whether that change occurs at the time of closing or opening the file is a moot point. Every time you open an ASCII file in one of these modes, the byte pointer will be repositioned to offset zero. If you open the file in append mode, the byte pointer will be positioned at the end of the file.

Example:

	A	B	C	D	E	F	G	H
1	NAME	MACRO				COMMENT		
2	----	-----				-------		
3	\A	{open "BGT1.PRN";"r"}				Open file in read mode		
4		{filesize SIZE}				Get size of file		
5		{setpos SIZE-10}				Goto 10 before end		
6		{readln LAST}				Read that line		
7		{close}				Close the file		
8		/fitBGT1~				Import file		
9		{quit}				Quit		
10								

Figure 15-3

using Sample.prn

On a blank worksheet, enter the following macro and assign it a range name. Assign the range name Size as well. After you run the macro, press the Return key to update the screen.

	A	B	C	D	E	F	G	H
1	NAME	MACRO				COMMENT		
2	----	-----				-------		
3	\A	{open "SAMPLE.PRN";"m"}				Open file in modify mode		
4		{filesize SIZE}				Get size of file		
5		{close}				Close the file		
6		{quit}				Quit		
7								
8								
9	SIZE					Store filesize		
10								

Figure 15-4

---

[39] Refer to the listing for the {open} command for an explanation of these modes.

{Close} can accept a filename as an argument, but the argument has no effect on the command. {Close} will close the currently open ASCII file, regardless of which filename you specify.

{ Filesize }

Purpose: Use {filesize} to determine and store the number of bytes of disk space occupied by a file.

Format: {filesize [location]}
    Where [location] is a cell. [location] may be a cell address, a range address, a range name, or in Release 2.2, a formula.

Sample: {filesize SIZE}

Complements: {open}

See also: {getpos}, {setpos}

Description: {Filesize} is one of the macro file manipulation commands that works reliably with *any* kind of file. Use it to determine the number of bytes a file occupies on a disk. Before you use the {filesize} command, however, you must first have used the {open} command to open that file.

{Filesize} is useful in two ways. First, if you are reading in lines from a file, you'll need to know when to stop. After reading each line, use {getpos} to obtain the current position of the byte pointer. Compare that offset to the result of the {filesize} command (see the reference for {getpos} for more information). Second, if you have been writing data to a file, you may want to move the byte pointer to the end of the file in order to write data there. Use the {setpos} command to set the byte pointer to the position returned by the {filesize} command (see the reference for {setpos} for more information).

If the specified file does not exist, the {filesize} command will fail, as will the {open} command that precedes it. Like other macro file manipulation commands, when the {filesize} command fails, macro control proceeds with the next command directly to its right—if any. If the command succeeds, control jumps directly to the cell below and 1-2-3 will not process any commands on the same line following the {filesize} command.

Example: Routine to read the last record in an ASCII file.

```
      A         B          C      D      E        F        G        H
  1  NAME       MACRO                             COMMENT
  2  ------------------------------------------------------------------
  3  READ_LAST  {open "REPORT.PRN";"r"}           Open file in read mode
  4             {filesize SIZE}                   Get size of file
  5             {setpos SIZE-10}                   Goto 10 before end
  6             {readln LAST}                     Read that line
  7             {close}                           Close the file
  8
  9
 10
```

Figure 15-5

using
Sample.prn

On a blank worksheet, enter the following macro and assign both of the range names. After you run the macro, press the Return key to update the screen.

```
      A         B          C      D      E        F        G        H
  1  NAME       MACRO                             COMMENT
  2  ------------------------------------------------------------------
  3  \A         {open "SAMPLE.PRN";"r"}           Open file in read mode
  4             {filesize SIZE}                   Get size of file
  5             {close}                           Close the file
  6             {quit}                            Quit
  7
  8
  9  SIZE                                         Store filesize
 10
```

Figure 15-6

{Getpos}

Purpose: Use {getpos} to determine the current position of the byte pointer in the file.

Format: {getpos [location]}
Where [location] is a cell. [location] may be a cell address, a range address, a range name, or in Release 2.2, a formula.

Sample: {getpos LOCATION}

Complements: {open}

See also: {setpos}

Description: {Getpos} stores, in the specified cell, the location of the byte pointer in the currently open file. The location will be stored as a value and can be referenced by the {setpos} command to reposition the byte pointer, or compared with the file size to determine when the byte pointer has reached the end of the file.

Example: Macro to read an ASCII file onto the worksheet

	A	B	C	D	E	F	G	H
1	NAME	MACRO			COMMENT			
2	-------	----------------			------------------			
3	READ_FILE	{open "REPORT.PRN";"r"}			Open file in read mode			
4		{filesize SIZE}			Get size of file			
5	LOOP	{readln M42}			+"{readln"&@cellpointer("address")&"}"			
6		{getpos LOCATION}			Store location			
7		{if SIZE=LOCATION}{QUIT}			If at end of file,stop			
8		{d}			Otherwise, blank cell			
9		{branch LOOP}			Repeat read operation			

Figure 15-7

You should press the {calc} key once you've positioned the cell pointer where you want 1-2-3 to begin writing the file on the worksheet. Alternatively, you could use a {recalc} command to recalculate the string formula in the Comment column. That command should appear just before the named range Loop in the macro. If you use this macro while the worksheet is in manual recalculation mode, make two changes. Just after the first {recalc} command, add another to recalculate the {readln} command in the Macro column. Second, name the cell in which the first {recalc} command resides Loop, instead of the cell the {readln} command appears in. In manual recalculation mode, both these formulas must be recalculated with every iteration of the macro.

If you are using Release 2.2, note that the string-formula command on row 5 could more simply be written as {readln} @cellpointer ("address")}.

using Sample.prn

On a blank worksheet, enter the following macro and assign it a range name. Also, assign the range name Loc1 to cell B8. After you run the macro, press the Return key to update the screen.

	A	B	C	D	E	F	G	H
1	NAME	MACRO			COMMENT			
2	-------	----------------			------------------			
3	\A	{open "SAMPLE.PRN";"r"}			Open file in read mode			
4		{getpos LOC1}			Get location			
5		{close}			Close the file			
6		{quit}			Quit			
7								
8	LOC1				Location of byte ptr			
9								
10								

Figure 15-8

{Open}

Purpose: Use {open} to open a file prior to reading it, writing to it, or ascertaining its size.

Format: {open ["filename"];["x"]}

Where ["filename"] is a string, a formula, a cell address, or a range name referring to a single cell; and ["x"] is the letter r, w, m, or a, or in Release 2.2, a range name, a cell address, or a formula evaluating to one of those letters.

Sample: {open "SPREAD.PRN";"w"}
or, with a pathname:
{open "C:\DBASE\PARTS.TXT";"r"}

Complements: None

See also: {close}

Description: Use {open} to open a file prior to ascertaining its size, reading it, or writing to it.

When you use 1-2-3 in interactive mode, you don't need to know of any distinction between an open and a closed file. When you retrieve a worksheet file with 1-2-3, the program automatically opens the worksheet file, reads a copy of the worksheet into memory, and closes the file. When you save a worksheet, 1-2-3 opens the worksheet file, writes a copy of the worksheet in memory over the worksheet file on disk, and closes the file.

When you use the macro file input/output commands to manipulate ASCII text files, you must perform each of these steps with separate commands. The {open} command opens the file, the {read} and {readln} command read from it, the {write} and {writeln} commands write to it, and {close} command closes it.

modes in which you can open a file

The mode in which you open the file determines what you can do with that file once it's open, and how 1-2-3 will change the file in response to the commands that follow.

You have a choice of four modes: read, write, modify, or append. Read mode enables you to read the file but not write to it. Write mode enables you to write to the file but not read it. Write mode also erases existing files before the macro does any writing. Modify mode enables you to read and write to the file interchangably. Unlike write mode, it will not erase an existing file before the macro writes to it. Append mode enables you to add new data to the end of an existing file but not read the file.

modify versus write mode

Although modify mode would seem to encompass write mode, when you issue {write} or {writeln} commands, the commands work differently depending on whether you have opened the file in modify mode or write mode. When you open an existing file in modify mode, if the byte pointer is positioned anywhere but at the end of the file, either command will overwrite existing bytes in the file with the new bytes written by these commands. The file will otherwise remain unchanged. In write mode, the entire file will be erased first. The macro will write to the file, but no matter the location of the byte pointer, nothing of the original contents of the file will remain. If the location of the byte pointer is anywhere but at the beginning of the file, 1-2-3 will fill the offsets preceding that one with random characters already present on the disk.

can't open a new file in append mode

You cannot open a new file in append mode. You can only open an existing file in append mode. If you try to open a new file in append mode, the {open} command will fail, and control will pass to the next command on the same line.

changing modes

After opening a file in one mode, you can at any time change modes by issuing another {open} command while specifying another mode. You don't have to close the file before doing so; 1-2-3 will do that for you.

Example: Changing the mode in which a file has been opened.

	A	B	C	D	E	F	G	H
1	NAME	MACRO					COMMENT	
2	----	---					---------	
3	\A	{open "TEST.PRN";"a"}					Open to append	
4		{writeln "This is the new last line."}					Append line	
5		{open "TEST.PRN";"r"}					Open for read	
6		{readln LINE1}					Read 1st line	
7		{close}					Close file	
8		{quit}					End	
9								
10								

Figure 15-9

byte pointer position

When you use the {open} command to open a file, the byte pointer is positioned at the first character in the file, which is identified as offset zero (not offset 1). You can reposition the byte pointer with the {setpos} command, or any of the following: {read}, {readln}, {write}, or {writeln}. (See any of those commands for descriptions of how their use affects the position of the byte pointer.) The {getpos} command will report the current position of the byte pointer.

writing the filename argument

Whether you supply it through a string, string expression, or a reference to a cell containing a string, the first argument must consist of, at a minimum, both a filename and an extension (that is, if the subject file has an extension; most do).

If the file is stored somewhere outside 1-2-3's current file default directory, then you must specify the path to that file with a valid DOS pathname preceding the filename. If you use a pathname you *must* enclose the pathname and filename in quotation marks or 1-2-3 will misinterpret the colons that name contains. It's good practice to always enclose literal text such as a filename in quotation marks,[40] but doing so is ususally optional. In this case it is mandatory.

The string may not be more than 64 characters in length. Should you not wish to specify such a path in the {open} command, you can use the / File Directory command or the / Worksheet Global Default Directory command to change the current directory to the one containing the file you wish to open. Once you have done that, you do not need to supply the pathname in the {open} command.

If you have changed 1-2-3's default punctuation (using the / Worksheet Global Default Other International Punctuation command) to **B (,..)** or **F (,.)**, you will have to enclose with quotation marks any filename that carries an extension. The aforementioned default punctuation settings interpret a period as an argument separator, and there's a period between a filename and its extension. Keep in mind that settings for default punctuation reside with each copy of 1-2-3, not with the worksheet file. If you suspect your application may be used with a copy of 1-2-3 which has been configured so that the period is an argument separator, you should always enclose any full filename in your {open} commands with quotation marks. This is one more reason for adopting such a practice as your standard operating procedure.

Following the filename and extension is an argument separator (a semicolon in this case). Directly following the argument separator is the second argument. Note that no space intervenes between the argument separator and the second argument.

You indicate which mode you wish to open the file in by including the letter that represents that mode as the second argument to the {open} command. R stands for read mode, W for write mode, M for modify mode, and A for append mode. For example, {open "TEST.PRN";"r"} will open a file called Test.prn in read mode.

Be sure there is no space between the argument separator (in this case, a semicolon) and the letter that follows it. For example, do *not* write {open "TEST.PRN"; "w"}. If there is a space after the separator, no matter what character follows that space, 1-2-3 will open the file in read mode. So, although it may be questionable form to do so—and you risk compatibility problems with future releases of 1-2-3 if you do—if you

---

[40] In the event there is ever a range name that duplicates that literal text, doing so will prevent 1-2-3 from construing the text as a reference to that range.

wanted to open a file in read mode, you could write either {open "TEST.PRN";"r"} or {open "TEST.PRN"; }.

Because 1-2-3 automatically supplies the worksheet filename extension when it saves and retrieves worksheet files, you may not be used to specifying filename extensions when you work with files. Take special note, then, that when you use the {open} command you must specify both the file name and its extension. Suppose that when you wanted to open a file named Test.prn you used the command {open TEST;w}. If no file named Test existed, 1-2-3 would create it and open it. If a file named Test did exist, 1-2-3 would open it in write mode. In either case, Test.prn—the file you really wanted—would remain closed. You must specify both filename and extension.

Example: Writing a line of data to a file.

```
     A        B         C        D         E         F          G        H
 1  NAME     MACRO                                  COMMENT
 2  ------------------------------------------------------------
 3  POST     {open "LIST.PRN";"a"}                  Append to List.prn
 4           {writeln "12,10,15,19,58"}             Comma separated values
 5           {close}                                Close the file
 6           {return}                               Return to main routine
 7
 8
 9
10
```

Figure 15-10

using Sample.prn

On a blank worksheet, enter the following macro and assign it a range name. Assign the range name Loc1 as well. After you run the macro, press the Return key to update the screen.

```
     A        B         C        D         E         F          G        H
 1  NAME     MACRO                                  COMMENT
 2  ------------------------------------------------------------
 3  \A       {open "SAMPLE.PRN";"r"}                Open file in read mode
 4           {getpos LOC1}                          Get location
 5           {close}                                Close the file
 6           {quit}                                 Quit
 7
 8  LOC1                                            Location of byte ptr
 9
10
```

Figure 15-11

{ Read }

Purpose: Use {read} to read a portion of a text or sequential data file.

Format: {read [count];[location]}
   Where [count] is a value and [location] is a cell.
   [Count] may be a number, a formula, a cell address, or a range name describing a single cell. [location] may be a cell address, a range address, a range name, or in Release 2.2, a formula.

Sample: {read 10;TARGET}

Complements: {open}

See also: {readln}, {write}, {writeln}

Description: From the currently open ASCII file, the {read} command reads from the current byte forward a specified number of bytes and copies the characters stored in those bytes into a specified cell.

If the location specified is a range encompassing more than one cell, 1-2-3 will enter those characters into the top left cell in that range. The entry will always appear as a left aligned label entry.

The {read} command differs from the {readln} command in that {read} can read forward any number of bytes from the current location, whereas {readln} will read only through the character directly preceding the carriage return that terminates the current line. See the beginning of this chapter for an explanation of the components of each line.

The {read} command differs from the / File Import Text (/FIT) command in that /FIT will read only the entire file onto the worksheet; {read} will read portions of the file. {Read} can also read portions of lines that are unreadable by /FIT. 1-2-3's /FIT command can't read any line longer than 239 characters. {Read} can't read more than 239 characters at one time either, but since {read} can select any portion of a line to read, as long as you don't request more than 239 characters at once, you can read lines longer than 239 characters by invoking {read} two or more times in a macro. [41]

read entire lines with {readln}, not {read}

Note that if you want to read an entire line, the {readln} command will do the job much more easily than will {read}. If you use {read}, you'll need to specify the number of bytes in the line; {readln} will automatically read from the current byte through the end of the line.

---

[41] If you are designing a macro in Release 3 that has to run in Release 2.x(2, 2.01, or 2.2), be aware that you should not use Release 3's higher limit, 511 characters per line, but the lower one that applies to Release 2.x.

prerequisite

The file to be read must already have been opened in read mode or in modify mode with the {open} command before the {read} command will succeed.

how many
bytes to
read?

{Read}'s first argument specifies how many bytes to read forward from the current position of the byte pointer in that file. The second argument specifies the cell in which 1-2-3 will store the label created from the string the {read} command produces.

Each byte in an ASCII file will store one character, so you must count the number of characters you wish to read from the file in order to specify the proper number as the first argument in the {read} command. Remember that blank spaces in that file each require one byte of storage as well, so include them in your count. In addition, if you intend to read past the end of a line, remember to count two bytes for the invisible carriage return and linefeed characters at the end of each such line.

You can easily map the byte locations of ASCII files (see the margin note "relating characters to byte positions" in the Overview and Introduction to New Concepts section at the beginning of this chapter) to help you pinpoint which bytes you want to read.

backing up
through the
file

effect of
negative
values in
{read}

If you specify a negative value for the number of bytes to read, 1-2-3 will interpret that as the maximum positive value: 240. If what you want to do is to read the preceding byte, you must first reposition the byte pointer to that byte. Use the {getpos} command to store the current position of the byte pointer as a value on the worksheet. For example, {getpos LOC} will store the byte pointer position in a cell named Loc. With the position of the byte pointer stored on the worksheet, use an expression in the {setpos} command to change the position of the byte pointer: {setpos LOC-1}. If the value 14 was stored in the cell named Loc, this {setpos} command will move the byte pointer to offset 13. With the pointer repositioned to the byte that you want to read, you can use a {read} command to read the current byte: {read 1;NEWCHAR}.

end of line
characters

There are two characters at the end of each line of the ASCII file that are normally invisible, yet each takes a byte. The {read} command can read those characters; the {readln} command normally cannot. For example, suppose the first line of an ASCII file named TEST.PRN consists of the string LITTLE MISS MUFFET. If 1-2-3 had opened TEST.PRN in read mode and read the command {read 18;LINE1}, 1-2-3 would store the string LITTLE MISS MUFFET in the cell named Line1.

If instead you wrote the command as {read 19;LINE1}, you'd get the same string with an extra blank space appended to it. If you then moved the cell pointer to the cell named Line1, pressed the Edit key, and looked in the control panel, you'd see a graphics character appended to the string. That's the hidden carriage return character that was stored at the end of the line.

If you wrote the command as {read 20;LINE1}, you'd get the same string with two blank spaces appended to it. If you again moved to the cell named Line1, pressed the Edit key and looked in the control panel you'd see two graphics characters appended to the string: one for the carriage return and one for the line feed, each of which terminates each line of an ASCII file.

To see these characters on the worksheet, do this quick exercise. On a blank worksheet, enter @CHAR(10) in cell A1 and @CHAR(13) in cell A2. Now select / Range Value, indicate A1..A2 and press Return. With the cell pointer on cell A1, press the Edit key and look in the control panel. Similarly, edit cell A2 and look in the control panel. The characters you see are the ones 1-2-3 will read as the carriage return (LICS 10) and linefeed (LICS 13).

Although there are circumstances under which 1-2-3 can display graphics characters, these graphics characters will not appear on the worksheet—you can only see them in the control panel if you edit the cell containing them.

testing for end of the line

If you want to test for those characters, you can do so with the @CODE function. @CODE will return the LICS code for the first character in a given string. The value returned by a reference to a cell containing a carriage return is 13, the value returned by a reference to a cell containing a linefeed is 10.

If those characters are the last ones at the end of a string you've read, you can use the @CODE and @RIGHT functions to identify them. If the string you want to test resides in cell C27, @CODE(@RIGHT(C27;1)) will return the LICS code for the rightmost character in that string. If you've read an entire line, that character will be the linefeed, or LICS 10 character. @CODE(@RIGHT(C27,2)) will return the LICS code for the second from the far right character in that string. If you've read an entire line, that will be the carriage return, or LICS 13 character.

reading through an entire file

If you want to read through an entire ASCII file, again, in most cases {readln} is a more appropriate command than is {read}. If you want to read the entire file onto the worksheet, chances are you want to divide that file into lines, and {readln} does so automatically; {read} does not. However, you can use {read} to read through a file, and you may find a situation that warrants it.

If you choose to use the {read} command to read through an entire file, you'll need to know when it has read to the end of the file. Unlike {readln}, {read} will not fail if it tries to read beyond the end of the file, it will merely continue to read the last byte in the file.

When the byte pointer is at the end of the file and the macro performs a {read} command, the macro will read the current byte. The only difference between that and when the byte pointer resides at any other position in the file is that the byte pointer will remain on the last byte. Repeated {read} commands issued from that position will result in repeatedly reading the last byte of the file on to the worksheet.

You can test for the end of the file using the advanced macro commands {filesize}, {getpos}, and {if}. {Filesize} will return the number of bytes in the entire file. {Getpos} will return the offset number of the current position of the byte pointer. When the offset number of the byte pointer equals the total number of bytes in the file, the byte pointer is at the end of the file. You can use the {if} command to test to see if that is true.

reading
through a
file of
indeterminate length

Before proceeding with testing for the end of a file, there's one other challenge to address. If you know the length of the file and at what position in that file you commence reading it, you can deduce the number of cells on the worksheet you'll need to store the file's data. You can then assign each {read} command to store its output in a different cell:

```
{read 5;CELL1}
{read 5;CELL2}
{read 5;CELL3}
```

However, if you don't know how much data you're going to read onto the worksheet, you'll need a device to automatically store the output from each {read} command in a new cell. There are several possible approaches. Here's one.

The macro will read the specified number of bytes from the file into the current cell (the location of the cell pointer), then move the cell pointer down one cell and repeat the operation until it has read the entire file.

Unfortunately, in releases of 1-2-3 other than Release 2.2 or higher, the {read} command can't accept expressions as arguments. In Release 2.2, you can write the operation rather easily with the commands:

```
{read 5;@cellpointer("address")}
```

The expression @cellpointer("address") returns the current location of the cell pointer, which is where you want to direct the output of the {read} command. Unfortunately, in Release 2 or 2.01, {read} won't evaluate expressions, and @cellpointer is an expression.

However, you can achieve the same effect using a slightly different approach. Here's an overview of the method we're about to present, by each row of the worksheet on which the macro appears. Begin by manually placing the cell pointer in the first cell in which you want data to be read. (1) opens the file in read mode, (2) stores the size of the file in a cell named Size, (3) freezes the control panel so subsequent changes to it don't display, (4) reads 5 bytes of the ASCII file into a cell named Ans, which is a temporary data-storage cell, (5) copies the contents of Ans to the current cell on the worksheet, (6) in a cell named Pos, stores the position of the byte pointer in the ASCII file (7) tests to see if the value stored in Pos is less than the value stored in Size. As long as Pos is the lesser value, then there remain bytes to be read. If Pos is the lesser value, the cell pointer moves down a cell to prepare to accept more data and the macro branches to Loop, where it reads another five bytes. If Size is equal to Pos, then the byte pointer has reached the end of the file and 1-2-3 reads the commands on the next line, (8) to close the file and (9) terminate the macro.

Here's the macro:

Example: Testing for End–Of–File with {Read}.

	A	B	C	D	E	F	G	H
1	NAME	MACRO			COMMENT			
2	------	----------------			-----------			
3	\A	{open "SAMPLE.PRN";"r"}			Open file			
4		{filesize SIZE}			Check size			
5		{paneloff}			Turn off menu display			
6	LOOP	{read 5;ANS}			Read five bytes into ANS			
7		/cANS~~			Copy ANS to current cell			
8		{getpos POS}			Check position			
9		{if POS<SIZE}{d}{branch LOOP}			If EOF, stop			
10		{close}			Close file			
11		{quit}						
12								
13	POS				Store position			
14	ANS				Store data			

Figure 15-12

This macro happens to read five bytes at a time; you can specify any number that suits you (up to a maximum of 239).

In Release 2.2, where {readln} can evaluate an expression, you should use {readln @cellpointer("address")} and {d} to do the job. Note that it makes for a simpler macro. Again, begin by placing the cell pointer in the first cell you want to accept data from the file.

	A	B	C	D	E	F	G	H
1	NAME	MACRO				COMMENT		
2	------	------------------------------------				----------		
3	\A	{open "SAMPLE.PRN";"r"}				Open file		
4		{filesize SIZE}				Check size		
5	LOOP	{read 5;@cellpointer("address")}				Read 5 bytes into current cell		
6		{d}				Move cellpointer		
7		{getpos POS}				Check position		
8		{if SIZE=POS}{branch END}				If EOF, stop		
9		{recalc LOOP}				Update {read} command		
10		{branch LOOP}				Branch to read more		
11								
12	STOP	{close}				Close file		
13		{quit}				End macro		
14								
15	POS					Store position		

Figure 15-13

reading
characters
from the
next line

Suppose you have a file containing two lines. The first line consists of the word Tom, the second consists of the word Tina. With the carriage return and line feed characters, the first line is 5 bytes long.

With the byte pointer at offset zero, the command {read 5;A21} would read the entire first line, including the carriage return and linefeed characters, into cell A21. If you edit that command to {read 7;A21}, the next time you activate the macro it will read all of the first line and two bytes from the next line of the file. The entire string that results will be entered in cell A21 and will look like this: Tom Ti.

Note that anytime you want to read all the remaining characters on the current line—excepting the carriage return and line feed characters—you can do so more easily with the {readln} command. The latter command will also omit reading of the two invisible characters at the end of each line. Those characters, although invisible, occupy two spaces in the text written on the worksheet and can be difficult to remove from that text.

reading
ASCII
graphics
characters

When 1-2-3 reads graphics characters from an ASCII file, it first passes them through a character translation table, which translates them into the Lotus International Character Set (LICS). 1-2-3 translates alphanumeric characters without changing them (an A is translated as an A). However, when 1-2-3 reads graphics characters, it translates each of them into a single other character. For example, a varied string of graphics characters would change to a string consisting of the same number of characters, but they'd all be the same character.

using
ASCII
screen
drivers

If you run the Install program, you can modify the current screen driver to change the way 1-2-3 handles graphics characters. In that case, 1-2-3 will show yet a different translation of the graphics characters you see in DOS.

To modify your screen driver, run 1-2-3's Install program, select Advanced Options, Modify Current Driver Set, and Text Display. Install will display a long list of screen drivers. Press the End key to see the last one; that should be Universal Text Display - ASCII - No LICS. Select that item, then select Save Changes and you'll see a prompt at the bottom of the screen that gives the name of your current driver set (probably 123—that's the default name). We recommend that you enter a new name (such as ASCII) in order to leave your current driver unchanged. Thereafter, when you want to run 1-2-3 with the ASCII screen driver, enter 123 ASCII at the DOS prompt, instead of entering 123.

With some experimentation, you may be able to use the {read} command with either driver to display a variety of graphics characters on your worksheets. Keep in mind, however, that it will be the screen driver in use at the time your macro is running that determines how 1-2-3 will display those characters. If you don't know that the ASCII driver is likely to be in use, we suggest you develop your application to work with the standard LICS drivers.

The {read} command begins reading at the current location of the byte pointer and reads forward the specified number of bytes. After the {read} command, the byte pointer will reside at the offset directly following the offset of the last byte read.

For example, if the byte pointer was at offset 16 before the command {read 5;ENTRY}, then it will be positioned at offset 21 after that command has been read by 1-2-3. Here's the logic it follows:

1. The byte pointer began at offset 16.

2. The read command instructed it to read 5 bytes. It begins reading at the current offset, 16, and advances to the next offset. It repeats that process 5 times, reading the bytes located in offsets 16–20, and now resides at offset 21.

The only exception to this rule occurs when the macro has just read the last byte in the file. There are no more bytes to read, so the byte pointer does not advance. If the macro does not reposition the byte pointer, subsequent {read} commands will continue to read a special invisible byte that demarcates the end of the file. There is no "wrap-around" effect back to the beginning of the file.

On a blank worksheet, enter the following macro and assign it a range name. Assign the range names Loc1, Read1, Loc2, and Read2 as well.

The macro will open the file in Read mode and report the position of the byte pointer in the cell named Loc1. That position will be zero because 1-2-3 always sets the byte pointer to offset zero when it opens a file in Read mode. It will then read the first three bytes of the file (the bytes located at offsets 0, 1, and 2) and store them in the cell named Read1. The macro will again report the position of the byte pointer (this time in the cell named Loc2). The byte pointer is now located at offset 3. Finally, the macro reads one more byte, which is the byte located at offset 3, and stores it in the cell named Read2.

Before running the macro, review the following diagram. The diagram contains the two lines from Sample.prn interspersed with a scale identifying the offset of each byte. Remember to regard zeros beyond the first one as the appropriate multiple of ten, so that, on line 1, the "s" in "simple" is located at offset 10.

```
This is a simple        <-- Line one of Sample.prn
01234567890123456?       <-- Byte numbers for line 1
sample ASCII file.      <-- Line two of Sample.prn
890123456789012345b?     <-- Byte numbers for line 2
```

```
         A       B        C       D      E       F       G       H
    1  NAME    MACRO                             COMMENT
    2  ---------------------------------------------------------------
    3  \A      {open "SAMPLE.PRN";"r"}            Open file in read mode
    4          {getpos LOC1}                      Get location
    5          {read 3;read1}                     Read 3 bytes
    6          {getpos LOC2}                      Get location again
    7          {read 1;read2}                     Read current byte
    8          {close}                            Close file
    9          {quit}                             Quit
   10
   11  LOC1                                       Location of byte pntr
   12  READ1                                      Data read from file
   13  LOC2                                       Location of byte pntr
   14  READ2                                      Data read from file
   15
```

Figure 15-14

{ Readln }

Purpose: Use { readln } to copy an entire line from an ASCII file on to the worksheet.

Format: { readln [location] }
   Where [location] is a cell. [Location] may be a cell address, a range address, a range name, or in Release 2.2, a formula.

Sample: { readln TAX }

Complements: { open }

See also: { read }

Description: In the currently open ASCII file, { readln } reads from the current position of the byte pointer to the end of the current line and enters that data into the specified cell. However, unlike the { read } command, { readln } will not read the invisible carriage return and linefeed characters at the end of the line.

If the location specified is a range encompassing more than one cell, 1-2-3 will enter the characters it reads into the top left cell in that range. The entry will always appear as a left-aligned label entry.
   Like the { read } command, { readln } begins reading at the current byte and moves the byte pointer to the offset directly following the last one read. However, whereas you must specify the number of bytes for { read } to read, { readln } almost always reads from the current byte

through the end of the current line. (For the exception, see the margin note "unusual circumstances", below.)

The {readln} command differs from the / File Import Text (/FIT) command in that /FIT will read the entire file on to the worksheet, {readln} will read individuals lines (or portions thereof) from the file.

effect on the byte pointer

After the macro has read a line with the {readln} command, the byte pointer in the ASCII file will reside on the first character of the next line. If the macro reads another {readln} command at that time, it will read the entire next line.

unusual circum-stances

Unlike the {read} command, the {readln} command ordinarily cannot read either of the two invisible characters that terminate each line (the carriage return and linefeed characters). However, if the byte pointer resides at the offset of the linefeed character in the ASCII file (which is the last character in a line) and the macro reads a {readln} command, 1-2-3 will read the linefeed character as a blank space and then read the entire next line. The net result entered on the worksheet is the next line of the file with a blank space preceding it.

testing for the end of the file

If you intend to read every line in a file and stop at the end, you could simply use the /File Import Text command. However, if you want to direct each line of the file to a different cell (instead of reading them into successive cells in a column), or if you want to begin reading somewhere after the beginning of the file, the / File Import Text command can't help. Use {readln} instead.

If you intend to use {readln} to read through the file, you need to know when you've reached the end of the file. After reading each line of the file, the byte pointer will move to the beginning of the next line. After reaching the last line of the file, the byte pointer will reside on a special byte that demarcates the end of the file. If the macro at that time reads another {readln} command, that command will fail.

As with all the file i/o commands, if {readln} succeeds, it immediately directs macro control to the next line of the macro, bypassing any instructions that may remain on the same line. If the command fails, control continues in normal fashion. If there are any instructions to the right of {readln}, the macro will read them.

With that in mind, you might wish to include a {branch} command directly to the right of the {readln} command. The {branch} command would direct control to the routine you want to start once 1-2-3 finishes reading the file.

Here is a sample application that tests for the end of the file. It opens a file and reads through it line by line.

Here's an overview of the method we're about to present, by each row of the worksheet on which the macro appears. Begin by placing the cell pointer on the first cell you want to accept the first line of data from the file. (1) Opens the file in read mode, (2) freezes the control panel so subsequent changes to it don't display, (3) reads a line of the ASCII file into a cell named Ans, which is a temporary data-storage cell; if the end of the file has been reached, the {readln} command will fail, and the next command on this line will be read, sending control to a routine, Stop, that terminates the macro (4) assuming that the {readln} command succeeded and there is data in Ans, copies the contents of Ans to the current cell on the worksheet, (5) the cell pointer moves down a cell to prepare to accept more data and the macro branches to Loop, where it reads another line of data from the file.

Here's the macro:

Example: Testing for End-Of-File with {Read}.

```
      A        B         C      D       E         F        G         H
  1  NAME     MACRO                    COMMENT
  2  ------------------------------------------------
  3  \A       {open "SAMPLE.PRN";"r"}  Open file
  4           {paneloff}               Turn off menu display
  5  LOOP     {readln ANS}{branch STOP} Read a line into ANS
  6           /cANS~~                  Copy ANS to current cell
  7           {d}{branch LOOP}         Move down, read more
  8
  9  STOP     {close}                  Close file
 10           {quit}
 11
 12  ANS                               Store data
```

Figure 15-15

In Release 2.2, where {readln} can evaluate an expression, you should use {readln @cellpointer("address")} and {d} to do the job. Note how it makes for a simpler macro. Again, begin by placing the cell pointer on the cell that you want to accept the first line of data from the file.

```
      A        B         C      D       E         F        G         H
  1  NAME     MACRO                    COMMENT
  2  -----------------------------------------------
  3  \A       {open "SAMPLE.PRN";"r"}   Open file
  4           {paneloff}                Turn off menu display
  5  LOOP     {readln @cellpointer("address")}{branch STOP}
  6           {d}{branch LOOP}          Move down, read more
  7
  8  STOP     {close}                   Close file
  9           {quit}
 10
```

Figure 15-16

reading
ASCII
graphics
characters

When 1-2-3 reads graphics characters from an ASCII file, it first passes them through a character translation table which translates them into the Lotus International Character Set (LICS). 1-2-3 translates alphanumeric characters without changing them (an A is translated as an A). However,

when 1-2-3 reads graphics characters, it translates them to other characters—many of them to the same character.

**using
ASCII
screen
drivers**

If you run the Install program, you can modify the current screen driver to change the way 1-2-3 handles graphics characters. In that case, 1-2-3
will show yet a different translation of the graphics characters you see in
DOS.

To modify your screen driver, run the Install program, select
Advanced Options, Modify Current Driver Set, and Text Display. Install
will display a long list of screen drivers. Press the End key to see the last
one; that should be Universal Text Display -ASCII- No LICS. Select that
item, then select Save Changes and you'll see a prompt at the bottom of
the screen that gives the name of your current driver set (probably 123—
that's the default name). We recommend that you enter a new name (such
as ASCII) in order to leave your current driver unchanged. When you
want to run 1-2-3 with the ASCII screen driver, enter 123 ASCII at the
DOS prompt, instead of entering 123.

With some experimentation, you may be able to use the {readln}
command with either driver to display a variety of graphics characters on
your worksheets. Keep in mind, however, that it will be the screen driver
in use at the time your macro is running that determines how 1-2-3 will
display those characters. If you don't know that the ASCII driver is likely
to be in use, we suggest you develop your application to work with the
standard LICS drivers.

**using
Sample.prn**

On a blank worksheet, enter the following macro and assign it a range
name. Assign the range names Loc1, Read1, Loc2, and Read2.

The macro will open the file in Read mode. At the time 1-2-3 opens a
file in that mode, the offset number of the byte pointer will always be 0.
The macro will then read the first line of the file (excluding the carriage
return and linefeed that terminate the line) and store it in the cell named
Read1. At this point, the byte pointer will be positioned at the beginning
of the second line of the file, which is located at offset 18. The macro will
then read the second line of the file and store that line in the cell named
Read2. There are just two lines to this ASCII file, so the macro has now
read through to the end of the file.

Before running the macro, review the following diagram. It contains
the two lines from Sample.prn interspersed with a scale identifying the
position of each byte.

```
This is a simple      <-- Line one of Sample.prn
01234567890123456?    <-- Byte numbers for line 1
sample ASCII file.    <-- Line two of Sample.prn
8901234567890123456?  <-- Byte numbers for line 2
```

```
         A       B       C       D     E     F       G       H
  1  NAME    MACRO                            COMMENT
  2  -------------------------------------------------------
  3  \A      {open "SAMPLE.PRN";"r"}          Open file in read mode
  4          {getpos LOC1}                    Get location
  5          {readln READ1}                   Read 3 bytes
  6          {getpos LOC2}                    Get location again
  7          {read READ2}                     Read current byte
  8          {getpos LOC2}                    Get location again
  9          {close}                          Close file
 10          {quit}                           Quit
 11
 12  LOC1                                     Location of byte pntr
 13  READ1                                    Data read from file
 14  LOC2                                     Location of byte pntr
 15  READ2                                    Data read from file
```

Figure 15-17

{ Setpos }

Purpose: Use { setpos } to change the position of the byte pointer in an ASCII file.

Format: { setpos [value] }
Where [value] is a number. [Value] may be a number, a formula, a cell address, a range name describing a single cell, or in Release 2.2, a formula.

Sample: { setpos 8 }

Complements: { open }

See also: { getpos }

Description: Use { setpos } to reposition the byte pointer in an ASCII file. You must have opened the file with the { open } command prior to using the { setpos } command.

If you want to set the position of the byte pointer to the end of the file, you can use the { filesize } command to place the number of bytes in the file into a cell. That number is also the number representing the offset of the last byte in the file, so you can then use the { setpos } command with a cell reference to the cell conaining the file size. Upon reading such a { setpos } command in a macro, 1-2-3 will move the byte pointer to the end of the file.

However, if the reason you want to move the byte pointer to the end of the file is to write something there, it is easier to simply open the file in Append mode: { open "SAMPLE.PRN";"a" } . Even if you already have the file open in some other mode, you can issue the above command to change to Append mode, and 1-2-3 will move the byte pointer to the end of the file.

If you constructed the macro as we instructed at the beginning of this chapter, you can easily add another line to it. Open the file in Append mode and use a {writeln} or {write} command. However, to add more text to the last line, you will need to do some more maneuvering to properly position the byte pointer. When you open the file in Append mode, the byte pointer will be set to the end of the file. To add to the last line, you will need to back up two bytes. To do that, you will need to use the {setpos} command.

The following macro will (1) open the file Sample.prn, (2) check the size of the file, (3) set the position of the byte pointer to two bytes before the end of the file, (4) write some new text at the end of the last line, and (5) close the file.

Before running the macro, move to an empty portion of the worksheet, select / File Import Text and specify Sample.prn. After running it, move to a blank space and repeat the File Import commands above and compare the two results. You'll see that the macro has written the sentence "This is new!" at the end of the second line of the file. Were you not to have repositioned the byte pointer with the {setpos} command, that text would have been written as a third line.

	A	B	C	D	E	F	G	H
1	NAME	MACRO				COMMENT		
2	-------	---------------------------------------				---------------		
3	\C	{open "SAMPLE.PRN";"a"}				Open file for both		
4		{filesize SIZE}				Determine file size		
5		{setpos SIZE-2}				Goto end of last line		
6		{write " This is new!"}				Write new text there		
7		{close}				Close file		
8								
9	SIZE					Store file size		
10								

Figure 15-18

{ Write }

Purpose: Use {write} to write a string of characters to an ASCII file.

Format: { write [text] }

Where [text] is a string of characters. [Text] may be a string, a formula, a cell address, or a range name describing a single cell.

Sample: { write "December 1988" }
or
{ write ENTRY }

Complements: { open }

See also: { writeln }, { read }, { readln }

Description: { Write } enables you to write one or more characters to the currently open file. { Write } will commence writing bytes at the current position of the byte pointer.

Suppose you open an existing file in modify mode, which is the mode in which you can write to an existing file without the macro erasing everything in it first. In modify mode, { write } will overwrite bytes already stored in the locations to which it writes. For example, suppose you have the following ASCII file:

```
Washers:   100   200   250
Faucets:    50    25    75
```

Let's superimpose our own offset counter above and below the file:

```
01234567890123456789Ø1234
Washers:   100   200   250
Faucets:    50    25    75
567890123456789Ø123456789
```

Let's further suppose that the byte pointer is at offset 10. Remember, you begin counting with 0, so offset 10 is actually the 11th byte in the file. In this case, that's the second "0" in the offset counter. If the macro reads the command { write "125 210 255" }, then the file would look like this:

```
Washers:   125   210   255
Faucets:    50    25    75
```

The string in the { write } command overwrites the bytes in the file, beginning with the current byte. If you attempted to write a longer string of characters, you'd begin to overwrite the hidden characters at the end of the first line, the carriage return and linefeed. If you overwrite the carriage return (the byte at offset 23) with a visible character, you'll eliminate the line break and the two lines of the file will merge into one For example, suppose the macro read the following two statements:

```
{setpos 23}
{write "0"}
```

The file would now consist of one long line, the "0" having overwritten the carriage return that formerly separated the two lines.

```
Washers:   125   210   2550 Faucets:   50   25   75
```

If you want to insert a line break in a file, write a carriage return character over the linefeed. With the file in the current position, the following macro command would resplit the lines. However since the macro is writing a new character to offset 23, and a 0 now resides there, it will overwrite that 0.

```
{setpos 23}
{write @char(13)}
```

Another carriage return written to the same byte would have no effect at all; it would merely overwrite one carriage return with another. However, if you now write a carriage return to the next byte, you will insert a blank line in the file.

You can do that by issuing just a {write} command. Since the macro last wrote to offset 23, the byte ponter now resides at offset 24. The current location of the byte pointer is where the beginning of the text contained in the next {write} command will begin.

```
{write @char(13)}
```

writing the argument

Quotation marks surrounding the string will ensure that it will be treated as a string. 1-2-3 will always attempt to treat a string not enclosed in quotation marks as a location. If the string cannot be treated as a cell address, formulaic expression, or range name (because the string is not a cell address or formula and no such range name exists), 1-2-3 will then treat it as a string. The danger in not enclosing a string of literal text in quotation marks is that someone may later create a range name that duplicates the string. The next time after such an event, the macro would malfunction.

A reference to a range containing a value will result in an error. 1-2-3 will display the error message "Invalid string value in WRITE...".

writing to empty files

If you open a new file and write to it, but do so at some offset from position zero, 1-2-3 will pad the opening of the file with a variety of random characters. These characters appear to come from the disk. This applies also if you open an existing file in write mode, which erases the current contents of the file before it begins writing the new data. To avoid that, include blank spaces in the string you write to the current line:

```
{open "NEW.PRN";"w"}
{write "     This line is indented five spaces"}.
```

If you wish to precede the current line with one or more blank lines, first use one {writeln} command with a null string for each blank line you wish to create. Used in that manner, the {writeln} command will enter a carriage return/linefeed (abbreviated together as CRLF) on each line, then advance the byte pointer to the next line.

For example, if you wanted to open a new file and write the string "Happy Birthday!" indented five characters to the left of the margin of the third line, you would use the following macro:

```
       A        B        C      D      E      F      G      H

 1   NAME     MACRO                            COMMENT
 2   ---------------------------------------------------
 3   \A       {open "NEW.PRN";"w"}             Open new file
 4            {writeln ""}                     CRLF
 5            {writeln ""}                     CRLF
 6            {write "     Happy Birthday!"}   Write a line
 7            {close}                          Close file
 8            {quit}                           Quit
 9
10
```

Figure 15-19

writing to files containing text or data

If you are writing to a file that already exists, you should open that file in Modify mode. In that mode, {write} begins writing at the current position of the byte pointer and writes over each succeeding byte until it has finished writing the specified string. If data was stored in any of the bytes written to with a {write} command, 1-2-3 will overwrite the data stored in those bytes.

writing ASCII graphics characters

When 1-2-3 writes graphics characters from an ASCII file, it first passes them through a character translation table which translates them into the Lotus International Character Set (LICS). 1-2-3 translates alphanumeric characters without changing them (an A is translated as an A). However, when 1-2-3 reads graphics characters, it translates them to other characters. Many translate to the same other character. That would change a varied string of graphics characters into a uniform string consisting of the same character.

using Sample.prn

The following macro will (1) open the file Sample.prn, (2) check the size of the file, (3) set the position of the byte pointer to the second offset before the end of the file, (4) write some new text at the end of the last line, and (5) close the file.

Before running the macro, move to an empty portion of the worksheet, select / File Import Text and specify Sample.prn. After running the macro, move to a blank space and repeat the File Import commands above and compare the two results. You'll see that the macro has written the sentence "This is new!" at the end of the second line of the file.

```
         A        B       C       D       E       F       G       H
1    NAME     MACRO                               COMMENT
2    -----------------------------------------------------------
3    \C       {open "SAMPLE.PRN";"m"}             Open file for both
4             {filesize SIZE}                     Determine file size
5             {setpos SIZE-2}                     Goto end of last line
6             {write "  This is new!"}            Write new text there
7             {close}                             Close file
8
9    SIZE                                         Store file size
10
```

Figure 15-20

{ Writeln }

Purpose: Use { writeln } to a write a complete line to an ASCII file.

Format: { writeln [text] }
   Where [text] is a string of characters. [Text] may be a string, a formula, a cell address, or a range name describing a single cell.

Sample: { writeln TEXT }

Complements: { open }

See also: { write }, { readln }, { read }

Description: If you open a new file and write to it, but do so at some offset from position zero, 1-2-3 will pad the opening of the file with random characters. These characters appear to be from the disk. To avoid such padding, include blank spaces in the string you write to the current line. This applies also if you open an existing file in write mode, which erases the current contents of the file before it begins writing the new data.

If you wish to precede the current line with one or more blank lines, first use one { writeln } command with a null string for each blank line you wish to create. Used in that manner, the { writeln } command will enter a carriage return/linefeed (abbreviated together as CRLF) on each line, then advance the byte pointer to the next line.

For example, if you wanted to open a new file and write the string "Happy Birthday!" indented five characters to the left of the margin on the third line, you would use the following macro:

```
        A         B         C         D         E         F         G         H
1    NAME      MACRO                                   COMMENT
2    -----------------------------------------------------------
3    \A        {open "NEW.PRN";"w"}                    Open new file
4              {writeln ""}                            CRLF
5              {writeln ""}                            CRLF
6              {writeln "     Happy Birthday!"}        Write a line
7              {close}                                 Close file
8              {quit}                                  Quit
9
10
```

Figure 15-21

writing the argument

Quotation marks surrounding the string will ensure that it will be treated as a string. 1-2-3 will always attempt to treat a string not enclosed in quotation marks as a location. If the string can't be treated as a cell address, range name, or formulaic expression, (because the string is not a cell address or formula and no such range name exists), 1-2-3 will then treat it as a string. The danger in not enclosing a string of literal text in quotation marks is that someone may later create a range name that duplicates the string. The next time after such an event, the macro would malfunction.

A reference to a range containing a value will result in an error. 1-2-3 will display the error message "Invalid string value in WRITELN...".

writing ASCII graphics characters

When 1-2-3 writes graphics characters from an ASCII file, it first passes them through a character translation table which translates them into the Lotus International Character Set (LICS). 1-2-3 translates alphanumeric characters without changing them (an A is translated as an A). However, when 1-2-3 reads graphics characters, it translates them to other characters. Many of them translate to the same other character, changing a varied string of characters into a uniform one.

using Sample.prn

The following macro will (1) open the file Sample.prn, (2) check the size of the file, (3) set the position of the byte pointer to the end of the file, (4) write a new line at the end of the file, and (5) close the file.

Before running the macro, move to an empty portion of the worksheet, select / File Import Text and specify Sample.prn. After running the macro, move to a blank space and repeat the File Import commands above and compare the two results. You'll see that the macro has written the sentence "This is a new line!" at the end of the file.

	A	B	C	D	E	F	G	H
1	NAME	MACRO				COMMAND		
2	----	--						
3	\C	{open "SAMPLE.PRN";"m"}				Open file for both		
4		{filesize SIZE}				Determine file size		
5		{setpos SIZE}				Goto end of last line		
6		{writeln "This is a new line!"}				Write new text there		
7		{close}				Close file		
8								
9	SIZE					Store file size		
10								

Figure 15-22

16

Accessing Add-ins

Overview and Introduction to New Concepts

Release 2 of 1-2-3 introduced the capability to serve as a host for separate programs, called add-ins, that work as part of 1-2-3. Add-ins comprise as diverse a group of programs as does software in general; databases, goal-seeking programs, and collections of specialized financial @functions are just several of many types of add-in software.

Add-ins can make good application adjuncts for three reasons: they can add considerable functionality to 1-2-3, in most cases they can be controlled by macros[42], and you can retrieve the memory they use at any time by detaching them from 1-2-3.

In order to transfer macro control from the worksheet to an add-in, you must first load 1-2-3 with the Add-in Manager (a program you receive with any add-in). In Release 2.2, the add-in manager is incorporated into 1-2-3, so you need load nothing separately. Provided the add-in was written to support 1-2-3 macros, you can then use a macro to:

---

[42] Many add-ins can be controlled through macros in exactly the same manner as you can control 1-2-3 with a macro. Other add-ins can be controlled with macros, but with reservations. For example, you might be able to use a macro to invoke the add-in and perform some operation as long as you do so from inside 1-2-3, not from within the add-in. Such variations are at the discretion of each add-in's developer, thus the need to evaluate each add-in individually.

• Display the add-in manager menu and either attach an add-in to 1-2-3 and assign the add-in to an Alt-function key, invoke the add-in, or detach the add-in from 1-2-3.

• Operate the add-in in the same manner in which macros can operate 1-2-3: by passing to the add-in keystrokes to enter data, navigate through the application, or execute commands.

• Customize operation of the add-in through advanced macro commands such as {menubranch}, {if}, and {getlabel}.

Since you can have more than one add-in attached to 1-2-3 at a time, you can transfer control between all the attached add-ins and 1-2-3 at will.

The key names {app1} through {app4} are the secret to controlling add-ins. The number included in the key name refers to each of the four Alt-function keys by which you access the add-in manager or add-ins themselves. However, it does not do so directly: {app4} does not refer to the F4 function key, it refers to the Alt-F10 function key. The details follow:

{App1}, {App2}, {App3}, {App4}

Purpose: When 1-2-3 reads {app1} through {app4} in a macro, it activates one of the four Alt-function keys associated with add-ins. Which key it activates depends on the number included in the key name:

Format: {app1}, {app2}, {app3}, {app4}

Sample: {app1}

Complements: None.

Description: When 1-2-3 reads {app1} through {app4} in a macro, it activates one of the four Alt-function keys associated with add-ins. Which key it activates depends on the number included in the key name:

{app} key names relate to alt-function keys

{app1} Alt-F7
{app2} Alt-F8
{app3} Alt-F9
{app4} Alt-F10

In Release 2 or 2.01, the Alt-F10 key always calls up the Add-in Manager menu; the function of the other keys depends on how you have configured 1-2-3. In Release 2.2, too, Alt-F10 calls up the add-in menu, but you can reconfigure it to call up an add-in. In Release 2.2, you can always call up the add-in manager menu from 1-2-3's main menu using the / Add-In command.

If you've attached an add-in to a particular function key, the corresponding key name (such as {app2} for Alt-F8) will display a menu for that add-in. Select items from an add-in menu just as you do from a 1-2-3 command menu—have the macro type the first letter of the command you wish to choose.

reading
unassigned
{app} keys

If the macro reads an {app} command corresponding to an Alt-function key to which no add-in is currently attached, 1-2-3 will beep, just as it will if you press any other key out of its proper context. (Note, however, that in Release 2.2 the Alt-F10 key is valid even with no add-in attached. In that case, it calls up the add-in manager menu.) For example, if you press Alt-F8 while in Ready mode with no add-in attached to that key, 1-2-3 will beep. Similarly, if you have the macro press Alt-F8 through the {app2} command and nothing is attached to that key, 1-2-3 will beep. 1-2-3 will not go into error mode, and accordingly, you can't trap detect anything with the {onerror} command. (Refer to the listing for {ifkey} in the chapter on Controlling Program Flow if you want to trap such events in a macro.)

when a
macro
controls an
add-in, it
must
conform to
the add-in's
command
structure

Once the add-in has been invoked, if that add-in supports macros (most add-ins do), all subsequent keystrokes will be directed to the add-in either until the macro ends or the macro, by invoking the add-in's own commands, terminates the add-in.

Just as you must write 1-2-3 keystroke macros to conform to the sequence and content of 1-2-3's command menus and its other operating characteristics, once you transfer macro control from 1-2-3 to an add-in, you must conform to the logical structure of the particular add-in you are using.

syntax
points

It is important to realize that {app1} through {app4} are not advanced macro commands, but key names. You should therefore write {app4} (with no spaces), not {app 4}. There is no space between the string "app" and the number that follows it. That number is not an argument; it's just part of the keyword. While you can create a variable {app} command using a string formula such as +"{app"&F10&"}", you cannot use a range name or cell address in the {app} command to provide the number (the command {appC14} won't work).

Since they are key names, {app1} through {app4} work with values that indicate the keystroke should be repeated. So if it made sense to

invoke an add-in repeatedly, you could do it as you would repeat any key. So {app1 10} would be the same as pressing Alt-F7 10 times.
Example:
Macro for Release 2.2:

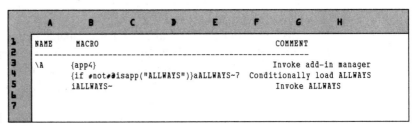

Figure 16-1

17

@Functions Commonly Used in Macros

Overview and Introduction to New Concepts

Macros work hand in hand with 1-2-3's spreadsheet. One manifestation of that close relationship is that macros often include the same @functions you'd use on the spreadsheet. All @functions return a value or a string, and you can use the information an @function provides as input to your macro. Here are some of @functions you'll most frequently use in macros:

Special functions:
@cell, @cellpointer: evaluate attribute of a cell
@hlookup, @vlookup: look up a value or string in a table

Date functions:
@now: current date and time
@time: define time setting

String functions:
@exact: detect precise matches
@find: locate position of character in string
@left, @right, @mid: extract substrings

@upper, @lower: convert to uniform case
@string, @value: convert from value to string or from string to value

Logical functions:
@iserr, @isna: detect presence of ERR or NA values
@isnumber, @isstring: detect type of entry stored in cell

The section that follows describes each of the @functions listed above. As you read, keep in mind that while we've used the same format to describe the @functions as we earlier used for the advanced macro commands, these are not macro commands. To include them in a macro, you have to include them within a macro command. The examples in each definition show the @function embedded in a macro command.

Special Functions

@cell

Purpose: @Cell enables you to determine any of several attributes of a designated cell.

Format: @Cell("attribute";cell address)
   Where attribute is any one of the following strings: contents, row, col, width, prefix, address, type, format, protect, or in Release 2.2, filename.

Sample: @cell("contents";C1)

Description: The @cell function enables you to determine any of a number of attributes of a cell. The following is a list of options for the first cell of the @cell function, followed by the result that argument will return:

- "contents": The current contents of the cell (the same result you'd receive from making a direct reference to the cell).

- "row": The number of the row in which it resides.

- "col": The number of the column in which it resides (where column A is represented as 1, column B as 2, etc.).

- "width": The width of the column in which it resides.

- "prefix": The label prefix that precedes the entry currently in the cell (returns nothing if the entry is a value).

- "address": The address of that cell (returned as an absolute address). If you've assigned the name Test to A4 @cell("address";TEST) will return A4.

- "type": The type of entry in that cell. The codes returned are v for value, l for label, or b for blank.

- "format": The type of format and number of decimal places assigned to the cell. The code returned is the same as the format code you see in parentheses in the control panel when you highlight a range-formatted cell. For example, C2 indicates currency format with two decimal places.

- "protect": The protection status of the cell. The codes returned are 0 for unprotected or 1 for protected. Remember that, by default, all cells have protected status. However, that protected status only becomes activated once you select / Worksheet Global Protection Enable. Cells are unprotected only after you use the / Range Unprotect command to assign unprotected status to them.

- "filename": The name of the file currently in memory. Release 2.2 returns in upper case the full drive, path, and filename of the file that is currently in memory. If the file is as yet unnamed, the @function returns a null string.

In macros, the various permutations of @cell are primarily useful in {if} statements, where you use @cell to determine whether a condition is true, then branch to another routine to either change the condition or leave things as they are. For example, if the current width of a cell is less than the length of the string that resides in it, the macro can branch to a routine to increase the width to that length (see the macro below).

	A	B	C	D	E	F	G	H
1	NAME	MACRO						
2	-----------	-----------						
3	\A	{if @cell("width";TEST)<@length(TEST)}{WIDEN}						
4		{branch NEXT}						
5								
6	WIDEN	{let SIZE;@string(@length(TEST)+1;0)}						
7		/wcs{SIZE}~						
8		{return}						
9								
10	SIZE							
11		{return}						
12								
13								
14								
15								

Figure 17-1

@Cell is the only function that can properly test to determine if a given cell is blank. If you want to determine if a cell named Test is blank, use an {if} statement such as {if @cell("type";TEST) = "b"}.

@cellpointer

Purpose: @cellpointer enables you to determine the attributes of the current cell.

Format: @cellpointer("attribute")
Where attribute is any one of the following strings: contents, row, col, width, prefix, address, type, format, or protect.

Sample: @cellpointer("contents")

Description: The @cellpointer function enables you to determine any of a number of attributes for the current cell. The following is a list of options for the first cell of the @cellpointer function, followed by the result that argument will return:

- "contents": The current contents of the cell.

- "row": The number of the row in which it resides.

- "col": The number of the column in which it resides (where column A = 1, column B = 2, etc.).

- "width": The width of the column in which it resides.

- "prefix": The label prefix that precedes the entry currently in the cell (returns nothing if the entry is a value).

- "address": The address of that cell (returned as an absolute address) If the cellpointer is on cell A4, @cellpointer ("address") will return A4.

  IF cell

- "type": The type of entry in that cell. The codes returned are v for value, l for label, or b for blank.

- "format": The type of format and number of decimal places assigned to the cell. The code returned is the same as the format code you see in parentheses in the control panel when you highlight a range-formatted cell. For example, C2 indicates currency format with two decimal places.

- "protect": The protection status of the cell. The codes returned are 0 for unprotected or 1 for protected.

- "filename": The name of the file currently in memory. 1-2-3 Release 2.2 returns (in upper case) the full drive, path, and filename of the file that is currently in memory. If the file is still unnamed, 1-2-3 returns a null string.

Like its companion, @cell, @cellpointer is useful in {if} statements, where you can use it to interrogate the status of the current cell and branch to an appropriate routine. For example, in the macro below, @cellpointer supplies the current row number. When the cell pointer has reached a certain row number, the macro terminates.

```
      A        B        C        D        E        F        G        H
1    NAME     MACRO                                        COMMENT
2    -----------------------------------------------------------------
3    \A       {let ROWS;@rows(LIST)+@cell("row";LIST)}     Check size of list
4    LOOP     {?}{d}                                       Enter data, down
5             {if @cellpointer("row")=ROWS}{quit}          End of list? If so, quit
6             {branch LOOP}                                If not, continue
7
8
9
10
```

Figure 17-2

@Cellpointer is the only function that can properly test to determine if the current cell is blank. If you want to know if the current cell is blank, use the {if} statement {if @cellpointer("type") = "b"}.

@Cellpointer is also useful in {let} statements. In line 3 of the following macro, the {let} statement uses @cellpointer to maintain a running total.

Example:

```
      A        B        C        D        E        F        G        H
1    NAME     MACRO                                        COMMENT
2    -----------------------------------------------------------------
3    \A       {let ROWS;@rows(LIST)+@cell("row";LIST)}     Check size of list
4    LOOP     {?}~                                         Enter data
5             {let TOTAL;+TOTAL+@cellpointer("contents")}  Running total
6             {d}                                          Down one
7             {if @cellpointer("row")=ROWS}{quit}          End? If so, quit
8             {branch LOOP}                                If not, continue
9
10
```

Figure 17-3

If you're using 1-2-3 Release 2.2, you'll find @cellpointer particularly useful in macros. It's common to need to refer to the current cell, no matter where the cell pointer is, and @cellpointer is the best way to do that. The following example illustrates a simple case:

```
        A       B       C       D       E       F       G       H
1   NAME    MACRO
2   --------------
3   \G      {getlabel "Enter a label: ";@cellpointer("address")}~
4
5
```

Figure 17-4

@vlookup

Purpose: @vlookup enables you to look up a value or a string in a table on the worksheet.

Format: @vlookup(key value,table range,column offset)
Where table range is the range containing a table of one or more columns, key value is the value you're using to locate an entry in the table, and column offset is the column in which the entry you wish to locate resides.

Sample: @vlookup(KEY;KEY_TAB;1)

Description: @Vlookup enables you to retrieve a value or a string from a table. In the following example, the table consists of two columns and is named Menu_list (however, the table could consist of any number of columns).

```
        A       B       C       D       E       F       G       H
1
2
3
4   MENU_LIST   1       exit
5               2       print
6               3       enter
7               4       save
8               5       labels
9               6       chart
10
```

Figure 17-5

@Vlookup takes three arguments: the value or string to use as a key, the table range, and the offset number of the column in the table from which you wish to retrieve a value or label. The key is a value or string that matches a value or string in the leftmost column of the table. The offset number designates the column from which to retrieve a value (zero is the leftmost column in the table, one the next column to the right, and so on).

@Vlookup will return the entry stored in the cell on the same row (but in the designated column offset in the table) as the match to the key value. For example, if you refer to the table shown above (in which the name Menu_List refers to the table stored in B4..C9), the formula @vlookup(4; MENU_LIST;1) will use the key value of 4 to match an entry in the leftmost column of the table named List, and return the entry located in the first offset column on the same row. So, 4 matches the value 4 located in cell B7, and the entry in the first column offset from B7 is in C7, which contains the label "save". @Vlookup(4;MENU_LIST;1) returns "save". Note that you will most frequently store the key value in a separate cell (so you can more easily change it) and use a range name to refer to it in the formula, such as @Vlookup(KEY; MENU_LIST;1).

@Vlookup works somewhat differently depending on whether the left column of the table (which contains the entries to be matched) contains strings or values.

If the left column of the table contains strings, then, with one exception, the key value must exactly match an entry in the left column of the table in order for @vlookup to return an entry from the table. So if the key value is John, there must be an entry John in the left column of the table (and with precisely that mix of upper and lower case letters). The exception occurs when the key is either blank or consists of a value entry. In that case, @vlookup will return the entry in the lowermost position in the designated column of the table (that's "chart" in our current example). If the key is a label that doesn't exactly match any label in the leftmost column of the table, @vlookup will return the value ERR. @Vlookup is case sensitive at all times, not just when you are using the ASCII Collating driver, so be sure to use the same case in a key as in the leftmost column of the table.

If the leftmost column of the table contains values, they must be arranged in ascending order going down the column. A key value will match the value in the leftmost column with which it is either exactly equal, or, if there is no exact match, the value which is the lesser value closest to the key value. For example, a key value of 2.9 will match the value 2 and return the entry "print" in the example above. If the leftmost column of the table contains values and the key is a label or, if the key is a cell reference and that cell is empty, @vlookup will return ERR.

Example:

```
        A       B       C       D       E       F       G       H
   1   NAME    MACRO
   2   --------------
   3   \A      {getnumber "Type number: ";ANS}
   4           {if @iserr(@vlookup(ANS;LIST;1))}{branch ERR}
   5           {dispatch @vlookup(ANS;LIST;1)}
```

Figure 17-6

@hlookup

Purpose: @lookup enables you to look up a value or a string in a table on the worksheet.

Format: @hlookup(key value,table range,row offset)

Where table range is the range containing a table of one or more rows, key value is the value you're using to locate an entry in the table, and row offset is the row in which the entry you wish to locate resides.

Sample: @hlookup(KEY;KEY_TAB;1)

Description: @Hlookup enables you to retrieve a value or a string from a table. In the following example, the table consists of two rows and is named List (however, the table could consist of any number of rows).

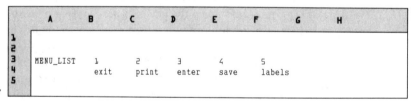

```
        A       B       C       D       E       F       G       H
   1
   2
   3   MENU_LIST   1       2       3       4       5
   4               exit    print   enter   save    labels
   5
```

Figure 17-7

@Hlookup takes three arguments: the value or string to use as a key, the table range, and the offset number of the row in the table from which you wish to retrieve a value or label. The key is a value or string that matches a value or string in the topmost row of the table. The offset number designates the row from which to retrieve a value (zero is the topmost row, one the next row to the right, and so on).

@Hlookup will return the entry stored in the cell on the same row (but in the designated row offset) as the match to the key value. For example, if you refer to the table shown above (in which the name List refers to the table stored in B3..F4), the formula @hlookup(4;LIST;1) will use the key value of 4 to match an entry in the topmost row of the table named List, and return the entry located in the first offset row on the same row. So, 4 matches the value 4 located in cell E3, and the entry in the first row offset from E3 is in E4, which contains the label "save". @Hlookup(4;LIST;1) returns "save." Note that you will most frequently store the key value in a separate cell (so you can more easily change it) and use a range name to refer to it in the formula, such as @Hlookup(KEY;LIST;1).

@Hlookup works somewhat differently depending on whether the top row of the table (which contains the entries to be matched) contains strings or values.

If the top row of the table contains strings, then, with one exception, the key value must exactly match an entry in the top row of the table in order for @hlookup to return an entry from the table. So if the key value is John, there must be an entry John in the top row of the table (and with precisely that mix of upper and lower case letters). The exception occurs when the key is either blank or consists of a value entry. In that case, @hlookup will return the entry in the lowermost position in the designated row of the table (that's labels in our current example). If the key is a label that doesn't exactly match any label in the topmost row of the table, @hlookup will return the value ERR. @Hlookup is case sensitive at all times, not just when you are using the ASCII Collating driver, so be sure to use the same case in a key as in the topmost row of the table.

If the topmost row of the table contains values, they must be arranged in ascending order going across the row. A key value will match the value in the topmost row with which it is either exactly equal, or, if there is no exact match, the value which is the lesser value closest to the key value. For example, a key value of 2.9 will match the value 2 and return the entry print in the example above. If the topmost row of the table contains values and the key is a label, or if the key is a cell reference and that cell is empty, @hlookup will return ERR.

Example: The following macros assume that you would also have written the routines named End and Err.

	A	B	C	D	E	F	G	H
1	NAME	MACRO						
2	--------------							
3	\B	{getnumber "Type number: ";ANS}						
4		{if @iserr(@hlookup(ANS;LIST;1))}{branch ERR}						
5		{dispatch @hlookup(ANS;LIST;1)}						
6								
7								

Figure 17-8

@isaaf

Purpose: Detects whether a given add-in @function is currently available.

Format: @isaaf("function_name")

Sample: @isaaf("custom")

Description: @Isaaf returns the value 1 if the add-in @function it names is currently available (that is, the add-in that contains it is attached to 1-2-3) and 0 if the @function is not currently attached to 1-2-3. @Isaaf is the only way to test for the availability of such an @function. @Isapp, an @function that tests for the presence of add-ins, will not detect the presence of an add-in that only contains @functions.

Exclude the @ sign itself when you write the name of the @function. So if the @function is called @custom, write @isaaf("custom"). Put the name in quotation marks, except if you store the name in a separate cell and refer to it through a cell address or named range; then use a string without quotation marks.

The following example assumes that an add-in named Finance.adn contains the add-in @function @Custom.

Example:

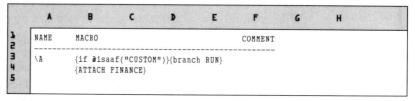

Figure 17-9

Logical Functions

@isapp

Purpose: Under certain circumstances, detects whether a given add-in is currently attached to 1-2-3.

Format: @isapp("add-in_name")

Sample: @isapp("ALLWAYS")

Description: @Isapp returns the value 1 if the add-in it names is currently attached to 1-2-3 and 0 if the add-in is not currently attached to 1-2-3. However, @Isapp works only for add-ins, such as Allways, that you can use the Add-In Invoke command to invoke. If the add-in does nothing but contain @functions, @isapp will not detect whether or not it is attached to 1-2-3 (see @isaaf).

You need not include the file extension used for the add-in; 1-2-3 will check the name only so far as the period separating filename from file extension. Be aware that some add-in products actually contain more than one add-in program, and that the file name of the add-in can differ from the name of the add-in on the product's box. So, for example, if the fictitious add-in ADD-IN PROFESSIONAL contained the add-in programs PRO_A.ADN and PRO_B.ADN, you should test for each of those add-ins separately, and you should use the actual names of the add-in files, minus the filename extension. In the case of the preceding example, you'd use the formulas @isapp("pro_a") and @isapp("pro_b").

Put the name in quotation marks, except if you store the name in a separate cell and refer to it through a cell address or named range; then use a string without quotation marks.

Example:

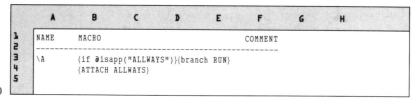

Figure 17-10

@iserr

Purpose: Detects the value ERR.

Format: @iserr(cell address)

Sample: @iserr(ANS)

Description: @Iserr returns the value 1 if the cell it evaluates contains the value ERR or 0 if the cell it evaluates contains any other value or is empty. Like the other logical functions, @iserr is useful primarily in {if} statements to determine the status of a given cell.

In {if} statements @iserr is used primarily to detect the presence of ERR, whereupon the macro will branch to an appropriate routine. For example, if in response to a {getnumber} prompt, the user merely presses the Return key without making an entry, 1-2-3 will enter the value ERR in the location {getnumber} designates. You may want to follow that {getnumber} statement immediately with an {if} statement to check for the presence of ERR. If it detects ERR, display an error message and reprompt for a valid entry.

You can't test for ERR through a conditional statement such as {if TEST = @ERR}. Such a test will always return a result of false. You must use @iserr.

Example:

	A	B	C	D	E	F	G	H
1	NAME	MACRO						
2	---------------							
3	\A	{getnumber "Enter number: ";TEST}						
4		{if @iserr(TEST)}{branch ERROR}						
5								

Figure 17-11

@isna

Purpose: Detects the value NA.

Format: @isna(cell address)

Sample: @isna(ANS)

Description: @Isna returns the value 1 if the cell it evaluates contains the value NA or 0 if the cell it evaluates contains any other value or is blank. Like the other logical functions, @isna is useful primarily in {if} statements to determine the status of a given cell.

Unlike the value ERR (which 1-2-3 will generate in response to any of a number of worksheet conditions), NA can appear on the worksheet only if you explicitly enter it there. Therefore, the circumstances under which you'll test for it are more limited in scope than those under which you might test for ERR.

However, if you do need to test for NA, you must use @isna to do so. You can't test for NA through a conditional statement such as {if TEST = @NA}. Such a test will always return a result of false.

Example:

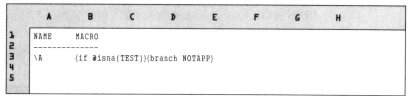

Figure 17-12

@isnumber

Purpose: Detects value entries.

Format: @isnumber(cell address)

Sample: @isnumber(ANS)

Description: @Isnumber returns the value 1 if the cell it evaluates contains a value or 0 if the cell it evaluates contains a string (label or string formula) or is blank. Like the other logical functions, @isnumber is useful primarily in {if} statements to determine the status of a given cell.

You can perform a similar kind of test by using the @cell function with its "type" argument (@cell("type";ANS)), but the @cell function will return a character instead of a value. For example, if in the preceding example, Ans contained a value, the @isnumber function would return a 1 (for true), while the @cell function would return a "v" (for value). Your choice between the two methods should be based on which kind of result—number or label—is more convenient for you to process.

There are two differences between the two approaches:

- @Cell will evaluate a string-valued formula as a value (and return a "v"); @isnumber will return a zero (for not a number) when it references such a formula.

- @Cell and @cellpointer are the only ways to test for a blank cell.

Example:

```
        A         B         C      D       E       F       G       H
    1  NAME     MACRO
    2  --------------
    3  \A       {if @isnumber(TEST)}{branch ROUT6}
    4
    5
```

Figure 17-13

@isstring

Purpose: Detects string-valued formulas or label entries.

Format: @isstring(cell address)

Sample: @isstring(ANS)

Description: @Isstring returns the value 1 if the cell it evaluates contains a label or string-valued formula or 0 if the cell it evaluates contains a value or formula that returns a value or if it is blank. Like the other logical functions, @isstring is primarily useful in {if} statements to determine the status of a given cell.

You can perform a similar kind of test by using the @cell function with its "type" argument (@cell("type";ANS)), but the @cell function will return a character instead of a value. For example, if in the preceding example, Ans contained a label, the @isstring function would return a 1 (for true), while the @cell function would return a "l" (for label). Your choice between the two methods should be based on which kind of result—value or label—is more convenient for you to process.

There are two differences between the two approaches:

- @Cell will evaluate a string-valued formula as a value (and return a "v"), while @isstring will return a one (for true) when it references such a formula. Beware that those responses are somewhat contradictory.

- @Cell and @cellpointer are the only ways to test for a blank cell.

Example:

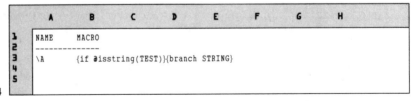

	A	B	C	D	E	F	G	H
1	NAME	MACRO						
2	--------------							
3	\A	{if @isstring(TEST)}{branch STRING}						
4								
5								

Figure 17-14

String Functions

@left

Purpose: Extracts a substring from the leftmost characters in a designated string.

Format: @left(cell address;n)
   Where n is the number of characters from the left edge of the string that will compose the substring.

Sample: @left(ANS;4)

Description: @Left returns a string that is a portion (or substring) of a designated string. @Left is primarily useful for either detecting the presence of a given substring (when you would use it in an {if} statement) or assigning a given substring to another cell (when you would use it in a {let} statement).

@Left will include in that substring the number of characters designated in the numeric argument. Blank spaces in the string count as characters. For example, @left("Christopher";5) returns the string Chris.
   Example:

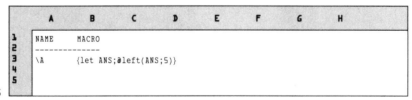

Figure 17-15

@right

Purpose: Extracts a substring from the rightmost characters in a designated string.

Format: @right(cell address;n)
   Where n is the number of characters from the right edge of the string that will compose the substring.

Sample: @right(ANS;4)

Description: @Right returns a string that is a portion (or substring) of a designated string. @Right is primarily useful for either detecting the presence of a given substring (when you would use it in an {if} statement) or assigning a given substring to another cell (when you would use it in a {let} statement).

@Right will include in that substring the number of characters designated in the numeric argument. Blank spaces in the string count as characters. For example, @right("New York City";4) will return the string City.

Example:

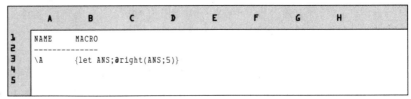

	A	B	C	D	E	F	G	H
1	NAME	MACRO						
2	--------------							
3	\A	{let ANS;@right(ANS;5)}						
4								
5								

Figure 17-16

@mid

Purpose: Extracts a substring from some number of characters in the middle of a designated string.

Format: @mid(cell address;start number;n)
Where start number is the number of the character position to begin with and n is the number of characters to include in the resulting substring.

Sample: @mid(ANS;4;3)

Description: @Mid returns a string that is a portion (or substring) of a designated string. @Mid is primarily useful for either detecting the presence of a given substring (when you would use it in an {if} statement) or assigning a given substring to another cell (when you would use it in a {let} statement).

@Mid will include in that substring the number of characters designated in the second numeric argument, beginning with the character located at the offset position designated in the first numeric argument. Blank spaces in the string count as characters. For example, @mid("Christopher";5;3) will return the string *top*. The "t" in Christopher is at the fifth offset (since offsets begin with zero, it's actually the sixth character), and, starting with that character, the next three characters in Christopher are t,o, and p.

Example:

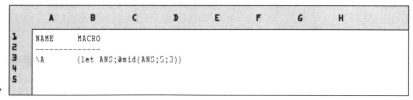

Figure 17-17

@string

Purpose: Converts a value into a left-aligned, string-valued number.

Format: @string(x;n)

Where x is a cell address, range name, formula, or value, and n is the number of decimal places you wish the resulting string to include.

Sample: @string(TEST;2)

Description: @String returns a left-aligned, string valued number from a designated value or formula. @String is primarily useful for converting a value into a string so you can test for the presence of a given substring (when you would use it in an {if} statement) or assign a given substring to another cell (when you would use it in a {let} statement).

@String enables you to incorporate a value into a string entry. You can choose the number of decimal places to include in the resulting string. One of the most common mistakes is to omit the argument that designates the number of decimal places. Even if you want to show no decimal places, you must indicate as much by including 0 as the second argument.

If you want to show fewer significant digits than there are in the value, you can't use a negative argument for the number of decimal places. Doing so will cause the @string function to return an error. Instead, nest the @round function within the @string function. For example, @string(@round(TEST;-2);2).

You can convert the result of an @string formula into a conventional label entry either by incorporating it into a {let} command (for example, {let TEST;@string(ANS;2)} will store a label entry in Test) or by copying it with the / Range Value command. However, if you place the cell pointer on an @string formula and press the Edit and Calc function keys to convert that formula to its underlying value, 1-2-3 will convert the formula to a value entry—not a label.

Example:

Figure 17-18

@value

Purpose: Converts a string that is a number into a value.

Format: @value(cell address)

Sample: @value(ANS)

Description: The @value function references a label entry consisting of a number, and returns a value. It's the complement to @string, which converts a value into a string. @Value is primarily useful for either detecting the presence of a given value (when you would use it in an {if} statement) or assigning a given value to a cell (when you would use it in a {let} statement).

While there would be no point in referencing a cell that contains a value with the @value function, if the string you are referencing changes to a value, @value will still process it (it will return the value it references). If you reference an empty cell, @value will return a zero.

Example:

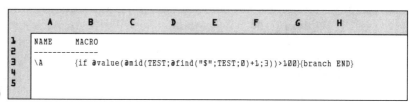

Figure 17-19

@find

Purpose: Returns the offset number of a character in a string.

Format: @find(character;string;starting offset)

Sample: @find("$";TEST;0)

Description: Returns the offset number of the first instance of a character within a string, beginning with a given offset. For example

@find("B";"BOB";0) returns 0, because if you begin at offset zero, the first instance of the character B occurs at offset zero. However, @find("B";"BOB";1) returns a 2 because if you begin at offset one, the first instance of the character B occurs at offset 2.

@Find is most often used in conjunction with one of the other string functions, particularly @mid. @Mid can use the offset number that @find returns to identify where in a given string @mid should begin extracting a substring.

Example:

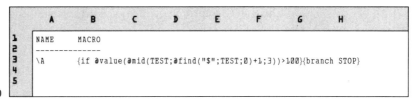

Figure 17-20

@exact

Purpose: Compares two strings and determines if they match exactly.

Format: @exact(string1;string2)

Sample: @exact(CODE;"034R61")

Description: @Exact will compare two strings and return a value of 1 if they are identical, or a value of 0 if they are not. It is primarily useful in {if} statements where you wish to know if one string is precisely the same as the other.

@Exact is case sensitive, so in the sample entry above, if the cell named Code contained an entry with a lower case "r" (which was otherwise identical to the second argument), the formula would still return the value 0.

@Exact is always case sensitive, not merely when the copy of 1-2-3 being used with it is installed with the ASCII Collating driver.

Example:

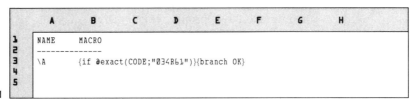

Figure 17-21

@lower

Purpose: Converts a string to all lower case.

Format: @lower(string reference)

Sample: @lower(TEST)

Description: @Lower converts a string to entirely lower case letters. It is the complement of @upper, which does the reverse, and a companion function to @proper, which converts a string to initial capital letters.

It is primarily useful in {let} statements, where it's used to convert a cell entry to all lower case.
Example:

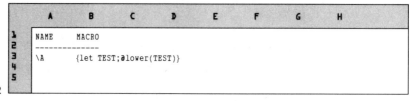

Figure 17-22

@upper

Purpose: Converts a string to all upper case.

Format: @upper(string reference)

Sample: @upper(TEST)

Description: @Upper converts a string entirely to upper case letters. It is the complement of @lower, which does the reverse, and a companion function to @proper, which converts a string to initial capital letters (Such As This).

It is primarily useful in {let} statements, where it's used to convert a cell entry to all upper case.

Example:

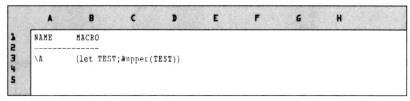

Figure 17-23

Time and Date Functions

@now

Purpose: Returns a serial number for the current time and date.

Format: @now

Sample: @now

Description: @Now returns a serial number which, when formatted with one of the Date or Time formats, can display a date or time on the worksheet.

It is primarily useful:

• In {wait} statements, where it can be used in a formula to set the amount of time for the macro to wait before proceeding. It's a good tool when you want to show someone a brief error message and then continue processing the macro.

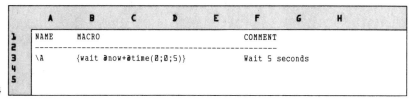

Figure 17-24

• In {let} statements, where it can date stamp the worksheet with the current date and time (each of the cells it stamps should have been previously formatted appropriately).

```
        A        B        C        D        E        F        G        H
  1 │ NAME    MACRO                              COMMENT
  L │ ▪▪▪▪▪▪▪▪▪
  3 │ \A      {let DATE;@now}                    Date stamp
  4 │         {let TIME;@now}                    Time stamp
  5 │
```

Figure 17-25

- In {if} statements, where it can be used to occasionally check the current time and, at the appropriate time, trigger an action (and do so without forcing 1-2-3 to wait motionlessly as {wait} statements do). The following macro statement could be run once at the end of any other macro routine. When it detects the time is after 12 noon, it will transfer control to an add-in program, which might be a communications program that would automatically download some files for you.

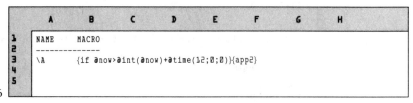

```
        A        B        C        D        E        F        G        H
  1 │ NAME    MACRO
  2 │ ──────────────
  3 │ \A      {if @now>@int(@now)+@time(12;0;0)}{app2}
  4 │
  5 │
```

Figure 17-26

@time

Purpose: Returns a serial number representing a given time.

Format: @time(hours;minutes;seconds)

Sample: @time(0;0;5)

Description: @Time is most often added to the @now function to define a future time. If you embed that formula in a macro command, you can use it as a timer to make an event occur some time in the future.

For example, {wait @now + @time(0;0;5)} causes the macro to wait five seconds before proceeding.

```
        A        B        C        D        E        F        G        H
  1 │ NAME    MACRO
  2 │ ──────────────
  3 │ \A      {wait @now+@time(0;0;5)}
  4 │
  5 │
```

Figure 17-27

Summary

The preceding list employs the category names (such as special functions, logical functions) used in the 1-2-3 documentation, but it includes neither the entire set of @functions that belong to each category nor every category of @functions. Now that you've seen some of the @functions that occur most commonly in macros, we encourage you to explore the remaining @functions on your own.

For a quick tour of 1-2-3's @functions, during a 1-2-3 session press the Help key, highlight the Help Index option and press Return, highlight @Functions and press Return, and then select any of the categories of @functions from the list you'll see. For more detailed explanations of any @function you encounter in the Help screens, consult the 1-2-3 documentation or any good 1-2-3 reference book.

18

Enhancing Existing Macros

Using the Advanced Macro Commands

Now that you've learned the advanced macro commands, you can begin using them to enhance your existing macros or to write entirely new macros. Let's begin by reviewing a variety of enhanced keystroke macros, then move on to several more powerful macros that enhance 1-2-3 worksheet commands.

The macros we'll discuss here are similar to the keystroke macros you've seen before, except they incorporate advanced commands to make them more effective. For example, the first macro moves the cell pointer down a specified number of rows on the worksheet. It could be written without any advanced commands by merely using a numeric argument to a {d} key name. However, by using the {if} command, you have 1-2-3 divide the work between the {pgdn} and {d} key names in order to speed up the time it will take to jump downward a considerable distance.

We'll present each macro in three ways: a brief statement of purpose, a more detailed description that includes any instructions needed to use it, and the macro itself. In each case, we'll assume you know how to properly name and activate it.

Purpose: Jumps down any number of rows.

Description: Prompts you for the number of rows downward on the worksheet you'd like to move the cell pointer from its current location. Interprets your response into the number of Pagedown and Downarrow keystrokes needed to most quickly respond. To repeat your last entry, press Alt J. This macro assumes you are using a 25-line display driver. If you're using a 43-line driver (for an EGA), wherever the number 20 occurs in the following macro, replace it with the number 38.

	A	B	C	D	E	F	G	H
1	NAME	MACRO						
2	-------------							
3	\D	{getnumber "How many rows down?" ;ANS}						
4	\J	{if ANS<20}{d ANS}{quit}						
5		{pgdn ANS/20}{d @mod(ANS;20)}						
6								
7	ANS							

Figure 18-1

Purpose: Maintains worksheet version number.

Description: Prompts you to determine the need to change the current version number. If you respond in the affirmative, increments version number by one. In any case, it saves the file under its current name.

	A	B	C	D	E	F	G	H
1	NAME	MACRO						
2	-------------							
3	\S	{getlabel "Change version number (y/n)? ";ANS}						
4		{if @upper(ANS)="Y"}{let VER#;VER#+1}						
5		/fs~r{esc}						
6								
7	VER#							
8								
9								
10								

Figure 18-2

Purpose: Time stamps worksheet and saves file.

Description: Enters current time into time-formatted cell and saves the file.

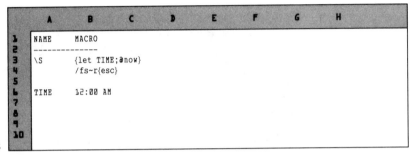

```
         A         B         C         D         E         F         G         H
  1   NAME      MACRO
  2   --------------
  3   \S        {let TIME;@now}
  4             /fs~r{esc}
  5
  6   TIME      12:00 AM
  7
  8
  9
 10
```

Figure 18-3

Purpose: Converts values to labels.

Description: Automatically converts a column of values into labels. Stops when it encounters an empty cell at the bottom of the column.

```
         A         B         C         D         E         F         G         H
  1   NAME      MACRO
  2   --------------
  3   \V        {edit}{home}'{d}
  4             {if @cellpointer("type")="b"}{quit}
  5             {branch \V}
```

Figure 18-4

Purpose: Converts labels to values.

Description: Automatically converts a column of labels into values. Stops when it encounters an empty cell at the bottom of the column.

```
         A         B         C         D         E         F         G         H
  1   NAME      MACRO
  2   --------------
  3   \L        {edit}{home}{del}{d}
  4             {if @cellpointer("type")="b"}{quit}
  5             {branch \L}
```

Figure 18-5

Purpose: Copies relative formula as if it were an absolute formula.

Description: Copies a single relative formula to any location as if it were an absolute formula. When the macro pauses, point to the cell that you wish to copy the formula to. We recommend that, before using this macro, you keystroke through it at the keyboard and observe the operation of the technique in the last line. It does not, as its appearance may suggest, convert the formula into a simple value. Instead, it converts a reference to a named range into the formula that named range contains.

```
       A       B        C        D       E      F      G       H
 1  NAME      MACRO
 2  --------------
 3  \R        {edit}{home}'~
 4            {let R_CELL;@cellpointer("contents")}
 5            {edit}{home}{del}~
 6            {?}+R_CELL{calc}~
 7
 8  R_CELL
 9
10
```

Figure 18-6

Purpose: Switches between automatic and manual methods of recalculation.

Description: If the worksheet is currently set on automatic recalculation, this macro will change it to manual and vice versa. This macro is a good example of how to control any global setting through a macro.

```
       A       B        C        D       E      F      G       H
 1  NAME      MACRO
 2  --------------
 3  \R        /wgr{if R_CALC}m{blank R_CALC}{quit}
 4            a{let R_CALC;1}{quit}
 5
 6  R_CALC
 7
 8
 9
10
```

Figure 18-7

Purpose: Combines a series of files beneath one another.

Description: Combines a copy of the file of your choice onto the current worksheet below any existing data, then presents a menu enabling you to continue combining files or terminates the operation. If you choose to continue, the macro will move the cell pointer one row beneath the lowermost data already on the worksheet and allow you to choose the next file to combine. Be sure to leave the fifth cell in this macro blank, or when you press Escape the macro will work improperly. You can change the method of file combination from copying to adding or subtracting by changing line 3 from /fcce{?}~ to /fcae{?}~ or /fcse{?}~, respectively.

```
        A        B        C       D       E       F       G       H

1     NAME       MACRO
2     ----------------
3     \C         {end}{home}
4                {d}{end}{l}
5                /fcce{?}~
6                {menubranch COM_MENU}{quit}
7
8     COM_MENU   Press Return to continue or Escape to quit
9                Press Return to combine another file, Escape to stop macro
10               {branch \C}
```

Figure 18-8

Purpose: Converts any zeros in a column of entries into empty cells.

Description: The macro tests to see if the cell is either blank or contains something other than a label. If the cell is blank, the macro terminates. If it contains a label, the macro skips over it. If the cell contains a zero, the macro erases the cell, moves down one, and repeats the operation.

```
        A        B        C       D       E       F       G       H

1     NAME       MACRO
2     --------------
3     \Z         {if @cellpointer("type")="b"}{quit}
4                {if @cellpointer("type")<>"v"}{d}{branch \Z}
5                {if @cellpointer("contents")=0}/re~
6                {d}{branch \Z}
7
8
9
10
```

Figure 18-9

Purpose: Jump to end of row or column menu.

Description: A collection of handy shortcuts for moving the cell pointer to the first or last entry in the current column or row.

```
       A        B          C        D        E        F        G        H
  1  NAME     MACRO
  2  --------------
  3  \J       {menubranch J_END}
  4
  5  J_END    Right     Left      Top       Bottom
  6           Jump to th Jump to th Jump to thJump to the bottom of this column
  7           {branch RI {branch LE {branch TO {branch BOTTOM}
  8
  9  LEFT     /wth{home}/wtc
 10
 11  TOP      /wtv{home}/wtc
 12
 13  RIGHT    /wth{end}{home}{r}{end}{u}{end}{l}/wtc
 14
 15  BOTTOM   /wtv{end}{home}{d}{end}{l}{end}{u}/wtc
```

Figure 18-10

Purpose: Allows you to enter dates in MM/DD/YY format and converts those dates to serial numbers.

Description: Prompts you for a date. You should enter a date in MM/DD/YY format (such as 9/25/88 or 10/3/89). The macro will automatically enter the date in the current cell as a serial number and format it as a date. To change the date format, change the number that is the second to the last character in line three of the macro. Substituting the number 2, 3, 4, or 5 for the 1 shown there will enable the formatted entry to display within a column of nine spaces.

```
       A        B          C        D        E        F        G        H
  1  NAME     MACRO
  2  --------------
  3  \D       {getlabel "Input date in MM/DD/YY format: ";D_ANS}
  4           {let D_ANS;@datevalue(D_ANS)}
  5           +D_ANS{calc}~/rfd1~
  6
  7  D_ANS
  8
  9
 10
```

Figure 18-11

Purpose: Enters Date or Time stamp as a label.

Description: Enters a date or time stamp on the worksheet, depending on the value contained in the cell named Type. If Type contains the value 114, the macro will enter a date stamp (in the format 27-Dec-88) in the current cell. If Type contains the value 120, it will enter a time stamp (in the format 09:31 AM) in the current cell. Either entry will be a label, so neither will change in the future. You can easily modify this macro so that it places a date and a time stamp in adjoining cells on the worksheet.

```
         A         B         C         D         E         F         G         H
  1   NAME      MACRO
  2   --------------
  3   \D        {let D_ANS;@now}
  4             {contents D_ANS;D_ANS;10;TYPE}
  5             +D_ANS{calc}{home}'~
  6
  7   TYPE      114
  8   D_ANS
  9
 10
```

Figure 18-12

Macros for 1-2-3 Release 2.2

The combination of Release 2.2's new macro and worksheet commands present a number of useful ways to enhance your macros. Used with Release 2.2's Macro Library Manager, you can store macros off the worksheet and use them with any worksheet.

Purpose: Saves the file whether or not it already has a name.

Description: If the file has no name, saves the file, clearing the current directory from the status line to clarify the prompt. If the file has already been saved, saves a backup copy (using Release 2.2's Backup option), assuring that you always have one previous version of the file in case you have to revert back to it due to a mistake that can't be undone.

```
      A       B       C       D       E       F       G       H
1  NAME    MACRO
2  ---------------
3  \S      {if @cellpointer("filename")=""}/fsx{esc}{quit}
4          /fs~b{quit}
5
6
```

Figure 18-13

Purpose: Toggles 1-2-3's Beep setting on and off.

Description: If the Beep setting is set to Yes, this macro changes it to No and vice versa. It permits you to eliminate the annoyance of needless beeps, but easily restore a source of feedback for those times, such as when debug macros, when you find the beep helpful.

```
      A       B       C       D       E       F       G       H
1  NAME    MACRO
2  ---------------
3  \B      /wgdob
4          {if [B_FLAG]}nq{blank [B_FLAG]}{quit}
5          yq{let [B_FLAG];1}{quit}
6
7  [B_FLAG]
8
9
10
```

Figure 18-14

Purpose: Formats a floppy disk in drive A.

Description: Uses the {system} command to pass a command to DOS. Assumes that the Format program is present in the 1-2-3 directory or, preferably, found in DOS's current search path. It stands as one simple example of the endless possibilities offered by {system}.

```
      A       B       C       D       E       F       G       H
1  NAME    MACRO
2  ---------------
3  \F      {system "FORMAT A:"}
4
5
```

Figure 18-15

Purpose: Copies the Autoload macro library to your worksheet.

Description: Prompts you whether or not to edit the macro library. If you respond by pressing "y", 1-2-3 copies the contents of the Autoload macro library to the worksheet, beginning at the location of the cellpointer. Since this action might overwrite data already on the worksheet, the simple prompt mechanism allows you to back out if you select this function inadvertently.

```
         A       B         C       D       E       F       G       H
1   NAME       MACRO
2   --------------
3   \M         Edit MLB now?  {get [ANS]}{esc}{if [ANS]<>"y"}{quit}
4              /aiMACROMGR~eAUTOLOAD.MLB~o~
5
6   [ANS]
7
```

Figure 18-16

Purpose: Invokes the Allways spreadsheet publisher add-in.

Description: Tests to see if Allways has been loaded. If not, it performs an application attach and assigns it to the Alt–F8 key. Then it invokes Allways, with which you can enhance a report.

```
         A       B         C       D       E       F       G       H
1   NAME       MACRO
2   --------------
3   \A         /a{if #not#@isapp("ALLWAYS")}aALLWAYS~8~
4              iALLWAYS~{quit}
5
```

Figure 18-17

Purpose: Displays all the named graphs in your worksheet, one after another.

Description: Creates a graph name table, then steps through the graphs, displaying each for 3 seconds until it gets to the last one. Be sure there are blank spaces in the rows below your cell pointer before you invoke this macro.

```
        A           B          C        D        E      F      G
   1  NAME       MACRO
   2  ---------------
   3  \G         /gnt~q
   4  [G_LOOP]   {if @cellpointer("type")="b"}{quit}
   5             {graphon @cellpointer("contents")}
   6             {wait @now+@time(0;0;3)}
   7             {d}{branch [G_LOOP]}
   8
```

Figure 18-18

Purpose: Ensures that, while you enter data, column widths will accomodate the longest label you enter.

Description: Stores the width of the current column, then tests the length of the most recent entry, widening the column if this new entry is longer than the current column width can display. Each time you place the cell pointer in a new column, you must re-invoke \E, to reset the counter for the new column's width.

```
         A          B          C        D        E      F      G        H
   1   NAME       MACRO
   2   ---------------
   3   \E         {let [WIDTH];@cellpointer("width")}
   4   [E_LOOP]   {?}~
   5              {let [LENGTH];@length(@cellpointer("contents"))+1}
   6              {if @iserr([LENGTH])}{quit}
   7              {if [LENGTH]>[WIDTH]}{[UPDATE]}
   8              {d}{branch [E_LOOP]}
   9
  10   [UPDATE]   {let [WIDTH];[LENGTH]}
  11              {let [LENGTH];@string([LENGTH];0)}
  12              /wcs{[LENGTH]}~
  13
  14   [LENGTH]
  15              {return}
  16
  17   [WIDTH]
  18
```

Figure 18-19

Purpose: Lets you change any label to upper, lower, or proper case.

Description: If the current cell is a label, displays a menu of case selections. To end the macro, point to a non-label cell and press Return.

```
         A          B            C           D       E      F        G          H

 1    NAME       MACRO
 2    ------------------
 3    \C         {if @cellpointer("type")<>"l"}{quit}
 4               {menucall [CASE_MENU]}{?}{branch \C}
 5
 6    [CASE_MENU] Upper-Case         Lower-Case          Proper-Case
 7                Make cell UPPER    Make cell lower     Make cell Proper
 8                {[UPPER]}          {[LOWER]}           {[PROPER]}
 9
10    [UPPER]    @cellpointer("prefix")&@upper({r}{l}){calc}~
11
12    [LOWER]    @cellpointer("prefix")&@lower({r}{l}){calc}~
13
14    [PROPER]   @cellpointer("prefix")&@proper({r}{l}){calc}~
15
16
17
18
19
20
```

Figure 18-20

Next

In the next chapter, you'll see how to develop even more powerful macros—ones that modify, replace, or qualify as entirely new 1-2-3 commands.

19

Writing Your Own Commands

Now that you're familiar with the purpose and syntax of each of the advanced macro commands, you're ready to begin using them to solve problems. The most accessible place to begin is by writing your own commands—commands you can use during interactive worksheet sessions or while you write macros. We call these customized commands "command enhancements."

There are three kinds of results that command enhancements can attain for you: They can add power to 1-2-3, abbreviate lengthy command sequences, and simplify complex commands. Let's review several command-enhancement macros, each of which attain one of these goals. They include:

- A macro to vary the widths of a range of columns and a macro to copy a range of relative formulas as if they were absolute formulas, neither of which are things you can ordinarily do in Release 2 or 2.01.

- A macro to abbreviate the commands required to freeze and unfreeze the screen in a macro and a macro to abbreviate the commands required to prompt a user for data entry.

- A macro to simplify the useful but complex {for} command.

Adding a Command to Vary the Width of a Range of Columns

In this example, we'll review one way a command-enhancement macro can enhance the power of 1-2-3.

1-2-3 can change the width of a single column (using the / Worksheet Column Set command) or of all columns (using the / Worksheet Global Column command), but Release 2.01 offers no commands with which to vary a range of columns. Release 2.2 contains a command, / Worksheet Column Column-Range Set, that duplicates the function of this macro. Even if you use that release, you may want to read about the macro: Its function won't be useful, but the principles you'll learn about macros will.

Suppose you are setting up an annual budget with one month of data in each column. Chances are you'll want each column in that series set to the same width. For a task such as that, you could write the following macro.

	A	B	C	D	E	F	G	H
1	NAME	MACRO					COMMENT	
2	------	------					------	
3	\A	{getnumber "Enter # of columns: ";COLS}					Get columns	
4		{getlabel "Enter width: ";SIZE}					Get width	
5		{for CTR;1;COLS;1;WIDEN}					Repeat	
6		{quit}					Stop	
7								
8	WIDEN	/wcs{SIZE}~{r}{return}					Widen	
9								
10	SIZE						Store size	
11		{return}						
12	CTR						Store counter	
13	COLS						Store # cols	
14								
15								

Figure 19-1

The macro begins with a {getnumber} prompt to enter the number of columns you wish to resize and stores the response in a cell named Cols. The macro assumes that the cell pointer resides in the first column of that range, and that the columns to be changed are the columns directly to the right of the current column (although you could easily change those assumptions). Line 2 of the macro prompts for the new width for the columns and stores the response in a cell named Size.

Line 3 uses a {for} command to initiate a loop consisting of the routine named Widen. The {for} command says, in essence, use the cell named Ctr as a counter, begin counting at 1 and end with the value stored in Cols (a value the user earlier supplied), count in increments of 1, and run the routine named Widen once for each count. Let's skip down to line 6 where Widen is stored, since that's where control moves at this point in the macro.

Widen begins with the keystrokes to set the width of the current cell (/wcs), then uses the cell named Size as a subroutine to supply the number of spaces wide for the current column (the value in Size, too, was earlier supplied by the user). The macro moves the cell pointer one cell to the right, completing one cycle of the {for} loop. Control returns to the {for} command, 1-2-3 increments the counter and repeats the routine until it has completed the prescribed number of iterations.

Now that you've had the basic version, lets spruce things up a little. We'll add three enhancements: The ability to type the number of spaces in the control panel or expand the cell pointer on the worksheet, the macro will return the cell pointer to its starting point when the macro has finished, and the macro will freeze the screen so you won't see it at work. The enhancements are reasonably simple; they add only one line to the macro's length.

	A	B	C	D	E	F	G	H
1	NAME	MACRO				COMMENT		
2	------	--						
3	\A	{getnumber "Enter # of columns: ";COLS}						
4		/wcs{?}~						
5		{let SIZE;@cellpointer("width");0)}						
6		{indicate "WAIT"}						
7		{windowsoff}{paneloff}						
8		{for CTR;1;COLS;1;WIDEN}						
9		{indicate}{windowson}{panelon}						
10		{1 COLS}{quit}						
11								
12	WIDEN	/wcs{SIZE}~{r}{return}				Widen		
13								
14	SIZE					Store size		
15		{return}						
16	CTR					Store counter		
17	COLS					Store # cols		
18								
19								
20								

Figure 19-2

The basic macro remains the same; here are the changes.

Line 2 now uses the / Worksheet Column-Width Set command with an {?} interactive command to set the width of the current column. Line 3 assigns that width to the cell named Size. Line 4 changes the Mode indicator to display the word Wait and line 5 freezes the screen while the macro works. After the {for} loop has finished, the macro returns the cell pointer to its starting point with the command {left COLS}. Cols stored the number of columns to change, so you can use that value as an argument to the {l} command to properly reposition the cell pointer.

Adding a Command to Copy a Range of Relative Formulas As Absolute

This macro enables you to copy an entire range of relative formulas as if they were absolute formulas. When the macro prompts for Source_range, point to or enter the range containing the formulas to copy. When the macro prompts for Target_cell, point to or enter the top left cell of the range to copy them to.

The underlying logic of this technique is as follows:

1. Move the source range to the target range. A Move command preserves all the formulas as if they were absolute.

2. Copy the target range to a working range. The working range now contains formulas that have changed because they were copied.

3. Move the range of formulas in the target range back to the source range. The source range now contains the original set of formulas.

4. Copy the working range back to the target range. This copy operation restores the formulas to their original form, which is identical to the formulas now in the source range.

Here's the macro.

```
        A        B           C        D        E        F        G        H
1   NAME      MACRO
2   --------------
3   \S        {paneloff}/rnc{panelon}Source_range:~{bs}{?}~
4             {paneloff}/rnc{panelon}Target_cell:~{bs}{?}~
5             {indicate "WAIT"}{windowsoff}{paneloff}
6             {let SOURCE;@cell("address";SOURCE_RANGE:)}
7             {let TARGET;@cell("address";TARGET_CELL:)}
8             {let S_ROWS;@rows(SOURCE_RANGE:)}
9             {let S_COLS;@cols(SOURCE_RANGE:)}
10            /rncWORKRNG~EZ8093~
11            /rncWORKRNG~.{d S_ROWS}{r S_COLS}~
12            /mSOURCE_RANGE:~TARGET_CELL:~
13            /cSOURCE_RANGE:~WORKRNG~
14            /mSOURCE_RANGE:~{SOURCE}~
15            /cWORKRNG~{TARGET}~
16            {blank WORKRNG}
17            /rndSOURCE_RANGE:~
18            /rndTARGET_CELL:~
19            /rndWORKRNG~
20            {windowson}{panelon}{indicate}{quit}
21
22  SOURCE
23            {return}
24
25  TARGET
26            {return}
27
28  S_ROWS
29  S_COLS
30
```

Figure 19-3

Now that you've seen the macro and know its functional strategy, let's focus on how this macro implements that strategy. Later, we'll look at some options for revising the macro.

```
{paneloff}/rnc{panelon}Source_range:~{bs}{?}~
```

The macro begins by freezing the control panel, selecting the Range Name Create command, and displaying a prompt to enter the Source Range. This operation involves some tricks, so let's discuss it for a moment. The {paneloff} command prevents 1-2-3 from displaying the Range Name Create menus or the prompt "Enter name:" that normally appears as the first step of the Range Name Create process.

The {panelon} command, which follows, enables 1-2-3 to begin updating the control panel again. The macro then types the string "Source_range:" in response to the invisible range name prompt. That string becomes the name of the range that 1-2-3 is creating, but it also acts as a prompt to the user. The macro presses Return to continue to the "Enter range:" prompt. It immediately presses Backspace to unanchor the cell pointer so the user will be able to move the cell pointer to any other cell to begin defining the range. 1-2-3 displays its normal "Enter range:" prompt and the macro pauses to allow the user to respond either by pointing or by typing. That range must include all the formulas to be copied.

```
{paneloff}/rnc{panelon}Target_cell:~{bs}{?}~
{indicate WAIT}{windowsoff}{paneloff}
```

Line two of the macro is very similar, but it requires that the user define only a one-celled range. The macro will later determine what the appropriate size of that range should be. Line 3 places a Wait indicator in the mode indicator and suppresses screen updating while the macro does its work.

```
{let SOURCE;@cell("address";SOURCE_RANGE:)}
{let TARGET;@cell("address";TARGET_CELL:)}
```

Lines 4 and 5 are maintenance operations. Because both the named ranges Source_range: and Target_cell: will later be invalidated (when the macro moves data on to one of their anchor cells), and the macro will need to move or copy data to each of these ranges, the macro uses a trick to preserve them.

You can specify the "Move to:" or "Copy to:" range by identifying just the top left cell of either range. Line 4 stores in the cell named Source the address of the top left cell of Source_range:. The @cell function will operate only on a single cell, so when the macro supplies it with the multi-celled range Source_range:, the function treats that range as if it were just the top left cell. Therefore, when you request the range's address, the function returns the address of the top left cell. With that address stored in the cell named Source, you can later use it as a Copy to: or Move to: address.

Line 5 does the same thing for the range named Target Range: as line 4 does for Source_range:.

```
{let S_ROWS;@rows(SOURCE_RANGE:)}
{let S_COLS;@cols(SOURCE_RANGE:)}
/rncWORKRNG~EZ8093~
/rncWORKRNG~.{d S_ROWS}{r S_COLS}~
```

Lines 6 though 9 automatically define the size of a range, Workrng, that will store formulas on an intermediate basis. The macro will later move the data stored in this range somewhere else. In order to specify that move properly, Workrng must be exactly the same size as Source_range:.

Lines 6 and 7 store values that represent the number of rows and columns in Source_range: in the cells named S_rows and S_cols, respectively. Those dimensions will later be used to define Workrng.

Line 7 creates the range named Workrng as cell EZ8093. EZ8093 is an arbitrary location, but a suitable one because it is far enough away from the top left portion of the worksheet to be likely to avoid any other data, yet has enough space below it and to its right to store a range of data as large as 100 columns by 100 rows.

Line 8 redefines that range. After selecting Range Name Create and entering the name Workrng, the macro anchors the cell pointer and expands it downward the number of rows stored in S_rows. The macro accomplishes that by using the key name {d} with S_rows as an argument. Since S_rows contains a value, {d S_ROWS} presses the Down-arrow key the number of times specified by that value. The {r} command uses the same strategy to expand the cell pointer to the right. The result of these four lines is a named range, Workrng, whose top left cell is EZ8093 and whose size is the same as Source_range:.

```
/mSOURCE_RANGE:~TARGET_CELL:~
/cSOURCE_RANGE:~WORKRNG~
/mSOURCE_RANGE:~{SOURCE}~
/cWORKRNG~{TARGET}~
```

Lines 10 through 13 perform the work described in the original synopsis above.

Line 10 moves the original formulas to Target_cell:. That move operation also moves the range name Source_range: to Target_cell: and, by moving on to the anchor cell of Target_cell:, it invalidates the range name Target_cell:.

Line 11 copies the range Source_range: to the intermediate range Workrng.

Line 12 moves Source_range: to the cell address stored in the named range Source. That address is the top left cell of the original location of Source_range: (where the formulas originated). The macro calls Source as a subroutine to type in the cell address in the midst of the Move command.

Line 13 copies the formulas from the intermediate range Workrng back to where you want them. It uses the same trick to supply the Copy to: range as the previous routine used to supply the Move to: range—this time using the cell address in Target.

The formulas have now been restored to their original location and have been copied to their new location as if they were absolute formulas; that is, the addresses and references of the copies are identical to the originals.

```
{blank WORKRNG}
/rndSOURCE_RANGE:~
/rndTARGET_CELL:~
/rndWORKRNG~
{windowson}{panelon}{indicate}{quit}
```

Lines 14 through 18 are the cleanup operation.

Line 14 erases the data stored in Workrng. Lines 15 through 17 delete the three range names. Line 18 reenables 1-2-3 to continuously update the screen and returns control of the mode indicator to 1-2-3.

Variation on the Macro

Here's a variation of the preceding macro that eliminates the need to always use the range below and to the right of EZ8093. Instead, it prompts the user for the top left cell of the range to be used as a work range. One difference of note in this macro occurs in line 14: It employs the Range Erase command instead of the {blank} command. This macro substitutes the name Working Cell: for the earlier macro's Workrng because here, that name must serve as a prompt. However, like many other advanced macro commands, the {blank} command won't work with a range name containing a colon. The Range Erase command has no such limit.

```
         A          B          C        D        E        F        G        H
 1   NAME       MACRO
 2   --------------
 3   \S         {paneloff}/rnc{panelon}Source_range:~{bs}{?}~
 4              {paneloff}/rnc{panelon}Target_cell:~{bs}{?}~
 5              {paneloff}/rnc{panelon}Working_Cell:~{bs}{?}~
 6              {indicate "WAIT"}{windowsoff}{paneloff}
 7              {let SOURCE;@cell("address";SOURCE_RANGE:)}
 8              {let TARGET;@cell("address";TARGET_CELL:)}
 9              {let S_ROWS;@rows(SOURCE_RANGE:)}
10              {let S_COLS;@cols(SOURCE_RANGE:)}
11              /rncWORKING_CELL:~.{d S_ROWS}{r S_COLS}~
12              /mSOURCE_RANGE:~TARGET_CELL:~
13              /cSOURCE_RANGE:~WORKING_CELL:~
14              /mSOURCE_RANGE:~{SOURCE}~
15              /cWORKING_CELL:~{TARGET}~
16              /reWORKING_CELL:~
17              /rndSOURCE_RANGE:~
18              /rndTARGET_CELL:~
19              /rndWORKING_CELL:~
20              {windowson}{panelon}{indicate}{quit}
21
22   SOURCE
23              {return}
24
25   TARGET
26              {return}
27
28   S_ROWS
29   S_COLS
30
```

Figure 19-4

Abbreviating Commands to Freeze/Unfreeze the Screen

In this example, we'll look at one way a command-enhancement macro can significantly reduce the amount of typing you have to do when writing macros.

It's common to want to use the {windowsoff} and {paneloff} commands as a pair to freeze the screen, later followed by the {windowson} and {panelon} commands to allow 1-2-3 to update the screen normally again. If you use these pairs often, you can effectively abbreviate them by creating a pair of new commands called {ON} and {OFF}. {ON} and {OFF} are subroutines; here they are at work in a routine that you don't want to show on the screen—the deletion of database records and subsequent updating of a named range that encompasses that database.

```
     A       B        C        D       E      F       G      H
1  NAME    MACRO                                COMMENT
2  ----------------------------------------------------------------
3  DELETE  {OFF}                                Freeze screen
4          /dqdd                                Delete records
5          /rncDATA~{bs}                        Redefine the
6          .{end}{r}~                              data range
7          {end}{d}~
8          {goto}DATA~{ON}                      Show data
9          {branch BROWSE}                      Allow to browse
10
11 OFF     {windowsoff}{paneloff}{return}       Freeze routine
12 ON      {windowson}{panelon}{return}         Thaw routine
13
14
15
```

Figure 19-5

Each subroutine consists of just three simple commands: { window-soff } or { windowson }, { paneloff } or { panelon }, and { return }. If you're using 1-2-3 Release 2.2, these routines are prime candidates to put into a macro library. Accordingly, you may want to rename them to be consistent with your own naming conventions. We suggest you enclose in square brackets range names that reside in a macro library to clearly distinguish them from on-sheet range names. So a range named [Sample] would be one that resides in a macro library, whereas a range named Sample would reside on the worksheet.

Irrespective of the naming conventions you employ, you'll find these routines simple to write, they'll be instantly available to any routine on this worksheet that cares to call it, and you'll save yourself from typing about 50 characters each time you use them.

Abbreviating Commands to Prompt for Input

Here's another case where you may want to shorten a command—or two commands—that are used frequently. The { getnumber } and { getlabel } commands are used for almost any kind of input-prompting. With a little help from another macro, you can improve them.

For example, a { getnumber } or { getlabel } statement (including the keyword, prompt, string, and location argument) can easily be long enough to be obscured if you place a documenting comment alongside it—even long enough so that it won't fit on one screen. That makes it difficult to clearly document those statements in a macro. However, except for the prompt string, you're often writing the command the same way repeatedly. The keyword is either getnumber or getlabel, and the cell in which to store the result is also often the same. [43]

For those times when that's true, you can shorten those statements from this:

{getnumber "Enter a value between 1 and 20: ";ANS}

{getlabel "Enter a letter between A and M: ";ANS}

To this:

{gn "Enter a value between 1 and 20: "}

{gl "Enter a letter between A and M: "}

Here's the macro to let you do that.

```
        A        B        C        D        E        F        G        H
1    NAME     MACRO
2    --------------
3    \A       {gn "Enter a value between 1 and 20: "}~
4
5    \B       {gl "Enter a letter between A and M: "}~
6
7    GN       {define GET1}
8             {let PROMPT;+"""&GET1&""";ANS}"}
9             {branch PROMPT}
10
11   GL       {define GET1}
12            {let PROMPT;+"""&GET1&""";ANS}"}
13            {branch PROMPT}
14
15   PROMPT
16            {return}
17   GET1
18   ANS
19
20
```

Figure 19-6

If you activate the \A macro, the instructions on line 1 will call a subroutine named Gn (for getnumber). That subroutine, which begins on

---

[43] In most cases, you'll temporarily store the entry in a cell (we often call it Ans for Answer) for some form of testing or conversion before using a {let} command to transfer it elsewhere.

line 5, stores the passed parameter in a cell named Get1, uses a string formula in a {let} statement to construct a complete {getnumber} command in a cell named Prompt, and branches to that cell. There it reads the full {getnumber} command (which now consists of {getnumber "Enter a value between 1 and 20: ";ANS}). After you've made your entry, it returns control to the calling routine in line 1. Since there are no further instructions in that calling routine, this macro terminates. The \B macro works the same way.

Simplifying the {for} Command

In this final example, we'll look at one way a command-enhancement macro can simplify a complex operation.

The {for} command, which automatically processes loops a specified number of times, is one of the most powerful available. Unfortunately, it's also one of the trickiest to write. Here is it's elusive syntax:

```
{for COUNTER_LOCATION;START_VALUE;STOP_VALUE;STEP_VALUE;ROUTINE}
```

The reason {for} is so complex is the number of choices it offers you—each of which you must deal with through an argument. However, if you make a few assumptions about how you'll apply {for} each time, you can narrow the field substantially. For example, let's assume you'll always use a cell named Ctr to store the counter and you'll always start counting with 1 and proceed in increments of 1. With these assumptions out of the way, all you have left to define with each {for} command are the name of the routine you wish to run and the number of times you wish to run it.

While we're at the game of simplifying, let's rearrange the order in which those two remaining arguments appear to mimic the order in which we just discussed them. Let's call our new command {repeat}. {Repeat} takes two arguments: the routine you want repeated and the number of times you want it repeated. So if you want to repeat the routine named Move 5 times, just write {REPEAT MOVE;5} instead of {for CTR;1;5;1;MOVE}. Now that's an improvement.

Here's the macro.

	A	B	C	D	E	F	G	H
1	NAME	MACRO			COMMENT			
2	--				---------			
3	\A	{REPEAT MOVE;5}			Repeat routine			
4		{quit}			End			
5								
6	MOVE	{r}{return}			Subroutine			
7								
8	REPEAT	{define FOR1;FOR2:v}{calc}						
9		{for CTR;1;FOR2;1;MOVE}			+"{for CTR;1;FOR2;1;"&FOR1&"}"			
10		{return}						
11								
12	FOR1	MOVE			{for} variables			
13	FOR2	5			{for} variables			
14	CTR	6			{for} variables			
15								

Figure 19-7

Line 1 shows the {repeat} command exactly as we just described it. Technically, it calls a subroutine named Repeat and passes to it two parameters: Move and 5. The routine named Repeat begins on line 8 and since macro control transfers to there at this point, that's where we'll pick up the description.

Repeat begins with a {define} command that tells 1-2-3 where to store the two passed parameters (in the cells named For1 and For2, respectively) and that the second parameter should be stored as a value. The effect of this command is to store the label Move in the cell named For1 and the value 5 in the cell named For2. The {calc} command is required to update the next line of the macro.

The instructions on the next line (row 9) execute a {for} command to set up a loop. This command is produced by a reference to the comment cell directly to the right. The comment cell contains a text formatted string formula. The object of the string formula is to integrate the string "Move" into the {for} command. (In 1-2-3 Release 2.01, you cannot reference the cell containing that string; that reference would be construed as a command to use that cell as the subroutine to run). However, in Release 2.2, as you'll see, there is a simple and elegant solution to this problem.

Notice that the range names For2 and For1 appear in the text formatted string formula, seemingly backward. That's because in order to present a more straightforward syntax, we changed the sequence in which the {repeat} command uses those arguments relative to the way the {for} command uses them. That means we have to switch them back in the {for} command (in the {for} command, the number of repetitions is the third argument and the routine to repeat is the last argument).

The {for} command repeats a routine called Move, which appears on row 6, five times. Move consists here of the commands {r} and {return}. The latter command provides an explicit terminator to the subroutine Move. The remaining cells, For1, For2, and Ctr, store values and strings used in the macro.

Release 2.2's ability to evaluate expressions in macro commands proves extremely useful in this macro—it lets us do away with a superfluous {calc} and a string formula, and adds only one character to the macro code. The following version illustrates this feat:

```
          A        B          C      D      E          F      G      H
  1   NAME     MACRO                      COMMENT
  2   ------------------------------------------------
  3   \A       {REPEAT MOVE;5}            Repeat routine
  4            {quit}                     End
  5
  6   MOVE     {r}{return}                Subroutine
  7
  8   REPEAT   {define FOR1;FOR2:v}
  9            {for CTR;1;FOR2;1;+FOR1}
 10            {return}
 11
 12   FOR1     MOVE                       {for} variables
 13   FOR2     5                          {for} variables
 14   CTR      6                          {for} variables
 15
```

Figure 19-8

Row 9 is now a label cell like all others. We achieved the indirect reference to the Move routine with the + sign which precedes For1. It indicates to the {for} command that For1 is part of a formula to be evaluated. Its result, Move, is the routine that is actually invoked.

We should also note that this is an instance where the requirements of good instruction and good programming conflict. In order to prevent any additional complexity from interfering with your understanding of the {repeat} command in the preceding explanation, we used a subroutine (named Move) that you wouldn't ordinarily employ in such a context.

Here's why. You don't need such an elaborate macro to run a subroutine that consists only of a key name (Move consisted of the key name {r}). Since macro key names can take numeric arguments to indicate how many times you wish to repeat them, you don't need a {for} loop to do that. Accordingly, you'd use a macro such as the one below, where the cell named Num contains the value representing the number of times you want to repeat the routine.

```
        A          B          C          D          E          F          G
1   NAME       MACRO
2   ------------
3   \A         {let NUM;5}
4              {r NUM}
5
```

Figure 19-9

If you try both this macro and the preceding one, you'll see that the macro using the {for} loop is significantly slower.

Command-Enhancement Summary

Even before reading this chapter, you already possessed the skills to write these kinds of macros. Our sole intent was to reveal some of the possibilities now available to you. The next time you encounter a situation where you need to add power to 1-2-3, to abbreviate excessive typing, or to simplify a complex operation, a command-enhancement macro may provide an excellent solution.

Incidentally, macros such as the ones just reviewed are prime candidates for inclusion in a macro library because you can reuse them on many worksheets.[44]

You'll find more command-enhancement macros in chapter 30— Development Tools. The macros in the "tool kit" are designed to shorten the process of writing turnkey macro applications.

Next

As a wrap-up to this section of the book, in the next chapter, we make a parting point about programming technique. It's an especially important point for those of us who cut our teeth on Release 1A macros, or were influenced by someone who did. And if you think about it, that's most of us.

---

[44] If you had no use for macro libraries when we introduced them in Chapter 5, you may want to return there for instructions for setting up a macro library after you begin using command-enhancement macros.

20

Release 1A versus Release 2 Advanced Macro Commands

If you read through all of the advanced macro command listings, you've noticed a number of them that have corollary commands that were introduced in 1-2-3 Release 1 or 1A (for example, /xg is the predecessor of {branch}). The older commands remain in 1-2-3 largely to preserve subsequent releases' ability to run macros written under Release 1 or 1A, not to encourage you to write new macros with them. [45]

However, if, in writing macros with Release 2, you only substitute the new commands for the old ones, you'll have missed a great deal of the power that the new commands offer. Often, using the new commands effectively means writing the entire macro routine differently, not merely substituting one command for another.

Here's an example. The following macros represent two ways to write a macro to perform the same operation. The first macro is written from the Release 1A standpoint. While it gets the job done, it is inefficient and slow. The second macro is written with a clear understanding of Release 2 macros, and is crisp and efficient.

---

[45] Athough at least one of those older commands, /xn, retains certain advantages over its successor. See the listing for the {getnumber} command for details on /xn.

```
         A        B        C        D        E        F        G        H
  1   NAME     MACRO
  2   --------------
  3   \D       {getlabel "Down how many rows? ";ANS1}
  4            /rncHERE~{bs}~
  5            {goto}ANS2~
  6            {{}down
  7   ANS1     8
  8            {}}~
  9            {goto}HERE~/rndHERE~
 10   ANS2     {down 8}
```

Figure 20-1

```
         A        B        C        D        E        F        G        H
  1   NAME     MACRO
  2   --------------
  3   \D       {getnumber "Down how many rows? ";ANS1}
  4            {d ANS1}
  5
  6   ANS1
  7
  8
  9
 10
```

Figure 20-2

If you've already learned the lesson of how to use Release 2 macros effectively, the first macro may seem contrived to illustrate a point. Actually, it's an adaptation of one we ran across.

Summary

In this section, you learned the purpose and syntax of each of the advanced macro commands, and saw one immediate application for them in command enhancement macros. Another excellent application for the advanced macro commands lies in the macros you've already written, many of which you can now enhance through the addition of these new commands.

Doing so will also help you grow more comfortable using the advanced commands. If those commands still seem unfamiliar, it's only because you haven't yet had sufficient experience with them. Some practice will remedy that. In time you'll become as familiar with them as you now are with other parts of 1-2-3.

Until then, when you encounter a question about those commands, here's how to get an answer.

Depending on what you need to know, there are several ways you should proceed:

- For detailed information about a particular command, refer to Chapter 10 to locate the page number on which the description of that command appears.

- For a quick refresher on the syntax of a command, use the tear-out Advanced Commands Reference Card included with this book.

- If you find that you know what you want to accomplish, but you don't know which command to use to accomplish it, follow these steps. (1) Read the section entitled Organization Of The Commands (located near the beginning of Chapter 10), which classifies all the advanced commands into functional groups. (2) Choose the most likely group and read its description, which directly follows the organizational chart in that section. That description summarizes the function of each command in the group. (3) Once you've identified one or more possible commands, refer directly to the description of each command.

Next

You now know the ins and outs of keystroke macros, and how to embellish them using the advanced macro commands. You can write your own commands and store them in macro libraries to customize your work with 1-2-3.

In the next section of the book, we'll introduce you to the techniques for writing turnkey macro applications. Turnkey applications entirely remake 1-2-3 in the image of some application (such as Accounts Receivable), so that a person can operate the application without any knowledge of 1-2-3. Such applications are more complex than the ones we've covered thus far, but they also build on everything you already know.

Section IV

Advanced Techniques

21

Introduction to the Advanced Techniques

This chapter consists of three main sections:

1. An introduction to turnkey applications, including a discussion of how to know when not to use 1-2-3, how to choose between interactive templates and macro-driven applications, and a review of the major elements of a turnkey application.

2. Instruction in the macros that make up those applications, including samples of the diverse techniques available for managing user input, for processing data, and for producing various forms of output.

3. Instruction in the process of developing those applications, including how to design an application to make maximum use of available memory and how to internationalize it, how to write macros in a structured manner that others can maintain, and how to use a host of simple techniques and ready-to-use tools that do such things as write macro code for you and help you debug your macros. [46]

---

[46] If you would prefer to learn about the process for writing these macros before learning about the content of the macros themselves, reverse the order in which you read these last two sections (either order works). We placed content ahead of process because we feel most people want to write some of these macros before stepping back to examine how effectively they're writing them (and it is with the latter concern that the process section helps).

385

In this section we'll build on your understanding of advanced macro commands by employing them in the development of turnkey macro applications. Turnkey applications, or macros that provide a ready-to-run solution to a particular business need, can be as varied as the needs of your business. Some of their more common applications include accounts receivable, departmental budget preparation and consolidation, financial reporting, ratio analysis, tax return preparation, and personal financial management. However, macros are just as capable of automating less mainstream applications such as animal husbandry feed-yield calculations or commodities pricing models. In fact, any application that might begin as an interactive 1-2-3 template is a candidate for a turnkey application. (We'll discuss how to decide whether it should be a template or a turnkey application in a moment).

We call the methods used to develop turnkey applications "advanced techniques," and once you begin using them you'll not only be able to construct your own turnkey applications, but also to modify such applications written by others.

Since we'll assume that you're already familiar with each of the advanced macro commands, we'll increasingly concentrate our explanations on the strategy behind each technique rather than on the individual commands that compose them. Accordingly, if you encounter a command you don't understand in these discussions, refer to the command description in the previous chapter for an explanation.

explore and experiment

We encourage you also to explore portions of this section that may not appear useful to you. The titles we've assigned to each portion describe only their most immediate application. In fact, using the skills you've learned in previous chapters, there are often other ways you can apply the macro. For example, some of the menu techniques presented in this section incorporate macros that you can easily adapt to move data around the worksheet.

what is a customized macro?

Before launching into those techniques, let's consider the characteristics of the applications we intend to build with them. Turnkey macros aspire to the same goals as do their less sophisticated counterparts: to achieve high levels of performance, ease of use, and maintainability. In other words, they should be powerful, easy to learn, simple to operate, and structured in such a way that they can be reliably modified by someone other than their author.

When To Use Customized Macros

Although customized macro applications have been effectively used to develop a dizzying variety of applications, at least some of those applications could probably have found a development environment more appropriate to their needs than 1-2-3 macros. Before writing a turnkey application, we recommend that you first consider whether 1-2-3 and macros are the best tools to use.

Whether it's your own time or that of an associate, someone's time will be used in developing the macro. You'll invest that time wisely if you precede development with some forethought.

is 1-2-3 the
right kind
of program?

We think applications that best use the underlying 1-2-3 environment are the ones that are likely to deliver the most value as custom macro applications. For example, a customized financial reporting system (which makes heavy use of 1-2-3's powerful @functions) will in most cases deliver more value than a macro-driven word processor (which doesn't get nearly as much native support from 1-2-3).

However, that's not to say that applications such as word processing are inappropriate subjects for macros; that determination is a question of circumstances.

For example, if you don't do a lot of word processing and the word processing you do isn't demanding, you may find loading a separate word processor to be more trouble than it's worth—perhaps you'd be perfectly happy with one you can write with macros. Or, if you need to track a small project, you may feel that your needs don't justify learning an entirely new program. A macro may offer enough functionality to suit your needs and be much easier for you to learn.

another
alternative:
add-ins

In both these cases, basing your comparison on performance alone might suggest you should buy a stand-alone program, but as you can see, other considerations could easily dictate otherwise.

When you have a continuing need for something that 1-2-3 does either poorly or not at all (say, relational database management), it may be worth your time to buy and learn a new product. If you do, we recommend reviewing the offerings among 1-2-3 add-ins. Add-ins are products developed by independent software vendors and comprise all the major horizontal categories—word processing, database management, graphics, and file transfer—and quite a few vertical categories as well. Because these programs attach themselves to 1-2-3 and operate in a similar manner, you may find one easier to learn and much simpler to share worksheet data with than a comparable stand-alone program. Further, you can automate most add-ins with 1-2-3 macros to create an application integrating the capabilities of both the add-in and 1-2-3. [47]

---

[47] We don't mean to endorse any particular add-in or add-ins in general. As is true of other types of programs, there are add-ins that are exceptionally well designed and crafted, and there are those that fall below that standard. We encourage you to evaluate with care any product you're considering—read reviews, talk to others who've used it, call and talk with the product's vendor—in order to increase the chances that the time and money you invest in it will bring you a good return.

developing
applications
with add-
ins, 1-2-3,
and macros

Add-ins use more memory than does 1-2-3 alone; how much more depends on the particular add-in. In most cases, you can detach the add-in at any time during a 1-2-3 session and reclaim all but about 20K of that memory. The 20K goes to the memory-resident Add-In Manager program used to attach add-ins to 1-2-3; in Release 2.2, since the Add-In Manager is integrated into 1-2-3 itself, you will reclaim all the memory that was used by the add-in. If you do detach an add-in to reclaim memory, you can later reattach that add-in should you need it again.

A macro can easily handle the attaching and detaching of add-ins. If you're working with large worksheets where available RAM is scarce, you might maximize your use of that memory by, before attaching the add-in, using a macro to extract to disk those portions of the worksheet you don't expect to use. Then recover those portions after you've detached the add-in. For more information about managing add-ins under macro control, see the "Working with Add-ins" section in Chapter 3. We'll cover the broader subject of maximizing resources such as available RAM in the section entitled Managing Resources later in this chapter.

are macros
the right
vehicle?

Another question to face is whether to fully automate an application with customized macros, automate only certain parts of the application with customized macros, automate only some keystroke sequences to facilitate interactive work, or develop a template that uses no macros at all.

Those choices represent a continuum of automation levels that runs from total automation through none at all. Since the farther up the automation scale you go, the more time you typically invest, consider when the additional investment will be a profitable one. Here are some questions and guidelines to help you know when that will be the case:

- *How much help do the applications' users need in its operation?* Are the users unfamiliar with 1-2-3? Macros can vastly simplify an application to the point where the user needs to know nothing about 1-2-3. Do the users constitute a group that will be difficult to train and support (perhaps because of high turnover or because they are geographically dispersed)? If so, macros are a good way to vastly reduce the training and support hurdles you face.

- *How much time will automating the application save?* Assess this element with the following formula: The amount of time the application takes to perform manually minus the amount of time the macro application will take to perform equals the amount of time the macro will save you each time you use it. Multiply that amount by how frequently you use the application in a given period (say, one month); then multiply that by the number of people using it. Finally, multiply that amount by the number of periods in its useful life. Compare that amount to the amount of time you expect it will take to develop and maintain the application. The more time you save, the better a return you'll get for the time you invest.

- *What are the costs of errors?* Can a macro significantly lessen the likelihood that they will occur? Are those errors difficult to detect if you don't prevent them with a macro? If errors are costly and macros can lessen their likelihood (they are often very effective at that), lean in favor of using a macro.

- *How long do you expect the application to last in this form or in some modified form?* The longer this application is likely to survive, the more return you'll get from the time you invest to develop macros.

We won't go so far as to prescribe any formula for the decision, but if you use common sense as you consider the aforementioned points, we think you'll arrive at the right answer.

you can blend modes: manual and macro-driven operation

As you consider your options, keep in mind that the decision to automate (or the converse) an application need not apply to the entire application. You might automate some parts of it and leave others for the user to operate on an interactive basis.

The 80/20 rule applies here. The last 20 percent of the automation job may require 80 percent of the effort, and that effort may yield insufficient returns to justify it. You might choose to designate that "20 percent" portion of the application for manual operation and provide whatever training and documentation users will need to perform those tasks with 1-2-3 interactively.

Another strategy is to selectively automate portions of an application. For example, consider a company-wide budgeting application. For department heads to just post numbers into a budget template, you might provide only an annotated template to use manually. However, the process of rolling up departmental budgets into divisions is a bit trickier, so you may decide to automate that portion of the application.

the real key is to get the application in use

Keep in mind that one of the keys to keeping productive is getting those applications in circulation. If you saddle yourself with totally automating every application that comes your way, you'll probably fall behind. If after an application has been in use for a while there's an apparent need for more automation, you can always add (more) macros to do the job. That kind of flexibility is one of the things that makes 1-2-3 such a popular development environment. In fact, after reading this book you may want to review your existing applications to identify ones you'd like to automate or automate further.

making
productive
tradeoffs

The implication of our discussion of blending macros with interactive templates is that there are tradeoffs to consider. For example, you can make a particular macro more maintainable, but you may have to work another two days to do it; you can add more extensive error handling, but it'll slow down the macro's performance; you might add hordes of help screens, but they'll use memory the application may require for other purposes.

macros
require
many small
decisions

Throughout this book we've suggested guidelines to help you navigate through the many choices that face you. Now we'll tell you that while you may try to follow an overall principle with respect to some issue (such as how much error-handling to supply in a macro), each time you write a macro, you must decide anew the optimal application of that principle for the macro at hand.

For example, you may decide that the reporting portion of a macro needs extensive error handling to prevent a printer error from aborting it, but the data entry portion of the macro under the control of the / Range Input command already seems pretty secure. You should vary your approach to suit each situation rather than adopting one rigid stance; you'll save time and still produce superb applications.

trading off
limited
resources

Aside from your time, available memory will probably be the other limitation you'll most often encounter. You can compensate for demands on memory made by one part of a macro by using less demanding techniques in other parts. For example, if you need a mistake-proof data entry system that requires an extensive amount of RAM, you might be able to compensate for the increased macro size by storing the help screens on disk instead of in the worksheet file itself. We'll address how to maximize memory in Chapter 28.

An Overview of the Content of an Application

This section will acquaint you with the broader issues you'll face when you set out to build a turnkey macro application. The issues we'll discuss will, to some extent, mirror the organization of the section on macro content to follow. If you are already an experienced application developer, you may now want to skip directly to that section.

We'll review the content of a turnkey macro application in terms of three general components: data entry, processing, and output. We don't mean to suggest that the process of developing an application proceeds from data entry routines, through data processing routines, and concludes with some form of output routine. The reality of building an application is closer to the process of weaving those types of macros into a mosaic. There are, however, common threads within each of those categories, and you will learn more easily about those techniques if we present similar techniques as a group.

Afterward, we'll discuss the need for design strategy, for several programming concepts, and for a tool kit with which to more rapidly fashion those applications. In short, we'll explain why you'll need everything that follows in this section.

User Interaction

writing macros for others is a different job than writing them for yourself

In previous chapters, we addressed the person using the macro primarily as "you," because most of those macros are ones you will write and use yourself. In this chapter you'll find that we've often changed that form of address to "the user" because the techniques presented here are ones you'll often employ to write macros that others will also use.

Writing macros for others is more challenging than writing the same macros for yourself. While you innately understand what the macro is trying to accomplish and how it is supposed to work, someone else who uses it won't. The less accessible you are (or wish to be) to the people using the macro (and the more of them there are) the more important it is to create an application that manages well all the interaction it has with its users. We'll present a multitude of techniques to help you succeed at that task, the major emphasis of which will lie with the job of entering data into the application and making menu choices.

Data entry encompasses data typed at the keyboard, data retrieved or combined from another worksheet file, data imported from some other kind of file (including files stored on CD ROM), or data continuously fed into the worksheet by analog-to-digital conversion devices (such as those used to monitor stock prices via FM broadcasts or those used to monitor equipment in a laboratory or factory.

When most people think of data entry, they think of just the data acquired through the aforementioned means—debits and credits, sales leads and active accounts, and the like. However, as a developer you'll see such entries in the broader scheme of managing all the interactions a person has with the application. Such interactions also include responding to prompts, entering filenames, defining report settings, selecting from menus, and so on.

If you approach each such task in a radically different way, you'll make the application harder to learn and use. Try to be consistent in your approach to the interactions the macro has with its user: prompt the person in the same place on the screen, use terminology consistently, and avoid clutter on the screen. We've combined the relevant techniques in the chapter on Managing User Input.

Processing Data

Processing data emphasizes the use of specialized macro commands such as {let}, worksheet commands such as Data Query Extract, or everyday formulas such as @index.

First and foremost, 1-2-3 is a spreadsheet, and most of the processing you do under macro control still consists of the spreadsheet recalculating numbers.[48] Macros can augment a spreadsheet application directly by controlling which parts of the worksheet 1-2-3 recalculates and when, by performing some trickier calculations (such as cumulative totals), by transferring data from one range to another, and by clearing that data at the end of a period.

1-2-3's database is another superb data processing tool built right into the worksheet. It's also one of the most fruitful areas for macro-automation because its utility is matched by the difficulty most people encounter learning to use it. Macros can remove that difficulty entirely by managing the variety of ranges (input, criterion, output, data-sort) that define a database, by eliminating the complexity of specifying criteria (single or compound; labels, values or formulas), and by eliminating the need to know 1-2-3's / Data commands.

Finally, data processing encompasses the techniques by which you handle errors in your application—and just as important, the techniques by which you can prevent some of the more common errors from occurring at all.

Output

Like data entry, output encompasses more than meets the eye. At its simplest level, output can consist of an onscreen display of data. Automating such displays entails such operations as navigating to a specified range, formatting cells, assigning column widths, and setting worksheet titles.[49]

---

[48] Since we'll assume you're proficient in those operations, we won't dwell on them, but don't interpret our lack of coverage to mean that they're less important to you than macros. They're more important than macros, because although you can almost always write an application without macros, you can almost never do it without worksheet formulas.

[49] We've organized the subject of Help Screens under Output. Even though an end user wouldn't regard a help screen as output, from a developer's point of view, creating a help screen is no different than creating any other form of screen output. The implication you should keep in mind as you read is that everything you learn about writing help screens applies to other forms of screen output as well.

Graphic displays are another important form of output. Unlike spreadsheet displays, which often require no more than showing data in the same format in which you calculate and store it, graphs may require considerable setup. Macros can help you store and retrieve catalogs of named graphs or enable users to define their own graphs quickly and easily.

Because 1-2-3 does not maintain named print settings and you are likely to have to print multiple reports from a single worksheet, macros can do that job for you. Not only do they make that process simpler and quicker, they can guarantee that you'll get comparable reports across different time periods.

The last kind of output we'll cover is writing files, be it in the form of a worksheet, ASCII, or PIC file. Macros can handle the tricky process of automating menus that sometimes say Cancel/Replace and other times return you directly to Ready mode. They can also write a variety of file formats directly from your worksheet. For example, you could write out a comma separated values file (also known as a CSV file or a comma delimited file) that dBASE programs can read without prior translation.

An Overview of the Process for Developing an Application

We've just reviewed the building blocks for an application (that was content); now we'll review how to convert those materials into a coherent application (this is process). As was true of our discussion of an application's content, this is a prelude to the indepth instructions we'll cover later in this section of the book, and is intended for you if you lack a sense of why those issues are important. Otherwise, skip directly to subsequent chapters later in this section where we introduce the techniques themselves.

Application Planning

Because turnkey macro applications are large, you develop them one routine at a time. It's as if you were writing many little macros—with one important difference. While you write each small routine, you must also coordinate it with every other routine.

Sometimes macro writers erroneously focus on a few fragments of the application without paying adequate attention to making the entire application work together. The more complex the application, the more important it will be that you coordinate its elements up front. Such inter-macro coordination has two dimensions, a technical dimension and a user-interface dimension.

Technical issues encompass structuring your macros so they share common subroutines and making those macros easy to revise in the future. Technical implementation also covers screen design, worksheet layout, execution speed, memory use, and inter-module links. Good technical implementation depends on thoroughly knowing both your application's requirements and the tools you have at hand to meet them.

User-interface issues encompass all the ways you create a consistently easy-to-learn and easy-to-use means for a person to use the application. Ignoring these subtle issues can have disastrous impact: It can turn the application you build into just another good idea that failed to work in practice.

That's why, if you don't already know, you'll need to find out how John the Accountant, Sue the Marketing Manager, and Isiah the Engineer (or whomever the application's users will be) work, so you can mold the application to their habits, not the reverse. Do they prefer to use the numeric keypad to key in a set of numbers quickly? If so, make sure the application allows them to. Are they already 1-2-3 literate? Then they're likely to become frustrated if the macro prevents them from exercising the kind of options they can when they use 1-2-3 interactively (one way to solve that problem would be to provide the option to use 1-2-3 either interactively or under macro control).

Once you know something about your user, you can use that knowledge as you decide how to prompt someone for a date (why not let the user enter it in in English and have the application convert it to an @date function?), where you place messages on the screen (in more-or-less the same place each time, please), whether to provide any printed instructions, onscreen instructions, or on-line help, and if so, how much.

Development Tools

Macro development is more art than science, and macro developers are artisans. As one of that group, you'll need a set of tools for your craft. Unlike the other techniques discussed, the macro-development tools we'll present (in the chapter on Macro Development Tips and Tools) don't become part of the final application any more than a hammer becomes part of the house you build with it.

These techniques will help you to evaluate the speed of alternative routines, navigate easily about the application during its development, quickly debug complex routines, and generally shorten the process of writing macros.

22

Managing
User Input

There are five kinds of user input you may be called upon to manage—single characters, labels, numbers, database records, and ranges—and the techniques for each kind differ. Before we review those techniques, let's take a quick look at the kinds of user input they're meant to manage.

- *Single Characters.* When you're accepting single characters, you most often want to trap and test them. For example, if you've posted a message on the screen that a person can press Q to quit (exit) the application, then you must test for the letter Q. If the next keystroke is a Q, the macro should terminate, and if it is some other keystroke, the macro should continue. This is one of the most common ways to arrange for users to convey their wishes to a macro run application.

  Trapping and testing keystrokes also enables you to completely redefine the keyboard. For example, you can disable certain keys and leave others active, or you can change the meaning of some keys (e.g., the function keys), so they support your application. For example, in a database application, you might redefine the F7 key so that it adds another record and the F8 key so that it edits the last record.

- *Labels.* The most common circumstance in which you'll be accepting labels is when you need to prompt a user for a single word or phrase, and where the number of choices exceeds the number you can display on a menu. For example, you might prompt the user for a report title or for a password with which to gain access to the application.

- *Numbers*. Since 1-2-3 is a spreadsheet, and spreadsheets are best at handling numbers, you'll probably find yourself developing more data entry routines for numbers than any other kind of data. It's common to need to make sure such numbers fall within allowable ranges. You might test an entry to see if it falls in the range of 100 to 1,000. If it does, the macro enters it. If it does not, the macro displays an error message indicating the acceptable range and once again prompts the user for a number.

- *Database Records*. This type of data entry is a collection of separate entries (perhaps individual characters, labels, and numbers) that will eventually wind up composing a single record in a 1-2-3 database. Multiple entries such as this frequently require that you allow them to be edited in free-form fashion.

- *Ranges*. Since so many 1-2-3 commands operate on worksheet ranges, it's common to have to supply the application with a range. Macros can define ranges themselves as long as they know what to define. When they don't, you'll have to involve the user in that process.

Let's review the approaches for achieving each of these objectives, one group at a time.

Single Characters

The {get} or {look} commands offer the best way to record individual characters. Both store on the worksheet one character from the keyboard buffer. In the examples that follow, we'll use the {get} command.

Typically, you'll want to record a character and test to see if it matches some predetermined character. For example, you might have a situation where if the user enters a Q, you want the macro to terminate the application; otherwise, the macro should continue.

Using {get}

The simplest of the possible scenarios is that one particular keystroke is of critical importance, and all the others are to be ignored. The following macro illustrates how this might be written.

	A	B	C	D	E	F	G	H
1	NAME	MACRO						
2	--------------							
3	\A	{get ANS}						
4		{if ANS="Q"}{quit}						
5		{branch OTHER}						
6								
7	ANS							
8								
9								
10								

Figure 22-1

{get ANS}

Row 1 of the macro causes the application to wait until the user types a key. As soon as 1-2-3 detects a keystroke, it stores it in the cell named Ans and the macro continues. In this case, the cell named Ans is B7.

{if ANS="Q"}{quit}

If the keystroke is an uppercase Q, the macro reads the command on the same line, {quit}, and terminates. Control returns to the keyboard. If the keystroke was anything other than an uppercase Q, the macro ignores the {quit} command and reads the command on the line below.

{branch OTHER}

If the keystroke entered was not a Q, the macro reads the {branch} command, which transfers control to a routine named Other. Other could be any routine that you wish to be processed in the event the user did not press the keystroke to terminate the application.

The only weakness of this method is that the character Q is embedded, or hard-coded, in the macro. Since it's not unusual to want to change such a macro to test for some other character, let's look at a technique that makes it easier to do that.

```
        A         B         C         D         E         F         G         H
  1  │ NAME      MACRO
  2  │ --------------
  3  │ \A        {get ANS}
  4  │           {if ANS=SPEC_KEY}{quit}
  5  │           {branch OTHER}
  6  │
  7  │ SPEC_KEY  Q
  8  │
  9  │ ANS
 10  │
```

Figure 22-2

In this version of the macro, a cell named Spec_key contains the character you want the macro to test for, Q. In the {if} command, that range name has replaced the Q. However, when 1-2-3 reads the {if} command, the effect will be the same because it will use the string value Q in place of the range name Spec_key.

Should you subsequently wish to test for some other character, all you need to do is enter it in the cell named Spec_key. The macro itself remains unchanged. This technique is a good one for any environment in which other people may be maintaining this macro. The variable Q is easy to identify and since you don't have to edit the macro itself to change the variable, there's less chance of introducing errors into the macro while revising it.

Case Sensitivity

Testing keystrokes involves comparing a string that the user has input to a string already stored in the macro. There are two factors that govern such comparisons in 1-2-3: case sensitivity and the interaction of values and labels.

case
comparison

1-2-3 usually—but not always—considers uppercase (or capitalized) letters as equivalent to their lower case counterparts. The exception occurs when the copy of 1-2-3 that is running the macro is using a driver set incorporating the ASCII collating sequence.[50] In that case, string comparisons will be case-sensitive.

Since the ASCII collating sequence is not a default in 1-2-3's Install program, most copies of 1-2-3 don't use it. Consequently, most copies of

[50] To set 1-2-3's collating sequence to ASCII, run the Install program by entering Install at the DOS prompt; then select Advanced Options, Modify Current Driver Set, Collating, ASCII, Return To Menu, and Save Changes; then either accept the current driver file name or specify a new driver file name, and press Return to exit Install. If you accepted the file name 123 for your driver set, you can run 1-2-3 as you normally do. However, if you specified some other driver file name, in order to run 1-2-3 with the newly created driver you must enter 123 driver_filename at the DOS prompt. So if you called your new driver Ascii, you'd enter 123 ascii.

1-2-3 will treat the same letters of different case as identical. However, you may have no way of knowing how the copies of 1-2-3 that will use your macro will be configured. A conservative policy is to guarantee your macros will be case-insensitive with any driver. To do that, have the macro convert all user entries to either upper or lower case before you test them.

Here's a macro that does just that.

```
        A         B         C       D       E       F       G       H
  1  NAME      MACRO
  2  --------------
  3  \A        {get ANS}
  4            {let ANS;@upper(ANS)}
  5            {if ANS=SPEC_KEY}{quit}
  6            {branch \A}
  7
  8  SPEC_KEY  Q
  9
 10  ANS
```

Figure 22-3

{let ANS;@upper(ANS)}

The change in this macro occurs on row 4, shown above. The {let} command contains a function, @upper, which will convert the input to be stored in Ans to all uppercase, irrespective of the case the user specified. Notice, too, that the letter stored in Spec_key, with which the user's entry will be compared, is in uppercase. If the user enters the proper letter but does so in lower case, and 1-2-3 is running under the ASCII collating sequence driver, 1-2-3 will still accept that character.

The cost of this technique is small—it takes a moment longer to write. There's no measurable difference in the time it takes 1-2-3 to convert the input string to all uppercase while the macro is running.

The {get} command always places a string in the destination cell, so even if the user types a numeral, you're assured of comparing a string with another string. Had you used the {getlabel} command instead of the {get} command to accept a keystroke, you'd also be assured that the user would enter a label, even if it was a numeral. However, if you are testing for one of the special keys such as Escape or a function key, {get} is the only command that will enable you to capture them properly.

If the user presses Escape or the Return key in response to a {getlabel} prompt, {getlabel} stores a single apostrophe (left-alignment label prefix) in the destination cell, whereas {get} will store their macro keyname ({esc} or ~). Use {getlabel} if you want to capture only alphanumeric keystrokes.

Disabling the Keyboard

The following macro technique excludes others from entering data into or otherwise affecting your application while you're away from the keyboard. Just have the macro disable Ctrl-break with {breakoff}, change the indicator to =OFF=, and test for an obscure key, such as a vertical bar character. Before you activate this macro, to keep secret the keystroke that will reactivate the keyboard, make sure the macro itself is off the screen. The macro below implements this variation.

	A	B	C	D	E	F	G	H
1	\A	{breakoff}{indicate "OFF"}						
2		{get ANS}						
3		{if ANS=SPEC_KEY}{indicate}{esc}{quit}						
4		{branch \A}						
5								
6	SPEC_KEY							
7								
8	ANS							
9								
10								

Figure 22-4

The macro in row 1 disables the Control-Break key and changes the mode prompt to =OFF=. Row 2 waits for a keystroke and stores it in the cell named Ans. Row 3 compares the stored entry with the character stored in Spec_key. If the two don't match, the macro ignores the remaining instructions on row 3 and reads the {branch} command on row 4 (which repeats the macro, causing it to wait for another keystroke). If the tested keystroke matched the one stored in Spec_key, the macro will restore the default mode indicator, cancel any further keystrokes that may be stored in the keyboard buffer, and return control to the keyboard.

Capturing Special Keys

If you want to capture and test non-alphanumeric, or special, keys such as Home, End, or Edit, you must use the {get} or {look} command. Other ways of accepting user input, such as the {getlabel} or {getnumber} command, interpret these keystrokes in other ways ({getlabel}, for example, will enter a single label-prefix character in response to the Escape key).

When you use either {get} or {look} to record such keystrokes, your macro must conform to the special ways in which 1-2-3 records special keys. There are two conditions to keep in mind:

1 {Get} and {look} record such keys in uppercase.

2. In cases where there are multiple forms of the keyname, 1-2-3 will record the key using only one of those forms.

Keep in mind that since you'll be testing for these keystrokes, you must test the keystroke against the exact form in which {get} or {look} will record them. If you test against an improper form, the user can enter the proper key and the comparison will still fail.

Uppercase Form

When {get} or {look} record a key such as the F7 {Query} key, 1-2-3 enters it on the worksheet as the uppercase string {QUERY}, so that's how you should enter the label you will test keystrokes against. Of course, as we said earlier, 1-2-3 will only distinguish upper from lower-case when it's running with a driver set incorporating the ASCII Collating driver. Entering the key name in uppercase covers you in any event, and if you develop applications for other people to use, you must account for that possibility.

In the example shown below, in the named range Spec_key, we've entered the key name we wish to test the user's keystroke against.

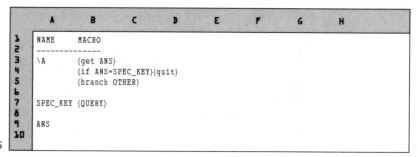

Figure 22-5

Proper Forms of the Keyname

You already know that a number of the special keys can be represented in more than one way in a macro (e.g., {esc} and {escape} both represent the Escape key). However, when 1-2-3 records a special keystroke with the {get} or {look} command, it will represent that key in only one way. If you test for one of the other ways you can represent that key, your test will find that the keystrokes don't match when they should.

Here's an example. In the macro above, suppose you want to test for the Escape key, so you've entered the label {ESCAPE} in the cell named Spec_key where you now see the label {QUERY}. You run the macro and the user presses the Escape key. However, 1-2-3 records the keystroke as {ESC}, so the comparison in line 2 in effect asks, "Is the string {ESC} the same as the string {ESCAPE}?" 1-2-3 says no, and the test that should succeed, fails.

The reason it fails is that although 1-2-3's macro interpreter will press the Escape key when it reads either {esc} or {escape}, 1-2-3's string comparison function doesn't regard them as interchangeable. It merely identifies them as two different strings. The moral of this story is when you are testing for any of the special keys, make sure you use the form of that key that {get} or {look} will return.

The following table lists all of the special keys that have more than one acceptable representation in a macro, and distinguishes which of those forms you must use if you are capturing keystrokes with {get} and testing them.

Table 22.1. 1-2-3 Special Keys That Have More Than One Form

The form that you must use if you are testing keys recorded with the {get} or {look} command	Alternate forms of each key also accepted by macros, but which fail if used with {get} or {look}
{UP}	{U}
{DOWN}	{D}
{LEFT}	{L}
{RIGHT}	{R}
{BACKSPACE}	{BS}
{ESC}	{ESCAPE}
{DEL}	{DELETE}

And, in Release 2.2 and 3 only:

{INSERT}   {INS}

It's probably easy to keep the representations for the arrow keys straight—the long form is the one recorded by {get} or {look}. Unfortunately, 1-2-3 follows no pattern. While it uses the long forms of most of the keys, the Delete key and Escape key are both recorded in their respective short forms, {DEL} and {ESC}.

Another potentially confusing usage regards the Insert key. In 1-2-3 Release 2 or 2.01, this key has no short form. So, although you can represent the Delete key as {DEL} or {DELETE}, you can represent the Insert key only as {INSERT}. In Release 2.2, things are a little different. You can use the short form {INS} while writing a macro. However, 1-2-3 records with {get} or {look} use only the longer form, so that is the form you must test against. Only {INSERT} works—in this or any other context in a macro.

Use the mnemonic "Delaware Eskimos are short" to remind yourself that the DELete and ESCape keys are the only keys that 1-2-3 records in their shortened form. All the others are in the long form.

If that method of recollection fails you, consult the quick reference card for the Advanced Macro Commands that accompanies the book. The acceptable forms are documented there as well.

Implementing a Key Table

The examples to this point have concentrated on a particular keystroke triggering some event (e.g., stopping the macro). Another common need is to test for various classes of keystrokes.

Consider the following scenario: You want to let a user enter data into a spreadsheet, you want to disable every function key except F2 (Edit), and you've placed a prompt on the screen to press F9 (Calc) when done.

Let's interpret this challenge in terms of what your macro must do. There are two keystrokes that should trigger separate events (F2 triggers editing, F9 terminates the macro). Another class of keystrokes is irrelevant and must be ignored (all other function keys). A third class of keystrokes must be passed through to 1-2-3 to work in their normal manner (normal data entry keys such as all alphanumerics and directional keys).

The following macro illustrates one way to do this.

	A	B	C	D	E	F	G	H
1	NAME	MACROS						
2		----------------						
3	\A	{get ANS}						
4		{if ANS=SPEC_KEY}{quit}						
5		{if @vlookup(ANS;KEY_TAB;0)+1}{branch \A}						
6		{ANS}{branch \A}						
7								
8	KEY_TAB	{ABS}						
9		{NAME}						
10		{GOTO}						
11		{WINDOW}						
12		{QUERY}						
13		{TABLE}						
14		{GRAPH}						
15								
16	SPEC_KEY	{CALC}						
17								
18	ANS							
19		{return}						
20								

Figure 22-6

```
{get ANS}
{if ANS=SPEC_KEY}{quit}
```

The {get} command waits for a keystroke and when it receives it, stores it in the cell named Ans. The macro in row 2 tests to see if the string stored in Ans is the same as the string stored in Spec_key. That string is the keyname for the F9 function key, {CALC}. If the keystoke is F9, the macro will read the command on the same line, {quit}, and the macro will end.

```
{if @vlookup(ANS;KEY_TAB;0)+1}
{branch \A}
```

The {if} command on row 3 performs another test, but this time it is testing to see if any of an entire group of keystrokes were the ones recorded in Ans. The keys that compose that group are stored in a table in cells B6..B12 (collectively named Key_tab).

The operation of this test revolves around some special properties of the @vlookup function when used with strings. The @vlookup function uses the entry in Ans as a key to locate an entry in Key_tab. The last argument in the @vlookup function, 0, indicates that the lookup should be performed on the first column in Key_tab (as it happens, there is only one column in Key_tab).

If the @vlookup function finds a match in Key_tab, the function returns the row position within the table of the match. For example, a match on {ABS} would return a 0, {NAME} would return a 1, {GOTO} a 2, and so on. If it finds no match, the function returns ERR.

If the @vlookup command returns either 0 or ERR, the {if} command will skip the remaining instructions on the current line and transfer control directly to the next line of the macro (that is also true of the value NA). Any other value will cause the {if} command to continue reading instructions on the same line.

In this case, if there is a match, we want the macro to continue reading instructions on the same line as the {if} command. All the positions except the first one in the table will return a value that will satisfy that condition. However, if the match is on {ABS}, the row position returned will be 0, which will have the opposite effect. That's why the complete formula adds 1 to the result of the @vlookup function. Therefore, if a match on {ABS} returns a 0, the formula will return a 1.

If the @vlookup function returns a 1 through 7 (the possible values returned by matches on the entries in the table), then the macro will read the {branch} command and transfer control to the beginning of the routine. Here's where the logic is tricky: The effect of such a branch is that the macro ignores any of the keystrokes found in Key_tab. When the {branch} command returns control to the top of the macro, the macro once again waits for another keystroke—without acting on the last one.

However, if the @vlookup function returned ERR (meaning that it did not find the keystroke in Key_tab), then 1-2-3 skips the remaining instructions and reads the line on row 4 of the macro.

```
{ANS}{branch \A}
```

The macro instruction on row 4 calls a subroutine consisting of the keystroke recorded in the cell named Ans.

```
ANS {edit}
    {return}
```

In this example, we'll suppose that the user had pressed the Edit key. The {EDIT} key representation would have been entered in the cell named Ans. 1-2-3 would read that key as a macro instruction to go into Edit mode. Then 1-2-3 would read the {return} command and return control to the next instruction following the subroutine call in row 4 of the macro. The next instruction, also on row 4, is a {branch} command to the beginning of the macro, which will wait for another keystroke. If 1-2-3 was in edit mode, the next keystroke would probably be some text, which 1-2-3 would also pass through, until the user pressed F9. When the user eventually presses F9, the {if} command on row 2 will terminate the macro.

An example will help to clarify the explanation. If a user presses F6, then the string {WINDOW} will be stored in ANS. The macro will compare this with the string stored in SPEC_KEY, determine that it is not equivalent, and will continue to the next line. In the next line, @vlookup searches the range KEY_TAB for a string that matches the entry in Ans, {WINDOW}. It finds a match in the fourth row of the table, so it returns the value 3, adds 1 to it, determines that this value is greater than zero, and branches back to \A. The macro will now get another keystroke without having done anything about the F6 keystroke. If another key had been pressed, the right arrow for instance, it would not have matched anything in the table, and the next line of the macro would have run. This macro line runs the subroutine called ANS. It simply sends "{RIGHT}" (the contents of Ans) through to 1-2-3, then goes to get another key.

Another, simpler way to write the macro is to extend the Key_tab table to include another column containing the letter Y. In this case, the

@vlookup function would lookup strings in the first column but return a result from the second column (offset 1). Then, you would only need to test for the result, Y.

```
       A          B          C        D       E        F       G       H
 1    \A        {get ANS}
 2              {if ANS=SPEC_KEY}{quit}
 3              {if @vlookup(ANS;KEY_TAB;1)="Y"}{branch \A}
 4              {ANS}{branch \A}
 5
 6    KEY_TAB   {ABS}      Y
 7              {NAME}     Y
 8              {GOTO}     Y
 9              {WINDOW}   Y
10              {QUERY}    Y
11              {TABLE}    Y
12              {GRAPH}    Y
13
14    SPEC_KEY {CALC}
15
16    ANS
17
18
19
20
```

Figure 22-7

Turning Off the Slash Key

If the point of your key-trapping exercise is to allow macro users some interaction but keep them from doing things that could cause trouble, you probably want to prevent them from invoking 1-2-3's command menu. If so, you can simply add the slash (/) to the bottom of Key_tab and extend the named range to include the new entry.

However, if you want to prevent them from getting at 1-2-3's menu, you should also prevent them from using the other method of doing so. If from Ready mode you hold down the shift key and press the less-than sign (<) key, 1-2-3 will display its menu. To prevent that, simply add the less-than sign to Key_tab and extend the named range to include the new entry.

Displaying Your Own Menu at the "/"

It's also possible to replace 1-2-3's menu with a menu of your own making. When the user presses the slash key, your menu displays. The following macro allows that to take place:

```
        A           B            C             D          E          F
1   \A          {get ANS}
2               {if ANS="/"}{menubranch MYMENU}{branch \A}
3               {ANS}{branch \A}
4
5   MYMENU      Copy         Move          Erase
6               Copy a cell  Move a cell   Erase a cell
7               /c{?}~{?}~    /m{?}~{?}~     /re{?}~
8               {branch \A}  {branch  \A}  {branch \A}
9
10
```

Figure 22-8

Displaying Your Own Help Screen at F1—A Release 2.2 Technique

Just as you can capture the slash key, 1-2-3 Release 2.2 enables you to also capture the F1 key, {Help}, and display your own help screen. The macro to accomplish this task looks very much like the previous macro.

```
        A           B            C             D          E          F
1   \A          {get ANS}
2               {if ANS="{HELP}"}{A_HELP}{branch \A}
3               {ANS}{branch \A}
4
5   A_HELP      {goto}HELP_SCREEN~{d}
6               {get ANS}
7               {home}
8               {return}
9
10
```

Figure 22-9

When the user of this macro presses F1, the macro calls the subroutine named A_help. A_help, a very simplistic help routine, displays a help screen, waits for a keystroke, and then places the cell pointer back in cell A1 before returning to the main routine, \A.

Be Careful of Curly Braces

The achilles heel of key-filtering macros is the { character. If the user presses the left brace, 1-2-3 will store it in Ans, and then try to run Ans as a subroutine. When it does, 1-2-3 interprets the left curly brace as the start of an incomplete macro keyword, halts the macro, and generates an error message. Like other such macro errors, this is not an error that the {onerror} command can trap.

You can prevent this kind of trouble by including the { character in the Key_tab table. The cost of that course is that if a user types that character, the macro will discard it. If you need to make that key available for users to type, insert the following line in the macro, directly after the {get} command:

```
{if ANS="{"}{{}{branch \A}
```

This line checks to see if the keystroke stored in Ans is the left brace. If it is, the macro uses the {{} command to type a left brace, and then branches to wait for another keystroke (avoiding the subroutine call to Ans altogether).

Although the right brace character, }, poses no problems, you do have to take special measures if you provide users the ability to type the tilde. Handle that with another {if} command, clustered with the other {if} commands; at any rate, before the {ANS} command.

```
{if ANS="~"}{~}{branch \A}
```

Usually, you want to protect the macro from crashing, but it isn't always necessary to provide total flexibility to users. Thus, you will probably want to trap the left curly brace, but unless the user is writing macros while under controlled data entry, or unless you have to guarantee that the macro won't crash, the tilde test may be unnecessary. In any case, here's the law enforcement special, fully bullet-proofed:

	A	B	C	D	E	F	G	H
1	\A	{get ANS}						
2		{if ANS="~"}{~}{branch \A}						
3		{if ANS="{"}{{}{branch \A}						
4		{if ANS=SPEC_KEY}{quit}						
5		{if @vlookup(ANS;KEY_TAB;1)="Y"}{branch \A}						
6		{ANS}{branch \A}						
7								
8	KEY_TAB	{ABS}	Y					
9		{NAME}	Y					
10		{GOTO}	Y					
11		{WINDOW}	Y					
12		{QUERY}	Y					
13		{TABLE}	Y					
14		{GRAPH}	Y					
15								
16	SPEC_KEY	{CALC}						
17								
18	ANS							
19								
20								

Figure 22-10

Generalizing the Curly Brace Test

If your goal is to block all but one or two of 1-2-3's special keys, you can simplify and generalize the keystroke test. The following macro allows the user to enter most keystrokes, to move down to another cell in the same column, and to stop the macro.

	A	B	C	D	E	F	G	H
1	\A	{get ANS}						
2		{if ANS=SPEC_KEY}{quit}						
3		{if ANS="{DOWN}"}{d}{branch \A}						
4		{if @code(ANS)=123}{branch \A}						
5		{ANS}{branch \A}						
6								
7	SPEC_KEY	{CALC}						
8								
9	ANS							

Figure 22-11

The heart of this macro—the reason it works—lies in row 4. Since the first character of each of the special keys is {, and since the @code function tests only the first character of a label, we can simply test for the ASCII value that corresponds to {, which is 123.

Embedding the Test in a Formula

As a rule, formulas recalculate faster when they are entered in a cell than when they are embedded in a macro label (such as the formula in row 4 of the above macro). The tradeoff you make if you enter the formula on the worksheet is readability: You'll generally have a more abstract macro if you remove the formula from the macro itself.

Here's a macro into which we'll insert a formula in the cell named Test, cell B3.

In order to create the correct formula, you must analyze the original macro to ascertain the logic to convert. The macro {if} and formula @if are similar in that both evaluate an expression and if it is true, pass control

	A	B	C	D	E	F	G	H
1	\A	{get ANS}{recalc TEST}{branch TEST}						
2								
3	TEST							
4		{branch \A}						
5								
6	KEY_TAB	{ABS}	Y					
7		{NAME}	Y					
8		{GOTO}	Y					
9		{WINDOW}	Y					
10		{QUERY}	Y					
11		{TABLE}	Y					
12		{GRAPH}	Y					
13								
14	SPEC_KEY	{CALC}						
15								
16	ANS							
17								
18								
19								
20								

Figure 22-12

to the statement to the right on the same line. They are different in the way they react when the expression is not true. The {if} statement passes control to the line below it. An @ function can't do that; it requires that all statements be on one line, separated by punctuation symbols (such as commas or semicolons).

The following table illustrates those differences. In each case, statement1 will be read if the expression is true; statement2 will be read if the expression is false.

Table 22.2. The Differences Between {if} and @

Type	Conditional Statement Format
Macro	{if expression}{statement1} {statement2}
Formula	@if(expression;statement1;statement2)

It's quite possible for statement1 or statement2 to be another "if" statement in order to introduce yet another level of testing. When you "nest" more than one test within either kind of "if" statement, that's called nesting.

The macro we're converting is the first version of the key filtering macro. That version used two nested {if} statements—one to test the keystroke against the string stored in Spec_key, and one to test the key-stroke against those stored in Key_tab. Neither the tests for the left brace character or the tilde are included; however, once you learn the formula-writing technique we'll use, you could write them into it.

In a macro, nested {if} statements can appear on different lines. In a formula, they must all appear on the same line in one formula. Here's the formula to be entered in the cell named Test in the macro shown above:

```
@if(ANS=SPEC_KEY;"{quit}";@if(@iserr(@vlookup(ANS;KEY_TAB;0));"{}";"{ANS}"))
```

This formula will return one of several possible string values—{quit}, {}, or {ANS}—any of which will act as a macro command. The first result will terminate the macro, the second does nothing except pass control to the next statement of the macro, the third calls the subroutine {ANS}. Now let's look at how those results might be derived.

```
@if(ANS=SPEC_KEY;"{quit}",
```

The first part of the formula tests to see if the string stored in Ans is the same as the one stored in Spec_key; if so, the formula returns the result of {quit}. If not, it continues reading with the next part.

```
@if(@iserr(@vlookup(ANS;KEY_TAB;0));"{}";
```

The second part of the formula tests to see if the @vlookup function returns the value ERR. That would mean that the value in Ans is not contained in the Key_tab table. If so, the formula returns the string {}. {}, also known as no op, because it performs no operations, merely passes control to the next instruction in the macro.

We've chosen the @iserr form of the macro because the way ERR is handled in a macro differs from the way it works in a formula. In a macro, ERR is equivalent to the value "False." This means the macro continues to execute. However, the formula hangs onto the special ERR value, causing the macro to halt execution.

```
"{ANS}"))
```

If none of the above conditions are true, then we know that the keystroke is neither the one stored in Spec_key, nor is it one of those stored in Key_tab. Therefore, the keystroke is deemed acceptable to be passed through to 1-2-3. The last string, {ANS} does that by calling Ans as a subroutine. As before, the macro will branch to the cell named Ans, read as a macro the keystroke it contains, and then return.

Accepting Label and Number Input

You'll recall from the introductory portion of this chapter that the most common circumstance in which you'll be accepting labels is when you need to prompt a user for a single word or phrase, and where the number of choices exceeds the number you can display on a menu. For example, you might prompt the user for a report title or for a password with which to gain access to the application.

There are four ways to manage the input of labels into the worksheet:

1. The {getlabel} command

2. The interactive command, {?}

3. The / Range Input command

4. A special application of the {get} command

Using {getlabel} To Manage Label Input

{Getlabel} stores a string in a cell identifed by a named range or cell address, and although you can arrange it so that {getlabel} stores the label in the current cell, it's also possible that it will store the label in a cell that isn't even on the screen at the time. That separation between the user's input and the effect of that input on the worksheet makes {getlabel} one of the least interactive of the data entry commands. {Getlabel} is most appropriate when the user doesn't need a lot of flexibility, or when you want to prevent the user from moving around the worksheet.

The following worksheet contains an entry form with three fields. Each of the entry fields has been assigned a range name. [51]

---

[51] Although you can use either a cell address or a range name with the {getlabel} command to describe where you want the label entered, we advise using range names. If you use cell addresses and later move the form even one cell on the worksheet, you'll have to revise three lines of macro code. If you instead use a range name, you won't have to change a thing. That advantage is especially important if this application will be modified by anyone but yourself—as such a person will be even less likely to know the consequences of such changes.

```
         A      B      C      D      E      F      G      H
1
2
3     First Name:
4     Last Name:
5
6     Soc Sec #:
7
8
9
10
11
12
13
14    \A       {getlabel "Enter First Name: ";FIRST}~
15             {getlabel "Enter Last Name: ";LAST}~
16             {getlabel "Enter Soc Sec #: ";SOC_SEC}~
17
18
19
20
```

Figure 22-13

Notice that one of the fields is labeled "Soc Sec #". Social Security numbers are significant because they are labels that begin with numbers. If, when you use 1-2-3 interactively, you fail to enter a label prefix before typing a social security number, 1-2-3 will treat the number as a formula, interpreting the dashes as minus signs. {Getlabel} provides the benefit of forcing 1-2-3 to store each entry as a label. Other strings that require such shepherding include telephone numbers, street addresses, and zip codes for the northeastern United States (which have a leading zero that 1-2-3 would drop if the string were stored as a value).

The macro shown above has a shortcoming in that it fails to move the cell pointer as data entry proceeds. Despite the explicit instructions contained within your prompt telling the user what to enter, that user could still become confused by the location of the cell pointer. You can remove this problem by moving the cell pointer to the next cell after an entry. Here's a revision to the above macro that does just that:

```
         A      B      C      D      E      F      G      H
14    \A       {goto}FIRST~{getlabel "Enter First Name: ";FIRST}
15             {d}{getlabel "Enter Last Name: ";LAST}
16             {d 2}{getlabel "Enter Soc Sec #: ";SOC_SEC}~
```

Figure 22-14

In Release 2.2, you could make the worksheet a little more efficient by deleting the last two range names. The range named First is required to position the cell pointer. But since arrow movement keys are used to place the cell pointer over the cells in which you wish to store data, there is no need to maintain the additional range names, as in the following example:

```
        A       B       C       D       E       F       G       H
 12 │\A       {goto}FIRST~
 13 │         {getlabel "Enter First Name: ";@cellpointer("address")}
 14 │         {d}{getlabel "Enter Last Name: ";@cellpointer("address")}
 15 │         {d 2}{getlabel "Enter Soc Sec: ";@cellpointer("address")}~
 16 │
 17 │
 18 │
 19 │
```

Figure 22-15

In 1-2-3 Release 2.2, the advanced macro commands have been enhanced to allow you to use formulas in place of macro arguments. That's the trick we're using here. {getlabel} is storing its output in the result of the expression @cellpointer("address"), which is, of course, whatever the cell pointer happens to be at the time.

accepting an existing entry

You may have wondered if there's a way to allow the user the option to accept the entry that already exists in the cell. That would come in handy if a person were updating a form in which entries already existed, some of which wouldn't change. Or, suppose that you want to supply defaults for certain entries on a form (if 98 percent of your customers are local, a default for state would save data entry time). However, you've still got to allow the user to change those items when the exception comes along.

The following macro does just that.

```
        A                       B                               C
 12 │NAME      MACRO                                   COMMENT
 13 │----------------------------------------------------------------
 14 │\A       {goto}FIRST~                             Position ptr
 15 │         {getlabel "Enter First Name: ";ANS}{TEST}  Prompt & test
 16 │         {d}                                      Down 1
 17 │         {getlabel "Enter Last Name: ";ANS}{TEST}   Prompt & test
 18 │         {d 2}                                    Down 2
 19 │         {getlabel "Enter Soc Sec #: ";ANS}{TEST}~  Prompt & test
 20 │
 21 │TEST     {if ANS=""}{return}                      If null, leave be
 22 │         /cANS~~{return}                          Else, enter Ans in
 23 │                                                      current cell
 24 │ANS                                               Store response
```

Figure 22-16

In this macro, the {getlabel} commands store the user's response in a cell named Ans. Since each of the {getlabel} commands works the same, we'll examine the first of them.

```
15    {getlabel "Enter First Name: ";ANS}{TEST}   Prompt & test
```

In row 15, the {getlabel} command stores the user's response in Ans and immediately runs a subroutine called Test, shown below.

```
21   TEST  {if ANS=""}{return}          If null, leave be
22         /cANS~~{return}              Else, enter Ans in
23                                      current cell
24   ANS                                Store response
```

The Test routine tests the entry the user has just made and does one of two things with it: either accepts the entry and stores it in the current cell or else discards the entry and retains the current contents of the cell. Here's how it works. Suppose there is already an entry in the current cell and the user decides to leave it unchanged. In response to the {getlabel} prompt, the user presses Return. The Return keystroke stores a single label-prefix character, the apostrophe, without anything following it, in Ans. That's also known as a null string.

The Test routine begins with an {if} command that evaluates if a null string, signified by the pair of quotation marks with nothing between, had been stored in Ans. In this case, that's true, so the macro reads the next command on the same line, {return}, and returns control to the calling routine above. Control resumes with the command on row 16, {d}. Notice that no entry was ever made in the current cell, so whatever was there will remain unchanged.

However, if the user had entered a first name at the {getlabel} prompt, then, instead of being a null string, that name would be in Ans. When the subroutine Test read the {if} statement, that statement would be false, the macro would skip the remaining commands on that line, and would read the Copy command on the next line. That command copies the label in Ans into the current cell.

Release 2.2 offers an alternate way to copy the contents into the current cell without using 1-2-3's menus. Instead of copying ANS to the current cell, you can use {let} to enter ANS into it. The following macro shows how that works:

	A	B	C
20			
21	TEST	{if ANS=""}{return}	If null, leave be
22		{let @cellpointer("address");ANS}{return}	Else, enter Ans in
23			current cell
24	ANS		Stop response

Figure 22-17

The only difference between this and the previous Test routine is row 22, which evaluates the expression @cellpointer("address") within the {let} command. This serves to copy the contents of ANS to the current cell, and has the advantage that the current cell will retain its current format and protection settings, overcoming a side-effect of the copy method.

Using {getnumber}

{Getnumber} exhibits many of the same characteristics and trade-offs as {getlabel}. However, if you want to allow the user the option to accept existing entries, you'll handle the testing a little differently.

Here's the new testing routine, written for {getnumber} as follows:

	A	B	C
12	NAME	MACRO	COMMENT
13		--	
14	\A	{goto}FIRST~	Position ptr
15		{getnumber "Enter April sales: ";ANS}{TEST}	Prompt & test
16		{d}	Down 1
17		{getnumber "Enter May sales: ";ANS}{TEST}	Prompt & test
18		{d 2}	Down 2
19		{getnumber "Enter June sales: ";ANS}{TEST}~	Prompt & test
20			
21	TEST	{if @iserr(ANS)}{return}	If null, leave be
22		/cANS~~{return}	Else, enter Ans in
23			current cell
24	ANS		Store response

Figure 22-18

Aside from the {getnumber} commands replacing the {getlabel} commands, the big change in this macro is that the {if} command in Test now tests for the presence of ERR instead of a null string. The reason for the change is that if the user decides to accept the existing entry and merely presses the Return key without typing anything, 1-2-3 will store the value ERR in the cell named Ans. If Ans contains ERR, the @iserr function will return a value of one, for true. The rest of the subroutine is identical to the previous macro.

An enhancement of the basic macro, and one you can apply to either this macro or the {getlabel} version, is to post a menu when the user has opted to accept the current entry. That menu will allow him to move the cell pointer one cell in any direction, to make another entry, or to terminate the macro.

	A	B	C	D	E	F	G	H
1	\A	{getnumber "Enter number: ";ANS}						
2		{if @iserr(ANS)}{branch MEN}						
3		/cANS~~{d}{branch \A}						
4								
5	ANS							
6								
7	MEN	{menubranch WHENCE}{quit}						
8	WHENCE	Number	Up	Down	Left	Right		
9		Enter a n	Move one	Move one	Move one	Move one cell right		
10		{branch \	{u}	{d}	{l}	{r}		
11			{branch M	{branch M	{branch M	{branch MEN}		
12								
13								
14								
15								

Figure 22-19

After you enter a number on the keypad and press Return, the cell pointer automatically moves down one row. If you want to reposition the cell pointer, instead of entering a number, press Escape or Return. 1-2-3 will present a menu containing choices for you to, with a single keystroke, move up, down, left, or right (if you need to go up 8 times, just press "u" eight times). The default choice, Number, returns you to data-entry mode.

If you want to terminate the routine altogether, anytime the menu is on the screen, press Escape. When you press Escape during a custom menu, control resumes with the command directly following the {menubranch} or {menucall} command that displayed the menu (it's a {menubranch} command in this case). The command directly following the {menubranch} command in this macro is {quit}, which terminates the macro.

The next enhancement is particularly effective if you use it with the numeric keypad engaged. The macro enables you to use the numeric keypad when you're entering data; when the menu appears you can use the same keypad to move the cell pointer, just as if the numeric keypad were disengaged—without having to do so. The macro uses the numbers that correspond to each arrow key to select menu choices, which move the cell pointer in the proper direction.

```
       A       B        C        D        E        F        G        H
 1   \A      {paneloff}{branch LOOP}
 2
 3   LOOP    {getnumber "Enter number: ";ANS}
 4           {if @iserr(ANS)}{branch MEN}
 5           /cANS~~{d}{branch LOOP}
 6
 7   ANS
 8
 9   MEN     {menubranch WHENCE}{quit}
10   WHENCE  Number          8-Up     2-Down   4-Left   6-Right
11           Enter a numbeMove one Move one Move one Move one cell right
12           {branch LOOP} {u}      {d}      {l}      {r}
13                         {branch M{branch M{branch M{branch MEN}
14
15
```

Figure 22-20

Not only does the macro relieve you from having to type u, d, l, or r to move the cell pointer, it eliminates any flashing in the control panel that would ordinarily occur when (in row 5) the macro copies Ans to the current cell. The first command, {paneloff}, freezes the control panel to perform that feat. Naturally, if you're using Release 2.2, you might be happier with the {let @cellpointer("address")} method, which obviates the need for {paneloff}.

Since {paneloff} doesn't need to be reinvoked each time you make an entry, we've placed it in a separate routine at the beginning of the macro (such a routine is called an initialization routine because it occurs only once, at the initiation of the macro). The next command is a {getnumber} command to prompt you for a value; even though the control panel has been frozen, the {getnumber} command will still display a prompt in the control panel.

The data-entry portion of the macro has been spun off as a loop (it begins on row 3), and it resembles the previous macro. If Ans contains ERR, control branches to a routine named Men, which in turn displays a menu.

This macro is not only useful and well structured, it's intuitive. When you write macros that score high on all three counts, you've got a winner.

Custom Prompts with Defaults

1-2-3's {getlabel} and {getnumber} command would be a lot more useful if they allowed you to specify a default value or string when you display that prompt—a default that the respondent could accept, edit, or replace. You can remedy that by creating a default prompt command yourself.

Once you've written the macro shown below and named the associated ranges, you can use the new {getdefault} command the macro creates to display a prompt and a default response and store the resulting entry as either a value or label.

The syntax for the {getdefault} command is as follows:

```
{GETDEFAULT [prompt string];[default string];[data type]}
```

Where the prompt string is a string of characters that form the prompt, the default string is a string you want to display as a default value, and data type is a "V" if you want 1-2-3 to store the entry as a value, or an "L" if you want it stored as a label.

	A	B	C	D	E	F	G
1	\S	{GETDEFAULT "Enter number: ";100;v}					
2							
3	GETDEFAULT	{define PROMPT;DEF;TYPE}					
4		{PROMPT}					
5		{DEF}					
6		{let RES;DEF}					
7	LOOP	{get ANS}					
8		{if ANS="{ESC}"{branch CLEAR}					
9		{if ANS="{BACKSPACE}"}{branch BACK}					
10		{if ANS="~"}{branch DONE}					
11		{ANS}					
12		{let RES;@s(RES)&ANS}					
13		{branch LOOP}					
14							
15	PROMPT	Enter number:					
16		{return}					
17							
18	DEF	100					
19		{return}					
20							
21	CLEAR	{blank RES}					
22		{esc}					
23		{PROMPT}					
24		{branch LOOP}					
25							
26	BACK	{if @length(RES)=0}{branch LOOP}					
27		{bs}					
28		{let RES;@left(RES;@length(RES)-1)}					
29		{branch LOOP}					
30							
31	DONE	{esc}					
32		{if TYPE="V"}{let RES;@value(RES)}					
33		~{quit}					
34							
35	ANS						
36		{return}					
37							
38	RES						
39		{return}					
40							
41	TYPE						
42							

Figure 22-21

This is one of the lengthiest command-enhancement macros you'll see, but it is also one of the most useful. Fortunately, once you've written this macro once, you won't need to again. Place it into a macro library and you can use it in as many worksheets as you like without retyping it.

The instruction on row 1 contains the new command; {getdefault} takes three arguments: the prompt string you want to display, the default value or string you want to display with it, and the type of the entry you want stored on the worksheet (value or label).

When you use this macro, it transfers control to a subroutine called Getdefault, the first line of which stores each of the three passed parameters in the cells named Prompt, Def, and Type, respectively. At this point, all three parameters are stored as labels, including the default parameter. If you want the worksheet entry that results from this operation to be stored as a value, the macro will do that, but later.

The instruction on row 4 calls the subroutine Prompt, which types the prompt string into the control panel as a label entry, but doesn't enter it. The prompt string remains in the control panel. The next line returns control to row 5, where the macro calls the subroutine Def. Def types the default prompt into the control panel. Let's suppose that the defaults were set as you see them in the {getdefault} command shown in the example macro. The control panel would now show the string "Enter number: 100".

The next line of the macro assigns the current value in Def (the label 100, in this case) to the cell named Res (for "Result"), and returns control to row 7.

Row 7 pauses until the user types a keystroke, then stores that keystroke in the cell named Ans. Rows 8 through 10 perform a series of tests on that stored keystroke to determine what the user wants done and respond accordingly.

The {if} command on row 8 tests for the Escape key. If that's the key stored in Ans, the macro branches to a routine, Clear, that will erase the default from the control panel. Clear, which begins on row 21, erases the entry in the cell named Res, clears both the prompt and the default from the control panel, and calls the subroutine Prompt to redisplay the prompt string (but not the default). The routine then branches to the cell named Loop on row 7, which pauses for another keystroke and conducts the same series of tests on it.

Let's suppose that the user types a letter this time. All of the tests on rows 8 through 10 fail, and the macro calls the subroutine Ans. Ans contains the letter the user types (remember that {get ANS} already stored it there), so the subroutine types that letter into the control panel and returns control to line 12. If the user typed a 2, the control panel now contains the string "Enter number: 2". If the user subsequently types two zeros, the control panel would display the string "Enter number: 200".

Let's suppose the user this time presses the Backspace key. The instruction on row 9 evaluates to true and the macro branches to the routine named Back—a routine designed to simulate the function of the backspace key.

Back begins with an {if} command that will test to see if there's no entry left to remove characters from. If there is, you don't want the macro to remove a character from the prompt string, so the macro merely branches to Loop and awaits another keystroke, in effect ignoring the backspace keystroke. If there are characters in Res, then the macro backspaces over the leftmost character in the control panel, removing it, truncates the leftmost character from the entry stored in Res, and branches to Loop to await another character.

Let's assume that the entry, which is now 20, is complete and the user presses the Return key. The instruction on row 10 evaluates to true and the macro branches to the routine named Done on row 31.

Done first clears the entire label (prompt and entry) from the control panel and checks to see if the entry is supposed to be stored as a value. If it is, the entry stored in the cell named type will be an upper or lowercase "v". The macro tests to see if the captialized equivalent of whatever is in Type is a "v". If so, the macro converts the entry in Res (the complete entry) from a label to a value. The instruction on row 33 presses the Return key to update the screen and ends the macro.

The implication of the conditional formula on row 32 is that, although we earlier stated that you had to enter the character "L" to designate the argument as a label, in fact any character except "v" or "V" will cause the macro to leave the entry as a label. [52] You could even omit the third argument, but you'd have to include the last semicolon even if no argument follows it—otherwise the {define} command (on row 3) that stores the passed parameters will cause an error.

---

[52] If you're running 1-2-3 with the ASCII collating driver (or if anyone who uses your application will run it with a copy of 1-2-3 using that driver), remember that upper and lowercase characters will not equate. To remedy the potential problem, you must eliminate case as a variable in your testing. Substitute the following for the instruction on row 32 of the macro:

{if @upper(TYPE) = "V"} {let RES;@value(RES)}

There are two ways in which you might enhance this macro. First, you might want to split this one command into two commands. Like {getlabel} and {getnumber}, each new command would be specific to one type of entry or the other. If you do, you can remove the third parameter altogether.

Instead, borrow code from the Done routine, making two versions—one for values and one for labels. Place the new instructions after the row that contains the define statement, as follows:

For numeric entries:	For label entries:

```
{define PROMPT;DEF:}{MAIN}     {define PROMPT;DEF}{MAIN}
{esc}                          {esc}
{let RES;@value(RES)}          ~{quit}
~{quit}
```

Notice that we've eliminated the test that Done performed in the previous example. In essence, you perform the test explicitly on behalf of the macro. The name of the routine called—Promptn or Promptl—determines whether you intended a number or a label. If you use Promptn, the label is converted to a value just before the macro ends.

The new macros use almost all of the {getdefault} macro shown above, though the routines have been restructured slightly to accomodate the new functionality. Since the new macros provide the same services as {getdefault}, you probably won't want to include both them and it in the same worksheet.

In the example that follows, the new macros are named {promptn} and {promptl} and you use them as direct corollaries of {getnumber} and {getlabel}—the arguments in each case are the same. Here's how they might look.

	A	B	C	D	E	F	G
1	\N	{PROMPTN "Enter number: ";100}					
2							
3	\L	{PROMPTL "Enter label: ";"10 Elm Street"}					
4							
5	PROMPTN	{define PROMPT;DEF}{MAIN}					
6		{esc}					
7		{let RES;@value(RES)}					
8		~{quit}					
9							
10	PROMPTL	{define PROMPT;DEF}{MAIN}					
11		{esc}					
12		~{quit}					
13							
14	MAIN	{PROMPT}					
15		{DEF}					
16		{let RES;DEF}					
17	LOOP	{get ANS}					
18		{if ANS="{ESC}"}{branch CLEAR}					
19		{if ANS="{BACKSPACE}"}{branch BACK}					
20		{if ANS="~"}{return}					
21		{ANS}					
22		{let RES;@s(RES)&ANS}					
23		{branch LOOP}					
24							
25	PROMPT	Enter number:					
26		{return}					
27							
28	DEF	100					
29		{return}					
30							
31	CLEAR	{blank RES}					
32		{esc}					
33		{PROMPT}					
34		{branch LOOP}					
35							
36	BACK	{if @length(RES)=0}{branch LOOP}					
37		{bs}					
38		{let RES;@left(RES;@length(RES)-1)}					
39		{branch LOOP}					
40							
41	ANS						
42		{return}					
43							
44	RES						
45		{return}					

Figure 22-22

The second change you might consider is to modify the macro so that it stores the resulting entry wherever the cell pointer resides at the time. To do that in the routine named Promptn, for example, insert a new row right in the middle of the subroutine—in row 7. In this new row, enter { recalc Nhere } . In the cell just below, which you should name "Nhere," enter the string formula:[53]

[53] Remember our earlier tip about writing string formulas. Enter the string formula in the Comment column to the right of the macro and format that cell as Text (select / Range Format Text). In the macro column directly to the left of the Comment cell, place a cell reference to the cell containing the Text-formatted formula. Because this is a long formula, it's unlikely to display in its entirety (like values, Text-formatted formula won't overwrite the cell to their right), but it will still make clear that the macro instruction to its left is a string formula, not a static label.

```
+"{let "&@cellpointer("address")&";@value(RES)}"
```

These two statements will assign the current value of Res to the current cell when the routine ends. A similar change, adding two rows to the Promptl command, would accomplish the same thing for labels. The first row would contain the {recalc} command and the cell below it would contain the following string formula:

```
+"{let "&@cellpointer("address")&";RES}"
```

If you're using 1-2-3 Release 2.2, the macro changes required are simpler still. There is no need for a {recalc} command, as {let} can evaluate formulas directly. Thus, row 7 of the original macro can be changed to this:

```
{let @cellpointer("address");@value(RES)}
```

Similarly, Promptl can be changed by adding only one line of macro code in row 12, like so:

```
{let @cellpointer("address");RES}
```

Using {?} To Accept Data Entry

One of the most flexible ways to accept data entry in a macro is to use the interactive {?} command. This command interrupts the macro and temporarily places 1-2-3 in interactive mode. 1-2-3 responds to keystrokes just as it does during interactive use with the exception of the Return key: Return terminates the interactive pause and returns control to the macro.

The following example is an interactive command adapted for use as a data-entry macro. It pauses to enable the user to type something, enters that data in the current cell, moves down one cell, and repeats itself. Because an interactive command ends when the user presses the Return key, we've included a tilde after the {?} command to supply the Return keystroke needed to enter the data that the user typed.

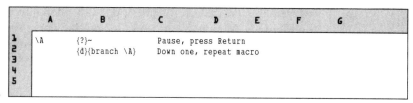

Figure 22-23

Although the above macro includes a command, {d}, to move the cell pointer, the user can supply that from the keyboard as well. Even with the numeric keypad engaged, the user can depress the Shift key to temporarily enable the directional arrows.

The chief advantage of the interactive {?} command is the ease with which you can enable the user to perform any 1-2-3 operation; but that's also a liability: you cannot prevent the user from inadvertently damaging the application. For that reason, this kind of routine is best suited for simple applications where mistakes are easy to correct—we recommend against using it in a turnkey application.

Another disadvantage to the macro shown above is that the user must terminate it manually with the Control-Break key sequence. The following enhancement remedies that shortcoming without sacrificing the economy of the previous version.

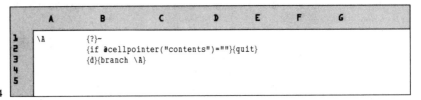

Figure 22-24

We've inserted a new line in row two containing an {if} command to test the contents of the current cell. If after an interactive pause, the current cell remains empty, the macro will terminate. If not, the macro moves the cell pointer down one row and repeats itself. So if you want to stop entering data, simply press Return without entering any data.

Using Range Input

As we explained in the section on keystroke macros, / Range Input is an interactive, data-entry command seemingly designed for use with macros.

When 1-2-3 reads the / Range Input command in a macro, macro control remains on that command and 1-2-3 goes into a special "Range Input" mode. Within any given range on the worksheet, it prevents the user from moving the cell pointer to all but the unprotected cells. It enables normal data entry-related functions such as cell pointer movement, typing, and editing, but restricts the user from accessing the 1-2-3 menu or using most function keys. This mode remains in effect until the user presses Return without having entered any data. At that point, macro control advances to the next instruction in the macro.

Altogether, it presents a very efficient way for you to include a data entry routine in your macro because without it, you'd have to write a great deal of macro code to accomplish the same thing.

The following macro implements the Range Input command in its simplest form.

	A	B	C	D	E	F	G
13	\A	/riFORM1~	Enter data into form				
14		{branch UPDATE}	Update database				
15							
16							
17							

Figure 22-25

In this macro, the Range Input command provides the data entry mechanism to allow the user to fill out a form located in a range named Form1. When 1-2-3 reads that command in the macro, the cell pointer will jump to the top left unprotected cell in that range and the user will be able to enter data, move to other unprotected cells in Form1, and edit existing entries in those cells.

One of the potential weaknesses of Range Input is that it so resembles 1-2-3's interactive mode (the mode indicator even changes to "Ready"), that it may leave users unaware of what you expect them to do. There are three ways around this.

1. Place a message on the worksheet in the Form range.

2. Use the mode indicator to prompt the user.

3. Place a message in the control panel.

Let's review each of these.

The Range Input command repositions the screen when you invoke it, so if you want to place a message on the worksheet, you should first perform a test to see where you should place the message in order for it to be in view. After you've unprotected the cells into which you want the user to enter data and you've decided on a range to specify, select the / Range Input command, enter the range that contains the unprotected cells (precisely as you intend to specify that range in the macro), and observe how the screen responds. Select a location for the message near the top of the screen where it will be more prominent.

The disadvantage to this technique is that there may not be room on the screen if you have a form displayed, or there may be so many entries there already that it won't be readily noticed.

One alternative is to use the mode indicator instead. Change the mode indicator to something like "Enter" just prior to the Range Input command, as in the following macro. Note that the macro contains two {indicate} commands: the one on row 13 sets the indicator to "Enter"; the one on row 15 resets the mode indicator.

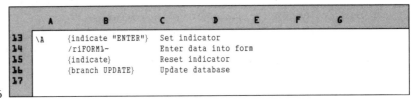

Figure 22-26

In Release 2.2, the indicator can display as many characters as your screen, usually 80, making it more obvious to users that they're in a special mode.

A third alternative is to place a prompt in the control panel via a {getlabel} or {menubranch} command. Here are examples of each method.

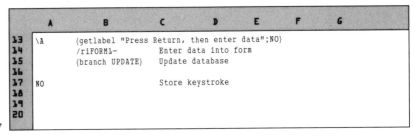

Figure 22-27

The only unusual feature of this macro is the range argument in the {getlabel} command, No. Although you want only to display a prompt, the {getlabel} command requires a range argument so that it can store whatever the user enters. Although you have no intention of using what the user enters, you must store it anyway, so we've used the range name

No to do that. In this case, the user will only press Return, which produces a null string (a single label prefix with nothing following it).

The {getlabel} method works well, but it provides only a brief prompt; too brief to tell you that you must press Return once without entering data when you are finished in order to terminate Range Input. For that, use the {menubranch} technique.

<table>
<tr><th></th><th>A</th><th>B</th><th>C</th><th>D</th><th>E</th><th>F</th><th>G</th><th>H</th></tr>
<tr><td>13</td><td>\A</td><td colspan="3">{menubranch ENTER}</td><td colspan="3">Display menu-prompt</td><td></td></tr>
<tr><td>14</td><td></td><td colspan="3">{branch \A}</td><td colspan="3">Loop if Escape</td><td></td></tr>
<tr><td>15</td><td>ENTER</td><td colspan="4">Press Return, then enter data...</td><td colspan="2"></td><td></td></tr>
<tr><td>16</td><td></td><td colspan="5">...when you finish, press Return to end.</td><td colspan="2"></td></tr>
<tr><td>17</td><td></td><td colspan="3">/riFORM1~</td><td colspan="3">Enter data into form</td><td></td></tr>
<tr><td>18</td><td></td><td colspan="3">{branch UPDATE}</td><td colspan="3">Update database</td><td></td></tr>
<tr><td>19</td><td></td><td></td><td></td><td></td><td></td><td></td><td></td></tr>
<tr><td>20</td><td></td><td></td><td></td><td></td><td></td><td></td><td></td></tr>
</table>

Figure 22-28

This menu has only one choice, and the prompt "Press Return, then enter data . . ." represents that choice. That menu choice will display an explanation line consisting of ". . . when you finish, press Return to end." After the user reads the prompt and presses Return, control of the macro proceeds to row 17 and Range Input begins. The {branch} command on row 14 is there in the event the user presses the Escape key while the menu displays; it will redirect control back to row 13 (refer to the chapter on Menus for more information about the effect of the Escape key on a macro menu).

Getting Help During Range Input

There's one other way out of Range Input, and you can use it to offer assistance to the users of your macro—as long as you do so carefully (we'll explain the caveat in a moment.) During Range Input, a user can activate another macro by pressing Alt and the letter of that macro. For example, suppose you'd written a macro to provide help; it moves the cell pointer to a help screen and pauses. If you placed a message on your Range Input form to "Press Alt-H for Help", the user could request help in the middle of filling out a form. Further, the last instruction in that Help routine could return control to the line in the interrupted macro that contains the / Range Input instruction, thereby returning users to Range Input mode after they have received help.

	A	B	C	D	E	F	G	H
13	\A	{menubranch ENTER}			Display menu prompt			
14		{branch \A}			Loop if Escape			
15	ENTER	Press Return, then enter data...						
16		...when you finish, press Return to end.						
17	INPUT	/riFORM1~			Enter data into form			
18		{branch UPDATE}			Update database			
19								
20	\H	~~			End Range Input			
21		{goto}HLPSCRN~			Display Helpscreen			
22		{get NO}			Pause			
23		{branch INPUT}			Return to Range Input			
24								
25	NO				Store keystroke			
26								
27								

Figure 22-29

We've added the Help macro in the screen shown above. The first job of this macro is to terminate Range Input mode; furthermore, it has to be flexible enough to do that under a variety of circumstances.

Suppose, for example, the macro has progressed to the point where the Range Input command has control of the application (row 17 in the above macro). Just after making an entry in the range named Form, the user presses Alt H for help. 1-2-3 terminates macro control on row 17 and activates the macro on row 20.

Here's an important lesson about macros: Although the first macro has terminated, the command that macro was executing hasn't. 1-2-3 remains under the control of the Range Input command. So the first job of the \H macro is to terminate the Range Input command. You know you can end Range Input by pressing Return once without entering any data; the macro carries that out by beginning with two tildes. If the user has just completed an entry before pressing Alt-H, the first of the two tildes on row 20 will terminate Range Input; the second one will have no effect. However, if the user has typed something and hasn't yet pressed Return, or has used the Edit key to edit an existing entry and is, before pressing Alt-H, in Edit mode then the first tilde will place the entry on the worksheet, and the second one will terminate Range Input.

Row 21 contains the commands to display a help screen contained in a range named Hlpscrn; row 22 uses the {get} command to force the macro to pause. Because {get} waits for a keystroke before it will allow 1-2-3 to continue reading the macro, the Help screen should prompt the user to press any key to continue. When the user does that, the {get} command will store the keystroke in the cell named No. The macro has no use for the keystroke so it'll never manipulate that entry; it just happens that {get} requires a location argument so you've got to provide one whether you intend to use the entry stored there or not.

You could have used the {?} interactive command instead, but {get} is often a better choice for that purpose because unlike the {?} interactive command, {get} prevents the user from moving the cell pointer or entering data on the Help screen.

Finally, in row 22 the macro reads a {branch} command to transfer control back to the Range Input command in the interrupted macro. Notice that in this macro we have named the cell containing the Range Input command so that the {branch} command can address it as a named range.

Now for the caveats we mentioned earlier about this technique. First, if any subroutine calls had been made and control had not yet returned to the calling routine at the time the user activates the new macro, 1-2-3 will no longer be able to return control to the calling routine(s). When the new macro begins, 1-2-3 cancels all subroutine nesting chains. Second, when the \H macro returns control to the line of the original macro containing the Range Input command, the cell pointer will return to the top left unprotected cell in that range (from where data entry always commences under Range Input), rather than to the cell pointer's location at the time the user requested help. If the person was filling out a particularly long form that could prove annoying and confusing—exactly the opposite effect you intend for a "Help" function. Accordingly, exercise discretion with this option.

Database Records

One of the best ways to store data is to place it in a 1-2-3 database. Once you've stored data there, you can use the powerful Data Query and Data Sort commands and the database statistical functions to manage and analyze it. However, while a database is for those reasons a good storage medium, the tabular form of a database isn't necessarily a good medium for data entry. Often an on-screen simulation of a paper form works better: It is familiar, provides instructional prompts, and demonstrates a clear sequence. If you choose to use an on-screen form, you'll need a routine to transfer the data entered there into the database.

If your form entries are all in contiguous cells located in the same column (that is, all the prompts appear in contiguous cells in one column, with the corresponding entries stored in the cells directly to the right of the prompts), you can simply use the / Range Transpose command to copy it from the on-screen form into the database (Range Transpose will tranpose the columnar data into a row). In the following example, column A contains the prompts, column B will contain the entries to be transferred to the database.

	A	B	C	D	E	F	G	H
1	CUSTOMER LIST FORM							
2								
3	First:							
4	Middle:							
5	Last:							
6	Title:							
7	Company:							
8	Street:							
9	P.O. Box:							
10	City:							
11	State:							
12	Country:							
13	Zip Code:							
14	Telephone:							
15								

Figure 22-30

Unfortunately, you'll probably find that you're unable to use such a straightforward approach when you design most of your forms. More likely, the data to be entered into the form must appear in a variety of columns and rows. Transferring to a database entries layed out in that manner requires two steps. First, in a range one row deep and as wide as the database, enter into each cell a cell reference to each successive cell containing data in the form. Further, those cell references should be stored in the same order as the data they reference should appear in the database. For example, if the first data entry cell in the form is cell L60 and the second is cell M63, and the row you will use to reference the data entry cells begins in cell R10, then the entry in cell R10 will be +L60 and the entry in cell S10 will be +M63.

	K	L	M	N	O
58					
59					
60	Enter Name:				
61		- - - - -			
62					
63	Enter street address:				
64			- - - - - - - -		
65					
66					
67					

Figure 22-31

	R	S	T	U	V	W	X
8							
9							
10	+L60	+M63					
11							
12							
13							

Figure 22-32

Second, use the / Range Value command to copy the range containing those formulas into the next empty row of the database. The Range Value command copies the current values of the formulas, (but not the formulas themselves), into the database.

The next challenge you face is finding a way to easily and quickly direct the output of the Range Value command to the next empty row in the database. In most cases, that will be the row below the last row you added to the database. The macro that follows does that job, and adds a few useful touches.

	A	B	C	D	E	F	G
12	NAME	MACRO			COMMENT		
13	--						
14	\A	{getlabel "Press Return, then enter data";NO}					
15	ENTRY	/ri{windowson}{panelon}			Range input		
16		FORM1~			and update screen		
17		{branch UPDATE}			Update database		
18							
19	NO				Store keystroke		
20							
21	UPDATE	{windowsoff}{paneloff}			Freeze display		
22		{goto}TOP~{end}{d}{d}			Move to bottom of dbase		
23		/rvFORM2~~			Copy formulas as values		
24		/cFORM0~FORM1~			Restore default template		
25		{goto}FORM1~			Return pointer		
26		{menubranch MEN1}			What's next?		
27							
28	MEN1	More entries			Print		
29		Enter more data			Print reports		
30		{branch ENTRY}			{branch PRINT}		
31							
32							

Figure 22-33

Before using the macro, you must create four range names that don't exist in the database:

- Form0 should contain a complete template of the data entry form, including data entry prompts, blank cells where the user will enter data, and default values in any data entry cells where you wish to offer the user the option of accepting or editing a default value. Further, all data entry cells, whether they contain defaults or not, should be Range Unprotected. Form0 should be placed somewhere other than the range in which you wish to have the user actually perform data entry.

- Form1 should contain a copy of Form0, and should be located where you wish to have the user perform data entry.

- Form2 should contain a series of cell references to each of the data entry cells in Form1. Form2 should consist of a range that mimics the structure of a record stored in the database: one row deep and as many cells wide as there are fields in the database. The formula in each cell should reference the cells in Form1 in the same order in which you wish those entries to appear in the database. If the user omits any entries when filling out Form1, the cell references currently in this form will return a zero for the empty cells. If you'd prefer to have a null string (a single label prefix) instead, place a null string in each empty data-entry cell in Form.

- Top should be a cell located just above the leftmost field name in the database, and you should enter a label-prefix into that cell. We'll explain why when we explain how the macro will use that cell.

The first line of the macro (row 13) places a prompt in the control panel to alert the user to what the macro will do next.

Row 14 contains instructions to put 1-2-3 into Range Input mode and to enable 1-2-3 to continuously update the screen and control panel displays. At the moment, the commands to update the screen are redundant since there have been no preceding commands to freeze the screen. Consequently, they have no effect. Those commands will come into play in subsequent iterations of the macro (we'll explain how in a moment). Row 15 completes the Range Input command by specifying Form1 as the range.

Row 16 contains instructions to transfer control to the routine named Update. The first line of Update freezes the screen to hide the cell pointer movement that will follow.

Row 20 freezes the screen display to hide the cell pointer movement to follow.

Row 21 moves the cell pointer to Top (remember, that cell contains a label-prefix and is located directly above the leftmost field name in your database). The commands {end} {down} will move the cell pointer to the leftmost field of the last record in the database. If the database has no records, they will move it to the leftmost field name. The final {down} command will move the cell pointer down to the cell that will contain the leftmost field of the next record of the database. The reason you were asked to place a label-prefix in Top is to enable the End Down key combination to move the cell pointer smoothly across Top and down the left column of the database. In most cases, if the cell pointer began its journey from the cell containing the field name below Top, the effect would be the same. The exception occurs when there are as yet no records in the database. Starting from the field name would place the cell pointer at the bottom of the worksheet, a far cry from where it should be. The current location of Top prevents that.

Row 22 uses the Range Value command to copy as string or numeric values all the formulas in Form2. The cell pointer is in the cell that will act as the left hand corner of the Copy To: range—the leftmost cell of the next record. Since the formulas in Form2 reference the entries the user has placed in Form1, this instruction effectively transfers those entries from the data-entry form to the database.

Row 23 copies the original data-entry template (stored in Form0)—complete with any default values you specified—to Form1. This step erases the last set of entries and readies the form for the next record.

Row 24 returns the cell pointer to Form1; that'll minimize disturbance of the screen in the moment between when the screen is unfrozen and when Range Input takes control of it again.

Row 25 presents the user with a choice of entering another record or printing a report (you could include any other choices in this menu). If the user chooses to enter more data, the macro transfers control to a cell named Entry, which contains the Range Input command. When the macro reads Range Input this time, the screen is still frozen. The {windowson} and {panelon} commands unfreeze it to enable 1-2-3 to show the fresh data entry form.

Incidentally, if you're working with databases under macro control, you'll also need to reset the various range settings (such as the Data Query Input range setting) associated with those databases. Consult the next section on defining ranges for information about how to reset your database ranges when you're finished updating the database.

Defining and Redefining Ranges

There are any number of circumstances in which you will have to enter—or readjust—a range. For example, if you need to enter a formula that sums a column of values, you'll need to specify the range to be summed. If you are adding records to a database, you'll have to reset such things as the Data Query Input range, the Data Sort Data-range, and the range contained in any database statistical functions you are using to analyze that database.

The cardinal rule for redefining any range is that ranges are defined by their upper left and lower right cell addresses. Whatever method you use, and there are many of them, should be directed toward redefining those two addresses. There are two basic ways to achieve that result: have the user do it (aided by the macro) or have the macro do it.

Method 1: Helping the User Redefine a Range

The first method employs a macro routine to enable the user to redefine the range. This method uses the same approaches that 1-2-3 does—the user can either type in the cell addresses or point to them.

Suppose you've got a formula, @sum(TOTAL), that relies on the range named Total. Let's look at a macro that, by changing the size of Total, enables anyone to change which cells are being added by this formula.

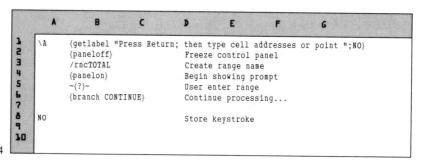

Figure 22-34

Here's an explanation of the macro:

```
{getlabel "Press Return; then point or type cell addresses";NO}
```

Row 1 of the macro displays an instruction in the control panel: Press Return; then point or type cell addresses. That prompt is generated by a simple {getlabel} command. Since {getlabel} is ordinarily used to store labels on the worksheet, you must give this one a range argument (in this example, that's No). When the user presses the Return key, the prompt disappears, 1-2-3 stores a null string in the range named No, and the macro proceeds to the next instruction.

```
{paneloff}
/rncTOTAL
{panelon}
~{?}~
```

The macro freezes the display of the control panel, then executes the / Range Name Create command to create what we will presume is an already existing range name. 1-2-3 would ordinarily show a prompt,

Enter name:, in the control panel along with the name Total. However, since the control panel is frozen, nothing will change.

The next instruction unfreezes the control panel, then presses Return to accept the name Test and pauses with an interactive command. Since the control panel has been unfrozen, 1-2-3 will display the next prompt. As soon as the Return key accepts the existing name Total, the cell pointer expands on the worksheet to highlight the existing range and, in the control panel, 1-2-3 displays a prompt, Enter range:, and displays the current range specification.

The macro next reads the interactive command and pauses to allow the user to either type a new range or use the pointer to redefine the existing range on the worksheet.

Rows 1 through 5 of the preceding macro qualify as a routine; in other words, you can use them in many different macros with little or no adaptation.

The following is a variation using the same routine that enables the user to, under macro control, enter in different cells a variety of @ functions referring to any range. This menu allows users to select which @ function to enter in the current cell; then the range-defining routine allows them to assign a range for the new formula.

	A	B	C	D	E	F
1	\A	/rncTOTAL~AA8192~			Assign name to cell	
2		{menucall FNCT}			Menu to choose function	
3		{getlabel "Press Return; then type cell addresses or point";NO}				
4		{paneloff}			Freeze control panel	
5		/rncTOTAL			Create range name	
6		{panelon}			Begin showing prompt	
7		~{?}~			User enter range	
8		/rndTOTAL~			Disassociate formula from name	
9		{branch CONTINUE}			Continue processing...	
10	NO				Store keystroke	
11						
12	FNCT	Sum	Average		Maximum	
13		Sum a range	Average a range		Find maximum value in a range	
14		@sum(TOTAL)~	@avg(TOTAL)~		@max(TOTAL)~	
15		{return}	{return}		{return}	

Figure 22-35

Let's take a moment to review the changes this macro introduces. Row 1 of the macro assigns the name Total to an unused cell elsewhere on the worksheet. This range name must exist when any of the functions are entered in the next step because those functions use Total as their range argument. If Total didn't exist at that time, the entry would culminate in an error.

Row 2 of the macro consists of a {menucall} command, which calls a subroutine to display and process a menu. That menu is stored in cells B12..D13. The menu choices execute routines that enter in the current cell a formula referring to the range Total. As soon as they do, macro control returns to the calling routine; specifically, to the instruction in cell B3. This initiates the range-defining routine. Since the new formula already refers to Total, when the user redefines Total, the formula will incorporate the new range as well.

The next variation occurs in cell B5, directly following the range-defining routine. After the user has defined the range argument for the formula, the macro deletes the name Total. This step disassociates the name Total from the formula, so that further changes to Total will no longer redefine the new formula. If the macro did not include this step, the next time you ran this routine and redefined Total, you'd also redefine every formula that you had entered with it.

Method 2: Using a Macro to Redefine a Range

There are other instances where you may want the macro to take complete control over the process of defining or redefining a range. For example, if you add records to a database, you might need to redefine the Data Query Input range, the Data Sort Data-Range, and the range referred to by any database statistical functions. In most cases you can completely automate this operation, in which case 1-2-3 will handle the operation more quickly and consistently than would be possible with the user's involvement.

There are two methods by which you can redefine a range; using the End key in combination with a directional arrow, or by inserting new rows and deleting existing ones within the range. Since both methods have their limits, we'll explain both and leave it to you to choose the most appropriate one for the situation at hand.

The first method, which uses the End key to redefine a range, is most appropriate for times when you have just one range to reset because it can only reset one range at a time. It requires that you organize your data in such a manner that every cell in either the far left or the far right column contains some kind of entry. The macro will cancel the existing range definition, position the cell pointer at either the top left or top right corner of the range, and expand the cell pointer across and down its borders to redefine it. With an entry in every cell along those two borders, the cell pointer will expand across the entire boundary. If one cell on either border is unoccupied, the cell pointer will stop at that cell before highlighting the entire range.

We'll use an example involving redefining a range containing a database, such as you might use if you were to redefine the Data Query Input range.

You can have the macro that transfers data from a data-entry form into the database make sure there is an entry in every field. In the example in the section on entering Database Records, we showed a portion of an intermediary range, Form2 (page 435), used to transfer data from the form to the database. That range mimics the arrangement of one row of the database. A portion of it appears below along with a portion of the data-entry form it references.

A portion of the range named Form2:

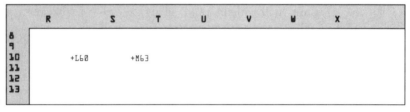

	R	S	T	U	V	W	X
8							
9							
10	+L60	+M63					
11							
12							
13							

Figure 22-36

A portion of the data-entry form:

	K	L	M	N	O
58					
59					
60	Enter Name:				
61		- - - - -			
62					
63	Enter street address:				
64		- - - - - - - -			
65					
66					
67					

Figure 22-37

Each cell in Form2 contains a cell reference to the cell in the data-entry form whose contents you want to store in the corresponding cell in the database. After the user has filled in a form, the formulas in Form2 will reflect the current entries in that form. The macro then uses the Range

Value command to copy the values from Form2 into the next empty row of the database. Since there is a formula in Form2 to correspond to each cell in a database record, and each of these formulas will always return some result, there will always be an entry in every field of every record.

For example, if the user fails to make an entry in cell L60, the formula in R10 will return a zero, and the Range Value command will copy that zero into the corresponding cell of the database. As a result, you can rely on the fact that every cell along the border of the database will be occupied.

If the prospect of storing a zero in a cell if the user leaves that cell blank isn't what you had in mind, you can instead store a null string. (Remember, a null string is a single label-prefix with nothing following it.) To do so, you must also create a template form that looks exactly like your data-entry form. In any blank in which you suspect the user may omit an entry, enter a null string. Before the user fills out the data-form, copy the entire template over the data-entry form. Then any entry that the user omits will contain a null string, and that's what the formulas in Form2 will reference.

Creating a blank template of your form and having the macro copy that template over the actual form after each record has been entered into the database is a good way to blank out the form after each entry.

Incidentally, when you use a macro to reset database ranges, make sure that you place those instructions outside your data-entry loop. Then the user will do all of the data-entry prior to the macro resetting the database ranges. If you were to have the macro do that with every record entered into the database, you'd unnecessarily repeat an operation that only needs doing once for each group of records entered or deleted.

The next method is appropriate for times when you add records to a database. This method can reset multiple ranges simultaneously (such as resetting both the Data Query Input range and a Data Sort Data-Range); however, it's of no use when you're deleting records from a database.

Earlier we proposed a way to transfer new records from a Range Input range to a database that involved referencing them with formulas placed in a second form laid out in the manner of a database record, then using the Range Value command to copy those values into the database. If you position the database so that no other data shares the rows in which it resides, you could instead insert a new row one row above the last row of the database. In so doing you'd be extending all the ranges (Data Query Input, Data Sort Data-range, and any range name referenced by database statistical functions) automatically. Then copy the existing record residing on the last row into the newly inserted row. Finally, use the Range Values command just as you did before—to copy the values returned by the formulas to the last row of the database.

```
        A        B         C        D        E        F        G        H
14  NAME     MACRO                        COMMENT
15  ------------------------------------------------
16  \A       {getlabel "Press Return to begin entering data";NO}
17  ENTRY    /riFORM1~                    Enter data into form
18           {branch UPDATE}              Update database
19
20  NO                                    Store keystroke
21
22  UPDATE   {windowsoff}                 Freeze screen
23           {goto}DATA~                  Move to last row
24           {end}{d}                      in database
25           /wir                         Insert new row
26           {d}                          To last record
27           /c{end}{r}~{u}~              Copy to new row
28           /rvFORM2~~                   Copy FORM2 to last row
29           {menubranch MEN1}            More data entry?
30
31  MEN1     More entries                 Print
32           Enter more data              Print reports
33           {windowson}                  {windowson}
34           {branch ENTRY}               {branch PRINT}
35
```

Figure 22-38

Associated Ranges

Whether you use these or any other method of resetting ranges, you can simultaneously adjust more than one range if those ranges are associated with one another. For example, if you created a range name named Data encompassing your database, and then used Data to specify the Data Query Input range and the range argument for a series of database statistical functions, those three range settings would be associated with one another, and a change to one will change the others. You could reset the Data Query Input range and all the database statistical functions simultaneously by redefining the range named Data. [54]

There's one important exception to the foregoing rule, and it applies only to ranges you have defined as a Data Query Input range. If you select / Data Query Delete Delete, 1-2-3 will delete any records in the Input range that match the current entry in the Criterion range. It will also automatically contract the Input range. However, even if you used a range name to define the Input range, that named range will not contract. If you used the range name as the argument for one or more database statistical functions, you'd have to have the macro redefine that named range.

---

[54] Note that in Release 3, things may work a bit differently. In that program, if you use the Range Name Create command to redefine range A, range B, with which it was formerly associated, won't change. However, if what causes the change is something such as a row or column deletion, then, of course, the Release 3 named range will contract.

Bounds Checking and Validity Testing

why perform such tests?

In the sections on capturing special keys (pages 401–404), we discussed how to test for a variety of keystrokes. In this section, we'll introduce you to variants of the same thing: bounds checking and validity testing. These two techniques enable you to test your keyboard input to catch some broad classes of inappropriate entries; either by comparing an entry with an allowable set of entries or by ascertaining that the entry falls within a given range. Here's an example of each.

Suppose you have an application that calculates pay using hourly input in increments of a quarter of an hour. However, you don't want the application to accept input of over 40 hours because you have a separate routine that selects the proper overtime rate based on the particular circumstances at hand.

Accordingly, you write a bounds checking routine to check the input of hours to make sure it is greater than 0 (no negative entries) but no greater than 40 (and if you were really picky you could test to make sure any fraction was a quartile).

In a mailing list application, if you know that a group of entries must begin with one of a number of strings of three digits, you can have the macro check for that fact. There are situations where the universe of possibilities is limited enough to include them on a menu, in which case you can have the user choose them from a menu. We're talking about situations where the range of choices is somewhat larger.

In either case, upon detecting an error the macro will branch to a routine to display an error message and prompt for a correct entry.

Since these techniques aren't designed to catch all incorrect entries, don't count on them to prevent inaccuracies. Their value lies in their ability to screen out gross errors, and thereby improve the overall accuracy of entered data.

when not to test

Incidentally, in most cases you shouldn't use these techniques for handling one-to-one matches. For example, if you are prompted for a date of birth at one point and for your current age at another, don't install a validity test to see that they match. Instead, derive one from the other. A person generally knows when he or she was born; prompt them for their birth date and have 1-2-3 calculate their age. The exception to this suggestion is if you suspect you may receive inaccurate information on such a question. In that case, it may be helpful to ask it again in another form and compare the responses for consistency.

testing
approaches
vary

Your approach to testing entries will largely depend on how you expect them to enter that data and what you must to test it for. We'll cover both issues here.

Bounds Checking

Let's begin by reviewing tests where you want the entry to fall within certain bounds.

We'll use the {getlabel} and {getnumber} prompts to acquire that data from the user. Both those commands force you to store the entry in some cell on the worksheet. In most cases, if you plan to test an entry you'll establish an intermediary cell—a holding tank of sorts—in which to store the entry while it's being tested. If it passes the test, you'll move it somewhere else; if not, you may issue an informative error message and prompt the person for another entry.

Here's a simple macro with a test for the proper first three digits of a zip code followed by a test to ensure that the number of hours being entered falls within a given range.

```
        A          B          C          D          E          F          G
1   \A         {getlabel "Enter Zip Code: ";TEST}
2              {if @left(TEST;3)<>"021"}{REJECT1}
3              {let ZIP;TEST}
4   HRS        {getnumber "Enter hours: ";TEST}
5              {if TEST<0#OR#TEST>40}{REJECT2}
6              {let HOURS;TEST}
7
8   REJECT1    {beep}{beep}{branch \A}
9
10  REJECT2    {beep}{beep}{branch HRS}
11
12  TEST
```

Figure 22-39

The macro shown above provides examples of tests performed on a string and on a value.

The first line of the macro prompts for a zip code and stores the input in a cell named Test. Test is acting as an intermediary cell—every entry to be tested will in turn be stored in Test. If the entry passes, it will be moved elsewhere; if not, the macro will sound a beep and re-prompt.

In this example, we've assumed that all of our addresses will be in eastern Massachusetts; therefore their zip codes should begin with the digits 021. We want the second line of the macro to test whether the left three characters in the string stored in Test are 021, but it actually does the reverse: It tests to see whether they are not 021.

The structure of an {if} command forces you to use a double negative, whereby finding an undesirable condition to be false means you got what you sought (conversly, finding an undesirable condition true means you have a problem).

In this case, the main sequence of macro instructions (prompting and testing, prompting and testing) should form the main routine. The exceptions (in the event an entry fails a test) should be handled by subordinate routines. Those routines handle the problem, then return control to the main routine.

Because the {branch} commands to transfer control elsewhere are located to the right of the {if} commands, and those commands will be read only if the {if} condition proves true, then the condition in the {if} command must prove false to allow the macro to continue reading the main routine.

The implication is that you should write a conditional statement that states exactly the opposite of the condition you want. Let's suppose you want zip codes beginning with 021, so you have written a statement that says the left three digits of the entry do not consist of 021: {if @left(TEST;3) < > "021"}.

Let's further suppose someone has just entered a correct zip code, say it's 02142. The result is that:

- The conditional statement in the {if} command evaluates to false.

- The macro ignores the {branch} command located to the right of the {if} command.

- The macro continues reading the main routine, copies the entry from Test to Zip, and prompts for the next entry.

On the other hand, if the entry is 02242, then:

- The conditional statement evalutes to true.

- The macro reads the {branch} command to the right of the {if} command.

- The {branch} command transfers control to an error-handling routine that beeps twice, then transfers control back to the line of the main routine that prompts for the entry.

The test statement uses a string function, @left, to test just the three leftmost characters from the string stored in Test. @Left is just one of 1-2-3's string @functions; we recommend that you familiarize yourself with the entire set of those functions—they are indispensable. (For a quick summary of those functions, press the Help key, then select Help

Index, @Functions, and String. This screen and the one that follows—select Continued—summarize those functions.)

If the string in Test passes the test, the {let} command in the next row stores the entry in a cell named Zip for the application to use. If the string doesn't pass, 1-2-3 beeps twice, then prompts for the same entry again.

Let's move on to the second prompt and test:

	A	B	C	D	E	F	G	H
2	NAME	MACRO						
3	---------------							
4	HRS	{getnumber "Enter hours: ";TEST}						
5		{if TEST<0#OR#TEST>40}{REJECT2}						
6		{let HOURS;TEST}						
7								
8								

Figure 22-40

The second prompt, stored in a cell named Hrs, is a {getnumber} command which stores a salary amount in Test as a value. In this case, we want the entry to be greater than 0 but not greater than 40. Accordingly, the macro tests for exactly the opposite. It says, in effect, Is the entry either less than 0 or greater than 40?

In order to do so, it has to test two conditions; the formula that does so is known as a compound formula. A compound formula contains two separate, complete statements—TEST<0 and TEST>40—welded together by the #OR# operator. Why #OR#? Because either condition would be cause for rejection.

Finally, the cell containing the {getnumber} command has been named in order to allow the routine named Reject2 to return control to that line after beeping to alert you of a problem.

Testing for Acceptable Entries

You can also test entries against lists of acceptable strings or values. However, the means for doing so vary depending on whether the entry you're testing is a string or a value. Let's deal first with the most common need, checking strings (label entries).

Testing Label Entries

Suppose that you have 35 department numbers in your company, one of which the operator must enter, and you want to be sure the operator enters a valid department number. That's too many options to offer

through a menu, but you can easily test the user's entry to see if its among
the entries on a preestablished list.

Make a list of the acceptable entries in a column on the worksheet, one
label entry per cell, assign the name List to the range containing them (use
the / Range Name Create command), then use the following three lines of
macro instructions to process the department number entry.

```
{getlabel "Enter department number: ";TEST}
{if @iserr(@vlookup(TEST;LIST;0))}{branch TRAP}
{let DEPT;TEST}
```

Line 1 prompts the user for an entry and stores it in a cell named Test.
Line two uses the "double negative" logic we earlier explained under
"Simple Tests for Strings and Numbers."

We want to know whether the entry stored in Test exists in the range
named List. The formula @vlookup(TEST;LIST;0) will return the vertical offset position of the entry if it occurs in the list. For example, if the
first entry in the list is the label 100, and Test contains the label 100, then
the formula will return the value 0, because 0 is the first offset in the list
(1-2-3 begins counting offsets with 0). However, if Test contains a label
that is not in List, the formula will return ERR (because it cannot report
an offset for an entry that doesn't exist).

Since we know ERR will result if the entry is invalid, we then use the
@iserr function to test the result of the formula. If the result is ERR,
then @iserr(@vlookup(TEST;LIST;0)) will be return the value 1, for
true. If the @vlookup function returns an offset value (meaning 1-2-3
found the entry in List), the @iserr formula will return the value zero,
for false.

At this point, it's time to embed the entire formula in an {if} command. If the formula is true, then the entry was not found among the
acceptable entries in List and we want to branch to an error-handling routine. If the formula is false, then the entry is in List and we want to transfer that entry from Test to some cell where the application will use it.
In the example above, that cell is named Dept, and the command
{let DEPT;TEST} does that job.

Testing Value Entries

The procedures for testing value entries vary from those for testing for
label entries because the @vlookup function we used to test for the existence of a listed entry returns a different set of results when the range

named List contains values instead of labels. When it tests values, it returns the offset of the nearest value in the list to the test value, so you never know if you have an exact match. Instead, you'll use the @dcount function. [55]

Begin with a fresh worksheet so the named ranges we'll use won't overlap the ones used in the previous example. Enter the label List in a cell and in the column directly below it, create a list of the acceptable values, one value per cell. Assign the name List to the entire list, including the label at the top. Copy the label List to a cell nearby, and make sure there is a blank cell just beneath the duplicate label. Assign the name Crit (for criterion range) to the cell containing the duplicate label and the cell directly beneath. Finally, assign the name Test to the blank cell in Crit (the one below the duplication label).

You now have a 1-2-3 database (named List) and a criterion range (named Crit) with which to test entries stored in that database. All you need now is a database statistical function, @dcount(LIST;0;CRIT), to determine if the entry in the criterion range exists in the database. If @dcount returns zero, the number in Crit does not exist in List. If it returns anything else, the number does exist.

In the following macro, we'll prompt for a value, enter that value in the cell named Test (that's the blank cell in the criterion range) and test to see if @dcount(LIST;0;CRIT) returns a zero. If it does, the entry does not exist and the macro will branch to an error-handling routine. Otherwise, the entry does exist and the macro will transfer it to a cell called Val and continue processing instructions.

```
{getnumber "Enter value: ";TEST}
{if @dcount(LIST;0;CRIT)=0}{branch TRAP}
{let VAL;TEST}
```

The @dcount function takes the arguments database range, offset number of the database column containing the entries to be tested against, and criterion range. The database is named List, the offset column number is zero (the column containing the entries to be tested against is the first—and only—column in this database), and the criterion range is named Crit.

---

[55] Unlike the @vlookup technique we just explained, the @dcount method works for both values and labels. The reason we explained the @vlookup method for identifying label entries is that it's simpler than the @dcount method. Because of that, when we can use the @vlookup method, we do. However, if what "simple" means to you is having only one method to remember, forget about @vlookup and stick with @dcount.

Summary

Testing for the existence of entries is a collaboration of spreadsheet formulas and {if} statements to test their results. If you have any doubts about how to write the formula itself or which formula to use, experiment by entering the formula in a cell on the worksheet. Once it works reliably, imbed it into an {if} statement in your macro.

Make sure that the {branch} statement to the right of the {if} statement expresses what you want to happen if the {if} condition proves true. The macro code that follows on the next line should express what you want to happen if the {if} condition proves false.

In order to accomplish that, when you write the {if} statement, you will sometimes need to use the double negative principle: Test for a condition you don't want. If the condition proves false, that means you got what you wanted. Therefore, the commands that appear on the line below the {if} condition represent normal processing of the macro, whereas the ones that the {branch} command direct the macro to represent an error-handling or exception-handling routine.

23

Menu
Systems

Menus are an important component of the interaction someone will have with your application. While 1-2-3's {menubranch} and {menucall} commands permit your macros to closely emulate 1-2-3's moving-highlight menu, circumstances may demand that your macros do more. In this chapter, we'll look at methods to implement the following:

- Prevent a user from inadvertently choosing an item that appears in the default position during a sensitive operation.

- Either disable the Escape key or transform it so that it works just as it does in 1-2-3 command menus—to back up through menus.

- Enable the application to supply its own menu items so that after an entry has changed on the worksheet, it shows up on the next menu as one of the items from which to choose.

- Construct a full-screen menu to handle a greater number of choices. (Further, you may want that menu to incorporate a moving highlight.)

The material that follows divides into sections on controlling menu responses (preventing inadvertent menu selection, disabling the Escape key, backing up through custom menus), dynamically modifying menus (how to create menus that change themselves), and displaying full-screen menus (a potpourri of single-key and moving-highlight menu-selection techniques).

There are a number of ways to implement full-screen menus. The reason there are so many ways is that no one way is versatile enough to satisfy all needs. If you are reading the section on full-screen menus for the first time, to avoid overwhelming yourself, we recommend that you begin by learning just one simple full-screen menu technique—and the one we suggest is the first you'll encounter—the {if}-list method. Use it for a while before returning to learn more. When you're ready, a near-encyclopedic array of methods will allow you to trade different combinations of speed of operation, ease of operation, error-handling strength, and relative simplicity to find the mix that best suits your needs.

The last section in the chapter explains how the new screen-control commands contained in 1-2-3 Release 2.2 can help draw attention to the full-screen menu you've created. In many ways,, full-screen menus can be considered a special category of "Using the Screen." If you've come here looking for ways to control the screen, refer also to Chapter 26, which is dedicated to that subject.

Controlling Menu Responses

Preventing Inadvertent Menu Selection

If you expect your application to be used by computer novices (whose lack of familiarity with a keyboard may lead them to inadvertently invoke the keyboard's auto-repeat function by holding down keys too long), or if you are including particularly sensitive operations (such as selecting which file to combine into the current file), you may need to take steps to prevent a user from selecting a menu choice inadvertently.

Since all 1-2-3 menus place the menu pointer on the far left item, and all you must do to select that item is to press Return, that's the choice a person is most likely to inadvertently select. You can prevent improper selection by transforming the far left menu item into a prompt.

You can do that in two steps: write the far-left menu item as a brief message instead of as a menu choice, and place macro instructions beneath that choice which will redisplay the menu.

```
        A           B               C           D           E
    1  TEST    {menubranch T_MENU}
    2
    3  T_MENU  Choose:                        Print       Save        Quit
    4          Point to choice & press Return Print data  Save file   Quit
    5          {branch TEST}                  {branch CL} {branch SV} {quit}
    6
    7
    8
```

Figure 23-1

In the macro above, the routine named Test displays the menu below. The far left menu item contains a prompt, while the explanation line below it contains a more descriptive message. Since the explanation line for the far left menu item will automatically display when the menu appears, you know the user will see it. If the user presses Return with the default item highlighted, control will branch to the instruction in cell B5, {branch TEST} which will, by returning control to the instruction in cell B1, redisplay the menu. That's the point of such a prompt; pressing Return while the menu pointer rests on it has no affect on the menu.

The user will instead need to either move the menu pointer and press Return, or type the first letter of one of the menu choices. And that brings us to an issue: If one of the menu items you wish to use begins with the same first letter as your prompt, the user will be unable to select that menu item by typing the first letter of the menu item.

Let's suppose that you wanted to include the choice "Clear" on the menu that appears above. If the user typed a "c", 1-2-3 would select the menu item that appears closest to the left side of the menu range; in other words, it would select the prompt (whose first word, Choose, begins with a "c").

You can fix that problem by inserting a space in front of the menu item "Choose:". Because a space will be the first letter of the far left menu item, if the user types a "c", 1-2-3 will select "Clear" instead. Incidentally, if you adopt that strategy, consider appending a space to the right side of that entry as well. Any spaces you add to the label will expand the menu pointer by an equal amount; a space on each side will eliminate any imbalance in the resulting prompt.

Disabling the Escape Key

Aside from their ability to display a menu, {menubranch} and {menucall} have one characteristic that sets them apart from {branch}, {} (subroutine), and other commands that change the normal flow of macro control. Each of the other commands transfers macro control immediately, while {menubranch} and {menucall} suspend the flow while the menu displays, and transfer it only after the user has made a menu selection. Because of that suspension, the user can interfere with the transfer of control and cause the macro to continue reading directly following the {menubranch} or {menucall} command.

In the following macro, if your user presses the Escape key while the menu appears in the control panel, macro control will resume with the next instruction following the {menubranch} command (in this case, that instruction is in cell B2). Since cell B2 contains a label entry, 1-2-3 will type that entry into the control panel. It will continue, typing the text that appears in the cell below (that is, the explanation line), and so forth, until it either encounters a tilde (which will enter one long, concatenated label in the current worksheet cell) or encounters an error.

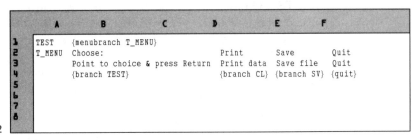

Figure 23-2

There are two ways to prevent this problem.

First, you can make sure there is a blank cell directly beneath the {menubranch} or {menucall} command. If the user presses Escape, the macro will read the blank cell and terminate.

Second, if you'd rather that the macro didn't terminate, you can effectively disable the Escape key by placing the same kind of {branch} command there as you placed beneath the default choice: one that causes the menu to redisplay. The following macro incorporates that design.

```
           A         B                    C             D           E
   1    TEST      {menubranch T_MENU}
   2              {branch TEST}
   3    T_MENU    Choose:                             Print       Save       Quit
   4              Point to choice & press Return      Print data  Save file  Quit
   5              {branch TEST}                       {branch CL} {branch SV} {quit}
   6
   7
   8
```

Figure 23-3

You could also have placed the new {branch TEST} command on the same line as the {menubranch} command; either location has the same effect as long as the {branch} command directly follows {menubranch}.

Backing Up Through the Menu Tree

You can use a variation of the preceding technique to enable your user to back up through your application's menus with the Escape key, just as you can back up through 1-2-3's command menus using that key.

Assuming this menu is at least the second in a series of menus, intead of using the {branch} command to redirect control to the statement that redisplays this menu, use it to redirect control to the command that displays the previous menu.

In the following macro, if your user selects Print from Menu_db, the macro will transfer control to the routine named Prt. The {menubranch MENU_PRT} statement in cell B27 will in turn display a menu called Menu_prt. If the user presses the Escape key while that menu appears in the control panel, the macro will read the {branch \D} statement to the right of the {menubranch} command in cell B27. {Branch \D} will immediately transfer control back to cell B21 which, since it contains instructions to display the first menu once again, accomplishes the effect of backing up from one menu to the preceding one.

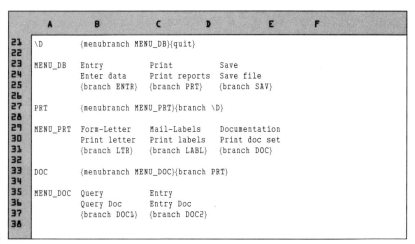

	A	B	C	D	E	F
21	\D	{menubranch MENU_DB}{quit}				
22						
23	MENU_DB	Entry	Print	Save		
24		Enter data	Print reports	Save file		
25		{branch ENTR}	{branch PRT}	{branch SAV}		
26						
27	PRT	{menubranch MENU_PRT}{branch \D}				
28						
29	MENU_PRT	Form-Letter	Mail-Labels	Documentation		
30		Print letter	Print labels	Print doc set		
31		{branch LTR}	{branch LABL}	{branch DOC}		
32						
33	DOC	{menubranch MENU_DOC}{branch PRT}				
34						
35	MENU_DOC	Query	Entry			
36		Query Doc	Entry Doc			
37		{branch DOC1}	{branch DOC2}			
38						

Figure 23-4

Dynamic Menus

The dynamic (or self-modifying) menu is a good tool for those times when you want to incorporate something in a menu that doesn't exist at the time you write the macro. For example, suppose you've designed a mortgage application that accepts input in the form of interest rates, term, and principal and provides output in the form of a monthly payment. You expect that users of the application will try out different combinations of the input items until they arrive at a monthly payment they're happy with.

You might include that monthly payment as part of the default prompt in your menu, and use the menu items to the right to allow the user to accept the current payment or try another combination.

The method for creating a dynamic menu is simple: either using the {let} command or a string formula, modify one or more of the labels that make up the menu items and/or their associated explanation lines.

Here's a sample macro illustrating the application we described above, albeit without the spreadsheet responsible for the mortgage calculations. The entry in cell B4 is the following string formula:

```
+"The mortgage payment is $"&@string(PMT;2)&" per month."
```

In the illustration below, we omitted the explanation lines for the second and third menu choices to allow you to see the first explanation line in its entirety.

	A	B	C	D	E	F	G
1	\S	{menubranch S_MENU}					
2							
3	S_MENU	Choose:	Yes	No			
4		The mortgage payment is $863.11 per month.					
5		{branch \S}	{branch YES}	{branch NO}			
6							
7	PMT	863.11					
8							

Figure 23-5

It isn't entirely necessary to use string formulas to engineer a dynamic menu. You may prefer to use {let} statements instead, particularly if you're sensitive to the need to make your applications as clear to others as possible. Here's a file-saving application that uses two {let} statements to create a dynamic menu.

```
         A          B            C           D      E      F       G
1    \S           {menubranch S_MENU}
2
3    S_MENU       SALES            New-Name
4    S_MENU2      Save as SALES    Save under new file name
5                 {branch F_SAVE}  {getlabel "Enter name for file: ";F_NAME}
6                                  {let S_MENU;@upper(F_NAME)}
7                                  {let S_MENU2;+"Save as "&@upper(F_NAME)}
8                                  {branch F_SAVE}
9    F_SAVE       {paneloff}
10                {onerror FILE_ERR}
11                /fs
12                x{esc}
13                {F_NAME}~
14                r{esc}
15
16   F_NAME       SALES
17
18
```

Figure 23-6

In the worksheet-saving macro pictured above, the menu item in cell B3 presents the previous filename assigned to this worksheet as the default, while the item to its right allows the user to specify a new name. Let's review how the routine beneath that second menu item works, because that's what's responsible for updating the first menu choice with the current filename.

The {getlabel} command in cell C5 solicits a file name and stores the resulting entry in the named range F_name. The {let} command on the next row assigns the label just entered into F_name to the cell named S_menu, and in the process converts the string to uppercase. S_menu is the cell that contains the first menu item. The second {let} command concatenates that name to the string "Save as " and enters it into the cell where the explanation line for menu item one resides. The {branch} command that follows transfers control to the routine named F_save in cell B9.

The routine named F_save freezes the control panel, designates an error-handling routine for errors that could occur in the process of saving a file, and saves the worksheet under the new name.

In that process, it handles a tricky problem. You want the macro to store the file in the current directory if the user enters no directory name. But you also want the user to be able to enter a drive and directory of their choosing. In order for 1-2-3 to respond properly to that input, the macro will have to cancel the existing drive and directory description that appear in the control panel as part of the File Save command. Then if the user enters no path, 1-2-3 will save the file in the current directory of the current drive. It also enables 1-2-3 to respond to any path that the user enters.

The challenge to making this work lies in using a method for cancelling the current path description whether or not a filename already exists.

For example, if after selecting File Save, you press the Escape key, 1-2-3 will either cancel only the filename (if the worksheet had previously been saved) or the path description (if the worksheet has never been saved).

The way to change 1-2-3's response so you can handle it uniformly is to have the macro first enter a filename of its own. That's the function of the ''x'' beginning the macro instruction in cell B12. Since you now know there is a new filename in the control panel, you can use the Escape key with the confidence that you know exactly how 1-2-3 will respond to it. It will clear the drive, directory, and file name from the control panel.

Before moving on, we should point out that were you to use this macro in an application, you should also supply the error-handling routine File_err to accommodate the possibility that the user will enter an invalid filename, directory, or drive description.

You might also want to check to see if the file already exists on the disk and prompt the user as to whether the file should be overwritten (for more information on that subject, see the heading ''Avoiding Errors'' in this chapter).

For the next example, we'll change back to a technique based on string formulas. As much as the example demonstrates the potential benefits of string formulas, it also makes clear the limitations those formulas impose.

	A	B	C	D	E	F
1	\A	{menubranch A_MENU}				
2						
3	A_MENU	Month	Growth-Rate	Run		
4		Specify a month;	ASpecify a growth	rRun analysis		
5		{branch MONTH}	{branch GROWTH}	{branch RUN}		
6						
7	MTH		8			
8	MONTH	{getnumber "Enter month number between 1 and 12: ";MTH}				
9		{let MTH;@int(MTH)}				
10		{if MTH<1#or#MTH>12}{beep}{branch MONTH}				
11		{branch \A}				
12						
13						
14	GRTH		12.00%			
15	GROWTH	{getnumber "Enter growth rate between 0% and 100%: ";GRTH}				
16		{if GRTH<0#or#GRTH>1}{beep}{branch GROWTH}				
17		{branch \A}				
18						
19						

Figure 23-7

The {menubranch} command in cell B1 posts a three-choice menu d through which you can specify the month, growth rate, and type of analysis to be performed.

If you select Month from that menu, the routine named Month prompts you for a month number and stores your response in the cell named Mth. The instruction on row 9 converts the value in Mth to an integer and checks to see if it is a number no less than 1 and no greater than 12. If it falls within that range, the routine branches back to \A to allow you to specify a growth rate or run the analysis.

Here's a snapshot of how the menu will appear in the control panel, with the menu-portion of the macro on the worksheet below.

```
A1: \A MENU
Month  Growth-Rate  Run
Specify a month; AUGUST now selected

         A         B              C             D           E        F

1    \A          {menubranch A_MENU}
2
3    A_MENU     Month            Growth-Rate     Run
4               Specify a month; ASpecify a growth rRun analysis
5               {branch MONTH}    {branch GROWTH}   {branch RUN}
6
7
8
```

Figure 23-8

You entered a number in response to the prompt for the month to analyze; the explanation line showing in the control panel not only incorporates that month, it expresses it as a word (August, in this example). The macro achieves such finesse through a string formula entered in cell B4:

```
+"Specify a month; "&@VLOOKUP(MTH;MTH_TABLE;1)&" now selected"
```

The formula references the lookup table containing, in its first column, the numbers 1 through 12, and, in its second column, the corresponding month names. The @vlookup function uses the month number to return the month name.

```
         A          B          C        D        E        F        G        H

24
25   MTH_TABLE
26           1    JANUARY
27           2    FEBRUARY
28           3    MARCH
29           4    APRIL
30           5    MAY
31           6    JUNE
32           7    JULY
33           8    AUGUST
34           9    SEPTEMBER
35          10    OCTOBER
36          11    NOVEMBER
37          12    DECEMBER
38
```

Figure 23-9

While the string formula works when you enter a month for the first time, a problem occurs when you change that number—the macro will continue to display the old month name in the explanation line of the menu (even if the worksheet remains set for automatic recalculation). The culprits in this case are the {getnumber} and {let} commands that store and transfer that new month value. Neither command updates the screen, so the string formula continues to reflect the old value.

The solution is to recalculate the cell (or cells) containing the string formula after those commands have done their work, but before the menu redisplays. Here's the revised macro with new commands in cells B11 and (since the explanation line in cell C5 also contains a string formula) B17. The command {recalc A_MENU} updates string formulas in B5 and C5 because, unlike the other range names shown in column A (which refer only to the cell directly to their left), A_menu refers to B3..D4.

	A	B	C	D	E	F
1	\A	{menubranch A_MENU}				
2						
3	A_MENU	Month	Growth-Rate	Run		
4		Specify a month; A	Specify a growth r	Run analysis		
5		{branch MONTH}	{branch GROWTH}	{branch RUN}		
6						
7	MTH		8			
8	MONTH	{getnumber "Enter month number between 1 and 12: ";MTH}				
9		{let MTH;@int(MTH)}				
10		{if MTH<1#or#MTH>12}{beep}{branch MONTH}				
11		{recalc A_MENU}				
12		{branch \A}				
13						
14	GRTH		12.00%			
15	GROWTH	{getnumber "Enter growth rate between 0% and 100%: ";GRTH}				
16		{if GRTH<0#or#GRTH>1}{beep}{branch GROWTH}				
17		{recalc A_MENU}				
18		{branch \A}				
19						

Figure 23-10

Perhaps you're thinking that you can place a tilde directly following the {let} or {getnumber} statements to more simply achieve the same result. That's correct, but only if 1-2-3's Global Recalculation is set to Automatic. If the worksheet happens to be set to Manual Recalculation, a tilde won't do the job because, although it will update the display of the value entry, it won't force the string formula to recalculate and respond to the new value.

There's yet another potential problem with using string formulas in menu ranges and because of it, you must prevent those formulas from returning the value ERR. While the recalculation problem could cause the explanation line to display out-of-date data, a string formula that evaluates to ERR anywhere in the menu range will cause the macro to terminate in an irrecoverable error (both the {menubranch} and {menucall} commands will respond to that circumstance with the error message "Invalid use of Menu macro command"). [56]

Let's examine what could cause the string formula to return ERR and then review a method to prevent it.

The {getnumber} command on row 8 enters your input into the cell named Mth. Remember, Mth is the cell that the string formula in cell B5 references (8 was the basis for the @vlookup formula returning the string AUGUST in the explanation line). If instead of entering number at that prompt, you merely pressed Return, you pressed the Escape key, or you entered a label (such as spelling out the number eight), 1-2-3 would enter the value ERR in Mth. Since the value ERR cascades through all formulas that reference it, the string formula in the menu range will also return ERR.

While you can't control what a person types at the {getnumber} prompt, you can test for the value ERR before allowing the macro to redisplay the menu and, if it detects ERR, prompt the user for a different entry to replace it. The instructions on rows 10 and 17 in the revised version below illustrate one approach, albeit a simple one. You could easily embellish the macro to include a branch to a routine that would display an informative error message before prompting the user for another entry.

	A	B	C	D	E	F
1	\A	{menubranch A_MENU}				
2						
3	A_MENU	Month	Growth-Rate	Run		
4		Specify a month; A	Specify a growth r	Run analysis		
5		{branch MONTH}	{branch GROWTH}	{branch RUN}		
6						
7	MTH		8			
8	MONTH	{getnumber "Enter month number between 1 and 12: ";MTH}				
9		{let MTH;@int(MTH)}				
10		{if @iserr(MTH)}{beep}{branch MONTH}				
11		{if MTH<1#or#MTH>12}{beep}{branch MONTH}				
12		{recalc A_MENU}				
13		{branch \A}				
14						
15	GRTH		12.00%			
16	GROWTH	{getnumber "Enter growth rate between 0% and 100%: ";GRTH}				
17		{if @iserr(GRTH)}{beep}{branch GROWTH}				
18		{if GRTH<0#or#GRTH>1}{beep}{branch GROWTH}				
19		{recalc A_MENU}				
20		{branch \A}				
21						

Figure 23-11

---

[56] If a string formula occurring elsewhere in a macro returns the value ERR, when the macro reads the cell containing the string formula, that macro will terminate and return control to the keyboard, but it will not do so in an error. 1-2-3 classifies ERR as a numeric value, and macros can't read values, so when 1-2-3 tries to read the cell containing ERR, it sees the cell as if it were blank and terminates. Because this situation does not result in an error of any kind, it is similarly untrappable. For that reason, you should make certain that any string formulas you do use are well protected from this problem.

Full-Screen Menus

You've seen ways to display your own menus in the control panel (using the {menubranch} and {menucall} commands). There are also ways to produce menus that display on the worksheet-portion of the screen. Because of their larger size, we call these menus full-screen menus. Since the {menubranch} and {menucall} commands are simpler to use than the techniques for producing full-screen menus, you'll generally use full-screen menus only in response to needs that macro-menu commands can't respond to. Here are several such needs:

1. The macro-menu commands limit each menu to eight choices. If you want to present more than eight choices at once, or if you think you may want to expand to more than eight in the future, a full-screen menu is the way to go.

2. The macro-menu commands not only limit the number of menu items on each menu, they limit the total number of characters you can use to represent those choices. A full-screen menu vastly extends those limits. [57]

3. Similarly, the macro-menu commands limit your explanation lines beneath each menu item to 80 characters, which may be insufficient to describe each of your menu items. A full-screen menu imposes no such limit; it even allows you to write more than one line of description about each menu item.

4. A novice user might overlook a two-line menu in the control panel. A menu occupying the worksheet-portion of the screen presents no such risk.

5. The manner in which you must write the macro-menu items and their associated explanation lines often results in a menu that is difficult to read and difficult to document. For example, note how the menu-item explanation lines overwrite one another in the preceding examples. A menu written for display on the worksheet portion of the screen doesn't suffer from those problems.

The following sections present techniques by which you can write full-screen menus, generally arranged in order of the level of macro-writing skill they demand of you, beginning with the simplest.

---

[57] The control panel is 80 characters wide. 1-2-3 automatically inserts two blanks spaces after each menu item (except the last one). Where ITEMS equals the number of items on the menu, the formula 80-(2*(Items-1)) calculates the total number of characters you can use in all of the items on that menu. So, for example, if you have 5 menu items, you are limited to 72 characters in total, or an average of 14.4 characters per menu item. If you have 8 items, the average must be 8.3 or less.

{ If } -List: A Simple Approach to Full-Screen Menus

Let's suppose you've created the following full screen menu and assigned the name Menu_scrn to cell J1.

```
          J        K          L         M         N
  1
  2                  CUSTOM ACCOUNTING APPLICATION
  3
  4       ˜
  5       1. Post accounts receivable    2. Run receivables report
  6
  7       3. Post account payable        4. Run payables report
  8
  9       5. Reconcile petty cash        6. Post general ledger
 10
 11       7. Trial balance               8. Income statement
 12
 13       9. Balance sheet              10. Exit and perform back up
 14
 15            11. Exit without back up
 16
 17
 18
 19            (C) 1990 by S&D Associates, Inc.
```

Figure 23-12

The following macro first displays the full-screen menu shown above and then prompts you to enter the numeral representing your choice from the menu.

```
       A      B          C          D       E      F      G      H
  1   \M     {goto}MENU_SCRN~
  2   LOOP   {getnumber "Enter a numeral and press Return. ";ANS}
  3          {if ANS=1}{branch ONE}
  4          {if ANS=2}{branch TWO}
  5          {if ANS=3}{branch THREE}
  6          {if ANS=4}{branch FOUR}
  7          {if ANS=5}{branch FIVE}
  8          {if ANS=6}{branch SIX}
  9          {if ANS=7}{branch SEVEN}
 10          {if ANS=8}{branch EIGHT}
 11          {if ANS=9}{branch NINE}
 12          {if ANS=10}{branch TEN}
 13          {if ANS=11}{branch ELEVEN}
 14          {getlabel "Invalid entry; enter 1-11 only. Press Return.";ANS}}
 15          {branch LOOP}
 16
 17   ANS
 18
 19
 20
```

Figure 23-13

On rows 3 through 13 the macro reads a series of { if } statements to evaluate your entry and, if your entry is among those it tests for, branches to the appropriate routine. If the macro fails to find a match, the macro will read the {getlabel} command in cell B14. That statement places a prompt in the control panel to explain the error, waits for a keystroke, and returns control to the cell named Loop (whereupon the macro reprompts you for another entry). This error-trap will handle entries that result in ERR (if you had in response to the {getnumber} command pressed Return, pressed Escape, or entered a label) as well as entries of any out-of-range numbers.

Though easy to comprehend and easy to debug, if you enter an out-of-range number (say, 12) and are running on an 8088-based computer, you'll notice a delay before 1-2-3 reads through all the {if} statements. Let's look at a slightly more complex, but more efficient way to do the same thing.

{Dispatch}: A Fast Approach to Full-Screen Menus

In place of the {if} commands in the previous example, the following macro uses a single {dispatch} statement containing an @vlookup function to direct the flow of macro control. Although the table Menu_list is long, the macro itself is very small. The @vlookup function does the work of all the {if} commands in the previous macro—and does it much faster.

	A	B	C	D	E	F	G	H
1	\M	{goto}MENU_SCRN~						
2	LOOP	{getnumber "Type number and press Return. ";ANS}						
3		{if @iserr(ANS)}{branch RECOVER}						
4		{dispatch @vlookup(ANS;MENU_LIST;1)}						
5								
6	RECOVER	{getlabel "Invalid response. Press return.";ANS}						
7		{branch LOOP}						
8								
9	MENU_LIST	-999	RECOVER					
10		1	ONE					
11		2	TWO					
12		3	THREE					
13		4	FOUR					
14		5	FIVE					
15		6	SIX					
16		7	SEVEN					
17		8	EIGHT					
18		9	NINE					
19		10	TEN					
20		11	ELEVEN					
21		12	RECOVER					
22	ANS							
23								

Figure 23-14

Since the heart of this macro is the {dispatch} command, let's skip directly to where it resides, on row 4. Remember that the difference between the {dispatch} and {branch} commands is that {dispatch} transfers control indirectly by way of another address; {branch} transfers control directly to the location named in its argument. In this example, {dispatch} will evaluate the @vlookup function (which will produce a range name), read the location stored in that range name, and transfer macro control to that location.

If we assume that the user entered 3 at the {getnumber} prompt, then the @vlookup function would search for a 3 in the first column of Menu_list (B9..C21) and return the entry one column offset to the right. The contents of the cell at that offset (which contains the label Three) identifies the destination to which macro control should branch (which implies that Three is the name of a range on this worksheet). {Dispatch} will transfer macro control to the cell bearing the range name Three, and 1-2-3 will begin reading as a macro whatever is stored there.

Both this and the previous macro compare a number entered by a user with a predefined list and transfer control to a corresponding named range. However, because 1-2-3 more quickly evaluates the single @vlookup formula in the {dispatch} command than it can evaluate an entire list of conditional formulas contained within {if} commands, this macro will operate more quickly than will its predecessor.

Let's return to the subject of error-handling. This macro has four defenses against errors; we'll first examine how the {dispatch} statement responds to three kinds of errors, then we'll discuss the {if} statement on row 3.

Note that the first value in the righthand column is -999 and that the routine name stored to its right is Recover. If the user enters a value less than the lowest value in an @vlookup table, @vlookup will return the value ERR. The value -999 is a trap for any low-ball entries (assuming, of course, that no one will enter anything less than that[58]); if someone were to enter a value such as zero, the macro will branch to the routine named Recover.

The table also contains a trap for errors that are too high. Since the largest valid entry is 11, any entry of 12 or more is invalid. @Vlookup will equate any entry greater than the highest entry in the table to the highest entry. So, whether someone enters 12 or 112, @vlookup will return the range name to the right of the 12 at the bottom of the table, and branch to the routine named Recover.

---

[58] If you want to be really certain this never causes an error, use the value -9.9E+99, which is about the largest negative value that 1-2-3 supports. It also displays nicely in general cell format with a default column width, and has no impact on performance.

Finally, the @vlookup formula automatically handles "imprecise" errors—such entries as 2.5. @Vlookup matches such entries with the next lesser entry in the table (so 2.5 equates to 2).

However, if the user presses Escape, presses Return, or enters a label instead of a value, 1-2-3 will enter the value ERR into the cell named Ans. No entry in the left column of the table can trap this entry (you cannot use @err in the left column of the table to match an ERR entry), so you'll have to trap that error before the macro reads the {dispatch} statement. That task falls to the {if} statement shown on row 3. Although your primary concern is to prevent @vlookup from returning the value ERR, there's no need to test the @vlookup function per se. Since the source of an Err in the @vlookup formula will be the entry in Ans, all you have to do is test Ans.

If your interests lean toward the most efficient possible macro, here's an alternative to the {if} command, and one that may work fractionally faster since it contains one less instruction. Replace the {getnumber} command with an /xn command (/xn, you'll recall, was the original prompt-for-a-number command introduced in 1-2-3 Release 1A).

Unlike {getnumber}, /xn will not accept any entry that results in ERR. If in response to the prompt you press Escape, 1-2-3 ignores the keystroke. If you press Return without entering anything or you enter a label, 1-2-3 will beep and display the error message "Invalid number input" on the status line. If you then press Return again or press Escape, it will automatically prompt you once again (and you don't even have to write a loop!).

There are some subtle limits associated with /xn that you should consider. First, it cannot display a prompt longer than 39 characters while ({getnumber} supports prompts of up to 72 characters), and because it begins with a slash (as do all of the old /X commands), it will momentarily display 1-2-3's command menu in the control panel prior to displaying the prompt. You'll experience that as a brief flash before you see the prompt. [59]

Here's the revised macro, without the {if} statement that you'll no longer need.

---

[59] This command also offers a simple way of entering data into the current cell; just omit the location argument: /xnEnter a number:~~.

```
        A        B         C         D       E       F       G       H
1     \M        {goto}MENU_SCRN~
2     LOOP      /xnType number and press Return. ~ANS~
3               {dispatch @vlookup(ANS;MENU_LIST;1)}
4
5     RECOVER   {getlabel "Invalid response.  Press return.";ANS}
6               {branch LOOP}
7
8     MENU_LIST  -999    RECOVER
9                  1     ONE
10                 2     TWO
11                 3     THREE
12                 4     FOUR
13                 5     FIVE
14                 6     SIX
15                 7     SEVEN
16                 8     EIGHT
17                 9     NINE
18                10     TEN
19                11     ELEVEN
20                12     RECOVER
21    ANS
22
23
```

Figure 23-15

Now that we've optimized the {dispatch} method for speed, let's compare it to the other means of processing entries made in response to a full-screen menu—the {if}-list.

The response time of the {if}-list method depends on how far down the list of {if} statements 1-2-3 must read before it finds a match for the user's entry. The farther down that list 1-2-3 finds a match for the entry in Ans, the longer it will take (whereas the {dispatch} method processes all entries in approximately the same amount of time). In selecting the twelfth choice from menus using either technique, the {dispatch} method processed the entry about one fifteenth of a second faster—a noticeable difference.

The {dispatch} method is also easier to revise since the table of numbers stands separately from the macro code itself. To add, delete, or revise entries on the menu, you need change only the table, not the macro code.

Speeding Up Full-Screen Menu Selections

One limitation of using either the {getnumber} or /xn command to process user input is that they require you to press Return after typing your entry. While that method allows you to edit your entry prior to pressing Return, it also slows down the process of making a menu selection. If this is a menu to be used frequently, you should consider eliminating the need to press Return after typing the character with which you select a menu item. You can do that with the {get} command.

One limitation of this technique, however, is that it demands that you use no more than one character to represent a menu choice, so you'll probably use letters (of which there are 26) instead of numbers (of which there are but 10 that have just one digit) to represent menu items.

Storing user input with the {get} command poses no problems for the {if}-list full-screen menu technique, but it does make the {dispatch} method more challenging to use. Remember that if the {dispatch} statement's @vlookup function returns a value of ERR, the macro will terminate in an irrecoverable error. {Get} will require you to do more work to prevent that function from returning ERR.

{Get} stores keystrokes as labels, so you'll need to construct a lookup table with labels in the left column. If the user enters a label that doesn't appear in that column, @vlookup will return ERR. However, unlike an {if} statement, @vlookup is sensitive to case, so if the user enters a lower case "a" and you've used an uppercase "A" in your table, @vlookup won't find it. You can solve that part of the matching problem by converting the string value returned by the reference to Ans to the same case as the entries in the table. For example, if the left column of your table contains entries in uppercase, convert the @vlookup formula's reference to Ans to uppercase, as shown in row 3 of the following example.

	A	B	C	D	E	F	G	H
1	\M	{goto}MENU_SCRN~						
2	LOOP	{get ANS}						
3		{dispatch @vlookup(@upper(ANS);MENU_LIST;1)}						
4								
5	ANS							
6								
7	MENU_LIST	A	EXIT					
8		B	ONE					
9		C	TWO					
10		D	THREE					
11		E	FOUR					
12		F	FIVE					
13		G	SIX					
14		H	SEVEN					
15		I	EIGHT					
16		J	NINE					
17		K	TEN					
18								

Figure 23-16

The @upper function eliminates case differences, but what if the user accidentally types a character that doesn't appear in the lefthand column of the table? Any such entries will cause @vlookup to return ERR. You could insert the {if} statement shown below before the {dispatch} statement. It tests to see if the @vlookup formula returns ERR and, if it does, branches to the Recover routine to inform the user of the mistaken entry and prompt for another entry by branching to Loop.

```
{if @iserr(@vlookup(@upper(ANS);MENU_LIST;1))}{branch RECOVER}
{dispatch @vlookup(@upper(ANS);MENU_LIST;1)}
```

Another option: Convert the characters the user types into their numeric LICS-code equivalent and test them as values. The advantage here is that you can prevent @vlookup from returning ERR without any testing (the reason is explained in our first discussion of {dispatch}-based menus).

	A	B	C	D	E	F	G	H
1	\M	{goto}MENU_SCRN~						
2	LOOP	{get ANS}						
3		{dispatch @vlookup(@code(@upper(ANS));MENU_LIST;2)}						
4								
5	ANS							
6								
7	MENU_LIST	-999		LOOP				
8		65	A	EXIT				
9		66	B	ONE				
10		67	C	TWO				
11		68	D	THREE				
12		69	E	FOUR				
13		70	F	FIVE				
14		71	G	SIX				
15		72	H	SEVEN				
16		73	I	EIGHT				
17		74	J	NINE				
18		75	K	TEN				
19		76		LOOP				
20								

Figure 23-17

This table contains an additional column composed of a series of @code formulas, each of which refers to the cell directly to its right (@code returns the LICS value of the character it references). The third argument in the @vlookup function is now 2 instead of 1, because the offset position of the right column of the table had shifted one column to the right. This macro entirely avoids the problems of matching letters, yet still enables you to use {get} to respond to single keystrokes.

One final note: Used in this way, {get} cannot properly respond if the user presses one of the non-alphanumeric keys (such as Uparrow or

Goto). Those keystrokes produce multi-character strings (such as {UP} and {GOTO}). When the @code function evaluates a string it returns the code number for only the first of those characters, and the first charac- ter of all the special keynames is the same: {. However, if you want your macros to respond selectively to those keystrokes, you can make them do so. Include 123 (the ASCII code for the left curly brace character) in the left column of your lookup table and place to the right of it the name of a routine that will examine the entire string stored in Ans, as in the follow- ing macro.

	A	B	C	D	E	F	G	H
7	MENU_LIST	-999		LOOP				
8		65	A	EXIT				
9		66	B	ONE				
10		67	C	TWO				
11		68	D	THREE				
12		69	E	FOUR				
13		70	F	FIVE				
14		71	G	SIX				
15		72	H	SEVEN				
16		73	I	EIGHT				
17		74	J	NINE				
18		75	K	TEN				
19		76		LOOP				
20		123	{	KEY_NAME				
21		124		LOOP				
22								
23	KEY_NAME	{dispatch @vlookup(ANS;KEY_LIST;1)}						
24								
25	KEY_LIST	{	LOOP					
26		{END}	ONE					
27		{DOWN}	TWO					

Figure 23-18

We've added two rows to the bottom of the lookup table. One (beginning with the value 123) activates the routine named Key_name, the other (beginning with the value 124) reactivates the routine named Loop.

The routine stored in Key_name will be activated if the string stored in Ans begins with an open brace, {. That routine contains another {dis- patch} statement that will look up the entire string stored in Ans, not just the LICS value of its first character. The table stored in Key_list will be fairly long, 24 rows or so—due to the number of keynames you'll need to test for. One way to use this list is to map the cell pointer keys to the numeric keypad, so that End is 1, Downarrow is 2, and so on. If you're using 1-2-3 Release 2.2, another way to use this list is to map the Help function key to your own help routine geared to the currently active menu.

Full-Screen Menus with a Moving Cell Pointer

The {menubranch} and {menucall} commands enable you to emulate 1-2-3's point-and-press-Return modus operandi, and you can have your full-screen menus do that, too. If you expect your application to be used by people who are unfamiliar with the keyboard, this method (also known as point-and-shoot) may speed their work and reduce errors. Unfortunately, you can't have your full-screen menus respond to both point-and-shoot and typing the first character of a menu item (and the latter is a quicker method for experienced users) so you'll have to choose one of these two methods to use.

The following sections present three methods for creating point-and-shoot menus and employ the following commands: {?} (interactive command), {get}, and / Data Query Find. Underlying all methods is the notion that the way to tell what item a user wants to select is by the row on which the cell pointer resides when the user presses the Return key. The following macro excerpt illustrates this idea.

	A	B	C	D	E	F	G	H
1								
2								
3		Consolidate worksheets from the disk						
4		Exit the application and use 1-2-3						
5		Exit the application and return to DOS						
6								
7								
8	TEST	{if @cellpointer("row")=3}{branch ONE}						
9		{if @cellpointer("row")=4}{branch TWO}						
10		{if @cellpointer("row")=5}{branch THREE}						
11								

Figure 23-19

The entries in rows 3, 4, and 5 represent menu items from which the user will choose. Test is the routine for selecting the routine to which the macro will branch in response to the user's selection.

We'll defer for the moment the discussion of the mechanism for selecting the appropriate cell (we've excluded it from the macro shown above) and focus momentarily on the Test routine. It works by determining the number of the row on which the cell pointer resides through the @cellpointer("row") formula. The rest of the macro is easy; it's no different than if the user had typed that number manually. Use any of the methods you already know to check the value of that number and branch on the result.

Perhaps the simplest approach, and the one we've employed in the above macro, is to enter the row numbers directly into the macro (that's known as hard-coding those numbers into the macro). However, if you move a menu item to a different row (even unintentionally by inserting a new row above the menu), you'll have to rewrite the macro.

A better way is to make what amounts to a relative reference to the row—not by a number, but by subtracting the number of the uppermost row of the menu range from the current row of the cell pointer. This makes your menu entirely portable; you can relocate it anywhere else on the worksheet without modifying your macro. Because, in the shifting world of most worksheets, that's an inherently more reliable approach, we'll employ it in upcoming macros.

The major differences in the macros that follow lie with their methods of cell selection. As always, there are tradeoffs, and you should consider those tradeoffs in light of the circumstances under which you intend the application to function.

{?} Moving Cell Pointer Menu

The simplest and quickest moving cell pointer menu uses the {?} interactive command. Construct a screen, like the one shown below, that contains a vertical list of menu selections.

```
        A       B          C          D         E        F

21
22
23
24              HIGHLIGHT SELECTION AND PRESS RETURN
25                  ONE        Macro Number One
26                  TWO        Macro Number Two
27                  THREE      Macro Number Three
28                  FOUR       Macro Number Four
29                  FIVE       Macro Number Five
30                  SIX        Macro Number SIX
31                  SEVEN      Macro Number Seven
32                  EIGHT      Macro Number Eight
33                  NINE       Macro Number Nine
34                  TEN        Macro Number Ten
35                  EXIT       Exit Macro
36
37
38
39
40
```

Figure 23-20

	A	B	C	D	E	F	G	H
1	\M	{paneloff}						
2		{goto}MENU_SCRN~{goto}MENU~{d}						
3		/wtb						
4		{?}/wtc						
5		{dispatch @cellpointer("contents")}						
6								
7								
8								

Figure 23-21

Line one of the macro freezes the control panel. Line two moves the cell pointer to Menu_scrn (cell A21) to position the screen so that the menu appears. The next instruction positions the cell pointer in C25, which is one cell beneath the top of a range named Menu. Menu encompasses cells C24..C35.

Row three locks the cell pointer out of the cells above and to the left of its current position. That's a partial safeguard to prevent the cell pointer from moving out of the range containing the menu descriptors; its obvious flaw is that it won't prevent the cell pointer from moving below or to the right of that range.

The {?} (interactive) command suspends macro processing and temporarily returns control of the application to the keyboard, where the user can press the Uparrow or Downarrow keys to highlight the descriptor associated with any menu item and press Return. The Return keystroke returns control to the macro, whereupon the macro clears the Worksheet Titles setting and, with the {dispatch} command on row 5, branches to a routine bearing the name of the selected descriptor. The routines to branch to don't appear on the screen above, but let's assume that each of the menu descriptor names (One, Two, Three, etc.) are also range names designating the first lines of a series of routines corresponding to the menu selections.

This approach is useful and very simple; its major limit is its lack of error handling. If the user moves the cell pointer to the right of the descriptor list or below it and presses the Return key, the {dispatch} command attempts to branch to a nonexistent address, and the macro will terminate in an irrecoverable error. The next macro corrects those deficiencies.

{Get} Moving Cell Pointer Menu

To prevent the cell pointer from moving outside the menu, the macro must trap keystrokes and act only on those that move within the menu range. In this example, we use the same menu as last time:

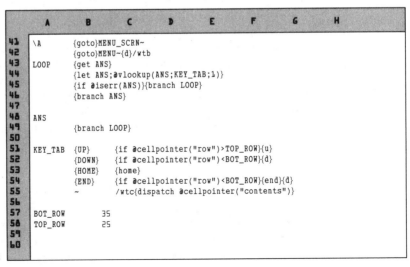

	A	B	C	D	E	F
21						
22						
23						
24			HIGHLIGHT SELECTION AND PRESS RETURN			
25			ONE		Macro Number One	
26			TWO		Macro Number Two	
27			THREE		Macro Number Three	
28			FOUR		Macro Number Four	
29			FIVE		Macro Number Five	
30			SIX		Macro Number Six	
31			SEVEN		Macro Number Seven	
32			EIGHT		Macro Number Eight	
33			NINE		Macro Number Nine	
34			TEN		Macro Number Ten	
35			EXIT		Exit Macro	
36						
37						
38						
39						
40						

Figure 23-22

The macro will act only on the keystrokes Uparrow, Downarrow, Home, and End for navigating among menu items, and Return for selecting a menu item. The macro combines three techniques: the key-table technique discussed in **Creating A Key Table** screens out selected keystrokes and acts on others, a relative-row referencing scheme enables you to prevent the user from moving above or below a given row within the menu range, and the technique from the previous macro enables you to branch to the appropriate routine for the selected menu item.

	A	B	C	D	E	F	G	H
41	\A	{goto}MENU_SCRN~						
42		{goto}MENU~{d}/wtb						
43	LOOP	{get ANS}						
44		{let ANS;@vlookup(ANS;KEY_TAB;1)}						
45		{if @iserr(ANS)}{branch LOOP}						
46		{branch ANS}						
47								
48	ANS							
49		{branch LOOP}						
50								
51	KEY_TAB	{UP}	{if @cellpointer("row")>TOP_ROW}{u}					
52		{DOWN}	{if @cellpointer("row")<BOT_ROW}{d}					
53		{HOME}	{home}					
54		{END}	{if @cellpointer("row")<BOT_ROW}{end}{d}					
55		~	/wtc{dispatch @cellpointer("contents")}					
56								
57	BOT_ROW	35						
58	TOP_ROW	25						
59								
60								

Figure 23-23

This macro is as complicated as any we've covered so far, so let's begin by separating the steps that go into it:

1. Displaying the menu screen.

2. Capturing and evaluating a keystroke typed by the user.

3. Moving the cell pointer within a restricted area (the range containing the menu descriptors).

4. Acting on a menu selection.

Displaying the Menu Screen. The macro begins as it did before: by positioning the screen, moving the cell pointer to the first descriptor in the list of menu items, and locking both horizontal and vertical titles to prevent the cell pointer from moving to the left or above its current location.

Capturing and Evaluating a Keystroke Typed by the User. The macro captures a keystroke from the user with the {get} command and stores it in the cell named Ans. In the next line, the macro changes the label in Ans to one of the five possible values. Those values are primarily string values, and they will either move the cell pointer down one cell, move it up one cell, move to the top of the list of menu descriptors, move to the bottom of that list, disregard the keystroke entirely, or execute a routine corresponding to the selected menu item.

That magic depends on the action of a look-up table called Key_tab. If the entry in Ans matches one of the labels in the left column of Key_tab, the macro instruction on row 44 will replace the current value of Ans with the corresponding label in the Key_tab's right hand column. If the entry in Ans matches none of those stored in the left hand column of Key_tab, the macro replaces the label stored in Ans with the value ERR.

Row 45 tests to see if the entry in Ans is ERR and, if it is, effectively ignores it by returning to the {get ANS} instruction to get another keystroke. If the entry in Ans is not Err, then the keytroke was one of those in the table and the macro branches to Ans to read the looked-up instruction newly stored there.

Moving the Cell Pointer Within a Restricted Area. If Ans was {UP} [60] (the label 1-2-3 stores if you press the Uparrow key),

---

[60] When you write this macro, take care to enter the keynames in the left column of Key_tab just as shown—in all uppercase. {Get} will store them that way and the @vlookup function we've used to look them up discriminates between upper and lowercase. For more information on that topic, refer to page 214.

then the lookup table will have returned the instruction {if @cellpointer("row")>TOP_ROW}{u}. This command is one of three designed to prevent the cell pointer from moving out of the list of menu descriptors.

The {if} statement checks to see if the number of the current row is greater than a predetermined row number (either a value, or preferably, an @cell formula stored in Top_row) above which you don't want the pointer to move. If the current row number is greater than (in other words, geographically below) Top_row, then the macro will read the {u} (or Uparrow) keyname. If not, it'll skip the instruction to press the Uparrow key. In either case, it will next read the instruction, {branch LOOP}, which will return control to row 43 to await another keystroke.

If Ans was {DOWN} (the label 1-2-3 stores if you pressed the Downarrow key), then the lookup table will have returned the instruction {if @cellpointer("row")<BOT_ROW}{d}. The {if} statement checks to see if the number of the current row is less than a predetermined row number (a formula stored in Bot_row) below which you don't want the pointer to move. If the current row number is less than (in other words, above) Bot_row, then the macro will read the {d} (or Downarrow) keyname. If not, it'll skip the instruction to press the Downarrow key. In either case, it will next read the instruction, {branch LOOP}, which will return control to row 43 to await another keystroke.

If Ans was {HOME}, the macro will press the Home key, causing the cell pointer to travel to the cell just beneath the locked rows at the top of the menu.

If Ans was {END} and if the cell pointer is not below the designated bottom row, the macro will press the End and Downarrow keys, causing the cell pointer to move to the bottom of the list of menu descriptors. We've assumed that, like the menu shown earlier, all the cells in the first column of the menu are occupied. If not, {end}{home} won't work, you'll have to substitute a command to {goto} the last cell in the list.

Acting on a Menu Selection.
If Ans is a tilde, then the user pressed Return to indicate a menu selection. The macro will reverse the locked title setting and branch to a range name corresponding to the contents of the cell on which the cell pointer resides (which is a menu descriptor such as ONE).

Once again, although we've haven't shown them on the worksheet, let's assume that each of the menu descriptor names (One, Two, Three, etc.) are also range names designating the first lines of a series of routines corresponding to the menu selections.

Let's take a moment to evaluate this menu macro. It provides the control lacking in the preceding pointer-activated full-screen menu macro.

However, it is fairly complex to write, and the keyboard response is a bit sluggish on an 8088-based computer (faster computers remedy the latter problem).

The reasons for the macro's performance problem divide into two categories. First, the macro is making two entries in Ans before responding in any way the user can see. Second, 1-2-3 refreshes the screen every time the cell pointer moves up or down, generating a distracting rippling effect and slowing response time further.

What's needed is a way to eliminate the problems of this macro while retaining its strengths. Fortunately, such a method exists, and one that is typical of the kind of creativity that often leads to the best solutions in advanced applications such as this.

Query Find Moving-Cell-Pointer Menu

For those of you reading this for hints on how you might not merely imitate the solutions we've found but apply the same kind of creativity to the resolution of other problems, let's begin with a brief review of the process we used to devise this routine (skip to the fifth paragraph down if you're in the market only for a full-screen menu solution).

We were searching for a way to restrict the cell pointer to a given range, to retrieve a specified value in response to the user pressing the Return key, to handle potential errors, and to do of all of those things very quickly.

The range of macro commands in 1-2-3 Release 2 or subsequent releases means that you can write almost any routine using those commands. However, as the preceding example proved, it may not be fast. Tapping the inherent speed of 1-2-3 often means finding worksheet-based methods of getting that work done. While you may have to write ten lines of macro commands to accomplish a given task, you may only need one worksheet command to do something very similar. The macro commands will be slowed by 1-2-3's ability to read and interpret each of those commands. If you can get the same work done with a worksheet command, chances are that placing that command in a macro will produce a very short macro that 1-2-3 can read and interpret very quickly.

On the basis of their ability to release limited control of the cell pointer to the user while restricting its movement to a given range, two commands present themselves for consideration: / Range Input and / Data Query Find.

Upon examination, / Range Input turns out to have a problematic limitation: Although you can restrict the user's movement of the cell pointer, there's no way of relating to a specific routine the location of the cell pointer when the user presses Return. When the user presses Return without first having made an entry during a Range Input command, the cell pointer returns to its location prior to the commencement of Range Input's control. Since Range Input allows for no intervention with a macro command, there's no way around this problem. Fortunately, any such troubles with Data Query Find yield to a little tweaking.

Once you've set the Data Query Input range and the Criterion range and selected / Data Query Find, 1-2-3 restricts the cell pointer to moving among cells in the Input range that match the criteria residing in the Criterion range. Although, like Range Input, Query Find will return the cell pointer to its place of origin when the command terminates control, Query Find will accept macro commands while it is in Find mode. That allows you to trap Return (or any other keystroke) before Query Find responds to it, store the cell pointer's location so you can use that location later, and then pass that keystroke through to 1-2-3 for a normal response. When Query Find terminates (which it will if you allow it to respond normally to a Return keystroke preceded by no data entry) you can use the stored location as the basis for branching to a routine.

The following macro illustrates how to construct a simple Query Find menu similar in structure to the previous ones.

	A	B	C	D	E	F
41	MENU_CRT	HIGHLIGHT SELECTION AND PRESS RETURN				
42		*				
43						
44	\M	{goto}MENU_SCRN~{paneloff}				
45		{goto}MENU_DB~{d}				
46		/wgpe				
47		/dqf{?}				
48		{let ANS;@cellpointer("row")-@cell("row";MENU_DB)}				
49		{esc 4}/wgpd				
50		{dispatch @vlookup(ANS;MENU_LIST;1)}				
51						
52	ANS					
53						
54						
55	MENU_LIST	1 ONE				
56		2 TWO				
57		3 THREE				
58		4 FOUR				
59		5 FIVE				
60		6 SIX				

Figure 23-24

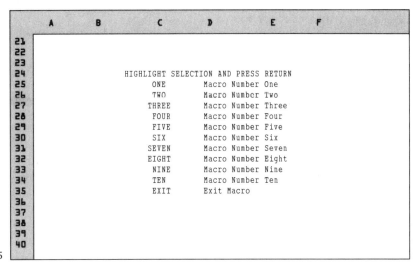

Figure 23-25

Let's begin with the macro instruction on row 44. The instruction {goto} MENU_SCRN~ positions the cell pointer in the top left corner of the screen shown above. The {paneloff} command suppresses the display of subsequent worksheet commands in the control panel.

The instruction on the next line positions the cell pointer one cell beneath the uppermost cell in Menu_db. Menu_db encompasses

C24..D35, so the cell pointer will reside in C25, on the label ONE. When you set up the worksheet, you should create the range name Menu_db and use it to define C24..D35 as a / Data Query Input range. Then assign to A41..A42 the name Menu_Crt (that range appears at the top of the macros screen shown above), select / Data Query Criterion range and enter Menu_crt. Menu_crt contains the field name for the left field of the menu-database and, beneath it, an asterisk so that any label will be selected during a Query operation. Were you to leave it blank, 1-2-3 would select values, labels, or blanks, reducing your flexibility to format the menu to your liking.

The instruction on row 46 enables global worksheet protection in anticipation of using Query Find. In 1-2-3 Release 2 and subsequent releases, users can edit database entries during Query Find mode. Since you don't want someone to be able to edit the menu, when you set up the worksheet, make sure none of the cells in Menu_db have been Range Unprotected (if so, select / Range Protect to reverse that). When this line of the macro enables global protection, it will prevent anyone from editing menu items during menu selection.

Row 47 selects Data Query Find to activate the moving-highlight menu. When 1-2-3 reads this instruction, the user will be able to move the menu highlight over each of the menu choices on the screen. During this operation, 1-2-3 will display the word Find in the mode indicator, so you may want to use the command {indicate "MENU"} to change that. In Release 2.2, you can use a longer and more descriptive string, even filling the top line of the display with instructions. The {?} (interactive) command will force 1-2-3 to pause before reading further.

As soon as the user presses Return, the {let} command on the following row will determine the number of the menu choice, through a technique you'll probably find many other uses for than this. The command subtracts the number of the row on which the cell pointer resides from the number of the top row of the range named Menu_list. The top of Menu_db is cell C24. Suppose the cell pointer is on choice number four, cell C28, when the user presses Return. Row number 28 minus row number 24 equals 4, and that's the number of the menu item the user selected. The beauty of this technique is that it works no matter where you relocate the menu on the worksheet. That number will be used in a moment to look up the appropriate routine for the macro to run in response to the menu selection.

The instruction on row 49 backs out of the Query Find menu with four Escapes. Since we used an {?} (interactive) command to force 1-2-3 to pause in Query Find mode, it's possible that the user could have pressed Escape several times and returned to Ready mode. The control panel is frozen so there'd be no indication of that to users, so it's unlikely that they'd pursue that further by trying to use 1-2-3 interactively. However, it is possible, and if the user had in turn selected some other set of commands, the four Escapes would act to cancel them just as it would act to cancel Query Find. We could have used a "q" to Quit from Query Find, but it wouldn't also extricate 1-2-3 from any other keystrokes the user might have issued during that interactive pause. If you're sure the application will be used with 1-2-3 Release 2.2, you can simplify matters and use the {break} advanced macro command, whose function is to put 1-2-3 into Ready mode. The keystrokes /wgpd disable global worksheet protection to return 1-2-3 to its original state (if you otherwise wanted worksheet protection enabled, skip that instruction).

The {dispatch} command on row 50 transfers control to one of the routines listed in the right column of the table named Menu_list (beginning in cell B55). Earlier we described a situation that would have stored the number 4 in Ans. In that case, the @vlookup function would return the string FOUR, and the {dispatch} command would transfer control to the routine by that name. We haven't shown that routine or those that support the other menu items, but they would typically appear several rows below the table stored in Menu_list.

Although Query Find seems an unlikely candidate for a full-screen menu technique, since Find mode takes care of the pesky job of moving the cell pointer and restricting it to the menu range, the macro code you need to supply is relatively simple. Furthermore, since you don't have to process pointer movement keystrokes (you only process a keystroke when the user actually selects something) the keyboard responds very quickly to the user's input. In our view, this is the best of the full-screen menu techniques.

Of course, you can further adjust it for safety, speed, or some combination of both. Earlier we mentioned the vulnerability imposed by using the {?} interactive command. One way to prevent the user from embarking on a spontaneous sidetrip is to test each keystroke with {get} and, since the Escape key is the only "illicit" way out of Find mode, ignore the Escape key. The following macros illustrate the {GET_KEY} subroutine in place of the {?} command.

	A	B	C	D	E	F
41	MENU_CRT	HIGHLIGHT SELECTION AND PRESS RETURN				
42	*					
43						
44	\M	{goto}MENU_SCRN~{paneloff}				
45		{goto}MENU_DB~{d}				
46		/wgpe				
47		/dqf{GET_KEY}				
48		{let ANS;@cellpointer("row")-@cell("row";MENU_DB)}				
49		{esc 4}/wgpd				
50		{dispatch @vlookup(ANS;MENU_LIST;1)}				

Figure 23-26

	A	B	C	D	E	F	G	H
71	GET_KEY	{get ANS}						
72		{if ANS="{ESC}"}{beep}{branch GET_KEY}						
73		{if ANS="~"}{return}						
74		{ANS}{branch GET_KEY}						

Figure 23-27

This type of protection is effective, but costly. Because the macro captures a key to the worksheet and then runs it as a subroutine, 1-2-3 refreshes the screen with each keystroke, resulting in a distracting rippling effect. On the other hand, this is barely noticeable on a 386-based machine.

Another problem may arise after the macro has been run. Because the menu operation functions through a Query Find command, that Query Find can be re-executed from Ready mode by a press of the Query key (the F7 function key). Having the screen change instantly back to the menu will confuse the user, not to mention the fact that the menu won't respond to keystrokes as it did before. You can prevent all of that by clearing the Data Query ranges after the user makes a menu selection. You'll need to modify the macro in two ways. After the menu selection has been made, clear the Query ranges with the keystrokes "/dqrq." Before the selection, you'll have to set the Input and Criterion ranges using the range names that refer to them. The following macro shows those changes on rows 47 and 50.

	A	B	C	D	E	F
41	MENU_CRT	HIGHLIGHT SELECTION AND PRESS RETURN				
42	*					
43						
44	\M	{goto}MENU_SCRN~{paneloff}				
45		{goto}MENU_DB~{d}				
46		/wgpe				
47		/dqriMENU_DB~cMENU_CRT~f				
48		{GET_KEY}				
49		{let ANS;@cellpointer("row")-@cell("row";MENU_DB)}				
50		{esc 4}/wgpd				
51		/dqrq{dispatch @vlookup(ANS;MENU_LIST;1)}				

Figure 23-28

If improving performance is really an issue, you won't want to use the Get_key variation. You might notice that, even without Get_key, we are still storing a keystroke on the worksheet. The {let ANS} statement, which creates the key value used in the {dispatch @vlookup} statement, causes the screen to redraw, slowing down the macro. Although it'll create a very long statement, you could incorporate the entire second argument of the {let} command in the {dispatch} statement in place of the argument Ans in the @vlookup formula. In this way, you never store a value in Ans, you merely calculate it at the time the macro evaluates the @vlookup formula as part of the {dispatch} statement.

If you're really looking to optimize performance, eliminate Get_key and combine the {let} statement and the {dispatch} statement to look somthing like the one below.

```
{dispatch @vlookup(@cellpointer("row")-@cell("row";MENU_DB);MENU_LIST;1)}
```

This lengthy macro command can be shortened by storing part of it in a cell on the worksheet. In the screen below, which represents the completed macro, Row_hi consists of the formula @cell("row";MENU_DB). Because the macro branches to another routine before it cancels the Query Find operation, we delete lines 49 and 50 and each subroutine (i.e., One, Two, etc.) must now begin with the {esc 4}/wgpd commands.

```
  ·     A          B         C         D         E        F        G       H
41   MENU_CRT   HIGHLIGHT SELECTION AND PRESS RETURN
42              *
43
44   \M         {goto}MENU_SCRN~{paneloff}
45              {goto}MENU_DB~{d}
46              /wgpe
47              /dqriMENU_DB~cMENU_CRT~f{?}
48              {dispatch @vlookup(@cellpointer("row")-ROW_HI;MENU_LIST;1)}
49
50
51   ROW_HI     24
52   ANS
53
54   MENU_LIST        1 ONE
55                    2 TWO
56                    3 THREE
57                    4 FOUR
58                    5 FIVE
59                    6 SIX
60                    7 SEVEN
```

Figure 23-29

While it uses a little more code to have each subroutine clear the Query Find, it's a small tradeoff if your objective is optimal performance.

Drawing Attention to Full-Screen Menus

One of the main objectives of the full-screen menu techniques is to focus the user's attention on the task at hand, namely, selecting a course for the macro to take. By reducing the amount of extraneous information on the screen, you can help the user of your macro focus. 1-2-3 Release 2.2 provides three commands that can help you in that endeavor.

Here's what a screen looks like when the corresponding macro uses these new commands:

```
                    M A I N   M E N U

         HIGHLIGHT SELECTION AND PRESS RETURN
            ONE         Macro Number One
            TWO         Macro Number Two
          THREE         Macro Number Three
           FOUR         Macro Number Four
           FIVE         Macro Number Five
            SIX         Macro Number Six
          SEVEN         Macro Number Seven
          EIGHT         Macro Number Eight
           NINE         Macro Number Nine
            TEN         Macro Number Ten
           EXIT         Exit Macro
```

Figure 23-30

What follows is the macro that produced the previous screen. For simplicity, we've chosen to enhance the simplest full-screen menu of the lot, the (!) Moving Cell Pointer Menu, but the same principles apply equally to all of the full-screen techniques. Here's the macro.

	A	B	C	D	E	F	G
1	\M	{frameoff}{paneloff "clear"}					
2		{indicate @repeat(" ";31)&"M A I N M E N U"&@repeat(" ";31)}					
3		{goto}MENU_SCRN~{goto}MENU~{d}					
4		/wtb					
5		{?}/wtc					
6		{dispatch @cellpointer("contents")}					
7							
8							
9							
10							

Figure 23-31

The first row of the macro uses the {frameoff} command to turn off 1-2-3's inverted "L" row-and-column frame. The next command, {paneloff "clear"}, clears the top three lines and the bottom line of the display and freezes them. Finally, {indicate} fills the top line of the display with a message announcing this as the main menu, with an equal number of spaces on either side.

When using this technique, you'll want to be sure to restore the worksheet frame and the indicator when the contents of the screen changes to display worksheet information. Here, we've assumed that the {frameon} and {indicate} commands, which restore those screen components, are in the routines run by {dispatch}.

24

Error Avoidance
and
Recovery

One of the finer points of the art of developing turnkey macro applications lies in dealing with events you have no way of predicting: Those are events that often cause errors. If you can deal with them, you can prevent those errors entirely.

One common and unpredictable situation confronts you when you want to save a file under macro control. If you wanted to save a worksheet with a macro, you'd either have to use the keystrokes /fsFILENAME~ (if you were saving the file for the first time) or /fsFILENAME~r (if you were replacing an existing file). The keystrokes for each situation differ, and although it might appear that you have to know whether or not the file exists in order to decide, there's a way to handle both situations with one macro.

The same challenge confronts you with respect to range names: If you are about to create a range name under macro control and you want to avoid overwriting an existing range name, how can you test for the existence of that name and, if it exists, assign a different name to the range?

In the macros that follow, we'll show you how to use macros to manage a few of the unpredictable elements of turnkey applications.

The {?} (Interactive) Command

As a macro tool, the {?} (interactive) command is a double-edged sword. It temporarily suspends macro control and returns control to the keyboard until the user presses the Return key. Unfortunately, while you as the macro developer probably have a very specific assignment you'd like the user to carry out during this interactive pause in macro control, the {?} command permits that person to do anything at all. That includes using the Escape key to back out of any 1-2-3 command menu the application may be in the midst of using. Once in Ready mode, although the macro is still in effect the user can do anything: press the slash key and select a command, press function keys, type entries, or move the cell pointer.

If you want to offset some of the interactive command's largesse, include in the macro a command to cancel any menu operations that the user may have engaged in during that pause. Since the Return key won't pass through to 1-2-3 during an interactive pause, the user won't in most cases have been able to complete those operations. A series of Escapes will cancel any menu 1-2-3 may be in the midst of.

Just for the record, the deepest menu in 1-2-3 is the one to select the time format for the Y-scale of a graph (/ Graph Options Scale Y-Scale Format Date Time): you'll need eight presses of the Escape key to cancel it. So if you want to be covered under any circumstance, use {esc 8}. If you're using 1-2-3 Release 2.2, you can eliminate the guesswork by using the {break} advanced macro command, which automatically returns 1-2-3 to Ready mode.

Dealing with Files

Let's begin with the simple all-purpose method for saving worksheet files whether or not they already exist, then we'll progress to a method you can use not only for worksheets, but for graph and print files as well.

In this example, let's suppose you wanted to save a worksheet named Stocks. The macro to save it under any circumstance is /fsSTOCKS~r{esc}. If the file does exist, the macro will select the Replace option to save it and return 1-2-3 to Ready mode. The {esc} key name will have no effect because pressing the Escape key in Ready mode has no effect. On the other hand, if you're saving the file for the first time, the macro will save the new file and return to Ready mode. Since there's not a Cancel/Replace menu, the "r" that follows will put 1-2-3 into Label mode and type an "r" into the edit line of the control panel. Finally, the {esc} key name will cancel the label and return 1-2-3 to Ready mode.

While you can use the preceding technique only with worksheet files (and that's likely to be the bulk of files you'll need to save), the next technique works with any of the three kinds of files 1-2-3 can save—worksheet, graph, and print files.

```
         A        B        C        D        E        F        G        H

 1     \F        {getlabel "Enter name of file to save: ";F_NAME}
 2               {open +F_NAME&".prn";"r"}{branch SAVE}
 3               {branch REPLACE}
 4
 5     SAVE      /pf{F_NAME}~gq{quit}
 6
 7     REPLACE   /pf{F_NAME}~rgq{quit}
 8
 9     F_NAME
10
```

Figure 24-1

Row 1 of this macro prompts for a filename and stores it in the cell named F_name. Row 2 attempts to open a print file by that name (note our use of a string formula to construct the filename argument in the {open} command).

If the {open} command succeeds, you can deduce that the file already exists. Remember, when any file manipulation command succeeds, control reverts immediately to the next row (yes, that's the opposite of the way {if} commands respond to a true condition). So if the file already exists, the macro skips the {branch SAVE} command and instead reads the {branch REPLACE} instruction on the next line.

The Replace routine saves the print file and, since 1-2-3 will display its Cancel/Replace menu, types an r to select Replace, then selects Go and Quit to complete the operation.

On the other hand, had the {open} command failed (meaning that the filename did not already exist), the macro would have read the Save routine. Save is identical to Replace, except Save omits the "r" because 1-2-3 will not display the Cancel/Replace option.

Another approach to accomplish the same result features an innovative use of subroutine commands. Since you already know how to handle the uncertainty associated with filenames, you may wish to skip to the next example, which demonstrates these techniques in the context of a file consolidation application.

The value of this alternative approach is twofold: first, it's an alternative you may prefer to the foregoing technique, and second, it demonstrates a use of the subroutine command that may help you in applications unrelated to saving files.

	A	B	C	D	E	F	G	H
1	\F	{getlabel "Enter name of file to save: ",F_NAME}						
2		{open +F_NAME&".prn";"r"}{branch SAVE}						
3		{let REPLACE;"r"}						
4	SAVE	/pf{F_NAME}~{REPLACE}rBUDGET~gq						
5		{blank REPLACE}						
6								
7	REPLACE							
8		{return}						
9	F_NAME							
10		{return}						

Figure 24-2

Rows 1 and 2 duplicate those of the preceding macro, so we'll assume you're already familiar with them and skip directly to row 3. The {let} command on row 3 assigns the letter "r" to the cell named Replace; that value will become significant in the next line of the macro.

Following the keystrokes to execute the / Print File commands on row 4, the macro reads the cell named F_name as a subroutine. That cell contains the name of the file to save, and the effect of calling it as a subroutine is to type that name as the name of the file to save. Control returns immediately to the next instruction on row 4, where a tilde enters that filename.

The next subroutine call is to the cell named Replace. Keep in mind that the macro has detected that a file exists with the name we want to assign to this file, and that since the macro has just entered the filename for the print file, 1-2-3 will display its Cancel/Replace menu. The subroutine call to Replace will type an r to select Replace from that menu, and the macro will continue on row 4 to specify the print range and save the print file.

The instructions on row 5 erase the cell named Replace to enable the next macro to set it anew.

Now let's suppose that the {open} command in row 2 succeeded, which means that no file already exists by the name we want to use. When the macro has detected no existing files, the {open} command will fail, so the macro will continue reading to the right of that command, and will branch to the routine named Save.

Save is the instruction on row 4. By jumping over the {let} command on row 3, the macro has left blank the cell named Replace. Keep in mind that because no file by the same name as the one we're using exists, 1-2-3 will not display its Cancel/Replace menu when the macro enters the filename. When the macro reads the {REPLACE} subroutine call directly after entering the filename, it will read nothing in Replace (in other words, the macro will not type any additional keystrokes) and return control to the next instruction on row 4.

By setting the value of Replace to correspond with the existence or absence of a file on the disk, you can easily make the macro respond appropriately to each of those conditions. That technique is applicable to many other circumstances where you need to carefully control the way the macro responds.

Finally, here's another version adapted for use in a file consolidation macro. It checks for the existence of the file you have asked to combine; if that file doesn't exist, it branches to an error message.

```
        A          B         C         D        E        F        G        H

1   \F         {getlabel "Enter name of file to combine: ";F_NAME}
2              {FILETEST}
3              /fcce{F_NAME}~
4
5   FILETEST   {open +F_NAME&".wk1";"r"}{restart}{branch FILE_ERR}
6              {close}
7              {return}
8
9   FILE_ERR   {beep 2}
10             ERROR! No file by the name if {F_NAME}.  Press any key.
11             {get ANS}{esc}
12             {branch \F}
13
14  F_NAME
15             {return}
16  ANS ~
17
18
19
20
```

Figure 24-3

Dealing with Range Names

Just as you might want to know whether or not a file name exists, you might also want to know the same thing about a range name. The technique for testing for the existence of a range name depends on two of 1-2-3's less-well known @functions, @@ and @iserr.

After storing the name of the range you want to test in a cell named Ans, this macro attempts to make a reference to the contents of that name. If the result is the value ERR, then the range name does not exist. Let's look more closely at the formula used to make this test.

Like the advanced macro command {dispatch}, the @@ function uses the location specified in its argument to identify a second location. The identity of the second location is stored in the first location. Let's suppose you wrote the formula @@(A1). If cell A1 contained the label B1, and cell B1 contained the value 100, then @@(A1) would return the value 100. If B1 contained the label Hello, then @@(A1) would return the string Hello.

Now let's use range names in that same scenario, and suppose you wrote the formula @@(ANS). If the cell named Ans contained the label Question, and the cell named Question contained the value 100, then @@(ANS) would return the value 100—and if Question contained the label Hello, then @@(ANS) would return the string Hello. However, if there was no such range name as Question, then @@(ANS) would return ERR.

With that in mind, let's consider the way you might construct an {if} command to detect the absence of a range name. If you return the value ERR, the {if} statement will evaluate to false and branch to the cell directly below. However, because the {if} command evaluates the results of a conditional formula numerically and labels are valued as zero, if the result of @@(ANS) is a string, the {if} statement will evaluate to false and macro control will once again branch to the cell directly below—even though the range name exists. You can't have a condition where the macro does the same thing whether the range name exists or not, so you'll have to modify the formula.

If you place the function @iserr outside the @@ function—@iserr(@@(ANS))—then you will in effect be asking only whether the result of @@(ANS) produces an error or not. Since the absence of a range name will cause the formula to produce an ERR, but a string result will not, you have a good test to use as the conditional statement in your {if} command.

There is one potential problem with this scheme. In the preceding example, if the entry in the cell named Question evaluated to ERR, then the result would be the same as if the range name did not exist. So if you use this method, keep that weakness in mind.

In the following macro, if the range name does not exist, the macro will branch to the routine named No; if it does exist, it'll branch to the routine named Yes.

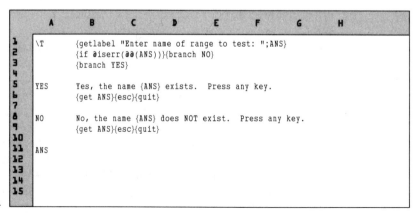

	A	B	C	D	E	F	G	H
1	\T	{getlabel "Enter name of range to test: ";ANS}						
2		{if @iserr(@@(ANS))}{branch NO}						
3		{branch YES}						
4								
5	YES	Yes, the name {ANS} exists. Press any key.						
6		{get ANS}{esc}{quit}						
7								
8	NO	No, the name {ANS} does NOT exist. Press any key.						
9		{get ANS}{esc}{quit}						
10								
11	ANS							
12								
13								
14								
15								

Figure 24-4

25

Testing Cells for Contents

Overview

It's quite common to need to know the contents of a given cell. The manner in which you test a cell depends on what you're looking for. The following is a quick rundown of the manner in which you might test for some of the more common things. In each case, the {if} statement has been written so that it will be true (branch to the right) if the cell contains the designated entry. Here's how you would evaluate a cell named Test to determine if it:

- contains a value: {if @isnumber(TEST)}

- contains a label: {if @isstring(TEST)}

- contains the value ERR: {if @iserr(TEST)}

- contains the value NA: {if @isna(TEST)}

- contains a given value, N: {if TEST = N}

- contains a given string, X: {if @exact(TEST;"X")}

- is blank: {if @cell("type";TEST) = "b"}

Testing for a Specific Label

potential
problem
with the
conditional
formula

If you want a conditional formula in an {if} command to check to see if two cells are identical, you must know in advance whether you plan to test labels, to test values, or to test two blank cells. The manner in which you write the testing formula depends on what pairs of entries you expect to test.

For example, if one cell is blank and the other contains a label, the formula {if CELL1 = CELL2} will improperly return a true result. Because the blank cell is valued as zero, 1-2-3 evaluates both entries as values, and since a label is also valued as zero, it finds the expression true. In that case, the formula {if @exact(CELL1;CELL2)} will work properly.

However, @exact is a string function and won't properly process values. If Cell1 and Cell2 contain the same value or if they are both empty (equal to value zero), the formula {if @exact(CELL1;CELL2)} will improperly return a false result (since @exact can't process values, it returns ERR, and {if} responds to ERR as if it were a false result). Keep in mind that if you use the @exact function, 1-2-3 will differentiate between upper and lowercase letters. {If @exact(@upper(CELL1);@upper(CELL2))} will eliminate such distinctions.

In some instances, you may need to use neither of those tests. If Cell1 contains an entry that you want to compare to Cell2, you can instead place that entry right into the macro. For example, if you know that you want to test to see if Cell2 contains the entry "Y", {if @exact(CELL2;"Y")} will always work no matter if Cell2 contains a label, a value, or is empty. If you want to make the same entry accept a lowercase Y as well as its uppercase counterpart, use {if @exact(@upper(CELL2);"Y")}.

If you are testing an entry that was stored by a {getlabel} command, you can always use the simpler test {if @upper(ANS) = "Y"}. [61] This test won't fail because {getlabel} will always store something in the target cell (which we've called Ans here). As long as any label entry (even the sole label prefix that 1-2-3 will store if the user merely presses Return in response to a {getlabel} prompt) resides in the tested cell, this simpler test will work.

All of these anomalies have nothing to do with the {if} command. They are instead the result of the manner in which 1-2-3 processes the

[61] Or use just {if ANS = "Y"} if you know your application won't be run with a copy of 1-2-3 that is installed with the case-sensitive ASCII collating driver.

conditional formula inside the {if} statement. You can see that by entering those formulas directly into cells on the worksheet and testing them.
That is, in fact, the best way to test the validity of any conditional formula
before you write that statement into a macro.

Maintaining Compatibility with Releases 2, 2.01, and 2.2

Release 2.0
versus
Release 2.01
and later

1-2-3 Release 2.0 will sometimes process a given {if} statement differently than will subsequent releases of 1-2-3. The {if} command works
the same in both releases; the differences arise from the way that the conditional formula (in the {if} command) evaluates references to labels.
Let's look at an example that could cause trouble if you run the macro
with both Releases of 1-2-3, then rewrite it so that it works on either release.

Suppose you have written a macro that processes a list of labels stored
in a column. With each loop of the macro, the cell pointer moves down
one row and tests to see if the cell is blank. If it is, the macro terminates; if
not, the macro processes the label it contains.

Example: A macro that will work in Release 2.0, but not in Release
2.01.

	A	B	C	D	E	F	G	H
1	\A	/rncTEST~~						
2		{if TEST=0}{branch STOP}						
3		[...do some processing on Test...]						
4		/rndTEST~						
5		{d}						
6		{branch \A}						
7								
8								
9								
10								

Figure 25-1

The key in this application is the manner in which the conditional
formula tests for the presence/absence of a label each time it moves down
another cell. The conditional formula shown above (in the {if} command) works fine in Release 2.0, because labels do not evaluate to zero.
The routine continues to loop until the macro encounters a blank cell at
the bottom of the list (or a cell containing a zero). However, in Release
2.01 and subsequent releases, references to labels do evaluate to zero, so
the preceding routine would stop upon encountering the first label.

What you need is a routine that works equally well in Release 2.0 and later releases. Here is one such routine:

```
{if @cell("type";TEST)="b"}{branch STOP}
```

Actually, if you're moving the cell pointer through the list one cell at a time, you can omit the naming of the current cell to identify it as the cell to be tested; just use the @cellpointer function:

```
{if @cellpointer("type")="b"}{branch STOP}
```

Another Compatibility Issue: Testing for Blanks

As we've already said, you should use either the @cell or @cellpointer function to test to see if a given cell or the current cell, respectively, is blank. One further note is in order. When you write an {if} statement to compare the results of either function, we recommend that you compare that result with the lowercase letter "b". Write {if @cellpointer("type") = "b"}, not {if @cellpointer("type") = "B"}.

If you enter either an @cell or @cellpointer function in a cell, specify the "type" parameter, and reference a blank cell (for example @cell("type";TEST) where the cell named Test is blank), 1-2-3 will return a lowercase b.

While in many cases, 1-2-3 will not discriminate between an upper or lowercase letter b when it reads the {if} statement, there are at least two situations where it will. If your application encounters either situation, and you've used an upper case B, the {if} statement won't work properly: 1-2-3 will detect a blank cell but your {if} statement won't respond to it.

Two situations will cause 1-2-3 to discriminate between uppercase and lowercase: (1) If the copy of 1-2-3 being used to run your application is itself running under the ASCII Collating driver. (2) If you happen to have used the @exact function in your formula {if @exact(@cell("type";TEST);"B")}.

26

Using the Screen

Introduction

Output takes a variety of forms; among them are screen displays, printed reports, and saved files. From a developer's point of view, there are some common threads that tie together all forms of output. For example, a help screen, although intended as a form of support to the user, is just another kind of screen output because the techniques used to produce it are essentially the same as those used to produce other forms of screen output.

Of all forms of output, the screen is the one your macro's user will probably spend the most time with. That makes the screen your primary means of communicating information to that person and one of your most important tools.

One of the chief limitations of macros in Release 1A was their poor control over the screen. As a result, a macro user was often forced to watch as the cell pointer raced madly around the screen, menus flashed by in the control panel, and a variety of largely irrelevant data occupied the screen.

No more. One of the subtler yet significant improvements to 1-2-3 came with Release 2's ability to suppress much of 1-2-3's normal screen activity; that control was in Release 2.2 extended to all of 1-2-3's normal screen activity. For example, in Release 2 and 2.01, you can now freeze the appearance of the control panel and the worksheet with the {paneloff} and {windowsoff} commands and, whenever you like, restore their normal function with the {panelon} and {windowson} commands.

In Release 2.2, you can not only freeze but clear the control panel (using {paneloff "clear"}), you can remove the inverted L from around the worksheet border (using {frameoff}).

You can easily place a message on the screen, freeze the appearance of the screen, then have the macro do whatever you'd like: The user will not see any of the activity that follows. When that activity finishes, move the cell pointer to the next relevant screen—perhaps for data entry—and allow 1-2-3 to update the screen normally once again.

Release 2.2 continued that trend, giving you even more control over what the macro user sees. For example, even 1-2-3's characteristic inverted-L frame can be suppressed; the indicator panel can accept as many characters as the screen can display; you can show a timed and automated sequence of graphs, with no interaction whatsoever required by the user.

Since the tools to control the screen are available, the question is, what do you want to do with them? Here are a few guidelines.

1. Keep the information on the screen relevant to the operation at hand. As the application progresses, remove information that's no longer relevant and replace it with something that is. For example, you can use the worksheet to store displays that you can show the user as the macro begins a new operation. If the first thing a user must do is to sign on to the system by entering a name and a password, you can place both the instructions and data entry blanks on the worksheet and display it at sign-on time. When the sign-on process ends and it's time to make some choices about what comes next, remove the sign-on screen immediately and substitute something else.

2. Use the screen to provide visual feedback to users with respect to their current actions, as well as their available options. Consider the following example. If the user is filling in an on-screen form, you can complete the entire operation with {getlabel} or {getnumber} prompts. But it may be helpful to also use the cell pointer to highlight the form's blank on the screen that will receive the data as yet another cue to the user as to what's happening.

3. Suppress the display of things that the user doesn't need to see. If you are updating a database with data that comes from an on-screen form, chances are there's no need for the user to see the database at all. So, if the operation would normally show the database when you're adjusting ranges or moving data, instead display a message and freeze the screen until the operation finishes.

4. Always keep the user informed about what's going on. For example, if the macro is doing something that requires the user to wait, post a message to that effect. If the user will have to wait quite some time, do one of two things: (A) Inform the person of the fact that the wait will be awhile (be specific about the length of time, if possible), so the user can opt to go off and do something else for that time. (B) Provide periodic feedback regarding the macro's progress. Let the person know that the macro is working properly and that it is progressing toward its goal.

   If the user must enter a particular kind of data, specify what kind of data the application expects.

5. Adopt conventions in the ways you communicate with a user and stick to them. Once you've established a certain part of the screen as the place in which to post messages, post all of your messages there.

The preceding set of guidelines can help you critique an application you've written. Ask yourself how effectively you've adopted each one, and where you might improve. You can also use them to guide you as you plan a new application.

As we present each of the screen-management techniques that follow, consider how you might use it to support one or more of the preceding objectives. Since the list of techniques is long and varied, we recommend that you choose just one or two of them for your use. There's no need to use them all, and doing so would remove any sense of order from the application. Once you've established some standards, vary from them only where special situations demand a change.

Message at the Top of the Screen

This routine is a gem—it's short, effective, and portable. It places a message in the control panel and waits for any keystroke, then clears the message and continues processing the macro. The message-display operation is a subroutine so you can use it with any main routine.

Here's the macro.

	A	B	C	D	E	F	G	H
1	\A	{SHOW "Place disk in drive A:"}						
2		/fsX{esc}A:FILENAME~						
3		[...the macro continues processing...]						
4								
5	SHOW	{define MSG}						
6		{MSG} Press any key.						
7		{get ANS}{esc}						
8		{return}						
9								
10	MSG							
11		{return}						
12	ANS							
13								
14								
15								

Figure 26-1

Row 1 of the main routine calls a subroutine named Show and passes to it a parameter consisting of a string. Control transfers to row 5, so we'll pick up there. The first row of the subroutine Show stores the passed parameter in a cell named Msg. Msg is a contraction—of the word Message—and is commonly used as a range name.)

Row 6 calls Msg (on row 10) as a subroutine. Remember, the string "Place disk in drive A:" is now stored in Msg. The macro types on that string, reads the {return} command on the next row, and returns control to row 6 with the next instruction to the right of the subroutine call. Another string, " Press any key." appears there, so the macro continues typing. The control panel now contains the string "Place disk in drive A:. Press any key." Since no tilde follows, 1-2-3 remains in label mode with the entry in the control panel.

The macro reads a {get} command (on row 7) and pauses. When the user responds with a keystroke, {get} stores it in Ans (although the macro has no use for it), presses the Escape key to cancel the entry, and returns control to the main routine (in this case, to row 2).

While the message displays in the control panel, 1-2-3's mode indicator contains the word Label. If you'd like to replace that with something else, use the {indicate} command to set the mode indicator before the macro types the message, and after it clears it (shown in the revision below).

```
        A       B           C           D           E           F           G           H
1       \A      {SHOW "Place disk in drive A:"}
2               /fsX{esc}A:FILENAME~
3               [...the macro continues processing...]
4
5       SHOW    {define MSG}
6               {indicate "PAUSE"}
7               {MSG}  Press any key.
8               {get ANS}{esc}
9               {indicate}
10              {return}
11
12      MSG
13              {return}
14      ANS
15
```

Figure 26-2

If you have Release 2.2, you might prefer a variant of the previous macro, employing a technique specific to 2.2.

```
        A       B           C           D           E           F           G           H
1       \A      {SHOW "Place disk in drive A:"}
2               /fsX{esc}A:FILENAME~
3               [...the macro continues processing...]
4
5       SHOW    {define MSG}
6               {indicate +MSG&@repeat(" ";66-@length(MSG))&"Press any key."}
7               {get ANS}{esc}
8               {indicate}
9               {return}
10
11      MSG     Place disk in drive A:
12              {return}
13      ANS     ~
14
15
```

Figure 26-3

The chief difference in this macro is that the {indicate} advanced macro command does most of the display work. As you recall, Release 2.2 permits formulas to be resolved in macro arguments and allows many more characters to be displayed by {indicate}. The formula in line 6 assures that the string in Msg ("Place disk in drive A:" in this example) is displayed in the far left of the central panel, and the "Press any Key" prompt is displayed in the far right. Note that this will not produce exactly the same effect with a 132 column screen driver. If you happen to be using one, simply replace the constant 66, which is simply 80 characters less the number of characters in "Press any key" with 118, or 132-14.

As the preceding macro superbly demonstrates, a macro need not be complex to do the job. Use this subroutine with any main routine.

Messages in Windows

1-2-3's ability to split the screen through the / Worksheet Window Horizontal or / Worksheet Window Vertical command provides an easy-to-use tool for posting messages.

For example, suppose you want to provide an optional set of instructions that will overlap part of a screen. You don't want the message on the current screen—that would make it mandatory. Instead, place that message elsewhere on a blank area of the worksheet.

Before we begin, let's detail a few assumptions and then outline a plan of action for this macro. We prefer to place messages at the top of the screen, rather than in the bottom of the screen. The top of the screen is the natural place for a person to look for a message, given that that's where 1-2-3's menus display. Here are the macro's objectives:

1. To store the location of the cell pointer, and to identify and store the location of the top left cell on the current screen. You'll need to know these locations later when you want to restore the screen to its original appearance.

2. To move the cell pointer upwards a number of rows equal to the number of rows that the message will occupy.

3. To split the screen into two windows, unsynchronize the two windows, and move the cell pointer in the upper window so the screen displays the message.

4. To wait for a keystroke, then move the upper window back to the former location of the upper left cell, clear the window, and return the cell pointer back to its original location. If your application depends on the Worksheet Windows being synchronized, you should also restore that setting.

The only real trick in this macro is the routine that identifies the top left cell on the screen. That routine is one you will probably use many times in your application—not just in this context, but any time you want to move the screen and precisely restore its former appearance—so we've written that part of the macro as a subroutine. That subroutine is named Setscrn.

```
        A         B         C         D      E      F      G        H
21                {SETSCRN MSG1}
22                [...the macro continues processing...]
23
24      SETSCRN   {define SET1}
25                {indicate "WAIT"}
26                {paneloff}{windowsoff}
27                /rncHERE~~
28                /wwh/wwu
29                {pgup}{d}{bigright}{bigleft}
30                /rncTOPLEFT~~
31                {goto}
32                {SET1}
33                ~{windowson}{panelon}
34                {indicate "HELP"}
35                {get KEY}
36                {indicate "WAIT"}
37                {windowsoff}{paneloff}
38                {goto}TOPLEFT~
39                /wwc
40                {goto}HERE~
41                /rndTOPLEFT~/rndHERE~
42                {panelon}{windowson}
43                {indicate}
44                {return}
45
46      SET1
47                {return}
48      KEY
49
50
```

Figure 26-4

Let's presume that the routine beginning on row 21 is the continuation of some other routine, perhaps a data entry routine, at which point the user has requested a screen of instructions. The command {SETSCRN} calls a subroutine that begins on row 24. Setscrn stores the information necessary to restore the current display and creates a window in which to display the message.

The {define} command on row 24 stores in a cell named Set1 the parameter passed with the subroutine call. The {indicate} command on the next row changes the mode indicator to WAIT and the commands that follow freeze the screen in preparation for some behind-the-scenes work.

Beginning with the instructions on row 27, the macro assigns the name Here to the current cell, splits the screen (placing the cell pointer in the bottom row of the top window) and unsynchronizes the two windows.

The instructions on row 29 automatically position the cell pointer in the top left cell of the original screen. Call it a fluke, but if after dividing the screen horizontally (as we've already done), you press the PageUp key, the Downarrow key, the Tab key, and the Backtab key (that's Shift-Tab), the cell pointer will reside in the cell that was in the top left corner of the screen a moment ago. [62] The macro then assigns the name Topleft to the cell so it can later be located.

Beginning on row 31, the macro moves the cell pointer to the location name passed to the subroutine from the calling routine—that's Msg1 in this case—then enables 1-2-3 to update the screen normally again to show the two windows (the upper one now shows a message) and pauses for the user to read the screen. The implication of the {get} command as a device to make the macro pause is that the message screen should include an instruction to "Press any key to continue."

After the user presses a key, the macro resumes, on row 36, reading instructions. It freezes the screen once more, returns the cell pointer to the original top left corner of the screen, unites the two windows into a single screen, returns the cell pointer to the cell from where it began its sojourn, deletes the temporary names Topleft and Here, unfreezes the screen, restores the original indicator, and returns control to the calling routine. If your application requires that the windows be synchronized, you should also include the macro string /wws at the end of the subroutine.

A Dynamic Menu

This macro enables you to combine the easy-to-use function of a {menubranch} command and the accessibility of a subroutine to generate error messages. Although a little complex to write, once this routine is in your macro library, you can use it to communicate with your users about all manner of errors.

---

[62] Due to the manner in which this technique moves the cell pointer, it requires that the original location of the top left corner of the screen be below the first row of the worksheet (or if / Worksheet Titles Horizontal are in effect, two rows beneath the lowermost locked row). It also requires that the cell be at least one full screen to the left of the right edge of the worksheet (but since few people place their data anywhere near column IV, that requirement usually won't affect you).

```
       A        B       C       D       E       F       G       H
1   \D          {getlabel "Enter SSN#: ";SSN#}
2               {if @length(SSN#)<>11}{ERR_VIEW "SSN";"SS_HELP"}{branch \D}
3               [...the macro continues processing...]
4
5   ERR_VIEW    {define ERR_NAME;ERR_NEXT}
6               {recalc ERR_MENU}
7   ERR_2       {menubranch ERR_MENU}{branch ERR_2}
8
9   ERR_\MENU                  ----> ERROR  <----
10              Problem with the SSN. Press Return for more information.
11              {dispatch ERR_NEXT}
12
13  ERR_NAME    SSN
14  ERR_NEXT    SS_HELP
15
16  SSN#        34
17  SS_HELP     SSN# must be 11 characters.  Press Return to continue.
18              {?}{esc}{return}
19
20
```

Figure 26-5

In this example, we'll use a social security number as the basis for the application. The most relevant form of error checking for a social security number is to evaluate the length of the entry—it should be eleven characters. The macro begins with a prompt and stores the resulting entry in a cell named Ssn#.

The {if} statement that follows contains a conditional formula to check if the length of the entry in SSN# is not equal to 11 (this is another example of the double-negative condition.[63] Essentially, this statement says, if the length of the social security number is anything but eleven characters, then run a subroutine called Err_view. Otherwise ignore the instruction to run Err_view and continue reading on the next line (where, presumably, the data entry routine would continue).

Since all the action lies with the subroutine Err_view, we'll assume that the entry was not eleven characters long and that the macro has read the instruction to the right of the {if} command. Note that the subroutine call also passes two parameters to the subroutine, Ssn and Ss_help.

The first line of the subroutine (which appears on row 5) stores the passed parameters in the cells named Err_name and Err_next. It then recalculates the range, named Err_menu, that contains the custom menu on rows 9 and 10. That should tip you that Err_menu contains a string formula; the {recalc} command updates that formula. Here it is:

```
+"Problem with the "&ERR_NAME&"; press Return for more information."
```

---

[63] For a thorough discussion of so-called "double-negative" conditional formulas, refer to the heading Error Trapping in the chapter Managing User Input.

This formula creates an error message by concatenating the string Ssn (which was the passed parameter stored in Err_name) into the middle of a sentence. That message forms the explanation line of the menu range that appears on rows 9 and 10. The very next macro instruction (on row 7) displays that menu. If, while the menu displays, the user presses the Escape key, the macro will read the {branch} instruction that follows and reread the {menubranch} command. That prevents the user from using the Escape key to break out of the menu.

The top line of the menu (row 9) is deceptive, because the label shown resides in cell B9 and extends across the screen. When you create a single choice menu like this, you want the inverse video menu pointer to extend across the entire control panel, with the message appearing in the middle as a prompt. Plan to use 76 characters total. Count the length of your message, subtract that from 76, and divide the difference in half. Edit the message label and insert the resulting number of spaces both to the left and to the right of the message (you should end up with a label 76 characters long). When the message displays, it'll be centered in a menu bar the width of the control panel.

The menu is a single-choice menu; a stroke of the Return key will execute the macro instructions on row 11.

Row 11 contains a {dispatch} command, which is uncommon enough to warrant a little more explanation. {Dispatch} is similar to {branch}; it transfers control to another location. However, unlike {branch}, {dispatch} transfers control not to the address specified as its argument, but to the address stored in the cell that its argument identifies. In this case, it transfers control to the location named in Err_next. Err_next was used earlier to store the second parameter passed to this subroutine, and it contains the label SS_HELP. That's the means by which the calling routine tells the subroutine where it should branch in order to supply more detailed error-correcting information to the user. As each calling routine can supply a different location, this subroutine can be used to handle any kind of error.

The range named Ss_help contains a label that 1-2-3 will type into the control panel. Since no tilde follows, 1-2-3 won't enter it on the worksheet. The next command is a {get} command that will force the macro to pause until the user enters a keystroke (as the help message instructs). After the {get} command stores the keystroke (although it'll never be used), the macro cancels the label entry in the control panel by pressing the Escape key, and returns control to the calling routine. Specifically, control returns to row 2 of the macro, just to the right of the subroutine call. The {branch} command located there transfers control back to the first line of the macro, which again prompts the user for a social security number. The macro then tests the entry again and, if this number is the proper length, the macro will continue reading on row 3 with the rest of the data-entry routine.

While this macro is useful and innovative, its mechanism is also a little obscure. If you're using Release 2.2, you can use a slightly simpler (but just as effective) technique.

	A	B	C	D	E	F	G	H
1	\D	{getlabel "Enter SSN#:";SSN#}
2		{if @length(SSN#)<>11}{ERR_VIEW "SSN#";"SS_HELP"}{branch\D}
3		[...the macro continues processing...]
4	
5	ERR_VIEW	{define ERR_NAME;ERR_NEXT}
6		{indicate" ----> ERROR <----
7		{getlabel +"Problem with the "&ERR_NAME&". Press Return for mo
8		{indicate}
9		{dispatch ERR_NEXT}
10	
11	ANS
12	
13	ERR_NAME	SSN#
14	ERR_NEXT	SS_HELP
15	
16	SSN#	34
17	SS_HELP	SSN# must be 11 characters. Press Return to continue.
18		{?}{esc}{return}
19	
20	

Figure 26-6

We've eliminated two range names and obviated the need to embed a macro command inside a string formula. {Indicate} and {getlabel}, by virtue of their new capabilities in 2.2, take the place of the {menubranch} command in this application, displaying a full-width indicator and displaying a dynamic prompt.

Showing a Message on the Screen

This technique provides a simple way to customize the display of an on-screen message. In the following example, we'll use a message that tells the user the name of the report that is being printed.

```
        A        B         C         D       E       F       G       H
1   \E      {PRN_MSG SUMMARY}
2           {quit}
3
4   PRN_MSG {define PRN_NAME}
5           {indicate "PRINT"}
6           {windowsoff}{paneloff}
7           {let MSG_SCRN;@repeat(" ";25)&"Printing "&PRN_NAME&" ..."}
8           +{home}{pgdn}
9           {windowson}
10          {windowsoff}{esc 3}
11          /ppr{PRN_NAME}~agpq
12          {windowson}{panelon}
13          {return}
14
15  PRN_NAME SUMMARY
```

Figure 26-7

The first command calls a subroutine, Prn_msg, and passes to it a parameter containing the string Summary. Control transfers to row 4 where a {define} command stores the parameter in the cell named Prn_name. That name will later be used to supply the name of the report in the message to the user.

Beginning in row 6, the macro freezes the screen, and assigns a label to the cell Msg_scrn. That label consists of 25 leading blank spaces, the word Printing, and the name of the report. The next command begins writing a formula by entering a plus sign and then pointing at a location. Although there's no indication of it from the macro code itself, the location the cell pointer is pointing to is the named range Msg_scrn. Since that screen contains the message, when in the next line the macro unfreezes the worksheet portion of the screen, that message appears highlighted.

The macro immediately re-freezes the worksheet portion of the screen (keeping the message on the screen), and cancels the formula entry (by pressing the Escape key three times).

The commands on row 11 print the report. The macro supplies the print range for the report by using the same label it already used to supply the report name in the screen message, but this time it uses that label in a new way. When the / Print Printer Range command prompts for a range to print (we are using the term "prompts" loosely; remember that because the screen is frozen you won't see 1-2-3's "Enter Print range:" prompt), the macro uses Prn_name as a subroutine: {PRN_NAME}. The subroutine types the label it contains as the print range, presses the Return key, prints the report and issues a form feed (using the commands Align Go Page Quit).

As soon as 1-2-3 regains control (and when that happens depends on whether you have a print spooler or print buffer, what size either may be, and how lengthy the report is) from the printing commands, the macro unfreezes the entire screen and returns control to the calling routine.

In Release 2.2, you might want to draw more attention to the screen by blanking out the row column frame and placing your message in the now-expanded indicator panel. The following macro lets you do just that.

	A	B	C	D	E	F	G	H
1	\P	{PRN_MSG "SUMMARY"}						
2		{quit}						
3								
4	PRN_MSG	{define PRN_NAME}						
5		{windowsoff}{paneloff clear}						
6		{frameoff}{indicate +"PRINT: Printing "&PRN_NAME&"..."}						
7		+{home}{pgdn}						
8		{windowson}						
9		{windowsoff}{esc 3}						
10		/ppr{PRN_NAME}~agpq						
11		{windowson}{panelon}						
12		{frameon}{indicate}						
13		{return}						
14								
15	PRN_NAME	SUMMARY						
16								
17								
18								
19								
20								

Figure 26-8

This macro still uses the positioning technique of its predecessor, but constructs its message by resolving a string formula in {indicate}'s argument. This also eliminates the need for the range name Msg_scrn.

Highlighting an Onscreen Message

Since the object of using the screen is often a question of attracting the user's attention, you'll want to have visually interesting techniques. One of the best highlights not just one cell, but an entire area of the screen containing a message. Macros like this, which can be used in many different settings, should be as portable as possible. They'll nearly always be written as subroutines so they can serve all the other routines that would benefit from their use.

Here's the macro.

```
        A       B       C       D       E       F       G
1  \A       {goto}CLEAR~
2           {paneloff}{windowsoff}
3           {goto}SCR~{goto}CTR~
4           /rncMSG{windowson}~
5           {windowsoff}~
6           {get ANS}
7           {home}{panelon}
8
9  ANS      ~
10
```

Figure 26-9

\A   {goto}CLEAR~
{paneloff}{windowsoff}

Row 1 of the macro moves the cell pointer to a cell that is empty and free from any formatting symbols that would clutter the control panel. Row 2 freezes the control panel and the screen.

{goto}SCR~{goto}CTR~

Row 3 moves the cell pointer to the top left cell of a screen you want to display. In the middle of the screen is a cell containing a message. The next command moves the cell pointer to the cell containing the message. You could omit the second { goto } command; it's only there for nit pickers. Its only purpose is to align the flashing cursor under the message string contained in the cell named Ctr. Without it, the flashing cursor will remain in the top left cell of the screen, where the cell pointer was last moved.

/rncMSG{windowson}~

Row 4 initiates a Range Name Create command, and specifies the name of a range that already exists. The cell named Ctr is at the center of that named range, which is three cells high and three cells wide. The next command on the same row unfreezes the screen, then presses the Return key to enter the name Msg as the range to create. The screen will respond to the existing range name by highlighting that range, which surrounds the cell containing the message. Since the control panel is still frozen, there's no visible prompt showing there from the Range Name Create command. This is an example of an advanced macro command's ability to intercede in the middle of a normal 1-2-3 command menu (in this case, in the middle of the Range Name Create command)—something nothing but an advanced macro command can do.

{windowsoff}~

On row 5, the macro re-freezes the screen, then presses the Return key to accept the current range definition for the named range Msg. However, since the screen was refrozen, the highlight remains on the screen even though the command has been completed.

{get ANS}

The {get} command makes the macro wait for a keystroke, effectively leaving the message on the screen as long as the user needs to read it. Since it will wait for a keystroke, part of the message should inform the user to press any key to continue. Since the {get} command requires that the keystroke be stored in a cell, Ans was designated for that purpose; however, the keystroke will never be used.

{home}{panelon}

After the user presses a key, the macro moves the cell pointer to the home location and reenables 1-2-3 to update the control panel once again.

This technique is a perfect candidate for enhancement with 1-2-3 Release 2.2. You can achieve an outstanding effect with some help from a couple of 2.2's new features.

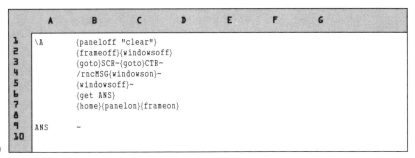

Figure 26-10

Since the first step was to clear the control panel, we've used the {paneloff "clear"} command. It's worth noting here that the "clear" argument, like all literal text, should be placed in quotation marks to ensure that 1-2-3 doesn't interpret it as a range name. (For example, if you don't delete the range named Clear, the macro will unceremoniously halt, as {paneloff} becomes confused.) The second step is to clear the worksheet frame with the {frameoff} command, leaving the screen completely clear except for the highlighted message in the middle of the screen. This can be a real attention-getter.

increasing portability

There are two steps you should take to make this routine work well as a subroutine. First, have the calling routine contain a {let} command to assign a message string to the cell named Ctr. In that way each calling routine can place whatever message it wants on the screen and use this routine to display that message. Second, exclude the {home} command at the end of the macro. Ideally, you would leave a blank line in the macro at that point, and use a {let} command to assign a location to which the cell pointer would return. The following is an example of the revision. Note that the calling routine is now named \A, while the message routine is now named Disp (for "Display").

	A	B	C	D	E	F	G
1	\A	{let CTR;"Working, please wait"}					
2		{let LOC1;"DATA1"}					
3		{DISP}					
4		{branch PRINT}					
5							
6							
7	DISP	{goto}CLEAR~					
8		{paneloff}{windowsoff}					
9		{goto}SCR~{goto}CTR~					
10		/rncMSG{windowson}~					
11		{windowsoff}~					
12		{get ANS}					
13		{goto}{LOC1}~					
14		{panelon}					
15		{return}					
16							
17	LOC1						
18		{return}					
19							
20	ANS	~					

Figure 26-11

While we've shown only one calling routine here, any number of the routines could call Disp as a subroutine. Each calling routine should contain {let} commands that assign a message string to the cell named Ctr, and that assign a location to which the cell pointer should return at the end of the subroutine.

The 2.2 version of the Disp subroutine would look like this:

```
     A         B          C         D       E       F       G
 7  DISP      {paneloff "clear"}
 8            {frameoff}{windowsoff}
 9            {goto}SCR~{goto}CTR~
10            /rncMSG{windowson}~
11            {windowsoff}~
12            {get ANS}
13            {goto}{LOC1}~
14            {panelon}{frameon}
15            {return}
16
17  LOC1      DATA1
18            {return}
19
20  ANS       ~
```

Figure 26-12

Managing Multiple Graphs

Graphs can be a highly effective way to present numeric information. Unfortunately, since they are difficult to automate, many 1-2-3 applications rely exclusively on worksheet displays. The graphics prospects are much more inviting with 1-2-3 Release 2.2, which includes the {graphon} command and its complement, {graphoff}. The technique that follows shows how you can make your applications both more informative and more visually exciting by creating a graph slide show. Later, a macro is presented which customizes a series of graphs one after another.

The screen below contains five years of financial data for the fictious "Amalgamated Industries Incorporated." Six graphs have been created which show various combinations of financial ratios. These graphs are numbered 001 through 006—the result of a numbering scheme you'll probably want to use over and over. It assures the correct sequencing of the graphs in an ordered list, so that graph 10 doesn't appear before graph 2. It also leaves plenty of room for future expansion—it's almost certain you'll never need more than 999 named graphs.

```
       A        B        C        D       E       F       G
 1  AMALGAMATED INDUSTRIES INCORPORATED      FIVE YEAR FINANCIAL REVIEW
 2
 3  Liquidity Measures:          1986    1987    1988    1989    1990
 4  Current Ratio                 1.5     7.1     1.5     2.3     1.7
 5  Rcvbls as % Curr Assets      44.4%   32.6%   60.4%   26.6%   34.6%
 6  Inv as % Curr Assets         22.2%   14.4%   25.0%   20.9%   25.2%
 7  Avg Coll Period (days)       41.1    33.3    49.7    31.3    29.1
 8  Avg Pmt Period (days)        83.1    88.8   102.7    81.6    81.3
 9
10  Debt Measures:
11  Times Interest Earned         2.7     2.8     3.6     4.2     4.8
12  Tot Debt as % Tot Assets     63.2%   67.4%   52.5%   51.3%   41.5%
13
14  Profitability Measures:
15  Gross Profit Margin          34.2%   38.1%   54.0%   63.2%   63.1%
16  Operating Profit Margin      11.4%   11.9%   14.3%   24.1%   22.3%
17  Net Profit Margin             5.0%    3.8%    5.2%   10.3%    9.6%
18  Return on Investment         10.5%   10.4%   13.2%   22.6%   17.6%
19  Return on Owner's Equity     21.9%   16.2%   14.4%   27.6%   15.9%
20
```

Figure 26-13

The macro below shows how these graphs can be displayed one after another. A graph name table (a feature of 2.2) appears in row 31; it describes each graph in the file. We explain the macros right after this screen.

```
        A        B         C        D       E       F       G
21  \G          {for ANS;1;6;1;G_VIEW}~
22              {quit}
23
24  G_VIEW      {graphon @right(@string(1000+ANS;0);3)}
25              {wait @now+@time(0;0;SEC)}
26              {return}
27
28  ANS         ?
29  SEC         2
30
31  NAME        TYPE        FIRST TITLE
32  001         Line        Profit Margins
33  002         Line        Current Ratio & Times Interest Earned
34  003         Bar         Collection vs Payment Periods
35  004         Stack-Bar   Rcvbls & Inv as % of Curr Assets
36  005         Bar         Return on Investment and Equity
37  006         Bar         Debt to Assets
38
39
40
41
```

Figure 26-14

Let's begin with \G. It does little more than employ a {for} loop to run G_view six times. That shouldn't be too surprising, as there are six graphs to view. Turning to G_view, note that it basically consists of a {graphon} command and a {wait} command. So it's not too difficult to discover that G_view displays the graph and pauses for a certain amount of time—2 seconds in this case. The real trick is using {for} to efficiently feed graph names into {graphon}. Let's examine the formula in {graphon} more closely.

```
{graphon @right(@string(1000+ANS;0);3)}
```

When G_view is first called, Ans is equal to 1. Adding 1000 gives 1001, and taking the rightmost three characters of the string "1001" yields "001", precisely the name of the first graph. Each time G_view is called, Ans is incremented, so the next graph to be viewed is "002". This procedure continues until each of the six graphs have been displayed.

{Graphon} gives you something you can't get with any other command in 1-2-3: the ability to continue running the macro while the graph is being displayed. In a slide show example like this one, you could probably get away with the 2.01 method, substituting the following macro sequence for G_view:

```
G_VIEW     {let TMP;@right(@string(1000+ANS;0);3)}
           /gnu{TMP}~
           {return}
```

If you're working exclusively in Release 2.01, this is the best you can do. The user will have to press a key to clear each graph, but they will see the same graphs that the Release 2.2 user would see, aside from the improvements in layout.

If, however, you're looking for the ability to change the attributes of a series of named graphs, you'll have to use the 2.2 method outlined below. Having to view each graph before the macro changes it defeats the purpose of the macro, and there's no close substitute for this functionality in 2.01. To illustrate this idea, consider the consequences of copying the .WK1 file to a laptop computer which has a monochrome LCD display. When color isn't available to distinguish graph ranges, graphs are best displayed in cross-hatching with the Black and White (B&W) option. The following macro makes the necessary changes in each of the named graphs.

```
          A         B         C         D         E         F         G
41   \C            {paneloff}
42                 {for ANS;1;6;1;G_CHANGE}~
43                 {quit}
44
45   G_CHANGE      {let G_NAME;@right(@string(1000+ANS;0);3)}
46                 {graphon G_NAME;"nodisplay"}
47                 /go
48                 bqq
49                 /gnc{G_NAME}~q
50                 {return}
51
52   G_NAME        006
53                 {return}
54
55
```

Figure 26-15

The \C macro uses the same technique as \G in the previous macro. The routine named G_change is called six times, one for each graph. You might notice that the name is calculated and stored instead of being used directly in {graphon}. This is because the name has to be used later to re-Create the named graph, thereby retaining its settings in the catalog of named graphs.

The next thing to notice is that {graphon} is being used with the optional argument "nodisplay". This prevents the graph from flashing up on the screen and permits the macro to go about the business of changing the graph to black and white and then creating it again. The operation of this macro is completely unobtrusive—you don't even notice it's running.

This same technique can be used to make any type of change to a series of graphs. For example, you might want to change the grid pattern on all the graphs, or you might want to set the Y-Scale to manual and set the same upper limit on the graphs, so even if they contain different highs and lows, they can be compared to each other without having to mentally re-scale the numbers.

Here's an example of another change you might want to make to the graph. If you'll recall, the screen which contained the data had the company name in cell A1. We can easily place "AMALGAMATED INDUS-TRIES INCORPORATED" in the second graph title by giving it a range name (like C_name) and plugging that name into each graph. That's exactly what the next macro does:

```
         A         B         C        D        E        F        G
41  \C        {paneloff}
42            {for ANS;1;6;1;G_CHANGE}~
43            {quit}
44
45  G_CHANGE  {let G_NAME;@right(@string(1000+ANS;0);3)}
46            {graphon G_NAME;"nodisplay"}
47            /gotsx{esc}
48            \C_NAME~qq
49            /gnc{G_NAME}~q
50            {return}
51
52  G_NAME    006
53            {return}
54
55
```

Figure 26-16

This macro is just like the previous one, but instead of changing from color to black and white, it selects the second title, clears it with the x{esc} technique, and inserts the range name C_name. The macro creates the graph again and goes on to the next one in the series.

Displaying Full-Screen Messages

There may be times when you'll want to break out of the familiar 1-2-3 screen to display a text message in full-screen mode. The effectiveness of the technique varies with the speed of the computer 1-2-3 is running on; the faster the computer, the better it works. Note that this technique is really most appropriate for 1-2-3 Releases 2.0 and 2.01, as Release 2.2 provides you the capability to clear the screen in the {frameoff} {paneloff "clear"} combination.

Try the following macro; we'll review its operation afterward.

```
         A         B         C        D        E        F        G        H
1   \A        {paneloff}
2             {indicate ""}
3             {open "CON";""}
4             {for COUNTER;0;34;1;LINE}
5             {writeln "                              DISK ERROR!"}
6             {write "                    Press any key to continue."}
7             {for COUNTER;0;10;1;LINE}
8             {close}
9             {beep 4}{beep 4}{beep 4}
10            {get COUNTER}
11            {panelon}{indicate}~
12
13  LINE      {writeln ""}
14
15  COUNTER
```

Figure 26-17

you can
treat the
screen like a
file and
write to it

The method uses the macro file manipulation commands, {open} and {writeln}. However, instead of manipulating a file, you'll use those commands to manipulate the screen. You can do that because just as you can address files by name with the file manipulation commands, you can use them to address the screen by a name—Con. Con is a contraction of the term console which, in DOS, refers to your computer's screen.

```
\A  {paneloff}
    {indicate""}
```

con is
another
name for
the screen

The first two rows of the macro freeze the control panel and remove the mode indicator.

```
{open CON;"m"}
```

Row 3 enables 1-2-3 to begin writing characters to Con, or the screen. Essentially, this command treats the screen as if it were a file and opens it in modify mode.

```
{for COUNTER;0;34;1;LINE}
```

Row 4 employs a {for} command to call a subroutine named Line. The {for} command will repeat the subroutine 34 times. (The technical breakdown of this {for} command is as follows: It will use a counter stored in a cell named Counter; the counter will begin at 0 and proceed to 34 by increments of 1 with each repetition of the subroutine named Line.) Since the subroutine Line is being run 34 times at this point in the macro, let's look at that next.

```
LINE {writeln ""}
```

The cell named Line contains a single {writeln} command that contains a null string as its argument (designated by two quotation marks with nothing between). The effect of this command will be to scroll downward one line (remember that {writeln} issues a carriage return/linefeed sequence) without writing anything.

One of the challenges of using file manipulation commands is that the action of the macro can change depending on the row of the screen on which the macro begins writing. When you use file manipulation commands to write to a file, the byte pointer establishes the location to which data will be written in the file. When those commands write to the screen, an invisible corollary to the byte pointer determines the screen location to which you will write characters. Unfortunately, the action of this corollary pointer is much more difficult to control, making it more difficult to control where on the screen you write data. Here's the problem—followed by the solution.

The first time you write anything to the screen in a given worksheet, you'll start writing at the top left corner of the screen. Each carriage return/linefeed sequence will advance the pointer down one row on the screen. When the pointer reaches the bottom row (that is, row 25, where 1-2-3's status line resides) and a carriage return/linefeed sequence occurs, the next line of data is written in row 25, everything else shifts upward one row, and whatever formerly resided on the first row of the screen disappears. If you continue to write new lines of data, eventually the entire worksheet display will have been pushed off the screen and replaced by whatever you've written through {write} or {writeln} commands. When you set out to create a full screen error message, that is exactly what you want to do.

However, before you write to the screen, you may wonder how many blank lines you'll need in order to clear the screen. The answer depends on where the pointer is. If you've already moved it to row 25 through previous {writeln} commands, then you only have to write 25 new lines to fully replace the current screen with you message screen. But if the pointer is on row 1, you'll have to write nearly twice that number, because you must first work your way down to row 25 before the screen will begin to scroll. So far, so good. However, if you ever display a graph, that automatically resets the pointer to row 1 of the screen.

Since you can never know where the pointer is, it makes sense to always write enough lines to the screen to begin from row 1 and completely erase the current screen. If the pointer is already at the bottom of the screen, those extra lines will only scroll off the screen.

Some of the lines you use to clear the screen can contain messages. If you precede the message with enough blank lines and follow it with enough blank lines, you can replace the worksheet screen with one containing your message.

This macro always issues enough line feeds (34) to begin from the very top of the screen. If the cursor is already at the bottom of the screen, they're superfluous: they take a moment more to scroll by but they don't adversely affect the macro.

```
{writeln "DISK ERROR!"}
```

The next line uses another {writeln} command to write a message ("DISK ERROR!") on the next line

```
{write "Press any key to continue."}
```

This line of the macro places another message on the line directly below the first message.

```
{for COUNTER;0;10;1;LINE}
{close}
```

This line adds 10 more blank lines, scrolling the message lines upward ten lines to the middle of the screen. The {close} command ends access to the console by the macro.

```
{beep 4}{beep 4}{beep 4}
{get COUNTER}
```

The three {beep} commands call the user's attention to the screen. The {get} command makes the macro pause and wait for a keystroke. Since the screen message tells the user to press any key to proceed, you can expect that once the user has read the message, a keystroke will be forthcoming. The {get} command has to store that keystroke, even though in this case there's no use for it, so it stores it in the cell named Counter. Since both {for} commands are finished running, there's no problem using Counter to store this keystroke. The next time you run the macro, the {for} command will overwrite the stored keystroke.

{panelon}{indicate}~

Finally, the {panelon} command restores 1-2-3's ability to update the control panel and {indicate} restores the default mode indicator to the screen. The tilde that follows it updates the screen so the worksheet displays once again.

There's an alternate approach you could use to eliminate the extra {writeln} commands on those occasions when the cursor already resides at the bottom of the screen.

Use a routine to change the value stored in a predetermined cell (we'll call that a flag) so that the value is zero if the cursor is at the top of the screen (before you've run the macro for the first time or after you've displayed a graph), and one when the cursor is at the bottom of the screen already (after you've run the macro at least once). Use a simple {let} command to assign the value of the flag after each such event. For example, if you name a cell Flag, after this macro has run, include the command {let FLAG;1}. In any macro that displays a graph, include the command {let FLAG;0}.

The {if} command in the rewritten macro below calls the subroutine named Addline to add the extra 24 lines needed in the event the cursor is at the top of the screen. If it's at the bottom already, just 10 are needed before the message and another 10 afterward.

	A	B	C	D	E	F	G	H
1	\A	{paneloff}						
2		{indicate ""}						
3		{open "CON";"m"}						
4		{if FLAG=0}{ADDLINE}						
5		{for COUNTER;0;12;1;LINE}						
6		{writeln "					DISK ERROR!"}	
7		{write "				Press any key to continue."}		
8		{for COUNTER;0;10;1;LINE}						
9		{close}						
10		{beep 4}{beep 4}{beep 4}						
11		{get COUNTER}						
12		{panelon}{indicate}~						
13								
14	LINE	{writeln ""}						
15								
16	COUNTER							
17								
18	ADDLINE	{for COUNTER;0;24;1;LINE}{let FLAG;1}						
19								
20								

Figure 26-18

You can make this macro a bit easier to revise if you place the message strings, currently written into the {writeln} command on row 6 and the {write} command on row 7, in separate cells and assign to each of those cells a named range. Here's the modified form; note the references to range names that appear in the commands on rows 6 and 7. The entries in cells D20 and B22, (the message strings) begin with quite a few leading spaces, so the entries may appear to reside several columns to the right, even though they do not.

	A	B	C	D	E	F	G	H
1	\A	{paneloff}						
2		{indicate ""}						
3		{open CON;"m"}						
4		{if FLAG=0}{ADDLINE}						
5		{for COUNTER;0;12;1;LINE}						
6		{writeln MSG1}						
7		{write MSG2}						
8		{for COUNTER;0;10;1;LINE}						
9		{close}						
10		{beep 4}{beep 4}{beep 4}						
11		{get COUNTER}						
12		{panelon}{indicate}~						
13								
14	LINE	{writeln ""}						
15								
16	COUNTER							
17								
18	ADDLINE	{for COUNTER;0;24;1;LINE}{let FLAG;1}						
19								
20	MSG1			DISK ERROR!				
21								
22	MSG2			Press any key to continue.				

Figure 26-19

A Full-Screen Message Using an XY Chart

Perhaps the most striking way to post a message on the screen is to do so with an XY chart—particularly if you have a color monitor. 1-2-3 has enough graphing options to allow you to create a message screen that contains both oversize and normally sized characters (see illustration).

In the following application, we'll assume that an error has occurred and use the message screen to deliver an error message. A step by step explanation of each macro follows the macros themselves. Here's a quick overview of how the pieces fit together.

1. \S: This is a set-up macro that will define the XY graph and store it under the name Msg. After running this macro, you should resave the worksheet to preserve those settings. Afterward, to display that

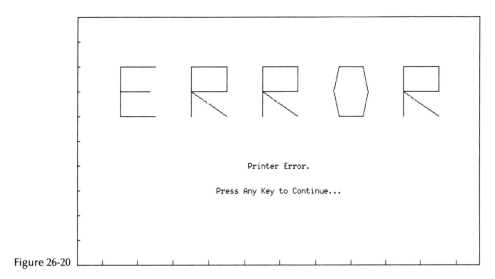

Figure 26-20

graph, just select / Graph Name Use and specify Msg. Since you'll only need to run the \S macro once, you can delete it from the worksheet once you have done so.

2. \P: This is the main routine you'll use to call the message-display and error-correction subroutines.

3. Err_view: This routine displays the error message and passes control to the error correction routine.

4. Err_next: The error-correction routine. Note that we haven't supplied the routine, it's merely implied, so if you try to run the routine, you'll get the error message "Macro: Invalid range in DISPATCH (B6)."

5. The values you see below the macros are the data from which the graph is constructed. Although once you've run the \S macro the graph will have been defined, the data itself isn't a part of those stored settings and must remain on the worksheet.

6. The range names referred to in the set-up macro are:
   Arange: B42..B80, Fdata: D42..D80, Frange: C42..C80, Xrange: A42..A80

	A	B	C	D	E	F	G	H
1	\P	{ERR_VIEW "Printer Error.";P_HELP}						
2								
3	ERR_VIEW	{paneloff}						
4		{define ERR_NAME;ERR_NEXT}						
5		/qnuMSG~q						
6		{dispatch ERR_NEXT}						
7								
8	ERR_NEXT	P_HELP						
9								
10								
11								
12	\S	{paneloff}/grgtxoc		(Setup Macro)				
13		symu1~fhqsxmu1~.1~fhq						
14		fglfnqdfFDATA~cqq						
15		xXRANGE~aARANGE~						
16		bARANGE~cARANGE~						
17		dARANGE~eARANGE~						
18		fFRANGE~ncMSG~q						
19								
20	XRANGE	ARANGE	FRANGE	FDATA				
21	0.6		0.3	Press Any Key to Continue...				
22	0.6		0.4	Printer Error.				
23								
24	0.25	0.8						
25	0.15	0.8						
26	0.15	0.6						
27	0.25	0.6						
28								
29	0.15	0.7						
30	0.235	0.7						
31								
32	0.35	0.6						
33	0.35	0.8						
34	0.45	0.8						
35	0.45	0.7						
36	0.35	0.7						
37	0.45	0.6						
38								
39	0.55	0.6						
40	0.55	0.8						
41	0.65	0.8						
42	0.65	0.7						
43	0.55	0.7						
44	0.65	0.6						
45								
46	0.835	0.6						
47	0.765	0.6						
48	0.75	0.7						
49	0.765	0.8						
50	0.835	0.8						
51	0.85	0.7						
52	0.835	0.6						
53								
54	0.95	0.6						
55	0.95	0.8						
56	1.05	0.8						
57	1.05	0.7						
58	0.95	0.7						
59	1.05	0.6						
60								

Figure 26-21

We'll skip the details of the graph-definition macro (you can keystroke through it if you want to see each of the settings it establishes) and concentrate on the macro you'll be using each time you want an XY graph-generated message.

The main routine in row 1 calls a subroutine, Err_view, and passes to it two parameters, the string "Print Error." and the string "P_HELP". The subroutine will use those parameters as part of the error message in the graph and to designate the routine to which control will transfer after this one, respectively.

The first line of the subroutine Err_view, in row 4, freezes the control panel. There's no need to freeze the worksheet portion of the screen as the only activity you'll want to hide will be the menu selections 1-2-3 uses to display the graph.

The {define} command on row 5 stores the passed parameters. In this case, 1-2-3 will store the string "Printer Error." in a range (cell D22) named Err_name. That range is a data-label range for the graph, so the string "Printer Error." will become a label on the graph. 1-2-3 will store the string "P_HELP" in a cell named Err_next. That cell will designate the location to which the macro will branch—possibly for error-correction assistance—after the graph displays.

Row 6 contains the heart of the subroutine: the keystrokes for displaying the graph itself. If you're unfamiliar with displaying graphs in macros, you should note that 1-2-3 will force the macro to pause when the graph appears on the screen—there's no need for an {?} (interactive) command or {get} command to do that. Release 2.2 gives you some more flexibility in this regard; the 2.2 version of the macro presented later uses some of this new capability.

The next row contains a {dispatch} command to transfer control to the position that is named in the range Err_next. {Dispatch} is an unusual command; it transfers control like a {branch} command, but it does so indirectly. The argument in the {dispatch} command identifies a location that contains yet another location name. {Dispatch} will transfer control to that last named location. In this case, {dispatch ERR_NEXT} transfers control to P_help, which is the location name stored in Err_next. (Although we haven't written an example macro for P_help, it should be specific to the error-correcting needs of the calling routine. Until you do supply a routine to branch to, Err_view will terminate in an error after displaying the graph.)

Observe how the structure of Err_view enables any other macro to use this subroutine. Once a calling routine passes parameters containing the specific error message and the name of the error-correcting routine to branch to, Err_view will customize itself to meet the calling routine's needs. That makes Err_view a versatile subroutine you can call from any main macro routine.

As you write the error-correcting routine to follow, keep in mind that, although separate from Err_view, both routines are part of the same subroutine. Accordingly, the error-correcting routine should either end with a {return} command to return control to the calling routine on row 1, or, if you don't wish to return control to the calling routine, with a {restart} command to cancel the subroutine nesting chain. If you choose to use {restart}, keep in mind that it will cancel all open subroutine calls, so if \P were a subroutine of some other calling routine, {restart} would cancel that relationship as well.

If you're using 1-2-3 Release 2.2, you might want to take advantage of the {graphon} command which, among other things, will let you display the "graph message" for a few seconds and then continue automatically to the next screen. This might be particularly helpful to novice users who might not notice the "Press any key" message in the graph. Here's the new macro, modified to accomplish that objective:

```
           A        B        C        D        E        F        G        H
1    \P          {ERR_VIEW "Printer Error.";P_HELP}
2
3    ERR_VIEW    {paneloff}
4                {define ERR_NAME;ERR_NEXT}
5                {graphon MSG}{wait @now+@time(0;0;2)}
6                {dispatch ERR_NEXT}
7
8    ERR_NEXT    P_HELP
9
10
11
12   \S          {paneloff}/grgtxoc          (Setup macro)
13               symul~fhqsxmul.1~1.1~fhq
14               fglfnqdfFDATA~cqq
15               xXRANGE~aARANGE~
16               bARANGE~cARANGE~
17               dARANGE~eARANGE~
18               fFRANGE~ncMSG~q
19
20   XRANGE      ARANGE   FRANGE   FDATA
21       0.6
22       0.6              0.4 Printer Error.
23
```

Figure 26-22

The major difference between this macro and the preceding one is that the /gnu command has been replaced by {graphon}. While both result in drawing the graph named Msg on the screen, the new command permits the macro to continue processing while that graph is displayed. Since the macro continues to run, there's no need for a message for the user to

"Press Any Key..." After two seconds have elapsed, as specified in the {wait} command, the macro branches to P_help.

It's important to realize that the graph will continue to display even after control is transferred to P_help, making it possible for P_help to display a graphical information screen. If your intention is to return to the worksheet display, it's a good idea to precede the {dispatch} command with {graphoff}, to update the screen before macro control is transferred.

Displaying Your Own Logo When the Worksheet Loads

Most professionally developed applications display a logo screen, often with a copyright notice. While achieving this effect with 1-2-3 and macros is not a simple task, you might be surprised to learn how impressive the display can be, as the screen below illustrates:

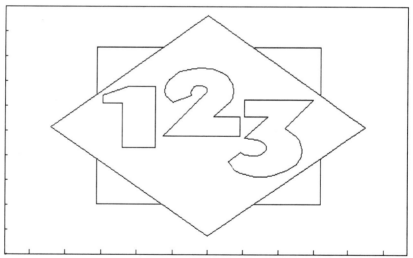

Figure 26-23

As you might have guessed, we use the same basic technique as the XY-graph error message in the previous macro. The difficult part is getting an appropriate set of data points. This data points for this graph were produced by laying graph paper on top of a 1-2-3 brochure and plotting the points manually. It took a couple of hours to complete, but it renders a display that is simply unavailable unless you're an assembly-language programmer and you're willing to write an add-in. The data set is too extensive to print in the book, but it's available on the optional disk in the same file that contains this macro.

	A	B	C	D	E	F	G	H
1								
2	\0		Press any key to see the 1-2-3 logo...					
3			{get ANS}{esc}					
4			{graphon "LOGO"}					
5			{wait @now+@time(0;0;3)}					
6			{graphoff}					
7			{branch NXT_STEP}					
8								
9	ANS		~					
10								
11	NXT_STEP		{quit}					
12								
13								
14								
15								

Figure 26-24

The autoexecuting macro, \0, is a typical macro to display a logo. It displays the graph named "Logo," pauses for 3 seconds, and continues on to the routine called Nxt_step, which in this case, just halts the macro.

When you see the logo graph in action, you'll notice that it has a slight animation effect. This is because the same numbers are repeated in more than one graph range, so they are re-drawn each time in a different color. Unfortunately, this is most noticeable on an 8088-based computer, whereas most macros work best with a fast machine. If you look closely at the graph definition for the Error Message Graph, you'll notice the same thing. The same range of numbers is defined for each of the A through F ranges, lending an animation effect.

Dressing Up Displays Using the ASCII-No LICS-Screen Driver

Now that you're acquainted with the fundamentals of screen control, let's venture a little further. Many of you won't find the techniques that follow useful for applications you develop for others because it assumes a configuration of 1-2-3 that few people use. If developing for others is your sole purpose you may want to skip to the next section. However, even if that's the case, you will find the reading worthwhile. The discussion will broaden your understanding of 1-2-3 and may surprise you with options you never knew existed.

This technique employs an alternate screen driver for 1-2-3 known as an ASCII (American Standard Code for Information Interchange) screen driver. But before we introduce the techniques themselves, let's review what a screen driver is and what makes an ASCII screen driver special.

A character (in other words, a letter, a number, or a symbol) is generally made up of a configuration of dots. While 1-2-3 tells your computer which character to display, your computer controls the actual appearance of that character.

1-2-3 tells your computer which character to display by sending it a certain value. A list of values and their corresponding characters are known as a character set. The ASCII character set standardizes the first 128 out of a possible 256 values and characters. [64]

ASCII uses only seven bits out of the possible eight bits to define its characters, which leaves 128 values unassigned to characters. Under ASCII, the characters corresponding to the values between 128 and 256 are left to the discretion of computer designers. On the IBM PC, these characters are a diverse mixture including international characters, the tops, sides, and corners of boxes, and many other characters, and are commonly referred to as the IBM graphics characters. Though most computers have implemented the same characters as the IBM PC, not all have. The original Wang PC, for example, displayed a different set of characters for the values from 129 through 256 than does the IBM PC.

By default, 1-2-3 uses a character set, called the Lotus International Character Set (LICS) that duplicates ASCII's first 128 characters and values. However, unlike ASCII, LICS assigns characters to bit values 129 through 256, overriding any hardware-based assignments for those values.

LICS uses the upper 128 values (from 129 to 256) to represent characters that provide support for multinational use of spreadsheets. For example, if your office is in the United States and you are creating a worksheet for use in an office overseas, you might avail yourself of the English pound symbol, £, or the Japanese yen symbol, ¥.

displaying the entire LICS character set

If you're intrigued by LICS and want to explore it further, try the following exercise. Begin with a blank worksheet and follow these instructions:

---

[64] Why 256 possible characters? The answer is a bit technical. 1-2-3 sends a single byte to your computer to tell it what character to display. A byte consists of eight bits (the word "bit" is a contraction of the words binary digit). Each binary digit can either represent the value zero or the value one (which is all the numbers in a base two, or binary, number system). Since each bit can be one of two values and there are eight bits in a byte, there are 256 possible combinations ($2^8 = 256$); therefore, there can be at most 256 different characters represented by such a system.

Select:	/ Data Fill
Type:	A1..A255
Press:	Return Return Return `
Move:	To cell B1
Enter:	@char(A1)
Select:	/ Copy
Press:	Return
Enter:	B2..B255

using
@char

    The formulas in column B return the characters included in LICS. Those formulas reference the numbers in column A—numbers that represent individual LICS codes. The first visible character you'll see is LICS 32, the exclamation mark. As you look toward the end of the list, you'll see a variety of special characters unassociated with any key on your keyboard. You can use the @char function to display them anywhere on your worksheet. However, before you adopt any of them, try printing them on your printer—not all printers can print these characters.

    Some of the characters that appear toward the end of the list you generated are repeats of characters represented by lower LICS codes. For example, the caret (^) appears as LICS codes 94, 130, and 146. Range names, when displayed on a range name menu, appear sorted in ascending order by LICS code. If you use in a range name a character represented by more than one LICS code, such as a caret, that range name will assume the position allocated to the lowest LICS code by which it is represented. For example, a range name beginning with a caret will be positioned according to LICS code 94, not 130 or 146.

using
@code

    Incidentally, the @code function is the complement to the @char function. If you want to know the LICS code for a given character, enter that character into a cell, then reference that cell with the @code function. For example, if you place a tilde in cell A1, if in cell B1 you enter @code(A1), you'll see the LICS code for a tilde, 126. Before proceeding, save your sample worksheet under the name Codes.

    Although 1-2-3 is configured to display LICS by default, you can use ASCII instead. Since the lower 128 characters, which include all of the alphanumeric characters, are the same in both ASCII and LICS, most of the time you won't notice any difference between the two. It's when you're using the characters over 128 that you'll see changes. When 1-2-3 uses the default LICS driver, it displays international characters for the values over 128. When 1-2-3 uses the optional ASCII driver, it displays the computer-specific characters. If you're running 1-2-3 on an IBM machine, those will be IBM's graphics characters.

Using the ASCII screen driver, you might employ some of those graphics characters to surround on-screen messages with boxes or borders. However, these characters are most suited for on-screen display only; most printers will not print them properly. Accordingly, if you use them we advise you to keep them outside of your print ranges.

The install program allows you to change between ASCII and LICS screen drivers. To do this, load Install and select Advanced Options, Modify Current Driver Set, Text Display, (be careful to get this next choice right) Universal Text Display -ASCII- No LICS, Return to menu, and Save Changes, then either enter a new driver name (such as ASCII) or press Return to accept the current driver name,[65] and choose Yes to exit Install.

Having installed the ASCII screen driver, load 1-2-3 with that screen driver. If you named the driver 123, you only need to load 1-2-3 in the normal manner. However, if you called the driver set something else, such as ASCII, then you must enter 123 ascii. Once into the worksheet, you can display the same characters that your computer assigns to the upper 128 characters. However, the method by which you do so differs. In DOS, you display graphics characters by holding down the Alt key and typing a value on the numeric keypad. In 1-2-3, you use the @char function. With 1-2-3 running with the ASCII screen driver, the function @char(199) returns the same character that DOS would produce if you held down the Alt key and typed 199 on the numeric keypad. Retrieve the Codes file you earlier created and notice the difference in the characters numbered 129-256.

Here's an exercise you can try with the ASCII screen driver in effect. On a blank worksheet, use the following steps to create an opening screen for an imaginary accounting application.

Move:	To cell C4
Enter:	@char(201)&@repeat(@char(205);35)&@char(187)
Move:	To cell C5
Enter:	@char(186)

---

[65] If you accept the current name, you will modify the current driver set. However, you can instead create a new driver set and leave your existing one intact. If the prompt now says 123, that's the name of the driver set file that 1-2-3 automatically uses unless you specify otherwise. Let that contain the settings you expect to use most often. If you've just modified the driver settings to include an ASCII screen driver, you might substitute the name ASCII for the current name. Then, when you want to run 1-2-3 with the ASCII screen driver, instead of entering 123 at the DOS prompt, enter 123 ascii.

Move:	To cell G5
Enter;	@char(186)
Select	/ Copy
From range:	C5..G5
To range:	C6
Select:	/ Copy
From range:	C4
To range:	C12
Move:	To cell C12
Press:	Edit (F2)
Change:	Change @char(201) to @char(200); change @char(187) to @char(188).
Move:	To cell D6
Enter:	Johnson Accounting
Move:	To cell D7
Enter:	Systems, Inc.
Move:	To cell D9
Enter:	ACCOUNT MANAGER
Move:	To cell A20
Enter:	© 1988 by Johnson Accounting Systems, Inc., All Rights Reserved

using
compose
key
sequences

Although the @char function will produce characters that have values above 128, you can also produce some of the more common ones by using Compose sequences. A Compose sequence consists of holding down the Alt key and pressing the F1 key, then entering a specified key sequence (the characters you can produce with Compose and their related key sequences are listed in the back of your 1-2-3 manual).

Now that you've seen some of the interesting things you can do with the ASCII screen driver, you should also know about its weaknesses. You already know that, oftentimes, you cannot print such characters. You are also unable to import or export them, and use of the ASCII screen driver presents a potential compatibility problem. Let's take the import/export issue first.

you cannot import or export graphics characters

You can neither import nor export graphics characters produced with the upper 128 characters. For example, were you to create such characters with Edlin (DOS's editor) and save them in a text file, when you import that text file on the worksheet (perhaps through the File Import commands or the {read} macro command), the characters will have changed. Similarly, if you create graphics characters inside 1-2-3 and export them (perhaps through the Print File command or the {write} macro command), when you view them in DOS they will have changed. Further, most printers won't print these characters. Instead, they print a variety of other characters that destroy the effect created by the graphics characters.

such characters may not be compatible with other copies of 1-2-3

Remember that all of the characters associated with values above 128 will vary depending on whether you are using the Universal Text Display-ASCII-No LICS driver or not (all of 1-2-3's other screen drivers use LICS). If you create the screen described above with an ASCII driver, save the worksheet, and then reload 1-2-3 using a LICS screen driver. The graphics characters will change to other characters. And therein lies the principal weakness of developing macros with the ASCII screen driver: what the user of your macro sees depends on what screen driver is in use, and most people don't use the sole ASCII screen driver; they use one of the many LICS drivers. Unless you are developing these macros for personal use or can guarantee that the copies of 1-2-3 that will run your application will be using the ASCII screen driver, avoid using them.

Using Custom ASCII Drivers

If you want the ultimate in control over the screen, you'll want to run 1-2-3 under one of the custom ASCII screen drivers that enable you to control the location of the cursor as you write to the screen. [66] These screen drivers will enable you to do such things as create pop-up boxes on the screen.

The secret to mining the wealth of these drivers is knowing how to erase portions of the screen, how to change screen attributes (such as blinking and reverse video), and how to position the invisible cursor (when you write characters to the screen, 1-2-3 sends them to the cursor's current position; move the cursor and you move where the next character you write will appear).

---

[66] The alternate ASCII screen drivers are available from the World of Lotus on CompuServe. While these drivers appear to work with Release 2.01, they do not seem to work with Release 2.2, and they do not work with Release 3.

You erase portions of the screen, change its attributes, and position the cursor with escape sequences. An escape sequence is a sequence of characters that begins with the escape character. For example, {Esc}[K erases from the cursor position to the end of the line. To send that sequence to the screen, you'd use the command { write @char(27)&"[K" }.

Here are all the ASCII escape sequences you can use and their effect on the screen.

Table 26-1. ASCII Escape Sequences

Positioning The Cursor

Escape sequence	Effect
Esc [A	Move cursor up 1 character.
Esc [B	Move cursor down 1 character.
Esc [C	Move cursor right 1 character.
Esc [D	Move cursor left 1 character.
Esc [numberA	Move cursor number of characters up.
Esc [numberB	Move cursor number of characters down.
Esc [numberC	Move cursor number of characters right.
Esc [numberD	Move cursor number of characters left.
Esc [rownumber; colnumberH or Esc [rownumber; colnumberf	Move cursor to a specified position (specified as the intersection of a rownumber and a columnnumber, where the top left corner of the screen is $0,0$).
Esc [s	Save the cursor's current position.
Esc [u	Return cursor to last saved position.
Esc [K or Esc [0K	Erase from cursor to end of line.
Esc [1K	Erase from start of line to cursor.
Esc [2K	Erase entire line.
Esc [J or Esc [0J	Erase from cursor to end of screen.
Esc [1J	Erase from start of screen to cursor.
Esc [2J	Erase the entire screen.

Using Display Attributes

Escape sequence	Effect
Esc [number]	Set one attribute.
Esc [number;number]	Set two attributes (and so on).

In the preceding escape sequences, number can have the following values:

0	Turn all attributes off.
1	Turn bold attribute on.
4	Turn underscore attribute on.
5	Turn blink attribute on.
7	Turn reverse attribute on.

notes on
using the
escape
sequences

Where you see the notations number, colnumber, or rownumber in the left hand column in any of the preceding tables, substitute the appropriate number. Both rownumber and colnumber are offset numbers. For example, row 1 of the screen is 0, row 2 is 1, column 1 of the screen is 0, and column 2 is 1.

In escape sequences 1-2-3 discriminates between upper and lowercase characters. Be sure to use the form of each character represented in the preceding tables.

The second escape sequence in the last table, Esc [number; number], can encompass yet more arguments. For example you could turn on bold, underscore, blinking, and reverse video attributes with the command { write @char(27)&"[1;4;5;7m" }. Characters that you write to the screen thereafter, up until you issue some other attribute, would possess those attributes. You cannot turn off attributes selectively, you must turn them all off and then reenable the ones you want to continue to use. To turn off all attributes for the characters you subsequently write, issue the command { write @char(27)&"[0" }. To change the attributes of an existing set of characters, write the escape sequence for the attributes you wish to use, then position the cursor and rewrite the characters you wish to change.

27

Help Systems

To make your applications easier to learn, it often makes sense to provide on-line help screens, just like 1-2-3's. While you can't make your help system look exactly like 1-2-3's, you can imitate it closely.

Basic Systems

A Help system can be very simple: You can merely store a few screens full of explanatory text somewhere on the worksheet and write a macro that displays each screen. The following macro provides an example.

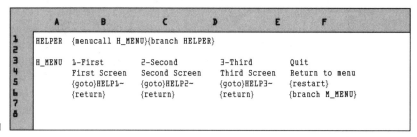

Figure 27-1

This macro might be called from another menu via a menu item named Help. It offers access to three separate help screens and can return to the main menu from which it was called. Each help routine positions

532

the cell pointer on the upper left cell of the help screen and redisplays the help menu (the {menucall} command will resume control after each routine ends). When the user finishes viewing the help screen, he or she selects Quit.

Another approach: To enable users of your macro to see both the help screen and the worksheet with which they need help, you might split the screen with the / Worksheet Window command. This technique is most valuable when the user wants help while performing some action, such as entering or viewing data.

There are three enhancements that you may want to make to the basic help model, relating to the following issues:

- *Memory Conservation:* Although the simplest place to store the text used in a help screen is right on the worksheet, you may need to reserve that space for data. So, instead of storing everything on the worksheet, a better method might be to store the information on another worksheet file or even in an ASCII file.

- *State Restoration:* The help macro usually moves the screen away from the work area. After the user has finished reading the help screen, the macro should restore the application to its former state— including redisplaying the former screen and reactivating the macro that was running prior to the help routine.

- *Context Sensitivity:* It's a safe bet that the topic on which the user desires help relates to the action the user is currently performing, or has just undertaken. There are a number of ways to read the context of the worksheet and automatically show the appropriate help screen.

In the balance of this chapter, we'll review techniques that respond to each of these concerns.

Minimizing Memory

File-Combine Method

Perhaps the most straightforward way to conserve worksheet space (and therefore memory) is to store most of the help information in another worksheet file. The macro transfers the help screens into the current worksheet with the / File Combine command as needed. The following macro illustrates the File Combine method of managing help information.

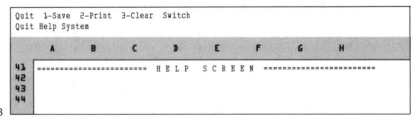

```
        A        B             C              D      E          F         G            H
1   HELPER   {goto}HELP_SCREEN~
2            {goto}HELP_RANGE~
3            {H_GET ONE}
4            {menucall H_1}
5            {blank HELP_RANGE}
6            {return}
7
8   H_GET    {define H_RNG}
9            /fccn
10           {H_RNG}~
11           x{esc}
12           C:\DATA\HELP.WK1~
13
14  H_RNG    SIX
15
16  H_1      Quit      1-Save          2-Print         3-Clear         Switch
17           Quit Help View Save help  View Print help View Clear help Help 2
18           {return}  {H_GET ONE}     {H_GET TWO}     {H_GET THREE}
19                     {menubranch H_2} {menubranch H_1} {menubranch H_1}
20
21  H_2      Quit      1-Total         2-Sort          3-Report        Switch
22           Quit Help View Total help View Sort help  View Report help Help 1
23           {return}  {H_GET FOUR}    {H_GET FIVE}    {H_GET SIX}
24                     {menubranch H_2} {menubranch H_2} {menubranch H_2}
25
```

Figure 27-2

Before we explain this help macro in detail, an overview is in order. When the user selects the Help item from a menu, control transfers to this routine. The routine displays a blank help screen, fills it with information from a help file on disk, and then displays a menu like the one below.

```
Quit  1-Save  2-Print  3-Clear  Switch
Quit Help System

        A        B       C       D       E       F       G       H
41  ====================== H E L P   S C R E E N ======================
42
43
44
```

Figure 27-3

This menu contains an option to quit, options for other help screens, and an option (Switch) to see another menu with other help screen choices on it. Each time the user selects a new help screen, the macro calls a subroutine and passes to it the name of a range to combine from the help file on disk. When the user finishes with help and selects quit, the macro erases the help screen in the current worksheet (to conserve memory) and returns control to the routine that called it.

Now let's look at this help system routine by routine. We have assumed that the routine named Helper is called from a main menu, and that when the user is finished with help, control returns to this main menu. The first thing Helper does is to move the cell pointer to the cell called Help_screen, then to the cell called Help_range. Helper then calls the H_get subroutine, so named because it imports the information from the file on disk.

The argument passed to H_get specifies the named range to be combined from the help file. The default is the range named One. Once the data from this range has been combined into the worksheet, the subroutine returns control to the Helper routine. The next command in Helper, {menucall H_1}, displays the first of the two menus depicted above. This menu system will manage a large number of help screens because you can add as many menus to it as you wish.

Read Method

Like the File-Combine method, the Read method reads help information into the application from a file that resides on the disk. However, because the Read method imports data from an ASCII file instead of a worksheet file, it's better suited to some circumstances than is the File-Combine technique.

Reading ASCII text into a worksheet with the Read technique is slower than importing text with the File-Combine method. That's because the {readln} command (which does the reading of the ASCII file) can read but one line at a time and because the destination cell on the worksheet must be reassigned with each successive line.

On the positive side, the Read technique does not require that 1-2-3 be in Ready mode when it's invoked. Because the Read technique relies on advanced macro commands (specifically, the file manipulation group), it can be used in the midst of any mode 1-2-3 happens to be in. As you'll see in the next section, that characteristic makes a particular help macro possible.

Restoring the Screen and Cell Pointer

To be useful, a help facility must be easy and rapid. For that reason, the macro must restore the application to its state at the time the user requested help. Here are four help techniques that do just that.

Capturing Cell Addresses

The following steps display a help screen and restore the original screen when the user is finished:

1. Store the address of the upper left cell on the screen. (In order to position the screen just as it appears when you request help, you will have to move the cell pointer to the cell that defined the top left corner of that screen.)

2. Store the address of the current cell. (After you've re-positioned the screen, you'll want to return the cell pointer to its original location.)

3. Display the help screen.

4. Wait for the user who is reading it to indicate he's finished.

5. Move the cell pointer to the stored top left corner cell location.

6. Move the cell pointer to the stored former location of the cell pointer.

The only catch in this process lies with the first step. There isn't any command to determine the location of the upper left corner of the screen, but there is a technique you can use. The following macro incorporates it.

```
        A          B         C         D       E        F        G        H

1    \H          {windowsoff}{paneloff}
2                {let INNER;@cellpointer("address")}
3                {bigright}{bigleft}
4                /wwh{pgup}{d}
5                {let UPLEFT;@cellpointer("address")}
6                /wwc
7                {goto}HELP_SCREEN~
8                {windowson}
9                {get ANS}
10               {goto}{UPLEFT}~
11               {goto}{INNER}~
12
13   INNER
14               {return}
15
16   UPLEFT
17               {return}
18
19   ANS
20
```

Figure 27-4

The macro begins by invoking {windowsoff} to suppress screen flashing, then storing the current location of the cell pointer in the range named Inner.

The next steps determine and store the location of the top left cell on the screen:

- The {bigright} {bigleft} combination always places the cell pointer in the leftmost column of the screen.

- The / Worksheet Window Horizontal command splits the screen horizontally and moves the cell pointer to the bottom of the window it has just created.

- The PageUp key followed by the Downarrow key places the cell pointer in what was the top left corner of the screen.

This sequence will always pinpoint that cell for you. It is, therefore, the kind of operation you'll want to store in a subroutine so you can call it from any macro. The macro then stores the location of that cell in the range named Upleft and reunites the screen into a single window. We suggest that you manually keystroke through the entire sequence to observe how it works.

With the status of the application stored, the macro is now free to display one or more help screens. This macro assumes the help screen is stored on the worksheet so it merely moves the cell pointer to the location of the help screen. The macro pauses for a keystroke (to enable the user to read the help message) and, upon detecting that keystroke, restores the previous screen with two {goto} commands.

This macro does have several restrictions:

1. When the cell pointer is on the bottom row of the screen, 1-2-3 beeps because it can't make a second horizontal window. Fortunately, the end result is still correct. Unfortunately, there's no way to eliminate the beep here.

2. When the cell pointer resides on a row above row 37 (on an 80x25 screen), depending on how the screen is oriented, there could be insufficient worksheet space above the cell pointer for {pgup} to function as this macro requires. Whether the macro works or not depends on how close the cell pointer is to the bottom of the screen. For example, if the cell pointer is on the second to the last line of the screen and that happens to be row 36, the macro will not work. Try it out so you can see for yourself. There does not appear to be a way around this limitation.

3. When column IU is on the screen, the macro will not work. It is possible to execute a {bigright} at any time except when the screen displays the last two columns. At that point, 1-2-3 decides that there isn't enough of a screen to the right to show. There does not appear to be a way around this limitation either.

We don't feel these restrictions are overly burdensome, however. If you need to use the File-Combine method of help information retrieval, this approach may be your best bet because it works in almost every case. It also leaves 1-2-3 in Ready mode once it arrives at the Help screen location, so you can use the File-Combine technique to import data if you need to.

The next method of screen restoration is a little cleaner and faster, but it will *not* work with / File Combine.

Mid-Formula

There is an interactive 1-2-3 operation you can use to restore the screen under some circumstances. As always, if it's possible to use an existing 1-2-3 operation to do some work instead of writing a macro routine, do so. Try it manually by pressing the plus (+) key to begin a formula, moving several screens away on the worksheet, and imagining that you're looking at a help screen. Now, press the Escape key and you'll see 1-2-3 restore the screen to exactly the same state it was in before you began your journey.

The technique goes like this: Freeze the control panel, press the plus key to begin a formula, move the cell pointer to the help screen, pause while the user reads the help screen, and abort the formula with Escape. The following macro implements those steps.

	A	B	C	D	E	F	G	H
1	\H	{windowsoff}{paneloff}				Freeze screen		
2		+{home}				Begin formula		
3		{pgdn 4}{d}				Position pointer		
4		{windowson}				Refresh screen		
5		{get ANS}				Pause for keystroke		
6		{esc 2}{quit}				Clear formula		
7								
8	ANS							
9								
10								

Figure 27-5

Since the macro displays a help screen by pointing, the first step (in cell B1) freezes the screen to hide the cell-pointer movement. The macro code in cell B2 begins a simple formula with " + ", then resets the screen to A1 to establish a consistent reference point for locating the help screen. Then it positions the cell pointer by, in cell B3 of the macro, paging down. When it has located the correct screen, it refreshes the screen with the {windowson} command (B4) and uses {get} to pause so the user can read the screen. After the user has pressed a key, the macro issues two Escapes (B6) to clear the formula.

Two limitations of this macro are that it requires navigation to the help screen by pointing, and it leaves 1-2-3 in Point mode (not Ready mode) while the user reads the help screen. These are fairly important limitations.

Having to point to the screen means the help screen isn't very relocatable on the worksheet. Every time you move it (by inserting or deleting columns or rows for example), you must change the macro that points to it. Being in point mode means that you can't perform a / File Combine to bring in more data from another file.

If your application is screen-oriented and not likely to change much, and if you have a fairly simple help system, requiring but one screen, this might be an excellent system to use. It is fast, efficient, and easy to program. If you need to make this help system refer to more than one screen, it is relatively easy to expand the help system to encompass more screens as long as they are all contained on the worksheet. The following macro illustrates how to do that.

	A	B	C	D	E	F	G	H
1	\H	{windowsoff}{paneloff}				Freeze screen		
2		+{home}				Begin formula		
3		{pgdn 3+H_MOD}{d}				Position pointer		
4		{windowson}				Refresh screen		
5		{get ANS}				Pause for keystroke		
6		{esc 2}{quit}				Clear formula		
7								
8	H_MOD	2				Help screen number		
9								
10	ANS							

Figure 27-6

The only difference between this macro and the previous one is the contents of cell B3. Here, the number of times to page down depends on the value stored in H_Mod. So if you need to maintain three help screens, you can vary the value in H_Mod, using a number between 1 and 3.

If you like this system, but need more data than you can store on the worksheet all the time, you can use the file management commands to construct a macro that reads data from the disk, one screen at a time. The following macro illustrates that approach.

	A	B	C	D	E	F	G	H
21	\H	{windowsoff}{paneloff}				Freeze screen		
22		{open + hulp window .lnn"; l"}				Open help file		
23		{for HELP_NUM;1;21;1;HELP_RD}				Read in help screen		
24		{close}				Close help file		
25		+{home}				Begin formula		
26		{pgdn 4}{d}				Position pointer		
27		{windowson}				Refresh screen		
28		{get ANS}				Pause for keystroke		
29		{blank A81..A100}				Clear help area		
30		{esc 2}{quit}				Clear formula		
31								
32	ANS	~				Storage cell		
33	FILE_NUM	1				File number		
34	HELP_NUM	22				FOR loop counter		
35								
36	HELP_RD	{recalc HELP_LN}				Recalc formula		
37	HELP_LN	{readln A102}				Read one line of help		
38								
39								
40								

Figure 27-7

This macro uses explicit cell addresses and string formulas, both of which make it more difficult to maintain. However, in 2.01. they are necessary evils—this macro can't exist without them. The corresponding 2.2 macro, which remedies these shortcomings, is presented a little later.

The macro begins (in cell B21) by freezing the screen. The next step is to open the help file and read in the help screen. The job of reading in the help data falls to a {for} loop. That loop repeats the Help_rd routine once for each line of help information. There are twenty lines of help information, so the {for} loop performs 20 iterations. (You have probably guessed that it uses a {readln} command to read each line of data in the help file).

```
23      {for HELP_NUM;1;20;1;HELP_RD}      Read in help screen
```

The sole function of Help_rd is to read in one line of help information at a time. The {readln} command it incorporates requires a cell address as an argument, so in order to read successive lines of the help file into successive cells on the worksheet, Help_rd must calculate that address anew with each line.

```
36      HELP_RD  {recalc HELP_LN}      Recalc formula
37      HELP_LN  {readln A102}         Read one line of help
```

The first line of Help_rd, contained in B36, recalculates the string formula in the cell below it. The string formula, reproduced below, calculates the cell-address argument by referencing the cell that stores the counter for the {for} loop (that cell is named Help_num). Each time the {for} loop executes Help_rd, it increments the value in Help_num.

And each time Help_rd runs, it recalculates the cell address used in the {readln} command based on the new value of Help_num.

```
B37: +"{readln A"&@STRING(80+HELP_NUM;0)&"}"
```

Let's suppose the {for} loop beginning in cell A24 runs Help_rd 20 times. The first time Help_rd runs, it reads one line of help information into cell A81. The second time it runs, it reads a line of help information into cell A82. This continues until it reads the twentieth line of help information into cell A100.

When it has finished reading lines of data from the file, this macro positions the screen with the formula method described earlier. When the user presses a keystroke, it erases the range that contained the help information, and clears the formula.

The Release 2.2 implementation of this macro shares many of the same concepts, but does so without resorting to explicit cell addresses and string formulas. Here's the new macro:

	A	B C D E	F G H
21	\H	{windowsoff}{paneloff}	Freeze screen
22		+{home}	Begin formula
23		{pgdn 4}	Position pointer
24		{open +"HELP"&FILE_NUM&".PRN";"r"}	Open help file
25		{for HELP_NUM;1;20;1;HELP_RD}	Read in help screen
26		{u 20}{close}	Close help file
27		{windowson}	Refresh screen
28		{get ANS}	Pause for keystroke
29		{blank HELP_AREA}	Clear help area
30		{esc 2}{quit}	Clear formula
31			
32	ANS	~	Storage cell
33	FILE_NUM	1	File number
34	HELP_NUM	21	FOR loop counter
35			
36	HELP_RD	{readln @cellpointer("address")}	Read one line of help
37		{d}	Move down for one line
38			
39			
40			

Figure 27-8

The major difference in the 2.2 version is that {readln} accepts a formula as its argument, instead of requiring a cell address or range name. If we had wanted to use a structure more parallel to the 2.01 example, we could have simply eliminated Help_In altogether and replaced Help_rd with {readln +"A"&@string(80+HELP_NUM;0)}. That would have overcome one stylistic weakness—using string formulas that resolve to macro statements.

However, by reading each line into the current cell pointer, we can eliminate the use of cell addresses as well, performing everthing by named ranges and by pointing. Thus, Help_rd is now {readln

@cellpointer("address")}, and the coordinate pair A81..A100 has been named Help_area.

So the macro navigates to the help area first, and then reads in one line of the help screen at a time, moving the cell pointer down after each line is read. When the entire help screen is in place, the macro repositions the cell pointer to the top of the screen with {u 20}.

A nice touch would be to add a {frameoff} command, just before the {windowson} command, to differentiate the appearance of the help screen for the user. If you wanted to get real fancy, you could also use the command {indicate @repeat("";25)&"HELP-Press any key when done"&@repeat("";25)}, which would center a message in the first line of the screen. If you use this technique, be sure to reset the screen with the {indicate} command when the formula is cleared and the macro ends.

The following macro implements a powerful help system. It has the ability to display many help screens, and it precisely restores the screen to the state it occupied before the user selected help. It's even possible to add the ability to select from a menu of help screens after the first one displays. The next macro shows how to modify the system for a menu of help screens.

	A	B	C	D	E	F
21	\H	{windowsoff}{paneloff}		Freeze screen		
22		{HELP_GET}		HELP_GET subroutine		
23		+{home}		Begin formula		
24		{pgdn 4}{d}		Position pointer		
25		{windowson}		Refresh screen		
26		{menucall HELP_MENU}		Display HELP_MENU MENU		
27		{blank A81..A100}		Clear help area		
28		{esc 2}{quit}		Clear formula		
29						
30	ANS	~		Storage cell		
31	FILE_NUM	1		File number		
32	HELP_NUM	21		FOR loop counter		
33						
34	HELP_GET	{open +"HELP"&FILE_NUM&".PRN";"r"}		Open help file		
35		{for HELP_NUM;1;20;1;HELP_RD}		Read in help screen		
36		{close}		Close help file		
37						
38	HELP_RD	{recalc HELP_LN}		Recalc formula		
39	HELP_LN	{readln A101}		Read one line of help		
40		{return}				
41						
42	HELP_MENU	Quit	1	2		
43		Leave help	Display screen 1	Display screen 2		
44		{return}	{let FILE_NUM;"1"}	{let FILE_;"2"}		
45			{branch HELP_MORE}	{branch HELP_MORE}		
46						
47	HELP_MORE	{HELP_GET}		Run HELP_GET		
48		{windowsoff}		Freeze screen		
49		{windowson}		Refresh screen		
50		{menubranch HELP_MENU}		Display menu again		
51						
52	.					

Figure 27-9

The first difference between the last macro for Release 2.01 and this macro is that a portion of it has been spun off as a subroutine. The part that opens the help file, reads each line, and closes it is now called Help_get. That routine is called in cell B22 and begins in cell B34. The next difference is in cell B26; instead of pausing to accept a keystroke after displaying the help screen, the macro displays a menu.

The menu text, which begins at cell B42, contains options for help screens other than the default. The routines that follow each of those options first store another character in the named range File_num. The Help_get routine will later concatenate that character with another string to form a unique help file name. Control next passes to the subroutine Help_more, which begins in cell B47. Help_more calls the Help_get subroutine, which in turn reads in the new help information and refreshes the screen before displaying the menu again. Because the {readln} command does not signal 1-2-3 to refresh the screen, we've included both a {windowsoff} and {windowson} command to refresh the screen (neither will do the job alone).

Although the menu shown above provides access to but two help screens, you can add many more such screens. You can have seven help screens on one menu. If you need more, you can daisy-chain help menus to offer yet more choices. Upon finishing with the menu, a user can simply press Return or Escape and the screen will again display what it did before help was requested.

If you're using Release 2.2, you'll want to apply the preceding concepts to the Release 2.2 method we showed earlier. Unfortunately, if you were to run this version of the help macro, you'd realize that freedom from cell addresses comes at a price. In this case, the screen refreshes with each line of the help file that's read in, due to the movement of the cell pointer. That can make the line-by-line reading of the help screen appear too obvious to the user.

Here's the revised macro which takes acccount of this behavior:

	A	B	C	D	E	F
21	\H	{paneloff}			Freeze panel	
22		+{home}			Begin formula	
23		{pgdn 4}			Position pointer	
24		{HELP_GET}			Run HELP_GET subroutine	
25		{windowson}			Refresh screen	
26		{menucall HELP_MENU}			Pause for keystroke	
27		{blank HELP_AREA}			Clear help area	
28		{esc 2}{quit}			Clear formula	
29						
30	ANS	~			Storage cell	
31	FILE_NUM	1			File number	
32	HELP_NUM	21			FOR loop counter	
33						
34	HELP_GET	{windowsoff}			Freeze Display	
35		{open +"HELP"&FILE_NUM&".PRN";r}			Open help file	
36		{for HELP_NUM;1;20;1;HELP_RD}			Read in help screen	
37		{u 20}{close}			Close help file	
38						
39	HELP_RD	{readln @cellpointer("address")}			Read one line of help	
40		{d}			Move down for next line	
41						
42						
43	HELP_MENU	Quit	1		2	
44		Leave help	Display screen 1		Display screen 2	
45		{return}	{let FILE_NUM;"1"}		{let FILE_NUM;"2"}	
46		{branch HELP_MORE}			{branch HELP_MORE}	
47						
48	HELP_MORE	{HELP_GET }			Run HELP_GET	
49		{windowsoff}			Freeze screen	
50		{windowson}			Refresh screen	
51		{menubranch HELP_MENU}			Display menu again	

Figure 27-10

We've changed the position of the {windowsoff} command so that it's contained in the body of Help_get. This means that the screen is frozen each time another help screen is selected from the menu. When the screen has been completely read into memory, the screen is refreshed. This method is much less disconcerting for its user.

Range Input

Like the mid-formula technique, the Range Input technique (based on the Range Input command) automatically returns the screen to where it was when help was invoked. However, the Range Input technique differs from the mid-formula technique both in that it is far simpler to implement and that it is appropriate only for help systems consisting of either one or two screens. The macro below shows how to implement the technique.

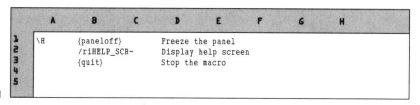

Figure 27-11

Thanks to the functions already built into the Range Input command, all this macro has to do is freeze the control panel and invoke Range Input.

The simplicity of the Range Input technique also has a cost. One of the properties of this method is that the macro stops running entirely until the user presses Return or Escape. This means additional help screens cannot be read in from the disk "on the fly." Another cost, though minor, is that each help screen itself must be structured in a specific way.

If you want to use only one help screen, make sure that it has an unprotected cell somewhere in the range named Help_scr. A further requirement is that the upper left corner of Help_scr must be the upper left corner of the help screen.

If you want to use two screens, then Help_scr must cover 40 cells, from the upper left corner of the top screen to the lower left corner of the bottom screen. So, for example, the macro above may display the two screens below it as help screens. If so, then the Help_scr range should be A21..A60, and the top and bottom cells of this range (A21 and A60) should be unprotected. This seems to be the only way to get Range Input to display full screens uniformly. If you use more screens, or if the unprotected cells are in different positions, then Range Input has the tendency to scroll up and down in half-screen steps.

Finally, place a message at the bottom of each screen. On the first, use the message "Press Downarrow for more information, Escape to continue." On the second, place the message "Press Uparrow to review prior screen, Escape to continue." (The Escape key will terminate the Range Input command and allow the macro to continue processing.)

Query Find

The fourth and final help method uses Query Find to position the screen
and cell pointer.

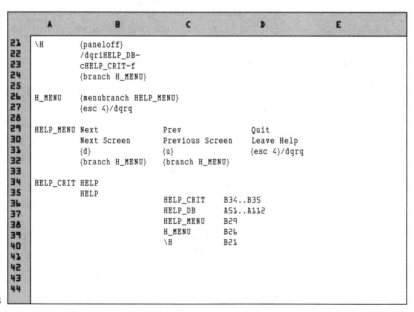

Figure 27-12

Rows 30 to 33 contain a range name table, to help clarify which ranges
are used and their respective locations. You can easily add a menu to this
macro, as the following adaptation shows.

Figure 27-13

(The range name table in the example above begins in cell C36.) You can also read in multiple help screens from the disk as follows:

	A	B	C	D	E
21	\H	{paneloff}		Freeze panel	
22		{HELP_GET}		Run HELP_GET subroutine	
23		/dqriHELP_DB~		Begin query find	
24		cHELP_DB~f		Complete query find	
25		{menucall HELP_MENU}		Display HELP_MENU menu	
26		{blank IU1..IU20}		Clear help area	
27		{esc 4}		Back out of query find	
28		/dqrq{quit}		Clear query settings	
29					
30	ANS	~		Storage cell	
31	FILE_NUM	1		File number	
32	HELP_NUM	21		FOR loop counter	
33					
34	HELP_GET	{open +"HELP"&FILE_".PRN";"r"}		Open help file	
35		{for HELP_NUM;1;20;1;HELP_RD}		Read in help screen	
36		{close}		Close help file	
37					
38	HELP_RD	{recalc HELP_LN}		Recalc formula	
39	HELP_LN	{readln IU21}		Read one line of help	
40		{return}			
41					
42	HELP_MENU	Quit	1	2	
43		Leave help	Display screen 1	Display screen 2	
44		{return}	{let FILE_NUM;"1"}	{let FILE_NUM;"2"}	
45			{branch HELP_MORE}	{branch HELP_MORE}	
46					
47	HELP_MORE	{HELP_GET}		Run HELP_GET	
48		{home}		Refresh screen	
49		{menubranch HELP_MENU}		Display menu again	
50					
51					
52					

Figure 27-14

The 2.2 adaptation might be as simple as replacing the Help_rd routine as follows:

	A	B	C	D	E
38	HELP_RD	{readln +"IU"&@STRING(HELP_NUM;0} Read one line of help			
39		{return}			
40					
41					

Figure 27-15

Context Sensitivity

The most useful help systems are context sensitive—that is, what they display depends on the current conditions in the application. How you implement context sensitive help screens depends on whether help is available only while in the menu system, or whether it is also available while operating free-form in the worksheet.

Individual Help Nodes in the Menu System

The simplest way to ensure that the help screen matches the context is to have each command menu contain its own help selection. Each help choice can then reflect the content of the menu it accompanies. The following menu macros illustrate how this might look.

	A	B	C	D	E	F
1	\D	{menubranch MENU_DB}{quit}				
2						
3	MENU_DB	Entry	Print	Save	Help	
4		Enter data	Print reports	Save file	Top Menu Help	
5		{branch ...}	{branch PR}	{branch ...}	{branch HELP1}	
6						
7	PR	{menubranch MENU_PR}{branch \D}				
8						
9	MENU_PR	Form-Letter	Mail-Labels	Documentation	Help	
10		Print letter	Print labels	Print doc set	Print Help	
11		{branch ...}	{branch ...}	{branch DOC}	{branch HELP2}	
12						
13	DOC	{menubranch MENU_DOC}{branch PR}				
14						
15	MENU_DOC	Query	Entry	Help		
16		Query Doc	Entry Doc	Print Documentation Help		
17		{branch ...}	{branch ...}	{branch HELP3}		
18						
19						
20						
21	HELP1	+{home}		Anchor pointer, reset screen		
22		{pgdn 3}		Position screen		
23		{get ANS}		Pause for key		
24		{esc 2}		Restore screen		
25		{branch \D}		Restore menu		
26						
27	HELP2	+{home}		Anchor pointer, reset screen		
28		{pgdn 4}		Position screen		
29		{get ANS}		Pause for key		
30		{esc 2}		Restore screen		
31		{branch PR}		Restore menu		
32						
33	HELP3	+{home}		Anchor pointer, reset screen		
34		{pgdn 5}		Position screen		
35		{get ANS}		Pause for key		
36		{esc 2}		Restore screen		
37		{branch DOC}		Restore menu		
38						
39						
40						

Figure 27-16

Each menu contains a selection named "Help." While a user is in the menu system above, pressing "h" at any level will display the appropriate help screen. The advantages to this system are twofold: The help display is immediate and it is easy to maintain. The disadvantages are that many similar help routines and range names are required, and Help is available only when in a menu. If you need a more sophisticated and flexible help system, the next section describes other ways to implement context sensitivity.

Context Sensitivity in Full-Screen Menus

While only a few keys have meaning when in a {menubranch} or {menucall} routine, full-screen menus can assign a function to nearly every key on the keyboard. With Release 2.2, you can detect if the user has pressed the F1 function key, as the string "{HELP}" is passed to the {get} command.

This makes it easy to implement context sensitive help screens that are activated the same way as 1-2-3's help system—via the F1 key. For users already familiar with or in the process of learning 1-2-3, this makes help easily accessible and intuitive.

Context Sensitivity from the Worksheet

There are two ways your help system can react to conditions in the worksheet.

The first is to have each macro, just before it finishes running, make a unique entry in a designated cell. When the help macro is activated, it evaluates that cell to determine which macro ran last and displays the appropriate help screen. For example, if the data entry macro was the last to operate, the help macro (when selected) can show the data entry help screen. The following macro demonstrates this principle in action. The /D, /E, and /R macros merely show the last lines of what would be longer macros.

	A	B	C	D	E	F	G	H
1	\D	{let HELP_NUM;1}			Store help screen number			
2		{goto}DAT_SCR~			Go to data entry screen			
3								
4	\E	{let HELP_NUM;2}			Store help screen number			
5		{goto}EXT_SCR~			Go to extract screen			
6								
7	\R	{let HELP_NUM;3}			Store help screen number			
8		{goto}RPT_SCR~			Go to report screen			
9								
10								
11	\H	{windowsoff}{paneloff}			Freeze screen			
12		+{home}			Begin formula			
13		{pgdn HELP_NUM+3}{d}			Position display help screen			
14		{windowson}{panelon}			Refresh screen			
15		{get ANS}			Pause for keystroke			
16		{esc 2}{quit}			Clear formula: thus restore screen			
17								
18	HELP_NUM	1			Number of additional pgdns for help			
19								
20	ANS	~			Null key storage			

Figure 27-17

Imagine that the first three macros are, respectively, simple data entry, data extract, and report macros. They store a pre-determined number that corresponds to an associated help screen and then continue on their way. From the value stored in Help_num, we can see that the data entry macro (\D) was the last to run.

When \H is activated, it displays the help screen specified by Help_num. The macro first freezes the screen (B11), then uses the mid-formula method of help display. It enters a plus sign and starts to point, with the cell pointer at the home position. The macro commands in B13 page down three times plus the number contained in Help_num. After arriving at the appropriate location, the macro refreshes the screen (B14) and pauses for a keystroke (B15). When the user has finished with the screen and presses a key, the macro restores the previous screen.

The second way is to have the help macro dependent on the cell pointer row or column. Consider, for example, a database application that is laid out vertically, so that the input screen is above the main database, which is above the extract range, and so on. When the help macro is activated, it tests the row of the cell pointer. If the cell pointer is in the extract range, then a help screen will be displayed that is appropriate to the extract function. If the cell pointer is in the database range, it will display a database help screen, and so on. The macro below shows how you might write this.

```
        A       B         C        D        E      F       G       H
   1   \H      {SCR_GET}                                Store screen, cellpointer
   2           {let ROW;@cellpointer("row")}            Store row
   3           {let H_RNG;@vlookup(ROW;H_TAB;1)}        Figure which help screen
   4           {goto}HLP_SCR~                           Go to help screen
   5           /fccn                                    File combine
   6           {H_RNG}~                                 Range for help screen
   7           x{esc}{H_FILE}~                          Help Filename
   8           {get ANS}                                Pause for a keystroke
   9           {SCR_BAK}                                Go to original screen
  10
  11
  12   ROW                                              Storage of row
  13
  14   H_RNG                                            Name of help screen range
  15           {return}
  16
  17   H_FILE                                           Name of Help file
  18           {return}
  19
  20
  21   H_TAB          41 INPUT
  22               61 DATABASE
  23              401 EXTRACT
  24              461 REPORT
  25
  26
```

Figure 27-18

The macro begins in cell B1 by calling a subroutine called Scr_get. This routine is not described in detail for reasons of simplicity, but its purpose is to store the upper left cell of the screen and the address of the cell pointer, so that the screen position can be restored with the corresponding subroutine, Scr_bak.

Next, the row of the cell pointer is captured, so that the macro can determine which help screen to display. In B3, it figures which help screen is appropriate by passing the row number through a lookup table called H_tab. While numbers have been hard-coded into H_tab, the application can be made more flexible if @cell("row";RANGENAME) formulas are used in place of numbers. The result is stored in the H_rng range. Each word in the lookup table corresponds to a range name in the help file.

Finally, the macro (B4) positions the cell pointer in the help screen, combines in the named range (B6) from the help file (B7), and pauses for the user to press a key (B8). When the user has seen the screen long enough and presses a key, the macro calls the Scr_bak subroutine, which restores the screen to its original position.

28

Application Design

Using Available Memory Efficiently

For those times when you need to conserve RAM, here are several tips you may be able to use to your advantage.

The most important thing to know is how 1-2-3 Releases 2.x (2, 2.01, and 2.2) manage memory. Release 1A consumed memory for every cell within a rectangle whose upper left corner was cell A1 and whose lower right corner was the intersection of the row containing the lowermost entry (or formatted cell or unprotected cell) and the column containing the rightmost entry (or formatted or unprotected cell).

Release 2.x uses what's known as a sparse matrix memory management scheme that doesn't consume as much memory under most circumstances. Nevertheless, there are some important things to know about it. Whereas Release 1A created an active range on the worksheet, Release 2.x creates an active range in any column containing entries. It consumes four bytes of memory for every blank cell between the uppermost and lowermost entries in any column.

Let's examine an extreme example to illustrate how to save memory with Release 2.x's memory scheme. If you have an entry in cell A1 and another in cell A8192 (note that both entries are in column A), you'd not only consume memory for each of those entries, you'd consume an additional four bytes for every blank cell between them. If you instead had entered the lower entry into cell B8192, you'd consume no memory in addition to that required for each of the entries. In the latter scenario, with the entries in separate columns, there are no intervening cells to occupy additional memory.

The guideline is simple: minimize the number of empty cells between the uppermost and lowermost entries in the same column. A column with a single entry in it or a column with one contiguous list of entries are both using memory at maximum efficiency. That means that 1-2-3 stores macros (which are generally written in a column with few intervening blank cells) very efficiently.

You should also know that a host of other factors affect how much memory you use. The first graph you define occupies 256 bytes. If you redefine the graph, you'll use no more memory. However, for every graph you create using the / Graph Name Create command, you'll consume 463 bytes of RAM. The most efficient way to handle graphs, therefore, is to write a macro to define each series of graph settings. Rather than store multiple graph settings with the / Graph Name Create command, store them in a macro label.

Range names occupy 33 bytes apiece—no matter how large the range is and no matter how many characters the range name contains.

In all cases, if you do something to recover memory—such as erase an entry, select / Range Protect to protect an unprotected cell, select / Range Format Reset to reset a formatted cell, delete a named graph, or delete a named range—you must also save the worksheet to disk and retrieve it before you will free the memory.

You can also save about 7K of RAM bytes if you load 1-2-3 by entering "123" instead of entering "Lotus" and then selecting 1-2-3 from the menu. In doing so you bypass the Lotus Access System, which uses the extra memory.

You should also know how Release 2.2's macro libraries use memory. Whereas Release 2.2's worksheet uses sparse memory memory management techniques and stores what it can in expanded memory, the Macro Library Manager can do neither. Library files reside exclusively in conventional memory (that is, memory below 640K). Libraries also encumber memory using the Release 1A upper left corner to lower right corner schema. Thus, the rules for efficiently using macro libraries are similar to those you'd apply in Release 1A: Keep cell entries close together, and crowd the upper left corner of the library. You do the latter by placing the entries to be stored in the library near to the upper left cell of the range you specify when you save a macro library.

If you're short on conventional memory, perhaps because you are running a terminate and stay resident (TSR) program, network software, or add-ins like Allways, you should keep your macro libraries lean. Store the macros you use frequently in one macro library and keep that loaded into memory. Group other macros by function and store them in separate macro library files. Then load each file only when you need it and unload it as soon as you finish.

Making Your Application Portable to Other Environments

If you work for a company with offices in other countries and want to develop templates that can be used in those countries as well as in your own, or if you are planning to market a macro-driven application internationally, there are some special concerns you must attend to. We've organized those issues into two groups: those having to do with hardware portability and those having to do with foreign languages.

Portability Across Computing Environments

Since portability, or the ability to use an application in a variety of computing environments, is one of the goals to which any macro-driven application aspires, we've woven techniques for attaining it throughout this book.

For example, when you write advanced macro commands that use arguments, use semicolons as your argument separators instead of commas. Semicolons are always valid argument separators, whereas commas are not (if you select / Worksheet Global Default Other International Punctuation, four of your six choices do not recognize the comma as an argument separator). If you use commas, anyone using a copy of 1-2-3 configured to a default that does not recognize commas as argument separators will be unable to run your macros without first changing all the argument separators they contain. Upon detecting any change in default punctuation setting, 1-2-3 will automatically convert the separators contained in formulas entered on the worksheet (so you need not use semicolons in those formulas), but it will not change separators in formulas contained in macros. For that reason, the same dictum applies to formulas used in macros—use semicolons instead of commas as argument separators. For example:

```
{let BONUS;@if(SALE>1000;SALE*.11;SALE*.1)}
```

While you might think that you can use commas as separators and instruct your users which defaults they must operate 1-2-3 under when they use the application, that's not a good solution. The settings that change argument separators also change the decimal and thousands separators, and it's a preference for those types of punctuation—rather than any preference for argument separators—that in turn invalidates commas as argument separators. So in forcing someone to switch to a setting using commas as argument separators, you'd also force them to view all their numbers punctuated in a manner that makes no sense to them. Instead, use semicolons as your argument separators and you'll never encounter that problem.

Since not all the computer systems that will run your application will support all of the application's features (such as on-screen graphs, which require a graphics-capable display adapter), you may need to include an installation routine to eliminate the incompatible option from the macro.

The following macro shows a menu including Set-up and Graph options. The Set-up option will store in the cell named Graphit either the label Do_graph or the label No_graph. The menu choice Graph executes the statement {dispatch GRAPHIT}.[67] If the named location Graphit contains the label Do_graph, control will transfer to Do_graph and the macro will display a graph. If the named location contains the label No_graph, the macro will branch to a routine that displays an error message and returns to the main menu.

	A	B	C	D	E	F
21	\A	{menubranch MEN1}{branch \A}				
22	MEN1	Enter	Graph		Set-up	
23		Enter data	Display graphs		Configure the application	
24		{branch ENTRY}	{dispatch GRAPHIT}		{branch SETUP}	
25						
26	SETUP	{getlabel "Can you display graphs? (y/n)";DECIDE}				
27		{let DECIDE;@upper(DECIDE)}				
28		{if DECIDE<>"Y"#and#DECIDE<>"N"}{branch SETUP}				
29		{if DECIDE="Y"}{let GRAPHIT;"DO_GRAPH"}{branch \A}				
30		{let GRAPHIT;"NO_GRAPH"}{branch \A}				
31						
32	DO_GRAPH	/gnuBAR1~q				
33		{branch \A}				
34						
35	NO_GRAPH	{getlabel "Graphs not available - press Return";ANS}				
36		{branch \A}				
37						
38	GRAPHIT	DO_GRAPH				
39	DECIDE					
40	ANS					
41						

Figure 28-1

---

[67] Remember that the {dispatch} command redirects macro control not to the location named as its argument, but to the named location stored in the cell that argument names.

You might enhance the manner in which the Set-up option works to have it automatically present the set-up routine the first time the macro runs.

Have an auto-execute macro containing an {if} command check the value of a cell named Installed. If the Set-up routine has not yet been run, the cell would contain a "N" and the macro would branch to that routine. The last instruction in the Set-up routine would assign the label "Y" to the cell named Installed. When you next use the application, this routine will again check the cell named Installed and detect a "Y", whereupon it will skip the Set-up routine.

If you do add this self-triggering routine, you should include the Set-up option on the main menu in the event a user later adds a graphics display adapter (or any other option that affects the performance of the application) or moves the application to another computer and needs to change those settings.

Here is the updated macro as it might appear before the application has been used—with an "N" in the cell named Installed (cell B43), and a new line of code (in cell B28) to change that to a "Y" when Setup runs.

```
        A         B                C               D          E           F

21   \0        {if INSTALLED="N"}{branch SETUP}
22   LOOP      {menubranch MEN1}{branch LOOP}
23   MEN1      Enter           Graph                     Set-up
24             Enter data      Display graphs            Configure the application
25             {branch ENTRY}  {dispatch GRAPHIT}        {branch SETUP}
26
27   SETUP     {getlabel "Can you display graphs? (y/n)";DECIDE}
28             {let INSTALLED;"Y"}
29             {let DECIDE;@upper(DECIDE)}
30             {if DECIDE<>"Y"#and#DECIDE<>"N"}{branch SETUP}
31             {if DECIDE="Y"}{let GRAPHIT;"DO_GRAPH"}{branch LOOP}
32             {let GRAPHIT;"NO_GRAPH"}{branch LOOP}
33
34   DO_GRAPH  /gnuBAR1~q
35             {branch LOOP}
36
37   NO_GRAPH  {getlabel "Graphs not available - press Return";ANS}
38             {branch LOOP}
39
40   GRAPHIT   DO_GRAPH
41   DECIDE
42   ANS
43   INSTALLED N
```

Figure 28-2

Converting the Application for Foreign Use

An application intended for use in a foreign country should incorporate the customary ways of performing the tasks that the application embodies, and use the language of that country. While you may be able to circumvent the language translation if you can ascertain that your audience comprehends the language in which you've written the application, you must still find out the linguistic version of 1-2-3 with which they intend to use the application. If that version differs from the version for which the macros were written, the macro instructions themselves will probably need to be translated.

Since the first letters of the menu choices in versions of 1-2-3 for other languages may vary from those of corresponding choices in the version for your language, and the syntax of the advanced macro commands will vary, you may need to change both the keystrokes and advanced macro commands those macros contain. However, if the version of 1-2-3 you wish to translate into happens to be for English, French, German, Spanish, or Italian, you can enlist the help of a Lotus utility called the 1-2-3 Macro Converter[68] (also known by its filename, Mactrans).

The Macro Converter will convert macro keystrokes and advanced macro commands into those of the version of 1-2-3 on which you want to run the application, although it cannot translate string formulas. You can probably circumvent that problem by rewriting string formulas into advanced macro command statements using {let} and {if} commands.

In Release 2.2, the latter restriction shouldn't be a problem. Since in Release 2.2 you can use a string formula for any macro argument, you won't need to calculate the entire macro label from a string formula. The former will translate, the latter won't.

There are several other items that the Macro Converter cannot translate; however, their incidence will in most cases be limited—so you may find those changes easy to make manually. They include:

1. The access mode argument in any {open} commands (r,w,m, or a).

2. The attribute argument in an @cell or @cellpointer function ("row", "col", "width", "prefix", "address", "type", "format", or "contents", or "filename").

3. The date string argument to an @datevalue command. The month name in that string may need to be translated.

4. Menu choices made through a series of directional arrow keynames, such as {r 3}. Since the menu items may not occupy the same positions on the foreign version's menu, this method of

---

[68] The 1-2-3 Macro Converter is available at no charge from Lotus Development Corporation.

selecting may lead the application astray. This is yet another compelling reason to avoid this method of menu selection. It may also create incompatibilities between your macros and future releases of 1-2-3, releases in which menu-item positions may change to accommodate new choices.

29

Structured Programming

An Introduction to Selected Programming Concepts

Although we never said as much, in the previous chapters we introduced you to a style of writing macros that we'll now call a structured style. As you undertake more ambitious macro projects, the importance of that style will grow proportionately. You'll need to know how to apply it to a more diverse mix of situations than we've covered here. This is a good time, then, to divorce your understanding of those techniques from any specific routine in which they may have appeared so you can better see how to apply them to any routine you may write.

Let's begin by clarifying the purpose of writing macros in a structured manner. A well-structured macro is both easy for someone else to understand and easy for that person to modify. In applications of any size, a structured macro will require significantly less time to develop and require both less time and less skill to test and debug. You will also be able to more readily transfer routines contained within that macro to other applications than you will the routines of its unstructured counterpart.

If you're writing macros and expect to be the only person to maintain them, structured techniques will save you time and frustration and reduce the amount of recoding you'll have to do each time you write a new application. If you work in an organization in which macros will be used by others, a structured approach is a key ingredient to protecting your organization's investment in those macros, and to ensuring that they will remain a productive asset for a long time to come.

If you work in an organization that fails to use structured methods of writing macros, those macros will be difficult to revise in the face of changes and successive macro-writers will impose upon them vastly different styles of problem solving—so much so that those applications will be nearly impossible to understand. In short, you will be in the business of short-term solutions.

The Methods of Structured Programming

The methods that follow fall into two groups:

- Things to do when you are writing a routine.

- Things to do when you are organizing the application into separate routines.

The simpler and shorter your macro is, the less need you have for principles by which you can organize the application into separate routines. Conversely, the more complex and lengthy the macro grows, the more attention you should give to an overall scheme for the application in addition to the details of the routines themselves.

In the topics that follow, we'll begin with those techniques that pertain to writing simple macros and progress to methods you'll only employ for use with complex applications.

Keep Each Line of the Macro Brief and Meaningful

Let's start on the level of an individual line in the macro. Restrict each line to encompass no more than one particular action, such as the keystrokes for printing a report. If that action encompasses more than one line, fine, but even if it doesn't fill an entire line, begin the next operation on the next line. That'll make your macro easier to document (the Comment for that line only has to describe one thing) and easier to revise (you can easily move an instruction that is isolated on its own line, and then close up the macro).

For example, although the keystrokes to save a file don't occupy a lot of space, they represent a distinct action you shouldn't mix with keystrokes that perform other actions.

```
/fs{FILE}~r{esc}                    Save/replace file
```

Use Variables

Rather than imbedding data and specifications within the macro itself, store that specific information in ranges on the worksheet and have the macro refer to those locations. You can easily change the data contained within each range without disturbing the macro itself. Here are two ways to use range names.

Create a range name referring to a range of the same dimensions as the print, database, or other kind of range you must set. In the macro, use that range name to convey the setting to 1-2-3. For example, if you create a range named Budget referring to A1..M35, you can write /ppr-BUDGET~agpq instead of /pprA1..M35~agpq. If you redefine the range that Budget refers to, your macro will respond to that change without any revision.

Suppose you have a setting (such as a column-width setting) in your macro that you'd like to vary. If you enter that setting as a label into a named range, and then call that range as a subroutine from your main macro routine, 1-2-3 will type the contents of the subroutine at that point in your macro. For example, if the cell named Width contains the label 25, then /wcs{WIDTH}~ has the same effect as /wcs25~. If you call the named range as a subroutine, you can revise the setting by entering a new label in the named range. You can only revise the setting in /wcs25~ by editing the macro label itself. Be sure to enter even numeric settings as labels in such subroutines. Remember, 1-2-3 can't read a value entry as part of a macro.

Use Range Names

The more complex your macros are, the more locations they reference. If those location references consist of range names instead of cell addresses and you later change those locations, you need not revise the ones that have moved. The range names will automatically adjust themselves to refer to the changed cell addresses.

On the other hand, one liability that accompanies the use of range names is that you must properly name all such references before running the macro. It's easy to write range names into a macro and then forget to actually create those range names on the worksheet. But if you forget even one, the macro will terminate in an untrappable error. For that reason, it's a good idea to scan your new or modified macro before you first use it to check that you've created each range name. One way to make that task easier is to write all your range names in the opposite case from the rest of the macro code. For example, write macro code in lower case and range names in uppercase:

```
/pprBUDGET~agpq
```

You can as easily do the reverse: Differentiate range names by typing them in lower case and the macro code in upper case. However, there are three reasons we recommend that you use uppercase for range names and lowercase for macro instructions:

1. To be sure all range names referenced in a macro have been assigned, we like to review those range names before running a macro for the first time. There are generally fewer range names than commands in a macro, and a few uppercase range names among a lot of lowercase commands are easier to identify than a few lowercase range names among a lot of uppercase commands. To help you decide which scheme you prefer, compare the macros below:

	A	B	C	D	E	F	G	H
1	\A	{windowsoff}{paneloff}				Freeze the screen		
2		/rvNEW_TOTAL~CUM_TOTAL~				Update cumulative total		
3		/pprBUDGET~agpq				Print budget report		
4	LOOP	{beep}				Alert user of end		
5		{wait @now+@time(0;0;5)}				Pause 5 seconds		
6		{look KEY}{esc}				Check for keystroke		
7		{if KEY=""}{branch LOOP}				If none, repeat beep		
8		{panelon}{windowson}				Turn on screen and		
9		{branch CONTINUE}				continue		
10								
11	KEY					Store keystroke		
12								
13								
14								
15								

Figure 29-1

	A	B	C	D	E	F	G	H
1	\a	{WINDOWSOFF}{PANELOFF}				Freeze the screen		
2		/RVnew_total~cum_total~				Update cumulative total		
3		/PPRbudget~AGPQ				Print budget report		
4	loop	{BEEP}				Alert user of end		
5		{WAIT @NOW+@TIME(0;0;5)}				Pause 5 seconds		
6		{LOOK key}{ESC}				Check for keystroke		
7		{IF key=""}{BRANCH loop}				If none, repeat beep		
8		{PANELON}{WINDOWSON}				Turn on screen and		
9		{BRANCH continue}				continue		
10								
11	key					Store keystroke		
12								
13								
14								
15								

Figure 29-2

2. If you sometimes use single letter range names for brevity, and you happen to include the letter L as a range name, the lowercase L looks too much like the numeral 1. On the other hand, the uppercase L is much more distinctive.

3. It's easier to press the Shift key to type an occasional range name in capital letters than to do the reverse.

Organize Common Actions into a Single Routine

Organize similar actions into a routine. This precept follows closely what we earlier told you about each line of the macro. Just as each line of the macro should perform one task, each routine should consist of a group of lines required to get some discrete job done.

For example, one line of your macro might contain the printing commands /ppcrrBUDGET~agpq. There may also be a variety of other tasks closely associated with those printing commands, for example, the application may need to redefine the named range Budget to reflect the new dimensions of the spreadsheet, to declare a new {onerror} statement to trap printer-related errors, to proffer a menu of print options (such as compressed print), to display a message during printing to let the user know that the keyboard will be unresponsive to input for a while, and so on. The commands to carry out those objectives all belong in the printing routine.

```
      A         B         C         D         E         F         G         H
 1  PRINT    {goto}PRT_MSG~                              Show message
 2           {windowsoff}{paneloff}                      Freeze screen
 3           /rncBUDGET~{bs}.                             Redefine print range
 4           {end}{l}{end}{d}~
 5           /ppcrrBUDGET~agpq                           Print report
 6           {windowson}{panelon}                        Unfreeze screen
 7           {branch START}                              Return to main menu
 8
 9
10
```

Figure 29-3

Routines such as this one, however, often evolve into routines that include other routines. For example, although the purpose of this routine is to print a report, you might want to add an option to select compressed print. If you do, you should present a menu that offers compressed print, normal print (return from compressed to normal width), and no-change (leave the current setting, whatever it is, alone).

Although this action is directly related to the printing that this routine is designed to perform, the alternate choices of compressed versus normal printing dictate that the instructions to establish those settings be organized separately from the main print routine. For all intents and purposes, you can regard such small subroutines as a part of the routine from which they spring. Here's the rewritten macro.

```
       A         B          C           D          E          F
 1  PRINT    {goto}PRT_MSG~                              Show message
 2           {windowsoff}{paneloff}                      Freeze screen
 3           /rncBUDGET~{bs}.                             Redefine print range
 4           {end}{l}{end}{d}~
 5  LOOP     {menubranch MEN1}{branch LOOP}      Font options menu
 6
 7  MEN1     Compressed    Normal       No change
 8           Change to com Change to nor Leave the current setting
 9           {COMPRES}     {NORM}        {branch PRT} Call subr for fonts
10           {branch PRT}  {branch PRT}
11
12  PRT      /ppcrrBUDGET~agpq                           Print report
13           {windowson}{panelon}                        Unfreeze screen
14           {branch START}                              Return to main menu
15
16  COMPRES  /ppos\015~qq                                Compressed mode, Epson
17           {return}
18
19  NORM     /ppos\027@~qq                               Reset to default, Epson
20           {return}
```

Figure 29-4

Segregate Dissimilar Tasks into Separate Routines

The corollary to organizing similar tasks into a single routine is to segregate dissimilar ones in separate routines. You do that by placing those dissimilar tasks into separate routines. For example, you might have an application that includes data entry, some what-if manipulation options, graphs, printed reports, and an exit operation that includes posting data to an external file used in the preparation of another report.

You'd probably transform each of those activities into a separate routine. If you do, it'll be much easier for you to revise each of those routines when the needs that gave rise to them change. And you may find that you can extract one or more of those routines to a disk file, and then combine the extracted routines into another worksheet that needs a similar routine.

That's one reason to write separate routines, but there is another: to avoid duplication. Suppose that five separate routines contain printing operations, and those printing operations are all more or less the same.

Consolidating the printing operations into one subroutine that can be called by all five routines would reduce the amount of macros you'll have to write, it will also help you to reduce errors in the macro.

For example, suppose each printing routine begins by moving the screen to display a message that will remain on screen while the printing ties up the computer, and that in the course of writing other routines, you decide to change the name you use to refer to the range containing that message. If you've imbedded the printing routines in other macros or merely repeated them once for each macro that prints a report, you'll now have to locate all such routines and make the change five times. 1-2-3 offers you no help in finding those routines, (except in Release 2.2, which incorporates a Search and Replace feature that enables you to replace the old name with the new one. However, if you've consolidated all those routines into one, that change would be simple to make; you wouldn't even need to use Search and Replace if you had it.

Make Subroutines Independent of Calling Routines

Although you may encounter situations where you can consolidate several subroutines without modifying them, it's more likely that you'll need to design the common subroutine somewhat differently from the originals. The common subroutine should be general enough to accommodate the needs of a variety of calling routines, each of which can pass parameters to the common subroutine parameters in order to specialize its action.

Suppose your application requires that the user enter a social security number, and you designed a routine to check for errors in that number. With the social-security error-checking in place, you realize that you have other potential data-entry errors to manage. Let's suppose the next item in the user's sequence of entering data is a zip code. With some thinking, you see that if you revise the error-handling routine you already have, it will manage the job for both entries.

You need to slightly rewrite how each data-entry routine calls the subroutine so that each passes to that subroutine parameters that will specialize the way the subroutine works with each of them. Initially, it's more work to design an error-correcting routine that works well with both data-entry routines, but the extra work yields tangible benefits:

- You avoid spending your time and 1-2-3's memory repeatedly writing similar error-checking routines.

- If you ever need to revise your error-correcting routines, there's now only one of the them (or if you've written more than one, fewer) to locate and revise. One change to a subroutine effectively modifies each routine that uses its services.

Before we leave this subject, there's one liability to consider. Suppose you have written a subroutine that is called by five routines. Let's further suppose that you decide to modify that subroutine, and it turns out that one of those five routines can't tolerate the change. The next time the macro runs that change will cause it to malfunction.

There is a guideline you can follow to reduce the incidence of this problem: Don't apply too rigidly what we've said about consolidating your subroutines. If you have to jump through hoops to get all the calling routines to use the services of a single subroutine you may be missing an important cue: That they really need different subroutines in order to prevent the kind of unintended problems alluded to above.

Set Up the Worksheet Manually

Don't Do It with Macros

If your worksheet will have any "set it and forget it" settings, don't establish them through a macro. Set them manually and then save the worksheet to permanently incorporate them into your application.

For example, if you never have to change the print headings on your reports, don't have the macro enter them anew each time you run a report—or even once when the application first starts. Instead, with the worksheet containing the macros loaded, select / Print Printer Options Header, enter the print headings by hand, and save the file. Once they have been saved with the file, there's no need for the macro to enter them. The fewer instructions your macro needs to read, the faster it will run.

Separate One-time Instructions from Recurring Instructions

You're already acquainted with writing loops. Now we'd like you to think about what should (and should not) reside within a loop. Since a macro will repeat a loop any number of times, you want that loop to contain only the instructions that need to be repeated. Otherwise, each iteration of the loop will take longer than necessary.

For example, consider the following macro.

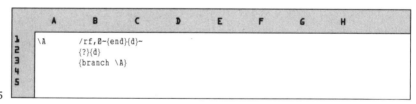

Figure 29-5

The macro formats a column of cells and then enables the user to enter data into cells in the column. However, the instructions on row 1 don't need to be repeated each time you enter data in another cell. Rewrite the macro to exclude row 1 from the loop, as shown below.

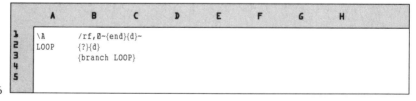

Figure 29-6

A variant of this guideline applies to circumstances where you should place an instruction in an initialization routine in order to prevent it from recurring in the instructions that follow. Consider the following routine, excerpted from a larger macro presented earlier.

```
        A         B         C         D         E         F         G         H
21   SETUP     {getlabel "Can you display graphs? (y/n)";DECIDE}
22             {if DECIDE<>"Y"#and#DECIDE<>"N"}{branch SETUP}
23             {if DECIDE="Y"}{let GRAPH_YN;"DO_GRAPH"}{branch \A}
24             {let GRAPH_YN;"NO_GRAPH"}{branch \A}
25
26   DECIDE
27
28   GRAPH_YN
29
30
```

Figure 29-7

The first row of the macro prompts for a one character response (either "y" or "n") and stores it in a cell named Decide. You don't know if the user entered that character in upper or lower case. Successive lines in the macro will test the entry to determine if it was a "Y" or an "N".

Conditional statements (such as those contained in the {if} commands on rows 22 and 23) don't discriminate between uppercase and lowercase characters (so, for example, "Y" = "y" would be true) unless you are running a copy of 1-2-3 with the ASCII Collating driver installed (in which case "Y" = "y" will be false). Let's suppose that you are developing an application that must work no matter which collating driver 1-2-3 is running under, so you have to have a way of testing not only for "Y" or "N", but for "y" or "n".

Rather than test each entry for all four characters, you decide that no matter what case the entry is, you should convert it into uppercase before you perform the test so you need test only for "N". You have a choice of doing that conversion in one of two ways, and depending on the particular macro at hand, one of those ways will be the more efficient.

For example, in the modified routine shown below, we've changed each reference to the range name Decide in the two {if} statements. The reference is no longer just to Decide, but to the uppercase value of Decide: @upper(DECIDE).

```
        A         B         C         D         E         F         G         H
21   SETUP     {getlabel "Can you display graphs? (y/n)";DECIDE}
22             {if @upper(DECIDE)<>"Y"#and#@upper(DECIDE)<>"N"}{branch SETUP}
23             {if @upper(DECIDE)="Y"}{let GRAPH;"DO_GRAPH"}{branch \A}
24             {let GRAPH_YN;"NO_GRAPH"}{branch \A}
25
26   DECIDE
27
28   GRAPH_YN
29
30
```

Figure 29-8

Let's suppose that you have numerous such tests to perform on the entry in Decide. In this case, there's a way to handle the conversion more efficiently than the technique we just presented. Rather than using @upper(DECIDE) in each test, you could precede all the tests with a single statement, {let DECIDE;@upper(DECIDE)}, that would convert the entry stored in Decide to uppercase. Thereafter, there's no need to write all those references as @upper(DECIDE), because the entry stored in Decide already is in uppercase. Here's the modified macro.

	A	B	C	D	E	F	G	H
21	SETUP	{getlabel "Can you display graphs? (y/n)";DECIDE}						
22		{let DECIDE;@upper(DECIDE)}						
23		{if DECIDE<>"Y"#and#DECIDE<>"N"}{branch SETUP}						
24		{if DECIDE="Y"}{let GRAPH_YN;"DO_GRAPH"}{branch \A}						
25		{let GRAPH_YN;"NO_GRAPH"}{branch \A}						
26								
27	DECIDE							
28								
29	GRAPH_YN							
30								

Figure 29-9

The lesson in this small example is that if you see a problem you will have to deal with repeatedly in your macro, look for a way to handle it once, just as the {let} statement does here.

Plan: How to Use Flow Charts and Pseudo Code

While the planning emphasis in smaller applications is devoted entirely to solving the technical problems associated with writing the routine at hand, in larger applications you must also plan the overall flow of the application, the different modules it comprises, and the relationships among those modules. There are two tools to help you plan larger applications: flow charts and pseudo code.

Drawing a flow chart will help you to describe the flow of the application. For example, it will tell you where each menu choice should lead, and what branches should proceed from a given {if} statement. Drawing a flow chart is generally a clearer, faster process than writing. As your applications become more complex, so will the flow charts you use to represent them.

If you wish, you can obtain a book on flow-charting and learn about the array of special symbols that have been developed for use in flow charts. We suggest you begin more simply. Establish the starting point (where the user is when the application begins) and the end point (or points, if there's more than one opportunity to exit). Now identify the first juncture at which either the application or the user will make a decision, note the options available, and draw lines showing the available routes to the next juncture. Use a pencil so you can change your work easily. When you've laid out the entire application, you may wish to review it with someone else who is knowledgable about the application. In any case, once you've accurately represented the application with the flow chart, you're ready to write pseudo code.

Pseudo coding enables you to describe what you want 1-2-3 to do without your becoming overwhelmed with the mechanics of actually doing it. For example, rather than write macro code to widen a column and include within it a subroutine call to supply the column width (for example, /wcs{WIDEN}~), you'd pseudo code that operation by describing the process in English (for example, "widen the column and allow for varying widths").

The relationship of pseudo code to flow charting is that pseudo coding fleshes out the operation described on the flow chart. Through pseudo code, you're saying, in effect, "Here are the steps I need to take to translate the general processes described on the flow chart into tasks 1-2-3 can carry out." Those tasks might include displaying a form for data entry, checking the entered data for errors, saving a file, widening a column, and copying a table of values from one range to another.

At the same time, you can lay out the worksheet, either on paper or on the screen. You must first have at least visualized the worksheet layout before you can write the pseudo code that expresses how to manipulate that worksheet. The person who writes the pseudo code should have a working knowledge of 1-2-3 in order to know what operations 1-2-3 will have to perform. On the contrary, the person doing the flow-charting needs to know very little about 1-2-3.

After writing pseudo code, review it to identify any common tasks, such as printing, that when you write the macro you will turn into subroutines. After you've made that review and noted the tasks that can be handled by a given subroutine, you're ready to translate your pseudo code into functioning macros.

Here's a summary of the process:

1. Draw flowchart.
   Note: Review results with someone else who knows the application.

2. Write pseudo code.
   Note: Identify common tasks to be handled by subroutines.

3. Write macro code.
   Note: Allow time to test and debug the application.

30

Macro Development Tips and Tools

Ironically, the process by which we craft fleet-footed, macro-driven applications is often entirely manual, and slow. However, there's no reason why some of the same tricks we use in our applications can't be applied to speed the process of developing those applications. This section presents a potpourri of time-saving tips and tools:

Toggling Between Two Files. Use this technique with Release 2.2 to quickly switch between two files and you won't have to rely on your memory to know what's in another worksheet that relates to your current project.

Navigational Aids. Since macros and the data on which they operate are usually located on separate areas of the worksheet, you'll often find your self shuttling back and forth between the two. These techniques can reduce the ardor of the journey.

Directory Switcher. This macro makes it easy to change your current directory so you can quickly find the information you need.

Learn Macro. In Release 2 or 2.01, model a macro and record it at the same time with this Learn macro.

Speedkey Macro. Use this macro to write any of the key names (such as {down} or {calc}) into your macros just by pressing those keys.

571

Benchmarks for your Macros. Performance is a key issue in most macro applications. Here's how to evaluate the relative merits of different approaches.

Run Macro. Use this macro to separately test each of the routines that makes up your macro.

Debug with { Indicate }. The { indicate } command offers a simple yet effective way to pin down where the trouble lies with a malfunctioning macro.

Debug with Step Mode. Release 2.2 provides a much-enhanced step mode that lets you trace through your macro, seeing each command just before it is carried out.

Range Name Documentor. Use this technique to document your range names so you can reinstate them if need be.

Protect your Macros. Use these techniques to prevent your work from being accidentally destroyed.

Updating an Application Already in Use. Plan for the revision of your macros from the start and that process can be a lot smoother.

Search and Replace. Find any string of macro code quickly and easily. Make revising names of routines and variables in your macros effortless.

User Macro. Instead of using backslash-letter names for your macros, use descriptive names, and use those names to run your macros.

Accelerator Keys. Provide routes by which you can directly run commonly used routines as an alternative to selecting those routines from menus.

Some of what follows are tips; some are macro tools. We recommend that you keep the macros in their own library file and combine them into your worksheet when you first begin to develop it. Keep them separate from the other macros you write so that, when you've finished your development work, you can easily erase them. If you have Release 2.2, you can use the Macro Library Manager add-in. Because the MLM makes these macros instantly available, it may become your single greatest productivity tool for developing macros. Since it takes only about 13K, we suggest you keep it installed all the time.

Toggling Between Two Files

When you write more advanced macros, it is not uncommon to need to refer to one or more worksheet files stored on the disk. Depending on how much memory you have available and how large the files are, you may be able to use Release 2.2's Undo capability to view them.

With Undo enabled, save the worksheet containing the macros you are currently working on. That step will prevent you from losing any work if you make an error while using Undo (more on that subject, shortly). Next, retrieve the worksheet you wish to review. Navigate around the worksheet in any way you want. You may use the arrow keys, Home, End, PageUp, PageDown, and the Goto command. When you want to see the worksheet containing the macros again, press Undo (Alt-F4). Provided there is sufficient memory, you'll instantly see the worksheet containing the macros.

Be aware, though, that while you are using the two files in tandem, you may not do anything besides move the cell pointer. Do not, for example, press the Calc key, edit a cell, or press the slash key. All such actions can be undone, and 1-2-3 will automatically replace the worksheet currently in the undo buffer with a copy of the current file as it was prior to your having initiated the undoable action. If the file that was in the undo buffer was the file containing the macros you had been working on, and you had not previously saved your work, you would have lost that work. That's why it is crucial that you save your file before using the Undo key for this purpose.

Navigational Aids

One of the challenges of writing macros is navigating between the area where you're writing the macro and the area where you have stored the data on which the macro operates.

Earlier we showed you how to split the screen horizontally (with the / Worksheet Window Horizontal command), unsynchronize the windows (with the / Worksheet Window Unsynch command), orient one screen to display your macros, orient the other half to show your data, and navigate between them with the Window function key (F6 on most computers).

There are several other quick solutions to the navigation problem. Let's suppose you want to write a line of macro code in which you need to reference a range. Leave the cell pointer in the macro-writing area, select / Range Name Create, and enter your range name. 1-2-3 will now allow you to point to the range. Press Backspace to unanchor the cell pointer, use the directional keys (such as Tab and PgDn, or Window) to move to the area containing your data, re-anchor the cell pointer by pressing the period key, highlight the range you wish to name, and press Return. 1-2-3 will immediately return the cell pointer to its original location, saving you 50 percent of the navigating work.

If while writing a macro you need just to look at the portion of the worksheet where your data resides, with your cell pointer in your column of macros, press the plus key, then use the directional keys to point to the location in question. If you've split the screen with the Worksheet Window command, you can also use the Window key (F6) to hop into the other window. Once you've observed what you needed to, press the Escape key. 1-2-3 will immediately return the cell pointer to the macro-writing area you started from. Pressing Escape again will clear the formula and restore 1-2-3 to READY mode.

If you use a lot of named ranges, as most macro developers do, you'll occasionally need to know the cell coordinates of a named range. The / Range Name Table command provides a table of all range names and corresponding range specifications, but when you need to know about only one named range, there's a simpler method. In Release 2 or 2.01, the quickest route is to select / Range Name Create, enter the name of the range, and observe the range specification that 1-2-3 displays in the control panel. In Release 2.2, you can simply press the Goto key and then twice press the Name key. You'll not only see a full screen of named ranges, as in Release 2.01, but in the edit panel you'll see the range specification of the range name that's currently highlighted. Once you have seen the specification, press Escape twice to return to READY mode.

Finally, if you merely need to know the contents of a cell and you either know its address or you know the range name assigned to it, press the plus key and enter the cell address or range name in question. If you now press the Calc key, 1-2-3 will display the value currently stored in the cell in question. Press Escape twice to return to Ready mode.

Directory Switcher

We find that there is no time when we are apt to change subdirectories more often than during the process of developing macros. If you need to select a file in a directory other than the current directory, or to select the parent directory to the current directory, 1-2-3 lets you use the Backspace key; to select a child directory, simply highlight the name of that directory and press Return, just as you would if you were selecting a file.

However, if you want to log onto another directory, you'll use the / File Directory command. That command offers no way to select a subdirectory visually, forcing you to type in the correct directory path and name without any prompts to help. That requirement can be overcome with a directory-switching macro like the one below. The macro displays up to eight subdirectories of your choice and lets you select one by highlighting it and pressing return.

	A	B	C	D	E	F
1	\[DIR]	{menubranch [DIR_MENU]}				
2		{quit}				
3						
4	[DIR_MENU]	123\	DISK\	TAX\	A:\	B:\
5		Make C:\123\	Make C:\DISK	Make C:\TAX\	Make A:\ the	Make B:\ the
6		/fdC:\123~	/fdC:\DISK~	/fdC:\TAX~	/fdA:\~	/fdB:\~
7						
8						
9						
10						

Figure 30-1

The directory switcher is straightforward. The main routine uses the {menubranch} command to post a menu of subdirectories. If you select a subdirectory, 1-2-3 will use the File Directory command to reset the current directory.

The name of the main routine, \[Dir], indicates that we feel this macro is a prime candidate for inclusion in a Release 2.2 macro library, and for subsequent invocation with 2.2's Run key (Alt-F3). Since the need to change directories isn't related to any particular worksheet, it makes sense to place this macro where you can use it at any time.

If some of your subdirectories begin with the same first character (for example \sales and \service), you may wish to change the macro so that you choose subdirectories by number. Doing so will circumvent the dual first-character problem, because even if five directory names start with the same character, the number that identifies each directory can still be unique. Here's the modified macro:

	A	B	C	D	E	F
1	\[DIR]	{menubranch [DIR_MENU]}				
2		{quit}				
3						
4	[DIR_MENU]	1-123\	2-DISK\	3-TAX\	4-A:\	5-B:\
5		Make C:\123\	Make C:\DISK	Make C:\TAX\	Make A:\ the	Make B:\ the
6		/fdC:\123~	/fdC:\DISK~	/fdC:\TAX~	/fdA:\~	/fdB:\~
7						
8						
9						
10						

Figure 30-2

For people who don't commonly log to the same directory each time they start 1-2-3, this macro has proven popular as an autoexecute macro. After 1-2-3 loads, it presents them with a menu of directories from which to choose.

Learn Macro

you can
model and
write the
macro in
one step

Modeling the operation you intend your macro to perform is a good way to cut development time because that practice reduces inaccurate keystrokes in the resulting macro. You can speed the development process further by using a technique that collapses the steps of modeling the macro and writing the macro into a single operation. 1-2-3 Release 2.2 has its own Learn command, and there is an add-in you can obtain for Release 2 and 2.01, Lotus Learn, that does the job in those versions. If neither of these are available to you, try the following Learn macro.

A Learn macro records as macro labels the keystrokes you type. For example, if you print a report, the Learn macro will write the label /ppagpq on the worksheet. The macro employs the {get} command to capture your keystrokes, then uses each captured keystroke twice. First the macro sends the keystroke to 1-2-3, which executes the keystroke as if it had been typed at the keyboard, then the macro writes the keystroke on the worksheet as a label. As you enter keystrokes at the keyboard with the Learn macro running, 1-2-3 acts just like it does in interactive mode, though you'll note it's a bit slower due to the extra steps used to simultaneously create a macro.

Here's the Learn macro.

	IU	IV
1	\L	{let ROW;21}
2		{blank IV21.IV8192}
3		{recalc LOOP}
4	LOOP	{get ANS}
5		{if ANS="{QUERY}"}{quit}
6		{if ANS="{"}{let ANS;"{{}"}
7		{ANS}
8		{let IV21;@s(!IV21)&ANS}
9	==>	{if @length(IV21)>30}{let ROW;ROW+1}{recalc LOOP}
10		{branch LOOP}
11		
12	ROW	21
13		
14	ANS	
15		{return}
16		
17		
18		
19		
20		

Figure 30-3

why
LEARN is
"ill-
behaved"

Because of some special circumstances, Learn violates precepts we've encouraged you to adhere to when you write macros, principles such as using range names instead of cell addresses and minimizing the use of string formulas. As such, it stands as a lesson in when to make exceptions to those rules.

After Learn captures a keystroke and has 1-2-3 execute it, Learn appends the character representing that keystroke to other such characters already stored in a cell on the worksheet. When the number of characters in a cell reaches a specified amount, Learn begins sending the keystroke characters to the cell below. It continues filling contiguous cells in the same column until you terminate Learn mode.

Learn employs an uncommon technique to shift the destination of the keystrokes as each succeeding cell fills. The more common technique for moving a destination cell is as follows. First, assign to the destination cell a range name and send the keystrokes to the named cell. When the cell fills, have the macro select Range Name Create, enter the range name, unanchor the cell pointer and move it down a cell, then press Return. The macro can then direct keystrokes to the same range name and they'll be stored in the new range. However, you can't use that technique in a Learn macro. The user may be in the middle of recording some other command sequence when it's time to use the / Range Name Create command upon which that approach depends.

Instead, each time Learn has to redirect keystrokes to the next cell down the column, it increments a row counter and, in two string formulas in the macro, concatenates the column letter(s) already written into the macro with the string value of the new row number to create the new destination cell's address.

We embedded 21, the starting row number, and IU and IV, the column letters, directly into the macro (a procedure referred to as "hard coding" those elements into the macro). IU and IV are good locations for storing keystrokes because they generally are not used in other ways. Since 1-2-3 Release 2 and higher incorporate a memory management schema that won't penalize you for using a worksheet range so far from cell A1, these columns are an ideal spot for storing keystrokes.[69] It's more work to write the macro so that it can be placed anywhere on the worksheet, so we'll discuss that variation later. Now let's dissect the operation of this macro routine by routine.

Initialize

```
{let ROW;21}              Initialize row counter
{blank IV21.IV8192}       Clear old macro
{recalc LOOP}             Update cell addresses
```

[69] For a detailed discussion of how to avoid unnecessarily encumbering memory, in Chapter 28 see the section on Using Available Memory Efficiently.

The macro begins by storing an initial value of 21 in a cell named Row. Since the macro will later increment that number as it calculates new cell addresses, you might call 21 an initial value, and placing it there is commonly referred to as initializing the row counter.

Learn then clears the contents of the range in which it will store keystrokes, IV21.IV8192 (that single period is no typographical error; either one or two periods serves as a valid ellipsis in a range description). The next {recalc} statement recalculates the range named Loop (B4..B9), which includes several string formulas in the macro.

As you might suspect from the irrelevancy of the name Loop to the string formulas it contains, Loop does double duty in this macro. The top cell in the named range of string formulas contains a macro instruction to which you'll want to branch repeatedly. Since a {branch} command will redirect macro control to the top left cell in any range, instead of using one range name to contain the string formulas and another to name the top cell in that range so the macro can reference it in a {branch} command, we've used just one name. Loop begins on the next line of the macro and covers the following five lines.

```
LOOP   {get ANS}                              Capture key
|      {if ANS="{QUERY}"}{quit}               Stop if Query pressed
|      {if ANS="{"}{let ANS;"{{}"}            Fix ANS for "{"
|      {ANS}                                  Echo key
|      {let IV21;@s(IV21)&ANS}                Concatenate ANS
|==>   {if @length(IV21)>30}{let ROW;ROW+1}   {recalc LOOP}
       {branch LOOP}                          Get another key
```

Beginning in row 4 the macro captures a keystroke, stores it in a cell named Ans, and performs two tests on it. The first of those tests checks to see if the keystroke is a key you've designated to use to stop Learn. That's the special key {QUERY} in this example; it could be any key you expect you will not press while recording keystrokes with Learn. If the macro detects that key, it terminates.

The second test is for a left curly brace ({) which, because of the way in which this macro passes keystrokes to 1-2-3, requires some special treatment. Specifically, that character has to be enclosed within a set of curly braces or, when the macro tries to record it as a label, the macro will instead interpret it as a macro instruction to be acted upon immediately.

The next instruction runs Ans as a subroutine. You'll recall that the {get} command stored the most recent keystroke in Ans and that you want to not only store the keystroke but pass it through to 1-2-3 so that 1-2-3 will respond to the user's keystroke. By running Ans as a subroutine, you will be sending the captured keystroke through to 1-2-3. If the user had just typed a W, the macro would have stored a W in Ans and a W would appear in the control panel just as if it had been typed without the Learn macro operating.

The next two cells of the macro, IU8 and IU9, contain string formulas. Those string formulas concatenate the column letters IV with the current value in the row counter to create a cell address. Cell IU8 reads as follows:

concatenation with string formulas

```
+"{let IV"&@STRING(ROW;0)&";@s(IV"&@STRING(ROW;0)&")&ANS}"
```

If Row contains 21, the resulting macro label would be {let IV21;@s(IV21)&ANS}. That statement concatenates the keystroke in Ans with whatever was already in cell IV21. The next row (IU9) is also a string formula:

```
+"{if @length(IV"&@STRING(ROW;0)&")>30}{let ROW;ROW+1}{recalc LOOP}"
```

If Row contains 21, the resulting macro label would be {if @length(IV21)>30}{let ROW;ROW+1}{recalc LOOP}. It checks the length of the cell entry in IV21 and, when the length of the entry is greater than 30 characters, increments Row by 1 and recalculates the range named Loop. In the next reading of this and the preceding statement, IV22 will be the destination Learn fills with keystrokes and tests.

The final row of the macro, {branch LOOP}, returns control to the top cell of Loop where the {get ANS} statement will await another keystroke from the user.

limitations

There are a several limitations to be aware of while using the Learn macro:

- Learn won't tolerate inserted or deleted columns or rows. Because the macro contains hard-coded cell addresses to locate data it requires, if you delete any columns to its left or insert or delete any rows above it, you'll change the location of that data and cause the macro to malfunction when it next runs. Because the macro resides in the rightmost column of the worksheet, if you attempt to insert columns to the macro's left, 1-2-3 will issue the error message "Worksheet full" (1-2-3 won't let you push data off the edge of the worksheet).

- Learn reserves certain range names. Learn uses the range names \L, ANS, RES, and LOOP, so you cannot use those names in the macro you are using Learn to write.

- Learn records what you do, not what you mean. Learn records keystrokes verbatim, so if you type "Jones," then press Backspace twice and type "as", the macro won't record "Jonas," it'll record "Jones{BACKSPACE} {BACKSPACE} as " Although the resulting macro will produce the label "Jonas," it'll type it just as you did, with two Backspace keystrokes. You can use the Edit key to remove extraneous keystrokes from the recorded macro after you finish recording.

- Learn records all keystrokes but one: The way it's written above, Learn will use any keystroke that you specify to terminate itself. Obviously, you can't include that keystroke in the macro you are using Learn to write. If that limitation bothers you, do one of two things. Either remove the statement {if ANS = "{QUERY}"} {quit} from the macro and depend on the Control-Break key sequence to terminate the macro or, instead of having the macro terminate when the designated key is pressed, have the macro post a menu. If you designated the Query key (F7) as the key to terminate the macro, then the two choices on the menu would be STOP and QUERY. STOP would, of course, terminate the macro. QUERY, however, would issue and record the {QUERY} keystroke, then return control to the Learn macro.

- Learn records keynames in long form. Since the Learn macro bases its output on the results of the {get} command, all of the keynames will appear in uppercase and in their long form (for example, {BACKSPACE} instead of {BS}), except for the Delete and Escape keys, which default to the short form. [70] Long keynames take longer for 1-2-3 to read than do short ones, so if your macro contains many such keynames you might want to speed it up by shortening them. A quick way to do that is to use a lookup table like the one in the second Speedkey macro, which appears next.

Speedkey Macro

Two keystrokes take the place of ten

As the macros throughout this chapter attest, the more advanced your macros become, the greater the proportion of advanced macro commands they will contain. Since Learn can only record keystroke macros, it's of little use when you're developing complex macros. That means you'll be writing such macros manually, but if you're not such a good typist or your memory for keyname-syntax lapses occasionally, you'll

---

[70] For a full explanation of how {get} records keynames, refer to the heading Capturing Single Characters in Chapter 22, Managing User Input, and read up to and including the table of 1-2-3 Special Keys That Have More Than One Form.

appreciate the Speedkey macro. This macro can reduce the work by writing for you any of the the keynames (such as {edit}, {esc}, and {right}). For example, if you were typing a macro in which you wanted to include the {bigright} keyname, you would ordinarily type out that name. With Speedkey, you'd press Alt-S and the Tab key and the macro would type {BIGRIGHT} for you.

Since you want to be able to invoke Speedkey in the midst of typing a macro label, Speedkey has to be able to type a key name into 1-2-3's edit line without executing that key name as a macro. Preventing that from happening constitutes the special challenge of this macro. Here's Speedkey.

```
       A        B           C          D         E        F          G
 1    \S      {get ANS}                                 Capture a key
 2            {if @length(ANS)=1}{quit}                 If letter, quit
 3            {let RES;@MID(ANS;1;@LENGTH(ANS)-1)}      Change key
 4            {{}{RES}                                   Run changed key
 5
 6    ANS     {BIGRIGHT}                                Storage - original key
 7
 8    RES     BIGRIGHT}                                 Storage - changed key
 9
10
```

Figure 30-4

Let's review how Speedkey works. After you invoke it, Speedkey waits for you to press the special key you want it to write. When press that key, the macro stores the keyname for that keystroke in a cell named Ans.

In the Speedkey macro's second row, it tests the length of the entry stored in Ans and terminates the macro if that entry is only one character long. If the entry contains a single letter, Speedkey assumes you mistakenly typed a single letter instead of a special key—there are no special keys with keynames of only one character—and returns you to interactive mode without taking further action. If the entry stored there does consist of more than one character, then the key you pressed was a special key and Speedkey creates a new entry derived from the keyname stored in Ans. That new entry is one that can be placed in the edit line.

The instruction in cell B3 creates the new entry, by removing the leading brace character from the keyname in Ans, and storing the resulting string in a cell named Res (for Result). You can see the effect of that action by, in the macro shown above, comparing the entry stored in Ans with the entry stored in Res. The absence of that leading brace "disguises" the

keyname so that 1-2-3 will not act on the keyname as an instruction when
the macro types it into the edit line. Here's how it works.

After the entry has been truncated and placed in Res, the macro types a
left brace character into the edit line, then types the truncated key name
stored in Res. Since the left brace is always the truncated character, in
total, those keystrokes together constitute the entire key name. However,
since the macro enters them as two separate strings, 1-2-3 won't treat
them as a macro command when Speedkey retypes them.

The job of retyping them falls to the final row of macro, which contains the left brace and a subroutine call to Res. Res, in turn contains the
remainder of the key name.

This preceding version of Speedkey records keystrokes in exactly the
same way 1-2-3 records them. Unfortunately, it runs contrary to some of
the macro conventions we've espoused: It writes key names in uppercase
instead of lowercase and uses the long version of keynames ({BACK-
SPACE} instead of {bs}). However, you can adapt Speedkey to work
the way you do. Here's how.

	A	B	C	D	E	F	G
1	\S	{get ANS}				Capture a key	
2		{recalc KEY_TAB}				Calc KEY_TAB formulas	
3		{if @length(ANS)=1}{quit}				If letter, quit	
4		{let RES;@vlookup(ANS;KEY_TAB;1)}				Change key via table	
5		{{}{RES}				Run changed key	
6							
7	ANS	{ESC}				Storage - original key	
8							
9	RES	esc}				Storage - changed key	
10							
11	KEY_TAB	{DOWN}	d}			Lookup table	
12		{LEFT}	l}				
13		{RIGHT}	r}				
14		{UP}	u}				
15		{BACKSPACE}	bs}				
16		{ESC}	esc}			String formulas	
17							
18							
19							
20							

Figure 30-5

The major difference between this and the previous version of Speedkey is the addition of a lookup table. The macro code in B4 uses the entry
in Ans as a key to look up an entry in the lookup table called Key_tab.
Key_tab is remarkable only in the sense that the entries in its bottom
row, in cells B16 and C16, are string formulas. The second command in
the macro recalculates Key_tab to update those formulas.

The formulas in Key_tab are very straightforward. B16 is a simple reference to Ans: +ANS. C16 changes B16 to lowercase and subtracts the leftmost curly brace. It reads as follows:

```
@LOWER(@MID(B16;1;@LENGTH(B16)-1))
```

In summary, this version of Speedkey captures a keystroke, recalculates the lookup table, retrieves the corresponding entry from the lookup table, and types the first left curly brace and then the retrieved entry into the edit line. If the recorded key is one of the five that 1-2-3 records in their long form (such as {BACKSPACE}), then the table yields the short form, in lowercase, without the left curly brace. The formulas at the bottom of the table produce the lowercase, truncated form of any other keyname.

If you are using Release 2.2, you may wish to add {INSERT} to Speedkey's conversion table between {BACKSPACE} and {ESC}. 2.2 supports the shorter keyname {ins} as well the longer {insert}. Like some of the other tools presented in this chapter, Speedkey is most useful when stored in a macro library. This will permit you to use it whenever you write a macro, without having to combine it in from another file.

Benchmarking Your Routines

As you learn more about macros, you'll frequently find yourself confronted with more than one way to write a given routine. If neither requires you to write string formulas, then the most common criteria for deciding between the two is speed. In this section we'll present techniques by which you can compare the speeds of alternate routines—a process commonly referred to as benchmarking.

As with the routines in question, in testing, too, there's more than one way to skin the cat. The best testing method depends on the approximate length of time it takes to run the routines you wish to test. For longer routines, use the technique we'll refer to here as single pass timing; for short ones, the method we call multi-pass timing is best. The latter approach compensates for rounding errors that occur with small time values.

Here's the method for single-pass timing.

Step 1. Create two one-celled named ranges called, respectively, Start and Stop. Format them with the command / Range Format Date Time 1 (if the column is narrower than 12 spaces, you will need to widen it to at least that size to display these formats). Do not format the cell directly beneath these named ranges. In that cell, enter the following formula:

```
@string(@minute(STOP-START);0)&":"&@string(@second(STOP-START);0)
```

The formula will calculate the elapsed time of the macro in minutes and seconds and express it as MINUTES:SECONDS.

Step 2. Revise the first routine that you wish to test to include two {let} statements—one as the first instruction of the routine and one as the last. The new instructions are:

- The new first statement: {let START;@now}

- The new last statement: {let STOP;@now}

If you used the Move command to move the macro code down to leave a blank cell for the new first instruction, you'll have to assign the new first cell a range name or the macro will begin with the second cell.

Now activate the macro.

Step 3. Press the Calc key to update the formula and use the / Range Value command to transfer the current elapsed time to a nearby cell while you test the second macro.

Step 4. Revise the second macro as described in step 2 and activate it. Press the Calc key to update the formula and compare the elapsed times of each of the routines.

The method for multi-pass timing is a bit more involved.

	A	B	C	D	E	F	G
1	\B	{let START;@now}				Record start time	
2		{for COUNTER;1;TRIALS;1;ROUTINE}				Repeatedly run routine	
3		{let STOP;@now}				Record stop time	
4		{calc}{quit}				Recalc time formulas	
5							
6	COUNTER		101			Temporary storage	
7							
8	ROUTINE	{dispatch RT_NAME}				Routine to run	
9	RT_NAME						
10							
11	TRIALS		100			How many times to repeat	
12							
13							
14	START	02:57:43 PM				Start time	
15	STOP	02:58:09 PM				Stop time	
16		0:26				Elapsed Min:Sec	

Figure 30-6

Begin by, in the cell named Rt_name, entering the name of the macro you wish to test and in the cell named Trials, entering the number of times you wish to repeat the macro. If the routine you're testing is short, use a high number (25, 50, or 100) of repetitions to reduce the impact of rounding errors on small time values. The longer you expect the routine to run, the fewer iterations you'll need.

Format cells B14 and B15 (named Start and Stop, respectively) with the / Range Format Date Time 1 command. Column B must be at least 12 spaces wide to accommodate that format). Do not format cell B16; in that cell, enter the following formula:

```
@string(@minute(STOP-START);0)&":"&@string(@second(STOP-START);0)
```

This benchmarking macro consists of four steps; explanations of each follow.

Step 1. Store the time of day:

```
{let START;@now}
```

The {let} statement stores the current time in the cell named Start. Since the {let} command translates any expression into a static value, Start will contain a value, not the @now formula (the latter would continue to change; the former won't). When the macro terminates, it will again record the time, but in a different cell, and determine the difference between the two times.

Step 2. Repeatedly run the macro routine:

```
{for COUNTER;1;TRIALS;1;ROUTINE}
```

As in any {for} statement, the range referred to in the first argument (Counter) stores the number of the current iteration of the routine specified in the last argument (Routine). The second and fourth arguments provide the starting and incremental values, respectively.

Because the {for} statement treats as a subroutine the routine that it runs, that routine must observe some restrictions.

For example:

- The routine cannot end with a {quit} command. Doing so would terminate the macro prematurely.

- The routine cannot contain a {restart} command. That would effectively change the {for} command's subroutine call into a {branch}. In that case, the macro would not read any further iterations or record an ending time.

- The routine cannot contain a {forbreak} command unless the tested routine precedes that {forbreak} with its own {for} statement. Otherwise, the {forbreak} command would prematurely terminate the loop that the testing macro operates.

- The routine should be written to accommodate repeated operations. If the routine depends on having the cell pointer at a certain cell at its commencement, include a command at its end to return the cell pointer to that spot for the next iteration.

Step 3. Store the ending time:

`{let STOP;@now}`

After recording a static time value in Stop, a worksheet formula will subtract the old time value in Start from the new one in Stop.

Step 4. Recalculate the worksheet:

`{calc}{quit}`

The calc command will update the formula that calculates the number of minutes and seconds the routine took to complete its specified number of iterations.

After the routine finishes, use the / Range Value command to copy the elapsed time from cell B16 to another cell for storage, or the next macro you run will change that value. You must use the Range Value command instead of the Copy command because Range Value will transform the dynamic formula, which will change with each macro you test, into a static value entry, which won't change.

You should compare the elapsed time only with a value you obtained by running another routine through this benchmark for the same number of iterations. If you divide this figure by the number of times you repeated the routine (to gain an average time), and then compare that average time with a single iteration of another routine that was not gained through this benchmark, you'll produce invalid results. The {for} command, by which this benchmark operates, delays each iteration of the routine it tests, so you can only properly compare the time you gain from it with the time gained by testing another routine run with this benchmark for the same number of iterations.

Run Macro

If you've followed the approaches we've used throughout this book, your larger macros consist of numerous small routines. While you're developing each of those routines, it pays to test them, too. As you finish each of the latter routines in a sequence of routines, you'll want to test just the routine you have just written, without running through all the preceding ones, too.

One way to do that is to assign a unique backslash/letter range name to the routine that you want to test, then activate it, and, when you've finished your test, delete the range name so you can use it with the next routine. Another solution is to run the routine using whatever name you intend it to have in the final macro. Since those names are typically such things as Enter, Print, and Error, and those names can't be activated with the Alt-Letter keystroke combination, you'll need some way to activate the routine.

If you are using Release 2.2, the Run key (Alt-F3) lets you run such routines. Here's how to do it. Press Run. If the file contains any named ranges, you'll see a menu of them; press Escape to put 1-2-3 in Point mode and thereby reactivate the cell pointer. Point to the cell containing the first line of the macro and press Return. The macro will run, but only when you use this technique from READY mode.

Whether you want to test routines that begin operating while 1-2-3 is in Menu mode, or if you are using Release 2 or 2.01 of 1-2-3, use the following Run macro instead. Just place the cell pointer on the cell containing the first line of the routine you wish to run and activate the macro shown below.

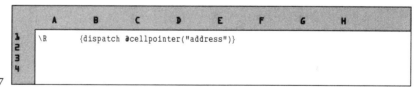

Figure 30-7

The macro relies on the ability of the {dispatch} command to use a formula as an argument. When you activate this macro, 1-2-3 will evaluate the formula to determine the address of the current location of the cell pointer (let's suppose that's the cell B5), and transfer macro control to that location.

The additional advantage of this macro is that you can use it to test portions of a routine or to test as yet unnamed routines.

Should you wish to run the macro with the cell pointer located not on it, but elsewhere in the worksheet, we'll show you how to do that when we explain the User Macro later in this chapter (pages 598–599).

Debugging with {indicate}

There are times when you won't have the luxury of testing each new routine by running it without first running the routines that precede it, because its predecessors provide vital input to it. That doesn't mean you'll have to sacrifice the ability to properly test that routine. If you run a test and the macro terminates improperly, you can use the {indicate} command to pinpoint the routine (or any portion thereof) that 1-2-3 was reading when the crash occurred.

Just insert the command {indicate "ROUTINE_NAME"} at the beginning of each routine in the macro, where, in Release 2.01, ROUTINE_NAME is up to five characters drawn from the name of the routine. Be sure each such five-character string is unique.

Run the macro again and, after it has crashed, the mode indicator will reveal the name of the culpable routine. If that routine is a long one and you have trouble identifying what portion of it caused the problem, you can further narrow your search. Remove the other {indicate} commands), then place a series of {indicate} commands in the form {indicate "SERIAL_NUMBER"} throughout the routine. Run the macro again and, after it's crashed, the serial number in the mode indicator will pinpoint the guilty portion of the routine.

This technique won't necessarily immediately lead you to the cause of the macro's problem; the real problem may lie with some earlier routine, but at least you have some evidence you can use to trace back to the cause of the trouble.

In Release 2.2, 1-2-3's Step mode is the technique of choice.

Debugging with Step

Release 2.2's Step mode is one of the best tools available for finding a problem in your macro. After you press the Step key (Alt-F2), 1-2-3 not only goes into Step mode, it displays in the lower left corner of your screen the current line of the macro, with a highlight on the instruction that 1-2-3 will read when you press the next keystroke. That mode continues until you press the Step key again to turn off this mode. The level of detail that Step mode provides is more precise than you could achieve with the {indicate} technique. But consider, too, that sometimes you don't want an approach that is so precise as this. Sometimes, {indicate} may narrow things down enough without using Step mode.

Range Name Table Documentor

managing range names

In applications of any size, you can easily end up with 25, 50, or 100 range names. Those range names are important; in many cases your macros reference ranges by name and won't function without those names.

What's more, those range names are at risk. Aside from such obvious threats as the Range Name Delete command (which deletes one name) and the Range Name Reset command (which, without further warning, deletes all your range names), there are yet more, and more subtle, opportunities for range-name related trouble.

how range names become corrupted

The key to a range name's survival are the cells that occupy the upper left and lower right corners of that range. Those cells are called the range's anchor cells. If you redefine that range, you'll see those cells' addresses in the control panel with two periods between them. If you use Point mode to redefine the range, you'll see that the cell pointer is anchored to each of those cells. If you change the location of either anchor cell, either by editing one of the cell addresses in the control panel or by pointing to another cell on the worksheet, 1-2-3 will redefine the range.

However, if you use the / Worksheet Delete Row (or Worksheet Delete Column) command to delete the row or column on which either anchor cell of the range resides, you'll corrupt that range definition. If you use the Move command and specify as the destination of that command an anchor cell, the same thing will happen.

When you corrupt a range name, 1-2-3 loses track of the associated range: Any name associated with the range becomes invalid, any formulas which reference that range will return the value ERR, and any command (such as / Data Query Input or / Print Printer Range) that stores that range will immediately lose its setting.

When a named range becomes corrupt through any of the actions described above, if you press the Goto and Name keys, you'll still see that range name in the control panel. If you select it, 1-2-3 will beep and display the error message "Invalid cell or range address".

If you then use the / Range Name Table command to write a list of range names and their associated ranges on the worksheet, 1-2-3 will still list the corrupted name, but it'll list the range associated with the corrupted name as ERR. If you save the file that contains that corrupt range

name and then retrieve the newly saved file from the disk, the range corner that caused the range to become corrupt will refer to IV8192 (the
lower right cell of the worksheet). If the original range was A1..C2, and
you'd moved something onto cell A1 (by which you corrupted the
range), then after saving and retrieving the worksheet, 1-2-3 will define
the range as C2..IV8192.

That makes it possible for you to use the / Range Name Table command to detect corrupted range names before they cause trouble. To do
so, before running your application, select the / Range Name Table command and scan the right column of the resulting table for range specifications that consist of ERR or that contain the cell address IV8192.

Another way to use the range-name table is to transform it into a more
lasting record of range names by adding a description in the column to the
right of the range specifications. The table below is an example of how
you might document your range names. The Range Name Table command will supply the leftmost two columns; you must supply the right
one and the column titles.

	A	B	C	D	E	F
161	=================		Range Name Table with Descriptions		====================	
162						
163		NAMES	ADDRESS		DESCRIPTION	
164		ANS	B135		Storage used by many macros	
165		DATA	B85..F92		Data input area	
166		MAIN	B125		Main menu (called by \M)	
167		MONTH	C71..D85		Monthly data	
168		NAMES	B164		Upper left cell of this table	
169		NUM	B114		Number of observations	
170		P_TEST	G43		Print test routine	
171		REPORT	I21		Report area	
172		TEST	G124		Cell to test keyboard entries	
173		\M	B122		Main menu macro	
174		\Q	C137		Quit macro	
175		\S	B132		File Save macro	
176						
177						
178						
179						
180						

Figure 30-8

This annotated range-name table is useful, but it won't adapt to
changes in the range names it documents. For instance, if you create a few
additional range names and recreate the table, the description fields won't
match the positions of the existing descriptions.

You can reorganize the table manually, but that process is time-con-
suming, and you can use a macro to do it instead. The updated table
(some new names have been added and others have been deleted) shown
below has been reconstructed with the macro, and is ready for you to fill
in the descriptions of the newly created range names.

```
          A        B          C        D         E          F
161   ================= Range Name Table with Descriptions ==================
162
163           NAMES      ADDRESS        DESCRIPTION
164           ANS        B135           Storage used by many macros
165           DATA       B85..F92       Data input area
166           LOWER      B43
167           MAIN       B125           Main menu (called by \M)
168           NAM        B29
169           NAMES      B164           Upper left cell of this table
170           NEW        B37
171           NUM        B114           Number of observations
172           N_SCREEN   A161
173           OLD        B40
174           ORDER      B31
175           REPORT     I21            Report area
176           TEST       G124           Cell to test keyboard entries
177           \M         B122           Main menu macro
178           \N         B21
179           \S         B132           File Save macro
180
```

Figure 30-9

The macro to automatically update the table appears below.

```
          A        B          C        D         E          F
21   \N       {goto}N_SCREEN~{goto}NAMES~
22            /c{LOWER}~{r 3}~
23            /re{LOWER}{r}~
24            /rntNAMES~
25            {ORDER}
26            {goto}NAMES~
27            /re{esc}{r 3}.{l 3}{LOWER}{r 3}~
28            {quit}
29   NAM
30
31   ORDER    {if @cellpointer("type")="b"}{return}
32            {let NAM;@cellpointer("contents")}{r 3}
33            {if NAM<@cellpointer("contents")}{branch NEW}
34            {if NAM>@cellpointer("contents")}{branch OLD}
35            {l 3}{d}{branch ORDER}
36
37   NEW      {l}/m{r}{LOWER}~{d}~
38            {l 2}{d}{branch ORDER}
39
40   OLD      {l}{d}/m{r}{LOWER}~{u}~
41            {l 2}{u}{branch ORDER}
42
43   LOWER    {if @cellpointer("type")="b"}{return}
44            {d}{if @cellpointer("type")="b"}{u}{return}
45            {u}{end}{d}{return}
46
47
48
49
50
```

Figure 30-10

Although it consists of five separate routines, the macro works on just a few principles. It positions the cell pointer, creates a new range-name table, transfers the descriptions from the old table to the new one, and erases any remaining entries. Now let's examine its operation in detail.

The first row of the macro positions the screen and moves the cell pointer to the top range name (cell B164) of the existing range-name table. The second and third rows copy all the existing range names to a column three columns to the right to preserve them, and erase the range names and cell addresses from the original range-name table.

The macro copies and erases the table with the help of the subroutine Lower. The instructions on row 22 select the Copy command, and in its midst invoke the subroutine Lower. Lower consists of two {if} statements designed to properly set the range to copy from. Remember the cell pointer is now located at the top of the old range-name table.

The first {if} command checks to see if the current cell is blank; if it is the subroutine immediately returns control to its caller without expanding the cell pointer at all, and the macro proceeds to copy only the current cell to a cell three columns to the right.

If the cell has something in it, the macro will continue reading the second row of the subroutine, which expands the cell pointer down one row and reads another {if} statement. As the cell pointer expands, the formula, @cellpointer("type"), in the {if} command that follows will evaluate the cell to which the cell pointer most recently expanded; if the original range to copy from was B164 and the new expanded range is B164..B165, then the cell being evaluated with the @cellpointer function is B165.

If B165 is blank, the macro presses the Uparrow key (contracting the cell pointer back to B164) and returns control to the caller, which copies just the entry in cell B164 to a cell three columns to the right.

If B165 contains an entry, the {if} command was false and control passes to the third and final row of Lower. The instructions on that row press the Uparrow key to contract the cell pointer. Since you know that cell B165 has an entry in it, you can reliably use the End-Downarrow key sequence to expand the cell pointer to the end of the list of entries—whether that list consists of one entry or one hundred entries. With the cell pointer expanded to the full length of the list of range names in the existing table, control returns to the main routine, which completes the Copy command, copying the list of names to the column three columns to the right.

Row 23 uses the subroutine Lower once again; this time to erase both the existing range names and the range specifications. Note that after the subroutine Lower runs, the main routine presses the Rightarrow key to expand the cell pointer one column to the right—that's how the macro includes the range specifications in the range to erase.

The next instruction, on row 24, creates anew the range-name table in the same location as the old one. Because the old table has been erased, if the new one is shorter than the old (because more names have been deleted than created), no residual entries will linger below the new list.

The next task is to reunite the existing range descriptions with the range names in the new table which they describe. That's the mission of the subroutine Order on row 25. Order proceeds down the description field, one cell at a time. It attempts to match an old range name with a new one. If it can't, it either opens up a new space in which you can later describe a new range name or deletes descriptions that apply to range names that no longer exist, and moves on to the next name in the list to repeat its action until arriving at the end of the list.

```
ORDER     {if @cellpointer("type")="b"}{return}
          {let NAM;@cellpointer("contents")}{r 3}
          {if NAM<@cellpointer("contents")}{branch NEW}
          {if NAM>@cellpointer("contents")}{branch OLD}
          {l 3}{d}{branch ORDER}
```

Order begins by performing an end-of-list test: It evaluates the contents of the current cell to see if that cell is blank. If it is blank, there are no names left in the table and the subroutine returns control to its caller. If an entry resides in the current cell, the next row assigns to the cell named Nam the contents of the current cell and moves to the right three columns (where the list of old range names resides).

Once in the column of old range names, Order compares the old range name in the current cell with the new range name three cells to the left (and now stored in Nam). Since 1-2-3 orders the range name table alphabetically, if the new range name in Nam would be alphabetically ordered before the old name [that's the effect of NAM<@cellpointer("contents")], then the new range name must not exist in the old list, and Order branches to the routine New to open a new description slot by moving the remaining descriptions and old names down one row. Here's the New routine.

```
NEW       {l}/m{r}{LOWER}~{d}~
          {l 2}{d}{branch ORDER}
```

If Nam comes after the current name in the alphabet, then the old name must be one that was deleted since the old range-name table was created, and Order branches to the Old routine to move the remaining descriptions and old names up one row (and in the process, delete the old range name). Here's the Old routine.

```
OLD       {l}{d}/m{r}{LOWER}~{u}~
          {l 2}{u}{branch ORDER}
```

Exhausting those two possibilities leaves but one other option: That Nam is equal to the current name, which means they are identical entries. In that case, the description is correct, and Order moves down to the next name and repeats itself. When the end-of-list test in the first line of Order eventually fails, it returns control to row 26 in the main routine, \N. \N then returns the cell pointer to the top of the range-name table, erases the column of old range names, and terminates.

Protecting Your Macros

In Release 2.2, you can protect macros by placing them into a macro library and assigning a password to that library file (refer to Chapter 5, Macro Libraries, for a complete discussion of this topic).

If you're trying to protect macros that are stored on the worksheet, whether that be in Release 2, 2.01, or 2.2, there aren't any sure-fire ways to protect your macros from those who'd like to view or modify them. However, if you want to discourage such prying, you can make the task difficult enough to dissuade most people. Unfortunately, because these releases of 1-2-3 don't offer any native method of macro protection, the tactics available to you involve modifying the style and form of your macro to make it difficult to read. While you may succeed in accomplishing that objective, unfortunately, you will also make the macro difficult for you to update.

With that caveat in mind, here's a set of stylistic standards that opposes everything we've heretofore mentioned about writing clearly structured macros. Use them only with appropriate caution.

1. Use meaningless range names. By removing any meaning from your range names, you'll remove any meaning from the references they supply in a macro. So instead of {branch PRINT}, you'd write {branch XYZ}. You could take that approach one step further and use {dispatch} commands instead of {branch} commands. Since a {dispatch} command's reference is once removed, those commands are harder to fathom than are {branch} commands.

2. Write self-modifying macro instructions. Specifically, try to use string formulas whose meanings change with each recalculation.

3. Scatter your macros around the worksheet. Rather than reserving one area for your macro code, embed it in widely scattered areas of the worksheet.

4. Use the Hidden cell format to obscure the macro from view on the worksheet. In addition to suppressing the worksheet display of the cell contents, Release 2.2 will even prevent the contents from being displayed in the edit panel whenever worksheet global protection is enabled.

5. Keep two versions of the worksheet file. One version with documentation and one without. Before you put the file into distribution, erase both the column containing range name identifiers to the left of the macro and the column containing comments to the right of the macro. When you do, use care to avoid erasing macro-menu items that may reside in the Comment column of the macro-writing area.

6. Break up the function of what could otherwise be a straightforward routine into many smaller subroutines and/or routines.

Incidentally, if you've removed the range-name documentation column from the worksheet and you find that you need to reinstate that column, there is a technique to help you do so. With the cell pointer located in the first blank cell of the Name column to the left of the macro, press the plus key and enter a reference to the macro cell to the right. Once you've entered that simple formula, select / Range Format Text and press Return. Copy the formula down the column as far as there are macro instructions in the corresponding cells to the right. You will see a column of cell references (such as $+B27$), some of which will appear as references to range names (such as $+\backslash M$). You may want to widen the column to accommodate all fifteen possible characters in each range name.

	A	B	C	D	E	F	G	H
1	+\S	{get ANS}						
2	+B2	{if @length(ANS)=1}{quit}						
3	+B3	{let RES;@MID(ANS;1;@LENGTH(ANS)-1)}						
4	+B4	{()}{RES}						
5	+B5							
6	+ANS	{BIGRIGHT}						
7	+B7							
8	+RES	BIGRIGHT}						
9								
10								

Figure 30-11

Updating an Application Already in Use

Updates are a way of life. Whether they are to extend the functionality of an application, update the data it contains, or simply fix bugs discovered after the application was put into use, many applications require some updating sooner or later. The question to consider is, how difficult will it be to update tomorrow what you and your coworkers are creating today?

If you're following the conventions for creating a well-structured application that we've presented in this book, you've already taken a big step in making your applications easier to revise. But even the best-structured application can be difficult to revise if that work has to be done by someone who knows little about macros in general, or the application at hand in particular. If you are creating a macro-driven application that is going to be used either by a large number of people or by someone whom you will have difficulty visiting, you might benefit by providing a way to automatically update that application.

The following technique is but one way to deal with the issue; we're sure it will spark you to think of others. Use whichever method works best for you and whichever method works best for you and whichever method works best with the application in question.

Imagine you have an application to which you want to add more macros. You provide a disk with a file containing just the changes. The user selects an option, Update, from his or her current macro menu and enters the name of the file that you provided. The current macro reads the Update macro, stores it in a preplanned location, and passes macro control to it. The Update macro assumes control over the entire update process—it revises the worksheet, names ranges, and so on.

The key to making such a scenario work is to plan for the update facility when you plan the application itself. Here's how such a facility should work: (1.) The application you originally develop should have within it an update routine a user can invoke through a menu choice. That routine has the ability to read a new macro onto the worksheet and to pass control to that macro. Aside from providing a blank range in which to import the new macro, that's all you have to build into the original application. (2.) The update macro you provide at the time of the update will have two components:

- A temporary set of routines designed only to revise the current worksheet to accommodate the changes and to import the permanent macro code that will support the new functions.

- The new, permanent macro routines, data, and/or formulas that the foregoing routine will import.

Here's a model for the portion of the Update macro to include in the application you build today—so you can automate its revision tomorrow.

```
     A          B              C      D       E      F       G
1   UPDATE     {getlabel "Enter update name: ";U_NAME}    Solicit filename
2              {U_CHECK}                                   Check filename
3              {paneloff}{goto}U_SCREEN~                   Display update screen
4              {windowsoff}                                Freeze screen
5              {goto}U_CODE~                               Position cell pointer
6              /fcce                                       File combine
7              {U_NAME}~                                   Type filename
8              {U_CODE}                                    Run UPDATE subroutine
9              {goto}U_DONE~{windowson}                    Display "done" screen
10             {get ANS}                                   Await a key
11             {quit}                                      Stop the macro
12
13  U_NAME                                                 Store filename
14
15  U_CHECK    {open U_NAME;"r"}{branch U_ERR}             If no file, show error
16             {close}                                     Otherwise, OK
17             {return}
18
19  U_CODE                                                 Place for new code
20
```

Figure 30-12

The update macro implements the approach outlined above with minimal involvement from the user. The only things the user needs to know are to copy the update file to the current file directory and to enter the name of the update file when the application requests it.

After soliciting the update filename from the user and storing it in a cell named U_name, the second line runs a subroutine, U_check, to check for the existence of a file of that name.[71] To control for such a time when a file by the specified name doesn't exist, write a suitable routine named U_err to inform the user of the problem. If the file does exist, the macro displays a screen with a message to wait while the operation proceeds.

The instructions on row 5 move the cell pointer to a location named U_code, where the combined file will be stored. The next three rows perform the consolidation and pass control to the first row of the combined macro. After control returns from that routine, the remaining rows of this macro complete the installation process.

The assumptions inherent in this macro are that you will structure the new worksheet so that the first row of the installation macro is in cell A1. Since that's the cell in the new worksheet that will land in the cell named U_code in this worksheet, and U_code is the location to which this macro later passes control, that cell must contain the first instruction of

---

[71] You might also assume that all your update files will be named Update, and code that name right into the macro. Then you would not need to solicit a name from the user.

the new macro. You should also place a {return} command as the last instruction in the new installation macro, so that control will return to the last few rows of the macro shown above. Instead of ending with a {quit} command, this macro could easily end by returning control to the menu from which it was invoked.

Among the other options you may consider for this application are the ability to read the update file from the disk of the user's choice (so users won't need to copy the file to the current directory, as the preceding approach requires) and to provide some form of access security to prevent accidental use or abuse of the update routine.

One form that security might take is to make Update an undocumented menu selection, to be explained only in the Update documentation accompanying the new worksheet. For example, in the macro code that implements a full-screen menu that shows a screen with choices which require the user to enter a number from 1 through 10, include an undocumented response (perhaps to the entry of the letter U) that activates the Update macro. That choice won't appear on the menu; you can reveal it in the instructions accompanying the update disk you distribute.

Another option is to require a password, either typed by the user or contained in a special text file on the macro disk—a text file that the application will always attempt to read before proceeding with an Update request. If that file is missing, the macro will refuse to continue the update.

Search and Replace

Release 2.2's / Range Search command makes it easy to find text anywhere in the worksheet, and that's useful for finding text in macros, too. For example, if you change a range name and want to find all the places in the macro that reference that range name, you can use Search command with its Replace option to ensure not only that you find them all, but that all of them are changed.

User Macro

We borrowed the name of the User macro from Lotus Symphony, which possesses a facility with an identical purpose: It allows you to enter the name of a macro in response to a prompt. When you press Return, the program will activate the specified macro.

Underneath the hood, the User macro is nothing more than the Run macro with a data entry front-end. Like the Run macro, User offers the benefit that it can invoke another macro even when you are in the middle of a menu sequence, something you can't do with Release 2.2's Run key.

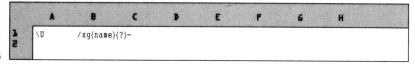

	A	B	C	D	E	F	G	H
1	\U	{getlabel "Enter name of macro to run: ";ANS}						
2		{dispatch ANS}						
3								
4	ANS	testmenu						
5								
6								
7								

Figure 30-13

This macro enables you to run a routine from anywhere on the worksheet, whereas the Run macro forces you to place the cell pointer on the first row of the routine you wish to run. Since a fair number of macros are dependent on the cell pointer's having been properly located prior to their commencement, you'll find you can use the User macro many times when the Run macro can't help you.

You can write a version of the User macro that allows the user to select the name of the macro from a list of available range names. While you can write that version using the {getlabel} command, it's easier to do with the / xg command.

	A	B	C	D	E	F	G	H
1	\U	/xg{name}{?}~						
2								

Figure 30-14

Accelerator Keys

If you expect the application you are writing to be used repeatedly by a knowledgeable user, consider including a way to accelerate that person's rate of selection of oft-used menu items. We call the means by which you do that, "accelerator keys."

For example, the menu below provides access to three routines—Ent, Prnt, and Grf. If you want a user to be able to access any of those routines more directly, simply assign the routine(s) in question a range name consisting of a backslash and a letter. Then place a message in that menu item's explanation line indicating which accelerator key to use to run that routine separately (or otherwise inform the user of that option).

```
        A           B              C                  D
  1   \M        {menubranch MAIN}
  2
  3   MAIN      Enter          Print              Graph
  4             Enter data (Alt-E)  Print reports (Alt-P)  Display graphs (Alt-G)
  5             {branch ENT}   {branch PRNT}      {branch GRF}
  6
  7   \E        {branch ENT}
  8
  9   \P        {branch PRNT}
 10
 11   \G        {branch GRF}
 12
```

Figure 30-15

You might think of this as a stepping stone user interface; it enables a user to modify the interface as he or she becomes more familiar with the application. The menu is always available, but it doesn't stand in the way when it isn't needed.

Conclusion

That sort of flexibility and responsiveness, along with proper structure and controls, are what effective use of macros is all about. We hope you'll let those principles guide your work with macros, and we trust that if you do, you'll find the results well worth the effort.

Index

A

Abbreviating commands
  to freeze/unfreeze the screen, 373-74
  to prompt for input, 374-76
Accelerator keys, 599-600
Activation of macros, automatic, 134-36
Add-in Manager, 327
Add-in programs
  accessing, 327-30
  {ifkey} command and, 263-64
  turnkey macro applications and, 387-88
Advanced macro commands, 175-381. *See also*
    specific commands
  benefits of, 177-78
  components of, 181-85
    arguments, 181-84
    keywords, 181
    separators, 184-85
  for controlling program flow, 237-74
    {branch} command, 246-47
    {define} command, 247-50
    {dispatch} command, 250-52
    {forbreak} command, 256-58
    {for} command, 252-58
    {if} command, 258-62
    {ifkey} command, 263-64
    {onerror} command, 265-67
    {Quit} command, 267-68

    {restart} command, 268-70
    {return} command, 270-71
    { } (subroutine call), 238-46
    {system} command, 271-74
  for data manipulation, 275-91
    {blank} command, 276-77
    {contents} command, 277-81
    {let} command, 281-84
    overview of, 275-76
    {put} command, 284-86
    {recalccol} command, 289-91
    {recalc} command, 287-89
  definitions of
    form of, 185-86
    organization of the commands, 186-91
  enhancing existing macros with, 354-64
  for file manipulation, 292-326
    {close} command, 298-301
    {filesize} command, 301-2
    {getpos} command, 302-3
    {open} command, 304-7
    overview of, 292-98
    {read} command, 308-15
    {readln} command, 315-19
    {setpos} command, 319-20
    {write} command and, 320-24
    {writeln} command, 324-26
  for keyboard interaction, 209-36
    {break} command, 211-12
    {breakoff} command, 212-13

{breakon} command, 213-14
{get} command, 214-16
{getlabel} command, 216-19
{getnumber} command, 219-22
interactive command {?}, 235-36
{look} command, 223-26
{menubranch} command, 226-30
{menucall} command, 210-11, 230-33
    overview and introduction to new
    concepts, 209-11
{wait} command, 233-35
overview of, 175-77
range names and, 179-81
Release 1A versus Release, 2380-82
for screen control, 192-208
    {beep} command, 192-94
    {bordersoff} command, 194
    {borderson} command, 194-95
    {frameoff} command, 194-96
    {frameon} command, 195-97
    {graphoff} command, 197
    {graphon} command, 198-99
    {indicate} command, 199-201
    {paneloff} command, 201-3
    {panelon} command, 203-4
    {windowoff} command, 204-6
    {windowson} command, 206-8
syntax of, 178-79
table of, 176-77
Advanced techniques. *See* Turnkey macro
    applications
Allways, 362
{App} key names, 328-30
Applications. *See* Turnkey macro applications
Arguments, 181-84
    contents of, 182-83
Argument separators, 184-85
ASCII collating sequence, case sensitivity and,
    399-400
ASCII escape sequences, 530-31
ASCII files, 292-94, 297-98
    {readln} command and, 315-19
    {write} command and, 320-24

    {writeln} command and, 324-26
ASCII graphics characters
    reading, 313
    {readln} command and, 317-18
    {write} command and, 323
    {writeln} command and, 325
ASCII-No LICS-screen driver, 524-29
ASCII screen drivers custom, 529-31
    {read} command and, 313-14
    {readln} command and, 318
Assumptions in macros, 159-61
Autoexecute macros, 134-36
Autoload macro library, copying to your
    worksheet, 362
Automated single step, 152-53
Automatic recalculation, turn on, 26
Automation features, 132-39
    activation of macros, 134-36
    data entry, 132-33
    loading macro libraries in Release 2.2,
        138-39
    loading worksheets automatically, 136-38

B

Backup file, save current worksheet and, 34
{Beep} command, 192-94
Beep setting, macro to toggle on and off, 361
Benchmarking routines, 583-86
Blank cells, testing for, 492
{Blank} command, 276-77
{Bordersoff} command, 194
{Borderson} command, 194-95
Bounds checking, 442-45
Braces, curly. *See* Curly braces
{Branch} command, 140-45, 246-47
    introduction to, 141-42
    range names with, 142-45
{Break} command, 211-12
Break key, interrupting a macro with, 79-81
{Breakoff} command, 212-13
{Breakon} command, 213-14

Byte pointer, 294, 300
{read} command and, 314

C

Case sensitivity, 492
    trapping and testing keystrokes for, 399-400
Cell addresses, range names versus, 142-44
@cell function, 332-34
Cell pointer
    full-screen menus with a moving, 469-82
    /Data Query Find moving cell pointer
        menu, 475-81
    drawing attention to full-screen menus,
        481-82
    {get} moving cell pointer menu, 471-75
    interactive command {?} moving cell
        pointer menu, 470-71
    placing at start of a macro, 101
@cell pointer function, 334-36
Cells, testing for contents, 489-92
Check register, 90-91
{Close} command, 298-301
@CODE function, 310
Column headings, freezing, 77-78
Columns, macro to jump to end of column
    menu, 359
Column widths
    command-enhancement macro to vary the
        width of a range of columns, 366-68
    macro to accomodate the longest label you
        enter, 363
    resetting
        range of columns, 24
    setting, 21
        range of columns, 24
    widen the current column, 24
Combining existing macros, 62-63
Combining files, macro for, 358
Command-enhancement macros, 365-79
    to abbreviate commands to freeze/unfreeze
        the screen, 373-74

to abbreviate commands to prompt for
    input, 374-76
to copy a range of relative formulas as
    absolute, 368-73
to simplify the {for} command, 376-79
to vary the width of a range of columns,
    366-68
Commands
    macros that enter, 51-54
    /Range Input command and, 132-33
    writing. See Command-enhancement
        macros
Comma separated files, 293-94
Compatibility, cross-release, 87
{Contents} command, 277-81
Contents of cells, testing for, 489-92
Context sensitive help systems, 547-51
Control panel
    characters appear in, instead of on
        worksheet, 156-57
    the macro-name letter appears in the control
        panel or on the worksheet, 155-56
    {paneloff} command and, 201-3
    {panelon} command and, 203-4
Copy(ing)
    another cell to the current cell, 26
    command-enhancement macro to copy a
        range of relative formulas as absolute,
        368-73
    /Copy command, interactive command
        {?} and, 104, 105
    Counter, {for} command and, 252-56
    Ctrl-Break, 85, 211-14
    Curly braces ({ }), 86, 181. See also
        subroutine call ({ })
    key-filtering macros and, 408-10
Currency
    format any range as, with zero decimal
        places, 33
    format current cell as with no decimal
        places, 33
Customized macros. See Turnkey macro
    applications

D

Database records, user input in, 431-35
Data entry. *See also* User input, managing
    automated, 132-33
    with interactive command {?}, 106-8
    interactive command {?} to accept, 425-26
Data manipulation, advanced macro
    commands for, 275-91
    {blank} command, 276-77
    {contents} command, 277-81
    {let} command, 281-84
    overview of, 275-76
    {put} command, 284-86
    {recalccol} command, 289-91
    {recalc} command, 287-89
/Data Parse command, 293
Data processing, 392
/Data Query Find command
    moving cell pointer menu using, 475-81
    screen and cell pointer restoration, 546-47
Date, macro to enter, in MM/DD/YY
    format, 359
@date formula
    input, 30
    rearrange, 30
@date function, {wait} command and, 234
Date stamp
    macro to enter date stamp as a label, 360
    as value, 31
Days of the week label, 23
Debugging macros, 150-63
    assumptions in macros and, 159-6
    1 with {indicate} command, 588
    prescriptions for common problems,
        153-59
    1-2-3 beeps and the macro does not run,
        153-54
    characters appear in the control panel
        instead of the worksheet, 156-57
    embedded spaces in a macro, 158-59

macro doesn't run; 1-2-3 doesn't beep,
    154-55
the macro-name letter appears in the
    control panel or on the worksheet,
    155-56
range names, underlying causes of
    problems with, 161-63
string formulas and, 170-71
{Define} command, 247-50
Deletion of range names, inadvertent, 161-62
Delimited files, 293-94
Directional arrow keys
    list of, 83
    names of, 22
Directory switcher, 574-75
{Dispatch} command, 250-52
    full-screen menus and, 462-65
    protecting your macros with, 594
Documentation, 66-71
    string formulas and, 170
DOS, {system} command and, 271-74
Dynamic code, 164-71

E

Edit command, in Macro Library Manager,
    125-26
Editing keys
    list of, 84
    names of, 22
Editing macros, 54-55
Embedded spaces in a macro, 158-59
Error avoidance and recovery, 483-88
    files and, 484-87
    interactive command {?}, 484
    range names and, 487-88
Errors, {onerror} command and, 265-67
Escape key
    capturing and testing, 402-3
    disabling, 451-53
    {menubranch} command and, 229
    {menucall} command and, 233

@exact function, 349

F

/File Combine command, macro libraries and, 114, 115
/File Import Numbers command, 292, 294
/File Import Text (FIT) command, 292, 293, 297
  {read} command versus, 308
  {readln} command and and, 316
File manipulation
  advanced macro commands for, 292-326
    {close} command, 298-301
    {filesize} command, 301-2
    {getpos} command, 302-3
    {open} command, 304-7
    overview of, 292-98
    {read} command, 308-15
    {readln} command, 315-19
    {setpos} command, 319-20
    {write} command and, 320-24
    {writeln} command, 324-26
  macro to combine a series of files beneath one another, 358
/File Retrieve command, 299-300
  macro libraries and, 114, 115
Files, toggling between two, 573
{Filesize} command, 301-2
@find function, 348-49
Flow charts, structured programming and, 569-70
Flow of control, 59
  advanced macro commands for changing the, 237-74
    {branch} command, 246-47
    {define} command, 247-50
    {dispatch} command, 250-52
    {forbreak} command, 256-58
    {for} command, 252-58
    {if} command, 258-62
    {ifkey} command, 263-64

    {onerror} command, 265-67
    {Quit} command, 267-68
    {restart} command, 268-70
    {return} command, 270-71
    {} (subroutine call), 238-46
    {system} command, 271-74
  {Forbreak} command, 256-58
  {For} command, 245, 252-58
    {forbreak} command and, 256-58
  simplifying the, 376-79
Foreign countries, converting applications for use in, 556-58
Formatting
  a floppy disk in drive A, 361
  a range, 51-53
Formulas
  command-enhancement macro to copy a range of relative formulas as absolute, 368-73
  key names used to write, 90-102
  libraries of, 117
  macros that enter, 48
  macro to copy relative formula as if it were an absolute formula, 357
  print range as displayed, then as, 30
  string, 166-71
    limitations of, 170-71
    numbers in, 168-69
    writing, 167-68
{Frameoff} command, 194-96
{Frameon} command, 195-97
Function keys, 11, 21
  list of, 83
@functions, 331-53
  logical functions, 340-44
    @isapp function, 340-41
    @iserr function, 341-42
    @isna function, 342-43
    @isnumber function, 343
    @isstring function, 344
  overview of, 331-32
  special functions, 332-40
    @cell function, 332-34

@cell pointer function, 334–36
@hlookup function, 338–39
@isaaf function, 340
@vlookup function, 336–38
string functions, 345–51
@exact function, 349
@find function, 348–49
@left function, 345
@lower function, 350
@mid function, 346–47
@right function, 345–46
@string function, 347–48
@upper function, 350–51
@value function, 348
time and date functions, 351–52
@now function, 351–52
@time function, 352

G

{Get} command, 214–16
{look} command and, 223–26
moving cell pointer menu with, 471–75
capturing and evaluating a keystroke
typed by the user, 473
displaying menu screen, 473
moving the cell pointer within a
restricted area, 473–75
trapping and testing single characters and,
398–99. *See also* User input, managing;
Single characters
{Getdefault} command, 420, 421
{Getlabel} command, 216–19
to manage label input, 413–17
{Getnumber} command, 219–22
to manage label input, 417–19
{Getpos} command, 302–3
Goto named range, 34
Goto key (F5)
sample macro for, 88–90
Graphics characters
reading, 313

{readln} command and, 317–18
{write} command and, 323
{writeln} command and, 325
{Graphoff} command, 197
{Graphon} command, 198–99
Graphs
macro to display all the named, 362
multiple, 509–13
+ / − , {contents} command and, 279

H

Help key (F1), 87
displaying your own help screen at, 408
Help screen
displaying your own, at F1, 408
during Range Input, 429–31
Help systems, 532–51
basic, 532–31
context sensitivity, 547–51
memory conservation, 533–35
restoring the screen and cell pointer, 535–47
capturing cell addresses, 536–38
mid-formula technique, 538–44
Query Find technique, 546–47
/Range Input technique, 545
Hidden cell format, protecting your macros
with, 595
Highlighting an onscreen message, 505–9
@hlookup function, 338–39

I

{If} command, 258–62
case sensitivity and, 492
testing for a specific label and, 490–91
{Ifkey} command, 263–64
{If} statements, full-screen menus and,
461–62
If-then-else construct
{if} command and, 258–59

{ifkey} command and, 264
{Indicate} command, 199-201
  debugging with, 588
Input, user. *See* User input, managing
Ins key ({insert} or {ins}), 84, 87
Interactive command {?}, 103-10, 235-36
  to accept data entry, 425-26
  applications of, 109
  data entry with, 106-8
  error avoidance and recovery, 484
  Return key and, 104-6
  testing macros with, 108-9, 151
Interrupting a macro, 79-81
@isaaf function, 340
@isapp function, 340-41
@iserr function, 341-42
@isna function, 342-43
@isnumber function, 343
@isstring function, 344

J

Justify text, 27

K

Keyboard
  advanced macro commands that allow
      interaction with, 209-36
    {break} command, 211-12
    {breakoff} command, 212-13
    {breakon} command, 213-14
    {get} command, 214-16
    {getlabel} command, 216-19
    {getnumber} command, 219-22
    interactive command {?}, 235-36
    {look} command, 223-26
    {menubranch} command, 226-30
    {menucall} command, 210-11, 230-33
  overview and introduction to new
      concepts, 209-11

  {wait} command, 233-35
  disabling, 401
Keyboard buffer, 210
  {look} command and, 223
Key names, 21-2, 82-102. *See also specific key*
      names
  {app}, 328-30
  avoiding duplication with macro range
      names, 180
  conventions for, 11-12
  formulas that point using, 90-102
  {ifkey} command and, 263-64
  number of repetitions of a keystroke
      represented by, 94-95
  saving time when you use, 93-95
  short forms of, 92-94
  spelling, 86
  splitting not possible, 85
  synonyms for, 97-98
  typographical errors, 86-87
Keystroke macros, 5-6, 15-81
  activating, 17-18, 23
  assigning range names to, 71-73
  detailed course, 35-36
  that enter 1-2-3 commands, 51-54
  that enter formulas, 48
  that enter labels, 36-42
    applications, 41
    if macro did not work, 40-41
    modeling the operation, 37-38
    naming the macro, 38-40
    writing the macro, 38
  that enter values, 42-46
  finding macros on worksheet, 74
  flow of control and, 59
  in Learn mode, 60-62
  multiple-line, 55-59
  Quick course on, 15-35
  revising, 54-55
  saving your file before activating, 17-18
  screen hopping, reducing, 75-76
  separating, empty cell needed for, 19
  stepping through, 79-80

steps for writing, 36
stopping, 79
style considerations, 64-73
  documentation, 66-71
  length of labels, 64-65
temporarily interrupting, 79-81
testing, 78-81
where to store on worksheet, 73-74
Keystrokes, trapping and testing. *See* User
  input, managing; Single characters
Key table
  implementing a, 404-7, 409
  for moving cell pointer menu, 473
Keywords, 178
  in advanced macro commands, 181
  avoiding duplication of, 179

L

Label(s)
  beginning with a number, 46-47
  keystroke macros that enter, 36-42
    applications, 41
    if macro did not work, 40-41
    modeling the operation, 37-38
    naming the macro, 38-40
    writing the macro, 38
  length of, 64-65
  macro to convert labels to values, 356
  macro to convert values to, 356
  managing input of, 413-26
  when formulas should not be, 92-93
Label prefixes, 18, 45-49
LEARN.ADN, 60
Learn macro, 576-80
Learn mode, 60-62
Learn-mode macros, 146
@left function, 345
{Let} command, 281-84
  {contents} command versus, 279
LICS (Lotus International Character Set),
  525-29

Links, refresh values of all, 33
Load command, in Macro Library Manager,
  124-25
Loading worksheets automatically, 136-38
Location arguments, 183
Logical arguments, 183
Logical functions, 340-44
  @isapp function, 340-41
  @iserr function, 341-42
  @isna function, 342-43
  @isnumber function, 343
  @isstring function, 344
Logo, displaying your own, when the
  worksheet loads, 523-24
{Look} command, 223-26
Loops, 140-47
  {branch} command and, 247
@lower function, 350

M

Macro libraries, 111-31
  assigning range names, 116
  creating separate macro library worksheets,
    114-15
  filename extensions for, 114
  file names for, 114
  formula, 117
  Release 2.2, 117-19. *See also* Macro Library
    manager (MLM) add-in program
  Release 2 and 2.01, 111-13
  retrieving, 115
  saving, 115
  segmenting, 115-17
Macro Library manager (MLM) add-in
  program, 118-31
  adding macros to a macro library, 128
  automatically loading macro libraries, 131
  consolidating macro labels into fewer cells,
    127-28
  editing a macro, 121-23
  main menu of, 124-26

methods of attaching, 119-20

minimizing memory use, 126-27

range names and, 128-30

saving a macro in a macro library, 121

security aspects, 130-31

writing, naming, and testing macros on worksheet, 120-21

MACROMGR.ADN. *See* Macro Library manager (MLM) add-in program

Macros

development tips and tools, 571-600

accelerator keys, 599-600

benchmarking routines, 583-86

debugging with {indicate} command, 588

debugging with Step key (Alt-F2), 588-89

directory switcher, 574-75

Learn macro, 576-80

navagational aids, 573-74

protecting your macros, 594-95

range name table documentor, 589-94

Run macro, 587-88

search and replace, 598

Speedkey macro, 580-83

toggling between two files, 573

updating an application already in use, 596-98

User macro, 598-99

example of how to write, 7-9

guide to using this book, 9-12

overview of, 3-7

overview of programming, 175-77

reasons for using, 3-5

types of, 5-7

Manual single step, 153

Memory

application design and efficient use of, 552-54

help systems and conservation of, 533-35

Menu, 1-2-3

macros to display, 84

{Menubranch} command, 226-30

{Menucall} command, 230-33, 245

subroutine calls and, 210-11

Menus, 449-82

controlling menu responses, 450-53

backing up through the menu tree, 453

disabling the Escape key, 451-53

preventing inadvertent menu selection, 450-51

dynamic, 454-59

screen management, 500-3

full-screen, 460-68

context sensitivity in, 549

{dispatch} command, 462-65

{if}-list, 461-62

speeding up selections, 465-68

full-screen, with a moving cell pointer, 469-82

/Data Query Find moving cell pointer menu, 475-81

drawing attention to full-screen menus, 481-82

{get} moving cell pointer menu, 471-75

interactive command {?} moving cell pointer menu, 470-71

individual help nodes in, 548-49

Menu slash, 84

Messages

full-screen, 513-18

using an XY chart, 518-23

showing, 503-5

at the top of the screen, 496-98

in windows, 498-500

@mid function, 346-47

.MLB extension, 114

MM/DD/YY format, 359

Mode indicator, {indicate} command and, 199-201

Months of the year, macro that automatically enters, 95-102

Move another cell to the current cell, 27

/Move command

inadvertently associating named ranges with, 162-63

inadvertently transferring a range name
with, 112.
Multiple-line macros, 55-59

N

Navigational aids, 573-74
Nesting levels
    {restart} command and, 268-69
    { } (subroutine call) and, 245
@now function, 351-52
Numbers
    as arguments, 182-83
    {getnumber} command, 219-22
    labels beginning with a, 46-47
    sum column of, 32

O

{Onerror} command, 265-67
    {dispatch} command and, 252
{Open} command, 304-7

P

{Paneloff} command, 201-3
{Panelon} command, 203-4
Passing parameters, 241-43
    {define} command and, 248-49
Password, Macro Library Manager, 130-31
Pathname, {open} command and, 306
Pie graph, making, 34
+/- graphs, {contents} command and, 279
Print(ing)
    alert when printing is complete, 29
    the current print range, 28
    new print range using the current settings,
        29
    range as displayed, then as formulas, 30

select new named print range and print it,
    29
Prompt for input, abbreviating commands to
    374-76
Prompts, custom, with defaults, 419-25
Prompt string, {getlabel} command and,
    216-19
Protect an unprotected worksheet, 25
Protected worksheets, unprotect, 25
Protecting your macros, 594-95
Pseudo code, structured programming and,
    569-70
Punctuation. *See also* Separators
{Put} command, 284-86

Q

Question mark (?). *See* Interactive command
    {?}
{Quit} command, 267-68
    introduction to, 148
    sample applications of, 148-49
Quotation marks
    arguments in, 182, 183
    around prompt string, 217, 221

R

/Range Erase command, {blank} command
    versus, 276
/Range Input command, 132-33, 209-10,
    426-31
    getting help during, 429-31
    screen restoration and, 454
/Range Name Create command, 38-39
/Range Name Labels command, 72-73, 93
/Range Name Labels Right command, 72-73
    macro libraries and, 112-13
/Range Name Reset command, 71-72
Range names, 38-40
    advanced macro commands and, 179-81

advantages over cell addresses, 142-44
assigning, 70-73
   macro libraries, 116
   Macro Library Manager, 120-21
  {Branch} command with, 142-45
documentation and, 70-71
error avoidance and recovery, 487-88
meaningless, protecting your macros with,
   594
problems with, 153-55, 161-63
Run key used to display, 18
speeding up screen switching with, 75-76
structured programming and, 561-63
style guidelines for, 145-47
table documentor, 589-94
/Range Name Table command, 71
Ranges, defining and redefining, 435-41
  associated ranges, 441
  helping the user redefine a range, 436-38
  using a macro to redefine a range, 438-40
/Range Search command, 598
/Range Value command, 100
{Read} command, 308-15
  byte pointer and, 314
  end of line characters, 309-10
  how many bytes to read forward, 309
  negative values in, 309
  reading ASCII graphics characters, 313
  reading characters from the next line, 313
  reading through a file of
    indeterminate length, 311
  reading through an entire file, 310-11
{Readln} command, 315-19
  {read} command versus, 308, 310
{Recalccol} command, 289-91
{Recalc} command, 287-89
Recalculation
  automatic, turn on, 26
  macro to switch between automatic and
    manual methods of, 357
  manual, turn on, 26
Refresh values of all file links in the
  worksheet, 33

Release 2.2
  advanced macro commands for Release 1 or
    1A versus, 2380-82
  autoexecute macros in, 135-36
  automatically loading macro libraries in,
    138-39
  automatic worksheet loading in, 136-38
  maintaining compatibility between Releases
    2.01, 2.2, and, 491-92
  screen displays in, 493-94
Remove command, in Macro Library
  Manager, 126
{Restart} command, 268-70
  {forbreak} command and, 257
{Return} command, 270-71
  {Quit} command and, 268
Return key (~~), 84
  interactive command {?} and, 104-6
  key name for, 87
@right function, 345-46
Rows
  macro to jump down any number of, 355
  macro to jump to end of row menu, 359
Run Key (Alt-F3), 18
Run macro, 587-88

S

Save (saving)
  current worksheet and maintain a backup
    file, 34
  macro to save a file whether or not it
    already has a name, 360-61
  macro to time stamp worksheet and save
    file, 356
Save command, in Macro Library Manager,
  125
Screen
  abbreviating commands to freeze/unfreeze,
    373-74
  advanced macro commands for controlling
    the, 192-208

{beep} command, 192-94
{bordersoff} command, 194
{borderson} command, 194-95
{frameoff} command, 194-96
{frameon} command, 195-97
{graphoff} command, 197
{graphon} command, 198-99
{indicate} command, 199-201
{paneloff} command, 201-3
{panelon} command, 203-4
{windowoff} command, 204-6
{windowson} command, 206-8
help systems and restoration of, 535-47
   capturing cell addresses, 536-38
   mid-formula technique, 538-44
   Query Find technique, 546-47
   /Range Input technique, 545
shift, to move current row to top, 28
in turnkey macro applications, 493-531
   ASCII screen drivers, custom, 529-31
   dressing up displays using the ASCII-No
      LICS-screen driver, 524-29
   dynamic menu, 500-3
   full-screen messages, 513-18
   full-screen message using an XY chart,
      518-23
   guidelines, 494-95
   highlighting an onscreen message, 505-9
   logo display when the worksheet loads,
      523-24
   message at the top of the screen, 496-98
   messages in windows, 498-500
   multiple graphs, 509-13
   showing a message on the screen, 503-5
Screen drivers
   {read} command and, 313-14
   {readln} command and, 318
Screen hopping, reducing, 75-76
Search formulas and labels in the worksheet
   for specified text, 27
Self-modifying macro instructions, 594
Self-modifying macros, 164-71
Semicolons, as argument separators, 184-85

Separators, 184-85
Sequential data files, 293
{Setpos} command, 319-20
Setting sheets
   {windowsoff} command and, 204-6
   {windowson} command and, 206-8
Sgrong functions, 345-51
Slash (/) key
   displaying your own menu at, 407-8
   turning off, 407
Sort
   current database, 32
   define and sort database, 32
Spaces. See also Separators embedded in a
   macro, 158-59
Sparse matrix memory management scheme,
   552
Special keys (non-alphanumeric keys), 82. See
   also Directional arrow keys; Function
   keys; Key names
   capturing and testing, 401-4
Speedkey macro, 580-83
Step indicator, 79, 80
Step key (Alt-F2)
   debugging with, 588-89
Step mode, 80-81, 154
Stepping through macros
   automated single step, 152-53
   manual single step, 153
Stopping a macro, 79
   {Quit} command for, 267-68
String formulas, 166-71
   limitations of, 170-71
   numbers in, 168-69
   writing, 167-68
@string function, 347-48
String functions
   @exact function, 349
   @find function, 348-49
   @left function, 345
   @lower function, 350
   @mid function, 346-47
   @right function, 345-46

@string function, 347-48
@upper function, 350-51
@value function, 348
String valued arguments, 182
Structured programming, 559-70
    methods of, 560-70
        flow charts and pseudo code, 569-70
        independence of subroutines from calling
            routines, 565-66
        keeping each line formula the macro brief
            and meaningful, 560-61
        organizing common actions into a single
            routine, 563-64
        range names, 561-63
        segregating dissimilar tasks into separate
            routines, 565
        separating one-time instructions from
            recurring instructions, 567-69
        setting up worksheet manually, 566-67
        variables, 561
    purpose of, 559-60
Subroutine call ({ }), 238-46
    without arguments, 245
    nesting limits and, 245
    passing parameters, 241-43
Subroutine calls
    {branch} command and, 247
    introduction to, 237-38
    {menucall} command and, 210-11
Subroutine chain (subroutine stack), 245
Subroutines
    names of, 239
    that do not work, 243-44
    that work, 244-46
Sum column of numbers, 32
/System command, 271-72
{System} command, 271-74

T

Table of files, create a formatted, 31

Testing. See also Debugging macros; Stepping
        through macros; User input, managing
    benchmarking routines, 583-86
    cells, for contents, 489-92
    with interactive command {?}, 151
    Run macro for, 587-88
    single characters. See User input,
        managing; Single characters
Testing macros, 78-81
    with interactive command {?}, 108-9
Text files, 293
Tilde (~), 84
    as text, 89
Time and date functions, 351-52
@time function, 352
    {wait} command and, 234
Time stamp macro, 356, 360
Toggling between two files, 573
Turnkey macro applications, 385-600
    design of, 552-58
        memory conservation, 552-54
        portability to other environments, 554-58
    error avoidance and recovery, 483-88
        files and, 484-87
        interactive command {?}, 484
        range names and, 487-88
    help systems, 532-51
        basic, 532-31
        context sensitivity, 547-51
        memory conservation, 533-35
        restoring the screen and cell pointer,
            535-47
    introduction to, 385-95
        add-ins and, 387-88
        output, 392-93
        overview of the process for
            developing an application, 393-95
        processing data, 392
        user interaction, 391-92
        when to use customized macros, 386-90
    menus, 449-82
        controlling menu responses, 450-53
        dynamic, 454-59

screen management, 500-3
full-screen, 460-68
full-screen, with a moving cell pointer, 469-82
individual help nodes in, 548-49
overview of the content of an application, 390-93
screen displays, 493-531
  ASCII screen drivers, custom, 529-31
  dressing up displays using the ASCII-No LICS-screen driver, 524-29
  dynamic menu, 500-3
  full-screen messages, 513-18
  full-screen message using an XY chart, 518-23
  guidelines, 494-95
  highlighting an onscreen message, 505-9
  logo display when the worksheet loads, 523-24
  message at the top of the screen, 496-98
  messages in windows, 498-500
  multiple graphs, 509-13
  showing a message on the screen, 503-5
structured programming for, 559-70
testing cells for contents, 489-92
TUTOR.MLB, 121-24
Tutorial Disk, Inside Lotus 1-2-3, 11

U

Undo key (Alt-F4), 18
Unprotect protected worksheets, 25
Unprotected worksheets, protect, 25
Unrecognized key/range name message, 87
@upper function, 350-51
User input, managing, 396-448
  bounds checking, 442-45
  database records, 431-35
  defining and redefining ranges, 435-41
    associated ranges, 441
    helping the user redefine a range, 436-38
    using a macro to redefine a range, 438-40
  label and number input, accepting, 413-26
    custom prompts with defaults, 419-25
    {getlabel} command, 413-17
    {getnumber} command, 417-19
    interactive command {?} to accept data entry, 425-26
    testing for acceptable entries, 445-46
  /Range Input command, 426-31
    getting help during, 429-31
  single characters, 396-413
    capturing special keys, 401-4
    case sensitivity, 399-400
    curly braces ({ }), 408-10
    disabling the keyboard, 401
    displaying your own help screen at F1, 408
    displaying your own menu when slash (/) key is pressed, 407-8
    embedding a test in a formula, 410-13
    {get} command, 398-99
    implementing a key table, 404-7, 409
    turning off the slash key, 407
  testing for acceptable entries against lists of acceptable strings or values, 445-47
User interaction, 391-92
User macro, 598-99

V

Value entries, testing, 446-47
@value function, 348
Values
  keystroke macros that enter, 42-46
  macro to convert labels to, 356
  macro to to convert values to labels, 356
Variables, 164
  creating
    through blank spaces, 165
    through string manipulation, 166-71
  formulas as, 93
  structured programming and, 561
Version number, macro to maintain, 355

@vlookup function, 336-38
   testing for classes of keystrokes and, 405-7

W

{Wait} command, 233-35
Window key (F6)
   eliminating screen switching with, 77-78
Windows
   eliminating screen switching with, 77-78
   messages in, 498-500
{Windowsoff} command, 204-6
{Windowson} command, 206-8
Worksheet titles, clear, 25
/Worksheet Titles Horizontal command, 78
/Worksheet Window Horizontal command, 77
/Worksheet Window Sync command, 77
/Worksheet Window Unsync command, 77
{Write} command, 299, 320-24
{WRIteln} command, 299, 324-26

X

/xg command, {branch} command versus, 247

/xi command, {if} command versus, 262
/xl command, 216, 218
   {getlabel} command versus, 218
/xm command, {menubranch} command and, 229-30
/xn command, {getnumber} command versus, 221-22
/XQ command, 268
XY chart, full-screen message using an, 518-23

Z

Zeros
   macro to convert any zeros in a column of entries into empty cells, 358
   set label for 1-2-3- to display in place of, 28

Extend Your Spreadsheet Skills
with
The Lotus Guide to 1-2-3, Release 2.3
by Nicholas Delonas and Daniel Gasteiger

The Lotus Guide to 1-2-3, Release 2.3 offers accessible, and engaging, instruction to the latest 1-2-3 release. Quick and thorough chapters guide you through the new functions of 2.3, plus expand your overall 1-2-3 capabilities. You will learn the essential formulas that are the heart of the spreadsheet, and how to manipulate and use data-analysis tools. Advanced chapters on macros will springboard you into more advanced applications with Release 2.3.

From the fundamentals of the spreadsheet to advanced applications, *The Lotus Guide to 1-2-3, Release 2.3* is the most up-to-date guide to the most up-to-date version of 1-2-3. This book covers all the latest functions including:

- Working with windows and desktop publishing with WYSISYG.
- Using the spreadsheet Auditor add-in and the file Viewer add-in.
- Formulas with Release 2.3 — @functions, extended Boolean expressions, conditional math, and business math.
- Advanced applications including generating a loan schedule, building a rolodex file, and short macro on simulating a horse race.

Forward by Eileen Rudden, General Manager for DOS Spreadsheets, Lotus Development Corperation.

Nicholas Delonas is a software developer, technical writer, and small-business consultant who keeps himself busy as the Macros Editor for LOTUS Magazine. Daniel Gastieger is a 1-2-3 and Symphony consultant, and also a contributing editor to LOTUS Magazine.

ISBN: 0-13-529371-5 $24.95

Look for this and other LOTUS BOOKS titles at your local book or computer store. To order directly call 1(800)624-0023. Visa/MC accepted.

LOTUS BOOKS
**An Imprint of Brady Publishing, a division of
Simon & Schuster, Inc. in association with Lotus Publishing**

Instructions for the Reference Cards

The attached reference cards are designed to be removed from the book and kept as handy aids in creating and using your macros. One card is for beginners and the other for advanced 1-2-3 users. Both are described below.

How To Write Your First Macro

Follow the instructions here to learn how to write a macro, even if you have never written one before. For more information about how to write macros, see Chapter 2 of *Inside Lotus 1-2-3 Macros, Revised and Expanded* (Brady Books, 1989).

A Quick Reference To The Advanced Macro Commands

Use this reference to remind yourself of the proper syntax for writing each of the advanced macro commands. For detailed information on the operation of each command, see Chapters 11-16 of *Inside Lotus 1-2-3 Macros, Revised and Expanded* (Brady Books, 1989).

Feel free to duplicate either or both of these cards and distribute them, as long as you meet the following two conditions: (1) The copy that you distribute must be complete (you may not omit portions of a reference card) and (2) you may not incorporate the copied card into other materials, although you may distribute the copied reference cards separately along with any other material.